To Roberta

VEXED AND TROUBLED ENGLISHMEN
1590–1642

BOOKS BY CARL BRIDENBAUGH

The Beginnings of the American People
I VEXED AND TROUBLED ENGLISHMEN 1590–1642

MITRE AND SCEPTRE:
Transatlantic Faiths, Ideas, Personalities, and Politics 1689–1775

CITIES IN THE WILDERNESS:
The First Century of Urban Life in America, 1625–1742

CITIES IN REVOLT:
Urban Life in America, 1743–1776

PETER HARRISON, FIRST AMERICAN ARCHITECT

THE COLONIAL CRAFTSMAN

SEAT OF EMPIRE:
The Political Role of Eighteenth-Century Williamsburg

MYTHS AND REALITIES:
Societies of the Colonial South

REBELS AND GENTLEMEN:
Philadelphia in the Age of Franklin (co-author)

GENTLEMAN'S PROGRESS:
Dr. Alexander Hamilton's Itinerarium, 1744
(edited, with an Introduction)

Vexed and Troubled Englishmen

Englishmen

1590 - 1642

CARL BRIDENBAUGH

New York
OXFORD UNIVERSITY PRESS
1968

Preface

THE ORDINARY MEN and women of any epoch of English history have seldom attracted the attention of historians. Yet there circulates in the land a much-quoted saying—almost a proverb—that history is about chaps. This book is focused on them. Many years ago I began trying to understand the nature and extent of the discontents, anxieties, fears—even the hopes—that impelled so many of the English to abandon their beautiful homeland and either to seek out the European continent and Ireland or to venture into the great unknown of the new world called America. This, it seems to me, is not only a fundamental question in English history but one of the primary questions to ask about the beginnings of the American people. Its importance is transatlantic. Another closely related question is what were the precise means by which these members of the Great Migration were aroused, recruited, assembled, and transported across the ocean from 1620 to 1642. What has emerged from my investigations, therefore, is virtually a social history of the English people during the half-century after 1590.

It is clear to me, and I hope will be to the reader also, that the England of the first two Stuarts had a quality, a style, a life of its own. It was far from being just the twilight of the preceding era. These men, and later the women, who went to live in Virginia, New England, and the West Indies were certainly not Elizabethans; they were the children of a new and different age. They were not the discoverers and explorers; they were settlers.

In any re-creation of past conditions, the author must ask of the reader this co-operation, that he endeavor for a time to live vicariously in the age under consideration.

Where the documents of an epoch preserve its thought and flavor, it is well to let them speak for it. Also, I believe that one should never lose sight of the individual, even in the chronicle of social forces. In attempting to recover something of the character of the people of these fateful fifty years of English life, I have drawn freely on what humble folk said for themselves and about one another. In so doing I have refrained from modernizing quotations or correcting spelling. It seems to me that the infinite, pre-Websterian resourcefulness in orthography, exhibited by high and low alike, and their quaint conceits of expression are essential to any comprehension of these Englishmen, and that the small effort required to read what they said and wrote is well worthwhile. Was it not Ben Jonson who declared that he had no time for a man who could not spell a word more than one way?

I also firmly believe that the truth about a period is more than the sum of the records it leaves behind. They are at best a tiny fragment of the whole. The feeling for an age, which long association with its physical and documentary remains imparts, leads to conclusions and generalizations which are logically sound and intuitively certain but for which no specific references or "statistical controls" may be adduced. This is particularly true of any work dealing with the pre-statistical period of history. Especially in the seventeenth century, ordinary folk had no sense of statistics, and in very few cases, given the present state of our knowledge and methods, can complete reliance be placed upon contemporary figures.

Whenever possible, I have made use of such reliable statistics as I could accumulate. It will be many years before court records (civil and ecclesiastical), town and borough records, and like manuscripts now gathering dust in county record offices and cathedral archives will become available for analysis. Even then the corpus will be fragmentary, and final unchallengeable conclusions will always remain impossible.

More than a century ago, the foremost American historian, Francis Parkman, taught that archival and library research must be pieced out and enlivened by a thorough knowledge of the stage-setting in which the men and women of former times performed. I have sought to follow his precept through what I like to call visual research. In my eagerness to reconstruct visually and imaginatively something of the half-century of life described in this volume I have motored up and down the byways of every county of England to familiarize myself with local conditions. I have sought out the surviving small structures, observed the lay of the land, the tiny villages and farms, as well as the towns and cities and the great houses. Likewise I have explored Brittany, Alsace, and the Black Forest of Germany, to compare the vernacular architecture of these regions with that of England.

When we consider the wonderful topographical variety of Britain, it almost seems that the only reliable history must be local history, but one must get on with the task and take the great risk of generalizing. In a work of this size it is impossible to deal adequately, in some cases to deal at all, with topics of genuine importance. I have written on some matters, such as education, office-holding, and culture, which prefigure developments in the colonies after 1642. I have, moreover, researched on many subjects about which I have not written—superstition, Puritan polity and theology, the Sabbath, literature, and constitutional change—to mention a few examples. With these limitations and others, of which I am painfully aware, I offer this book as a venture into a neglected, rich, and fascinating field of historical investigation.

Providence, Rhode Island   CARL BRIDENBAUGH
January 1968

Acknowledgments

INEVITABLY in this venture into Anglo-American history, which has been in preparation for a decade or more, I have turned to many people for assistance, and with singularly few exceptions, it has been generously bestowed. I take genuine pleasure in thanking them here at the same time that I absolve them wholly from any responsibility for what I have written.

In my own country at the University of California at Berkeley, four former students aided me in exploiting its fine collection of the sets of English local history societies, which are so rich in personal materials: Professor Carlos Allen of Pennsylvania Military College, Professor John Beattie of the University of Toronto, Professor Martin Lodge of Temple University, and David Corkran of Berkeley. For timely aid in procuring copies of manuscripts or articles and for gifts of books, I am beholden to Professor Mildred Campbell of Poughkeepsie, New York, Mr. Philip Barbour of Newtown, Connecticut, Professor Lawrence Stone of Princeton, and Professor Larzer Ziff of the University of California at Berkeley. Professor Carleton Sprague Smith of New York University led me to useful references about music; while at Yale University Miss Marjorie Wynne of the Beinecke Library once again placed me greatly in her debt. At my own university, Professors William F. Church, Ernest Frerichs, Bryce Lyon, and John Workman helped out on several occasions, as did Mr. Grant Dugdale of the Brown University Press with editorial problems. As always over the many years, Miss Jeanette Black came to the rescue of her former teacher.

Professor Louise Hall of Duke University made a vital contribution by unsnarling the biographical details about Samuel Vassall; the account given here is pretty much as she wrote it.

In England I met frequently with understanding and substantial aid. Mr. F. G. Emmison, County Archivist of Essex, supplied everything I asked for and more, including the hospitality of his own home. Professor D. B. Quinn of Liverpool, a loyal friend of many years' standing, gave me one of my best quotations and drew my attention to several important topics. Mr. William Kellaway of the Institute for Historical Research came to my assistance at a critical moment by procuring copies of documents from the Guildhall Library and the British Museum. Likewise Mr. P. M. Cadell, Assistant Keeper of Manuscripts at the British Museum, helped me with a difficult bit of seventeenth-century handwriting. Similarly, I wish most gratefully to thank Professor Charles Wilson of Jesus College, Cambridge, for counseling a total stranger and forestalling a serious blunder. An exchange of letters with Dr. Valerie Pearl enabled me to run down an important quotation.

At the University of London, the library officials kindly allowed me to read a number of excellent unpublished masters' and doctors' theses, most of which are cited in the footnotes, but I wish again to thank their learned authors and to express the hope that like Messrs. Davies and Everitt they will be able to publish their useful findings.

The widely known *Short-Title Catalogue* was my principal bibliographical guide, and I succeeded in locating nearly every entry that I needed in the following libraries: in England I visited the Bodleian (where Mr. D. M. Merry made my long stay a joy), the British Museum, the Goldsmith's Library at the University of London, and Dr. Williams's Library in Gordon Square; in the United States, the Houghton Library of Harvard University, the Folger Shakespeare Library of Washington (presided over by the always helpful Louis B. Wright), the New York Public Library, the Library Company of Philadelphia, and the Massachusetts Historical Society in Boston. Dr. Ray A. Billington and Dr. John E.

Pomfret sent me materials from the Henry E. Huntington Library at San Marino, as did Dr. Lawrence E. Towner of the Newbury Library in Chicago, the John Hay Special Collections and the John Carter Brown libraries of Brown University. At the John D. Rockefeller Library of Brown University the entire staff sought in every way to ease my labors and provided me with a secluded study.

During the year 1958–59 I spent most of my time at the Institute for Historical Research in London, where Mr. Taylor Milne and his assistants went out of their way to help a novice; and the Director, Professor Sir Goronwy Edwards, thoughtfully offered me an opportunity to try out some of my findings in an Institute Lecture. In my travels around England, I discovered useful local histories at the public libraries of Norwich, Exeter, and Dorchester, and dozens of kind countrymen and citizens willingly answered a traveler's questions—I recall the exceptional courtesy of one man who, seeing me gazing at an old house in Norwich (now a gentleman's club) offered to take me inside to view the antique furnishings.

For permission to quote from *Western Star* (Holt, Rinehart and Winston, Inc., Copyright 1943, by Rosemary Carr Benét) my thanks are due to Stephen Vincent Benét's literary agents, Brandt & Brandt.

To the John Simon Guggenheim Memorial Foundation I am deeply indebted for fellowships that enabled me to visit England twice, and to Vice Chancellor James D. Hart and the University of California at Berkeley for generously making research assistants and funds available to me.

Note on Documentation

IN ANY WORK of social history, documentation becomes a serious problem because of the large number of authorities to be cited merely for one paragraph, often just for one sentence. Moreover, certain statements made in the text rest upon conclusions arising from the entire study which therefore cannot be fully documented. I have tried, as Thomas Prince said in 1736, "to cite my Vouchers for every quotation, date, or statistic." I have read many tracts and other works that are not indicated. As far as possible, at the end of each paragraph, the principal sources are cited in the order in which they were used with this exception: where a quotation appears in a footnote, the first reference following it gives the authority for this quotation. Because I have quarried thoroughly the records of the courts of quarter sessions and the voluminous and long-titled publications of many county record and local history societies of England, short titles have been used to save space in the footnotes. Lists of these follow below, together with a list of abbreviations for the libraries and repositories in which I have met with so much co-operation and visited with such profit.

After this book was sent to the publisher, there came into the author's hands the important Volume IV of *The Agrarian History of England and Wales* (Cambridge, England, 1967), which covers the years 1500 to 1640. The chapters by Mrs. Joan Thirsk, Alan Everitt, and M. W. Barley contain a mass of illustrative material, most of which tends to support the major conclusions in the present work pertaining to farming, farm laborers, marketing of agricultural produce, and rural housing. Significantly, however, there is but one reference to the colonies (on early housing in New England) in its 870 pages; yet emigration was certainly a concomitant of rural dislocation. The comments of the authors mentioned above concerning the insufficiency of objective sources and the impossibility of developing "statistical controls" are especially relevant.

GENERAL ABBREVIATIONS

Barnstaple Recs. J. R. Charter and T. Wainwright, *Reprint of the Barnstaple Records* (Barnstaple, 1900).

CSM Colonial Society of Massachusetts, *Publications.*

CSP, Col. Calendar of State Papers, Colonial. America and West Indies.

CSPD Calendar of State Papers, Domestic.

CSP, Venetian Calendar of State Papers, Venetian.

Camden Camden Society, *Publications* [title varies].

DAB Dictionary of American Biography.

Dartmouth Recs. MSS Deeds and Documents in Exeter City Library; also Court Minutes [1558–1642 ff.] Also typed Calendar of above Deeds & Docs., but Court Minutes are not calendared.

DNB Dictionary of National Biography.

Ec. Hist. Rev. Economic History Review.

EHR English Historical Review.

Force, *Tracts Tracts and Other Papers, Relating to the Origin, Settlement, and Progress of the Colonies in North America,* comp. Peter Force (Washington, 1837).

HMC Historical Manuscripts Commission [followed by Report number or title].

Maidstone Recs. Records of Maidstone (Maidstone, 1926).

NEHG Reg. New England Historical & Genealogical Register.

NEQ New England Quarterly.

Pevsner *The Buildings of England* [followed by name of county].

Plymouth Recs. R. N. Worth, *Calendar of Plymouth Municipal Records* (Plymouth, 1893).

RHS Trans. Royal Historical Society, *Transactions.*

Reading Recs. Reading Records: Diary of the Corporation ed. J. M. Guilding (Oxford, 1896), v. III, 1630–40.

Southampton Recs. Southampton Record Society, *Publications.*

STC Short Title Catalogue, ed. Pollard and Redgrave. [The indispensable bibliographical work for a subject of this kind.]

VCH Victoria County History [followed by name of county].

WMQ   William and Mary Quarterly.

   All other authorities are cited by the full bibliographical reference the
first time they are used and, thereafter, by a recognizable short title, *e.g.:*
Chamberlain, *Letters;* or *Winthrop Papers.*

COURTS OF QUARTER SESSIONS RECORDS

Hamilton, *Quarter Sessions*   A. H. A. Hamilton, *Quarter Sessions* [Devon]
   from Queen Elizabeth to Queen Anne (London, 1878).

Essex Sessions   Calendar of Essex Sessions Rolls, XVIII–XX (1600–
   1642), comps. M. M. Emmison & C. Baker (Microfilm at University of California, also originals, and some mimeographed copies).

Essex Arch.   Extracts from Essex Archdeaconry Court Records, in 12
   vols., by a reliable antiquary. All of these Essex Records are in the
   Essex Record Office at Chelmsford.

Essex Assize Rolls   Assize Rolls of county Essex, *ca.* 1558–1650 (Microfilm at University of California, Berkeley).

Hertfordshire Sessions   Quarter Sessions Books, 1619–1657, Hertford
   County Records, vols. V, VI, 1928.

Middlesex Sessions   Middlesex County Records, ed. J. C. Jeaffreson (London, 1887–1892).

Middlesex Sessions, n.s.   *Calendar to the Sessions Records (Middlesex),
   New Series, 1612–1618,* ed. William Le Hardy (London, 1935–
   1941).

*Northampton Sessions   Quarter Sessions Records of the County of North-
   ampton, 1630, 1657, 1657–8,* ed. Joan Wake (Hereford, 1924).

North Riding Sessions   North Riding of Yorkshire Quarter Sessions (North
   Riding Record Society, 1883–1884), I–III.

Somerset Sessions   Quarter Sessions Records for the County of Somerset
   [1607–1660]. ed. E. H. Bates-Harbin, Somerset Record Society,
   XXIV (1908).

Somerset Assize Orders   Somerset Assize Orders, 1629–1640, ed. Thomas
   G. Barnes, Somerset Record Society, LXV (1959).

Sussex Sessions   Quarter Sessions Order Book, 1642–1649, Sussex Record
   Society, LIV (1954).

Warwick Sessions   Warwick County Records [Quarter Sessions], I–VIII
   (1625–1690) [Warwick, 1935–1953].

West Riding Sessions   West Riding Sessions Rolls (Yorkshire Archaeological and Topographical Association, Record Series), I–II.

Wiltshire Sessions   Records of the County of Wilts [extracts from Quarter
   Sessions of the Seventeenth Century], ed. B. Howard Cunningham
   (Devizes, 1932).

   "Wiltshire Quarter Sessions Records," in *HMC Various,* LV, I
   (1901).

Worcestershire   Calendar of Quarter Sessions Rolls (in *Worcester County Records*, ed. J. W. Willis-Bund).

COUNTY HISTORICAL AND RECORD SOCIETIES

Bedford   Publications of the Bedfordshire Historical Record Society.

Bristol & Gloucester   Bristol & Gloucester Archaeological Society, Transactions.

Buckinghamshire   Records of Buckinghamshire . . . of the Architectural and Archaeological Society for the County of Buckinghamshire.

Chetham   Remains Historical and Literary connected with the Palatine Counties of Lancaster and Chester.

Devon & Cornwall   Devon & Cornwall Notes & Queries.

Devonshire   Transactions of the Devonshire Association for the Advancement of Science, Literature, and Art.

Hampshire   Hampshire Field Club and Archaeological Society, *Papers and Proceedings.*

Kent   Kent Archaeological Society, *Archaeologica Cantiana.*

Lancashire & Cheshire Trans   Transactions of the Historic Society of Lancashire and Cheshire.

Lincolnshire   Lincolnshire Notes and Queries.

London   Transactions of the London and Middlesex Archaeological Society.

Norfolk   Norfolk Record Society, *Publications.*

Norfolk & Norwich   Norfolk and Norwich Archaeological Society, *Norfolk Archaeology.*

Northampton   Northampton Archaeological Society, *Publications.*

Oxfordshire   Oxfordshire Archaeological Society, *Publications.*

Somerset   Somerset Record Society, *Publications* [title varies].

Somerset & Dorset   Somerset and Dorset Notes and Queries.

Suffolk   Suffolk Archaeological Institute, *Publications* [title varies].

Surrey   Surrey Archaeological Society, *Collections.*

Surtees   Surtees Society [Durham], *Publications* [title varies].

Sussex   Sussex Record Society, *Publications* [title varies].

Sussex Arch.   Sussex Archaeological Society, *Collections.*

Western Antiquary   The Western Antiquary; or Devon and Cornwall Notebook.

Wiltshire   Wiltshire Archaeological and Natural History Society, *Magazine.*

Yorkshire   Yorkshire Archaeological Journal.

LIBRARIES AND REPOSITORIES

BM   British Museum.

Dr. Williams's Library   Gordon Square, London [strong on Puritan MSS].

Bodleian   Bodleian Library, Oxford.

ERO   Essex Record Office, Chelmsford.

Folger   Folger Shakespeare Library, Washington, D.C.

General Library & Goldsmiths' Library   University of London, Senate House.

HCL   Harvard College Library (Houghton Collection of Rare Books).

Huntington Library   Henry E. Huntington Library and Art Gallery, San Marino, California.

JCB   John Carter Brown Library of Brown University, Providence, R.I.

JH   John Hay Library, Special Collections, Brown University, Providence, R.I.

LC   Library of Congress, Washington, D.C.

LCP   Library Company of Philadelphia.

NPYL   New York Public Library.

PRO   Public Record Office, Chancery Lane, London.

Contents

There was a wind over England, and it blew.
(Have you heard the news of Virginia?)
A west wind blowing, the wind of a western star,
To gather men's lives like pollen and cast them forth,
Blowing in hedge and highway and seaport town,
Whirling dead leaf and living, but always blowing,
A salt wind, a sea wind, a wind from the world's end,
From the coasts that have new, wild names, from the huge
    unknown.

                 Stephen Vincent Benét, *Western Star*

VEXED AND TROUBLED ENGLISHMEN
1590–1642

Westward the Land Was Bright

TIMOTHY SNAPE of the parish of St. Saviour in Southwark, designating himself a yeoman of London, made his will in September, 1624. He was about to embark on a perilous voyage to Virginia, which he might not survive, and he wished to bequeath his effects to his sister Hannah, the wife of John Barker, citizen and haberdasher of the City. In 1629, like many another young Englishman who followed the western star, Snape died before he had made a real start in the New World. Some years later, William Moulle, a Virginia planter who had crossed the Atlantic to sell his tobacco, wrote from Plymouth to his brother in London that he was about to sail back to the colony, "And I leave this (if I should dye att sea and not bee taken [prisoner]), that you should have the little I take with mee to sea. . . . And if please God that this bee, Helpe our Deare Mother and our goode Sisters and Brothers if there be any occasion; for I give you it with this intent, And I doubt no lesse of you . . . the seas are so troublesome that I dare not venter to take my Sister Dorothy over with me. . . ."[1]

Timothy Snape and William Moulle were but two of thousands of men, women, and children who were caught up in the fateful Westward Movement which began in their native island. Within a year or so after the accession of King James I, his subjects began

1. Henry F. Waters, *Genealogical Gleanings in England* (Boston, Mass., 1901), I, 20; *WMQ.*, XIV, 102–3.

to gaze longingly at the setting sun and then to sail out toward it. The flow of emigrants began in 1607 as a mere trickle, increased to a recognizable stream after 1620, and after 1629 became a mighty flood. Some of them were lured away from home and country, more were driven out for one reason or another, and a very large number of them looked upon their departure as a belated response to a divine injunction.

When the leaders of the Pilgrims in Leiden debated removal to America in 1619, some of them alleged that though it was "a great design"—and desperate—it was also "subject to many unconceivable perils and dangers." They had read in Hakluyt's accounts and some of the other collections of voyages and discoveries about the difficulties and inconveniences of an ocean crossing. No traveler could hope to avoid the "casualties of the sea," women and older persons would be weakened, there might be encounters with enemies. And when they reached the western shores, dread savages, famine, disease from drinking impure water (for there would be no beer or cider), and many other menaces would threaten their well-being if not their very existence. "Surely," said William Bradford, "it could not be thought but the very hearing of these things could not but move the very bowels of men to grate within them and make the weak to quake and tremble." [2]

Whether the English intended to go forth to Virginia, the islands of the Caribbean, or Massachusetts Bay, the mere prospect of venturing on the high seas, though alluring, surpassed in formidableness anything that they could imagine and frightened humble folk who never before had been out of sight of land. The ordinary English who planned to emigrate by families or in groups and who gave rational thought to what they were contemplating were beset night and day by all sorts of doubts and fears. Youthful men and women, who had accepted a drink or perhaps a shilling and signed to go to some plantation, knew very little about what was in store for them, and usually they displayed little concern until it was too late.

For most people, the seriousness of their commitment became clear as they boarded their ships—at London, Ipswich, Southampton, Weymouth, Plymouth. The first large contingent of Puritans

2. *Of Plymouth Plantation, 1620–1647, by William Bradford, Sometime Governor Thereof,* ed. Samuel E. Morison (New York, 1952), 26.

sailed from Southampton in the vessels of the Winthrop Fleet in 1630. One of the passengers aboard the *Arbella,* Edward Johnson, penned a moving and memorable account of the final, tearful parting of the emigrants from their friends and relatives. "Among this company, thus disposed, doth many Reverend and godly Pastors of Christ present themselves, some in a Seamans Habit, and their scattered sheepe comming as a poore Convoy loftily take their leave as followeth, 'What dolefull dayes are these, when the best choice our Orthodox Ministers can make is to take up a perpetuall banishment from their native soile, together with their Wives and Children; wee their poore sheepe they may not feede, but by stoledred [stealth] should they abide here.' " [3]

In early Stuart times there were between 12,000 and 14,000 English merchant ships, whose owners, with a singular lack of inventiveness, gave their vessels certain names over and over again: *Ann, John, Mayflower, Gift of God, Hope,* etc. Those selected for carrying passengers and cargo to America were ordinarily from 200 to 350 tons burthen, and 50 to 200 people would be crowded on board what Thomas Shepard called "a close ship." Traveling conditions were inevitably grim, even in the best of them, for master, passengers, and crew alike. As more people made the crossing, however, prospective settlers who could afford some extras learned what to take to add a little comfort during the voyage. In *New Englands Prospect* (1634), William Wood included "a few lines from the Pen of experience." Each passenger was usually allowed to take five pounds of provisions, such as salted beef, pork, and fish; also butter, cheese, pease, water-gruel, "Biskets, and six-shilling Beere." Wood urged them to take some conserves, good wine to burn, and "Sallet-oyl" in addition—all for seasickness—and for relief from the salt diet, sugar, eggs, bacon, rice, some poultry, and a wether sheep. Most important was lemon juice to cure or prevent scurvy. Passengers had to supply their own pans for cooking and their own bedding, and long coats were recommended for wear during storms.[4]

When the company and their goods were safely stowed, and the

3. *Johnson's Wonder-Working Providence, 1628–1651,* ed. J. Franklin Jameson (New York, 1910), 50–54, especially p. 53.
4. Marsden, in *RHS Trans.,* n. s., XIX, 310–36; *CSM,* XXVII, 354; Gabriel Debien, *Les Engagés pour les Antilles, 1634–1715* (Paris, 1952), 92; William Wood, *New Englands Prospect* (1634) 49–50.

tide and winds right, the crew weighed anchor, hoisted the sails, and the tiny craft got under way. For all hands this was the crucial moment, one of which they were acutely sensible. One pious exile, who had been inordinately harassed, nevertheless recalled "having tasted much of gods mercy in England, and lamenting the losse of our native cuntry when we tooke our last view of it. . . ." As England faded out in the mist and the vessel was hull-down over the horizon, one and all "betooke them to the protection of the Lord on the wide Ocean." [5]

"It is too common with many to feare the Sea more then they neede, and all such as put to Sea, confesse it to be less tedious then they either feared or expected." William Wood here took the favorable view required of the writer of a promotion tract, but he was correct in saying that ships seldom overset or sank out at sea. They did rock like cradles, however, and nearly everyone on board suffered from seasickness. Captain John Smith tells of the ships of the first Virginia voyage in 1606 being detained in the Downs "in the sight of England" for six weeks; "all which time Maister Hunt our Preacher, was so weake and sicke, that few expected his recoverie." Robert Hunt kept manfully at his pastoral task despite "making wild vomits into the black night." Master Thomas Shepard, the Puritan, was more fortunate than the Anglican: "the Lord was very tender of me and kept me from the violence of sea sickness." During a rough passage, broken bones and bruises were not uncommon among a ship's company. Margaret Shepard and her baby narrowly escaped serious injury when, by the "shaking" of the ship *Defense* in a blustering storm, she struck her head on an iron bolt.[6]

Some emigrants enjoyed a more or less calm and pleasant crossing. Sir Henry Colt, a Roman Catholic and a former soldier who had fought for the King in the Netherlands, made Barbados in the *Alexander* in five weeks and five days out of Weymouth. None of the company developed any sickness or distemper in the tropical waters, and all of them, miraculously, arrived safely. "Who cann without notable Ingratitude but carry this favour and benefitt of

5. *CSM,* XXVII, 383; *Johnson's Wonder-Working Providence,* 56.
6. Wood, *New Englands Prospect,* 49–50; *Travels and Works of Captain John Smith,* ed. Edward Arber and A. G. Bradley (Edinburgh, 1910), I, 90; Philip L. Barbour, *The Three Worlds of Captain John Smith* (Boston, 1964), 109; *CSM,* XXVII, 383–4.

thine oh God perpetually fixed in our hearts," was this gentleman's fervent prayer of thanks for a good passage. "I was a little sicke, but had my health in a competent manner," Edmund Browne reported of his voyage to New England in 1639 aboard the *Thomas and Frances,* even though the smallpox did break out in the ship. Aboard the *Arbella,* which had a reasonably smooth crossing, Johnson observed: ". . . you see weakly Women, whose hearts have trembled to set foote in Boate, but now imboldened to venter through these tempestuous Seas with their young Babes, whom they nurture up with their Breasts, while their Bodies are tossed on the trembling Waves. . . ." More than a few women were safely delivered of babies somewhere out on the Atlantic. According to William Wood, women and children bore up at sea as well as the men, and many of them perked up from breathing the clean salt air.[7]

All mariners feared the fierce Atlantic gales, and the emigrants of nearly every ship had occasions when they prayed that their bark might ride out the storm. Thomas Shepard, his pregnant wife, and son Thomas sailed for New England from Harwich on October 16, 1634. They had been at sea but two days when their vessel was almost wrecked on the sands. They managed to get into Great Yarmouth, but little Thomas became very ill getting from the ship to the shore and died within two weeks. Not until the next August did the Shepards embark again. This time the ship was "very rotten and unfit for such a voyage" and sprung a bad leak in the first storm. Dirty weather persisted for the entire trip, "but after many sad stormes and wearisom dayes and many longings to see the shore," the *Defense* reached Boston on October 3, 1635. Master Shepard's days of rejoicing were numbered, for his wife, sick and weak after months of raw, cold weather, died of "consumption" toward the end of the winter.[8]

The ships carrying servants to the Chesapeake and West Indian colonies provided the poorest accommodations; the long passage in one of them must have been a protracted nightmare. George

Sandys wrote to John Ferrar of the Virginia Company in April, 1623: "It would wel please the Countrye to heare that you had tak[en] revenge of Dupper [a brewer of Southampton] for his stincking beare; which with what succeeded by their contagion, in my conscience hath been the death of 200." Another letter contained the charge that ". . . our Shipp was so pestered with people and goodes that wee were so full of infection that after a while we saw little but throwing folkes over boord. . . ." Early in 1624, the Council in Virginia reminded the Company "how the ships are pestered Contrary to your agreementes, Victualed with mustie bred the reliques of former Vioages, and stincking beare, heretofore so earnestly Complayned of, in greate parte the cause of that mortalitie, which is imputed alone to the Countrey. . . ." The plague "(or as killing a disease)" struck Barbados so severely one year "that the living were hardly able to bury the dead," and there were those who were convinced that it was "brought thither in shipping." Ship fever was to continue a threat to colonial health for more than a century.[9]

It took from five weeks to several months to cross the Atlantic, depending upon the natural vagaries of wind and wave. Quick passages such as those of six weeks and a little more than eight weeks made by Colonel Colt and Master Browne ordinarily enabled all hands to arrive in good health. Not many were so fortunate, however. One ship, bound from London to Boston, took twenty-six weeks ("between land and land eighteen weeks"). Her beer had been all consumed within a month, and the passengers had to drink stinking water mixed with a little vinegar. Continually storms buffeted the vessel, and the fog off Cape Ann forced the master to sail into port by compass. "Yet," said John Winthrop, "through the great providence of the Lord, they came all safe on shore, and most of them sound and well liking." [10]

Some experiences during over-long voyages proved to be frightful. Such was the grisly tale of the *Virginia Merchant,* 300 tons, Captain John Locker, which sailed for Virginia by way of the

9. *Records of the Virginia Company of London,* ed. Susan M. Kingsbury (Washington, 1935), IV, 109, 232, 451; Richard Ligon, *A True and Exact History of the Island of Barbados* (1673), 21.
10. *CSM,* VII, 76; *Winthrop's Journal,* ed. J. K. Hosmer (New York, 1908), I, 199–200.

Western Isles in 1649, with Colonel Henry Norwood and some other Royalist gentlemen and a total list of 350 passengers. It took twenty-three days to make Teneriffe, and water ran very low. Thereafter the passage to Bermuda and thence to the coast of Carolina was uneventful until the ship lost her mainmast in a terrific storm off Cape Hatteras. For eleven days tempests lashed the crippled ship before she arrived off Cape Henry, where, disastrously, "our mortal enemy the north-west gale" kept her from entering Chesapeake Bay. The food supply soon ran dangerously low, and famine threatened the poorer passengers. "Women and children made dismal cries and grievous complaints," Colonel Norwood recalled when he was writing about his experience. "The infinite number of rats that all the voyage had been our plague, we now were glad to make our prey to feed on; and as they were unsnared and taken, a well grown rat was sold for sixteen shillings as a market rate. Nay, before the voyage did end . . . a woman great with child offered twenty shillings for a rat, which the proprietor refusing, the woman died." Somewhere along the Maryland coast Captain Locker agreed to put Colonel Norwood and a party of the weakest ashore. To their dismay it turned out to be an island. One of the three frail women with them died, and Norwood advised the two surviving ones "to endeavour their own preservation by converting her dead carcass into food, as they did to good effect. The same counsel was embrac'd by those of our sex; the living fed upon the dead; four of our company having the happiness to end their miserable lives." Rescued finally by some friendly Indians, they were taken to York River on February 17, 1650, after a terrible and terrifying journey of twenty-two weeks' duration.[11]

Fearsome as the natural obstacles to a quick and pleasant Atlantic crossing might be, every ship's company dreaded equally the possibility of capture by their fellow men. Though the *Thomas and Frances* ran into only two severe storms on her trip out to New England in 1639—one of the fastest crossings on record—Master Edmund Browne told Sir Simonds D'Ewes that "Wee were often put into some feare of pyrates or men of warre, but our God pre-

11. Colonel [Henry] Norwood, *A Voyage to Virginia* (n. d. [*c*. 1650]), in Force, *Tracts*, III, No. X.

served us." Divine aid did not succor every ship, however. "Dunkirkers" often boarded vessels while they were still in the English Channel. Along the southern route to America in 1637, the *Elizabeth* was surprised by war ships from the Spanish West India Fleet, and her 120 passengers were carried to Spain and imprisoned. Parliament learned that they were still held in confinement in 1660! In 1636, a Mr. Armitage, a woolen draper of Cannon Street, London, sent fifty men and boys and seven women to Virginia for servants in the *Little David,* James Hogg, master. On the high seas, only thirty-five miles off Land's End, they were all taken by a "Sallee-man" and sold for slaves, according to the story published by John Dunton, mariner. His son, aged nine, was one of the company, and Dunton himself was sold to one Obigolant, who ordered him to pilot a Sallee pirate ship in the Narrow Seas "for taking English women," because they brought high prices in the Mediterranean slave markets.[12]

When all of these hazards are taken into consideration, it is something of a miracle, even to a godless age, that so few ships were actually lost on the westward passage, and that such a large proportion of the individual Englishmen who decided to risk their lives in a new land ultimately reached the American shore.

The first glimpse of the New World evoked strange sensations in the minds of all of the English, many of them far from favorable. Relief at being once more on *terra firma* often yielded to dejection, sometimes to despair. Lewis Hughes, a clergyman in Bermuda, informed Sir Nathaniel Rich that "some of the new comers are almost at a stand, and do sigh to see how many trees they have to fell and how their hands are blistered." And well they might have sighed, for very few of them knew how to wield an axe. William Bradford's account of the arrival of the Pilgrims at Cape Cod in late fall is both poignant and touching: "Being thus passed the vast ocean, and a sea of troubles before in their preparation . . . they had now no friends to welcome them nor inns to entertain or refresh their weatherbeaten bodies; no houses or much less towns to repair to, to seek for succour. . . . Besides, what could they see

12. *CSM,* VII, 76; *Proceedings and Debates of the British Parliaments Respecting North America,* ed. Leo F. Stock (Washington, 1924), I, 286; *CSPD, 1636–7,* p. 141; John Dunton, *A True Journal of the Sally Fleet* (1637).

but a hideous and desolate wilderness, full of wild beasts and wild men. . . . For summer being done, all things stand upon them with a weatherbeaten face, and the whole country, full of woods and thickets, represented a wild and savage hue. If they looked behind them there was the mighty ocean which they had passed and was now as a main bar and gulf to separate them from all the civil parts of the world." Nevertheless, sustained by their faith, these humble families sturdily faced their tasks, and the Lord looked after them.[13]

William Wood, who crossed to Massachusetts Bay in 1634, commented somewhat contemptuously about the reactions of some of the new arrivals: "I have my selfe heard some say that they heard it was a rich land, a brave country, but when they came there they could see nothing but a few Canvis Boothes and old houses, supposing at the first to have found walled towns, fortifications and corne fields, as if townes could have built themselves. . . . These men, missing of their expectations, returned home and railed against the Country." [14]

Not everyone who found America either forbidding or disappointing could do anything about it, let alone return to England. Homesickness is a real and bitter affliction. George Thorpe was persuaded that in Virginia "more doe die here of the disease of theire minde than of theire body. . . ." One of these was Richard Frethorne, formerly of London. His parents had sold him to the Virginia Company for a servant. In 1623 he wrote home that "I yor Child am in a most heavie Case by reason of the nature of the Country is such that it Causeth much sicknes, as the scurvie and bloody flix [dysentery], and divers other diseases. . . ." Since he came off the ship he has had nothing to eat but pease and loblollie (water-gruel), yet he has to work hard "both earlie, and late." It "is most pitifull if you did knowe as much as I, when people crie out day, and night, Oh that they were in England without theire lymbes and would not care to loose anie lymbe to be in England againe, yea though they beg from doore to doore, for wee live in feare of the [Indian] Enimy everie hower. . . ." Ten are dead out

13. HMC Manchester (8th Report), Appendix, No. 252; Of Plymouth Plantation, ed. Morison, 61–2; CSM, XXII, 49–50.
14. Wood, New Englands Prospect, 47.

of his group of twenty, and of last year's twenty at this place, only three remain alive. Goodman Jackson, who lives ten miles away in Jamestown, "much marvaild that you would send me a servant to the Companie, he saith I had better beene knocked on the head. . . ." If you love me, he writes piteously, redeem me and let me come home. "O that you did see my daylie and hourelie sighes, grones, and teares, and thumpes that I afford mine owne brest, and me, and Curse the time of my birth with holy Job. I thought no head had been able to hold so much water as hath and doth daylie flow from mine eyes. But this is Certain I Never felt the want of Father and mother till now, but now deare frendes full well I knowe and me[an] it although it were too late before I knew it." [15]

And yet—most of the English men and women remained in the strange new lands, and eventually, those who survived the first years also prospered and shared in the creating of a new society. Late in the seventeenth century, Puritan ministers in New England used to ask the people: "What went ye out into the wilderness to see?" Today we ask more. We want to know what these Englishmen were like, and what their land was like, and what happened there to make them abandon that pleasant isle, cross the tempestuous Atlantic, and venture their all in the wilderness.[16]

15. *Recs., Va. Co.*, II, 417; IV, 41.
16. Cotton Mather, *Magnalia Christi Americana* (London, 1702), bk. III, p. 6.

I

The People of England

G OD IS ENGLISH!" So John Aylmer, flushed with piety and patriotism, informed his countrymen as he set out for England in 1558, after years in exile. In *An Harborowe for Faithfull and Trewe Subjects,* a spirited defense of Queen Elizabeth against the trumpeting of John Knox, the good clergyman identified the English Church and the English people as one, an elect nation under divine blessing and guidance. Experience born of his forced sojourn on the continent of Europe had made this patent to him, and he enthusiastically expatiated to Englishmen of all degrees on how much better off they were than the French, Germans, Turks, Scots, or Spanish. "You have God, and all his army of angels on your side," Aylmer asserted as he exhorted his countrymen to manliness in the wars. "If you lose the victory: he must lose the glory." [1]

The subjects of other princes did not acknowledge this preference for the English on the part of the deity. On the contrary, from distant St. Augustine in America, Pedro Menéndez de Avilés wrote to King Philip of Spain to urge him to master the lands to the north of Florida lest other nations seize them, colonize

1. In commenting upon puritans in 1573, Archbishop Parker asked Lord Burghley: *"Where Almighty God is so much English as he is,* should we not requite his mercy with some earnesty to prefer his honour and true religion"? (Italics mine.) John Bruce (ed.), *The Correspondence of Matthew Parker, D. D.* (Parker Society, Cambridge, Eng., 1853), 419. On Aylmer's tract (*STC,* 14390, Folger) and the concept of the divinely favored England, see William Haller, *The Elect Nation* (New York, 1964), especially pp. 87–8, 113, 232.

there, and make common cause with the Indians. Later conquest and rule would prove most difficult, "especially should the French or English settle it, as they are Lutheran peoples, and because they and the Indians are nearly of one faith"! And to many another Castillian official, the English were nought but "barbarous foreigners." [2]

In the scepter'd isle itself, however, the Queen's subjects, fortified by the sanctions of their faith, credited the reports of their own travelers and ignored such foreign criticisms as reached their eyes and ears. "What country in Europ comparable to England? what more wonderfull than London"? boasted Thomas Johnson in 1596. By 1618 so firmly rooted was the conviction of their own superiority that the English bought and read, without sensing its unconscious irony, *The Glory of England: A True Description of many excellent prerogatives and remarkable blessings, whereby She Triumpheth over all the Nations of the World,* in which Thomas Gainsford unequivocally placed his country in the van of all nations, past and present—"not that I meane to rippe up the bowels of antiquity." On the eve of the Great Civil War, after a tour of southern England and Wales, Peter Mundy, whose firsthand familiarity with India, China, and Japan, as well as with continental Europe, was unsurpassed, wrote the following comment in his journal:

> In conclusion: More to bee enjoyed, More to bee seene at Home in [our] owne land (take itt in the generall) than in any one country beesides in the whole worlde, both for conveniency and delightt.

Certainly the average Englishman of the early seventeenth century, in a mood of soaring, uncritical pride, took a larger view of his country and his countrymen than they deserved. Yet, in the main, he was right.[3]

2. David Beers Quinn (ed.), *The Roanoke Voyages, 1584–1590* (Hakluyt Society, 2d ser., CIV, 1955), II, 717, 772.
3. Mundy also suggested: "Hee that desires to know more of Englands excellencies, let him read Thomas Gainesford, Of the Glory of England." Thomas Platter, who, like most Germans, thought otherwise, offered a more restrained estimate of the stay-at-home English in 1599. "Nowadays the common people are still somewhat coarse and uncultured, especially those who never get away

Here was a land of astonishing vitality; England was fast becoming one of the foremost nations of the globe. The ultimate test of a society may be its capacity to produce leaders of ability and judgment, and these early Stuart England did breed in abundance in all spheres save that of kingship; its success, however, lay in the superior quality of the mass of Englishmen. It was the people, not the constituted leaders, who initiated the most far-reaching undertaking of modern times, the planting of "a nation, where none before hath stood." Properly then, in this inquiry, we turn not to the nobility, not to the gentry, and not to the great merchants of London and the outports, but to the ordinary people who raised them up and sustained them, for as Robert Reyce of Suffolk expressed it in 1618: "When I consider the degrees and severall callings of our country inhabitants, I think it fit to begin with the poorer sort, from whom all other sorts of estates doe take their beginning." [4]

II

It was from the several generations of Englishmen who were born after 1590 and attained manhood before 1641 that the emigrants to America were drawn. Though reliable figures are lacking, recent authorities calculate that between 4,200,000 and 4,460,000 people were living in the realm itself; of the numbers of Welsh, Scots, and Irish we know still less. By 1640 the English and Welsh had risen to about 5,460,000, an increase of almost 30 per cent in spite of the staggering number of deaths from accidents, mounting undernourishment, famine, and pestilence, not to mention the perennial high mortality among infants and mothers. [5]

from home, and believe the world beyond England is boarded off, and that no nation can compare with the English for *virtue* or *comeliness*. . . . Hence so soon as they see a handsome man they say he is an Englishman, or if they believe him a foreigner they say it is a pity he is not English." Peter Mundy, *Travels* (Hakluyt Society, 2d ser., 1946), IV, 50–51; Thomas Platter, *Travels in England,* ed. Clare Williams (London, 1937), 15, 183; Thomas Johnson, *Cornucopiæ* (1596), sig. F 2r; Thomas Gainsford, *The Glory of England* (1618), 304, 207–9.

4. "Newes from Virginia," in C. H. Firth (ed.), *An American Garland* (Oxford, 1915), 13; Robert Reyce, *Suffolk in the Seventeenth Century,* ed. Lord Francis Hervey (London, 1902), 56.

5. The "very rough calculation" for 1603 by W. K. Jordan, *Philanthropy in England 1480–1660* (London, 1959), 26, 63, is used here, as is his estimate of an

In England, as in all Western Europe, the uneven distribution of the population was striking. Perhaps three-fourths of the people lived on the soil amid rural conditions, and four-fifths of these resided south of a line running south-westward from the Wash to the Bristol Channel. We are told that the Thames Valley contained about 20 per cent of all Englishmen, and that the most densely settled counties were, in order, Surrey, Gloucestershire, Somersetshire, and Kent.[6]

Wherever they lived, north or south, in the country or in town, the English found themselves ranged in clearly defined groups. To each of them, such a permanent disposition of men, women, and children into rich and poor, gentle and simple, seemed both right and divinely ordained. The famous apostrophe to the hierarchical ordering of society that William Shakespeare put into the mouth of Ulysses is but the most familiar of many statements on the theory of degrees uttered by such contemporaries as William Harrison and Richard Hooker. These heirs of the late Middle Ages could conceive of no other way to assort individuals in civilized life. "Equality of persons," proclaimed Archbishop Whitgift, "engendereth strife, which is the cause of all evil." [7]

Using the estimates made by Sir Thomas Wilson in 1600, we can distribute English society into the following ranks or degrees: "the men which do not rule"—copyholders, cottagers, urban shopkeepers and artisans, mariners, and displaced persons popularly known as rogues and vagabonds—or, in modern phrase, the "lower classes" (a term which they would not have understood). Altogether these made up about one million heads of families. Then there were those who did rule, the "upper classes" in our parlance: they consisted of some 85,000 yeomen (many of them poor, some rich with £300 to £500 a year from their farms) and the landed gentry, embracing the esquires, knights, bishops, and nobles, that numbered about 16,500. In these pages the concern is

increase of about 30 per cent by 1640. B. H. Slicher Van Bath, *The Agrarian History of Western Europe* (London, 1963), 80, 88; H. C. Darby, *Historical Geography of England* (London, 1963), 435–6, 442.

6. Darby, *Geography*, 360n.

7. "Take but degree away, untune that string,/ And, hark, what discord follows." *Troilus and Cressida*, I, iii, 101–10; Marchette Chute, *Shakespeare of London*, (New York, 1950), 45.

not so much with the over-recorded privileged orders as with the middling and lower sorts of Englishmen.[8]

Notwithstanding the prevalence of this inherited, stratified society, which was based on the still unquestioned belief that family, wealth, and education should determine social position, members from one order were constantly rising or falling into another. What some historians call social mobility existed to a marked degree under the early Stuarts, especially in comparison with the situation in contemporary Continental countries. This ease of moving upward, or downward, had its origin in the British Isles; later, in America, it was merely given ampler scope by transplanted Englishmen.

In London and the great towns, as well as in the countryside, individuals of different ranks freely intermingled—at church, in the market place, at school, in the tavern, before the courts, on the highroad, and at the theater. Familiarity without intimacy with one's betters or inferiors was an experience common to all; today a considerable feat of imagination is required for one merely to grasp at this potent truth. The true snobbery of that age is discovered far more readily in the attitude of most Englishmen toward foreigners than in their behavior toward their own countrymen.

The inhabitants of Albion were a mixture of nearly a dozen ethnic stocks. Commercial relations between Picardy, Normandy, and Brittany and the British Isles induced many French traders to move to London and the ports of the southern coast from Dover and Rye to Plymouth and Fowey. By the 1630's, the growth of the Gallic traffic to Devon alone warranted the formation of a "Society of French Merchants of Exeter" to exercise the trades of merchants and retailers of French commodities. Their leader was Israel Mauduit, whose descendants would play a prominent role in the history of pre-Revolutionary Massachusetts.[9]

---

8. Thomas Wilson, "The State of England Anno Dom. 1600" in *Camden Miscellany,* 3d ser., XVI (London, 1936), 18–23; Sir Thomas Smith, *De Republica Anglorum* (1583), in William H. Dunham and Stanley Pargellis, *Complaint and Reform in England, 1436–1714* (New York, 1938), 212.

9. By the eleventh century, two Mediterranean elements had been added to the basic Upper Paleolithic men of Britain and Ireland: first the Celts (as truly "Nordic" as Anglo-Saxons); then the Danes, Norwegians, Jutes, and Norman French. *CSPD, 1635–6,* p. 235.

The insular position of England served to attract far more than to discourage a steady influx of aliens, a movement that increased after 1560 because of the persistence of conditions disturbing for the ordinary people of Western Europe. Dutch, Walloon, and Flemish artisans and their families had fled to England in the latter part of the sixteenth century from the "Spanish Fury" in the Low Countries; in the seventeenth century they immigrated merely to procure work. In like fashion, persecution in France and the Spanish Netherlands drove Huguenots across the Narrow Seas. "The coast townes of Kent are full of French women and children that come over dayly for feare of troubles in those parts" was the report reaching London in August, 1615. Soon the men were arriving also. By 1635 the French Calvinist Church in Canterbury had nine hundred communicants, most of them Walloons.[10]

Immigration in such numbers inevitably generated new issues —religious, economic, and political. From the English bays- and say-makers of Colchester in 1605 came the age-old complaint of the nativist that the "Dutch strangers" engrossed their trades and practiced the crafts of weaving and roving without serving the legal apprenticeships. On the other hand, as early as 1611 some alien merchants at London petitioned the Earl of Salisbury for a free market outside the City, because they and some traders in the new drapery at Norwich and Colchester suffered unfairly at the hands of the freemen of London who would allow none but freemen of the City to buy or sell in the metropolis.[11]

The Archbishop of York reported in 1636 that the drainers of Hatfield Chase employed "altogether Frenchmen, and a few Dutchmen" on their new lands and maintained a plantation of two hundred families, who worshiped in a barn on the Lincolnshire border under the tutelage of Peter Bontemps, a minister from Leiden. It was the Archbishop's view that these foreigners were of "very mean condition" and had become "vipers nourished in the bosom, that take the bread out of the mouths of English subjects by over-

10. *The Letters of John Chamberlain*, ed. Norman E. McClure (Philadelphia, 1939), I, 612; *Sussex Arch.*, XIII, 200; *CSPD, 1619–23*, pp. 261, 270; *1635*, pp. 69, 283, 408; *VCH Kent*, III, 350–51.
11. *CSPD, 1603–10*, p. 229; *1611–18*, p. 107; *1633–4*, p. 575.

bidding them in rents, and doing more work for a groat than an Englishman can do for sixpence." [12]

The native artisans chiefly resented the fact that strangers were permitted to work in the several crafts without serving as apprentices for the required seven years. The Privy Council learned from a census of aliens in 1616 that there were 1,343 of them exercising 121 different trades in London; the immigrants in Westminster and Middlesex, where they tended to locate, were not included, nor were musicians, painters, "picture-drawers," dancers, and the like. By 1635 the total had risen to 2,547.[13]

"Commissioners for Aliens," appointed in 1621, were instructed by King James to take a yearly count of strangers. Foreign wholesale merchants might continue in business, but all retailers and craftsmen were to be suppressed unless they submitted to the apprenticeship laws, paid quarterage in the several companies, as the English did, and gave bond for compliance.[14]

A year later the Privy Council ordered a general search throughout the kingdom into the numbers, condition, and trades of all strangers and their children. From surviving listings, we find that at Sandwich in Kent in 1622 there was a total of 70 aliens, 2 denizens, and 108 English-born sons of immigrants from the Continent; and that by trades they were makers of bays, serge, and linsey-woolsey, as well as gardeners, tailors, basket-makers, and whitesmiths. The much larger town of Colchester contained 234 alien householders, 379 householders born of "Dutch" parents, 798 children belonging to these families, and 124 servants born out of England. Most of these people were weavers or bays- and say-makers. Similar reports came from Canterbury, Rye, Dover, Norwich, and London. Twelve years later, in the ecclesiastical province of Canterbury, the French and Dutch supported ten Calvinist churches, which Archbishop Laud "knew full well" had to

12. *CSPD, 1636–7*, pp. 13–14.
13. In 1635, Bishopsgate contained 873 "foreigners," most of them weavers who were crowded into small tenements hastily made in large, old houses. They formed a French enclave in the Spitalsfields neighborhood. Newcomers, arriving daily from Dover, had difficulty finding housing. *London*, n. s., VI, 273; *CSPD, 1611–18*, pp. 377, 397; *1625–6*, p. 524; *1635*, pp. 456–7, 591–4.
14. *CSPD, 1619–23*, pp. 280, 304.

be reduced to "a communion with the Church of England" before his plans for reform of the Church itself could be carried out.[15]

By the close of the period, many of these strangers had spread over the eastern and southern counties of England. Their offspring not only ranged about more freely than had their parents, but, by marriage, they had already associated themselves with the English and lost their "foreign" identity just as hundreds of thousands had done in previous centuries.

From the west, across St. George's Channel, came the Irish— Roman Catholics in search of a subsistence they could not gain at home. They made good cargo for the ship owners of the West Country, who sniffed handsome profits from the immigrant traffic. In the summer of 1605, men, women, and children arrived from Erin "in great numbers" and dispersed throughout London and Middlesex. Alarmed, the Privy Council paid to have them rounded up and shipped home again from Bristol, Barnstaple, and other ports of entry.[16]

A series of famines in Ireland induced further importations that reached serious proportions in 1628. Ship owners brought in scores of them to Wales at 3s. a head according to the justices of the peace, who requested an order from the Council to enable them to stop it. The year following, the Corporation of Bristol sought to stay the flow at the source by exporting corn to the stricken land. At the same time, "a multiplicity" of Irish men, women, and children plagued Essex, but the perplexed justices could not apply the poor law because they did not know at what port the Irish had landed. Shropshire also experienced an influx. Devon authorities moved decisively with an order to the constables to take up, punish, and send away "the Irish rogues with which the countrey swarmes." [17]

Obviously the English of the seventeenth century were a mixed breed. A learned scholar of 1635 asserted that twelve languages were spoken in the British Isles, and until that year, at least, immi-

15. *HMC Exeter*, 114–15; *CSPD, 1619–23*, pp. 381, 417; *1635*, p. 275; Peter Heylyn, *Cyprianus Anglicus* (1671), 262, 265.
16. *CSPD, Addenda, 1580–1625*, p. 468.
17. *CSPD, 1628–9*, pp. 358, 442, 495–6; *Shropshire*, 4th ser., II, 48–9; A. H. A. Hamilton, *Quarter Sessions from Queen Elizabeth to Queen Anne* (London, 1878), 105; *Barnstaple Recs.*, II, 135.

gration continued at an excessive rate and created a host of new
social and political problems. Conversely, the French, Walloons,
and Dutch contributed much to English life: they introduced new
words to the language and new patronymics to be mispronounced;
they added sorely needed fruits and vegetables to the monotonous
English diet; and a few contributed capital and taught new methods of finance and engineering. They brought in their strange but
exciting customs, and they altered architectural styles in Kent and
Essex. Eventually some of their children betook themselves and
their different folkways to the new world of America.[18]

It may startle some readers to be told that the strangers in the
land during the decade before the great civil conflict were so numerous, when so many people of old English origin were forsaking
Britain, for one reason or another, to seek prosperity or security
on the continent of Europe or in America.

III

Although, naturally, most rural Englishmen remained rooted on
their holdings, the legend that the men, women, and children who
comprised the farm and laboring families stayed put on any given
farm or village generation after generation is demonstrably facti-
tious. Rather they were a peripatetic lot, shifting here, moving
there, traveling along the roads in incredible numbers. Furthermore, they had been changing locations ever since serfdom began
to disappear in the fifteenth century.

Evidence of this mobility of population can be found in a study
of the villeins who left the Norfolk manor of Forncett, twelve
miles from Norwich, between 1400 and 1565, and settled in sixty-
four different places. Sixty-seven of them moved to thirty-six
neighboring villages within ten miles of Forncett; thirty-eight went
to sixteen communities as much as twenty miles distant; whereas
twenty-one located still farther away in twelve large towns along
the eastern coast of Norfolk, among them Yarmouth and Lowestoft. Most important of all, twenty-two peasants from Forncett
settled down in the great city of Norwich. There is little reason to

18. C. V. Wedgwood, *The King's Peace, 1637–1641* (New York, 1956), 24; E. E.
Rich, in *Ec. Hist. Rev.*, 2d ser., II, 259–62.

suppose that Forncett was not typical in kind, if not wholly so in degree, of many manors that lost population from the fifteenth century right on down to the outbreak of the Great Rebellion. The novel element in these early years of the seventeenth century was that a greater proportion of the population was involved.[19]

The number of Midland families cut adrift now increased as the enclosures, begun in the sixteenth century, continued. More and more hedgerows appeared in those shires and in the Home Counties where, at one time, open fields had been omnipresent. When the displaced farm laborers had to move their families from their old locales, they usually tried to find shelter and employment as near at hand as was possible; at first the search for a livelihood might lead to an adjacent small town, and later, perhaps, to a large country town. For some of the most enterprising, the next move might be to a city such as Norwich, Bristol, or Exeter. One must not fall into the very great error of assuming that all roads led to London, for they did not. Clothworkers, for instance, tended to circulate from one center of their trade to another in Suffolk and Essex, in Kent, or, in the West Country, from Gloucester southward as far as Taunton.[20]

Often overlooked is the effect that marriage and death had on what we may term the normal spreading of population over England. Parish and quarter-session records of most counties yield abundant evidence of this—there were thousands of marriages of people from widely separated communities. The death of a father frequently necessitated the breakup and dispersal of his family. The justices of Woodbridge in Suffolk made provision in October, 1639, for the family of Robert Dawson of Great Bradley. His widow, Anne, came originally from Stambourne, Essex, where her brother, John Levett, followed the trade of a tailor. Anne's youngest child was placed with William Fineham, a cook of Great Bradley (the parish paid half the charge), and the justices sent the

19. Frances G. Davenport, *The Economic Development of a Norfolk Manor, 1086–1565* (Cambridge, Eng., 1906), 97.

20. Waters presents an unusually full and convincing mass of information about the shifting of those rural families whose members migrated to America. At a tithe suit in Merton, Oxfordshire, in 1590, four of the witnesses, who had lived there from eleven to fifty years, had left the parish; the fifth, who farmed in the neighborhood, came from Warwickshire (*Gleanings*, II, 904). *VCH Oxfordshire*, V, 227; M. V. Barley, *The English Farmhouse and Cottage* (London, 1961), 129; Essex Sessions, XVII, 162.

widow and her oldest daughter to live with her brother in the adjoining county. In its very provisions for widows and orphans, the poor law itself served to encourage a considerable movement of population. In the counties of the East and South to which the Continental foreigners came, their children, as we have seen, were very much on the move.[21]

The exigencies of a transformed and expanding economy impelled many a person to change his residence. Towns, cities, and particularly the great metropolis of London required ever more laborers, and their populations mounted through immigration from the country rather than from the birth rate. In this movement the system of apprenticeship played an important role. In 1615 Richard Mitchell, weaver of Witney, Oxfordshire, sent his son Richard to London for seven years' service in the tape-weaver's trade under Libeus Crafte of East Smithfield, whose other 'prentice was Robert Walden, son of a local laborer. John Lay, son of a miller of East Budleigh, was the second lad from the Devon village to be bound before the Corporation of Dartmouth to John Trecky to learn the shipwright's trade. In Hertfordshire in 1641, John Sweeting of Albury, butcher, apprenticed his son Richard to Benjamin Lunt, tailor of nearby Manuden.[22]

Depositions made at the port of Southampton, from whence so many emigrants departed for the colonies, reveal an astonishing movement of individuals between 1600 and 1640. Mariners and sea captains congregated there from all over Britain, and from that port they made their ways homeward after a voyage. Every week Flemings, Dutch, Picards, Normans, and Bretons sailed into the harbor to trade, and carriers took imported goods out over inland routes to exchange for exportable freights. There chapmen filled their packs with articles designed to take in unsuspecting yokels at roadside taverns, town marketplaces, fairs, and at isolated farmsteads. London traders ventured southward in quest of traffic, and country clothiers crowded into Southampton from places as far off as the Midlands and Cornwall.[23]

Commercial needs occasionally induced members of a mercan-

21. *Suffolk*, XV, 153.
22. Slicher Van Bath, *Agrarian History*, 82; *Middlesex Sessions*, n. s., III, 191, 236. Dartmouth Recs., Nov. 27, 1623, *et passim;* Essex Sessions, XX, 545; *Sussex Arch.*, XVI, 26.
23. *Southampton Recs.*, I–IV, *passim.*

tile family to locate in widely separated trading centers. From Guernsey the Jourdaines crossed the Channel to Devon, where they settled at Lyme Regis, Topsham, and Exeter. Before long Ignatius Jourdaine (now Englished to Jordan) went up to London, and in 1620 John Jourdaine made the long voyage to the East Indies. Later connections by marriage of Ignatius can be found at Boston in Massachusetts Bay: John Coggan, its first shopkeeper, the merchant John Hill, and probably Henry Jordan who lived in Charlestown, Massachusetts, and who was the son of Henry Jordan, citizen and cutler of London, belonged to the same family. A combination of trade and religion furnished the incentive for the father of the famous Thomas Shepard to take the radical step of moving his grocery business, inherited from his father-in-law, to Banbury in Oxfordshire from Fossecut, near Towcester, Northamptonshire, because there was "no good ministry in the town." [24]

An arresting note savoring of modern tourism and the building trades was sounded at Southampton in 1639 by John Bodle from Hailsham, Sussex. He had been living high for a month at the Crown when he voluntarily disclosed to the puzzled Mayor and Common Council that he had an inheritance of £10 from Hailsham "and is by profession a bricklayer and that hee doth not use to worke at his profession in the winter time, but doth use to goe abroade to see fashions and confesseth that hee brought to this towne in money about £10 with a mare, but will not discover what he hath spent." No puritan he, who made his mark both by his manner and by his hand.[25]

The story of uprooted persons who wandered about the countryside, burdened the poor rates, annoyed and angered the inhabitants, and aroused the fears of the citizens in the towns is a tale that requires no elaboration. Described variously as sturdy beggars, rogues, and vagabonds, these unfortunates constituted but another element in the internal migration of the English. The brute fact, which must be kept firmly in mind, is that, far from being a settled, stay-at-home folk, Englishmen of all kinds not only were on the move in large numbers before 1640, but nearly all of them

24. Waters, *Gleanings*, II, 1071–4; *Aspinwall Notarial Records* (Boston [Mass.], Rec. Com., XXXII, 1903), 56, 112, 119, 120, 215, 293; *CSM*, XXVII, 357.
25. *Southampton Recs.*, IV, 1.

had come to look upon migration and travel, whether occasional, seasonal, or permanent, forced or voluntary, as a normal accompaniment of their age. It almost seems as if nearly everybody took to the highways at sometime or other. Those who contend that where people are moving about there can be no order should observe the comparative orderliness of early Stuart England.

The extraordinary mobility of the people of the United States in the present century is customarily interpreted as a uniquely American phenomenon, but that this is far from so is made overwhelmingly clear to anyone who studies the local histories of seventeenth-century England. The beginnings of American mobility are in Stuart England.

IV

In families of every degree in the early seventeenth century the birth rate was high, but the death rate was also very high. The average Englishman could look forward to a life span of only thirty to thirty-five years, about the same expectation of a Southeast Asian today and less than half that of his modern descendant. Death was such a frequent occurrence that everyone grew inured to the experience, accepted its inevitability, and never thought of avoiding its presence. People silently agreed with Robert Hegge that one must "digest these common crosses of mortalitie . . . [for] in this world we are but Tenants at will and no man has a lease of his life for a tearme of yeares." The heaviest incidence of death fell upon newborn infants and tiny children; infant mortality appears to have mounted from 1600 to 1640. William Whiteway noted in his diary that the winter of 1619 turned out "very sickly for all sorts of persons, especially of young children. A great number have died since the first of January." [26]

The vital statistics for this period are very meager, but one can say with confidence that there was considerable local variation in death rates and in the virulence of the periodic epidemics. Ordinarily, if a child lived to the age of four, he had a reasonable chance

26. Louis I. Dublin, A. J. Lotka, and M. Spiegelman, *Length of Life* (New York, 1949), 32; Slicher Van Bath, *Agrarian History*, 82; *The Oxinden Letters, 1607–1642*, ed. Dorothy Gardiner (London, 1933), 46; *Dorset*, XIII, 59.

of attaining maturity unless he later fell a victim to one of the diseases that ravaged the land—smallpox and the bubonic plague appeared with alarming frequency and carried off thousands of persons. In addition many women died in childbirth. Little doubt whatever exists that the ratio of deaths to births narrowed, and that, as a consequence, the growth of population slackened in contrast to its marked increase during the reign of Queen Elizabeth.[27]

Everywhere the public betrayed a deep curiosity about long-lived people, and provincial pride burst forth when the chroniclers assured their readers of the salubrity of their native regions. The air of Cheshire is very wholesome, so claimed William Webb of that county; disease is rare, the physicians have no patronage, and the people live to be very old there. At Middlesex Quarter Sessions in August, 1614, the judges excused Thomas Bromley of St. Giles in the Fields for being late for jury duty, because he was "aged almost a hundred yeares." But every such instance of longevity was more than counterbalanced: a man of Kinton in Warwickshire had twenty-seven children between 1639 and 1664, "most of them born alive, yet not one of them lived above a month." It is always possible to cite extreme cases, but death made deep inroads at all levels of age.[28]

In Stuart times many diseases such as scurvy, kidney and bladder stones, and dental decay, all of them caused by vitamin deficiencies and malnutrition, took a heavy toll. Hunger and the frus-

27. Dame Hester Temple of Stowe, Buckinghamshire, had 700 descendants "extracted from her body." With 7 to 16 or more children born to one family, only a high child mortality could have kept the population so low. Thomas Fuller, *History of the Worthies of England* (London, 1811), I, 145; For one populous county, see *Somerset & Dorset*, XV, 75; XX, 148; also Hoskins in *Past and Present*, IV, 57, for a rural parish outside of Exeter; and K. E. Burley, The Economic Development of Essex (Ph.D. Thesis, London, 1957), 22–3, for the unhealthiness of the marsh belt in that county; Slicher Van Bath, *Agrarian History*, 83; Joan Thirsk, *English Peasant Farming* (London, 1957), 140.

28. Mary Waters of Markehill, Essex, died at age 93 in 1620. She had been a widow for 44 years, had borne 16 children, had 114 grandchildren, 228 in the third generation, and 9 in the fourth—a total of 367 descendants, or one for every day in a leap year and one left over. Fuller, *Worthies*, I, 511; William Webb, "Description of Cheshire, 1621," in Daniel King, *The Vale-Royal of England* (London, 1656), 16; *Middlesex Sessions*, n. s., II, 62; *Diary of the Reverend John Ward, 1648–79*, ed. Charles Severn (London, 1839), 98; Daniel Lysons, *The Environs of London* (London, 1792), II, 432, 587; III, 160, 239.

trations of poverty led to widespread alcoholism. Somewhere near half of the population lived on or slightly below the level of subsistence, and they could offer little resistance to communicable diseases. In particular, large numbers of girls and young women between the ages of fourteen and twenty died from tuberculosis; the appalling loss of two-thirds of all infants and children before they reached their fourth year may be attributed in large measure either to tubercular mothers or to the mother's starvation, or both. Nor were the gentry spared these heavy losses: "My niece [Elizabeth] Stukeley was lately brought to bed of a sonne," John Chamberlain wrote to Sir Dudley Carleton, "but the joy lasted not longe, for they both vanished soone thereafter." [29]

The historians of these years have concerned themselves primarily with the affairs of the captains and the kings; very little attention has been given to the women, young girls, and small female children who comprised a substantial majority of the people of England. Though the predominance of males in court circles was pronounced, the women of London outnumbered the men thirteen to ten. This is not surprising, for the women who survived infancy and childbirth lived longer than most men and proved to be tougher physically, even though generally they were not as well nourished. The men often succumbed to the peculiarly male hazards of life at sea or died in the wars or were killed in the amazingly frequent industrial and field accidents. This explains in part the numerous widows in the seaports and other cities and towns as well as in the rural parishes. If we are to recover imaginatively something of the reality of existence in early Stuart England, the stronger and more numerous sex must be accorded its proper place in the scheme of things.[30]

The subordination of women under feudalism and the Christian Church throughout the Middle Ages proved to be so complete and so effective that few challenges to this immutable order occurred much before the accession of Elizabeth. The first treatise explain-

29. Slicher Van Bath, *Agrarian History*, 84–5, 91; Alice Clark, *Working Life of Women in the Seventeenth Century* (New York, 1920), 86–7; Wallace Notestein in *Studies in Social History*, ed. J. H. Plumb (London, 1955), 90–91; Chamberlain, *Letters*, I, 133.
30. Alfred Harbage, *Shakespeare's Audience* (New York, 1941), 76.

ing the complicated and restricted status of the fair sex, assembled
in Tudor days though not published until 1632, was *The Lawes
Resolutions of Women's Rights*. Because of Adam's sin, the compiler held, half apologetically,

> Women have no voyse in Parliament, They make no Lawes,
> they consent to none, they abrogate none. All of them are
> understood either married or to bee married and their desires ar
> subject to their husband, I know no remedy though some
> women can shift it well enough. The Common Law here
> shaketh hand with Divinitie. . . .

Thus, in most instances, did man-made society deny to woman any
part in public life or control of her property. Years later, 1642,
Thomas Fuller could still insist that "the house is the woman's centre," as he elucidated the attitude of his countrymen, for in Jacobean and Caroline times, men in general deeply resented the intru-
sion of women into the hitherto forbidden spheres of trade and the
intellect.[31]

It was the growth and change in the economy that opened more
places for women in business life, and education raised many of
them socially and culturally as their worldly wealth accrued. Puritanism proved a tangible aid in their gradual emancipation. As in
former years, the women helped to educate England's children and
managed households; they aided their spouses in agriculture or
trade, and they nursed them through their illnesses. Soon they
would embark with them, however reluctantly, in the great English
adventure of colonization. The women gave the *coup de grâce* to
the Middle Ages; they were the makers of a modern England. In
succeeding pages we shall observe them in the slow but inexorable
process of carrying out a revolution in the position of their sex—
surely the most far-reaching change of modern times, one which
makes the men's Great Rebellion appear relatively insignificant.

31. Marriage makes a woman and a man one legal person, "Baron and Feme";
"That which the Husband hath is his own," in Section VIII; "That which the
Wife hath is the Husbands," in Section IX. *Lawes Resolutions,* 6, 116, 129, 130;
Thomas Fuller, *The Holy State, and the Profane State* (London, 1841), 2;
Dorothy Stenton, *The English Woman in History* (New York, 1957), 30, 57, 61–
4, 66; Carroll Camden, *The Elizabethan Woman* (Houston, Texas, 1952), 19, 35.

V

We cannot stress too often the small scale of existence in the seventeenth century. This was an era when civil society was little more than a congeries of many very small units, and if we desire a fuller understanding of the mighty part English women were coming to play, we must look for it in the tiniest yet the most important of these—the family. Speaking of this institution, Thomas Gataker declared, "this societie is the first that ever was in the world." In the new order which was slowly forming after the Reformation, the household began to take on an importance that it had never been accorded in feudal days. Its influence reached out into the fields of industry and trade, into religion and education, and eventually into administration and politics; and in many ways it supplanted the old monastic, manorial, and court institutions.[32]

As one might expect, the hoary concept of rank prevailed in the smallest unit of English life. "Within doores there are degrees also," said Gataker, but the classic definition came from the great William Perkins in 1609: "A Familie is a naturall and simple Societie of certaine persons, having mutuall relation one to another, under the private government of one." He held that it takes at least three persons to make a family, "because two cannot make a societie." Inasmuch as most families were large, however, his comment had little reference to actual conditions; a household usually consisted of the husband, wife, and children, the parents and other relations. Frequently servants, apprentices, journeymen, and hired laborers were included. Though Holy Writ emphasized the submission of the wife to the husband, few contemporaries contested the dictum that "shee is a great Officer in the little Common-wealth of the House." If she did not rule by the time-proved devices of indirection, she was conceded to be second in command by the writers on matrimony and the family; they ranked her ahead of the sons, just as the sons came before the daughters and

32. William and Mallevile Haller treat this theme brilliantly in "The Puritan Art of Love," in *Huntington Library Quarterly*, V, 235–72; and another fine study is Chilton L. Powell, *English Domestic Relations, 1487–1653* (New York, 1917); Thomas Gataker, *Marriage Duties Briefely Couched Together. . .* (1620), 3.

the servants. The secret of the well-being of all England, not merely Essex, as the rhyme went, was that the land was "full of good housewives." [33]

As legacies from the medieval Church, all the problems and issues pertaining to the family descended to the English clergy. During the reigns of Elizabeth and James, the presses issued a spate of special writings on the subject. Drawing their authority from the Scriptures, the clerical writers debated and defined the rules and conduct of what they called "Holy Matrimony," by which they meant the married state and the life of the family. In a marriage sermon, Thomas Gataker enumerated the "benefits" a man derived from the society of a good wife:

> The best Companion in Wealth;
> The fittest and readiest Assistant in Worke;
> The greatest Comfort in Crosses and Griefes;
> The only warrantable and comfortable Meanes of Issue and
> posteritie;
> A singular and soveraigne Remedie ordained by God against
> Incontinencie;
> And the greatest Grace and Honour, that can be, to him that
> hath her.

Few men of the day, however, profited so much out of matrimony as Mr. Emmanuel Badd of the Isle of Wight, who, "by God's blessing and the loss of five wives, grew very rich." [34]

Puritans were not the only ones who debated the problems relating to women, marriage, and the family. The heavy emphasis on the godliness of the civil society in this period was both Protestant and English, and it contrasted sharply with the stress on monasticism of the Middle Ages. The Puritans' * concern with the issues

* Throughout this work, *puritan* will be used to designate an *attitude* toward God, the church, morals, and behavior; whereas *Puritan* will refer to a *party* or radical wing of the Church of England.

---

33. Thomas Gataker, *A Good Wife God's Gift* (1623), 3; William Perkins, *Christian Oeconomie* . . . (1609), 2; William Scott, *An Essay of Drapery* . . . (1635), 147.
34. On the Puritan development of the idea of civil marriage, consult Powell, *English Domestic Relations*, 2, 25–6, 42, 48, 51; Thomas Gataker, *A Wife in Deed* (1623), 1–26, 39–40; Christopher Hill, *The Century of Revolution, 1603–1714* (Edinburgh, 1961), 16.

was merely more intense and more persistent, differing in degree but not in kind from that displayed by the Anglican clergy. One has but to compare the elaborate, standard Puritan treatises, such as William Gouge's *Of Domesticall Duties* (1622, 1626, 1634) and Daniel Roger's *Matrimoniall Honour* (1641, 1650) with *The House Holder's Helpe for Domesticke Discipline* (1615), a manual by R. R., and the anonymous *Discourse of the Married and Single Life* (1621), to discover that the only difference between these Anglican treatises and the Puritan models is not the omission of a high moral tone, but their refreshing brevity.

When lay writers of the Anglican persuasion took up the subject, their audience was formed of all Englishmen, and not just Puritans. It is evident that Sir Thomas Overbury addressed himself to a gentle audience. Defining a good woman as "A very, very Woman," he professed that "A Good Woman is a comfort, like a man." About the same time Barnabe Rich addressed his tract on women to all "honorable and worthy Dames, as well wives, widowes, maides, of all estates and degrees, whosoever or whatsoever." Shallow and derivative though he was, Gervase Markham mirrored perfectly the prevailing views about the "English Hus-wife" and her family in his *Country Contentments,* which was first published in 1615, reached a fifth edition by 1638, and was still a standard manual in 1657. These and similar popular works by laymen enjoyed a great and prolonged vogue and unquestionably reached a wider audience than the treatments of the family by either the plays of London or the printed sermons of the Puritan preachers.[35]

During the half-century from 1590 to 1640, the family became ever more influential in charting the course of English society. To

35. "Our English Hus-wife," this paragon who is the mother and mistress of the family, "who has employment indoors generally," said the demanding Markham, "must bee of chast thought, stout courage, patient, untyred, watchfull, diligent, witty, pleasant, constant in friendship, full of good neighbour-hood, wise in discourse, but not frequent therein, sharpe and quicke of speech, but not bitter or talkative, secret in her affaires, comfortable in her counsels, and generally skilled in the worthy knowledges which doe belong to her vocation. . . ." Gervase Markham, *Country Contentments, or the English Huswife* (1623), 4; Sir Thomas Overbury, *A Wife Now the Widdow of Sir Thomas Overbury, Being a Most exquisite and singular Poem of the Choice of a Wife* (1614), n. p.; Barnabe Rich, *The Excellency of Good Women* (1613); Alexander Nichols, *A Discourse of Marriage and Wiving. . .* (1615), in *Harleian Miscellany* (London, 1808), II, 156–86; Scott, *Essay of Drapery*.

be sure, it had always been economically and socially essential, but it grew steadily more so. The cumulative effect of the Reformation, together with Scriptural authority, gave the family a religious role that enabled it virtually to challenge the Church. For this reason there can be no understanding of the English people apart from their religious life.

The bases of this divinely ordained household are to be found in the husband and the wife. *The Geneva Bible,* the book of the Puritans, taught that "Masters in their houses ought to be as preachers to their families, that from the highest to the lowest they may obey the will of God." William Gouge spoke not merely for Puritans but for all of England when he described the family as "a little Church, and a little common-wealth . . . whereby triall may be made of such as are fit for any place of authoritie, or of subjection in Church or common-wealth. Or rather it is as a schoole wherein the first principles and grounds of government and subjection are learned: whereby men are fitted to greater matters in Church or common-wealth." [36]

Such sentiments as these, as well as injunctions for family prayers and catechizing, appear in the Anglican devotional literature of the time, notably in the thirty-six or more editions that Bishop Bayly's *The Practise of Piety* went through between 1612 and 1636; and none other than the judicious Hooker told Englishmen that "to fathers within their private families Nature hath given a supreme power; for which cause we see throughout the world even from the foundation thereof, all men have ever been taken as lords and lawful kings in their own houses." [37]

36. The Hallers and Mr. Hill both emphasize the Puritan element in "the spiritualization of the household," and I agree with them, but it seems to me that they overlook the vital fact that many Anglican families passed through much the same development despite the official designation of the parish as the lowest unit for religious discipline. The Roman Catholics also had perforce to make more of the family in England than their hierarchy recognized. See Christopher Hill, *Society and Puritanism in Pre-Revolutionary England* (London, 1964), chap. XIII, and especially pp. 446–7, 454; marginal note to Genesis, 17:27, *Geneva Bible* (London, 1608); Haller and Haller, "Puritan Art of Love," 246; William Gouge, *Of Domesticall Duties* (1622), 18.

37. Lewis Bayly, *The Practise of Piety* (1622); Helen C. White, *English Devotional Literature [Prose], 1600–1640* (Madison, 1931), 13, *et passim;* Richard Hooker, *Of the Laws of Ecclesiastical Polity* (Everyman's ed., London, 1907), I, 191.

The family being under divine ordinance, it followed that it should be formed with the greatest care. To the Protestant mind, celibacy was both popish and unsuited to a civilized community, and dwelling apart from others was bad for both religion and morals. "Marriage fills the Earth, and Virginity Heaven," wrote Scott, adding a note, "how should Heaven be filled, if the Earth were empty." Whatever their rank in society, the English all agreed about the desirability of the married state. "Pray if my sister Elizabeth may marry well in London, not to neglect itt," Henry Oxinden of Kent urged his mother in 1639, "for good husbands are hard to bee got here." Many families thus reached out from their counties for partners for their daughters and thereby further contributed to the movement of population.[38]

One has the impression that, save for the very poor, most English marriages in town as well as country were arranged, at least in part, by the parents. In 1641 Henry Best described the fashion "att our Country Weddinges" in Yorkshire. First, the young man, or his father, wrote to the maid's father; and if his suit was approved, he called twice to "see howe the mayd standeth affeckted." If she was "affeckt" and willing on his first visit, he gave her ten shillings in gold or a ring, or perhaps as much as 20s. in gold. On the second visit he brought gloves worth 6s. 8d. or 10s. After that, each time he called he brought along some toy or novelty of less value until the wedding. The parents treated about the dowry and set the wedding day. Clothes were assembled, the dinner prepared for, and gloves (paid for by the groom) were sent to close friends. The wedding day was a gala occasion and full of earthy merriment accompanied by a heavy consumption of "love wine." [39]

Once a match had been agreed upon by the parents of both parties, the betrothal (a verbal pledge before witnesses) took place. Betrothal was a most serious matter, and, once effected, it could not be broken legally except on the authority of a bishop for reasons of proved fornication (especially by either party with kindred of the other), disease, or violent casualty making one unfit for

38. Scott admitted that marriage was an impediment to great enterprise and that the best works of merit proceeded from the unmarried, who had more liberty, but he concluded that it was commendable for a citizen to marry. Scott, *Essay of Drapery*, 148–9; *Oxinden Letters*, 144.

39. Henry Best, in *Surtees*, XXXIII, 116–17; *HMC Buccleuch*, III, 366.

generation. Customarily marriage followed shortly after the betrothal, for, as Moll Barnes declaimed in *The Two Angry Women of Abington:*

> Short wooing is the best, an howre, not yeares,
> For long debating love is full of feares.

Sometimes a contract covering the dowry and property of the bride was involved, which not infrequently led into court. The marriage contract of the diarist William Whiteway, Jr., and Eleanor Parkins of Dorchester was concluded on April 6, 1620. On May 4, "in my father Parkins his hall about 9 of the clock at night," the betrothal ceremony was celebrated in the presence of Master John White,* the parents, and relatives. Mr. White married the couple on June 14 at Holy Trinity "in the presence of the greatest part of the town." [40]

Whatever the duration of the courtship, good taste decreed that the lovers should act becomingly. As for the young man, Richard Brathwaite taught that (in striking contrast with our own day):

> He may expresse his love with modestie,
> Yet never coll and kisse in open place,
> For I should deeme such love hypocrisie
> Or some such thing; if I were in her case.
> And better is love showne in privacie
> Then 'fore the eies of men. . . .[41]

---

* During the decades covered in this volume, the adjective *Reverend* was never placed before a clergyman's name. He was called Master (abbreviated Mr.) because with few exceptions he was a Master of Arts.

---

40. George Raven of Swanton Morley Parish was excommunicated for having "lewdlie ran awaie" after contracting to marry Marie Lincolne in 1597. *Norfolk,* XVIII, 54; for details on marriage negotiations and an agreement in 1651 (but which had not changed since 1642), see *Surtees,* XLII (II), 62–80; *Lawes Resolutions,* 55–60, Henry Porter, *The Two Angry Women of Abington* (1599), in *Tudor Facsimile Texts* (1911); *Dorset,* XIII, 59.

41. It would be interesting to know what Mr. Brathwaite would have had to say about the lack of taste displayed by a woman referred to in an account of January, 1639: "A gentleman carried his wife to London last week, and died about 8 at night, leaving her £500 in land. The next day before 12 she was married to a journeyman woollen-draper that came to sell mourning to her"!! *HMC Gaudy,* X, 172; Musophilus [Richard Brathwaite], *The Good Wife, or a rare one amongst Women* (1618), n. p.

There were some marriages then, as always, of couples who dispensed with the formalities. Alice Smith of Wimbourne Parish, Dorset, procured from an ecclesiastical court in 1599 an affirmation of marriage. When she and Robert Yates agreed to marry, he said: "Heare; Alice, I doe give thee my faithe and trothe to marrye with thee, and do take thee to my wieffe; and I will never marrye with any other but thee whilst I live." To which she replied, "And I doe take you to my husband and doe give you my faithe and trothe." Then they kissed and shook hands without benefit of parents or clergy. When families proved intractable, abduction or elopement was resorted to. In 1607 Joan, wife of a laborer, Christopher Ward of Hogsden, stood charged in the Middlesex Quarter Sessions "with consentinge to take away a young gentlewoman from her parentes by night." She and her husband were bound in £20 and £30 to appear at the next sessions, all of which proves that such actions took place in real life as well as in plays.[42]

Although the marriage counselors and immemorial custom dictated that the parents arrange all matches out of policy, sensible writers, like William Gouge, wanted young men and women to marry for love. The ideal was a well-planned love match. In urban communities young people had more of a choice than in the rural regions. Timothy's remark that he must consult his friends before starting a courtship drew only contempt from Plotwell in *The City Match:*

> How! Friends; consent? that's fit
> For none but farmers' sons and milkmaids.
> You shall not debase your judgment.
> She takes you for a wit. And you shall
> Match her like one.[43]

As more people moved into the cities and towns or became rootless wanderers about the countryside, such marriage arrangements as described above became impossible, and the number of unsuitable and unhappy unions created mounting concern. Writer after writer, Puritan and Anglican, lay and clerical, published tracts on

42. Fletcher in *Dorset*, XLVII, 44–5; *Middlesex Sessions*, II, 30.
43. Camden, *Elizabethan Woman*, 66; Jasper Mayne, *The City-Match* (1639), II, vii, in R. Dodsley (ed.), *Select Collection of Old Plays* (London, 1825).

courtship and marriage. Mainly they counseled prospective husbands to proceed with the utmost caution in choosing a mate. "It is
not evill to marry, but it is good to be warie," or, as an old
proverb put it, "There belongeth more to marriage than two payre
of bare leggs." Deftly weighing the pros and cons of marriage, the
author of *A Discourse of the Married and Single Life, Wherein the
Misery of the One, is plainely declared the felicity of the other*
sought to steer between "Scylla and Charibdis." His comments are
often acid, and he presents a dismal picture of the married state:

> Sometimes at marriages Walnuts are scattered up and downe;
> which sheweth that a woman is like unto a Walnut, that hath a
> great shell; faire without, but rotten within: to pull off the first
> barke, we use to bruise them in our handes, and to breake the
> second, wee indanger our teeth.
>
> What fruit maketh more noyse than a Walnut when it is
> broken? [44]

On page 115, however, marriage finally triumphs.

In general, the writers seemed more concerned that the man
choose a good wife than that the woman find a suitable husband.
Robert Furse of Moreshead, Devonshire, in his testament to posterity enjoined the greatest care about marriage. One should select
a wise and prudent woman, and should inquire diligently what her
mother's "quallytis and maners" were like, for like mother, like
daughter. Barnabe Rich warned: "It is a hard matter therefore in
this age to distinguish betweene the good woman and the bad," because they all "pranck up themselves in their light and gaudy attire." He found many a woman to be "impudent, immodest,
shameless, insolent, audacious, a night walker, a company keeper,
a gadder about the streets." Gataker prophesied that utter ruin will
come where women "affect mastership; seek to rule and overrule"
their husbands. Such forwardness is on the rise, and every woman
must "learne to know her place and her part." The whole of matrimony is a godly business, and a man can never be too circum-
spect.[45]

44. Gataker, *A Good Wife*, 7; Proverb quoted by Camden, *Elizabethan Woman*,
79; *A Discourse of the Married and Single Life. . .* (1621), 11, 96.
45. *Devonshire*, XXVI, 172; Rich, *Good Women*, 5–6, 32; Gataker, *Marriage
Duties*, 10.

In a more positive vein, Gervase Markham declared that a prospective wife must be "of an upright and sincere religion, and in the same both zealous and constant. . . . I doe not meane that herein shee should utter forth that violence of spirit which many of our (vainly counted pure) women do, drawing a contempt upon the ordinary Ministerie, and thinking nothing lawefull but the fantazies of theire owne inventions, usurping to themselves a power of preaching and interpreting the holy word, to which merely they ought to be hearers and beleevers, or at most but modest persuaders, this is not the office either of Hous-wife or good woman." Next to sanctity and holiness, the infallible marks of a good woman were modesty, bashfulness, silence, abstinence, and sobriety. Such virtues were fundamental, because, as Gataker held, the wife's duties were to begin at the lower tasks and progress to the higher, always to give way first, and, especially "to shew the inferioritie of the wife in regard of the husband." [46]

Thus was early Stuart society securely founded upon the family, and kinship was the sure key to success for all ranks of Englishmen. Marriage came much later for the English peasant than for the people in town, because the countryman could not marry and set up a home until the family holding passed to him. Children soon arrived to take their proper and subordinate places in the little commonwealth and church. The birth rate was high and families were large in spite of the high mortality among infants. James Herriott, Esq., who married Elizabeth Josey, a gentlewoman of Bermondsey, in 1625, was one of forty offspring of a Scottish father.[47]

Anglican and Puritan families alike sought to raise their children according to Holy Writ. The sanctions of the state Church buttressed family discipline and worship. We shall note in detail later that strictness prevailed, and little hands were given tasks to perform: Thomas Shepard at the mere age of three years "was put to keepe geese and other such cuntry worke" by his grandparents. Then, as now, parents may have taken infinite pains with their offspring, but some of them were obstreperous, unruly, and even vicious. At the Deanery Court of South Malling, Sussex, in 1614

46. Markham, *Country Contentments*, 2–4; Gataker, *Marriage Duties*, 5, 7.
47. Lysons, *London*, 555.

and again in 1620, the churchwardens presented John Beldam for "abusing of his parents and seeking the means of vexation of his neighbors." When the Anglican priest Nehemiah Rogers preached on "The Parable of the Lost Sonne," he held that many parents were deficient in respect to education, and if the children proved lewd, though it was the Devil's work, still the parents must not despair but continue to work hard at their duty.[48]

Despite the steady growth of puritan temper and the power of the household, the historian can perceive a slight but progressive undermining of the traditional life and ways of the little commonwealth in the decades before numbers of Englishmen left their homeland and went out to America. The records of the local courts reveal that the enclosures and other agrarian difficulties resulted in the dispossession of many rural families and augmented the shifting of population. Even when householders stayed on their land, it was normal for sons to go off to other villages, towns, or cities to earn a living; sometimes they ran away to sea to escape parental control. Daughters too departed occasionally. Thomas Richardson of West Mill, Hertfordshire, husbandman, bequeathed sums of money to each of three sons but left nothing to a fourth son, Ezekiel, because he had migrated to New England against his father's wishes. Periodic visitations of the plague possibly dealt the family its severest blow by carrying off the members indiscriminately, leaving survivors to shift for themselves. Differences over religious affairs were more and more dividing parents and children—even husbands and wives—into Anglicans, Puritans, or Separatists.[49]

There were other strains on family ties. With woman's rise in importance and self-respect, she did not always display the submissive attitude taught by the books; the aggressive female had begun to march. Gataker had warned that the worst evil of marriage was "a contentious woman," and he went on to say that "an

48. For a New England Puritan tract on this subject, see Thomas Cobbet, *A Fruitful and Useful Discourse Touching the Honour due from Children to Parents and the Duty of Parents Toward their Children* (London, 1656); *CSM*, XXVII, 358; *Sussex Arch.*, L, 42–3; Nehemiah Rogers, "The Parable of the Lost Sonne," in *The True Convert* (1631), Part III, 6; Hill, *Society and Puritanism*, 454–5.
49. *NEHG Reg.*, LVII, 298–9.

evill wife is as the raine dropping in thorow the tiles, that maketh him weary of the house, that vexeth him so that it driveth him out of doores." William Gouge deplored the fact that there were many wives "who thinke themselves every way as good as their husbands, and no way inferior to them." [50]

Denied divorce by law, except in rare instances, many an Englishman, convinced that he suffered from an evil wife, seized the first opportunity to get away from her and his family responsibilities. Some of the men of Norfolk who had been divorced—and even a few who were married—took second wives in defiance of the law. The churchwardens of Birchington in Kent presented Thomas Smith "for dwelling in our parish and having a wife and not living with her according to law." The hundred jury of Tendring, Lexden, Winstree, and Thurstable presented John Johnson of Wivenhoe, carpenter, to the Essex Quarter Sessions in 1627 "for keeping away from his family and neglecting to relieve them for the space of 5 years, and [because he] hath frequented an alehouse all this time, William Harvey's of Wivenhoe." In addition it was alleged that Johnson kept a greyhound, ferrets, and a net, and yet did not have lands worth forty shillings a year. He had also dug "a sawpit" in the middle of the street, an annoyance for 5 years," and laid timber there! [51]

Tiring of marriage was not confined to men; as the years passed, many women found ways and means to escape the tyranny of the smug male. At Essex Archdeaconry Court, Catherine Key de-

50. A marginal note on Gouge's *Domesticall Duties* reads: "Of all that are inferiours, the wife cometh neerest to a paritie," 271; Camden, *Elizabethan Woman*, 35; Gataker, *A Good Wife*, 4–8.

51. Unlike the rich, poor people could not afford to seek divorce in such instances where it was permissible. G. Feilding wrote to Lord Feilding in 1635: "your sister, my Lady Desmond, is now suing a divorce of your brother, accused of that I have hard few Feildings guiltie of, insufficiencie to please a resonable woman." *HMC Denbigh*, Pt. V, 14; Mr. Kettel, a schoolmaster of Ramsey, was haled before the Archdeaconry Court in 1604 for living in Essex apart from his wife and family, "for setting up debate between neighbours, and for being a tale carter." The court ordered him "to live with his wife where she is or else bring her to live with him and that he is not to teach any more in the parish." Essex Arch., X, 72b; *Kent*, XXV, 12; Essex Sessions, XX, 104; *CSPD, 1637–8*, p. 313; *Middlesex Sessions*, n. s., I, 172, 173, 378; and for "speeches" at a remarriage of a husband and a wife (who had taken a second husband) in 1604, see Lysons, *London*, I, 554–5.

more knowledge and pleasure through the ear than by the eye. At London and in the provincial cities, Englishmen thronged to plays. Everywhere in the land the men, women, and children listened to sermons, those inclined toward Puritanism most of all; they heard the Bible read daily at family worship. In taverns and at the market crosses—in dozens of ways—men heard the latest gossip and advices. If the playgoing apprentices at the bankside became half-intoxicated on the gorgeous rhetoric of *Tamburlaine,* thousands of less sophisticated folk felt the compelling excitement of religious exhortations from a thousand pulpits and pieced out with their imaginations what they were told about the New World.

The speech of London and the Thames Valley was, by 1611, well on its way to becoming the crisp, clear English used by King James's scholars in translating the Bible. When the King James Version first appeared, an old laborer of Northamptonshire told Thomas Fuller that it "agreeth perfectly with the common speech of our country [county]." Already the Londoner could be distinguished from the countryman by his speech, and, moreover, a person's place in society became apparent with the first words he uttered. When Rosalind sought to pass as a native lad in the Forest of Arden, Orlando exclaimed: "Your accent is something finer than you could purchase in so removed a dwelling." [57]

Though the Scots, Welsh, and Cornish conversed in tongues few Englishmen could understand, and in Yorkshire and other remote counties the local dialects proved well-nigh incomprehensible, good usage was spreading rapidly throughout the south of England. In 1618 Robert Reyce asserted that the "gentility and learned scholars" of rural Suffolk spoke the same English as their kind elsewhere, without a characteristic dialect or idiom:

> Howbeit I must confesse our honest Country toyling villager to expresse his meaning to his like neighbour, will many times lett slip some strang different sounding tearmes, no wayes intelligible to any of civill education. . . . Butt this being only of the ruder sort, the *artificer of the good townes,* scorneth to follow them when he naturally prideth in counterfitt imitation of the

57. Fuller, *Worthies,* II, 157; *As You Like It,* III, ii, 359–60.

best sort of language, and therefore noe cause to observe any therein.[58]

One quality of the everyday vernacular was the persistence of medieval rural habits of thought and expression in picturesque metaphors and figures of speech—agricultural, feudal, military— to which Biblical and nautical terms were continually being added. Shakespeare knew very well that his city audience would understand when the servant in a play remarks of his master's greed: "Sir, for a quart d'ecu he will sell the fee-simple of his salvation, the inheritance of it, and cut the entail from all remainders, and a perpetual succession for it perpetually." Thomas Fuller saw nothing strange in a man of the cloth characterizing some people as those "who would sooner creep into a scabbard then draw a sword." [59]

In the West Country, the steward of Berkeley, John Smyth of Nibley, collected and lovingly set down "Phrases and proverbs of speech proper to this hundred." With pride, all spoke of "We hundreders." A "y" was always inserted between consonants, as in "sit y downe," and "my mal is a good y wenche." "Thick and thuck" for this and that "rush out with us at every breath." [60]

A feature of early seventeenth-century speech that most strikes the modern student is the extensive use of proverbs, many of which had a medieval origin. When this listening people did speak, they usually drew on the hundreds of sayings which pithily embodied current forms of folk wisdom. Every plain country fellow and his dame, John Earle discovered, "has some thrifty hobnail proverbs to clout his discourse." Such clichés performed a very useful task, for most Englishmen contented themselves with the authority of the saying, leaving more sophisticated and argumentative talk to their cultivated betters. Many of the proverbs, universally known and repeated almost daily, tell us much that we would like to know

58. On the widespread use of the Cornish language as late as 1600, see *Western Antiquary*, III, 115–16; Reyce, *Suffolk*, 55 (italics mine).
59. *All's Well that Ends Well*, IV, iii, 311; Fuller, *Holy and Profane State*, 148.
60. John Smyth of Nibley, *The Berkeley Manuscripts. The Lives of the Berkeleys . . . from 1066 to 1618, with a Description of the Hundred of Berkeley* (Gloucester, 1883–5), III, 22–3.

about simple, mundane matters. John Ward, for instance, deemed it significant enough to record in his diary in 1661 his realization that "Our English proverb which expresses women's lyin-in, by being *in the straw,* argues that feather beds are not auncient." [61]

Learned writers drew inspiration from the sayings of "the rude multitude" just as the great romantic musicians levied upon folk tunes for symphonic themes. Proverbs served Shakespeare amply and well in the speeches of his ordinary characters. "Some rise by sin, some by virtue fall." "Pitchers have ears." "There's small choice in rotten apples." "Wives may be merry, and yet honest too." The epigrams of Francis Bacon owed much to the proverbs: "There is a cunning which we in England call 'the turning of the cat in the pan' which is when that which a man says to another, he lays it as if another had said it to him." In compiling his *Worthies of England,* Fuller thought it worthwhile to quote one or more of the proverbs characteristic of each county. "A London jury; hang half, save half." Nottingham: "Many talk of Robin Hood, who never shot in his bow." Enterprising John Heywood gathered *Three Hundred Epigrammes, Upon Three Hundred Proverbs,* which he published at London, confident that there would be a good sale for such an anthology. The proverbs are numbered, and many are printed without any gloss, such as "Poore men have no soules, have riche men anie?" [62]

In many of the proverbs, the extreme earthiness and barnyard gaminess so characteristic of the rural English comes out unabashed. "He that's cooled with an apple, and heated with an egge, over me shall never spread his legg," was termed by John Smyth, steward of Nibley, "a widowe's wanton proverb." He also interpreted "Its merry in the hall when the beards wag all," one of the most widely quoted proverbs, to mean that when the men are eating the women are dancing. [63]

61. Huizinga, *Middle Ages,* 229–30; John Earle, *Microcosmography* (1628), ed. Harold Osborne (London, 1933), 53; Ward, *Diary,* 113 (italics mine).
62. Fuller, *Worthies,* 5, 54, 57, 59, 205; John Heywood, *Three Hundred Epigrammes, Upon Three Hundred Proverbs* (1598), 2, 10, 167.
63. John Heywood thought it necessary to clean up the proverb in a fashion that probably would have made John Smyth smile:

It is merry in the hall when beards wagge all.
Husband for this, these Wordes to mynd I call:

That the ordinary countryman fully realized the value of proverbs is seen in their widespread use as house mottoes set over hearths or in some equally prominent place. In Buckinghamshire there is one which reads:

> If thou speakest evil of thy neighbour
> Come not nigh the door of this house.

And it is followed by a postscript:

> Peace on earth, good will towards Women.[64]

In the years from 1620 to 1640, many English men and women sought their own new worlds across the broad Atlantic, and, as part of their mental outfit (in Edward Eggleston's classic phrase), they took with them their folk wisdom in proverbial form. Much of this survived and nourished the culture of a new people. But it is not in *Poor Richard's Almanac,* in which Benjamin Franklin distilled so many of these proverbs, that one reads:

IMPROVE THE TIME

This motto, which Franklin revised to "Remember that TIME is Money" in his *Advice to a Young Tradesman* (1748), can still be made out on the south side of the beautiful tower of the decorated Gothic Church of St. Dionysius at Market Harborough in Leicestershire.[65]

> This is ment by men in their merry eating
> Not to wag their beards in brawling and threatening.
> Wife, the meaning hereof differeth not two pinnes,
> Between wagging of men's beards and womens chins.

Heywood, *Epigrammes,* No. 2; *Berkeley Manuscripts,* III, 26–33.
64. *Country Life,* XIII, 107.
65. Copied by the author on the spot in August, 1962; *The Papers of Benjamin Franklin,* ed. Leonard Labaree (New Haven, 1961), III, 306–8.

II

Country People

IN A TRACT of 1618, Nicholas Breton has *A Countryman* discourse with *A Courtier* in Vergilian vein about the comforts and satisfactions of life in the English countryside: "We have good husbands and honest widows; pure virgins and chaste batchelors; learned churchmen and civil townsmen; wholesome fare, full dishes, white bread, and hearty drink; clean platters and fair linen; good company, friendly talk, plain music and a merry song: and so when God is praised and the people pleased, I think there is no course where a man may be better contented." To a city-bred man, the country appeared to be naught but "the great Circumference of London [and] . . . the Emblem of the City in Folio." Hyperbolic as both of these statements are, the country was the scene that most Englishmen knew best and loved most. John Milton evoked nostalgic memories for all his readers when he wrote of Satan, who:

> Forth issuing on a summer's morn to breathe
> Among the pleasant villages and farms
> Adjoined, from each thing met conceives delight:
> The smell of grain, or tedded grass, or kine,
> Or dairy, each rural sight, each rural sound. . . .[1]

1. Nicholas Breton, *The Court and Country* (1618), in Dunham and Pargellis, *Complaint and Reform*, 460; Donald Lupton, *London and the Country Carbonadoed and Quartered* . . . (1632), 97; "Paradise Lost," ix, 444–51, in *The Poetical Works of John Milton* (New York, n. d.), 207.

Though no precise figures are available, we may estimate that, from 1590 to 1640, more than 70 per cent of all the English lived in the country in tiny village communities, or, in some counties, on isolated farms. Moreover, of those who dwelt in the many small market towns, provincial cities, or in the great metropolis itself, a considerable majority had been born and reared in rural surroundings. In every respect, the English were a pastoral folk that "discovered loveliness only where they could discern fruitfulness." [2]

The outstanding trait of all the country people was provinciality. Their intense love of their own locality came down from the Middle Ages, and the rural Englishman rightly thought of himself as being to the manor born. The very complex geological formation of the country lent itself to localism: the terrain (much more varied than that of any country of comparable size in Europe) and the diversity of rocks and subsoil deposits all combined to produce local dissimilarities in agriculture, building materials, institutions, and in the people themselves. One had but to travel a few miles in any direction to be aware of these differences, even in areas of small compass. Thomas Fuller singled out Kent "for its local attachments and prejudices," but such qualities and attributes could be ascribed to virtually every county, and to certain districts within the larger ones. Lincolnshire's location isolated its inhabitants, particularly the fen dwellers, from the outer world; in their ignorance they took an aversion to foreigners—"the natives' first inclination was to throw a stone at them." [3]

Although localism was conspicuous in early Stuart England, there also existed accompanying uniformities which, if overlooked, would result in a distorted history. The country as a whole, for in-

2. W. K. Jordan thinks it "probable that in 1600 at least eight of every ten Englishmen were rural dwellers . . . if we may include . . . those living in some scores of small market towns which belonged to the countryside on which they had grown. . . ." *The Charities of Rural England, 1480–1660* (New York, 1962), 17; "They perceived no romantic beauty in wildness and solitude; to be barren was a disfigurement." Eva G. R. Taylor, *An Atlas of Tudor England and Wales* (London, 1951), 8.
3. Alec Clifton-Taylor, *The Pattern of English Building* (London, 1962), 21, and especially the two end-maps; F. J. Fisher, "The Sixteenth and Seventeenth Centuries: The Dark Ages in English Economic History," in *Economica*, n. s., XXIV, 9; Fuller, *Worthies*, I, 531; J. W. F. Hill, *Tudor and Stuart Lincoln* (Cambridge, Eng., 1956), 7.

stance, was enjoying a marked prosperity that had evolved from widespread economic changes. More than anything else, these changes were undermining English local life and institutions without supplying the ordinary people with the necessary understanding or skills for coping with the new conditions. Again, general as the prosperity was, it was not universally experienced. Thus, even in this investigation of conditions common to all of the king's subjects, local variations must be taken into account.[4]

II

With the opening of the seventeenth century came a renewed interest in country life that developed, possibly, as a reaction to the unprecedented urban growth of England. Most writers enthusiastically discussed the country gentleman and the yeoman, but Thomas Powell, in 1631, stated the case for the husbandman. He argued that "for the happy content of the life and the honest gain which it brings with it," the occupation of a husbandman should appeal to "a good man's son." Minimizing the hardships and glossing over the particulars, Powell laid down certain requisites: a judicious mixture of the gentle and the rustic, for "if the clown be predominant, he will smell all brown bread and garlic. Besides, he must be of a hardier temper than the rest of his brethren, because the unhealthfullest corners of the kingdom are the most profitable for farmers." [5]

The peasants, who constituted about 80 to 90 per cent of the entire rural population, were neither the highest nor the lowest in the social order. They did not question the concept of the arrangement or think of it in theoretical terms at all. From time out of mind there had always existed a few at the top who enjoyed wealth, privilege, and power, and, at the bottom of society, "the mutable, rank scented many." This stratification was apparent to all, even to the inhabitants of small village communities; indeed it seemed to them but a fitting and proper expression of the actual

4. While according local variety its proper place, the writer has tried studiously to steer a middle course between easy, inaccurate, low-level generalizations and no generalizations at all.
5. Thomas Powell, *Tom of all Trades* (1631), in Dunham and Pargellis, *Complaint and Reform*, 573.

facts of existence. Philip Kinder, writing of Derbyshire, insisted that "the common sort of people out of a genuine reverence, not forced by feare or institution, doe observe those of larger fortunes; courteous and readie to shew the waye to helpe a passenger." [6]

Only a small minority of the agricultural population were free-holders, and their land did not produce the forty shillings a year required for suffrage. The great body of the peasantry, landless men whom contemporaries described as "poor husbandmen," included numerous copyhold and leasehold tenants along with the cottagers living as tenants-at-will on plots of four acres or less. Below them ranged the many day laborers who worked for wages on the lands of the yeomen and gentry. The rural artificers, such as tailors, shoemakers, carpenters, bricklayers, masons, and the craftsmen who worked in the growing cloth industry of the countryside, were aligned with the hired workers. All these, the rude, inferior sort of people, had "neither voice nor authoritie in the commonwealth," as William Harrison made clear, but were "to be ruled, and not to rule other" men.[7]

Across the land, the proportions of landholders and landless persons differed widely. Between 1610 and 1640 at Weyhill, an open-field village of Hampshire, forty-four inhabitants held their land "by copie of the court roll," and about forty had no land at all. William Lambarde thought that Kent contained fewer copy-holders than the West Country and not so many "feeble tenants" as in the North of England. Reporting on Devon, Westcote deemed that the "meaner husbandman" and the rustics who labored for a daily or annual wage, such as hedgers, ditchers, reapers, shepherds, and herdsmen, formed a very large class. The trend which a writer noted in Devonshire in 1632 applied pretty generally to the entire countryside: "The meanest sort of people also will now rather place their children to some of these mechanical trades than

6. Unlike most Continental countries, England had few bondsmen or villeins, and no slaves. For the survival of villeinage in the seventeenth century, see Savine, in *RHS Trans.*, n. s., XVII, 236–86; *CSPD, 1603–10*, p. 111; Hill, *Century of Revolution*, 43; William Harrison, *A Description of England . . .* [1577, 1587], ed. F. J. Furnivall (New Shakespeare Society, London, 6th ser., 1877), Pt. I, 134–6; Philip Kinder, *Historie of Derbyshire*, ed. W. G. D. Fletcher (London, 1883), 181.
7. Hill, *Century of Revolution*, 43; Harrison, *England*, Pt. I, 134.

to husbandry." A well-informed authority has recently concluded that in the countryside as a whole, "at least one man in three was a wage-earner." [8]

These husbandmen of the inferior sort and the laborers must be classed among the poor of England. The "hireling, as meanest," so Westcote said, "is last remembered"—long hours in the fields, low wages, uncertain and seasonal employment, and, always, very hard work were the lot of the plain country fellow. No wonder Earle described him as one who "manures his ground well, but lets himself lie fallow . . . for his conversation is among beasts. . . . His hand guides the plough, and the plough his thoughts, and his ditch and landmark is the very mound of his meditations." This fellow says "Gee" and "Ree" better than English.[9]

Personal histories of peasants are hard to come by. Now and then we catch a glimpse of one of them in the records when he is snared by economic conditions and falls from his station into the great classless multitude of the unemployed and unemployable "wanderinge persons." Though a healthy husbandman and able to work, Gray Fitch of Bocking had neither land, nor a master, nor a lawful craft to work at in 1611. Because he belonged "to the inferior sorte of people" and seemed indisposed to give up "his roguish kynde of life," the justices ordered him apprehended as a "sturdy beggar" along with two laborers, Stephen Worste of his village and Thomas Wayte of Chelmsford, and several others of the same stripe. Not a few of the more reckless ones took recourse to stealing. At the Michaelmas Session in 1637, the Essex justices had Thomas Fuller from Upminster whipped for the theft of fourteen "wheat sheves" worth a mere five shillings; whereas John Sturt of

8. Sumner Powell, *Puritan Village* (Middletown, Conn., 1963), 8, 14, 173–5; William Lambarde, *A Perambulation of Kent* [1576] (Chatham, 1826), 7; Thomas Westcote, *A View of Devonshire in 1630* (Exeter, 1845), 50, 62; Kenyon, in *Sussex Arch.*, XCIII, 80; Tristram Risdon, *A Survey of the County of Devon, 1630* (London, 1723), I, 8; W. G. Hoskins, "Provincial Life," in Allardyce Nicoll (ed.), *Shakespeare in His Own Age* (Cambridge, Eng., 1964), 14, 17; T. C. Caldwell, Devonshire from the Accession of Queen Elizabeth until the Civil Wars (Ph.D. Thesis, Yale University, 1934), 43–4.

9. Westcote, *Devonshire*, 52; Hoskins, in Nicoll, *Shakespeare*, 17–18; Earle, *Microcosmography*, 52. For the use of the term "husbandman" both to denote rank and occupation, see Mildred Campbell, *The English Yeoman Under Elizabeth and the Early Stuarts* (New Haven, 1942), 29–32.

Grays Thurrock, because he had no chattels and called for the Book and read, got off with a branding for stealing seven ewes, three lambs, and a wether, valued at £3 9s.[10]

In 1640, it has been said, one-quarter of the inhabitants of most English parishes were poor, miserable people lacking any means of subsistence except at harvest time. The unavoidable conclusion is that women and young girls, the wives and daughters of "poor husbandmen" and wage earners, accounted for a majority of these unfortunates. Estimating a family's average weekly income at 3s. 2 d., out of which came rent, clothing, and food for all, Alice Clark adjudged that "The full misery of the labourer's lot was only felt by the women." Most of them tried to earn a little money by spinning at home; others worked at the same hard tasks that the men performed—at Lambourne, Essex, during the harvest of 1608, Grace Gage and her sister were employed by Goodman Peacock to tread the "haymowe." Working as hard as she could, however, the wife of a husbandman could earn little more than a shilling a week plus meat and drink.[11]

These deprivations may well explain why Sarah Beale of Braintree, spinster, fit for work but having no land or mystery to live by, went to the House of Correction three times for lewd and ungodly behavior. At Godstone in 1608, Justices Bostock Fuller and John Evelyn of Surrey witnessed the whipping of two women and two male rogues for stealing ducks; passports were then made out and one of these vagrant couples was sent back to Devonshire, the other to Somerset. A week later, Justice Fuller caused "2 stoute Rogues called Marye Rendoll a widowe, and Ann Marks a wyfe, to be whipped" and then dispatched to their place of origin in Essex.[12]

Orphans and the abandoned children of dispossessed persons and vagrants, and there were many of them, could do little more than beg their way around the country; only an occasional sidelight illumines the life of these pitiful waifs. Christopher Levett, "His Majesties Woodward of Somersetshire," relates an incident

10. Essex Sessions, XIX, 17–18; XX, 434.
11. *Considerations Touching Trade, with the Advance of the King's Revenue* (London, 1641), 15; Coleman, in *Ec. Hist. Rev.*, 2d ser., VIII, 283; Clark, *Working Life of Women*, 67–8, 86; Essex Sessions, XVIII, 284.
12. Essex Sessions, XIX, 137, 145; *Surrey*, IX, 175, 178.

which reveals that little food and no bed of their own was their portion. One night in 1623, in his "Wigwam" located somewhere on the coast of Maine, Levett was telling stories to his men to overcome their wilderness discomforts: "And then came into my minde an old merry saying, which I hearde of a beggar boy who said if ever he should attaine to be a King, he would have a brest of mutton with a pudding in it, and lodge every night up to the eares in drye straw. . . ." [13]

Naturally many husbandmen, by dint of frugality and fruitful toil, did prosper modestly. John Carter of Coryton, Essex, in addition to providing for his wife and two daughters, left 80s. in 1612 to his brothers and sisters; another husbandman, Tristram Tucker of Brampford Speke, Devon, had his lease all paid up when he died and could bequeath animals, cloth, and utensils worth £58 1s. 4d. to his wife, Dorothy. In Surrey, John Potter of Thorpe, "farmer," left 10s. in apparel and ready money, two yearling bullocks, two calves, five horses, a cart, five pigs, seventeen acres in corn, and £4 10s. in furniture and household articles. His entire estate came to £35 5s. A less prosperous husbandman, Philip Petors of Rackenford near Barnstaple, willed his apparel to his eldest son, and two shillings each to two other sons, two platters to his daughter Margaret, and a bushel of rye to her husband. The residue of this tiny estate of only £9 5s. went to his wife, Joan. However, William Harrison states that such men as these, respected by their fellows, were often called upon for public service.[14]

Occasionally a few fortunate peasants moved up with the yeomen, and some achieved social distinction. A good example of the latter was John Leach, who left his brother Symon, the village blacksmith of Credition, far behind him when, by diligence and learning, he became the first rector of Arlington in North Devon and, ultimately, chancellor of the Cathedral of Exeter. Such success stories so caught the imagination of the people that the writers of the day were prone to fix upon these exceptions and to overlook the manifold instances of personal failures and genuine tragedies.

13. Christopher Levett, *A Voyage into New England* . . . (London, 1628), 5.
14. Waters, *Gleanings,* II, 1408; Charles Worthy (ed.), *Devonshire Wills* (London, 1896), 14, 62; *Surrey,* XXIII, 79; Harrison, *England,* Pt. I, 134.

In truth the members of the peasantry were seldom the picturesque lot so frequently portrayed in play or pamphlet; not only did they not benefit very much from their country's prosperity, but, as a group, they suffered marked economic distress and misfortune.[15]

"The English yeomanry," according to Thomas Fuller, lived "in the temperate zone betwixt greatness and want; an estate of people almost peculiar to England." Other observers of the time and most historians since then have concurred in lauding the yeoman as "the backbone of old England." In the process they have painted an idyllic picture of the man and his condition, but his actual history is far less roseate. Depressed or flourishing, still the yeomen command our special attention, because they not only composed the most dynamic group in rural England, surpassing even the gentry in this respect, but they also made the most significant and enduring contribution to the settling of the colonies in America.[16]

Ranking midway between the gentry and the peasantry, yet not separated by impassable barriers from either, the yeomanry shared public authority with the former and fear of an insecure future with the latter. Unusually serious and determined to forge ahead in the community, the yeomen worked hard, saved conscientiously, and bought land whenever they could. Of the land-hungry, none was more acquisitive than the yeoman, and, as Miss Campbell has so clearly demonstrated, he was not always a freeholder, but rather more often a copyholder who enjoyed better terms of tenure than those below him. Having "systematically underspent," the yeoman was able to take advantage of land transfers made by his betters who had overspent and had to sacrifice their holdings.[17]

In describing Essex, John Norden expressed first surprise and then admiration that "so manie sufficient yomen could growe

15. Beatrice F. Cresswell, Fifty Years in a Country Town, Crediton, Devon, 1551–1599 (Typescript, Muniment Room, Exeter Library), 146; W. G. Hoskins and H. P. R. Fineberg, Devonshire Studies (London, 1952), 426.
16. Fuller, Holy and Profane State, 106.
17. In The English Yeoman, Mildred Cambell has written the classic account of the kind that is very much needed on the gentry and the merchants. W. G. Hoskin's notice of Miss Campbell's book, in Ec. Hist. Rev., XIV, 193–6, supplies a valuable commentary, as does Wallace Notestein in The English People on the Eve of Colonization . . . (New York, 1954), chap. VII; Breton, Court and Country, in Dunham and Pargellis, Complaint and Reform, 459, 475–6; Harrison, England, Pt. I, 133.

amonge so manie of greater state . . . and are Lordes of their
owne dwellings. Or at leaste ferme them in such easie manner, that
they paye their ferm and increase in wealth." Such a man was Benjamin Elliott of Nazeing. He had not confined his acquisitions of
land to Essex, but had reached over into Hertfordshire for more
acres at Widford, Hunsdon, Eastwick, and Ware. At his death in
1622, his land was producing more than the annual allotment of
£8 that he willed should be paid toward the support of his son at
Cambridge. Norden attributed such prosperity to the fact that the
gentlemen of Essex, unlike those of many other counties, did not
engross the land by retaining "more fermes in their own manur-
ance" than they needed for maintenance.[18]

Broad generalizations can lead to error; it must be kept in mind
that the wealth, numbers, manner of living, and holdings of the
yeomen varied greatly from one region to another. The yeomen of
East Anglia enjoyed the same economic position as their Essex
brethren. Numbers of them engaged in the cloth industry in addition to their agricultural pursuits, and, as a result, they harnessed
their well-being to the rise and fall of that trade. The typical Norfolk yeoman possessed about two-thirds of the wealth of an average gentleman of Yorkshire. Even so, the Norfolk yeomen did not
always prosper. In 1628 the Commissioners of the Subsidy in that
shire reported "That some of them doe owe unto their Landlords
two years Rent, many of them one yeares, and very few or none
but are in some arreares with them. . . ." Though this distress
proved temporary, it occurred at a most critical time in the history
of the region. The Kentish yeomen bore "away the bell for wealth
from all of their ranck in England." In Hampshire and Dorset
more of them farmed copyholds than freeholds. In the West Country, yeomen had not yet attained the wealth of those in East
Anglia, Essex, and Kent.[19]

18. A most yeomanlike bequest was made in 1625 by George Kinge of Woodham
Mortimer to his son-in-law William Vassall, of "my instruments and tools for
measuring and plotting of land." Waters, *Gleanings,* II, 905, 1315; John Norden,
A Chorographical Description of the several Shires and Islands of Middlesex,
Essex, Surrey, Hampshire, Wiltshire, Werdate, Garnsey and Jersey [1594]
(B. M. Add. MSS., 31852), 12; John Norden, The County of Essex [1595]
(Add. MSS., 33769), 10.
19. Nearness to London produced in Middlesex, according to Norden: "Another
sort of husbandmen or yeomen rather there are, and that not a few . . . who

Devonshire revealed marked differences in culture and estate. The yeomen were described as men "free, by law, nature, and disposition," holding their lands by inheritance or lease, and every man was reputed to be of "aspiring Mind," but they ranged from the coarse, ignorant, and superstitious constable of Stockton Pomeroy Hundred on the one hand to the Furse family of Dean Prior on the other. The Furses moved rapidly upward from their humble start as "sympell and unlernede men off smalle possessynes, substance, habillytye or reputasion" in the sixteenth century to become members of the lesser gentry by the opening of the seventeenth. Though originally from a poor family of Dorset, George Hoskyns removed to Stoke Abbot, where he became a rich yeoman. He could read, write, and play the treble viol. After he married Margaret Pulman, the daughter of a prosperous Devon yeoman, Hoskyns settled at Axmouth and lived in Devon for a quarter of a century.[20]

A single case can never be typical. Yet the life of John Carter of Denham, Buckinghamshire, who died in 1635, does epitomize the careers of the ablest, most ambitious, and most fortunate of the yeomanry. Goodman Carter had begun his life as a husbandman, "the lower of the two ranks of farmers." He rose by virtue of his increasing wealth, which eventually amounted to the tidy sum of £821. Among his valued possessions was Rusholtes, a spacious two-story farmhouse well stocked with country furniture and a fine supply of linen. A small tract called Red Hill and Rusholtes Farm, which he occupied by copyhold, totaled 150 acres; he owned no

---

wade in the weeds of gentlemen. . . . These only oversee their husbandry and give directions unto their servants or not at all setting their hand unto the plough, who have great feedings for cattle and good breed for young often use Smithfield and other like places with fat cattle, where also they store themselves with lean. And thus they often exchange, not without great gain." Quoted by Michael Robbins, *Middlesex* (London, 1953), 33–4; Jordan, *Charities of Rural England*, 21; *Norfolk Archaeology: State Papers Relating to . . . Norfolk*, ed. Walter B. Rye (Norwich, 1907), 140; Fuller, *Worthies*, II, 484.

20. Miss Campbell gives an excellent description of the Devonshire yeoman; see also Risdon, *Devon*, II, 6; Westcote, *Devonshire*, 48; *Devonshire*, X, 315–29; XXVI, 169–71; *Devon & Cornwall*, XXI, 241–8; XXII, 162–4; N. S. B. and Ethel C. Gras, *The Economic History of an English Village* (*Crawley, Hampshire*) (Cambridge, Mass., 1930), 111–12; for the less prosperous yeoman of Yorkshire, consult especially R. Parkinson, *The Life of Adam Martindale*, in *Chetham*, IV; and Adam Eyre, *A Dyurnall . . .* in *Surtees*, LXV.

land in fee simple and accordingly was not a freeholder, though he died a freeman. His son was called a yeoman, and his grandson styled himself "gentleman." [21]

Though the average yeoman, like "Old Carter" in *The Witch of Edmonton,* was content to be called *goodman,* many contemporaries were becoming aware of the upward thrust of rich yeomen. Sir William Vaughan complained that "the Yeoman doth gentilize it." "Now of late they have entred into the trade of usurye," charged John Hooker of Devon in 1599, "biyenge of clothes and purchasinge and merchandises clymminge up daylye to the degree of gentlemen and do bringe up their children accordingly." In *The Ordinary,* a gentleman remarks, "These yeomen have no policy i' the world." Apparently he did not acknowledge the yeoman's running with Englishmen of all ranks in the upward-and-onward race to be a policy, but others believed it to be so. A restless, aspiring, sometimes too ambitious lot, these yeomen strove for security and position by increasing their posessions. Yet at the very same time, many of them stood on the brink of failure, faced with the grim possibility of sinking down to the level of cottagers and laborers. This was one more of the prime anomalies of English life.[22]

Upon being asked "What's your parentage"? Viola, disguised as a young man, replied simply, "Above my fortunes, yet my state is well: I am a gentleman." To be a member of the gentry, "whome their race and bloud, doo make noble and knowne," meant that one belonged to the privileged orders of England. Persons of inferior rank all instinctively looked up with genuine respect to their gentle betters, whose authority to rule locally came from commissions issued by the Crown to justices of the peace. In their official capacities as justices, in their private family lives, and in their dealings with the peasantry, the country gentlemen set the standards for and gave the tone to their society.[23]

About 16,500 heads of families made up the gentry of this pe-

21. *Buckinghamshire,* XVI, Pt. I, 83–94.
22. *The Witch of Edmonton,* in Fredson Bowers, *The Dramatic Works of Thomas Dekker* (Cambridge, Eng., 1958), III, 498 (I, ii, 2–8); Sir William Vaughan, *The Golden Fleece* (1626), "To the Reader"; *Devonshire,* XLVIII, 341–2; William Cartwright, *The Ordinary* (1634), III, ii, in Dodsley, *Old English Plays,* XII; *VCH Oxfordshire,* V. 87.
23. *Twelfth Night,* I, v, 297–9; Harrison, *England,* Pt. I, 128; Dorothy Ross, in *History,* n. s., XXVIII, 148–56.

riod. As with other ranks, their distribution over the countryside
was noticeably uneven: the spacious county of Devon contained
from 360 to 400, compared to the 800 to 1,000 in much smaller
Kent, where the group profited by its proximity to London. In
1595 John Norden found Essex "well stored with noblemen, and
gentlemen of accompte and manie stately dwellings they have,
which beawtiefies the face of the Country." [24]

"Those which wee call Esquires," said Sir Thomas Wilson, "are
gentlemen whose ancestors are or have bin Knights, or else they
are heyres and eldest of their houses and of some competent quantity of revenue fitt to be called to office and authority in their
Country where they live." Also accepted as gentlemen were graduates of universities, captains home from the wars, physicians,
lawyers, and, according to Barnabe Rich, anybody that "can live
without manuell labour, and thereto is able and will beare the
port, charge, and countenance of a gentleman, he shall [for monie
have a cote and armes bestowed upon him by heralds (who in the
charter of the same doo of custome pretend antiquitie and service . . .) and thereunto being made so good cheape] be called
master, which is the title that men give to esquires and gentlemen."
There is an element of sarcasm as well as truth in the widely
quoted proverb that "gentility is nothing but ancient riches." [25]

Possession of a sufficient landed estate to enable the owner to
live off its income identified the country gentleman. Here again the
estimates of what was sufficient varied: "Northward and farr off"
this indicated £ 300 to £ 400 a year, but in the neighborhood of
London and the adjacent counties, where the price of land had
soared, one was not "counted of any great reckning" unless his income exceeded £ 1,000.[26]

24. Hoskins and Fineberg, *Devonshire Studies*, 334; A. Milner Everitt, Kent and
Its Gentry, 1640–1660 (Ph.D. Thesis, London, 1957), ix; Norden, Chorographical Description, 12.
25. When a Somerset herald visited Burford in Oxfordshire in 1634, the rector
of the parish, Thomas Wyatt, inquired of him about his own social position: "I
. . . said I gave no arms and challenged. He said I was a gentleman by my
degree and questioned me no further." Quoted by Mark Curtis, *Oxford and
Cambridge in Transition, 1558–1642* (Oxford, 1959), 271; Wilson, "State of
England," 23; Barnabe Rich, *Roome for a Gentlemen* (1609), 13, who follows
Harrison, *England*, Pt. I, 128–9, almost verbatim. Rich is quoted by Campbell,
Yeoman, 34–5; *HMC Portland*, IX, 5.
26. Wilson, "State of England," 24; Emmison, in *Bedford*, XX, 42.

No real gulf existed between the upper yeomanry and the lesser gentry. More than one rich yeoman not only disdained to become gentle by purchase but saw no advantage worth the charge; frequently, moreover, his daughters married gentlemen and his sons espoused the daughters of squires. Nicholas Breton's father held of the true member of the rural gentry that "if he could speak well, and ride well, and shoot well, and bowl well, we desire no more of him. . . ." A more noticeable difference pertained between a rustic country gentleman and his urban counterpart. Consider the amazement of Thomas Fuller when, near Lewes, he beheld a Kentish lady being drawn to church in her own coach by six lumbering oxen. Certain it is that the English gentry, flexible, growing, and prospering, displayed much snobbery, but none of the castelike rigidity of the privileged orders on the Continent.[27]

We may ascribe certain traits as common to the gentry; yet its members included a number of distinct types. Anthony Kingscote, Esq. of Kingscote in the Barony of Berkeley was typical of the ancient squirearchy. "Hee and his lineall ancestors have continued in this little manor nowe about 500 yeares, never attainted nor dwellinge out of it else," John Smyth noted, "nor hath the tide of his Estate higher or lower flowed or ebbed in better or worse condition." John Bruen of Cheshire returned in 1579 from a gay life of hunting, hawking, and cockfighting as a gentleman commoner at St. Alban's Hall, Oxford, and resolved to lead a more religious life at Bruen Stapleford. A "moderate Episcopalian," Bruen might be labeled a doctrinal Puritan. Besides supporting twenty-one boarders in his house (not including his children and servants), he maintained the old-fashioned hospitality by feeding anyone in the county at two meals a week.[28]

The economy of the gentlemen of Norfolk was not so stable as that of Mr. Kingscote or Mr. Bruen, as the Lords of the Council

27. Fuller wrote: "Sure I am in Kent there is many a yeoman of great ability, who, though no gentleman by descent and title, is one by his means and estate; . . . also by his courteous carriage. . . ." Fuller, *Worthies*, II, 485; Campbell, *Yeoman*, 33, 48, 50, 55; Breton, *Court and Country,* in Dunham and Pargellis, *Complaint and Reform,* 460; George Roberts, *Social History of the People of the Southern Counties of England* (London, 1856), 487.
28. *Berkeley Manuscripts,* III, 252; William Hinde, *Life of John Bruen* (New York, 1857), 16–17, 85; *Chetham,* XIV, xv–xx.

learned in 1628 from a subsidy agent: "that gentlemen and most part of those of the best and ablest estates . . . live at the armes end of their fortunes, And that (besides what hath in these late times for Aydes, for Subsedies, for Benevolences and Loanes, and other Contributions passed from them) they find all their owne charges increased, and their revenues and other commodities made incertayne and much abated. . . ." In 1616, fresh from Emmanuel, Thomas Knyvett had discovered this for himself when he succeeded to his father's estate and debts in Norfolk. As one of the "prime gentry," he was summoned to receive the Order of the Bath at the coronation of Charles I in 1625, but "ever sensitive of social gradations," he astutely evaded the honor and the payment of £500 to £600 by reviving a dormant family claim to the greater dignity of the Barony of Berners.[29]

From 1630 to 1640 Knyvett actively carried out his local responsibilities. As a justice of the quorum, he attended at Quarter Sessions at Bury St. Edmunds, where he became acquainted with "the generall voice of this towne amongst the vulgar sort." Recreation and social life were not lacking: hawking, entertaining scholars who came to consult the excellent library inherited from his father, and invitations to the Court where he viewed Inigo Jones's masques—all fitted into the role he played as a country gentleman.[30]

East Anglian gentlemen understandably enjoyed more contact with the Court and the City than those of the West Country or the Midlands. Country gentlemen such as Oliver Cromwell of Huntingtonshire and John Winthrop of Suffolk lived a somewhat homespun existence for the most part, though Winthrop, a thoroughgoing Puritan, practiced law in London to augment his income from the Manor of Groton. Notwithstanding his appointment in 1626 as an attorney for the Court of Wards and Liveries, however, he found himself in serious financial straits.[31]

29. *Norfolk Arch.* (1907), 139; *The Knyvett Letters,* 1620–1644, in *Norfolk,* XX, 19, 22, 27.
30. *Knyvett Letters,* 19, 29, 84, 88.
31. "I was by birth a gentleman living neither in any considerable height nor yet in obscurity." For Cromwell, see Sir Charles Firth, *Oliver Cromwell and the Rule of the Puritans in England* (World Classics, London, 1958), 1–46; *The Winthrop Papers* (Mass. Hist. Soc., Boston, 1929–47), I-III (1498–1637).

More fortunate was Herbert Pelham of Lincolnshire, an emigrant to Massachusetts Bay about 1635, who was first treasurer of Harvard College and a kinsman of the third Lord De la Warr, governor of Virginia. Above the English town of Boston on the river Wytham at Dogdyke, Pelham owned 480 acres, which his father had enclosed in return for surrendering all of his rights in other parts of Holland Fen. The income Herbert Pelham derived from this and other holdings in England enabled him to live as the first known gentleman-at-large in the English colonies.[32]

The upper gentry and the nobility, however great their importance in the life of the period, need not long detain us. They lived in great houses like the one belonging to Lord Savage at Long Melford in Essex, which the sophisticated and widely traveled Oxonian James Howell describes: "I never saw yet such a dainty Race of Children in all my life together: I never saw yet such an orderly and punctual attendance of Servants, nor a great House so neatly kept; here one sees no dog, nor a cat, nor cage to cause any nastiness within the body of the House. The Kitchen and Gutters and other Offices of noise and drudgery are at the fag-end; there's a Back-gate for the Beggars and the meaner sort of Swaines to come in at; the Stables butt upon the Park, which, for a chearful rising Ground, for Groves and Browsings for the Deer, for rivulets of Water, may compare with any for its highness in the whole Land; it is opposite to the front of the Great House, whence from the Gallery one may see much of the game they are a-hunting." [33]

Everywhere and at every level of the ruling class, from copyholding yeoman to duke, the majority of men and their families struggled to move ahead in wealth and degree. Much to the annoyance of the older families, the several ranks of the gentry filled with risen men. Earle lampooned the upstart country knight whose "father was a man of good stock, though but a tanner or usurer; he purchased the land, and his son the title. He has doffed off the name of Country Fellow, but the look not so easy, and his face bears still a relish of churn-milk. He is guarded with more gold

32. John Langdon Sibley, *Biographical Sketches of Graduates of Harvard University in Cambridge, Massachusetts* (Cambridge, Mass., 1881), II, 416; Thirsk, *English Peasant Farming*, 38.
33. James Howell, *Familiar Letters* (London, 1903), I, 106–7; for deer parks in Devon, see *Western Antiquary*, IV, 21–3, 49, 72.

lace than all the gentlemen of the country, yet his body makes his clothes still out of fashion." [34]

The first two Stuarts sold titles to get sorely needed funds; such aristocrats as John Chamberlain referred contemptuously in 1616 to King James's setting "the mint of new dignities" to working; six years later he advised a friend overseas that baronetcies might be obtained for £200 to £250. When King Charles sought to raise money in 1630 by selling knighthoods, the ballad makers in Hallamshire satirized both King and commoners:

> Come all you farmers out of the country,
> Carters, plowmen, hedgers, and all.
> Tom, Dick, and Bill, Ralph, Roger, and Humphrey,
> Leave off your gestures rusticall;
> Bidd all your home spunne fashions adew,
> And sute your selves in the fashions new.
> Honor invites you to delights,
> Come to Court, and be all made Knights.[35]

III

The England of 1630 was divided into the City of London, the Cinque Ports, and forty counties (including Bristol and Durham), each of which had its county town where the life of the shire focused. Over the centuries every county developed a certain individ-

34. In *King Richard III*, I, iii, 70–74, Gloucester says:

> . . . the world is grown so bad,
> That wrens make prey where eagles dare not perch:
> Since every Jack became a gentleman,
> There's many a gentle person made a Jack.

Earle, *Microcosmography*, 43.
35. Chamberlain, *Letters*, II, 10; *CSPD, 1619–23*, p. 418; Joseph Hunter, *Hallamshire: The History and Topography of the Parish of Sheffield*, ed. Alfred Gatty (London, 1869), 133n. For the purposes of this work it is not necessary to assay the views of Messrs. Tawney, Trevor-Roper, Hexter, *et al.*, concerning the gentry save to note that the gentry as a whole cannot be correctly described as in serious straits financially before 1640. See J. H. Hexter, "Storm over the Gentry" in *Reappraisals in History* (Evanston, Illinois, 1961), 117–62; for East Anglia, Alan Simpson, *The Wealth of the Gentry, 1540–1640* (Chicago, 1961); and Mary E. Finch, *The Wealth of Five Northamptonshire Families, 1540–1640* (Northampton, XIX, 1956); and especially Lawrence Stone, *The Crisis of the Aristocracy, 1558–1641* (Oxford, 1965).

uality that set it off from the rest—a fact that local topographers proudly pointed out. *A Helpe to Discourse,* published in 1631, thus characterized some of them:

> Cheshire for men,
> Berkshire for dogs,
> Bedfordshire for naked flesh,
> And Lincolnshire for bogs.
>
> Derbyshire for lead,
> Devonshire for tin,
> Wiltshire for hunting plomes,
> And Middlesex for sin.[36]

The endowment and manner of life of any agricultural people is both directly and subtly affected by the climate and the weather. To anyone motoring over England in all seasons, this fact becomes immediately evident, and it did not escape the notice of the early seventeenth-century travelers. "Although so far north and though the sun rarely shines in its full splendour for a whole day, yet the air is temperate," the Venetian ambassador reported back to the Signory in 1622; and Fynes Moryson testified that "the ayre of England is temperate, but thicke, cloudy, and misty." Nicholas Assheton of Lancashire filled his journal for 1618 with notations like these: January 2, "A foule rainie day; noe stirring," and November 7, "A verie foule, raynie, stormie daye." [37]

Strong winds and storms often lashed the coasts, disrupted shipping, and ruined crops. In 1607 mighty floods inundated portions of Somersetshire, Norfolk, Bedfordshire, Huntingtonshire, Lincolnshire, and Kent, "destroying many thousands of men, women, and

36. Michael Dalton, *The Country Justice* (4th ed., 1630), 192 [The Bodleian copy of this useful work (Antiq. d E $\frac{1630}{1}$) is carefully annotated by a seventeenth-century hand and prefaced by useful notes, dated 1633 and 1635; also on the front and back blank pages are further notations. John Batson gave this book to "Walter Wrothesly Armiger," February 1, 1635]. *Western Antiquary,* V, 262. In Taylor's *Atlas* are reproduced forty plates of Christopher Saxton's county maps as published for Speed in 1627, together with useful thumbnail sketches by Professor Eva G. R. Taylor.

37. *CSP Venetian, 1621–3,* p. 423; Fynes Moryson, *An Itinerary containing his ten yeares travell . . . ,* ed. J. Maclehose (New York, 1907–8), IV, 165; *Chetham,* XIV, 73, 113.

children, overflowing and bearing downe whole townes and villages, and drowning infinite numbers of sheepe and other cattle." In January and February, 1617, contrary winds kept more than three hundred ships in the Downs, and during the years 1626, 1627, 1637 and 1642, storms raged for long periods. On the other hand, in some years droughts brought despair to the farmers, as in 1605 in the region between Bristol and Bath, "where there was last year twenty load of hay, there is not now four load of hay." [38]

Englishmen experienced mild winters generally: extreme cold seldom occurred, and, in southern England, snow never remained long on the ground. Nevertheless "hard frosts" and protracted spells of uncomfortably cold weather caused real distress. In the five weeks of cold weather that began shortly before Christmas in 1607–8, "victuals were so frozen they would take no salt," and a Devon farmer told of roasting a piece of beef on New Year's Day and keeping it some time; "then I was driven to take a spit and put the end thereof in the fire, and heat it red-hot, and so got him in the flesh." Many of his cattle perished for want of fodder. But even if the Englishman escaped bitter cold winters, he had to endure a raw, damp climate that kept him miserable most of the winter months because the habitations of persons of all degrees, but particularly the poor, had inadequate heating arrangements. Even in summer, on the many sunless days, the English expended much of their energy in merely keeping warm.[39]

38. Darby, *Geography*, 391n, 392, and Fig. 65, p. 391, for a graph giving wet and dry years, 1600–1640; *A True Report of Certaine Wonderfull Overflowings of Waters . . .* , ed. Ernest E. Baker (Weston-super-Mare, 1884); *Chetham,* I, 177; for Titania's vivid description of an English storm, *A Midsummer Night's Dream,* II, i, 88–99.

39. William Whiteway of Dorchester, who lived most comfortably for that day, recorded in January 1634/5: "This yeere we had an extreme hard winter with much frost, severe haile, cold raines, so that the Thames was frozen and men went and rode over it. 22 Jan. the ink did freeze in my pen while I did write. Countreymen could not labour, and therefore 1 Feb. there was an extrardinary collection in this Towne to relieve the extraordinary necessities of the poore. Many dround [perished] in the snow." Thomas D. Murphy, The Diary of William Whiteway of Dorchester, County Dorset, from the year 1618 to the year 1635 (Ph.D. Thesis, Yale University, 1939), (fol. 221), p. 252; *Western Antiquary,* III, 223; Platter, *Travels,* 184; *Devonshire,* XV, 456; Darby, *Geography, 392n;* and for life on the frozen Thames at London in 1619, John Stow, *Annales, or a Generall Chronicle of England . . . augmented . . . by Edmund Howes, Gent.*

An aerial survey of the English landscape in 1590 would have disclosed three general types of land: numerous forests and wooded tracts; extensive areas of waste, swamps, and fens; and a vast expanse of cultivated open fields. Today it is impossible to state even approximately the proportion of each type of land.[40]

On one point contemporaries all agreed: many districts suffered from a scarcity of wood. In 1614, a Londoner who, perhaps, recalled the forests as they had once been and was appalled at the attrition, exclaimed: "such hath beene the plenty of wood in England for all uses that within man's memory, it was held impossible to have any want of wood in England." Now even the royal forests were disappearing. The policy of the first two Stuarts of selling oaks for revenue accelerated the destruction of timberlands begun under Queen Elizabeth. Reports of 1600 had it that around country villages near the seacoasts "most of the woods are consumed and the ground converted to corn and pasture"; hedgerows were taking the place of broad oaks. "Extreme waste" of wood in the manufacture and burning of brick and tile further diminished the woodlands, especially in the Weald and the Forest of Dean. Sherwood Forest still covered a large part of Nottinghamshire in 1640, though bit by bit encroachments by local lords for deer parks or grazing lands threatened this great stand of timber.[41]

More Englishmen lived on the fens than in the forests and woods. In Lincolnshire, Norfolk, Huntingtonshire, and Cambridgeshire, projects for drainage had been undertaken by act of Parliament, and they made headway after 1634 with the hiring of the Dutch engineer, Cornelius Vermuyden, by the Earl of Bedford.

(1631), 1034; *CSPD, 1619–23,* p. 321; G. Utterstrom, "Climatic Fluctuations and Population Problems in Early Modern History," in *Scandinavian Economic History Review,* III, 3–47.

40. The Ordinance Survey Office published a *Map of XVII Century England* (Southampton, 1930). The plates were casualties of World War II, and it is to be hoped that this map will be reissued. See also the many helpful maps in Darby, *Geography,* and the endpapers of Clifton-Taylor's *Pattern of English Building.*

41. A survey of all royal forests, parks, and chases (which omits the forests of Dean and Wychwood) is printed in Darby, *Geography,* 398–9; Stow, *Annales,* 1025; Robert G. Albion, *Forests and Sea Power: The Timber Problem of the Royal Navy* . . . (Cambridge, Mass., 1926), 127; *HMC Salisbury,* XIV, 330–31; Alfred C. Wood, *Nottinghamshire in the Civil War* (Oxford, 1937), 1–2; *Winthrop Papers,* I, 297.

Nevertheless, prior to 1640 not enough land had been reclaimed to have any significant effect on English agriculture.[42]

Champion, as the topographers and antiquaries called the unenclosed countryside—where "the lands of the freeholders, farmers, and tenants lie in common"—dominated the landscape south of a line extending from the East Riding of Yorkshire southwestward to Shropshire and Hereford, then due south to Dorset. John Norden described Dorsetshire, Wiltshire, Hampshire, Berkshire, and Northamptonshire as typical champion. The same could be said of the Midlands, where the most extensively cultivated counties of England were located. Buckinghamshire and Oxfordshire remained among the most completely agricultural of the southern and Midland Counties, whereas the field system of Middlesex had already taken on "hybrid" qualities. Open fields persisted in Norfolk and the western half of Suffolk, and even in parts of Essex that bordered on Suffolk and Hertfordshire. Graphic proof of this is to be found on William Sands's Map (1600) of the Manor of Great Henny and Bulmer. The manor is situated on the river Stour about two miles from Sudbury, the Suffolk town that sent so many Puritans to New England. Open-field farming had disappeared in Devon and Cornwall, and in Kent for the most part save in a few places like the Manor of Wye.[43]

William Harrison had noticed in 1577 that the farmhouses always stood close together in the champion country; the compact village not only best met the requirements of strip-farming and common grazing but also provided a social center for the copyholders. Always on wooded or hilly terrain unsuited for open-field husbandry, the houses stood apart on the owners' land, as in the

42. H. C. Darby, *The Drainage of the Fens* (2d ed., Cambridge, Eng., 1956), 28–64; *CSPD, 1603–10,* pp. 290, 536; *1619–23,* p. 104.
43. For the extent of the open fields, see map in C. S. and C. S. Orwin, *The Open Fields* (Oxford, 1938), 61–5; and Darby, *Geography,* figs. 66, 67; *HMC Buccleuch,* III, 102; Norden quoted by Byrne, *Elizabethan Life in Town and Country* (London 1957), 108, 110; Jordan, *Charities of Rural England,* 23, 27; Robbins, *Middlesex,* 31; William Sands, Map of the Manor of Great Henny [and] Bulmer, 1600 (Essex Record Office, Chelmsford), D/Dc 332/9a; Taylor, *Atlas,* 14; F. G. Emmison, "Types of Open Field Parishes in the Midlands," *Hist. Assn. Pamphlet,* No. 108 (1937); A. C. Edwards, *Elizabethan Essex* (Chelmsford, 1961), pl. 3, for Chrishall, where in 1593, two-thirds of the manor was still farmed in strips.

United States at a later date; and when land was enclosed, owners preferred to live on their own acres. Consequently, as the yeomen left their little villages, more and more isolated farms began to dot a landscape that formerly was characterized by open fields.[44]

England thus presented to the traveler a countryside of manors and farms. A manor, the popular *Surveyor's Dialogue* informs us, "is of Lands, Wood, Meddow, Pasture, and Arable: It is compounded of demeisns and services of long continuance," and, again, John Norden thinks of the manor as a little society "whereof the Tenants are members, the Land the body, and the Lord the head." The lord lived in the manor house, and his tenants in the manorial village or hamlet.[45]

Just as every county had its individual features, so did each manorial village vary noticeably from even its nearest neighbors in size, arrangement of buildings, materials used for construction, and appearance. Yet they all more or less fitted into a general manorial pattern. Most manors contained one or more hamlets, ordinarily without churches, and a larger village consisting of a collection of dwellings and farm structures, usually adjoining or situated not far from the manor house and its outbuildings.

All of the institutions and arrangements of the manor—physical, agricultural, religious, legal—served to support what St. Thomas Aquinas designated the inclination of men "to know the truth about God and to live in communities." This idea and fact of neighborhood, this mere living together in close proximity with little individual privacy, was probably the most important single inbred characteristic of the English, one which they took with them in one form or another to the New World, for those who eventually left their land had experienced neighborliness in the villages where they had been born and reared.[46]

About nine miles north of Newark-on-Trent is Laxton, close by the Manor of Laxton that the colonizer Sir William Courteen, rich son of a Flemish refugee risen to merchant prince, purchased from the Duke of Buckingham in 1625. Less altered by time than

44. Harrison, *England*, Pt. I, 237; Howard L. Gray, *English Field Systems* (Cambridge, Mass., 1915), 272.
45. John Norden, *The Surveyor's Dialogue* [1607], 3d ed., (1618), 27, 39.
46. *Summa Theologica*, quoted by R. H. Tawney, *Religion and the Rise of Capitalism* (New York, 1947), 25.

nearly any other Midlands village, Laxton Town fits all of the conventional notions of an open-field community. In 1635 this compact Nottingham village contained eighty-seven dwelling-houses of all kinds, forty-three of them cottages, all fronting on either side of the main east-west highway or on a side road winding southward to the hamlet of Laxton Moorhouse. With the exception of two windmills on high ground, not one of the dwellings or outbuildings stood beyond the village limits, and the manor house itself and all its appurtenances actually joined the cottages on the south. At the center, where the highroad turns to the west, towers the parish church of St. Michael, its lavish fifteenth-century clerestory almost overwhelming the tiny structure beneath.[47]

East of the Woods of Oriel College lay Studley Manor. George Sergeant drew a beautiful survey of it in 1641, and he inserted a map of the great house set in "The Mannour Yards" and the adjoining village in the upper-left-hand corner. The village consisted of about twenty-five structures along the north side of the "Shyre Way" leading to Boarstall and Oakley; each farmer's cottage had an enclosed garden strip in the rear. Though no church is shown on the map, the community boasts a handsome almshouse erected in 1639 by Sir John Croke, lord of the manor. A place of no great distinction, Horton-cum-Studley, like its immediate neighbor Beckley, may stand as a good example of a typical manorial village.[48]

Far to the west, remotely situated sixteen miles from Gloucester

47. In 1625 Sir William Courteen sent settlers to Barbados, the first English colony in the Caribbean; one of his ships had discovered the island the previous year. *DNB*, XII, 333. On Laxton, see J. D. Chambers, *Laxton, The Last English Open Field Village* (London, 1964), 7–23; and the fine study of the Orwins, *Open Fields*, 82–3, 115, pls. 13, 14, 20, 22, and Maps I, II, at end of volume; Pevsner, *Nottinghamshire*, pl. 21 and p. 95; Victor Bonham-Carter, in *The English Village* (Harmondsworth, 1952), supplies the general historical background, 15–51.

48. Horton-cum-Studley retains much of its seventeenth-century appearance. George Sergeant, A Plot and True Description of the Mannour of Studley in the County of Oxon and Bucks . . . admeasured Anno 1641 [Map Room, Bodleian, C 17 49 (92)]; *VCH Oxfordshire*, II, 56. In the Library of Wendover, Bucks, is "A Topographicall Inscription and vertical mensuration of the *Mannors* of Wendover. . . ." The survey is in color and depicts all of the buildings in elevation with red tile roofs. *Buckinghamshire*, XIII, Pt. 2, pp. 69–70; and for Fenny Stratford, *ibid.* XII, 6; for John Norden's very detailed map of Atherington Manor, see *Sussex Arch.*, XLIV, 147.

and three from the river Severn, which washed the manor's shores, was "the burgh, Burrowe or Market towne of Berkeley" that contained eighty households between 1618 and 1639, and the "Castle adjoyninge." A few miles off lay the dependent hamlet of Nibley. Cowley manor and parish, with the Church of St. Bartholomew, served the entire Hundred of Berkeley; in 1639 the "hamblet" had only about 1,000 souls and 162 houses and cottages besides the baronial castle. "Of this parish it may be said," its steward John Smyth of Nibley proudly recorded for posterity, "that if it were enclosed round from all other society and commerce of men, it would abundantly suffice for the sustentacon and well beinge of the inhabitants, without supply from other places that the mind of man could necessarily desire." [49]

One other manor further illustrates the almost infinite variety of manorial villages. On the north bank of the Thames, lying about a mile and a half from the river at Purfleet, is "the antient Mannor of Avethlie." Its maritime location and nearness to London once spelled both profit and pain to the residents: "there being within the precynct of this mannor a poore (if not a Rude) Towne, where . . . the market is kept" weekly, a survey of 1625 relates. To Aveley came the "men of Kent" once a week to buy in and often to forestall the market. Less acceptable was an influx of beggars and other suspected persons, "many of them being of lewd sort as whores, scoldes, lazye and Idle people [who] have brought horrible and not to be named syns and wickedness into the towne." [50]

It is still possible to recreate in the mind's eye what a seventeenth-century hamlet must have been like by visiting any number of small communities. Even today, despite the common presence of one or more long streets lined with timber-framed houses and Gothic churches, or more rarely Norman, and many an outbuilding, all of these towns testify in their varied aspects to the rural prosperity of earlier days. The community remains often make better sources for the historian than the parchments reposing in county record offices, priceless though such documents may be.

49. *Berkeley Manuscripts,* III, 84–5, 151, 261.
50. Survey of the Manor of Aveley, *c.* 1625 (Essex Record Office), D/D Th; also pp. 1–10 in Mimeograph No. 58, pp. 1–3, 6.

In a day's motoring, one can inspect a dozen or more Suffolk villages, such as Woodbridge on the North Sea, Framlingham, picturesque Bildeston, and ever-attractive Kersey, not one like another. Or again, beginning with Dedham in Essex, it is possible to visit communities that, in the seventeenth century, belonged to both open and enclosed country. West Bergholt, the Horkesleys (Great and Little), untouched Pleshey, High Roding, and Hatfield Broad Oak—all were villages of Jacobean and Caroline England and still retain much of their early structures and outlines.[51]

The inhabitants of many villages of Suffolk, Essex, and Hertfordshire took justifiable pride in the possession of the public greens on which their houses faced. Having been formed irregularly by forking roads, they seldom were large and rarely square. The largest and most attractive Essex green may still be viewed at Writtle, near Chelmsford; though more spectacular is the elongated triangle of the Suffolk town of Long Melford with the impressive brick Melford Hall and, at its northern end, "one of the most moving parish churches of England," built of freestone c.1460. Nikolaus Pevsner rightly terms this green unforgettable. In the small, virtually untouched Essex village of Matching, one may see a large polygonal green.[52]

The greens of other counties are generally less impressive, though still quite pleasing to the eye. In the limestone belt, the traveler who ventures off the main highway from Oxford to Henley may stumble on Marsh Baldon, a delightful, unspoiled village with a well-kept green of twenty-four acres bordered by cottages—a rare survival of the sixteenth century. A neighborly mile away, Toot Baldon maintains a smaller irregular green on which the "gentlemen" of the place still play cricket on the morning of a Bank Holiday; they stop only for lunch, not for rain.[53]

If next one travels in the West Country from Salisbury as far as Chagford on the hither edge of Dartmoor, he will observe that the landscape bears little resemblance to that of the Midlands. Com-

51. In *The Midland Peasant* (London, 1957), W. G. Hoskins discusses the recently rebuilt Wigston in Leicestershire, a typical village of the stone-belt counties. Professor Pevsner's *Suffolk* and *Essex,* together with the *Quarter-Inch Ordinance Survey Map of East Anglia* (1930, Sheet 9) are indispensable.
52. Pevsner, *Essex,* 14, 270; Pevsner, *Suffolk,* 12, 316–17, 321, and pl. 52.
53. *VCH Oxfordshire,* V, 30–31; visit to the Baldons, 6 August, 1962.

pact villages, with houses often set well back on all sides of an open square into which the roads converge, are to be found, but they are quite different and fewer in number than in the Midlands. Here and there is a hamlet, but in the seventeenth century this was a region of small, isolated, enclosed farms and small stone or cob farmhouses with thatched roofs. The terrain was hilly with small valleys like those of the Teign and the Dart. Stone fences abounded and many were the hedgebanks so high that one could not see over them to either side of the road.[54]

Emphasis on the openness of the English countryside in this era has all too frequently obscured the presence of hedgerows sufficient to elicit both favorable and damning comments. "Love your neighbour, yet pull not down your hedges," George Herbert advised. In the middle of the sixteenth century, John Leland said that thick hedges had long been growing in Cornwall and Devon, and in other western counties such as Somerset and Gloucester; Lancashire and the Weald also had their hedgerows. While traveling in the Malvern Hills and the Forest of Dean in August, 1639, Peter Mundy noticed "greatt store off good Fruit trees on the hedges in and by the high waies." These were the years when England was irrevocably sliding from the old into the new, and the hedge became a sort of outward and visible sign of that great transition.[55]

IV

The many kinds of structures that sheltered the English countryfolk in 1590 were mostly old relics that had been erected a century or so earlier in the indigenous, medieval tradition without any conscious thought of style. Shelter rather than housing, and often inadequate at that, was all that most of the rural population had ever known. The records of Leicestershire include a report that a "poor

54. Hoskins and Fineberg, *Devonshire Studies*, 291–2, 293, 324, 330; W. G. Hoskins, *Devon* (London, 1954), 96; W. G. Hoskins, Ownership and Occupation of the Land in Devonshire, 1650–1800 (Ph.D. Thesis, London, 1938).

55. Hedge breakers plagued many a manor court, as at Scrooby in Nottinghamshire; in 1627 the pledgemen declared "William Hobson is a common hedge breaker of his neighbor's hedges. Accordingly he is in the lord's mercy. 12*d*." *CSM*, XLII, 187, 189, 195; *Jacula Prudentum* (1640), in Robert Aris Wilmott (ed.), *The Works of George Herbert* (New York, n. d.), 306; Darby, *Geography*, 345–6; Mundy, *Travels*, IV, 24.

man, a wisket maker," put up "for his own succor," a cote of
"Stickes and turffes" at Whitwick in 1604. Only a few of these
primitive habitations have survived—the hut of a charcoal-burner
in south Yorkshire and that of a bark-peeler at High Furness, Lancashire. Both are made out of branches and wattle, and are covered with earth and sod. It is altogether possible, of course, that
this type of refuge was warmer and snugger in winter than the de-
caying one-room hovels occupied by poor laborers on many of the
manors.[56]

During the reign of Elizabeth, the gradual shift in land use from
the raising of cereal crops to grazing resulted in the eviction of laborers and poor husbandmen from their dilapidated quarters.
These hapless people faced a housing shortage, already acute as a
result of the marked increase of population in the sixteenth century. Some of them resolved their plight by renting cottages from
freeholders; others squatted on the waste land and hastily put up
crude cotes measuring about fourteen by sixteen feet and pat-
terned after familiar medieval models. Writing of the people of
Cheshire in 1621, William Webb tells us that "in Building and Furniture of their Houses, till of late years, they used the old manner
of the Saxons: For they had their fire in the midst of the house,
against a Hob of Clay, and their Oxen also under the same roof." [57]

Judging from contemporary accounts, thousands of these miserable cottages must have been erected. John Earle describes such
an abode in 1625 when writing about "A Plain Country Fellow":
"His habitation is some poor thatched roof, distinguished from his
barn by the loop-holes that let out smoke, which the rain had long
since washed through but for the double ceiling of bacon inside,
which has hung there since his grandsire's time, and is yet to make
rashers for posterity." To this we can add the more vivid comments made by Thomas Nash a few years later: the common cot-

56. A detailed study of the housing of the Tudor and Stuart poor is both needed
and feasible. *Leicestershire Arch. Trans.*, XV, 248; Photographs of the North
Country huts in both C. F. Innocent, *The Development of English Building
Construction* (London, 1916), figs. 1–2; and Fiske Kimball, *Domestic Architecture of the American Colonies and of the Early Republic* (New York, 1927),
figs. 1–2; Davenport, *Norfolk Manor*, 103.
57. G. E. Fussell, *The English Rural Labourer* . . . (London, 1949), 10, 12;
Wiltshire Sessions, 102; King, *Vale–Royal*, 19.

tage "hath no other windowes than to serve to let out the smoke, no other hangings, than what the spider affords, no other bed-steads, or table-bords, than the bare earth, no other bedding than plaine strawe, . . . no other Couches, or Chaires, or stooles, or fourmes, or benches, or Carpets, or Cushions, than what Nature hath wrought with her owne hands, the groundwork being the earth, and the greene grasse. . . ." Such a habitation was that of John Taylor: ". . . very unfit, by reason it hath neither chimney, nor flue, nor stone wall about it above the height of four feet, being a thatched house without a loft, and hath already once or twice been like to set the town on fire." [58]

Here and there some of the poor husbandmen made out well enough in that era of rising prices to provide somewhat better ac-commodations for their families. Robert Reyce relates that in Suffolk, a poor cottager "whose purse will nott serve to bestow much, thinkes hee doth very well if hee can compasse in his man-ner of building to raise his frame low, cover it with thatch, and fill his wide pannells (after they are well splinted and bound) with clay or culme enough well tempered, over which it may bee of more ability both for warmth, continuance and comliness toe be-stowe a cast of haire, lime and sand made into mortar and layd thereon, rough or smooth as the owner pleaseth." In Sussex modest prosperity enabled some of the inhabitants, as in the parish of Kindford, to make some of the crude dwellings more comfortable, and a like improvement went on in Kent. Windows continued to be an unhoped-for luxury; only the rich could afford glass panes before the Civil War; "copyholders and ordinary poore people had none." The majority of the householders would have felt a kinship with Chaucer's widow:

> Full sooty was hir bour, and eek her halle,
> In which she eet ful many a sclendere meel.[59]

A decade before the opening of the seventeenth century, Parli-ament, aware of the desperate state of the homeless poor and, also,

58. Earle, *Microcosmography,* 52; Thomas Nash, *Quaternio, or a Fourfold Way to a Happie Life* . . . [1633] (1639), 12; *HMC Various,* I, 95.
59. Reyce, *Suffolk,* 51; *Sussex Arch.,* XCIII, 86; Everitt, *Kent,* 6, 17; Campbell, *Yeoman,* 228–9; *Country Life,* II, 381; John Aubrey, *Brief Lives,* ed. Andrew Clark (Oxford, 1898), II, 329; Geoffrey Chaucer, *The Canterbury Tales,* ed. Walter W. Skeat (Modern Library, New York, 1929), 241–2.

of the chicanery of landlords, passed an act that made it unlawful to erect a dwelling or to convert a building for use as a house on any plot of ground less than four acres. Records of county courts reveal that many gentlemen and even more yeomen breeched this law regularly. Responsibility for the infractions cannot be levied entirely against the landlords, however, for many a poor husbandman or laborer connived with them to acquire shelter. Two weavers of Bocking not only built a cottage in 1623 without the legal four acres, but they had no license from the justices and no permission of the lord or the parish. Four men in Hertfordshire violated the four-acre rule—a laborer, a husbandman, a bricklayer, and a collarmaker. A fine of £10 was the standard penalty for breaking this statute.[60]

Various subterfuges and attempts to flout the law can be turned up in every county. Geoffrey Martin of Stanway, Essex, chiseled by covering over a small barn "and making it a dewelling howss and nott laying 4 ackers of feere land according to the stattutt," and Edmund Aylesbury did the same thing at Ballsall, Warwickshire. The parishioners of Weeley presented Thomas Greene to the Essex Quarter Sessions in 1631 for holding the grounds of several farms of the parish in his own hands and letting houses to the poor at a dear rate, which both wronged them and impoverished the parish. Others pulled down "fair dwelling houses" and their outbuildings and in their place erected cottages for the poor that brought in a greater profit—an instance of this at Luton in Bedfordshire in 1618 prompted the Privy Council to order an investigation of such practices.[61]

Not insensitive to the needs of the peasants, the lords of the manors often granted permission for the building of cottages on the common land. In the single Middlesex parish of Enfield, forty-three new cottages went up on the waste between 1615 and 1635. Occasionally, as in Somerset at West Permard, overseers of the

60. Danby Pickering (ed.), *Statutes at Large,* 31 Eliz., c 7 (Cambridge, Eng., 1763), VI, 409–10; Essex Sessions, XIX, 499, 529; XX, 13; *Sussex Arch.,* LVIII, 17; *North Riding Sessions,* IV, 35; *Middlesex Sessions,* n. s., II, 15, 32; *Extracts from the Court Rolls of the Manor of Wimbledon,* ed. P. H. Lawrence (London, 1866), 199; *Hertfordshire Sessions,* V, xx, 150, 277; *Sussex Sessions,* LIV, xxxi.
61. Essex Sessions, XIX, 384; XX, 286; *Warwick Sessions,* VI, 1, 3; *CSPD, 1611–18,* p. 545.

poor licensed the location of a cottage on the waste without providing the required four acres; that particular one was to shelter
William Walter and his family, he "beinge growne poor and impotent." It appears that usually the justices of the peace bowed to
the patent fact of insufficient housing; but this did not excuse Edward Wymble of Chrishall, Essex, for "erecting a cottage on the
Lord's waste. . . . therein, as it is supposed, keeping a house of
bawdery and thievery." [62]

Indubitably the ordinary people felt the rural housing shortage
most severely, but the ever-expanding number of families of both
copyholding and freeholding yeomen and the lesser gentry were
also cramped for living space. Substantial savings from augmented
incomes produced by high prices for agricultural products enabled
most of the members of these two aspiring orders to provide both
for more room in their living quarters and to acquire finer furnishings in emulation of their betters. Reyce spoke disparagingly of
the low standards of craftsmanship and materials, asserting that
the workman who can "doe his work with most beauty, least
charge (albeit nott so strong) hee is most required." Beginning
about 1580, a remarkable transformation and improvement in ap-
pearances, conveniences, and efficient use of farm dwellings went
forward in the eastern, southern, and some of the western counties; it reached its peak during the next half century, and by 1640,
a veritable revolution had occurred in vernacular * building, visible signs of which existed everywhere south of Yorkshire.[63]

This conspicuous activity in housing rural Englishmen took

---

* When architectural historians speak of the *vernacular,* they mean the results
achieved by people who built as they spoke, without any realization that some
other mode of expression might exist and be better. There is, today, in England
an active Vernacular Architectural Society.

---

62. Thomas Griffin of Calne, Wiltshire, a shoemaker "destitute of a house to
dwell in, and haveinge a wief and fower poore children," sought and received
permission to build a cottage on a plot of ground on parsonage land. *HMC
Various,* I, 81–2; Lysons, *London,* II, 316; *Hertfordshire Sessions,* V, xxi–xxii, 8;
Somerset Sessions, II, 5, 24; Essex Sessions, XIX, 393.
63. Mr. M. W. Barley wisely points out "that in 1600 it was already as difficult
as it is today to distinguish precisely between a house and a cottage. What
mattered was not the size of the dwelling, nor the standards of the occupants,
but how much land went with either." *English Farmhouse,* 54, 59, 60; Reyce,
Suffolk, 50.

three readily observable forms: a rebuilding of existing medieval cottages and "great halls" and the overlaying of their exteriors with modern features; the tearing down of old and often decayed or dilapidated structures to provide space for the raising of new ones; and the erecting of a large number of new buildings on newly acquired sites to accommodate more families of yeomen and lesser gentry. The course that construction followed in any one region was governed largely by the availability of building materials and of land upon which to seat the dwellings. Taken in its entirety, all of the brisk activity may be labeled most accurately *The Great Housing Boom,* for, as William Harrison proudly stated in 1577: "if ever curious building did florish in England, it is in these our yeares, wherein our workemen excell." [64]

Within the reaches of London, refurbishing of old rather than the construction of new edifices was the rule. The prosperous farmers of East Anglia, Essex, Hertfordshire, Middlesex, Surrey, and Kent expended their considerable energies and ample purses in building chimneys and fireplaces, cutting walls in order to put in casement windows—"because glasse is come to be so plentifull" —and dividing great halls, where they existed, by the insertion of a ceiling to make two floors. Each room had a special name indicating its purpose (parlor, solar, buttery, chamber, kitchen). Often the workmen added wings to an existing structure for servants' quarters, so that four- and six-room houses became common in the east and south, though in a county like Bedford, one- and two-room cottages still predominated.[65]

64. C. F. Innocent first called attention to this "great rebuilding" by all classes in 1916, and W. G. Hoskins has brought together recent scholarship in two articles: "The Rebuilding of Rural England," in *Past and Present,* IV, 44–57; and "The Great Rebuilding," in *History Today,* V, 104–11. See also Barley, *English Farmhouse,* 63, 67. Other works are Harry Batsford and Charles Fry, *The English Cottage* (3d. ed., rev.; London, 1950); Martin S. Briggs, *The English Farmhouse* (London, 1953); and particularly Olive Cook and Edwin Smith, *English Cottages and Farmhouses* (London, 1954); Harrison, *England,* Pt. I, 238.

65. In Dorset, Devon, Cornwall, and Somerset there was also much rebuilding of old houses. Harrison, *England,* Pt. I, 233–40; for the restoration and enlarging of a typical mid-Suffolk farmhouse in 1580, see the drawings and photographs in *Suffolk,* XXIV, 14ff; for Robert Furse's house in Devon, see *Devonshire,* XXVI, 181; and for Robert Loder's house in Berkshire, reconstructed in 1618, see *Camden,* 3d ser., LIII, 157–8; also Emmison, in *Bedford,* XX, 7–8.

The years 1603–40 constitute "the most important period of all for English vernacular building." One really should not think of the cottages and farmhouses as *architecture,* but rather as the construction of a basic type common to most of northwestern Europe —what we may label the International Vernacular. In Brittany at Dinan, and in Normandy at Bayeux and Honfleur, and to the east in Strasbourg and Colmar, as well as in such tiny Alsatian communities as Obernai, Riquewihr, and Kaysersberg, and all the way across Germany through Nagold in the Black Forest, to Osterode and Goslar in the Harz Mountains, and as far as distant Königsburg, one may observe the same kind of exposed half-timbering and jetty construction that characterizes the houses along Myddleton Place and Bridge Street in Saffron Walden, or those that line the loveliest thoroughfare in all East Anglia, at Kersey. We do not know the names of any of the men who erected them, but we applaud their unconscious skills in achieving a most satisfactory harmony of building and environment. And fortunate indeed were those of their time who could take the concepts and techniques of the new construction with them to America, where they sought, literally, to build a new England.[66]

The rural workmen of the seventeenth century clung to traditional medieval plans and arrangements. A typical specimen of the medieval variety still stood as recently as 1905, at Shorne, near Gravesend. Constructed for a yeoman in the fifteenth or early sixteenth century, it measured 45½ feet by 20 feet, and the second story projected two feet on the front only. A hipped roof of thatch surmounted a box frame made from local oak. The heavy timbers, shaped with axe and adze close to the spot where the great oaks had been felled, had warped and twisted because they had not been properly seasoned; hence the slanting floors and picturesque deformities the modern tourist admires so greatly at Lavenham and other East Anglian towns. To save money, the builders had used the cheapest filling: earth, sand, straw, and sticks or reeds, better known as *wattle and daub.* Only a few of these homesteads remained after the rebuilding that characterized The Great Hous-

66. The French call half-timbering *colombage,* the Germans, *Fachwerk.* Most of this paragraph is based upon actual viewing of the structures on the Continent, and eighteen photographs in the author's possession.

ing Boom, and one would err greatly if those truly medieval houses were to be confused with the newly built Jacobean and Caroline houses portrayed in modern works as "Renaissance architecture." [67]

In centuries past, particularly in southeastern England (notably the Weald of Kent), and widely too in Essex, but less often in Middlesex, Hertfordshire, Cambridgeshire, and Buckinghamshire, houses and farm buildings had been constructed of wood. Builders had made extensive use of weatherboarding for sheathing, but now the mounting scarcity of wood in the entire southeastern part of the country forced men to make substitutions. Daub and other cheaper and less satisfactory building materials were used instead of the stronger and more durable "bords," and houses made wholly of wood were seldom erected anywhere in the kingdom. Boards for siding and for wainscoting the interior walls were often imported from the Baltic. Nevertheless, because a large proportion of the people who went out to America in the Great Migration came from these counties where wood construction had been the custom, they reverted to it, especially in New England, where there was a superabundance of timber.[68]

Wastage of building materials forced "the witt of this latter age to devise a new kind of compacting, uniting, coupling, framing, and building with almost half the timber which was wont to be used, and far stronger as workmen strike not to affirm, butt," as Reyce points out, "the truth is not yet found out soe." The majority of structures built according to this new method were half-

67. A surveyor said in 1566 of the central portion of the present Chignall Hall, Essex, built in the mid-sixteenth century: "It standeth nakedly without any defence from the wynde and buylded moostly with grene tymber as it semeth. For the howses yelde and shrinck in every part. . . . And certenly if yt be not pulled downe, the greater part thereof will fall downe or (ere) yt be longe." Yet the structure still stands, though much added to. Quoted in *Essex Homes. 1066–1850* (Chelmsford, 1958), pls. 10, 11; *Kent,* XXVII, facing pp. 193, 196; Hannah, in *Sussex Arch.,* LXXI, 107–33; Reyce, *Suffolk,* 49–50.

68. For the meaning of *clapboard* in England and New England, see William Bradford, *History of Plymouth Plantation, 1620–1647,* ed. Worthington C. Ford (Mass. Hist. Soc., 1912), I, 235, 235*n.* Harrison, *England,* Pt. I, 233; Clifton-Taylor, *English Building,* 31–2, 51, 54–5; Hugh T. Morrison, *Early American Architecture* (New York, 1952), 15, 30, and fig. 21; G. D. Ramsay, *English Overseas Trade During the Centuries of Emergence* (London, 1957), 97; Best, in *Surtees,* XXXIII, 110–12.

timbered, with a steep roof, usually of thatch, resting on a frame-
work of vertical posts and horizontal beams—an arrangement
known today as a *box-frame*. A striking external feature of many
box-frame houses was a second story, and often a third, projecting
one or two feet on the front of the building and sometimes on the
sides. The English call this a *jetty;* the Americans, an *overhang*.[69]

Workmen could choose from several kinds of filling when they
made the walls for half-timbered buildings. Ordinarily they constructed a light wooden core of sheathing from wattles or sticks, or
of stronger laths, which they covered with daub or plaster, or else
they left the timbers exposed, to weather into a lovely soft gray.
Less frequently, they put in a nogging of expensive bricks that they
arranged in herring-bone and other patterns, as in the famous Pay-
cock House at Coggeshall, Essex, and in many Kentish dwellings.[70]

In the southern and eastern counties, the scarcity of stone as
well as of wood explains the popularity of brick in the more pre-
tentious houses; it proved too costly for small cottages. It also
turned out to be the favorite material for the many new chimneys—in the limestone region at Oxford, the city council decreed
in 1632 that all future leases should require all houses to be "slat-
ted" and chimneys to be of brick or stone. The skilled bricklayers,
now in great demand, joined with the carpenters and initiated the
moving of the massive chimney stack from the gable-end to the
center of the house and built a winding stairway alongside it, customarily between the stack and the "porch" entry. Such an arrangement permitted the introduction of back-to-back fireplaces
(and often a third) and warmed the stairwell, a great asset in

69. The endless debate about the origin of the jetty is sensibly reduced by Mr.
Clifton-Taylor to three reasons, any one or all three of which sufficiently
explains any case: (1) the overhang probably originated in the cities and towns
and was imitated in the country; it was simply to gain more floor space in the
upper storeys; (2) the jetty did serve as a protection from damp, which is
"perhaps a more likely explanation"; and (3) the jetty may be purely structural,
a method of producing a cantilever effect. Clifton-Taylor, *English Building,*
36–9, and for a view of a stripped house at Somersham, Suffolk, showing the
box-frame construction, consult pl. b facing p. 42; Reyce, *Suffolk,* 51; Barley,
English Farmhouse, 29.

70. Clifton-Taylor, *English Building,* 42, 45; Pevsner, *Essex,* fig. a, pl. 46.

damp East Anglia and later a prime necessity in cold New England. Emigrants from the southeastern counties of England to the Chesapeake country, finding excellent salt-saturated clays and an ample supply of oyster shells for burning into lime, turned intuitively to the construction of brick houses.[71]

Devon, too, contained little satisfactory building stone, but few brick houses appeared there in this period; the cob house remained the standard. A mixture of moist, stiff clay and chopped straw, called *cob,* was pitched into position with a fork; it made a durable, hard wall if a well-thatched roof protected it from the rain. And, as hundreds of West Country cottages bear witness, a most pleasing effect could be obtained with a plaster coating and a white- or cream-wash.[72]

The Great Housing Boom gave work to the members of the thatcher's craft. The difference in the relative prosperity of the several counties can be gauged to some degree by the wages paid to thatchers. In Essex a skilled workman earned 7s. 6d. a week; in most parts of the country the pay was sixpence per day and meat; in Yorkshire the men had only fourpence, because the employers gave them three meals a day in addition. A Yorkshire farmer reported in 1641 that "Wee usually provide two women for helpes in this kinde, *viz.*; one to draw thacke, and the other to serve the thatcher"; and "shee alsoe is to temper the morter, and to carry it up to the toppe of the howse. . . ."[73]

Tile roofs were not uncommon in Essex and Kent, and could be found in parts of Hampshire, Berkshire, and Hertfordshire, but tile-hanging was not truly popular until the mid-seventeenth century and hence the emigrants who set out for the New World did not know much about it. Possibly they had heard that searchers for

71. Clifton-Taylor, *English Building,* 214–15; The first brick building went up in Leeds in 1628, but for the next fifty years little more occurred there. Fussell, in *Agricultural History,* VII, 187n; M. G. Hobson and H. E. Salter (eds.), *Oxford Council Acts, 1625–1655* (Oxford, 1933), 40; Barley, *English Farmhouse,* 67–71, pl. IIIb; Martin S. Briggs, *Homes of the Pilgrim Fathers in England and America, 1620–1685* (Oxford, 1932), 42, 51–6.
72. Hoskins, *Devon,* 267–9; Clifton-Taylor, *English Building,* 272–9.
73. *VCH Essex,* II, 340, 342; Clifton-Taylor, *English Building,* chap. 13; Best, in *Surtees,* XXXIII, 138.

"tyles" in Essex in 1595 and 1596 had found forty-six tile kilns to be defective and the tiles wanting in size, whiting, and annealing, and for this reason they abstained from trying them out in the colonies.[74]

In the rural England of the late Middle Ages, the great barn located on the manor or the monastic estate was the most important building to the people of the community, for in it the corn they harvested was threshed and stored. When the monasteries were torn down, the tithe barns usually remained to serve the needs of the entire area. Thus, in the seventeenth century, the great manorial barns and the great monastic barns furnished the models for the yeomen and lesser gentry who desired to erect structures of a smaller scale on their freeholds.[75]

Monastic tithe barns were commonly built of stone, but weatherboarding was widely used, particularly for smaller barns, in those regions where it was available. Very few of these smaller barns exist today, but from those that have survived we can trace their descent from the great barns and reconstruct what kind of notions about barns the emigrants took to the colonies. On Leigh's Farm, at a crossroads just outside of the Essex town of Felsted, there is a small barn surrounded by a moat. It is about fifty feet in length and twenty feet wide, windowless, and is entered at the center of the long side through a porch with a truncated gable. The whole is sheathed with weatherboards. Resembling this structure basically (though much modernized), is the Josselyn barn at Little Horkesley. Built c. 1500, to go with a superb farmhouse, the barn, as well as the house, is roofed with thatch. At Sutton Mandeville in Wiltshire there is another weatherboard barn, also thatched, and of about the same size. A barn of this type in Sussex, with two bays

---

74. Briggs, *Farmhouses,* 66; Batsford, *English Cottages,* 77; Essex Sessions, XVII, 25–6.

75. Well-preserved examples of great barns may be seen in Essex at Little Coggeshall (Grange Farm) and Cressing Temple Farm, High Rodding; at Bradford-on-Avon in Wiltshire; also in the excellent series of photographs in Cook and Smith, *English Cottages,* 10–11, pls. 201–16, from Berkshire, Dorset, Wiltshire, Somerset, and Gloucestershire; and in the superbly illustrated and learned study by Walter Horn and Ernest Born, *The Barns of the Abbey of Beaulieu at its Granges of Great Cogswell and Beaulieu St. Leonards* (Berkeley, Calif., 1965). See also Pevsner, *Essex,* pls. 46b, 47; *Middlesex,* pl. 34; *Surrey,* pl. 5; *Country Life,* VIII, 294–6; LI, 902.

and measuring twenty-three feet by eighteen feet, bears the inscription "Johnny Killingbeck 1610." [76]

By 1640 many new barns had been erected, but from the scanty evidence to be found on maps and surveys, it seems that most of the produce of the small farms was still stored in the great manorial barns. The barns that were put up were beginning to be used for more than threshing and storage. Some landlords had converted old barns into several tenements in order to circumvent the four-acre act; certainly as originally constructed they were scarcely habitable, for most of them lacked windows, and their grayed weatherboarding let in much cold and damp. Occasionally a well-to-do husbandman took pride in decorating his farm buildings, for the records of Great Tey state that in 1623 William Stebbing had opened a claypit a rod wide in the highway in order to "new daub and flower [embellish]" his barns. A year passed before the Essex justices ordered him to fill in the pit! What kinds of shelter the husbandmen afforded their fowls, hogs, and other animals must remain largely to conjecture.[77]

The improvements in shelter and appearance accompanying The Great Housing Boom had their counterparts in convenience and the amenities of living. The wider use of glazed windows, even with their small leaded panes, made for far better lighting of interiors, and the division of the medieval halls into rooms with fireplaces assured greater warmth and dryness during cold and wet weather for those who could afford the fuel. These changes and additions in turn had a beneficial effect on the health of the inmates of the house.

The vogue for cutting up the interiors of existing dwellings, inserting second and third floors with several rooms at each level, and constructing new wings to provide additional space stemmed in part from what has been described as "the filtering down" of a

76. Some idea of seventeenth-century barns may be gained from examining the twelve representations on John Walker's colored map of Chelmsford (1591), of which the Essex Record Office has published a reduced facsimile. The writer personally inspected in 1962 most of Essex and East Anglian barns mentioned. See also *Journal of Architectural Historians,* XI, 7–8 (for Wiltshire); Hannah, in *Sussex Arch.,* LXXXIII, 30–31.

77. Cook and Smith, *English Cottages,* 10–11; *Country Life,* LXI, 223; LII, 736–42; Essex Sessions, XX, 5.

sense of privacy. Admittedly privacy was a relative matter, the degree of enjoyment being dependent upon the wealth of the householder and the size of the family. Heretofore the priceless opportunity of being able to withdraw from a group and to be alone was enjoyed only by the upper classes. Now members of large families that lived in small cottages at least had the satisfaction of separating the sleeping, cooking, and living activities in a house having two rooms on the ground floor and a sleeping garret overhead, and this was a marked advance over what their forefathers had known.[78]

There can be no doubt that already this intangible development, this blessing of privacy, incomplete as it was, was affecting the psychology of the middling and lower sorts. And it is most important to realize that those Englishmen who attempted to transfer their civilization across the Atlantic Ocean employed both the concept of privacy and the prevailing house plans for implementing it in the first permanent houses they built in the New World.

78. Lewis Mumford first drew attention to the idea of privacy in *The Culture of the Cities* (New York, 1938), 29, 40, 115, 118; Hoskins, in *History Today*, V, 110; and in *Past and Present*, IV, 54; for a somewhat contrary and less convincing view, see Barley, *English Farmhouse*, 60–61, 124–5.

III

Countrymen Day by Day

To THOSE ENGLISHMEN who ventured across the Atlantic during the 1620's and 1630's, the greatest shock proved to be the absence in the new lands of community existence. Throughout the entire English countryside, but particularly in the thirty-four counties south of Yorkshire and Lancashire, very few hamlets remained truly isolated. Always the essential feature of farm and village life had been its local and communal nature. A relationship which was intensely personal conjoined the members of this vigorous, lusty village stock—an interdependence that was, more or less, an extension of the comings and goings of a country family.[1]

This tiniest unit of society conducted activities that were at one and the same time productive and sociable. Its hierarchical composition had evolved over the years out of the hard facts of daily urgency. All matters pertaining to the land, shelter, and field husbandry became the responsibility of the man, whatever his degree. If he were a prosperous husbandman or yeoman, he personally directed all of the agricultural laborers, tenants, and male servants or apprentices in their daily tasks. To the housewife fell the management of all indoor affairs and those of the dairy, barnyard, and kitchen garden, and the orchard where such existed. As the husband and his wife strove without letup to fulfill their personal obli-

1. N. S. B. Gras has pointed out, for instance, that such an out-of-the-way village as Crawley in Hampshire was never really isolated, and the same held true of most farming communities. *Economic History of an English Village*, 2; also Clark, *Working Life of Women*, 42.

gations, they also developed a strong sense of duty toward the whole household.

The traditional family solidarity and *rapprochement* attributed to the more favored villagers cannot be claimed for the miserably poor and landless denizens. Indeed it would be remarkable if such feelings and attitudes could have developed amid the rigors of a poor husbandman's existence. Sunrise found him trudging off to work in the fields, where he toiled until sunset for a wage insufficient to support his family in decent circumstances. There could have been little time, let alone the heart or energy, for recreation or social activities. It is hard to believe that the ballader who wrote

> But 'tis a Husband-man's delight
> To worke all day, and sleepe all night.

had any firsthand knowledge of the "delight" of long hours of exhausting labor.[2]

The only occupants of the peasant's cottage during daylight hours were his wife and those of his children who were too young to go out to work. The older boys labored in the fields alongside their father, and the girls of the family were employed by the day in the neighborhood or went into yearly service if there were any opportunities for it. Sometimes the boys also lived in the households of their employers, where they fared better than they would have in their own homes; a monotonous diet and a one-room house that more often than not was cold, damp, and inescapably grimy were all they could look forward to at the end of a day's work.

The "Huswifery" celebrated by the writers of the day rarely manifested itself among the rural poor. Food preparation was so limited by supplies and custom, and the houses were so sparsely furnished, that indoor duties took up little time. Nevertheless the peasant's wife had no leisure. If the dwelling were situated on the required four acres of land, her husband expected her to make it productive. It was her obligation to cultivate the garden plot and look after any poultry or livestock the family owned. After she

2. *The Roxburghe Ballads,* eds. W. Chappell and J. W. Ebsworth (Hertford, 1871), I, 303; Byrne, *Elizabethan Life,* 133–9; Clark, *Working Life of Women,* 86.

completed her work out-of-doors, or when the weather made those chores impracticable, she mended or made clothes for the family or else she spent whatever time was left of the daylight hours in spinning yarn to stretch the family's meager income. The only relieving feature for the toilworn woman was that ordinarily she had enough plain food and hours of outdoor labor to make her muscularly strong, and consequently her babies had a better chance of surviving than those born in the cities.[3]

The lack of leisure for a poor, overworked peasant and his spouse, the absence of any privacy or of the amenities for a complex household, and the impossibility of acquiring any proper education or of conducting religious worship in the home circle more than explain their apathy and want of family feeling. Physically and spiritually life was barren. With little hope for better days, the meaner sort of husbandman and his family lived out their lives amid conditions of drudgery, dirt, and almost overwhelming poverty.[4]

The chronicle of England's poor bears no resemblance to that of the thriving husbandman or yeoman. Fortunately for this history, the majority of the emigrants to New England, and not a few of those who went to the West Indies or the Chesapeake, were recruited from the middling people of the countryside, about whom more information survives. It is possible, therefore, to examine the kinds of family arrangements they carried with them that so profoundly affected the development of English civilization in the New World.

The families of those of greater rank or fortune commonly embraced more members than the mere conjugal group; the presence of several elderly or dependent relations, together with male and female apprentices and servants who lived in, often made a very numerous household, or *family*. The late R. H. Tawney has shown that *hospitality* literally meant *housekeeping* for "a miniature co-operative society, housed under one roof, dependent upon one industry, and including not only man and wife and children, but servants and labourers, ploughmen and threshers, cowherds and

3. Alice Clark's *Working Life of Women* is one of the few adequate treatments of the English poor. See especially pp. 43, 50, 67–8.
4. Clark, *Working Life of Women*, 58.

milk maids" who lived together, worked together, and played together.[5]

Religious observance of some kind figured prominently in the
daily round of rural being, whether the family was Anglican or
Puritan or Roman Catholic. Since the Reformation, the head of
the family had assumed certain diurnal duties that made his family
truly "a little Church, and a little common-wealth." Generally the
master read passages from the Geneva Bible (revised Great Bible)
of the Puritans or, in an Anglican household, from the Bishops'
Bible, or from the Book of Common Prayer and from the new
King James Version after 1611, together with such other devotions
and prayers as were thought suitable. The principal difference between the Puritans and Anglicans was not whether they practiced
devotions, but their precise nature and the amount of time spent
on them. Thus, from hearing the Bible read aloud repeatedly, and
simply expounded, either willingly or by compulsion, children and
youthful servants and apprentices absorbed a considerable body of
biblical lore and teachings whose practical worth served them
throughout their lives and which supplied to the English people as
a whole a priceless fund of common culture.[6]

It was the mistress of the household, however, who inspired the
lines attributed to Thomas Parr:

> May England's few good hous-keepers be blest
> With endlesse Glory and eternall Rest;

One can readily understand why only a "few" merited the plaudits
of this "old, old, very old man" when the wide range of routine
work demanded of the wife of a prosperous yeoman is considered. Besides bearing babies annually, she alone saw to the nur-

5. R. H. Tawney, *The Agrarian Problem in the Sixteenth Century* (London,
1912), 233.
6. The expelled Puritan vicar of Felsted, Ezekiel Culverwell, advised the elder
John Winthrop about his children in 1618–19: "And to this end make it (as
you doe) your cheefe studye to trayne them up in the nurture and admonition
of the Lord, which I understand from their infansy to nurse them up in
knowledg and practise of christianity as their capacity will bear." Many of the
household manuals stressed the responsibilities of masters for the proper religious
instruction of their servants, even supplying prayers for family use, as in the
thirty-six or more editions of Bishop Bayly's *The Practise of Piety* issued between
1612 and 1636. *Winthrop Papers*, I, 234.

ture, training, and disciplining of the children; from birth through adolescence she was their schoolmistress. Preparing meals, baking, cleaning, washing, malting, and "dinner matters," all of which had to be finished by noon each day, were her responsibility. When male and female apprentices and servants actually lived with the family, they too came under her surveillance: they had to be fed, clothed, and directed in the proper performance of their daily chores. Good "Huswifery" also required her to perform or supervise the brewing, dairy work, gardening, nursing, and doctoring, and, not infrequently, to spin flax or wool in her spare time. Physical endurance and toughness, ingenuity and industry were requisites for the mistress of a farming family merely to keep abreast of her many assignments. Her success or failure in carrying out these many tasks really determined her husband's success or failure:

> For husbandry weepeth,
> Where housewifery sleepeth,
> And hardly he creepeth,
> Up ladder to thrift.[7]

The working day of the housewife paralleled that of her husband. Governed by the insufficient lighting common to the age, she arose at four or five and woke the maid; at night she retired according to the season:

> In winter at nine, and in summer at ten,
> To bed after supper, both maidens and men.

So many exhortations were addressed to the housewife to keep busy—"Always be doinge of some good werkes, that the dyvell may fynde thee ever occupied"—that one must assume that many wives fell short of the standards set up for them by their masculine preceptors.[8]

---

7. John Taylor, "The Old, Old, Very Old Man," in *Works,* I, No. 2, p. 19; Thomas Tusser, "The Points of Huswifery, United to the Comfort of Husbandry," in *Five Hundred Points of Good Husbandry as well for the Champion or Open Country as for the Woodland or Several* (London, 1812), 129, 140–41, 236, 253–64; Clark, *Working Life of Women,* 5, 9, 50, 94–5, 145.
8. Tusser, "Huswifery," 247, 268–9; *The Book of Husbandry by Master Fitzherbert,* ed. W. W. Skeat (English Dialect Society, VIII, 1882), 94.

Comments and advice were freely offered. George Herbert warned that "A gentle house-wife mars the household." In *The City Madam,* the daughter of a London merchant admits reluctantly that her country sister is a good business woman—she knows the price of corn in the market, can estimate the cost of beef per stone, or figure out when to raise goslings—but is not qualified to be a life partner for a country gentleman. From the clerical ranks, Nehemiah Rogers sententiously asserted that "Domesticall business is for the woman's employment. God hath not (ordinarily) given them that capacity and judgement he hath to men," and he counseled the men to "honour Women as the weaker vessels." Less sanctimonious and more practical were the numerous household hints entitled "Points of Huswifery" that Thomas Tusser appended to the second edition (1561) of *Five Hundred Points of Good Husbandry,* a work so widely approved that seventeen reprintings or revisions were published before 1638.[9]

Managing the servants, who often numbered as many as ten, turned out to be the most trying task for the housewife. Young girls entered the family as apprentices or as servants; they had to be disciplined, supervised at work, and constantly instructed during all the daylight hours. In *Jacula Prudenta,* Herbert maintained that "one eye of the master sees more than ten of the servants," and Tusser urged that the housewife "Declare after supper—take heed there unto,/What work in the morning, each servant shall do," and further,

> Make maid to be cleanly, or make her cry creak,
> And teach her to stir, when her mistress doth speak.

There could be no letup, not even at mealtimes, and teaching table manners to country louts and ill-bred lasses called for both fortitude and patience. Custom enjoined that no servant be permitted to talk saucily at the table lest he or she develop the habit of impudence at other times, and most mistresses tried to enforce the convention of

9. Herbert, *Works,* 303; Philip Massinger, *The City Madam* (1632) Act II, Scene ii, in *The Best Plays of Old Dramatists* (New York, n. d.), II; Nehemiah Rogers, *The Good Housewife with her Broome and Candle: or an Exposition on the Parable of the Lost Groat,* in *The True Convert* (1632), Sermon No. 2, p. 5.

> No lurching, no snatching, no striving at all;
> Lest one go without, and another have all.

From this couplet it is clear that the boardinghouse-reach plagued the mistresses of Tudor and Stuart households and was not exclusively a phenomenon of nineteenth-century America.[10]

It would be unfair to brand all domestic servants as uncouth. If a serving maid were intelligent and willing to learn, and if her training were resourcefully administered, "she wan the love of all the house." Thomas Churchyard has vividly described such a paragon who worked in a household of the lesser gentry, but she could just as well have resided with a yeoman's family. Up with the lark every morning, she performed her duties with cheerfulness, thoroughness, and dispatch; and she "did herselfe esteeme" as she moved quickly and silently about the house all day long. Moreover she was a good cook and skillful at dressing meat. Once a year, usually at Easter time, she went into town, all pranked up in garments upon which she had lavished her hard-earned wages, and with a very much prized purse hanging from her neck on a green ribbon "welbeseene." Responsibility and tireless industry, however, exacted their tolls from this slender girl. In cold weather her hands turned blue, and "her lippes were red but somewhat chapped," and exposure to the open air in winter and summer caused her tender skin to peel. The stitch in her side, a result of heavy work, caused her the most distress, however, and it made her short-winded.[11]

For many a country wench the time spent with a large farming family brought rewards beyond her wages. Those who worked in yeomen's households had one advantage over those who worked for the gentry, in that daily, during work or play, they associated with young men of their own rank, and thereby widened their acquaintance with possible suitors. Usually the experience moulded a young woman from a poorer background into a thrifty house-

---

10. Many girls went to work as maid servants for Adam Winthrop at the Manor of Groton in Suffolk: In 1606 Alice Reignold agreed to work for wages of 33s.4d. per annum; and the next year Margaret Winthrop wrote to John: "I have maydes anow ofered me." *Winthrop Papers,* I, 43, 47, 52, 56, 124, 161; Tusser, "Huswifery," 251, 266, 267; Herbert, *Works,* 324.
11. Thomas Churchyard, *The Firste parte of Churchyardes* (1578).

keeper, and not infrequently it enabled her, through marriage, to move upward in society.[12]

Indubitably, many serving girls and boys chafed at household regulations and worked no harder than was necessary unless the mistress was nearby and watching them. Nevertheless their lot was not an unhappy one: they enjoyed an ample diet, a dry bed, and, as a rule, healthy though hard work indoors and out. Milkmaids earned such a national renown as eager, tireless dancers and singers of ballads that Martin Parker and other versifiers, knowing them to be ballad-buyers, extolled them in many a song.[13]

There was also a dark and dangerous side to the experiences of the pretty and buxom female servant, for more than one found the men of the household either demanding or willing to test her virtue. All counties can be included in William Webb's conclusions about Cheshire: "Likewise, be the Women very friendly and loving, painful in [daily] labour, and in all other kind of Hous-wifery expert, fruitful in bearing of Children, after they be married and sometimes before." The Essex Archdeaconry court had a typical case come before it in 1591: Alice Colleton of Birch Magna alleged that her master's son, Richard Nooth, "had lyen with her." In Much Munden in 1624, it was the father, a poor husbandman already burdened with many children, who brought the charge that his daughter had been got with child by William, son of her master, John Sell, gentleman. Because William had absconded, the justices directed the inhabitants of Much Munden to care for the child until the father could be found. Sometimes a fellow-servant was implicated, as in the case of Elias Marmsell of Great Haddam, who had got Elizabeth Douce pregnant when they both worked in Thomas Kitchen's family. Few households were so loosely conducted, however, as that of William Richman, which the judges of the Somerset Assizes ordered investigated in 1632 because thirteen maids were reported to have borne children there in fourteen years.[14]

Other court cases revealed that some masters and their dames

12. Notestein, in Plumb, *Social History*, 95.
13. *Roxburghe Ballads*, I, 165–7; II, 114–19.
14. King, *Vale-Royal*, 19–20; Essex Arch., XII, 16a–b; *Hertfordshire Sessions*, V, 36–7, 48; *Somerset Assize Orders*, 19.

were guilty of harsh, ruthless, and inhuman treatment of the servile members of their families. "Sibbell" Clarke, servant of a yeoman, Thomas Kenton, had to go all the way from Hadley to the Middlesex Sessions to lodge a complaint about her master's "hanging a horslocke upon her legge." The justices were so incensed that they ordered him to pay her 20s. in addition to the ten weeks' wages he owed her, and then released her from his service. In Suffolk, at Woodbridge, the authorities freed Elizabeth Chapman from her apprenticeship to Mr. Robert Ose of Stratford upon learning of the "diverse abuses" she suffered at his hands; and the courts heard numerous cases in which barbarous beatings had resulted in the permanent injury and even death of a servant. It should not surprise any one that, rather than submit to chastisement, spirited wenches and lads preferred to run away and "rogue" it up and down the countryside.[15]

II

In the country, "Rusticus" asserted in 1632, "we seldome eat to please the palate, or satisfie appetite; onely eate to live, give nature her due, not overburthen her; for we hate to be accounted any of Epicurics." Speaking of "the meaner sort of husbandmen," Harrison stated it much more baldly: "divers of them living at home, with hard and pinching diet, small drinke, and some of them having scarce inough of that." Nor did the poorer peasant eat regularly at a set meal in the manner of the gentry or city people: "the Poorest sort . . . generallie dine and sup when they may." [16]

The diet of the average husbandman consisted almost exclu-

---

15. One maid-servant at Burbage in Wiltshire was beaten so severely in 1607 that her "kennel-bone" [collarbone] and two of her ribs were broken. There were, of course, some maidens who proved to be both immodest and unruly and deserved some kind of discipline. After all, not a few of these girls were involuntary apprentices who had been bound out, as orphans, by the churchwardens or justices to persons who would have them until they reached twenty-one to twenty-five years of age. *HMC Various,* I, 79; *Surrey,* VIII, 249–50; Coldridge [Devon] Churchwardens Accounts (Muniment Room, Exeter City Library), 83; *Middlesex Sessions,* II, 39; *Suffolk,* XV, 152, 164, 168; Conyers Read, ed., *William Lambarde & Local Government* (Ithaca, 1962), 43; Essex Sessions, XIX, 278, 320.
16. Nash, *Quaternio,* 23; Harrison, *England,* Pt. I, 152–3, 166.

sively of bread and cheese, which he moistened with cider, perry, and occasionally homemade ale or beer. This kind of fare caused the callous Londoner to inquire: "What makes the peasant grovel in his muck, humbling his crooked soul, but that he eats bread just in colour like it? Courage ne'er vouchsaf'd to dwell a minute where a sullen pair of brown loaves darken'd the dirty table; Shadows of bread, not bread. You never knew a solemn son of bag-pudding and pottage made a commander, or a tripe-eater become a tyrant. He's the kingdom's arm that can feed large and choicely." Thomas Parr of Salop, who attained a very great age, waxed strong on this diet, however, and without complaint:

> Hee was of old Pithagoras opinion,
> That greene cheese was most wholesome (with an onion)
> Course Mesclin bread, and for his daily swig,
> Milk, Butter-milk, and Water, Whay, and Whig;
> Sometimes, Metheglin, and by fortune happy,
> Hee sometimes sip't a Cup of Ale most nappy,
> Syder, or Perry, when hee did repaire
> T' a Whitson Ale, Wake, Wedding, or a Faire,
> Or when in Christmas time hee was a Guest
> At his good Land-lords house amongst the rest:
> Or (at the Alehouse) husse-cap Ale to taste.[17]

This dark bread, which was the staple food of most of the peasants, was made from recipes that varied according to the grains available in the area. Up in Yorkshire, "Poor folkes putte usually a pecke of pease to a bushell of rye; and some againe two peckes of pease to a frundell of massledine, and say that these make hearty bread," Henry Best recorded, but for "the browne bread bakinge" on his own farm, he used one-third rye, one-third pease, and one-third barley in the winter; in the summer the amount of barley was reduced. In 1623, a poor year, the farmers of one Suffolk hundred baked bread of maslin flour (half rye, half wheat); thirty Devon parishes used only barley flour. "In times of dearth," which occurred nearly everywhere sooner or later, inferior brown bread, adulterated with pease, beans, oats, and "some acorns," was almost the sole fare of the poor, and of many yeomen too. Kinder

17. Cartwright, *The Ordinary,* II, i; Taylor, *Works,* I, No. 2, p. 20.

attributed the "fair, long, broad teeth" of the Derbyshire people to masticating their favorite oaten bread. White bread appeared only on the tables of gentlemen and citizens; when William Lilly arrived in London in 1620, he ate white bread for the first time; he remarked that it was "contrary to our diet in Leicestershire." [18]

The austere diet of the cottager was made more palatable by the daily swig. Harrison conceded that "our maltbags lug at alepots like pigs at their dames teets," and there can be no doubt but that ale and beer of varying strengths and quality slaked the English thirst more satisfactorily than any other drink. In Devon, Kent, Sussex, and Worcestershire, apple cider or pomage was the great country beverage; a "swish-wash" of honey and water with a dash of pepper or other spices found favor with Essex housewifes, but it no more resembled delicate metheglin than "chalk did cheese." As originally concocted in Wales, genuine metheglin (spiced or medicated mead, made from honey) was a fine drink. It is the belief of some writers that the ordinary peasant was not accustomed to heady drafts, and they cite his disposition to "verie much babbling" and becoming "cupshotten" at Whitsun ales and on feast days as proof. It can be observed in support of the assertion that Shakespeare's bibulous tavern scenes seldom include the simple countryman.[19]

Of other kinds of food now widely consumed, the ordinary people tasted very little. According to Harrison, vegetables that had once been produced and then neglected were again being cultivated "among the poore commons . . . melons, pompions, gourds, cucumbers, radishes, skirets, parsneps, carrets, cabbages, navewes, turneps, and all kinds of salad herbes." Fruits were slowly spreading from Kent, where they had recently been introduced from the Low Countries. "White meats"—milk, butter, cheese, eggs—were eaten in large quantities by the gentry and the middling sort, and in some regions by the poor. Modest households

18. Best, in *Surtees,* XXXIII, 103–4; Sir William Ashley, *The Bread of Our Forefathers* (London, 1928), 2, 29, 38–9, 40, 52, 59; Harrison, *England,* Pt. I, 153–5; Kinder, quoted in Steven Glover, *History of the County of Derby* (Derby, 1829), I, 314; *William Lilly's History of His Life and Times, from the Year 1602 to 1681* (London, 1822), 25.
19. Harrison, *England,* Pt. I, 152, 161, 295; William Crossing, *Folk Rhymes of Old Devon* (Exeter, 1911), 122–3.

in Bedfordshire, for example, had stored away as many as thirty or forty cheeses, and in Shropshire, all countrymen were accustomed to milk and "good Butter." Along England's extensive seacoasts and up the river estuaries, fish of many kinds—eels, lampreys, and various kinds of shellfish—might be had in plenty and were cheap; at inland markets, salt and dried fish and smoked North Sea herring (sprats) sold in considerable quantities.[20]

A widely held myth persists that the staple food of all and sundry was the "Roast Beef of Old England," a phrase used by Richard Leveridge in a song made famous by Hogarth in his "Gate of Calais." That lyric, however, was referring to the mid-eighteenth century. It is true that Thomas Tusser urged the serving of "Twice-A-Week Roast" in his advice to housewives as early as the 1580's:

> Good plowman look weekly, of custom and right
> For roast meat on Sundays, and Thursdays at night.
> Thus doing and keeping such caution and guise,
> They call thee good huswife,—and they love thee likewise.

Thomas Fuller, also, testified that in 1642 at a Kentish yeoman's board "you shall have as many joints as dishes; no meat disguised with strange [French] sauces; no straggling joint of a sheep in the midst of a pasture of grass, beset with salads on every side, but solid substantial food." Moreover an Essex family of seventeen persons bolsters the tradition: John Greene, Esq. of Bois-Hall, Navestock, set down in his accounts "that wee doe expend almost 10 stone [140 lbs.] of beefe one week with another, and about 3 quarters of mutton and a quarter of lamb." Along with this generous fare of "butcher's meate" costing only £1 15s., he also served one barrel of beer, and bread, milk, butter, oatmeal, cheese, rabbits, and chickens. "And I doe beleeve we doe spend about 10/ per weeke more in salt, oatmeale, rootes, pease, sugar, spice, and such other things as wee have from London." It cost Greene a total of

20. Harrison, *England*, Pt. I, 324; Emmison, in *Bedford*, XX, 29; *Coach and Sedan Pleasantly Disputing* (1636), C-3. For fish, Wedgwood, *The King's Peace*, 25–6; *Western Antiquary*, II, 89; X, 161–3; *CSPD, 1619–23*, p. 123; *1635*, pp. 3, 92, 136, 155 (on trawling); Taylor, *Works*, I, No. 21, pp. 17–18.

£3 10s. a week to feed the seventeen people! Surely none of them could complain that something more than a pound a day of the roast beef of Old England was short rations.[21]

All this evidence notwithstanding, it is extremely doubtful if the ordinary countryman ever ate much beef, or any other kind of meat; a little bacon now and then was about all a man could be sure of. All meat, and especially beef, was both expensive and scarce; the entire country did not contain enough beef cattle to supply many tables on the scale of John Greene's. Country gentlemen and citizens, and frequenters of inns, ate heavily of meat—Sir Andrew Aguecheeck attributed his lack of wit to his being a great eater of beef—but the average farmer seldom saw any on his own table. He looked forward to public feasts for a taste of it, but usually all he got was mutton or pork. Some few peasants in each county remedied the meat shortage by poaching, for numerous complaints reached the Privy Council about "the inferior sort who do continually spoyle and destroy all manner of game, as well as deers, hares, pheasants, partridges, herons, and other fowle with gunns, nets, doggs, crossbowes, stone bowes and all other ways and means they can invent." [22]

Because of the local nature of agriculture and the inadequacy of transport facilities for corn and hay crops, a community whose crops failed might starve in the midst of general plenty. Everywhere rural inhabitants lived very close to the subsistence level, and the fear of famine possessed them all; in fact it became a common psychosis and actually led to violence on occasion. The diary of Walter Yonge of Plymouth reveals that in three successive years, beginning in 1607, severe frosts or heavy rains caused an "extreme dearth of corn." At some places in Devonshire, the price of hay rose to 2s. 6d. per 32 pounds, and consequently cattle had

21. Richard Leveridge's "The Roast Beef of Old England," written early in the eighteenth century, was echoed by Fielding in *The Grub Street Opera*, III, ii (1731). Tusser, "Huswifery," 273; Fuller, *Holy and Profane State*, 106; "Diary of John Greene," ed. E. M. Symonds, in *EHR*, XLIII, 600.
22. The diet of the rural Frenchman was even more limited: "The tables of the poor never saw, good years or bad, any but a vegetable diet." See the comment of Robert Mandrou, *Introduction à la France Moderne* (Paris, 1961), 14–35; Fussell, *English Rural Labourer*, 28–9; *Sussex Arch.*, XLVIII, 7–8; *Somerset & Dorset*, X, 71; Pickering, *Statutes at Large*, VII, 138–41.

to be slaughtered; these straits periodically plagued the farmers all over England.[23]

The threat of widespread starvation materialized when nature failed the entire country. Such a disaster occurred in the winter of 1623, and the corn shortage was felt everywhere. The Privy Council fumblingly attempted to limit the amount of barley used in Wiltshire for brewing, because this "grayne being usuallie the cheapest is in tyme of scarcity the Bread Corne of the poore." A royal order was also issued to suppress unnecessary alehouses and to regulate the strength of the ale and beer in the remaining ones, so as to conserve barley. In Suffolk the millers were directed not to sell meal to the poor in smaller quantities than they could buy in the markets, but the justices had to relax the enforcement of that order "for fear of a mutiny among the poor"; they did, however, order the mixing of buckwheat with barley for flour. Everywhere, but particularly in Norfolk, Somersetshire, Lincolnshire, Nottinghamshire, and East Anglia, complaints about the scarcity of grain and high prices haunted the authorities, but regulatory measures failed to alleviate the sufferings of the poor.[24]

An even more serious threat of famine came in 1630 and was not surmounted until 1633. In March, 1630, food supplies were so short in Suffolk that several times the authorities reported that the poor were on the verge of rioting because buckwheat was being exported. In June the Privy Council tried to stop the grain shipments, to limit the quantities allotted for brewers' malt, to cut down the number of alehouses, and to enforce the laws against badgers, engrossers, and forestallers. "These times," said Lord Montagu, "brings nothing out but fears—fear of sickness, fear of famine . . . but I hear of no fasting [?] and prayers to prevent these judgements." A "libel" found on the porch of the minister of Wye, read, in part:

23. Sporadic efforts were made by the Lords of the Council to anticipate grain shortages; in 1619–20, they directed the authorities in Lincolnshire "to provide a magazine for storage of corn during the present plenty." *HMC Rutland*, XII, IV, 456; Walter Yonge, "Diary," in *Camden*, XLI, 16–18, 94.
24. *Some Annals of the Borough of Devizes*, ed. B. Howard Cunnington (Devizes, 1925), 70; *CSPD, 1619–23*, pp. 481, 484, 492, 532, 548, 553, 578, 580. See William B. Willcox, *Gloucestershire, 1590–1640* (New Haven, 1940), 135–9, for a full treatment of one county.

> The corn is so dear,
> I dout mani will starve this yeare. . . .

To which was added:

> The Poore there is more
> Than goes from dore to dore
>
> You that are set in place
> See that youre profession you doe not disgrace.[25]

No community in the land escaped distress, and "the complaints of the poor" about their "miserable wants" continued. The fears of public servants at Newbury that disorders might break out were realized in November, 1630, when a dozen or more "poor ragged women, many of them aged," attacked some carters leaving for Reading with loads of grain. Five of these pitiable creatures were whipped, seven were sent to the House of Correction, and watches were immediately set to prevent "like tumults." The King's orders accomplished nothing, nor did the local authorities succeed in keeping prices down or in providing relief for the starving. A bailiff of Buckinghamshire said that the inhabitants complained more of the weekly taxation to aid the poor than the poor did of the restraint on begging. In the summer of 1631 all the barns in Nottingham were empty, and at York measures were initiated to suppress the infinite numbers of beggars. Still the export of grain went on, for in September, 1632, one Andrew Humfrey complained to Secretary Coke about the multiplicity of licenses

> Granted to carry away our grain
> But it will never return from Spain;
> The mealman, the merchant, and the clown
> Strive to pull our State down,
> And then they may run clean out of town,
> And buy them a velvet gown.[26]

25. *CSPD, 1629–31*, pp. 387, 545; *VCH Sussex*, II, 194–5; *HMC Buccleuch*, III, 349–50, 352; *HMC Exeter*, 68.
26. On the great Midford Hill Riot, November, 1630, when more than one hundred angry people attacked the licensed carriers of corn from Wiltshire to Bristol, see Thomas G. Barnes, *Somerset, 1625–1640* (Cambridge, Mass., 1961), 3, 11, 13, 50, 174–5, 175n; *CSPD, 1629–31*, pp. 403, 410, 473, 474, 486; *1631–3*, pp. 4, 10, 16, 17, 18, 24, 25, 414; Cooper, in *Sussex Arch.*, XVI, 27–9.

Thus in the very years when the tide of the Great Migration to America was running at the flood, malnutrition, fear of hunger, and actual starvation made a vast body of the English more than usually attentive to the fascinating talk of peddlers and to tales told in taverns of the lands across the sea where every man might have a full belly, yea, and meat in large store. In the words of the old radical song, they sniffed "The Pie in the Sky."

III

Cold, dampness, heat, poor lighting, and bad air rendered indoor country existence thoroughly uncomfortable in all but the three months of summer. When the raw, penetrating cold of the unkind winter had passed, the ordinary Englishman of Stuart days had then to put up with constant chilling rains and the unavoidable damp of his cottage, even when he had fuel to burn in the fireplace. Few countrymen could keep consistently warm; like the industrious housemaid, they went through the winter with blue fingers and chapped lips. Even in the houses of the well-to-do the temperature indoors was never stable. Farmers offset the absence of lighting and good air by being outdoors most of each day and retiring soon after sundown, but they too spent much energy in merely keeping warm. As for the many undernourished creatures, sensitivity to dampness and cold caused true suffering, and almost the only protection anyone could devise was to wear heavy clothing all year, which, in itself, was far from hygienic.[27]

The "deare times of fuell" came in with James I, and all of England suffered as a result of them. The cutting of ever larger quantities of timber for charcoal to fire the iron and glass furnaces, the greater demand for ship timbers, The Great Housing Boom, and similar needs produced a real crisis. J. U. Nef has shown that the enclosures of common fields did more injury to the peasant by depriving him of free firewood than by the cutting down of the grain supply. Between 1612 and 1633, when general prices rose about 15 per cent, the price of firewood soared around 119 per cent.[28]

27. Compare the similar, though more acute, problem of France, Mandrou, *Introduction à la France*, 40–43.
28. Substantial yeomen, aware that fuel shortages would worsen rather than improve, made provisions in their wills for their heirs to be given loads of wood:

The families of gentlemen and rich yeomen could afford enough firewood for culinary purposes and ordinarily for their fireplaces, but for the mass of rural people the fuel shortage was a problem of veritable magnitude. As early as the 1570's, as John Leland pointed out, poor inhabitants in the districts, "already scant of wood," burned "turf, furze, or ling, or even cow-dung for fuel." As the seventeenth century advanced, Norden reported that, in addition to those substitutes for wood, the poverty-stricken people in parts of Wiltshire and Lincolnshire, and in the Isle of Portland, were using heath and broom as well. In 1636, the Earl of Huntington wrote from Newcastle-under-Lyme that "a black moorish earth is the fuel of most of the common people." [29]

In his *Five Hundred Points of Good Husbandry,* Tusser urged the rural inhabitants to start in August to get in firewood for the winter: it would be cheaper at that time and the weather would be fair. A court order of the Manor of Scrooby in Nottinghamshire instructed all the farmers to "prepare fuel for winter" during the summer months, but the husbandmen either would not or could not comply, for in 1622 George Mylnes and John Fitch each had to forfeit 6s. 8d. to the lord for failing to do so. In the villages and towns, local authorities did what they could to alleviate suffering; but numerous as philanthropists were in this age, very few of them seem to have given money to supply fuel to the needy. One conspicuous exception was in the parish of Berkhamsted, where in 1625 the officers were able to distribute fifty-eight loads of wood among seventy-two families; they purchased the fuel with a gift of £100 donated by the King.[30]

Robert Ward of Lexden, near Colchester, willed that his mother-in-law should have sixteen loads of firewood; and Samuel Sherman, a clothier of Dedham, stipulated that his wife should have ten loads of wood annually from a seven-acre lot called "Catts Rent." From Devon, in 1610, came a report that "tymber for buyldinge and other necessaries for husbandrie are alreaddy growen soe extreame deare" that wood had to be imported from Ireland, Wales, and Flanders. Waters, *Gleanings,* II, 1144, 1178; Harleian MSS, 6832, No. 32, quoted by John U. Nef, *The Rise of the British Coal Industry* (Chicago, 1932), I, 158, 159, 190, 191; *Bibliotheca Lindesiana,* ed. R. R. Steele (Oxford, 1910), I, No. 1011, p. 117; Vaughan, *Golden Fleece,* 4–5; *Knyvett Letters,* 98; *Winthrop Papers,* I, 297.
29. Taylor, *Atlas,* 9; Norden, *Surveyor's Dialogue,* 222; Norden, Chorographical Description, 14; *HMC Hastings,* IV, 338; Fuller, *Worthies,* I, 399, 445; II, 1.
30. Tusser, *Husbandry,* 189; *CSM,* XLII, 185; Powell, *Puritan Village,* 32.

Not only was the price of firewood too high for the poor husbandman, but so many frauds were practiced on the unwary that
in 1601 Parliament revised the assize of fuel and stipulated the size
of wood and billets. It is not surprising, in view of shortages and
high costs, that impoverished people who were cold and hungry
helped themselves to the wood on the commons or wherever they
could find it. In 1619, after twelve years of experimenting with
regulations, the manor court of Wimbledon set a fine of ten shillings for anyone who should "privately or openly possess or carry"
any wood, or pollard tree, or any other fuel in carts from the common lands. Proclamations restricted the cutting of wood in the
royal forests, and after 1634 the Forest Courts forcefully administered the laws against encroachments.[31]

Some of the cases brought before county courts involved such
paltry sums that the justices must have taken cognizance of the
grim need that drove people to this kind of pilfering. In 1631 the
Essex Quarter Sessions listened to charges that George Beikson of
Upminster was both a nightwalker and "a woodstealer"; they fined
John Parker of Little Badow, laborer, twopence for taking six
pieces of wood. Some years later the court tried Thomas Roughton, a laborer, for stealing a large parcel of firewood worth five
shillings from Sir Thomas Wiseman, and tried his father, Elias
Roughton of Little Coggeshall, for knowingly receiving it. Similarly in Warwickshire in 1634–35, a rash of cases of theft of billets and faggots came before the court. Sneaking into the close of
Walter Overbury, Esq., a tailor and a laborer of Barton-on-Hill
carried off "half a load of wood," and a laborer of Stratford-on-
Avon named Edward Pigeon not only broke into John Hem-
minge's close, but, in order to get the wood he carried away, he
had topped all the trees. None of these cases was as pathetic, however, as that of Alice Whittaker, wife of a laborer, who was
brought into court for stealing a faggot worth only one penny.[32]

31. Coal, which was a boon to people of seaports, was too costly for inland
country dwellers. Taylor, *Atlas*, 8–9; *Extracts from the Court Rolls of the Manor
of Wimbledon*, 177, 178, 181–2, 185, 205; *Bibliotheca Lindesiana*, I, No. 1073,
p. 126; No. 1164, p. 137; Pickering, *Statutes at Large*, VII, 67–8; *Statutes of the
Realm*, IV, 981; *CSPD, 1634–5*, p. xxxii; John Rous's grievances, "Diary," in
Camden, LXVI, 93.
32. Essex Sessions, XX, 288, 291, 339, 421, 491, 526; *Warwick Sessions*, VI, 18,
22, 25, 26.

Tales of the year-round warmth of the Caribbean isles and of the lush forests of Virginia "where wasting of Woods is an ease and benefit to the Planter" must have awed the perennially cold Englishman. Though Francis Higginson candidly admitted that the first settlers at Naumkeag (Salem) in 1629 found the Massachusetts winter unexpectedly severe, he emphasized at the same time the pertinent fact that "here we have plentie of Fire to warme us, and that a great deale cheaper than they sell Billets and Faggots in London; nay all Europe is not able to afford to make so great Fires as New-England. A poore Servante here that is to possesse but 50 Acres of Land, may afford to give more wood for Timber and Fire as good as the world yeelds, then many Noble Men in England can afford to doe." And how compelling his next line must have been for many a shivering peasant: "Here is good living for those that love good Fires." [33]

IV

The Somerset Court of Quarter Sessions, held at Ilchester in April, 1628, heard a petition from the inhabitants of Ashwick alleging that "by reason of a late lamentable visitation of sicknesse in which the greatest part of the most sufficient and able persons of their . . . parish then Dyed leaving many poor and impotent people and fatherlesse children," the parish could not "releive their poore." Though this is an extreme instance, still it brings home forcefully the precarious state of health of most of the rural English.[34]

Ill-housed, seldom warm, generally undernourished, the English countryfolk offered little resistance to afflictions and disease. Only a small fraction of them escaped annual colds—men, women, and children all exhibited the badge of that common ailment, the runny nose. In like fashion, the bloody flux (as dysentery was called) spared very few. People expected to suffer from a variety of undes-

33. Mr. Higginson also wrote that, though tallow candles did not exist, an abundance of fish afforded ample oil for lamps which, of course, guaranteed better lighting than English farmers enjoyed. *New England's Plantation* (1630), reprinted in Force, *Tracts*, I, No. XII, 11; Edward Waterhouse, *A Declaration of the State of the Colony and Affayres in Virginia* (1622), 4.
34. *Somerset Sessions*, II, 62.

ignated fevers, or "humours"; measles was one of the most dangerous. John Chamberlain remarked somewhat snobbishly that the spring of 1610 proved to be a time of bad colds and many fatal infirmities among the mass of the people, but that "these popular diseases kill few of the better sort." Yet only two years later, in November, he found out that the Crown Prince had died of "none other than the ordinare ague that hath raigned and raged allmost all over England since the later end of sommer." Rheumatic disorders afflicted nearly everybody sooner or later, and the sight of people with "deformed Bodies, crooked Legs and Feet, wry Necks" was a common one. Widespread consequences of malnutrition, such as the prevalence of tuberculosis among women and the susceptibility of children to rickets, have already been mentioned. By way of contrast, very few people ever experienced the ills resulting from our modern rich and ample diets, or from overeating.[35]

He was a rare individual in early Stuart days who did not have to nurse along a chronic disability in addition to contracting some kind of fever and a number of other maladies. In his old age, Richard Baxter retailed all of his youthful ailments. He suffered first from what he called "a consumption" because of the inexperience of his Shropshire physician; when he was seven a good doctor brought him through the measles, and at fourteen, through the smallpox. Too soon after his recovery from the latter, he went bathing in a brook and contracted a severe cold and catarrh. He often spit blood; he suffered abdominal pains—he gradually realized that free eating of raw apples and plums did him no good— and finally, at the age of seventeen, this future divine concluded that he was not afflicted with the scurvy as he had thought but really was a victim of a "hypochondriac melancholy." [36]

Curiously, medical historians seldom comment on two impediments to well-being of which there is the most eloquent testimony in the records. One is the frequency of skin diseases and a variety of sores, particularly on the legs—an understandable affliction where very little washing and bathing took place and people wore filthy clothing. Scurvy, scrofula (the King's Evil), and other erup-

35. Chamberlain, *Letters*, I, 300, 388; *London Gazette*, June 1, 1668.
36. Richard Baxter, *Reliquiæ Baxterianæ* (1696), 9–10.

tions, manifestations in part of a poor diet, lack of sanitation, and nervous difficulties, or of venereal disease, were common complaints. Equally conspicuous, as one leafs through records, are the number of farm accidents. It would seem that few husbandmen lived out their lives without breaking one or more bones at work or play. Lifting and other heavy labor brought on hernias or, as contemporaries explained: "ruptures, or broken Bellies, or bearing down in their privy parts." If strangulation of the hernia ensued, which was not infrequent, death inevitably followed. What with the maimed soldiers back from the wars and those crippled by ordinary accidents, the English scene presented an inordinate number of physically broken men and women.[37]

Visitations of infectious diseases, the most grievous being smallpox, reached epidemic proportions periodically. Some persons assumed a certain fatalistic resignation toward it; they were "of opinion that the pox, bringing out so much corruption to the surface of the bodie, helped to cleare it inwardly," but even to a people inured to health hazards, any outbreak of the disease in the community must have aroused fear approaching panic. Those who survived (and the mortality rate was high) were badly pockmarked as a rule, which was a real personal tragedy for many a pretty young woman.[38]

The general lack of sanitation and squalid housing conditions provided a hotbed for disease. Contrary to general opinion, some farms did have a kind of privy on the premises: Thomas Tusser listed their cleaning as a night chore for "November's Husbandry"; yet they still remained pestiferous and odorous. The free ranging of dogs and other animals in and out of a cottage gave rise to swarms of fleas, and the only preventive which Tusser could suggest was to strew the chambers with wormwood. As for other vermin, little could be done except to deaden the "stink" with strong-

37. For skin ailments, see *CSPD, 1634–5*, p. 216; *Barnstaple Recs.*, II, 139; J. J. Keevil, "The Seventeenth Century English Medical Background," in *Bulletin of the History of Medicine*, XXXI, 416, 417. Not until the advent of newspapers after the Restoration do we begin to have evidence of the great number of hernia cases through the advertisements for trusses, but obviously they existed in the beginning of the seventeenth century. *London Gazette*, June 1, 1668; March 7, 1669 [70]; *Orange Gazette*, February 1, 1688/9.

38. *Chetham*, IV, 20; *Somerset & Dorset*, XX, 124; Chamberlain, *Letters*, I, 140.

scented rue. Personal hygiene was rudimentary; it could not have been otherwise when everybody wore the same, heavy, unlaundered clothes for months on end. If the fastidious Samuel Pepys had to be combed for lice every night, it requires little imagination to picture the "thick plantations" carried about by untrimmed, unwashed peasants. The greatest carrier of disease, however, was the omnipresent rat.[39]

The most dreaded and deadliest of all epidemics was the plague. A popular term without precise definition, the plague could have been bubonic, pneumonic, or some form of typhus. The visitation usually came after periods of serious drought and famine, for then the rats practically competed with men for food. Generally it struck first in isolated rural spots and then fanned out with the never-ceasing movement of population. Everyone recognized it as a great leveler which infected and carried off rich and poor alike. The epidemic of 1603 had a greater effect upon the English people than the death of Queen Elizabeth or the accession of King James. [40]

Preceded by a drought in 1602, the plague, characteristically, broke out in scattered communities in Cheshire, Derbyshire, and Lincolnshire before it attacked the metropolis. Spreading over the North and Midlands, the epidemic struck Wigan in Lancashire in April, and by August sixty-eight deaths had occurred when thirty were normal. Pycombe Village and Fletching Parish in Sussex lost many inhabitants, and the mortality in Devonshire exceeded anything that anyone could remember. The presence of the plague in many of the Wiltshire villages resulted in the loss of work for the weavers and necessitated a weekly expenditure of large sums for their relief. All of rural England knew "theise dangerous tymes of Infection." [41]

Although the plague subsided in London (the city recovered rapidly after 1603), it continued to affect many country areas for long periods thereafter. In parts of Devon, farm villages passed through six years of travail; the people of Tiverton and its environs

39. Tusser, *Husbandry,* 52, 172; Essex Sessions, XX, 259.
40. Charles F. Mullett's *The Bubonic Plague and England* (Lexington, Ky., 1956) is a superb study; see especially pp. 2, 4, 9n. See also *Lancashire & Cheshire Trans.,* 39.
41. Mullet, *Bubonic Plague,* 105, 108; *Lancashire & Cheshire Trans.,* 40; *HMC Various,* I, 73; *Sussex Arch.,* IV, 235, 276.

suffered a prolonged epidemic from 1608 to 1619. The parish records of tiny Abbas Comlie in county Somerset show that in July and August, 1611, eighteen persons succumbed to the plague. An almost equal number, of the 112 that had bravely remained in the village and "fled not from the infection," contracted the disease but survived it.[42]

The second disastrous epidemic of the century began in 1625, and again it broke out in communities that had suffered most severely from crop failures. Starting at Plymouth in December, 1624, it moved northward to Okehampton and then progressed along the road to London. Local authorities strove heroically to prevent it from invading their communities. In July, 1625, orders went out from Westminster to all justices of the peace to suppress all alehouses "as much as is possible," and to restrain people from receiving any new inhabitants from London as inmates or lodgers; or, if persons had already come from there, they should not be allowed to "resort to London." In January, 1625/6, the Bishop of Exeter wrote to Sir John Coke that because the sickness is "dispersed into diverse places in this country," he was "constrained to debar them of sermons in their churches, for avoiding the combining of the sick and the whole which caused a reviving of the infection and a great death of many." At their Trinity session in 1626, the justices of the peace of Warwickshire forbade "the general meeting and concourse of people at feasts, wakes, May games, morris dancing, bear-baiting, and like assemblies." Whether because of these measures or other circumstances, this scourge did not exact as great a toll of lives as the epidemic of 1603.[43]

The next plague years, 1630–31, were particularly fatal in Devonshire and Essex, but there was no general visitation in the decade after 1625. Then again, from 1636 to 1640, the epidemic raged in the very counties from which so many Englishmen were in the process of emigrating to America: Devon, Dorset, Sussex, Essex, and East Anglia. Though the plague seldom winnowed the population of the rural districts the way it did that of the large towns, many obscure villages lost more than half of their working

42. Mullet, *Bubonic Plague*, 108, 112, 114–16, 119; *Somerset & Dorset*, V, 91; *CSM*, XXVI, 357.
43. Mullet, *Bubonic Plague*, 143, 156; *Devon & Cornwall*, VI, 198; *HMC Various*, 343; *HMC Coke*, XII, I, 249; *Warwick Sessions*, I, 35.

populations, and the vivid horrors of the epidemic for those who lived through it disturbed both individuals and whole families, unsettling them emotionally if not making them openly hysterical. The historian who writes of rural England can no longer pass over the profound social and economic consequences of these periodical scourges in unhinging the minds of the countryfolk. Their effect was national as well as local, and yet few chroniclers have sought to relate the plague to the general history of the age. As Charles Mullett ironically wrote: "Pages for ship money, not a word for pestilence." [44]

When one or more members of a farming household of any degree suffered an accident, an ordinary affliction, or an infectious disease, the housewife immediately took charge of the patient and administered generous doses of home remedies as a part of her kitchen physic. She always kept herbs and other specifics on hand from which she brewed or concocted such medicines as she needed. When home remedies failed them, many women, and men too, not infrequently resorted to quacks. Mrs. Margaret Neale of Aldeburghe, Suffolk, created a sensation in 1597 by curing diseases by prayer and "therefore hath recorse of people to her farre and nighe." When the justices heard her confess that after a "washe," she recited a prayer to God, then a paternoster, and lastly another devised prayer, they ordered her to perform penance in church with a white rod in her hand and to wear a paper on which was to be written in capital letters: "WITCHCRAFT AND ENCHANTMENT." The same charge might have been levied against William Willett in 1630 for sending to Secretary Edward Nicholas a box containing a mermaid's hand with a rib which was said "to be good to make rings for cramp and to stop blood," with some other virtues. It was Thomas Tusser's advice, however, that housewives should

> Ask Medicos counsel, ere med'cine ye make,
> And honour that man for necessity's sake.

44. In the tiny community of Milton Abbas, Dorset, between August, 1638, and March, 1638/9, forty-five males and thirty-six females were buried. John Hutchins, *History of Dorset* (Westminster, 1868), IV, 382; *HMC Kenyon,* XIV, IV, 45; Roberts, *Southern Counties,* 289–90; Justices' Order, April 18, 1637, Essex Record Office, Q/SB; *North Riding Sessions,* IV, 99; *Sussex Arch.,* XCIII, 81; Mullett, *Bubonic Plague,* 176–7.

> Though thousands hate physic, because of the cost,
> Yet thousands it helpeth that else should be lost.[45]

There were a sufficient number of practitioners for the house-wife to consult if she had been so inclined. Of particular impor-tance for the rural people was the fact that the doctors were not all concentrated in the large towns; enough of them lived in villages and served a "riding practice" to "give England adequate medical care." Such a doctor was John Symcotts, who had an extensive practice in Huntingdon and Bedfordshire. He attended the nota-bles, among whom were the Cromwell family, and the most hum-ble and those in between, as well as prescribing for many others by correspondence.[46]

All aspirants to the medical profession, according to statute, had to be licensed by the bishop of the diocese, who was assisted by the consistory court in enforcing the law. Recruited chiefly from the families of rich yeomen and county merchants, about a third of the applicants for a license had attended one or the other of the two universities, and some of these had medical degrees. The greater majority prepared for their examinations by apprenticing themselves to an established physician or surgeon. Apothecaries were sometimes permitted to practice as doctors. The licensing was so diligently supervised that the general excellence of England's medical services was second to none.[47]

45. Tusser's twelve essential home remedies were aqua vitae, tart vinegar, rose-water, treacle, cold herbs, white endive, succory, spinage, water of fumitory, liver, conserves of barberry and quince, and sirops. Tusser, "Huswifery," 274–5; *Norfolk*, XVIII, 133–4; *CSPD, 1629–31*, p. 237.

46. Mr. Notestein estimated that England had one physician for every 8,000 people. *English People*, 101; John H. Raach, *A Directory of English Country Physicians, 1603–1643* (London, 1962); see also Raach, The English Country Doctor in the Province of Canterbury, 1603–1643 (Ph.D. Thesis, Yale Uni-versity, 1941), viii–ix, xv–xvi, 118; Keevil, in *Bulletin History of Medicine*, XXXI, 409; F. N. L. Poynter and W. J. Bishops (eds.), *A Seventeenth Century Doctor and His Patients: John Symcotts, 1592?–1662 (Bedford, XXXI)*, ix–xxx.

47. Of the 814 doctors listed in Raach's *Directory*, 179 had no university train-ing. Occasionally a minister sought a license to practice medicine, like the vicar of Barnstaple, John Trinder, or the Puritan John Fiske, who, "havinge preached mooche, seinge the danger of the tymes, he changed his profession of Divinitie into physicke." At Salem, however, John Fiske resumed his former profession and doubtless practiced what Cotton Mather termed the "angelic conjunction" of spiritual and physical healing. Given the age, England had a fine record of medical service, and the spirit of medical science crossed to America in the custody of

Complaints about the high cost of medical attention were many.
Earle wrote about "A Mere Dull Physician" who always pronounced a "disease incurable but by an abundant phlebotomy of
the purse." A versifier made public the fat income of Rogers, a
Kentish apothecary:

> So that he did receive two hundred pound
> By each yeeres practice, as it cleere was found.

The doctors, for their part, had a very high social position to maintain and accordingly charged well for attendance, which is the reason why more than half of the population had to confine their
medication to home physic or to risk advice from unlicensed practitioners of illiterate quacks.[48]

Resetting a broken arm or leg was recognized as a problem beyond the housewife's abilities, and a busy bonesetter was called in.
At South Creake, Norfolk, in 1597, Giles Michell practiced bone-
setting; his competitor was Mrs. Bridget Dike, and neither of them
had ever been licensed. When Secretary Nicholas's son broke his
arm at school in 1633, the master, Mr. Pinkney, and Burgis, an
unlicensed bonesetter, "a plain country man whose only skill is
much experience," successfully cared for him.[49]

Women doctors were very rare, but there are records of one at
each of the Norfolk towns of Barney, Swaffham, Wells, and Yarmouth. Outside of the household, the only medical training open
to women was through apprenticeship to midwives. The handling
of obstetric cases in the countryside had long since been the sole
prerogative of the midwife, and only at London and a few other
large cities did one encounter a "man-midwife." One skilled in the
practice seldom lacked for employment, and people would send for
her from great distances. Like doctors, midwives were supposed to
be licensed by ecclesiastical authority; ordinarily a committee of

---

Mr. Fiske, Giles Firman, and other emigrants. Raach, *Directory of English
Country Physicians*, 14, 15; Keevil, in *Bulletin History of Medicine*, XXXI,
409–10; 411, 414, 422; *Winthrop Papers*, III, 394; *Norfolk*, XVIII, 27, 36, 44;
Devon & Cornwall, XV, 81; XXVI, 96; *Hertfordshire Sessions*, V, 296; Essex
Sessions, XIX, 190; Essex Arch., X, 29b.
48. Raach, *Directory of English Country Physicians*, 11, 15; Earle, *Microcosmography*, 16; *Roxburghe Ballads*, III, 2.
49. *Norfolk*, XVIII, 83; *CSPD, 1633–4*, p. 57.

"discreet women," together with a physician, acted for the bishop. The applicants had to take an oath to serve the poor as well as the rich, not to substitute one infant for another, not to employ any sorcery or incantation, nor to cut off the head, nor to dismember or hurt any newborn child, as well as to use pure water and the official christening words for the sacrament of baptism. Midwives also had to give information on oath at court about cases of bastardy when they had been present at the travail of the mother, and on other occasions, at the request of the court, they made examinations for the judges. Theirs was a task of great responsibility, and, for the most part, they lived up to their oath.[50]

V

This depressingly somber account of rural life, though true, must be modified by reference to some of the more carefree and joyous activities of the country people. Robert Herrick of Dean Prior in Devon neatly summed up the traditional pleasures in "The Country Life":

> For Sports, for Pagentrie, and Playes,
> Thou hast thy Eves, and Holydayes:
> On which the young men and maids meet,
> To exercise their dancing feet:
> Tripping the comely country round,
> With Daffadils and Daisies crown'd.
> Thy Wakes, thy Quintels, here thou hast,
> Thy May-poles, too with Garlands gra't:
> Thy Morris-dance; thy Whitsun-ale;
> Thy Sheering-feast, which never faile.
> Thy Harvest-home; thy Wassaile bowle,
> Tht's tost up after Fox i' th' Hole.
> Thy Mummeries; thy Twelfte-tide Kings
> And Queenes; thy Christmas revellings:

50. *Norfolk*, XVIII, 27; Clark, *Working Life of Women*, 269, 275, 276–7; *Kent*, XXV, 17; XXVI, 41; XXVII, 228; *Oxinden Letters*, 24; the midwife's oath is reprinted in Daniel Neal, *History of the Puritans. . .* (London, 1754), I, 413; *North Riding Sessions*, IV, 37, 49; Essex Sessions, XX, 319–20.

Thy Nut-browne mirth; thy Russet wit;
And no man payes too deare for it.[51]

No pastime met with such universal enthusiasm as dancing; at
every opportunity, when a piper could be located, people of all
ages and both sexes gathered to dance upon the green, in a nearby market house, on the village common, or around a Maypole.
The young people smiled and kissed at every turning while their
elders laughed—and checked. Dances varied according to region
and achieved fame for their dramatic and spontaneous features
which, besides much kissing, called for shaking of hands, clapping,
stamping, snapping of fingers, peeping, and wiping of the eyes.
Very popular were the "longways" dances for four, six, or eight
persons; square dances for eight; round dances for six, eight, or
more. May dances revolved around the pole, and the performers of
morris dances fastened bells around their legs. Individuals essayed
hornpipes and jigs; there was a dance for everyone and they all
joined in.[52]

Village dancing provided the ideal opportunity for flirting and
matchmaking, and also for high merriment, considerable drinking,
and less innocent pleasures as excitement mounted under the spell
of the almost barbaric squirls of the pipes, the shrill squeaking of
the fiddle, and the rhythm of the tabor. Sometimes the dancing
went on for hours. In Lancashire, Adam Martindale's eldest brother fell in love with "a young wild airy girle, betweene fifteen and
sixteen yeares of age; an huge lover and frequenter of wakes,
greenes, and merrie-nights, where musick and dancing abounded."
She had only £4 for her portion, and his aspiring yeoman family
opposed the match, but after the marriage his parents agreed that
"she proved above all just expectations not onely civill, but religious, and an exceeding good wife." But frolics did not always end
felicitously: in 1640 on St. John's Day at Broad Chalk, Wiltshire,
a "dancing match" lasted all night, and one young woman was

51. *The Poetical Works of Robert Herrick,* ed. L. C. Martin (London, 1956),
230. (Italics mine.)
52. Devon had a "Furry Dance," and Cornwall had its "Geese-Dancing" (from
the French: *déguiser*). *Western Antiquary,* II, 8, 19; Camden, *Elizabethan
Woman,* 168; Breton, *Court and Country,* in Dunham and Pargellis, *Complaint
and Reform,* 462.

supposed to have been outraged by a youth who termed himself "the bishop." [53]

These were years of song and music for all Englishmen, and those who lived in the country probably heard more secular music than their descendants did until the days of the B.B.C. Whitsun ales and weddings always called for music of some kind. Thomas Fuller, a popular Norfolk fiddler, "useth to come to Sheringham and draweth resort of youth together," and John Aubrey recalled that in his childhood "the tabor and pipe were commonly used, especially Sundays and Holydayes, and at Christnings, and Feasts." Robert Milbourne from Terling in Essex regularly sallied forth on a round of nearby alehouses on Sabbath days and paid for drink by playing his pipe and tabor. Viewed with a certain suspicion as possible vagabonds, many indifferent performers known as minstrels wandered about the provinces singly or in small groups, and without patrons; still these people supplied much of the music heard in rural England. Stopping off at "a poore Ale-house" on the road from York to Tadcaster in 1638, "The Water Poet" was pleased to have the entertainment provided by "a Tinker who made pretty musique with his Banbury Kettle-drum." For some people, at least, life seemed to be offering something more than just work.[54]

53. *Chetham,* IV, 16; *HMC Various,* I, 107.
54. In his character of "A Poor Fiddler," Earle wrote: "A new song is better to him than a new jacket, especially if bawdy, which he calls merry, and hates naturally the Puritan, as an enemy to his mirth. A country wedding and Whitsun ale are the two main places he domineers in, when he goes for a musician, and overlooks the bagpipe. The rest of him is drunk, and in the stocks." Among the "new songs" was "The Country Farmer's Vain-glory, in a new song of Harvest Home: Together with an Answer to their Undecent Behaviour":

> Our oats they are how'd, and our barley's reap'd,
> Our hay is mow'd, and our hovel [canopied stack]'s heap'd.
>   Harvest Home, Harvest Home.
> We'll merrily roar out our Harvest Home.
>   *   *   *
> We cheated the Parson, we'll cheat him again,
> For why shou'd the Vicar have one in ten?
>   One in ten, one in ten,
> For why should the Vicar have one in ten?
>   *   *   *
> We'll drink off our liquor while we can stand,
> And hey for the honour of old England,

When a nation attains affluence, its inhabitants of all ranks no longer find contentment in the simple and wholesome pleasures they had enjoyed in poorer times. In these years the country as a whole was thriving, and this prosperity was accompanied by a rapid and little-understood transformation of English society. In 1618 John Norden sensed this shifting in attitudes and values when he wrote of the farmers and their wives of earlier days who contented themselves with:

> a meane dyet, and base attyre, and held their children to some austere government, without pride, haunting Alehouses, Tavernes, dice, cards, and vaine delights of charge, the case is altered: the Husbandman will be equal to the Yeoman, the Yeoman to the Gentleman, the Gentleman to the Squire, the Squire to his superiour, and so the rest, everyone so far exceeding the course held in former times, that I shall speake without reprehension, there is at this day thirty times as much vainly spent in a family of like multitude, as was in former ages; whereof I speake . . . to tel you truly both Lord and Tenant are guilty in it.[55]

This change appeared first among the gentry. "When we do not hunt, we hawke," Viscount Conway told a friend in 1638, "the rest of the time is spent in tennis, chesse, and dice, and in a worde we eat and drinke and rise up to play; and this is to live like a gentleman; for what is a gentleman but his pleasure." And play they did, as long and as hard as their station in life allowed.[56]

Nicholas Assheton of Downham was one of the lesser sporting

Old England, old England.
And hey for the honour of old England.

Earle, *Microcosmography*, 39; *Roxburghe Ballads*, III, 610–11; and on ballads in general, Sir Charles Firth, in *RHS Trans.*, 3d ser., VI, 27–8; *Norfolk*, XVIII, 79; Aubrey, *Brief Lives*, 11, 319; *Essex Sessions*, XIX, 240; *HMC Various*, LV, I, 77; Walter A. Woodfil, *Musicians in English Society from Elizabeth to Charles I* (Princeton, 1953), 109, 127, 131–2, 135; Taylor, *Part of this Summers Travels* (1639), 26, in *Works*, I, No. 3.
55. F. J. Fisher in *Economia*, n. s., XXIV, 3; Norden, *Surveyor's Dialogue*, 13–14. "Plus ça change, plus c'est la même chose": see recent comments of a like nature on the new British leisure in the "Colored Supplement" of *The Sunday Times* (London), Sept. 16, 1962.
56. *HMC Portland*, XIV, II, 52; *Oxinden Letters*, 12, 106.

gentry of West Lancashire; he meticulously kept a diary of his junkets. During the two years 1617–18, he never missed the two Sunday services, listened to forty sermons, three of them by different bishops, and thought he had acquitted himself very well with his maker. In the same period he also participated in sixteen fox hunts, ten for stags, two for bucks, two for otter, two for hares, and one for badgers, besides spending four days each shooting grouse and fishing, and two with the falcons. Out-of-doors he shot with the long bow, ran foot races, and raced his horses. On Sabbath evenings, Assheton and his wife frequented an alehouse and saw no sin in it, nor did the many male and female companions who joined them there. Indoors his recreation consisted chiefly of playing at shove-groat or dice with his pious cronies (once all night), or at some "other friendlie sports." He could get "very merrie with dancing" at the Abbey or an occasional "masking." Once he was "somewhat to busie with drink," eleven times "merrie," once "very merrie," once "more than merrie," and another time as "merrie as Robin Hood." Strangely, though, he never mentioned cards or bowling; yet many gentlemen did bowl. Others gaily went boating "to laugh and sing, and drink old sherry." Thomas Knyvett warmly applauded the pleasures of his Norfolk neighbors; though he was unwilling to join them in their "bowlinge after the sunn be gon to bed, for fear of catchinge coulde." "In sports and journies," as George Herbert declared, "men are known." [57]

As yeomen prospered and could afford the time and money for diversion, many of them took up some of the gentry's pastimes and vices; indeed they made them their own, though they centered them in the village alehouses and inns. Hundreds of sporting yeomen attended and wagered on the outcomes of cock mains and bull- or bear-baiting in the yards of their favorite public houses. "Wee all Pressed to a cocking," Nicholas Assheton set down for June 2, 1618, and Peter Mundy glowed with pride when he thought of the "Invincible courage off our Mastives and Fighting Cockes, Mayntenyning their duell oftentymes till death." [58]

57. *Chetham*, XIV, xxvi, 1n, 3n, 73, 88, 122; *Seventeenth Century Songs and Lyrics Collected from the Original Music Manuscripts*, ed. John P. Cutts (Columbia, Missouri, 1959), 2; *Knyvett Letters*, 90; Herbert *Works*, 314.
58. Public houses all over the English countryside could be quickly recognized by the "Ivy-bush" invariably used for a sign. The number of rural drinking

No sooner did husbandmen and others of the lower orders learn about the thrills of tavern gambling than many of them, especially young, single farmers, sought to join with their betters in amusements they could ill afford; and before long apprentices and servants also caught the fever. For some, this meant missing divine service; for others the loss of hard-earned shillings and pence. Unscrupulous taverners employed every device to lure simple louts into their establishments to have a try at cards. The constables at Thirsk presented Matthew Toppin, laborer, and the Tawfert brothers, yeomen, "for coseninge and cheating in play at cards and fraudulently winning £10." More enterprising laborers tried to earn a little money on the side by illegally keeping forbidden greyhounds for yeomen and gentlemen.[59]

Both royal and local officials joined with the clergy and some of the privileged orders in frowning at the tendency of the poorer sort to disport themselves in the manner of the gentry and to play away their substance. Definite class legislation can be detected in the proclamation of King James I prohibiting artificers, husbandmen, laborers, mariners, fishermen, watermen, and all apprentices and servants from playing at an unlawful game anywhere at any time except at Christmas, and then only in their own houses and with permission from their masters. Moreover, no man (of any rank) might play at "bowles" publicly out of his own garden or orchard. Also forbidden were morris dances or open dancing, bear-baiting, "common Players," and fencing in public. The games listed as unlawful at public houses clearly reveal the entertainment provided by those establishments: dice, cards, table games, bowls, quoits, curling, loggat, shove-groat, tennis, casting the stone, and football. Besides the loss of money and immoderate tippling, such pastimes, the authorities held, led to all kinds of difficulties with working men and tended to draw irresponsible youth "to an idle and disordered course of life." [60]

establishments varied from county to county: the Essex hamlet of Moulsham had twenty-two alehouses and seven inns in 1628. Essex Sessions, XX, 199; Norfolk was a great sporting shire; there, in 1607, George Wilson of Wretton wrote *The Commendation of Cockes and Cockfighting. Chetham,* XIV, 99; Mundy, *Travels,* IV, 50; Lysons, *London,* II, 587–8.

59. *North Riding Sessions,* III, 129; *Warwick Sessions,* VI, 53, 57; Robert Burton, *Anatomy of Melancholy* [1621] (New York, 1886), I, 383–5.

60. Ordinarily noblemen and gentlemen severely restricted the pleasures of their servants: at Rye, in 1613, Lord Montagu allowed his servants to play cards only

Strict Puritans, a few proper gentlemen, and imitative yeomen probably agreed with the observation of the Bishop of Lincoln that "walking and discoursing, with men of liberal education, is a pleasant recreation; it is no way delightsome to the ruder sort of people, who scarce account anything a sport which is not loud and boisterous." We are told about young men who would "endure long and hard labour in so much that after twelve hours hard work they will go in the evening to football, stoole ball, cricket, prison-base, wrestling, cugel throwing, or some such like vehement exercise." Most Englishmen not only approved of outdoor sports (some argued that the time devoted to them might otherwise be spent in tippling), but one and all indulged in them wholeheartedly, and none would deny that noise and turmoil often accompanied them. In 1617 and again in 1633 the first two Stuarts not merely permitted but fostered recreation in the Declaration of Sports, formidable opposition notwithstanding.[61]

Enclosure of the common lands, which deprived numerous communities of "their onely place of exercise and recreation," added to the problems facing the clergy, for the churchyards then remained the sole places of resort for those who wanted to participate in games. There were those who would engage in strenuous exercises after a day's work, but the large majority of husbandmen and laborers counted on Sundays for recreation. For the rank and file, holy days were probably more precious for the leisure time in which to play than for worshiping. When divine services were con-

---

during the Christmas festivities. *VCH Sussex,* II, 197; Dalton summarized the law against games in common houses as it stood in 1630. *Country Justice,* 63–4; *North Riding Sessions,* III, 259; IV, 33n; Hamilton, *Quarter Sessions,* 115–16.

61. After echoing the sentiments of Robert Sanderson, Bishop of Lincoln, Thomas Fuller, in 1643, went on to say: "It is no pastime with country-clowns that cracks not pates, breaks not shins, bruises not limbs, tumbles and tosses not all the body. They think themselves not warm in their gears, till they are all on fire; and count it but dry sport, till they swim in their own sweat." In Fox i' th' hole, part of the company hopped about while the others would beat a man's up-raised leg with leather thongs; another popular and rough game in Cornwall was "hurling." Fuller, *Holy and Profane State,* 175; Robert Sanderson, *The Case of the Sabbath,* quoted in W. W. Whitaker, *Sunday in Tudor and Stuart Times* (London, 1933), 136; Chamberlayne, *Angliæ Notitiæ,* in Fussell, *English Rural Labourer,* xi, *Western Antiquary,* IV, 132; *Devon & Cornwall,* XI, 4; *King James's Declaration to his Subjects, concerning Lawful Sports to be used* (1618), in *A Collection of Scarce and Valuable Tracts . . . of the late Lord Somers,* ed. Walter Scott, Esq. (London, 1809), II, 53–5; *Harleian Miscellany,* V, 75–7.

cluded, male and female alike repaired to the churchyards for merriment and sport; some ungodly enthusiasts skipped the services altogether. A number of Yorkshiremen, for instance, greatly impeded the minister's reading of the afternoon service on an Easter afternoon at Cleveland when they played a game called Trippett; in Essex a jury presented four men for playing at bowls on Sunday.[62]

Individual cases, lapses, and misdemeanors could be dealt with, but a riot such as the one in and around the churchyard of Newnton, Wiltshire, on Trinity Sunday, 1641, posed a serious problem for the justices of the peace. Forty to eighty persons, armed with staves, came from Malmesbury and joined in a fight over a Maypole garland which was carried by the young men of Newnton. When a fencer named David Tanner spied John Comyn of Newnton bearing a garland, he bade him and the company to stand. Comyn retorted: "Wynn it and weare it, come threescore of you, you are but boies to wee." Thereupon a great melee occurred and many men of Newnton were sorely beaten.[63]

Some of the privileged orders sided with those members of the Anglican clergy who took steps to curb rural pastimes on Sunday. Particularly did they deplore the mingling of gentlemen with "many of inferior rank." They chided them for:

> their stout and strong abetting of so sillie vanities amongst hundreds, and sometimes thousands, of rude and vile persons, to whom they should give better, and not so bad example and encouragement, as to be idle in neglecting their callings; wasteful in gameing and spending their meanes; wicked in cursing and swearing; and dangerously profane, in their brawling and quarreling.[64]

More countrymen played football than any other sport or game, and spectators crowded to the Sunday matches. Always a favorite

---

62. Cricket was played in churchyards on Sunday. *Sussex Notes & Queries*, XII, 65; *Norfolk*, XVIII, 136; *Bibliotheca Lindesiana*, I, No. 1209, p. 143; *Maidstone Recs.*, 63–4; Essex Arch., XII, 5a, 25b, 26a; Sussex Arch., XLIX, 64; *North Riding Sessions*, III, 136, 199; Essex Sessions, XIX, 316; Hinde, *Bruen*, 17.
63. *HMC Various*, I, 107–8.
64. *Chetham*, XIV, 18n; *Surtees*, XCV, 223.

game in medieval times, it had been prohibited in 1349 in order to encourage the spending of more time at archery, but in the early seventeenth century it again became a most popular sport. It was often called *camping*. Parish officers usually overlooked its illegality, because everyone enjoyed the rough-and-tumble pastime. At Coldridge, Devon, in 1600, the churchwardens went so far as to pay out eightpence for a "foote Ball," and near Petworth Village, Sussex, two fields were set aside on the common land for football and bowling. On March 2, 1600, John Chamberlain wrote to his good friend Dudley Carleton, urging him to visit at Knebworth in Hertfordshire: "You may do well yf you have any ydle time to play the good fellow and come and see our matches at football, for that and bowling wilbe our best entertainment." [65]

Many were the injuries resulting from scrummages; broken bones and severe lacerations commonly occurred. So violent had the sport become by 1617 that King James renewed the prohibition of the game, but the dictum was flagrantly ignored. "Brand broke his leg at footebal," Adam Winthrop noted about one of his Groton husbandmen in 1627. Even the death of some players did not deter the enthusiasts of the game. At Aston on Trent in Derbyshire, a great multitude gathered in June, 1624, to see the inter-county "footeball play" between Aston and Castle Donington of Leicestershire "where a man was slayne," and there are records of deaths in hotly contested matches in Sussex and Devonshire. Worcestershire justices proceeded against some violators of the ban in 1633, and the Corporation of Kendal set a fine of 12*d.* for breaking the law, but they showed more concern for property owners, for they levied a fine of 3*s.* 4*d.* against persons convicted of breaking a window when playing football in the borough's streets.[66]

Rural England under James and Charles presented scenes of strong contrasts: back-breaking toil, insufficient diet, poor housing, and bad health afflicted most of the lower orders; their superiors lived on a better plane. The ordinary people, however, managed to

65. *Devon & Cornwall*, XVII, 131; *Sussex Arch.*, XCVI, 74; Coldridge Churchwardens Accounts, 91; Essex Arch., X, 8a, 9b, 10a; Chamberlain, *Letters*, I, 91.
66. *Winthrop Papers*, I, 216; Essex Sessions, XIX, 168; *HMC Hastings*, IV, 206; *VCH Sussex*, II, 32; *HMC Various*, I, 307; *HMC Kendal*, X, IV, 316; Hutchins, *Dorset*, I, 38–9.

be a sturdy stock who loved a good time and played even harder than they worked when they had the chance. One can only admire the tremendous store of energy in these lusty countrymen who, on Sundays, after six days of hard labor, felt the desire and had the vitality to play at football and other "unlawful games" or to go brawling in their own or adjacent villages.

IV

Townsmen and Citizens

T HE ESSENTIAL RURALNESS of England in the first half of the seventeenth century has already been indicated, but in emphasizing its all-pervasive parochial character, we must not ignore the decisive role of the more closely settled communities. They gave the countryside form and focus, and provided connections with the outside world. In England, as in the great civilizations of the past, from those of the Indus Valley and the vales of the Tigris, Euphrates, and Nile down to our own time, the economic, social, cultural, and political activities were centered in the cities. London has received its due from the chroniclers, but the manifold contributions of the towns and lesser cities of England are usually passed over or denigrated or misunderstood.

England displayed none of the remarkable urban concentrations of the Netherlands—Holland, especially, was unique on the continent of Europe. Nevertheless more than one-quarter of all Englishmen lived in large towns, cities, and the metropolis of London. If we accept the highest reliable estimate of the population of London in 1634 as 339,824, there still remained more than 910,000, or 18 per cent, of the subjects of King Charles I who lived in other urban communities.[1]

1. The figure of 339,824, estimated with great care by Charles Creighton in "The Population of Old London," in *Blackwood's Edinburgh Magazine*, CXLIX, 447–96, is accepted by Gras, Nef, Jordan, and other authorities. The latest estimate by Stone (*Aristocracy*, 386), is 320,000. Creighton's figure should be compared

In describing England and Wales in 1600, Sir Thomas Wilson stressed that they contained 25 episcopal cities, 641 great market and shire towns, and 9,725 village communities or parishes (thirty years later someone counted 512 market towns in England alone, and their names crowded the contemporary maps of Saxton and Speed). In Sir Thomas's view, 289 of his 641 towns appeared in no way "inferior in greatness" to most of the cities; and some of the rest, "albeit they be not walled," he thought surpassed many of the cities in population and riches. He also declared that many places that ranked as country towns actually housed more than three or four thousand communicants "besides the younger sort under 18 yeares of age." By immemorial custom, many a community having a population of but one thousand to fifteen hundred considered itself a town, though it might lack any legal town or borough status.[2]

Travelers generally accorded British towns great distinction in their accounts. "In England particularly I have seen a country of great beauty and fertility, and very populous," the Venetian ambassador Foscarini wrote to the Signory in 1613 after a journey from London to Scotland. Almost incredulously, he reported that every eight or ten miles "I have found a city, or at least a town comparable to the good ones of Italy," and in them collectively, "a quantity of most beautiful churches so numerous as to pass belief."[3]

During the sixteenth century many people left their manorial villages or open farms to settle in some larger place near by. Ordinarily the impetus for this internal migration, symbolized by the enclosures, is discovered on the land. Almost as important, how-

---

with the more recent smaller estimates of 225,000 and 230,000 for the 1630's by J. I. Archer (The Industrial History of London, 1630–1640 [M.A. Thesis, London, 1934], 47) and Woodfil (*Musicians in English Society*, 5). If we accept 230,000, then the proportion of the population living in London amounted to about 4.2 per cent and that of the other urban centers around 20.8 per cent of the total of 5,460,000 (as estimated by Jordan, *Philanthropy in England*, 63). Paul Zunther, *Daily Life in Rembrandt's Holland* (New York, 1963), 14, 15, 26.

2. Wilson, "State of England," 11–12; *CSPD, 1633–4*, p. 366.

3. "And for our townes and villages, such as they are, considering the use and necessity of travell," Gainsford patronizingly insisted, they "surmount by farre the Hostelries and deformed villages of other nations." *Glory of England*, 254–5; *CSP Venetian, 1613–15*, pp. 40–41.

ever, was the urban lodestone. To many a man, woman, or youth, the lure of town life as they glimpsed it on market days or during the visits to annual fairs sooner or later became irresistible. Year by year the attractions grew more compelling, socially quite as much as economically. Whatever the respective merits of the town and country as debated by the pamphleteers might be, a host of inarticulate, unlettered countryfolk decided in favor of the town. At the least, many a "queen of curds and cream" employed feminine cajolery to sway the family's decision to move townward, for "Rusticus" frankly confessed "they are our wives that first sollicite and perswade us to come to your Cities." The tracing of these people in transit is a fascinating exercise and reveals nearly as much about the course of later American history as about the Britons themselves.[4]

II

From 1600 to 1640, urban England offered prospects every bit as varied as those of its rural counterpart. Though now largely dissipated, a pronounced individuality then distinguished each community. For the average person, the strikingly different mode of living offered, the size, and the function of an urban center, rather than its form of government or whether it could properly be designated a town or a city, determined its drawing power. Unless a town was favored with a maritime situation or a location near a mine, it served principally as an adjunct to the surrounding countryside—each was an *urbs rure*. The services rendered by every little community were dictated by the nature of the locality and its products, though some of the towns gained additional importance because of the administrative activities centered in them.

Typical of these small market towns that existed south of Yorkshire was Petworth in West Sussex, a community of 918 inhabitants in 1641. Here was the marketing and trading center for farmers living within a radius of six or eight miles; and here, too, the Court of Quarter Sessions met periodically. An abundant supply of timber, stone, lime, and clay from the Downs was available for new construction; and surplus corn and livestock from the

4. *The Winter's Tale,* IV, iv, 160; Nash, *Quaternio,* 7, 8–9.

productive land rendered the parish practically self-sufficient. Few counties could boast of more market towns than Devon; and in the level shire of Essex, John Norden discovered in 1595 that in addition to the tri-weekly markets at Colchester, nineteen other places held scheduled one-day markets every week.[5]

Along the most heavily traveled roads, certain market towns attained additional affluence from their services to the passing traffic. "Those townes that we call thorowfares," explained Harrison, "have great and sumptuous innes builded in them, for the receiving of such travellers and strangers as pass to and fro." The main street of Woodbridge in Suffolk is called THOROUGHFARE today. Where the Great North Road crossed the river Witham in Lincolnshire, the market town of Grantham had long been a noted thoroughfare, and the Angel at the north end of the High Street (one of the few medieval hostelries still surviving) could have inspired Harrison's comment. Through their associations with the sojourners, the inhabitants of the thoroughfares kept up with the news and activities of the larger cities and London; Richard Baxter believed that in Kidderminster, the "constant converse and traffic with London doth much promote civility and piety among tradesmen." [6]

5. "What makes A Citty whether a Bishoprick or any thing of that nature? Resp: it is according to the first Charter which made them A Corporacion; if they be incorperated by the name [Civitas] then they are a City; if by the name [burgum] then they are A burrough." In most parts of the country, the towns grew during the years 1560–1640, but in Lincolnshire "depopulation" aroused such concern that a royal inquisition was initiated in 1607. The Corporation of Boston petitioned in 1635 that the county be directed to pay half of the town's share of ship money because of the decayed condition of the borough. John Selden, *The Table Talk of John Selden*, ed. Sir Frederick Pollock (London, 1927), 30; Hill, *Tudor & Stuart Lincoln*, 140–41; Gould, in *EHR*, LXVII, 392–6; *VCH Lincolnshire*, II, 332; *CSPD, 1635–6*, p. 8; Norden, Chorographical Description, 14–15; Kenyon, "Petworth," in *Sussex Arch.*, XCVI, 36, 44, 47–50, 60; Hoskins, *Devon*, 317–522. For selected towns, see Hoskins, in Plumb, *Social History*, 38–9 (Leicester); *Camden*, LXXIV, 14 (Bewdley); *Somerset & Dorset*, XI, 250 (Shaftesbury); Cook and Smith, *English Cottages*, pl. 190. A visit to Stanton St. John, an Oxfordshire stone-built town, does much to evoke an image of the small-town past.

6. On the Ordnance Survey's *Map of XVII Century England*, the thoroughfares are clearly marked. Harrison, *England*, Pt. I, 107; *CSPD, 1603–10*, p. 115 (Grantham); *1619–23*, p. 408; *Reliquiæ Baxterianæ*, I, 89; Darby, *Geography*, 361n, 363.

The heavy travel from the Channel ports up to London supported a dozen or more Kentish towns, such as Dartford, Ashford, and Sandwich, having populations of one thousand to twelve hundred, and many smaller places of five hundred to eight hundred souls. Tonbridge, at the junction of the main highway from Rye to London and the road from Maidstone, was one of these smaller towns. Its box-frame houses of two-and-a-half stories crowded the hundred yards from the river Medway to the market cross (merely a roof set on posts) and up the High for another hundred. Carriers bringing fish to London or travelers to Dieppe and Le Havre had a choice of inns—The Bull, The Rose and Crown, The Swan, and The Angel. The small sums the wayfarers left behind helped in some measure to lighten the burden of this poverty-stricken community whose Friday market, few shopkeepers, and depressed artisans could barely maintain half of the population above the level of subsistence.[7]

In the southern and eastern counties, no sizable market town lacked a numerous body of artisans engaged in the cloth trade. An Italian traveler of 1603 expressed great surprise that broadcloths, "and especially kerseys, are made all over the kingdom in the small hamlets and villages, and not in the big towns only." Spinning wheels, warping frames, and looms produced the bulk of many a community's annual income. Colchester's cloth trade, preeminent since the thirteenth century, had suffered a decline, but it revived in the sixteenth century with the immigration of many Flemish weavers, and by 1604 it stood second only to the city of Norwich among East Anglian cloth centers in the manufacture of bays and serges. The clothworkers, in turn, supported other artisans: in Suffolk at Sudbury, out of a population of about 3,000, 1,600 adults practiced forty-five different trades.[8]

In the West Country, too, as Lieutenant William Hammond perceived in 1635, small cloth towns were to be found every few

7. *Kent,* LXXVI, 152–62, especially the map on p. 155; for a list of 226 persons passing from Rye to Dieppe in eight months of 1635-6, see *Sussex Arch.,* XVIII, 173–9.

8. *CSP, Venetian, 1603–7,* pp. 104–5; *VCH Essex,* II, 328–34; *Diary of John Evelyn,* ed. H. B. Wheatley (London, 1906), II, 85; for Sudbury, see Powell, *Puritan Village,* 42; *Suffolk,* VII, 1; for Thaxted, see Cook and Smith, *English Cottages,* pl. 53.

miles. Some of them were poor and run-down, others well-built
and quite prosperous. Among Devon's many fine towns, Tiverton
stood out because "multitudes resorted hither for employ"; a ru-
mor of 1608 credited the place with supporting 8,000 people in
the making of woolens. In that same year, an "occupational census" of Tewkesbury, Gloucester, and Cirencester indicated that
nearly 50 per cent of the adult inhabitants of these towns worked
at the cloth trades, 15 per cent were laborers and carriers, and
19.3 per cent were dealers or retail shopkeepers. In Devon were
some stannary towns, with Chagford in the lead, which owed their
wealth to the moorland tin mines.[9]

Within the orbit of London, Peter Mundy could think of no
"handsomer and cleanlier place" than Maidstone, a town that had
driven a great trade in thread ever since the Walloon refugees had
introduced it in 1590. Standing by the Medway in the midst of the
rich hop-growing country of Kent, the town had four "established
companies" consisting of mercers, drapers, artisans, and "Vitlers."
Each had its own court for enforcing the orders governing apprentices and journeymen of many specialized crafts. The Victuallers,
for instance, supervised all maltsters, innkeepers, badgers, brewers,
butchers, millers, husbandmen, and "common labourers not being
artificers." [10]

The greatest thoroughfare of each county was generally the
shire town, where the presence of administrative and judicial
authorities, the county records, weekly markets, and annual fairs
produced much of the bustle and liveliness that so attracted the
peasants. Lieutenant Hammond found the shire town of Somerset
to be "A pleasant, and dry Place, the Streets hansome and fayre,

9. Peter Mundy accounted Worcester about as large as Gloucester and praised its
"Faire and well paved streetes, high into the middle with kennells on both sides;
Many Cloathiers. . . ." Travels, IV, 22; [William Hammond] "A Relation of a
Short Survey of the Western Counties . . . in 1635," in Camden Miscellany,
3d ser., XVI, passim; H. M. Dunsford, Historical Memoirs of Tiverton (Exeter,
1790), 35–8; Tawney, in Ec. Hist. Rev., V, 36; Hoskins, Devon, 495–7, 504–8
(Totnes), 360–62 (Chagford); Pevsner, South Devon, 283–5, 295–7, pls. 18a,
66a.

10. The goldsmiths, physicians, and "all petty chapmen," belonged to the Mercers; smiths, joiners, carpenters, and cutlers belonged to the Cordwainers. In
1637, the Corporation ordered that every freeman's widow "shalbee as free as
her husband was dureing her widdowhood." Maidstone Recs., 63, 68, 79, 80, 106;
Mundy, Travels, IV, 40.

and well built, with a sweet River [the Tone] gliding through her, grac'd with a fayre Church and a stately Steeple, with a sweet and tunable Ring of Bells." From John Walker's map of Chelmsford of 1591 one can obtain a clear impression of the county town of Essex, which John Norden described as "a verie proper towne and a great thorough-fare." It lacked the distinction of Ipswich, the elegant seat of neighboring Suffolk East, which lay six miles upriver from Harwich. John Evelyn described Ipswich as "doubtless one of the sweetest, most pleasant, well built townes in England," and he particularly admired its twelve medieval parish churches, more than any town of like size could boast. A "gallant towne and rich," a great market for corn, a center of shipbuilding, noted for the manufacture of fishing nets, and for the staple of "the chiefest Merchant Adventurers of All England, for the Suffolke Cloathes," Ipswich came as close to being an all-around town as any in the entire country.[11]

The shire towns also had their ups and downs, which reflected the economic well-being of the times. In the good years during the reigns of the first two Stuarts, most of them flourished: men of many professions as well as artisans and tradesmen were drawn to them, new houses went up, and old ones were renovated. "Dorchester (as it is well knowne) is one of the principall places of traffick for westerne marchants, by which meanes it grew rich and populous, beautified with many stately buildings, and faire streetes, flourishing full of all sorts of tradesmen and artificers." There were times, however, when this town of 3,000 could barely hold its own. Lincoln, once the fourth city of England, was but a "corpse" of a town in 1637.[12]

11. *Camden Miscellany*, 3d ser., XVI, 72, 78; John Walker, *Chelmsford in 1591* (facsimile of original in Essex Record Office); also reproduced in *Elizabethan Essex* (Chelmsford, 1961), pl. 11; Evelyn, *Diary*, II, 85–6; Tobias Gentleman, *England's Way to Win Wealth* (1614); Tusser, *Husbandry*, 158; Norden, Chorographical Description, 14; see John Speed, *The Theatre of the Empire of Great Britain* (1611), *s. v.* Suffolk; R. G. Hedworth-Whitty, History of Taunton under the Tudors and Stuarts (Ph.D. Thesis, London, 1938); Pevsner, *South and West Somersetshire,* 310–20, pl. 17; Pevsner, *Suffolk,* 265–83.
12. With the decline of Lincolnshire, Boston fared badly as a seaport, and its famous St. Botolph's Fair lost out to that of Sturbridge. In like fashion, Grimsby lapsed into desuetude. Charles Brears, *Lincolnshire in the 17th and 18th Centuries* (London, 1940), 5–6; Speed, *Theatre of the Empire of Great Britain,* for a map of Dorset and a pleasing view of Dorchester in 1610; John Hilliard, *Fire from Heaven* (1613).

Shipping, fisheries, the making of salt, piracy, and other maritime means of livelihood, licit and illicit, supported about as many of the inhabitants of the island kingdom as did agriculture, the cloth trade, and industrial and mining pursuits combined. Any seventeenth-century map reveals hundreds of fishing hamlets as well as dozens of small maritime towns such as Boston, King's Lynn, Lowestoft, Wivenhoe, the Cinque Ports, Lyme Regis, East Looe, and Fowey. On a hillside in North Devon, on the west bank of the Torridge estuary, lay Bideford, whose main access was by a bridge of twenty-four pointed stone arches, erected in the fifteenth century. Under the patronage of the influential Grenville family, this little haven doubled its population as it moved beyond fishing to a lucrative piracy. At the behest of Sir Richard Grenville, the Queen granted the town its charter of incorporation in 1573. With the development of the Virginia and Bermuda tobacco trade, Bideford's fanatically puritan townsmen successfully challenged their larger neighbor, Barnstaple. By the time of Charles I her local merchants were importing Spanish wool for the Devonshire clothiers and reaching out for commerce with the Low Countries, Brittany, and the Mediterranean.[13]

The persistent refrain of the Cinque Ports (Hastings, Rye, Seaford, Pevensey, Winchelsea) re-echoed from all the coastal communities in 1614: London hath engrossed the trade of the kingdom. At the same time, they complained that the Dutch and French monopolized the fisheries of the Channel and the North Sea. It was in this same year, however, that Tobias Gentleman published *England's Way to Win Wealth,* which demonstrated that his native place, the east coast port of Great Yarmouth, had not only grown rich in this age, but could increase its share of the Dutch herring catch, which amounted to £2,000,000 a year. Frenchmen, Flemings, Dutch, Zealanders, and the Easterlings of the Hanse thronged to the yearly Yarmouth Fishing Fair, where they mingled with men from the lesser ports of eastern and southern England and trafficked "aboute the takinge, sellinge, and

13. Henry J. Hillen, *History of the Borough of King's Lynn* (Norwich, 1907); Wedgwood, *King's Peace,* 25; Hoskins, *Devon,* 113, 335–7; *Devonshire,* IV, 404–7, XLVII, 310; R. G. Granville, History of Bideford (Typescript, Muniment Room, Exeter Library). The mayor of Barnstaple reported the town's population to be "well near 8,000" in 1634. *CSPD, 1634–5,* pp. 172–3.

buying of herrings." Blessed with "brave buildings" and noted for its 140 curious narrow passage ways or streets (known to the natives as rows), which were lined with the tiny houses of fishermen and mariners, Yarmouth was indeed a bustling place. In addition to the thousands of codfish and hundreds of hogsheads of herrings, large quantities of Norwich cloth, Norfolk wheat, malt, barley, and rye were shipped off in the coastwise trade and to London each year.[14]

Four large maritime towns situated along the southern and western shores of Britain ranked ahead of Great Yarmouth (eleventh) in the ship-money assessments of 1619. These communities —Plymouth (third), Dartmouth (fourth), and Barnstaple (fifth) in Devon, and Southampton (eighth) in Hampshire—owed their wealth and importance to the increasing overseas traffic to the Iberian Peninsula and the Mediterranean, to the vigorous activity in the Greenland and Newfoundland fisheries, and to new ventures to the distant East Indies, North America, and the Caribbean. "Upon the British coast, what ship yet ever came/That not of Plymouth heares"? was merely a rhetorical question asked by Michael Drayton. Excitement could be easily sensed in the four towns as they became the principal bases at which merchants and trading companies mounted most of the "western designs" and the ports of embarkation for thousands of their fellow-countrymen who sailed away, voluntarily or under compulsion, for another try at life in a new world. To "That loftie place at Plimmouth call'd the Hoe," the finest maritime prospect in the entire land, Devon men, women, and children flocked in 1583 to view the departure of Sir Humphrey Gilbert for Newfoundland, in 1584 of Sir Richard Grenville for Raleigh's Roanoke, in 1609 of Sir George Somers for Virginia, and in 1620 of the Pilgrim Fathers in the ship *Mayflower* for New England.[15]

---

14. *Sussex Arch.*, XVII, 137–40; Gentleman, *England's Way to Win Wealth*, 10–11, 12–14, 26, 44; I. R., *The Trades Increase* (1615), 26–52; Charles J. Palmer, *A Perlustration of Great Yarmouth* (Great Yarmouth, 1874), I, 17, 18–19, 118–20; II, T. S. Willan, *The English Coasting Trade, 1600–1750* (Manchester, 1938), 129.

15. Samuel R. Gardiner, *History of England . . . 1603–1642* (London, 1883), III, 288n; Michael Drayton, *Poly-Oblion. . .* [1622] (London, 1889), I, 6, 12; *Western Antiquary*, II, 4–5; VII, 122–3; A. E. Stevens, Plymouth Harbour and

Six major provincial centers collectively made prime contributions to the nation's life during the first four decades of the seventeenth century. Varying in size from eight to twelve thousand inhabitants, Bristol, Norwich, Exeter, Salisbury, York, and Newcastle rapidly gained importance after 1500 as regional capitals remote from London. Each of them was a city, that is, the seat of a bishop and the diocesan administration. Each possessed a royal charter conferring upon its corporation certain powers of self-government. Each also profited from the existence within its limits of industrial and commercial facilities that accounted for most of its wealth; and, with the exception of Norwich and Salisbury, each had either its own harbor or access to the sea through a seaport close by. Year after year, too, each of these provincal cities increased in social distinction as more of the upper gentry chose to leave their country seats in the winter season and occupy town houses.[16]

Bristol, having been set apart from Gloucestershire in 1373 by King Edward III, and in keeping with its role as the metropolis of the West Country, enjoyed the status of a county. "Bristoll is even a little London for Merchants, shipping, and great and well furnished Marketts, etts., and I think second to it in the kingdom off England for these perticulers and others" was Peter Mundy's opinion after a visit in 1639. Its merchants extended the old Bristol-Ireland shipping to include the ports of Dublin, Galway, and Coleraine; and commerce with Spain, long quiescent, began to flourish again after the peace of 1604. By 1610 the traffic with Spain, Portugal, and the Atlantic Islands equaled that of the 1550's, and energetic merchants also discovered new sources of gain in a three-cornered trade to Newfoundland for codfish, which their ships carried to markets in the Peninsula and the Mediterranean, and thence returned with spices, fruits, olive oil, and wine ("Bristol Milk" was already well known in 1634). Further evidence of the venturesomeness of the citizens could be observed

Port in the Sixteenth and Seventeenth Centuries (M.A. Thesis, London, 1936–7); R. N. Worth, *History of Plymouth* (2d ed., Plymouth, 1890); Edwin Welch, *Southampton Maps from Elizabethan Time: An Introduction to 24 Facsimiles* . . . (Southampton, 1964).
16. Plumb, *Social History,* 38.

after 1620 when cargoes of tobacco from Virginia and the Caribbean, together with cotton and indigo from the latter region, came up the Avon in ever-larger quantities; and, after 1637, the refining of raw West Indian sugar became a prominent industry in the city. By 1640 Bristol was unchallenged as the greatest English seaport after London.[17]

Manufacturing played its part in Bristol's rising prosperity. The making of cloth, which had accounted for much of the city's advance during the Middle Ages, had declined rapidly after 1550, but starting about 1620 cloth again began to figure prominently in export cargoes. Fabrics woven locally from Welsh wool and, even more, those collected from villages of South Gloucestershire made up most of the outbound shipments. The Kingswood coal pits supplied fuel for the manufacture of brass pins, and from 1612 onward, the processing of sugar from the Atlantic Islands and the Caribbean not only added another source of income for the city, but increased the demand for coal. Olive oil from southern Europe and train oil from the Newfoundland fishery were imported for the use of eleven soap houses; these flourished until a royal order of 1633 limited the city to an annual production of a mere 600 tons.[18]

All of this feverish enterprise called for both labor and leadership. The result was that Bristol attracted workers from the adjacent western counties, South Wales, and the Marches, and, occasionally, lads even came from the Eastern Counties, the Midlands, and London to serve apprenticeships. A census of 1607 gave the city 10,549 inhabitants, and those of the out-parishes raised the number to around 12,000. Sir William Brereton noticed in 1634 that this "rich city" was "exceedingly thronged with Londoners, Irish, and others, who resorted to Bristoll fair" semian-

17. Sir John Stafford referred to Bristol in 1611 as the second city in the kingdom. *CSPD, 1611–18,* p. 79; Mundy, *Travels,* IV, 11; Ramsay, *English Overseas Trade,* 133–44; Bryan Little, *The City & County of Bristol* (London, 1954), 108, 113–14; P. V. McGrath, "The Merchant Venturers and Bristol Shipping in the Early Seventeenth Century," in *Mariner's Mirror,* XXXVI, 69–80; N. C. P. Tyack, Bristol and Virginia in the Seventeenth Century (M.A. Thesis, Bristol, 1930), 55–60.
18. Little, *Bristol,* 115–16.

nually in January and July, and concluded that it "may well deserve in my judgment to be reputed inferior to few [cities] except London." [19]

The urban population of Devon, stimulated by a general prosperity arising from increased activity in fishing, the pursuit of overseas commerce, and the making of cloth, underwent a remarkable expansion in the second half of the sixteenth century. A more than ample share of this growth accrued to Exeter, its county town. Although the new economic and social gains began to transform the city, in 1635 Lieutenant Hammond thought that Exeter still outwardly displayed a medieval aspect, and contemporary views bear him out. "The City is inviron'd about with a Wall, about 2. Mile in Compasse, with 5. Gates, and some watch Towers, and on the out parts thereof she is guarded about with pleasant walkes and diverse Bowling Grounds." Within the ramparts he found that "the Buildings and Streets are faire, especially her high Street from East to West Gate." Ranking next to Bristol among the cities of the West Country, Exeter contained something more than ten thousand people in 1638.[20]

In a model urban study, Professor MacCaffrey has pointed out that Exeter's magnates, by the "bold, skillful, and successful exploitation of every vantage point and the creation of new ones," guided their city to the wealth and power it possessed in 1640. The town's markets, the shire administrative business, the ecclesiastical affairs, and the manufactures of the artisans of the eleven incorporated companies made it "the emporium of the western parts." As the terminus of an excellent network of highways, Exeter served as the principal place of export for the cloth produced in the Southwest. The shallowness of the Exe, however, impelled the

19. Tyack, Bristol and Virginia, 63–4; City of Bristol, Apprentice Books, 1600–31 (Typescript, B. M. Edgerton, 2044); Little, Bristol, 112–13; Chetham, I, 176; John Latimer, The Annals of Bristol in the Seventeenth Century (Bristol, 1900), 34; CSPD, 1636–7, pp. 343–4; 1637, pp. 51, 147.
20. Dartmouth nicely illustrates the growth of urban Devon; one-half of the names of the residents of 1643 were unknown there a hundred years before. Percy Russell, Dartmouth (London, 1950), 82, 92; Caldwell, Devonshire, 67–71; Camden Miscellany, 3d ser., XVI, 77; and in particular, Wallace T. MacCaffrey, Exeter, 1540–1640 (Cambridge, Mass., 1958), 7, 11–13, and the view of Exeter c. 1600, frontispiece; also insert on map of Devon in Speed's Theatre of the Empire of Great Britain.

city's merchants to develop and control the haven of Topsham four miles downstream at the head of the estuary, where seagoing vessels could lie at anchor and be unladed by lighters.[21]

Larger than Exeter and almost rivaling Bristol in size, land-locked Norwich, the shire town of Norfolk, derived its riches from the usual administrative and marketing services its inhabitants performed for the populous county. Most of the town's 1,283 rate-payers of 1634 engaged in work connected with the cloth industry, which, with all its ramifications, flourished not only within the community itself but throughout all of East Anglia. Norwich depended almost entirely upon the high roads for transport and communication; the nearest seaport, Great Yarmouth, though but eighteen miles distant as the crow flies, could be reached only by a highway route of twenty-four miles, and the haven of Ipswich lay fifty miles away to the south. This walled town, with its many thatched roofs, won praise from Thomas Fuller, who avowed that "Norwich is (as you please), either a city in an orchard or an orchard in a city, so equally are houses and trees blended in it; so that the pleasure of the country and populousness of the city meet here together. Yet, in this mixture, the inhabitants participate [in] nothing of the rusticalness of the one, but altogether of the urbanity and civility of the other." [22]

III

Not a few Englishmen of the seventeenth century were acutely aware of Fuller's distinction between *rusticalness* and *civility*. Allusion has been made to the popular, literary debate of the time; in

21. MacCaffrey, *Exeter*, 22; W. B. Stephens, *Seventeenth-Century Exeter* (Exeter, 1958), 126–36, 160–73; Westcote, *Devonshire*, 135, 152.
22. Norwich also received and dispatched yarns and cloth through King's Lynn. It is not clear from the meager and confusing evidence whether much use was made of the river Yare prior to the end of the seventeenth century, when the channel was widened between Norwich and Great Yarmouth. For a fine view of a walled city, showing watch towers and churches, see *The North East Prospect of the City of Norwich* (n. d.) in Anon., *History of Norwich* (Norwich, 1768), folding frontispiece; and for modern scenes inside the city, E. C. Le Guie, *Norwich City* (Norwich, 1956); Fuller, *Worthies*, II, 487, 489; *Norwich Rate Book from Easter 1633 to Easter 1634*, ed. Walter Rye (London, 1903), 9–85; A. D. Bayne, *A Comprehensive History of Norwich* (Norwich, 1869).

addition, a study of the role of cities occupied Continental Europeans and attracted attention in England as well, where the phenomenon of urban growth was more recent. Sir Thomas Wilson, among others, was familiar with the pioneer study of the limitations on an indefinite increase of population made by the Italian Giovanni Botero in *Della Cause della Grandezza delle città* (Rome, 1588), which Robert Peterson of Lincoln's Inn translated and published in 1606 as *A Treatise, Concerning the Causes of the Magnificence and greatness of Cities.* A second edition came out in London in 1635.[23]

Signor Botero carefully differentiated the hamlet, the village, and the town from the city, which he defined as "an assembly of people, a congregation drawn together, to the end they may thereby the better live at ease in wealth and plenty." For him, a city's greatness resided not in the size of the site nor the circuit of the walls, "but the multitude, and number of the Inhabitants and their power." Cities grow, he maintained, "partly out of the vertue generative of men, and partly out of the vertue nutritive of the Cities." It should prove instructive to review in some detail the English experience in urban living in the light of Signor Botero's comprehensive analysis, and to note the effect of a compact environment on the people born in a town or city and upon those who exchanged their rural residences and ways for the radically different career of the townsman and citizen.[24]

Anyone and everyone, countryman or townsman, is moulded to some degree by his environment. Inwardly in views and attitudes, and outwardly in appearance and relation to their fellow citizens, English townsmen adapted themselves to their artificial surroundings. When they left their houses or shops, they stepped out onto man-made streets—seldom did they resort to the fields and woodlands. Their very houses, unlike those on the isolated farms and in the country villages, stood crowded together, close upon the streets. The shortage of building lots, particularly in walled towns, had made this necessary. This pressing need for space had led to the adoption of party walls, the use of the jetty, or overhang, for

23. Wilson, "State of England," 16; *Encyclopedia of the Social Sciences* (New York, 1930), II, 647; Botero, *Greatness of Cities,* 89–90.
24. Botero, *Greatness of Cities,* 1–2, 91.

the second and third stories on the front of the house, and the not infrequent digging of a cellar, something rarely done in the country. Even in that "rich Marchant and sweet Maritime Towne" of Southampton, where 4,200 inhabitants lived inside the walls, seven to a house, a traveler commented on its "pretty well compacted Streets and Buildings." [25]

Little is known about the precise course of The Great Housing Boom in the towns and cities; nevertheless it took place there, and, apparently, earlier there than in the rural parts. At Dartmouth in Devonshire, builders erected about a hundred "handsome houses" before 1642, half of them on the higher and lower streets and connecting lanes, and the other fifty on ground reclaimed from the mud flats along the harbor's banks. Yarmouth, Shrewsbury, Oxford, and Leicester were typical centers of the new building, as were Plymouth and Exeter. [26]

The townsmen had to be guided by the same conditions and limitations that surrounded the countrymen who were erecting new buildings; they made use of local materials, if they were cheaper, and when possible substituted new methods of construction for the old styles. At Oxford and in the Cotswold towns, limestone went into most of the buildings, and slate upon the roofs. "All the howses in Witney and Burford are built of stone," Richard Symonds found in 1644, and the same held true for the great cloth town of Chipping Camden, as well as for Bibury, Bourton-on-the-Water, and Castle Combe, lesser communities so much visited these days. In Bristol, as in many other places, oak was cheaper than stone or brick, even though limited in supply. Houses were built of heavy timber frames with rough-cast plaster or tiles covering the fronts and backs. Thomas Fuller adjudged the framed dwellings of the Bristol merchants "generally very fair," and pointed out that their entries might be unusually narrow, but they led into "high and spatious Halls, which Form may mind the Inhabitants . . . of their passage to a better place." We learn of the

25. *Camden Miscellany*, 3d ser., XVI, 56–7; John D. Wilson, *Life in Shakespeare's England* (Harmondsworth, 1951), 117; Welch, *Southampton Maps; Southampton Recs.*, Pt. I, xvii; *Suffolk*, VII, 1.
26. See the plan of Dartmouth, pl. II of frontispiece in Hugh R. Watkin, *Dartmouth*, Vol. I. *Reformation* (Parochial Histories of Devonshire, No. 5, 1935); Russell, *Dartmouth*, 95–6; Hoskins, in *History Today*, V, 104, 106.

common fate of monastic buildings and ancient ruins from the case of Thomas Till of Coggeshall, who faced charges at the Archdeacon's Court in Essex in 1598 "for carrying out a great . . . stone from the porch of the church and applying the same to his own use." That he had only to return it to its place seems a woefully insufficient penalty.[27]

Some of the new construction went up on vacant sites; occasionally old houses were demolished completely and replaced; in other instances, medieval structures were enlarged or modernized. Everywhere the richest merchants lived in three-story houses of ten to fifteen rooms; the most prosperous tradesmen inhabited four or five rooms on two floors. Because party walls, which served two buildings, could not be breached for windows, light entered a town house from the front and rear only. Consequently, in urban rebuilding after 1600, there was widespread replacement of latticed windows by glazed ones to insure not only better lighting but better ventilation, an important consideration to the townsmen, who spent more of their days indoors than did their rural neighbors. The house of a retailer often had a large "shop window" covering most of the front of his place, and if there were a pent-roof above it, it could be removed in the morning to open the shop to passing customers. Fire hazards prompted the Exeter authorities to proscribe thatched roofs in 1603, and subsequently slate and tiles began to replace the picturesque and familiar thatch in new houses, but many of the old roofs remained intact for decades.[28]

The fact that many new or rebuilt private houses graced every

27. For the haphazard growth of England's second city, see *A Plan of Bristol*, by Jacob Millerd (1673), in Walter Ison, *The Georgian Buildings of Bristol* (London, 1952), pl. 1; Richard Symonds, "Diary," in *Camden*, LXXIV, 18; Clifton-Taylor, *English Building*, 95–7; Fuller, *Worthies*, II, 294; *The Burford Records*, ed. Richard H. Gretton (Oxford, 1920), 188, 211; Roberts, *Southern Counties*, 296; Essex Arch., XII, 25a.

28. Hoskins, in *Past and Present*, IV, 55. Hentzner said of the English towns in general: "Their houses are commonly of two stories, except in London, where they are of three and four, though but seldom of four; they are built of wood; those of the richer sort with bricks, their roofs are low, and where the owner has money, covered with lead." Quoted in Wilson, *Life in Shakespeare's England*, 20, 117; *First Ledger Book of High Wycombe* (Bucks Rec. Soc.), II, 105; Dartmouth Recs., DD 62393; J. Alfred Gotch, in *Shakespeare's England* (Oxford, 1916), II, 63; Richard Izacke, *Remarkable Antiquities in the City of Exeter* (London, 1724), 12.

city and large town did not drastically alter their medieval appearance. The High Street of Exeter illustrated the transition in the principal provincial cities from the accession of King James to the calling of the Long Parliament. Nearly all buildings were of timber construction; only here and there was there a stone structure; most of the roofs were of thatch, the law notwithstanding. The two- and three-story buildings, low-pitched, small, far from convenient, and crowded together, were only occasionally relieved by some substantial merchant's fine residence—a spectacle of the rich and poor living side by side.[29]

The traveler who strayed away from the principal streets of any town quickly became aware of the fact that The Great Housing Boom had not succeeded in providing England's burgeoning urban population with either sufficient or adequate housing. Congested, decayed, residential areas, harboring most of the humbler people, persisted. Coventry had many good streets lined with fair buildings, but, as John Taylor discovered in 1639, "a great number of the inhabitants (especially the poorer sort) doe dwell in vaults, holes, or caves, which are cut or digged out of (or within) the Rocke." At Nottingham, too, John Evelyn saw that "divers" lived in the rocks and caves; Leicester, he conceded was well situated but an "old and ragged citty . . . despicably built, the chimney flues like so many smiths-forges." Similar descriptions can be found for some of the Devon communities: Honiton was "a very poore built towne," according to Symonds, who also branded Crediton, "vulgarly called Kirton," a "great lowsy towne." Colchester was not alone in 1609 in having not a single house available for rent or purchase at any price. Some denizens of walled cities escaped the depressed areas by settling beyond the ramparts in out-parishes: Bristol, for instance, developed genuine suburbs at Clifton and across the Avon.[30]

Poor buildings and party walls were not solely responsible for the blight of English towns. The almost sterilized neatness and orderliness of present-day Norwich's Elm Hill and the Butterwalk at

29. *Western Antiquary*, II, 159; *CSPD, 1619–23*, pp. 116, 118; Hoskins, in Plumb, *Social History*, 53–8 (Leicester).
30. Taylor, *Works*, I, 15; Evelyn, *Diary*, II, 63–5; *Camden*, LXXIV, 37, 40; Philip Morant, *The History and Antiquities of the County Essex* (London, 1768), I, 77, note A.

Totnes bear little resemblance to their seventeenth-century states. Only the main streets in the principal cities were paved in those days, and all manner of living things—dogs, cats, pigs, geese— roamed at large, a menace to passers-by and a persisting public nuisance. Furthermore, it was the general practice of most citizens to cast garbage, refuse, and filth of every description into the streets (often from upper stories, to the peril of pedestrians), there to remain until removed by an underpaid "Raker" on his weekly round. Everyone, particularly old people and children, was in constant danger of being knocked down by hard-riding horsemen or by carts and wains with careless drivers. Sidewalks being unknown, the phrase "giving the wall" connoted providing safety as well as offering courtesy. Rank and privilege availed nothing; all who went abroad on the streets were faced by the same sights, smelled the same noisome odors, and were exposed to the same dangers. Civic pride had yet to be born.[31]

In the city and town, as on the farm, the bulk of Englishmen and their families lived very simply. They had as yet slight awareness or at least little acquaintance with the amenities and fixtures of comfortable living. Because of the bulk and weight, their few pieces of furniture, fashioned from oak, were assembled inside the houses by joiners, for these were the days of the carpenter and joiner; the cabinetmaker did not make his appearance until the Restoration. Planks laid upon trestles formed most tables, and benches served as seats for all but the head of the house, or, later, the group—hence the word *chairman*. An inventory from a town in Essex in 1635 mentions "one joyned Table and six Joyned stooles," also one "Chayre" and one cushion. The closest approach to a comfortable seat was a bench-like settle, and when householders spoke of a hall being "benched," they referred to built-in benches, which were seldom mentioned in inventories. Only a modicum of decorating was attempted in humble residences; a rare exception is the mantelpiece which Gabriel Harvey of Saffron Walden carved and embellished to illustrate his craft of ropemaking.[32]

31. One can acquire a feeling for these conditions by leafing through Latimer's *Annals of Bristol* for the years 1600–1640.
32. In general see Christina Hole, *English Home Life, 1500–1800* (London, 1947); and Ralph Dutton, *The English Interior, 1500 to 1900* (London, 1948).

The more prosperous citizens, like the aggressive yeomen, were gradually acquiring better furnishings. The living rooms of their houses, new or rebuilt, were paneled with English oak or with wainscot "brought hither out of the east countries," whereby, according to a contemporary, they are "not a little commended, made warme, and much more close than otherwise they would be." Sometimes the owners hung their walls with tapestries, arras work, or with painted cloths. Upstairs, a massive bedstead might be covered with a feather bed, bolster, blankets, and a "Coverlyd" (Harrison considered the improved bedding one of the greatest changes in the domestic arrangements of his day), but other than this, bed chambers had little else in them save a chest or two.[33]

William Harrison must have been thinking of the great city merchants and the richest gentry when he wrote that "the furniture of our houses also exceedeth, and is growne in maner even to passing delicacie," but surely he exaggerated when he added that "costlie furniture . . . is descended yet lower, even unto the inferiour artificers and manie farmers, who . . . have, for the most part, learned also to garnish their cupboards with plate, their joyned beds with tapistrie and silke hangings, and their tables with carpets and fine naperie, whereby the wealth of our countrie . . . dooth infinitelie appeare." Henry Gandy, a middle-class brewer of Exeter, was one of the few who attained these luxuries. He died in 1603, and left a three-story house having three rooms on the ground floor—hall, parlor, and kitchen; on the floor above, two bed chambers and "a little room"; and on the next floor, under the roof, a garret or loft. His inventory lists basins, ewers, and other pewter, weighing 204 pounds; six dozen wooden trenchers; twelve spoons either pewter or iron; and fifty ounces of silver plate, consisting of five bowls and a gilded salt (forks were not known in England for another decade). The five dozen table napkins listed

---

Francis W. Steer, *Farm and County Inventories of Mid-Essex, 1635–1749* (Colchester, 1950), 71, 75; Emmison, in *Bedford*, XX, 12–23; *Country Life*, LI, 840. The Harvey mantlepiece is in Saffron Walden Museum. English housing and furnishings still lagged behind those of the Low Countries. See Owen Feltham, *A Brief Character of the Low Countries* (London, 1659), 18, 19–20; Nash, *Quaternio*, 10.

33. Harrison, *England*, Pt. I, 235, 240.

suggest a touch of new refinement, but all of this seems a bit incongruous with the keeping of fourteen pigs in a congested neighborhood.[34]

Whatever architectural distinction the towns attained was ordinarily exemplified by public buildings rather than private houses. Although a market shambles frequently amounted to nothing more than a roof set upon wooden pillars to protect the butchers and their customers from the rain, like the fifteenth-century timber shed close by a rebuilt market cross at Shepton Mallet, some ambitious towns built market houses of two or three stories. The Market Hall with a double-gabled roof at Chipping Camden is one of the handsomest of these, but the much-photographed three-story jettied Guildhall and Market at the head of Town Street in Thaxted, Essex, is more in character. The ground floor of these halls was kept open as a shambles; the enclosed upper stories served town and county affairs, as in the case of the red brick Shire Hall of Woodbridge in Suffolk, which is overlaid and embellished with Dutch strapwork of the early seventeenth century.[35]

Some of the buildings used for the manufacture and sale of cloth are interesting for their design and construction. The unique Yarn Market in Dunster, Somerset, has a stone core and a lean-to roof with windowed dormers raised one story on heavy beams, and faces the Market Square where the shambles once stood. At Lavenham the Guild of Corpus Christi erected a splendid hall, notable for its ground-floor oriels and ornate exterior carvings, which far outshone the cloth halls of Biddenden and other Kentish towns but took second place to the checker-patterned stone and flint Guildhall (1421) at King's Lynn.[36]

Generous bequests from the rich men of this age built and endowed schools and almshouses in their native towns. These insti-

---

34. The comments of William Harrison are not based on personal inspection of the sites mentioned; they are taken from documents which he perused. Born in London, educated at Oxford and Cambridge, he traveled only between those cities, but his source material is considered reliable for the most part. *England*, Pt. I, 238–40; *Western Antiquary*, VII, 1–5.

35. *Country Life*, XL, 603–4; LI, 340–47; LXXIV, 239; LXXX, 239; Pevsner, *Shropshire*, 266; Pevsner, *Essex*, 350, pl. 44; Pevsner, *Suffolk*, 464, pl. 552.

36. *Country Life*, IV, 343–5; XVII, 50; Pevsner, *South and West Somerset*, 158, pl. 2a; Pevsner, *North-West and South Norfolk*, 230, pl. 49a.

tutions were created to carry on the functions that had formerly been performed by monastic orders. The Grammar School of Shrewsbury (1590), Blundell's School in Tiverton (1604), and Lord Knyvett's Free School at Stanwell (1624) were visible signs of this liberality that provided charity and lent distinction to the towns. The granite loggia of Penrose's range of almshouses, erected at Barnstaple in 1627, is better executed than that of the well-known almshouses of Moretonhampstead, built ten years later.[37]

The true glory of English architecture, however, lay in the churches. Many a traveler concurred with Signor Foscarini in commending them before mentioning other public buildings. Who could visit Boston without being overwhelmed by the monumentality of St. Botolph's, the largest parish church in the land; or how could anyone fail to exclaim over perpendicular Gothic churches as far apart as Ottery St. Mary in Devon and Lavenham in Suffolk? Without the walls at Bristol stood St. Mary Redcliffe, dubbed by Queen Elizabeth "the fairest, goodliest, and most famous parish church in England," and St. Stephen's, within the walls, with its tall, proud tower rivaled the Cathedral in the quality of its perpendicular mode. Though most small towns had but one "very fair" church, large towns had many: Ipswich could very well have boasted of spectacular St. Margaret's and eleven other parish churches, but Norwich probably led all provincial cities, with something more than fifty medieval edifices within its walls.[38]

A wayfarer soon learned that in each of the principal cities of England, whether the city itself was externally impressive or not, he would find a cathedral and chapter house both dignified and elegant. The cathedrals of Norwich, Exeter, and York stood out, though they could be challenged by some of the smaller bishops' seats and such wonderful structures as those at Salisbury, Wells, and Ely. Without question, any architectural merit the English

37. Pevsner, *North Devon*, 48, pl. 42; Pevsner, *South Devon*, 208, 285, pls. 64a, 64b; Pevsner, *Middlesex*, 150, pl. 43a; Pevsner, *Shropshire*, 268, pl. 46a.
38. Pevsner states that Norwich has thirty-two parish churches that have survived, four are ruined, and that Sir Reginald Blomfield knew of an additional twenty— "all medieval." *North-East Norfolk and Norwich*, 234–5, 270, pl. 1; Le Guie, *Norwich City*, 18; Pevsner, *South Devon*, 218–23, pl. 66a; Pevsner, *North Somerset and Bristol*, 359, 371–86, 395–6; Pevsner, *Suffolk*, 296–9, 316–20; Evelyn, *Diary*, II, 86.

towns and cities possessed was chiefly ecclesiastical and medieval.[39]

There is no evidence that the ordinary townsmen took much interest in the architectural changes in their communities. In a time when the mingling of the old and the new in domestic and civic, if not ecclesiastical, styles was producing a far from satisfactory urban scene, citizens appeared to be either unaware of or indifferent to the fact that they were living in the midst of a transitional period of architectural taste and building construction.

IV

In spite of the fact that a townsman could always get into the country merely by taking a short walk, the artificiality of urban existence made a lasting impress on individuals of all conditions and degrees. Those persons who were born and raised in the city thought of busy streets and structures with party walls as normal and natural. In the compact, congested urban centers, more opportunities occurred for sociability with one's neighbors; and it was possible, in a city, to find individuals with common interests, or to remain anonymous, if that seemed desirable.

The composition of the urban population differed radically from that of the rural. A much greater proportion of the inhabitants of both sexes and all ages were foreign-born, and there were many more young, single males than in manorial villages. In 1632 David Lupton lamented the loss to the city of the venturesome and eager younger sons who saw no future in agriculture. The earnestness with which the town fathers stressed the godliness of civil society and the wickedness of remaining single or living apart from one's fellowmen was not uniquely a puritan attitude; it was an urban one.[40]

The family was the fundamental social institution of the town as well as of the country, though it developed significant variations. As a rule, it was smaller, both in the size of the actual conjugal group and in the total number of individuals who occupied one

39. See Pevsner's volumes for ample descriptions and plates illustrating the great cathedrals.
40. Lupton, *London and the Country*, 97; Chute, *Shakespeare of London*, 55; Nash, *Quaternio*, 6–7.

house or tenement: eight to a house appears to be a more or less constant figure for this period. Strikingly fewer children and old people lived under the same roof. In the seaports, fishermen and mariners absented themselves from the family board much of the time, and the wives of men long away—sometimes for years— encountered serious problems of subsistence and morality; widows of those lost at sea or by industrial accidents abounded. Because town dwellings offered greater indoor privacy and a refuge from outsiders, family solidarity, long submerged by the overwhelming social pressures of the manorial village, began to crystallize in the larger cities and towns.[41]

The distribution of townspeople into ranks and degrees also differed markedly from the rural hierarchy. Those labeled as "persons of inferiour rank" formed a motley group in every urban community. Recent studies indicate that they made up "fully 80 per cent" of the entire population of the provincial cities and larger towns. Most artisans ("mechanical men of the meanest quality," as they said in Norwich), and such native laborers as porters, carters, and longshoremen, who worked for pittances, formed the core of the lower sort. To these people, others were constantly being added: "hempen home-spuns" like Bottom and his "crew of patches"; droves of victims of enclosures from the country villages; hundreds of idle, thieving rogues and vagabonds, both male and female; poverty-stricken Irish imports; discharged or maimed soldiers and sailors—all of them ostensibly seeking work, but many of them mere beggars.[42]

Of the partially free individuals, covenanted servants, and apprentices, some would ultimately reach the middle group. Ability to read and write, and to speak correctly, separated persons of recognized rank from the lower orders quite as effectively as did clothes. In a play, Master Barnes of Abington asks about a letter his servant Nicholas Prouverbs is fumbling with: "Why read it,

---

41. See Mrs. Joan Thirsk's suggestive review article, "The Family," in *Past and Present*, No. 27 (April, 1964), 120–22; *Somerset & Dorset*, I, 70–71; for a significant study of the contemporary French family, see Philippe Ariès, *Centuries of Childhood* (New York, 1962).

42. *Midsummer-Night's Dream*, III, i, 79; III, ii, 9; V, i, 72–4; *CSPD, 1603–10*, p. 359; *1619–23*, p. 60; *1627–8*, p. 348; *The Elizabethan Underworld*, ed. A. V. Judges (New York, 1930), xv–xx; Jordan, *Philanthropy in England*, 329.

canst thou read?" and Nicholas replies, "Forsooth though none of
the best, yet meanly." John Mortimer of Exeter, a humble weaver,
husbanded his resources and, at his death, bequeathed a small estate to his wife, left a large loom to his cousin and a small one to
his own son, Peter, and—a rarity in those days for one of his degree—willed *The Plain Man's Pathway to Heaven* to John Bayle,
and to his two sisters, a Testament and *The Sufferings of Christ*.[43]

In nearly every town the middling sort, composed of tradesmen,
master craftsmen, and their families, turned out, as a group, to be
every bit as ambitious and grasping as their yeoman counterparts,
and they too sent members up to join the better sort. Many a
tradesman thought of himself as a merchant in the rough, whom
time, application, and patience would elevate to a superior station.
Occasionally his spouse, coveting the same clothes, sights, and
entertainment as her betters, ostentatiously attempted to climb pre-
maturely. In 1635 Sir William Brereton visited Hereford:

> Here we observed a smith's wife in a loose bodied gown, gentle
> womanlike, walking in the streets, whom the boys followed,
> hooting, shouting, and jeering after her, who was in a mighty
> perplexity and distraction, one pulling her by the arm, another
> by the gown, another by her loose sleeve, whose pride and arro-
> gance was most justly rewarded with shame, reproach, and
> scorn.[44]

A few gentle families possessed and occupied town houses, but
for the most part they were seasonal transients. The mercantile society, characterized by constant, hard work and the saving of
money, contrasted sharply with the country gentry with its open-
handed expenditures, conspicuous display, and comparative idleness, the waning of the old hospitality notwithstanding. Many a
town merchant aspired to broad acres and a gentle status, but few
attained them. The persistent quest for a higher station revealed itself in the amount and richness of household furnishings of the
otherwise frugal merchant and in the elegance of the apparel of his
proud "Shee Citizen" and her daughters. Respectability and gentle
conduct also signaled the new degree. When his wife forgot her

43. Worthy, *Devonshire Wills*, 176; Porter, *Two Angry Women of Abington*, n. p.
44. *Chetham*, I, 186.

manners and raged at Mistress Coursey, Mr. Barnes hastened to reprove her: "What will the neighbring country vulgar say,/When as they heare that you fell out at dinner?" The measure of the citizen's status was, however, first and foremost, wealth—wealth in ships, in goods, and, above all, in money.[45]

A natural consequence of this mingling in close proximity of all sorts and conditions of men and women from town and country and from foreign nations, and of their intermarriage, was that at every level the old medieval exclusiveness faded away. At the same time, however, the disparity between the patrician families and those of lesser influence was starkly evident in an urban setting, because the rich merchant, the middling tradesman, and the poor man frequently dwelt side by side on the same street. Living in close quarters, the townsmen saw much of each other and really did rub shoulders, but though they encountered more people daily than ever before, they knew them less well. Each tended to associate with only his own kind, and much of the rural sense of neighborliness was lost. People retreated to anonymity, and impersonality prevailed in human relations. Few features of this period are more appalling than the callousness displayed by most of the citizens of that age toward the misery and wants of the creatures they branded as "the disorderly poor."

Opportunities beckoned to enterprising men of all ranks, for urban society was unusually fluid; in a scale graduated according to money, a man could rise—or fall. Every year many of the men who came to the cities from manorial villages made good and rose to both commercial and civic leadership. Faced by constantly changing and swelling populations, local corporations could no longer maintain their vaunted species of urban particularism. Gradually a cosmopolitan spirit pervaded men's minds; the countryman became a citizen—a profound psychological transformation experienced every year by larger and larger numbers of Englishmen.[46]

45. See Wilson, "State of England," 12, for a country gentleman's annual expenditures; Porter, *Two Angry Women of Abington.*
46. Barnes, *Somerset,* 19, 21.

V

The inhabitants of England's towns and cities encountered all of the stimulations accompanying rapid growth and prosperity, yet their lives were far from being unalloyed rounds of success and pleasure. Swarming of population and physical expansion brought in their trains a series of critical problems which, if they did exist in the country, were more intensified in urban settings, and the civic authorities, save in a few matters, signally failed to cope with them.

Timber houses with thatched roofs, when combined with chimneys that often fouled and belched sparks, made tinder boxes out of every structure along the crowded streets. Citizens were understandably obsessed with fear of fire, for municipal measures intended for fire prevention were either ineffective or only fitfully enforced. In petitioning in 1624 for the revoking of John Taylor's license to brew and bake, the parishioners of Wyllie, a small Wiltshire town, declared that the community had almost been set afire twice because Taylor's house had neither chimney nor flue, nor stone walls above four feet in height, and that the roof was thatched without a loft. One can construe the miserable state of housing for the poor as well as fire risks from the petition against Taylor, and in the presentment of Otilwell Johnson or his tenants before the Court Leet of Manchester for using a fire despite the lack of a chimney in his hovel "to the Terror and feare of Henry Kelley and others of his neighbors." [47]

When fire did break out, extensive conflagrations could scarcely be avoided, especially if there were a strong wind. The history of Tiverton offers a sorry record of such catastrophies. In four hours on a market day in 1598, some fifty people lost their lives in a blaze that also destroyed over 400 houses, 300 pairs of looms, and an "abundance of kersies," plus a number of market horses. The town had not much more than recovered in 1612 when another fire consumed 600 houses; the losses then amounted to £350,000. Those who lost their homes and all their possessions departed to

47. *HMC Various*, I, 95; Essex Sessions, XX, 261; *Court Leet Records of the Manor of Manchester* (Manchester, 1886), III, 8.

seek a livelihood elsewhere. Although neighboring villages sent contributions, the town never completely recovered. In writing up an account of a serious fire in Dorchester, Stow remarked that he would fill many sheets of paper if he set down all of the fires in England in 1613 "as is evident by the incessant collections throughout all Churches of this Realme, for such as have been spoyled by fire." [48]

All over Europe fire-fighting was in its infancy, but certain of the British municipal authorities were endeavoring to discover methods to reduce the havoc caused by conflagrations. Some ordered that leather buckets be kept in parish churches for conveying water from its source to the blaze; others acquired poles, hooks, and chains for "the pullinge downe of howses" to prevent the spread of fire; still others procured ladders that would enable them to reach flaming chimneys and burning roofs. One measure universally adopted, though seldom properly enforced, required that all chimneys be cleaned regularly to forestall blazing at the top. Devizes was one of the few English boroughs whose mayor ordered the purchase of "an Engine for the prevencon of the danger that may hap to arise by fyer." The main obstacle, however, in dousing fires was the shortage of water. [49]

As the urban communities expanded, the need to increase the water supply grew critical. In small towns like Braintree and Bocking, the inhabitants had always depended on "the common towne pumpe" for drinking and household water, and, in event of fire, the bucket-lines had formed there. In time the pumps in many

48. The town clerk of Barnstaple wrote of the holocaust of 1598 at Tiverton: "The report goeth that the rich men of the town were unmerciful to the poor and suffered them to die in the Streets for Want and so it might be Digitis Dei." Bishop Bayly subscribed to this theory of divine judgment in his *Practise of Piety*. Philip Wyot's Diary, April 4, 1598, in Richard Wood, Notes, Extracts . . . Barnstaple (MS, Muniment Room, Exeter City Library, n. p.) *Western Antiquary*, II, 168–9; III, 2, 12; X, 147; Edwin S. Chalk, *History of St. Peter's Church, Tiverton* (Tiverton, 1905), 21; Dunsford, *Tiverton*, 42–3; *Wofull Newes from Tiverton* (1612); *CSPD, 1611–18*, p. 206; *Somerset & Dorset*, I, 71; III, 104; Hamilton, *Quarter Sessions*, 19, 90; *The Lamentable and Fearfull burning of the towne of Dorchester* (1613); Frances Rose-Troup, *John White* (New York, 1930), 28–9; Stow, *Annales*, 892, 1003; *Municipal Records of the Borough of Dorchester, Dorset*, ed. C. H. Mayo (Exeter, 1893), 538–9.
49. *HMC Lincoln*, XIV: VIII, 91: *Sussex*, XLVII, 54, 66; *Chetham*, n. s., XLVI, 23; *Oxford Council Acts*, 104; *Devizes Recs.*, 98.

places fell into decay or disrepair, and the laundresses, who by custom did the community's weekly washing in troughs close to the pumps, polluted the water supply. Enterprising corporations of a few towns moved to bring in water from the outside: "This yere the towne builted some of the Conduytts," the Plymouth records for 1592 state; twelve years later Walter Mathews added a new conduit at his own charge. In 1600 John Moore, "plumber," of Exeter contracted to lay new lead pipes for the two conduits leading from two cisterns in the parish of St. Sidwell beyond the walls; and it is plain that by 1604 Dartmouth's inhabitants got their water from pipes, for they were prohibited from washing at the conduits or in the streets any longer. Early in the century Bridgewater in nearby Somerset used wooden water pipes, and in 1616 the Oxford Council authorized the University to open the streets for laying lead pipes to convey water to Carfax. The Council also directed the construction of a conduit "to be bewtified and adorned as an ornament of the city with three several cocks fayerly set out to run water three several ways." In spite of these efforts, however, about all that can be said is that few urban issues proved more lasting than those connected with fire and water.[50]

Problems having to do with food distribution and public health confronted the townsfolk daily. Every borough found it necessary to have surveyors of the market, who, prodded occasionally by the grand jury, saw to the proper management of the shambles, adjusted minor disputes, and inspected the measures and quality of the food exposed for sale. Ordinarily only flesh was sold at the structures we know as markets or shambles, though this included chickens, turkeys, and other fowl. Once a week, or sometimes oftener, the butchers would stand in their stalls ready to cut and sell meat. The survival of medieval customs was evident when the butchers were indicted for selling meat in the Sudbury market that "hadn't been chased enough by the dogs" or that was "unbaited" [51]

Town authorities set aside locations for other markets, which required different regulations concerning hours, custom, and meas-

50. Essex Sessions, XIX, 519–20, 537; *HMC Exeter*, 26, 285; *HMC Hereford*, XIII: IV, 341; *Plymouth Recs.*, 20, 23; Dartmouth Recs., D. D. 61710; *Somerset & Dorset*, XVI, 14; Anon., *History of Norwich*, 243; Izacke, *Exeter*, 12, 16; Mundy, *Travels*, IV, 23; *Oxford Council Acts*, 253.
51. Powell, *Puritan Village*, 45; *Devon & Cornwall*, XXVII, 217.

ures. There was a meal market in most towns, and, on the coast, the fishmongers congregated near the waterside. Butter and other white meats (dairy products, such as cheese and, occasionally, eggs) were sold by women in some appointed sheltered place, like the loggias known as Butterwalks at Totnes and Dartmouth. Milk and products not displayed in the markets were huckstered up and down the streets, and everywhere tradesmen's shops dispensed cooked and processed foods. Most of the bread consumed in Great Coggeshall in 1626 was baked by the Widow Rose Blighton, who typified the goodwives who ran most of the bakeshops in all the towns. Some women bakers specialized in cakes and the ever-popular gingerbread. A poor householder who had limited cooking facilities could arrange to have meat roasted or other food cooked at victualing houses, cook shops, or inns.[52]

Except in times of dearth or famine, the city people had enough to eat. Though the poorer element tasted of meat but rarely, still the town of Dorchester could support eleven butchers in 1620. The chief item in the diet of the great mass of the people was fish: John Ward recalled that "Sprats are proverbially called the Weaver's beef of Colchester." It was remarkable how far inland the carriers traveled to deliver Colne River oysters, Yorkshire salmon, and lobsters from the Cinque Ports. Godfrey Goodman attested to this traffic when he deplored men's desire for certain foods only when they were scarce and costly: "When we live in the Inland countries, then we begin to long for sea-fish. . . . Me thinks the Colchester Oysters never taste so well, as when they are bought in Northampton: fresh Salmon at Newcastle is meat for servants and colliers, for no man of worth will respect it." The greatest dietary deficiency came from a lack of vegetables and fruits. Produce from market gardens continued to be almost unknown save in Essex, Kent, and Surrey. Samuel Hartlib reported that cabbages, turnips, carrots, and parsnips came in from Holland and Flanders until well past 1605, when the "Art of Gardening began to creep into England, into Sandwich and Surrey, Fulham, and other places," but as late as 1637 a "famous town" within twenty miles of London "had not so much as a mess of Pease" but

52. *Warwick Sessions*, VI, 41; *Bedford*, II, 170; *Manchester Court*, III, 215, 320; Essex Sessions, XX, 101.

what came from the metropolis. The pippins that Shakespeare had Sir Hugh Evans eat with his cheese may have been "of my own graffing," but other men had to rely on imports.[53]

The many single persons or journeymen with families who lived in the town had to be lodged and fed. Sojourners could sleep at an inn on flax or canvas sheets, if they had the means, or at an ale-house with lesser accommodations. A few could find lodgings in a tradesman's house; mostly they took their meals in one of the innumerable victualing or alehouses which sprang up everywhere. The county of Leicester licensed 309 bonded public-house keepers in 1609, and the city of Oxford, to the puzzlement of King Charles, had 300. If an employer agreed to supply meat and drink to his workmen, wages were adjusted accordingly: in Essex in 1607, a "masterless" bricklayer received a daily wage of 8*d*. "with meat and drink," otherwise he got 14*d*. When the justices of the peace set the wages for artisans and handicraftsmen in the borough of Dartmouth in 1630, they provided that a master carpenter or hellier (tiler or slater) was to receive 7*d*. a day with "meate and drinke" or 14*d*. without them; apprentice shipwrights with three years of service were to have 16*d*. without and 8*d*. with food.[54]

Ale and victualing houses varied widely in quality and service. Fynes Moryson implied that all English inns were exemplary; Sir William Brereton was more restrained; he assessed The Crown at Berwick-on-Tweed as "an honest inn," and found that others offered only ordinary mean entertainment. In contrast, so distaste-ful did the Water Poet find the drunken host, the bread-and-water fare, and the revolting chamber-pot stench of The Rose and Crown where he spent a night that, upon reaching Dunster the next day, he expressed his views in a bitter rhyme:

53. Hutchins, *Dorset*, II, 339; Ward, *Diary*, 112; Godfrey Goodman, *The Fall of Man, or the Corruption of Nature* . . . (London, 1616), 190; Fuller, *Worthies*, I, 31; *Oxinden Letters*, 21: *North Riding Sessions*, IV, 101, 109; Evelyn, *Diary*, I, 9; [Samuel Hartlib], *S. Hartlib, his Legacy of Husbandry* (1655), 8–10; *Merry Wives of Windsor*, I, ii, 12–13.
54. For an excellent, detailed description of the public and sleeping rooms, furnishings, and supplies of Goodman's inn at Petworth in 1619, see *Sussex Arch.*, XCVIII, 86–7; *CSPD, 1603–10*, p. 434; *1634–5*, pp. 431–32; Essex Sessions, XVIII, 189; XIX, 166; XX, 27; Hutchins, *Dorset*, 339; *A Catalogue of Taverns in ten Shires about London* (1636); Dartmouth Recs., DD 62257, DD 62420.

> From nasty Roomes, that never felt broomes,
> From excrements, and all bad sents,
> From childrens bawling, and caterwawling,
> From grunting of hogs, and barking of dogs,
> and from byting of Fleas, there I found ease.

In quiet communities, like Barnstaple, which licensed only thirty-six a year on an average from 1634 to 1641, public houses came under strict regulation, but there can be no question that clean, inviting establishments serving good food were in the minority.[55]

The price of firewood, a major concern for all Englishmen, rose everywhere, but particularly in seaports like Dartmouth—this is not strange considering that it took 2,500 trees to build a ship. Early in the reign of Charles I, Bulstrode Whitelocke looked upon firewood and timber as the most expensive articles to be sold in that town. In all the coast towns, however, the situation was being relieved by the importation of coal from Newcastle. Even so, the poor people who lived beyond the limits of navigation and could not benefit by cheap water carriage were unable to afford the added costs of cartage. Inasmuch as the town-dwellers usually had better protection against the excessive cold and dampness of the stormy seasons, they probably suffered less from pulmonary infections, influenza, and chronic colds.[56]

The real threat to the public's health in all the cities arose from the unsanitary conditions. Crowded areas were seldom clean, and the customary provision for cleaning streets was typified by Lyme Regis's borough ordinance directing every householder on Saturday night before dark to "cleanse the street over against his dwelling-house" and to remove all dung and dirt or suffer a fine of one shilling. But such orders for a once-a-week cleanup failed to produce an even tolerable condition by modern standards. Inhabitants tossed rubbish and ordure out of their doors and windows without restraint; at Warwick a man went so far as to lay a dunghill in the

55. *Chetham*, I, 189–91; Taylor, *Works*, I, No. 21, pp. 8–9; *Barnstaple Recs.*, I, 37; *Worcestershire*, II, 345, 567.
56. *CSPD, 1635*, p. 73; Nef, *Coal Industry*, I, 163, 193, 196; *Memoirs of Bulstrode Whitelocke*, ed. R. H. Whitelocke (London, 1873), 46; Stow, *Annales*, 1024–5; A. Leigh Hunt, *The Capital of the Ancient Kingdom of Thetford, East Anglia* (London, 1870), 127n; *HMC Exeter*, 68; *HMC Various*, IV, 286.

middle of a watercourse, and the authorities at Weymouth hoped to prevent children of seven or over from "filthing the streets" by fining their masters 6*d.* for such offenses. Pestilential rats, proverbial tenants of the waterfront, spread out to the unswept streets and propagated in manure piles, refuse heaps, and privies. The celebrated odors of the Near and Far East once suffused the atmosphere of all English towns to such a degree that even the constant rains never entirely erased them. The average townsman could have agreed with Coleridge's comment on Cologne:

> I counted two-and-twenty stenches
> All well defined, and several stinks.[57]

Townsfolk suffered most of the afflictions experienced by the men of the country, and communicable diseases often brought greater disaster to the towns because congested living conditions facilitated their course. Smallpox raged periodically nearly everywhere and carried off many citizens and left survivors marked for life. At Dorchester in 1624, the heaviest incidence of this disease fell upon the children. From the little evidence available it would seem that only the regular consumption of beer and cider could have prevented periodic epidemics of typhoid fever. Hentzner noticed in 1598 that "they are often molested with scurvy": too much salt meat and fish and not enough fresh fruits doubtless favored this ailment, which inevitably ravaged crews on ships long at sea. Some Devonshire ports maintained lazarettos. At Totnes in 1626, Nicholas Harris, for forty years a foot-postman, was maliciously accused of being a leper. Denied admission to the almshouse, the wretched old man walked all the way to London to procure a certificate from the Governors of St. Bartholomew's Hospital of his freedom from the disorder and then walked all the way home again before he could obtain admission.[58]

57. Roberts, *Southern Counties,* 277, 281; *Warwick,* VI, 19. Discussing medical service, Urban says, in Nash's *Quaternio,* that he believes that "we mostly outstrip you in health." (pp. 44–5)
58. The many accidents are largely attributable to specific urban causes, such as traffic injuries or many kinds of industrial accidents. Wilson, *Life in Shakespeare's England,* 20; Whiteway, Diary, pp. 10 (fol. 20), 65 (fol. 74). For a table of mortality at Manchester, 1625, see *HMC Kenyon,* XIV, IV, 31–2; *Western Antiquary,* XI, 74; Izacke, *Exeter,* 20.

By far the greatest inroads of the successive visitations of the plague occurred in the centers of concentrated populations. In the first and deadliest outbreak of the period, 1603–5, Bristol's plague victims totaled around 3,000, Norwich's 3,076, and York's about 3,500; smaller towns lost proportionately. From 1608 to 1619, in addition to its fire, Tiverton went through a kind of "persistent epidemic," and one historian has estimated that at the city of Cambridge, the plague appeared every five years through the seventeenth century. Richard Whiteway has left a record of how the terrible scourge of 1624–25 ran from place to place: at its height in the city of London, the week of July 18th, 5,205 people died, and 4,000 more succumbed in the suburbs of Westminster and Stepney. Thence it "was dispersed into divers quarters of this kingdome, as to Oxford, Exeter, Winchester, Bath, and all the towns about London, Reading, Abington, Southampton, the Isle of Wight," and of course it reached Dorchester and the towns in Dorset. "It reigned long and continuously at Exon all the while," where the fever had broken out the previous year, and carried off an estimated "four Thousands of Persons." After 600 persons had died during the severe epidemic of 1637 at Bury St. Edmunds, the chief inhabitants withdrew into the country, leaving 4,000 people "unvisited," 103 families shut up, and 117 sick of the sores and under care, besides 439 who were recovering. By December the city had already disbursed £2,000, and its weekly charge for caring for plague victims ran to £200.[59]

Local officials pursued every means known to combat the epidemics and take care of the stricken poor. Sometimes the measures taken cut two ways: they forbade strangers from places of known infection to enter the town, and they shut the houses where only one person was known to be sick, thereby preventing all of the inmates from earning their livings. All markets and fairs were suspended, which to some degree cut down on the spread of the disease but also brought about a critical food shortage—Salisbury reported in 1627 that "more people are like to perish by famyne than by the infeccious disease or sickness." To provide necessary

59. Little, *Bristol*, 112; *Norfolk & Norwich*, I, 184; Mullett, *Bubonic Plague*, 109, 143–4, *et passim* for the entire period; *Plymouth Recs.*, 23; Whiteway, Diary, pp. 93 (fol. 101), 97 (fol. 105); Izacke, *Exeter*, 20; *VCH Cambridge*, II, 101; *Suffolk*, I, 40.

relief, special taxes were levied. In Sandwich, in 1610, where only 39 out of 139 infested householders were able to take care of themselves, it took 30 to 40 shillings a day for relief, and many of those taxed had their own cases of sickness to look after.[60]

Whenever the plague invaded a town, all normal activities immediately slowed down; and if its stay was prolonged, trade and daily life were totally disrupted. Death broke up families and left the towns with a larger number of unattached people than ever before. If employers died or fled the town to escape the scourge, their journeymen, apprentices, and servants found themselves adrift. In the Essex cloth town of Hadleigh, most of the chief merchants and clothiers deserted the place, and 200 families became wholly dependent upon the town's charity. The labor force, itself decimated, was helpless; some of them managed to regroup, but many wandered about in a veritable daze, a reservoir of homeless, rootless souls of both sexes to whom adroitly worded suggestions about leaving England made a great appeal. To such as these, America appeared as a land of hope.[61]

By the standards of the day, the towns had a sufficient number of well-trained and properly licensed doctors. Many accusations of high charges and malpractice have been made against them, but they too had their grievances. One of them declared that "if the patient find not cure or ease as soon as he expects then forthwith he changes his physician and applies himself to another, and loudly lays the fault on his former physician." Non-payment of bills plagued most of them: Bartholomew Chapell, "medicus," sued Thomas Lidsam in the borough court at Plymouth in 1603 for refusing to pay for the treatment of "quadam informitate in naso suo." Cities and towns usually appointed one or more physicians to treat certain of the dependent poor and all prisoners. Late in the sixteenth century, the Guildhall Feoffees at Bury St. Edmunds began to pay traveling female practitioners for treating persons having incurable cases of fistulas, sores on the limbs, and like ailments. This use of women seems to have been unique in county

60. "Near 2000 needy people" suffered from the plague at Colne, Wiltshire, in 1640, most of them clothworkers and tradesmen. *HMC Various*, I, 81, 96–7, 106; Bayne, *Norwich*, 214–15; *CSPD, 1627–8*, pp. 36, 39; *1637–8*, pp. 395–6; *Western Antiquary*, X, 125; *HMC Exeter*, 176; *Maidstone Recs.*, 255–6.
61. *CSPD, 1637*, p. 161.

Norfolk, but it is significant as an entering wedge for the sex in a man's profession.[62]

Lincoln, Norwich, Canterbury, Exeter, Bristol, and the big boroughs of Leicester and Ipswich became famous medical centers. No finer practitioner could be found in England than Dr. Thomas Browne, author of *Religio Medici*. Educated at Winchester, Oxford, Montpellier, and Padua, and a graduate of Leiden, he settled down to practice at Norwich in 1637, a city counterpart of Dr. John Symcotte of Bedfordshire. In addition to physicians, one or more surgeons (Barber-Chirurgions) practiced in each community. In 1639 at Gloucester, John Deighton took over his father's medical library of 121 books, his surgeon's chest, and a box of twenty-three "Capitoll instruments" among which were a trepan with four bits to bore the skull, an iron head-probe, forceps, catheters, and "dividers" for opening the mouth. Thus equipped, he was ready and willing to set broken bones, remove bullets, and perform amputations.[63]

The ceaseless thronging of rural people into the urban centers, small or large, exacerbated the problem of keeping the peace; violence, petty cruelty, abuse of the unfortunate, and major crimes increased in these unstable years. In the past, social control had been achieved through the head of the family, but in this age no public agency had developed that could cope with the mounting number of inhabitants who were outside any parental discipline. The constable, who represented law and order, said Earle, "is a Viceroy in the street, and no man stands more upon't that he is the King's Officer," but after sundown, on the unlighted streets, it was practically impossible for him, alone, to maintain public order, detect perpetrators of disturbances, and prevent crime.[64]

The town rulers soon realized that they must take measures to protect their citizens. In 1561 Exeter notified the proprietors of all inns and taverns that they must hang lights at their doors, and each citizen, in order, was to do the same every third night. Bristol acquired its first lighting in 1604 with the hanging of a few candle

62. Raach, English Country Doctor, 115; *Plymouth Recs.*, 231; Keevil, in *Bulletin of Medicine*, XXXI, 422; *Suffolk*, I, 262; *Warwick Sessions*, I, 20.
63. Raach, English Country Doctor, 118; *DNB*, VII, 64; *Bristol & Gloucester*, LXIV, 71–88.
64. Earle, *Microcosmography*, 47.

lanterns. Though the Common Council had already (1601) appointed a "beadle of the beggars" and a "beadle of the rogues," the city had no regular night or constable's watch before 1621, when the town sergeant warned thirty-two citizens to patrol the streets each night. Officers of smaller towns, such as Halstead in Essex, thought it sufficient to appoint one to five regular watchmen who, carrying a lantern and a "grayned staff" (a symbol of office), went on nocturnal rounds.[65]

Appointment of a watch did not assure the towns of a surcease of crime. When Shakespeare has Dogberry charge his watch, one of them, voicing the opinion of his fellows, replies, "We will rather sleep than talk; we know what belongs to a watch." The Grand Jury of Dartmouth in 1624 presented "Daniell Boone for sleeping in his watch and letting his halberd be taken from him on January 5th last." (Had his celebrated namesake not been more alert, the English-speaking peoples would be lacking a great folk-hero.) More than once the watch itself was guilty of misdemeanors, as when Constable Soda of Chelmsford "withdrew his watchmen to drinking," and later they were all embroiled in an affray with the watch of Moulsham. There were times, however, when both awake and alert, they were abused or beaten up by "Gentlemen-rankers out on the spree," or by gangs of local toughs or vagrant criminals. When all allowances are made for the dangerous and thankless services performed by the constables and watchmen of urban England, their institutional insufficiency is patent.[66]

VI

Edward Chamberlayne pointed out in the first edition of *Angliæ Notitiæ* (1669) that the country and the city enjoyed many sports and diversions in common: "The Citizens and Peasants have Hand-Ball, Foot-Ball, Skittles, or Nine Pins, Shovel-Board, Stow-Ball, Goffe [?], Trol Madam, Cudgels, Bear-baiting, Bull-baiting, Bow and Arrow, Throwing at Cocks, Shuttle-cock, Bowling, Quoits, Leaping, Wrestling, Pitching the Barre, and Ringing of Bells, a

65. *Devon & Cornwall*, XIX, 148–9; Latimer, *Annals of Bristol*, 13–14, 31, 77; Essex Sessions, XVIII, 167; MacCaffrey, *Exeter*, 91.
66. *Much Ado About Nothing*, III, iii, 39–40; Dartmouth Recs., Jan. 10, 1624; Essex Sessions, XX, 193, 248.

Recreation used in no other Country of the World." He ought to have mentioned morris dancing and other terpsichorean forms, maypoles, tennis, horse-racing, and games of chance, for with green fields and groves so near at hand, the youths of the towns could participate in the pastoral pleasures. The opening of a dancing school at Oxford by John Bosely, musician, and Thomas Clarke, is an indication of urban sophistication.[67]

The differences Chamberlayne observed in amusements were not those of town versus country, but of rank or degree. Cockfighting might seem "too childish and unsuitable for the Gentry, and for the Common people Bull-baiting and Bear-baiting may seem too cruel, and for the Citizens Foot-ball very uncivill and rude." When George Wilson of Wretton published *The Commendation of Cockes, and Cock-fighting* in 1607, he asserted that finebred cocks were to be seen in the covered pits of the urban centers of Norwich and Bury St. Edmunds. Public baiting of bulls occurred in the large towns several times a week, because an old law stipulated that every bull must be baited before being butchered to ensure more tender flesh.[68]

Such games as bowling or tennis were not at all uncommon. At Dorchester bowling greens could be found outside the city's walls; at Gloucester, John and Henry Payne received a royal license in 1604 to erect "a sign post in the street" stating that they kept a tennis court and bowling alley; and ten years later, Anne, Roger, and James Wright won a life permit to keep a tennis court at the sporting town of Bury St. Edmunds. There were restrictions, however, as shown by cases heard at an archdeacon's court in 1623 against persons who bowled at Taunton "upon divers Saboth daies" and another instance when the ecclesiastical officials presented John Street "for playing at Tennis in the Churchyard on the Saboth daie." [69]

67. Chamberlayne, *Angliæ Notitiæ* (1669), 46; (1671), 57–8; *CSPD, 1611–18,* p. 50; *Oxford Council Acts, 1583–1626,* p. 309.
68. Chamberlayne, *Angliæ Notitiæ* (1669), 46–7; Wilson, *Commendation of Cockes,* Dedication & chaps. V & VI; *Devon Notes & Queries,* IV, 16; *Plymouth Recs.,* 145.
69. Three men of Taunton played "fives against the church wals upon Sundayes and holydayes." *Collecteana,* II, 82, 83, 97; *CSPD, 1603–10,* pp. 78, 144; *1611–18,* p. 230; *Somerset,* 82–3, 97.

Artificial conditions existing inside the cities altered the character of old recreations and furthered new ones that proved to be great attractions for visiting countrymen. Among the most exciting of city diversions were the performances of Elizabethan and Jacobean comedies and dramas given by troupes of "stage players." Sooner or later these strolling players came to all the cities and many of the larger towns. Armed with papers from the Master of the Revels authorizing them to act under the sponsorship of the King, the Queen, the Prince, or some nobleman like the Earl of Worcester, they came under civic or ecclesiastical supervision. Before a company could set up its stage, however, it had to obtain the mayor's permission; ordinarily the request was granted after a special showing for the Aldermen and Council. Men and boys played all of the parts, which explains why one manager could be sure that the audience would understand when he apologized for a delay in the start of a play—"the queen was shaving." [70]

No community outside of the metropolis possessed a regular theater; the guildhall or town hall was adapted for the production —Southampton's Corporation refused to permit plays in its hall after one dire experience when the courtroom furniture had been "broken or spoyled." More often than not the Thespians set up a temporary stage on trestles in the open yard of some large inn. The audience, composed of country squires, city merchants and their families, citizens, apprentices, and servants all gathered there; the rich sat on covered seats in the permanent galleries of the hostelry, and the common people stood. R. Willis remembered that, when he was a lad in Gloucester, his father had taken him to see a play "and made mee stand betweene his leggs, as he sate upon one of the benches, where wee saw and heard very well. . . . The Cradle of Security. . . . This sight tooke such an impression in me, that when I came towards mans estate it was as fresh in my memory, as if I had seen it newly acted." [71]

Puppet shows were also extremely popular. Sometimes the servants and children in the audience became so disorderly that the

70. For a warrant of 1624 from the Master of Revels, see *HMC Exeter*, 171; *Reading Recs.*, III, 37, 76; *Norfolk & Norwich*, III, 1–8; *HMC Reading*, XI: VII, 185.
71. *Somerset & Dorset*, III, 104; *HMC Southampton*, XI: III, 28; Chute, *Shakespeare of London*, 193, 195; R. Willis, *Mount Tabor* (1639), 110, 113.

more sedate inhabitants of the towns protested, and, as so often happens, a few puppeteers gave the entire tribe a bad name. Thomas Smith was taken up by the watch as a drunkard and bound over to the Middlesex Quarter Sessions because he "hath noe trade, but liveth by goeinge about the country with Puppet-plays." In Bridport, in 1630, town authorities expelled eleven men charged with putting on blasphemous shows and sights late in the night "by way of puppet playing." [72]

"Tumblers and people of leike disposition" could also make a living touring the provincial cities, and they too drew the ire of influential citizens, who labeled them a "hinderans of good Rule and order and to the meantenans of all disorder and loseness to the great displeasure of God Almightie." Here and there these entertainers picked up a few shillings by agreeing not to put on a performance: John Jones prayed to show "feats of activity" in Plymouth in 1623, but he was willing to depart and forfeit any box-office receipts on payment of ten shillings by the town; it cost the inhabitants of Lyme Regis only two shillings to rid themselves of this same performer. The people of Kidderminster, "having been formerly eminent for Vanity, had yearly a Shew, in which they brought forth the painted forms of Giants, and such like foolery to walk about the Streets with." When such entertainment was offered, who can blame servants and children for sneaking out of the house to join the crowds going to the show? [73]

Minstrels, who had been so popular prior to the seventeenth century, were losing their town audiences to paid musicians, or *waits*. Professor Woodfil has listed over seventy communities that had companies. Clad in liveried coats and wearing silver badges, the waits won the support of the townsmen for their performances at all public and private festivities; they also received protection from the competition of itinerant minstrels. The four musicians of Plymouth, enormously proud of the fact that their "wayteship" was instituted by "that never to bee forgotten knight Sir Francis Drake," protested that the £10 a year and the "escouchions" and "Clokes," which they received at public charge, were far inferior to

72. *Middlesex Sessions*, II, 142; Roberts, *Southern Counties*, 41–2; Whiteway, *Diary*, 159 (fol. 156).
73. *HMC Exeter*, 321; Roberts, *Southern Counties*, 41–3; *Devonshire*, XV, 462; *Reliquiæ Baxterianæ*, 24.

the awards the waits in other places of the same importance were given. Some of the companies fell far short of excellence, if we can believe Lieutenant Hammond, who categorized "all the Towne Musicke they Have" in a town near Ely to be like "the divellish stinging of their humming Gnatts." [74]

Opposition to the theater began in most of the cities in the early years of King James's reign. Contrary to popular belief, it was not wholly the consequence of the growing puritan criticisms, though these did exert pressure. Rather, it was the common complaint that, because the performances were given at night, the constables had trouble with "the great concourse" of people and the attending disorder. Exeter's rule that all stage performances must end before five o'clock in the winter and six o'clock in the summer was copied elsewhere; Salisbury set seven o'clock as the closing hour for plays given at the George in High Street, under penalty of 40 shillings. Opponents of the theaters also took the stand that shows lured the poorer tradesmen and apprentices to spend their substance frivolously, inculcated wrong notions in the minds of the audience, and, in general, lowered the moral tone of the community.[75]

By 1630 the town fathers had come to frown not only upon the theater but on all kinds of diversions. The students at Oxford might entertain Archbishop Laud with a play, and a comedy might be performed in Latin in the Deanery at Canterbury, but the provincial theater was dead because urban sentiment opposed such vanities now so intimately linked with London and the Court. King James's Book of Sports (1618), reissued by King Charles (1633), the rising puritan feeling, and the prudential sentiments of borough and city corporations combined to suppress the supposed immoral consequences of frivolity. Merry England was to be no more.[76]

---

74. Now and then the waits got out of line: the fiddlers of Staines and Windsor were "so lewd" in their songs that they merited the punishment of libelers in 1627. *CSPD, 1627–8*, p. 233; *Camden Miscellany*, 3d ser., XVI, 90; Woodfil, *Musicians in English Society*, 56, 58–9, 74, 79, 89, 108; *Plymouth Recs.*, 203; *Southampton Recs.*, II, 118–19.

75. *HMC Exeter*, 321; *HMC Various*, IV, 237; *Essex Sessions*, XVIII, 79.

76. There were times when it would seem that the English were in danger of losing their collective sense of humor. An instance in point was related by the noted polemicist Henry Burton in 1641: a company of young men at Dartmouth "went to the country to fetch home a May-pole with Drumme and Trumpet . . .

The only institution dedicated to merriment and diversions that survived and prospered throughout these fifty years was the tavern. The best place to seek out sociability in cold weather, or bad, was the alehouse:

> For a Song or a Tale
> Ore a Pot of good Ale,
>   To drive cold winter away.

Many a "pot knight" went daily to his favorite alehouse down the street, even when alewives were known to "mix rosin and salt in their ale." Every town had a drinking place for individuals of any purse or station: Bideford had twenty-four; so did Shaftesbury; and Plymouth had 134 for a population of 7,000 (one for every fifty-two persons). These statistics refer to licensed houses only; William Neale insisted in 1620 that he could point out forty unlicensed houses in Chelmsford and Moulsham, and it is fair to conclude that these communities were not the only ones where such a situation existed. Indeed it would be difficult to refute the charge that drinking was the major sport of all Englishmen, whether in town or country.[77]

In making a charge to a grand jury, William Lambarde described what actually went on in the public houses: quaffing, drinking, and gluttony. Such establishments ordinarily opened at six o'clock, "the sweet time of the Morning," when "the Ale knight is at his cup ere hee can well see his drinke." By eight o'clock more than one of these regular topers was already drunk; toward high noon, journeymen, apprentices, laborers, chapmen, and others dropped in, and gaming often commenced despite the laws forbidding it. When the "heat was on" the public houses, gamblers diced,

---

the Pole being thus brought home and set up, they began to drink healths about it, and to it, till they could not stand so steady as the Pole did, whereupon the Mayor and the Justice bound the ringleaders over to the Sessions." When one of the youths died shortly afterward, Burton pronounced it to be God's punishment, and further asserted that the May-pole incident gave occasion for the profanation of the Lord's day a whole year after, "it was sufficient to provoke God, to send plague and judgment among them." Henry Burton, *God's Judgement upon Sabbath-breakers, and other like Libertines, in their unlawfull Sports* (1641), 9–10; *Oxinden Letters*, 134; Whiteway, Diary, 57 (fol. 67).

77. *Roxburghe Ballads*, I, 86; Harrison, *England*, Pt. I, 161; *CSPD, 1635*, p. 246; *1635–6*, p. 255; Worth, *Plymouth*, 355; Essex Sessions, XIX, 372.

played cards, or shuffleboard in private dwellings. The Mayor's Court at Barnstaple listened to many cases involving feltmakers, tailors, tuckers, and even a scavenger, William Voysey, for illegally playing at cards or shuffleboard in the houses of other artisans.[78]

VI

In England's provincial centers, from 1600 to 1642, a remarkable growth and transformation took place that had both environmental and psychological elements. Trade, industry, and commerce, carried on in compact, congested surroundings, inexorably fostered new and different standards of living and implanted new attitudes in the minds of the English population. This more complex, sophisticated, and pulsating existence in a great town or city, where new and strange ideas circulated, and where people from many counties and even distant countries, both called foreigners, mingled together daily, has frequently been labeled bourgeois—and with some reason. But much more properly, it may be designated *urban,* which, along with *urbane* and *urbanity,* we derive from *urbs.* The longshoreman, the carrier, the artisan, the comfortable tradesman, their womenfolk and children, these set the tone of town life quite as much as the wealthy merchants (the bourgeois), most of whom, be it observed, rose from lower ranks, or from the parallel rural yeomanry. In any case, the impress of all of these urban people upon the thinking of the English as a whole was rapidly becoming paramount in this period. In many respects the great metropolis itself was but the provincial city writ large; and we must now go up to London, "the staple of English civilitie."

78. Read, *Lambarde & Local Government,* 73, 78; Hamilton, *Quarter Sessions,* 72; Nicholas Breton, *Fantastickes* (1636), n. p.; *Plymouth Recs.,* 156, 157; *HMC Various,* I, 93; *Barnstaple Recs.,* I, 50, 53.

V

London: The Staple
of English Civilitie

"I HOPE TO SEE LONDON once ere I die," Justice Shallow's servant Davy told Bardolph, and he was not alone in his desire; all over the island of Britain thousands of people shared his aspiration. In this age Englishmen just could not speak or think of their metropolis in anything but superlatives: "What more wonderfull than London?" Thomas Johnson exclaimed, and Donald Lupton asserted that "She's certainly a great World, there are so many little Worlds in Her: She is the great Bee-hive of Christendome, I am sure of England; She swarmes foure Times in an yeare, with people of all Ages, Natures, Sexes, Callings. . . . She seems to be a Glutton, for shee desires always to be Full. . . ." Like the American West two centuries later, London simply defied the imagination.[1]

For most of the would-be travelers, there was neither reason nor need for them to withstand the tremendous lure of the capital. The

---

1. London's reputation with Englishmen was unquestionedly great as early as the twelfth century. A contemporary of Tristram once said: "London is a right rich city, a better not in Christendom, nor a worthier nor a better esteemed nor a better garnished of rich folk. Much they love largess and honor, and lead their life in great pleasaunce." Quoted by R. L. Loomis (ed.), *The Romance of Tristram and Ysolt by Thomas of Britain* (New York, 1931), 274; *King Henry IV* (Pt. II), V, iii, 61; Johnson, *Cornucopiæ*, sig. F 2r; Lupton, *London and the Country*, 1–2.

paralyzing hardships of a peasant's life and the rural conditions
that loosened and often broke the bonds that held men and women
to their native villages made the towns seem all the more attractive. Nor did the pastoral existence seem idyllic to all of the middling and better sorts, who lived more comfortable lives than the
lower orders. Real though invisible forces were inexorably expel-
ling them from farm and manor house and propelling them townward and cityward. Though all roads did not lead to London,
nevertheless, between 1600 and 1642, vast numbers of Englishmen—the adventurous, the ambitious, the determined, the seekers,
the discontented, the restless, and the discouraged—set out for the
metropolis, the poor to make money and the rich to spend it, both
anticipating exciting experiences.

The men and women who composed this horde that besieged
London came from every part of the realm; the great majority of
them traveled the long, hard way in desperation. They poured into
the City seeking refuge, escape, shelter, possibly a chance to start a
new life. Lupton believed that others, such as cashiered soldiers,
poor country curates with no place to stay, and multitudes of tenants-at-will, shifted localities in the winter quarter: "London is one
of the freest places for their aboad, without [anyone] questioning
them what they are, for if they pay for their lodging or other
charges, they need not remove." In Botero's words, these individuals looked upon the City by the Thames as a "sanctuarie" wherein they might find a "moderate libertie and a lawful place of
safetie." [2]

Reports that work might be found in the city lured many a
countryman; there he hoped to find a job in one of its handicrafts,
or work in the shops or on the wherries, barges, and ships. Youths
and maids went to be educated as apprentices, or into domestic
service. Jane Martindale, over the objections of her yeoman parents, left rural Lancashire for London; she lived there for two
years, married a gentleman, and kept an inn. Returning home at
the time of her mother's death, she contracted smallpox and died
August 5, 1632. The possibility of making a quick shilling by levying for maintenance on newly arrived gentlemen attracted "many
rascals and tall yeomen" from neighboring counties. The unskilled
countrymen, however, outnumbered the employable persons to

2. Botero, *Greatness of Cities*, 31–2; Lupton, *London and the Country*, 112–15.

such a degree that the House of Lords drafted an act in 1621 to restrain agrarian migration. Trained craftsmen, those who had served out the required seven years as apprentices, and anyone possessing an estate sufficient to sustain them might settle in the City; otherwise the authorities were directed to expel any newcomer and send him back to his native parish lest he become a public charge.[3]

Tales told in provincial taverns and by chapmen along the roads of the astonishing wonders of the city convinced those yeomen and thoughtful and imaginative men who were chafing at rural "inconveniences" that London was a Never-Never-Land where one could exchange the boredom of the country for urban excitements. From these same peddlers, literate countrymen bought ballads and pamphlets praising urban existence. Even the puritans brightened up at the prospect of hearing the best preaching in the land at the Sabbath services or weekly lectures in the fine parish churches of St. Antholin or St. Stephen, Coleman Street. The likelihood that every known diversion and recreation would be spread dazzlingly before all citizens was doubtless questioned, but one and all were sure that they would find a richer and more varied life in London than in Norwich, Bristol, or Exeter.

Although expectation of material gain was the primary motive of all outsiders moving to London, anticipation of pleasure was common to all, particularly the members of the gentry. Botero expressed it thus: "Men are also drawen to live together in Society through the delight and pleasure that . . . the art of man doth minister and yield unto them." Those persons who were weary of "Boores and Peasants" fled the tedium of the country: for the noblemen and politicians, the Court at Westminster was the ultimate goal; for the citizens, there was the grand spectacle of the Court and courtiers which could be viewed daily. Robert Rich, Earl of Warwick, imparted the sentiments of the ladies he knew: "Weemen love themselves best, and London next." "Society," as one who escaped to the city recalled in later years, "I considered, was the very marrow and comfort of my life." [4]

3. *Chetham,* IV, 6–8, 18; Ludovich Barry, *Ram-Alley or Merry Tricks* (1611), I, i; Jordan, *Philanthropy in England,* 104.
4. Breton, *Court and Country,* in Dunham and Pargellis, *Complaint and Reform,* 458; Stone, *Aristocracy,* 386–8, 391; Botero, *Greatness of Cities,* 9, 11; Nash, *Quaternio,* 42–3, 50.

Life in the city was not all beer and skittles, as the newcomers quickly discovered. So you are going to London, Lupton, in a sense, exclaimed, and warned every visitor to beware of the place: "Shee is the Countrymans Laborinth, he can find many things in it, but many times looseth himselfe"; and Abraham Cowley, admitting that he preferred pastoral solitude to "the monster London," this "foolish city" which laughed at him and his kind, heartily agreed. One gentleman wrote with seething indignation to his wife in Wiltshire about "that expensive town and [its] hell hound tradesmen," whose chicanery "sticks plaguely in the gizard of mee." [5]

So many pitfalls faced the unwary, whether of high or low degree, that the celebrated compiler of do-it-yourself manuals, Henry Peacham, published a most timely work in 1642, *The Art of Living in London; or a Caution how Gentlemen, Countreymen, and Strangers, drawn by occasion of Business, should dispose of Themselves in the thriftiest Way; not only in the Citie, but in all other populous Places, and also a Direction to the poorer Sort, that came hither to seek their Fortunes.* Clear, concise, informative, this tract offered some sound advice to the poor, but, alas, the cost probably prevented them from ever benefiting from it. "Here is employment for all hands that will work," so go and get a job at once, Peacham taught. You young men, avoid all whores; and you young women, avoid becoming such; "poverty of itself is no vice." [6]

As the hopeful migrants approached the city and gazed across the Thames at the skyline of the metropolis, they saw the panorama of the greatest thoroughfare in England just as C. J. Visscher sketched it in 1613, or Mathew Merian in 1638. According to the best recent estimates, the population of greater London grew from 224,275 in 1605 to between 320,000 and 339,824 in 1634. By 1640 it may have reached 350,000, half again as large as it was four decades before; and the proportion of the city's people to the total for all England and Wales rose from 5.3 to 6.4 per cent.[7]

5. Lupton, *London and the Country,* 4; T. H. Ward (ed.), *The English Poets,* (New York, 1924), II, 269; Stone, *Aristocracy,* 393.
6. Peacham, reprinted in *Harleian Miscellany,* IX, 84–9.
7. See footnote 1 of Chapter IV; also W. K. Jordan, *The Charities of London, 1480–1660* (London, 1960), 15–16.

The composition of London's population was constantly changing. There were, of course, many like those whom Captain John Smith of Lincolnshire described as having "lived fortie yeeres in London, and yet have scarce beene ten miles out of the Citie." These were true Londoners, many of them "born within sound of Bow-bell and . . . sufficiently ignorant in Country business." The signal rise in numbers came not from a natural increase of the basic native element (the high death rate prevented that); it was the result of the large increment from without, the people we have been describing—peasants, yeomen, ministers, craftsmen, gentlemen, rogues—men and women from all over England. Descending on London, they contributed their skills to the enhancement of the life of the city, and they also figured in the records of Middlesex Court of Quarter Sessions.[8]

Prominent too, especially in the clothmaking sections of the metropolis, were the refugees from France and the Low Countries. These "foreigners" began to settle in the out-parish of St. Martin Le Grand about 1563, because the authority of the City did not reach into that liberty. Most of those that followed also located there and in the other liberties and suburbs, but enough of them lived in the City itself to give London a cosmopolitan air. When the foreigners were added to the country yokels, their combined numbers were enough to overwhelm the Cockneys.[9]

Day in and day out London harbored a host of transients, who may have amounted to 8 per cent of its population. Constantly coming and going at stated intervals were the postriders and carriers with their wagons. Hundreds of other carriers—drovers, pack-horsemen, petty chapmen—and a large assortment of other people, such as visiting tradesmen and provincial merchants, arrived and departed less regularly. Lawyers and their clients attended the business of the courts at Westminster, and the relatively large number of foreign visitors from the Continent must not be forgotten. Students made up another substantial part of this floating population. Finally, along the waterfront from Deptford and Limehouse up to London Bridge, mariners by the thousands—

8. Smith, *Travels and Works,* II, 704; Fuller, *Worthies,* II, 55–6.
9. Stow, *Survey of London,* ed. Strype (1733), bk. III, 111–12; Stow, *Annales,* 868; *CSPD, 1635,* pp. 283, 456–7, 592–4, 613; Valerie Pearl, *London and the Outbreak of the Puritan Revolution* (New York, 1961), 15.

watermen, bargemen, fishermen, and seagoing sailors—some bred
locally, more from other parts of England or from foreign lands,
came and went daily.[10]

These birds of passage made fundamental additions to both the
economic and social life of the city. As transients, they provided a
steady custom for inns, alehouses, victualing houses, and lodging
houses; they also patronized the theater and purchased from artisans and tradesmen luxury articles as well as staple goods. The
correspondence of John Winthrop, Esq., of the Manor of Groton
in Suffolk affords a glimpse of several aspects of the life of a temporary London resident. As an attorney for the Court of Wards,
Winthrop went to the City periodically, traveling up and down
either on horseback or by private coach. For the transporting of
his womenfolk, or of articles purchased in town, he used various
wagons including those of "Hobson the Cambridge Carrier"
(made famous by Milton's epitaphs). He usually lodged with his
brother-in-law Mr. Emmanuel Downing at the sign of the Bishop [!]
in Fleet Street over against the Conduit, but his son John preferred the Three Fauns in Old Bailey.[11]

II

The lower and inferior sorts of Englishmen and foreigners made
up a larger proportion of the population in London than they did
in the smaller cities and large towns. "Possibly 90 per cent" of the
inhabitants of the capital were "artisans and urban poor." Of
these, about 13 per cent were young men and women who hired
out as domestic servants in families ranging from a simple tradesman's to that of a rich nobleman, and in the process they created a
kind of servile hierarchy within as well as outside of the city
households. A host of wage laborers assisted carpenters, masons,
bricklayers, plasterers, and plumbers in building the new houses or

10. In 1637, more than 200 scheduled wagons, carriers, and foot posts arrived at
designated taverns and inns every week, and with them came many passengers.
Most women traveled with the carriers. John Taylor's directory, *Works*, II, No. 3;
Harbage, *Shakespeare's Audience*, 76n; Platter, *Travels*, 149; Stow, *Annales*, 867;
Taylor on Thames-Isis, in *Works*, I, No. 1, pp. 16–18; Stow, *Survey of London*,
bk. I, 3.
11. *Winthrop Papers*, I, 237, 257, 336, 338, 346, 348; II, 87.

on the King's Works (where wages were often twelve months in arrears).[12]

"In the Chequer," one day in 1602, John Manningham heard that there were about 30,000 "idle persons and maisterless men" in the city. Precisely who composed the "idle" is a matter for debate: some were unemployed, some unemployable, for chronic unemployment always existed in this great human reservoir despite the remarkable growth of the City and the suburbs; the inferior sort, understandably, suffered most keenly from it. Not to be confused with these unfortunates was a shiftless, indigent, idle crew at the very bottom of society, made up of disorderly rogues, vagabonds, and criminals with their "doxies." This tribe proved to be as burdensome to the orderly, honest poor quite as much as they were to the sober citizens and the gentry.[13]

The great majority of the "maisterless" men were unskilled. Their brawn being the only commodity they had for sale, they toiled at pick-and-shovel jobs, or on the wharves and docks, or as porters, carrying all kinds of goods and articles from place to place. If such a man had any backing or small means, he might be a carman, distinguishable by his "Canvas frocke, a red cap, [and] a payre of high shoes." Several thousand men, many of them from Somerset, Gloucester, and Wiltshire, "who generally are esteemed the strongest, and most active men of England," earned their livings by rowing passengers up and down the river. These men, together with the fishermen, bargemen, and miscellaneous longshore

---

12. Jordan, *Charities of London*, 81; Jordan, *Philanthropy in England*, 329; Harbage, *Shakespeare's Audience*, 76n; *CSPD, 1611–18*, p. 537.

13. The frequently unpaid crews of His Majesty's naval vessels and soldiers discharged from the wars were often in desperate conditions, and their wives and children were starving. When they were reduced to beggary, they pitifully tried to distinguish themselves from the professional rogues. A maundering soldier in one of Martin Parker's ballads cries out:

> To beg I was not borne, sweet sir.
> . . . .
> For I am none of those
> That roguing goes . . .

Roxburghe Ballads, III, 111; *RHS Trans.*, 3d ser., VI, 20; *Camden*, XCIC, 73; *CSPD, 1611–18*, p. 208; R. H. Tawney and E. Power, *Tudor Economic Documents* (New York, 1924), II, 335–6; *Middlesex Sessions*, n. s., IV, 143.

laborers, all "nourished by the Thames," numbered "above 40,-000," according to John Norden.[14]

Artisans, handicraftsmen, and mechanics, the very numerous body of London's citizenry interchangeably called artificers in the Statute of 1563, were always linked with the urban poor and generally looked down upon from above with contempt. The handicrafts were not all "mean trades," however, and all artisans did not belong on one humble level of society; rather they formed a vertical segment, which extended from the rich goldsmith at the top, who lent money to the King, down to the lowly tailor. The kindly Fuller had this to say about the craftsman, whom he conceded was "a necessary member in the commonwealth":

> He seldom attaineth to any very great estate. Except his trade hath some outlets and excursions into wholesale and merchandise; otherwise, mere artificers cannot heap up much wealth. It is difficult for gleaners, without stealing whole sheaves, to fill a barn. His chief wealth consisteth in enough, and that he can live comfortably, and leave his children the inheritance of their education.[15]

Some craftsmen had had thorough training and exhibited rare skills, as samples chosen almost at random illustrate: compass-makers, spectacle-makers, bugle-makers, map-makers, coach-makers, yea, even dice-makers, who probably essayed other work in ivory. Though ranked inferior to the specialists, excellent craftsmen practiced "the Art and Mistery" of the locksmith, the tobacco-pipemaker, the bookbinder, the gilder, the girdler, the tierwoman (milliner), and the pasteboard-maker.[16]

Just below the skilled craftsmen came the common artificers

14. *Coach and Sedan, Pleasantly Disputing,* sig. E; Norden, County of Essex, 12; *Middlesex Sessions,* III, 29.

15. In 1650 "tailor" was a term of contempt, which may have originated both from the lowly status and great number of these artificers. "It is not easily credible, what may be said of the preterpluralities of Taylors in London: I have heard an honest man say, that not long since there numbered between Temple-barre and Charing Crosse, eight thousand of that trade." Nathaniel Ward, *The Simple Cobler of Aggawamm in America* (4th ed., 1647), 30–31; Fuller, *Holy and Profane State,* 109, 110–11.

16. As late as 1616, Erasmus Fynche worked at the trade of a "cross-bowmaker." *Middlesex Sessions,* n. s., III, 214; for the crafts mentioned in the text and many more, see *Middlesex Sessions,* n. s., *passim.*

who knew little more than the rudiments of their trades: carpenters, masons, bricklayers, founders, smiths, and coopers. A host of "labourers," yeomen, and other unskilled individuals took advantage of the relaxed conditions in the burgeoning metropolis to practice some of these trades in which they had not served a regular apprenticeship; in 1613 Thomas Bird of Whitechapel, Richard Mann of Stepney, and Richard Bromley and Isaac Wilson of St. Clement Danes, all laborers, were indicted at the Middlesex Sessions for illegally "using" the trades of bricklayer, plasterer, and carpenter, respectively. There were, besides, numberless laborious services requiring the daily labor of artisans possessing varying degrees of training and skills; among them were scriveners, hackneymen and coachmen, paviors, chimneysweepers, hairdressers, and barbers. In addition, dozens of crafts connected with the two great urban industries of clothmaking and leatherworking employed countless individuals. Lastly, certain tradesmen belonged in this category of common artificers: confectioners, cooks, bakers, victuallers, butchers, aquavite-stillers, and oatmealmakers.[17]

The women of London may have outnumbered the men thirteen to ten, but the refusal of the guilds and most trades to accept women as apprentices prevented them from becoming journeymen and obviously narrowed their opportunities to work at a craft. Spinsters were exceptions; girls were taken on as apprentices, but they earned meager pay as journeymen. Thomas Powell warned men to avoid "housewives trades (as brewer, baker, cook, and the like), because they be the skill of women as well as of men and common to both"; probably this explains, in part, the low wages in those employments. Fewer restrictions upon retailing existed in London than in the provinces; a young girl often bound herself to a shopkeeper and, when she became a freewoman, received a license to sell. This avenue was restricted somewhat in 1631 when the Common Council forbade selling in the streets by "divers unruly People," among whom were listed "Sempsters, Oyster wives, Herbe wives, Tripe wives and the like." By far the greatest number of young women apprenticed themselves as domestic servants, as chambermaids for gentlewomen, or at inns. In all probability,

17. *Middlesex Sessions*, n. s., I, 84, 86; *CSPD, 1611–18,* p. 197; *Archaelogia*, XXIII, 121.

women seeking employment other than as domestics fared better in the suburbs, where the city guilds exercised little control.[18]

Steady work was essential for survival of the common working people of London, for nearly every penny they earned went into shelter, clothing, and, most of all, food; few of them could save for lean times. The slightest dislocation in the economy or interruption of their work promptly brought on distress. Some discouraged artificers, like the "very servisable fellowe, and very good Taylor," whom Thomas Knyvett offered to send to his wife in Norfolk, welcomed an opportunity to go back to the country. A young woman whom Jane Martindale knew in 1630 "had thoughts to sell her haire, which was very lovely," because her money "grew so neare to an end." Corporate support for craftsmen was available to some degree through the guilds of London, but such aid went only to a few out of the many who were in desperate straits.[19]

A profound transformation of the London economy was well under way at the opening of the seventeenth century. Crafts and trades were dividing and subdividing, and luxury articles that required specialized skills were in demand, with the result that hundreds of new occupations opened up. Furthermore, the guilds were splitting into producers and purveyors, and the latter were gaining almost complete control of the industries.[20]

Those artificers who could not afford to join a guild or to rent a house or shop within the City moved out to the suburbs in such numbers that those areas became the principal seats of their industries. Only forty leather dressers still remained in the City in 1619, whereas at least 3,000 had located south of the Thames in Lambeth, Bermondsey, and Southwark. The shifting of location did not necessarily carry with it a decline in the quality of craftsmanship; Low-Country foreigners who had become journeymen without having served apprenticeships frequently made valuable contributions to the quality and variety of English manufactures.

18. Harbage, *Shakespeare's Audience*, 76; Clark, *Working Life of Women*, 10, 200–202; Powell, *Tom of All Trades*, in Dunham and Pargellis, *Complaint and Reform*, 571; Mayne, *The City-Match*, III, ii; *Middlesex Sessions*, n. s., III, xii, 152.
19. *Knyvett Letters*, 60; *Chetham*, IV, 8; Powell, *Tom of All Trades*, in Dunham and Pargellis, *Complaint and Reform*, 572.
20. N. Brett-James, in *London*, n. s., V, Pt. IV, 383.

Thomas Fuller had nothing but praise for the Dutch handicrafts-man who, "by his ingeniousness he leaves his art better than he found it." [21]

The native artisans and members of the London guilds, how-ever, did not suffer these competitors gladly. A petition of 1632 complained that in the suburbs "great numbers of traders and handicraftsmen do enjoy, without charge, equal benefit with the freeman and citizens of London." Not until February 24, 1636/7, did a Royal Proclamation incorporate all tradesmen and artificers within three miles of the capital who had served a regular seven years' apprenticeship and prohibit those not free of the company from practicing their trades. No others were to pursue their crafts after November 1. As might be expected, those unfavorably affected bitterly resented the severe, if intermittent, official regula-tion of crafts and the royal prodigality in granting monopolies. A tract of 1640 epitomized the anger of these people in two sen-tences:

> . . . No Freeman of London, after he hath served his yeares, and set up his Trade, can be sure long to [enjoy] the Liberty of his Trade, but whether he is forbidden to use it, or is forced at length with the rest of his trade to purchase it as a Monopolie, at a deare rate, which they and all the Kingdome pay for. Wit-ness the Sope-business.

Hard lives, official meddling, and contempt from their betters made many London artificers desperate enough after 1625 to lis-ten attentively to facts and fancies about a new land across the sea where a more promising life beckoned.[22]

Much celebrated in song and story, the 'prentices, some of whom were born in the City and liberties but many more of whom came in from the country and distant towns, formed a large ele-ment of London's population. Here and there was doubtless one who merited the description in *The Cities Advocate:* "He goes bareheaded, stands bareheaded, waits bareheaded before his mas-

---

21. N. Brett-James, in *London,* n. s., V, Pt. IV, 383; Fuller, *Holy and Profane State,* 110, 112; *CSPD, 1611–18,* pp. 4, 62.
22. N. Brett-James, in *London,* n. s., V, Pt. IV, 387; *CSPD, 1611–18,* p. 62; *1619–23,* p. 334; *Bibliotheca Lindesiana,* I, 209; *England's Complaint to Jesus Christ against the Bishop's Canon* (1640), B2.

ter and mistress, and whiles as he is yet the youngest apprentice he doth perhaps (for discipline sake) make old leather over-night shine with blacking for the morning, brusheth a garment, runs of errands, keeps silence, till he have leave to speak." 'Twas such a one that the merchant in *The City-Match* had in mind when he declared his nephew to be "as dutiful as a new apprentice." To these humble lads, the seven years of service must have been a long and uninspiring experience.[23]

Most of the wordage and stories about apprentices were concerned with the vocal, exuberant, and often unruly youths who shirked their tasks, stole from their masters, and harassed the night watches, but in their defense it must be said that these lads were also subjected to long hours, heavy work, and not infrequently brutal correction for derelictions in duty. In 1605 George Lorryman of Ratcliffe "flogged with whippes his apprentice," John Woodfall, so that he "became and still remains a lunatic"; a smith of Tottenham, Thomas Thorp, was charged in Middlesex Sessions with several instances of breaking the heads of his apprentices with "a slice of iron." Similar cases involving inhuman treatment crop up in every county's records. Nor did bound girls escape corporal punishment. The court admonished Moses and Mary Smith of Rosemary Lane not to beat or abuse their apprentice "other than with due and orderly correction by a birch rodd, not giving her above six stripes at any one tyme." [24]

Court records also disclose that some masters failed to live up to their agreements. Articles of indenture usually provided for the instruction and decent care of the apprentices. From a husbandman's household in Edenbridge, Kent, arrived Thomas Treppe to

23. E. M. Bolton, *The Cities Advocate* (1629), 26–7, 40; Mayne, *The City-Match,* I, i; A[braham] J[ackson], *The Pious Prentice, or the Prentice's Piety* (1639).
24. Innumerable cases in the Middlesex Court of Quarter Sessions of 1616 can be cited for examples of the idle apprentice. William Burch of St. Mary le Bow, apprentice to Henry Boxe, grocer, was summoned to answer and give evidence that Elizabeth Tue persuaded him to embezzle money from his master; also against William Pryme, a cook of St. Martins in the Fields, for giving Elizabeth Tue a charm to "inveigle" Burch; and against John Batchford for carrying Burch drunk into a bawdy house; and finally against two master tailors for harboring Elizabeth and William. *Middlesex Sessions,* n. s., III, 118; 332; I, 182; II, 238; *Middlesex Sessions,* II, 14; Essex Sessions, XX, 160–1; Fuller, *Holy and Profane State,* I, 106; B. P., *The Prentises Practise in Godlinesse* (1608).

learn the mystery of embroidering with Leonard Terry of Westminster. After four years the justices ordered him released, because Treppe testified that Terry had employed him only in selling tobacco and never gave him any instruction in the craft. Such misuse of apprentices also occurred in higher trades. In a petition asking the Common Council to cancel his indentures, Henry Norris testified that his father, Sir William Norris of Lancashire, had paid £110 when he bound him to a merchant to learn that trade, arithmetic, and the keeping of accounts; so far he had learned nothing about his master's business, ciphering, or the keeping of books. It was not lack of instruction, however, that convinced the court that it should cancel the indenture of Thomas Thomas, an apprentice to a tailor of Ratcliffe; it was Thomas's complaint that his master "hath not maynteyned him with sufficient apparell as an apprentice ought to have, but kepte him full of lyce." [25]

The institution of apprenticeship underwent a remarkable change in London during the reign of Queen Elizabeth. The discovery that many apprentices were "persons of good quality," sons of gentlemen, provoked an animated debate over their status under apprenticeship. Some persons believed that such apprentices paid "the barbarous penaltie of losse of Gentry," and quoted Erasmus who had branded the system "a kind of bondage." Sir Thomas Smythe concurred, but called it "voluntary bondage." Edmund Bolton stoutly contested this position in *The Cities Advocate, In this Case or Question of Honour and Armes: Whether Apprenticeship Extinguisheth Gentry?* in 1629. Gentlemen's sons usually served apprenticeships under master-merchants by sea, assurers, wholesalers, "and some such few others which may more specially stand in the first class of the most generous mysteries in which the wit or minde hath a farre greater part than bodily labour." Such a status, Bolton insisted, was not unseemly for them, and any idea to the contrary was odious and uncivil. The young gentlemen did not don the uniform of blue, russet, white, and "sheep's colour" or fabrics of fustian, canvas, sackcloth, leather, and wool; nor did they fancy wearing the familiar, flat, round caps of the ordinary apprentice. Instead they affected costly apparel, wore weapons, and

25. *Middlesex Sessions*, n. s., IV, 167; *Chetham*, IX, 10–12; *Middlesex Sessions*, II, 47.

frequented "schools of dancing, fencing, and music" to the degree that the Common Council saw fit to forbid those practices.[26]

Whatever their vaunted intelligence, their newly assumed privileges, their discipline (or lack of it), the fact remains that thousands of London apprentices spent their years of service in a transitory status. Like their masters, they formed a distinct hierarchy according to the dignity and status of the trade to which they were bound, and according to whether or not their parents had paid to have them bound. When a faithful apprentice came out of his indentures, ready to work as a journeyman, his best move was to marry his master's daughter. So many lads succeeded in advancing by this means that the playwrights and authors of tracts rang the changes on them.[27]

Journeymen coming from gentle or wealthy families had few worries about getting started in a trade, but the poor apprentice seldom had any means of acquiring "a sufficient trading competence." On the average, a young man needed a stock worth £70 to set up as a merchant, and £30 as a tradesman. Some London companies supervised the distribution of funds bequeathed by "divers benefactors of their societies" for setting up "young beginners," and recent researches have demonstrated that there was enough available capital to launch 800 to 1,000 new careers. At the time, however, serious criticisms were made about the administrations of the funds: in praising the spirit behind the bequests, Thomas Powell nevertheless observed "(how faithfully [they are] disposed of I leave to their own consideration), but surely the poorer sort complain much of the misemployment of it generally." He proposed that a list of benefactions be printed "that the meanest might thereby be able to call their grand masters to account if they abuse the trust." The truth is that the loans did go to favored apprentices. The great mass of newly freed journeymen found employment only with difficulty, for they had to compete with artificers from the rural areas and with persons who had not served full terms as apprentices. Only a very small percentage of erstwhile apprentices eventually rose to become masters; the others re-

26. Stow, *Survey of London,* II, 453–4; Bolton, *The Cities Advocate,* Dedication, 9, 13, 15, 26.
27. Sir George Clark, *Three Aspects of Stuart England* (London, 1960), 41; Jonson and Marston, *Eastward Hoe* (1605), II, i.

mained journeymen and spent their lives as part of the wage-earning London poor.[28]

The ordinary little tradesman, who had to operate on a slim margin of profit, frequently found an able assistant in his wife. Indeed, many a woman participated fully in the conduct of her husband's business. When living quarters were above the shop, a common arrangement, she scheduled her household tasks so that she could watch over the master's custom—and keep an eye on the apprentices, who did not always appreciate her supervision, as a letter written by Valentine Pettit to his cousin Richard Oxinden indicates: Mr. Pettit had just visited the shop of a Mr. Newman where young Richard Oxinden had started to work with the idea of becoming an apprentice. The youth admitted that he liked his master, "but his Mistress was . . . a strange kynde of woman." From the other 'prentices, Pettit learned that Mr. Newman had changed since his marriage: "they all say, that through her dyssuadinge him, hee is brought to such a pass that hee will beate them for any small occasion." Furthermore, when the master and mistress dined out, which they did frequently, the food was even skimpier than usual. In fact Richard was sure that he did not want to live the next seven years in the Newman household and thought that he should break off immediately before he was completely enrolled.[29]

The constantly shifting economic situation and the revolutionary social changes in London and its suburbs inevitably transformed conditions determining arrangements about rank and place. Although the hierarchical conception remained unquestioned in the minds of all citizens, the actualities of existence had altered. The ordinary people, 90 per cent of the population, lived apart from those who counted and ruled. They were also differentiated among themselves by their mysteries and crafts and lived in little trade enclaves. Even within these groups, new social distinctions emerged; Harrison ranked citizens and burgesses who were freemen of their towns among those next to gentlemen. Certainly

28. Powell's criticism in *Tom of All Trades*, in Dunham and Pargellis, *Complaint and Reform*, 572, seems to have been overlooked in Professor Jordan's detailed discussions of "Loan Funds" in his *Charities of London*, 172–7; and in his *Philanthropy in England*, 266–7.

29. *Oxinden Letters*, 40–41.

in this vast agglomeration of London wealth proved to be far more of a social solvent than it was in any of the smaller centers, where, in turn, it had facilitated change more rapidly than in the country.[30]

Though few in number, the citizens divided easily into "the great merchants," and "the lesser," according to their wealth and influence. The lesser merchants, a somewhat formless element, embraced shopkeepers and retailers, members of the less influential city companies, and men of miscellaneous callings, such as iron and brass founders, the keepers of the larger inns, grocers, chandlers, haberdashers, and the like. Purveyors rather than producers, these tradesmen displayed the same energetic, acquisitive, and often greedy traits of their counterparts in the smaller cities and their yeoman brethren in the countryside. Some of the lesser merchants and the great merchants and their families might be termed the urban gentry. William Harrison tells us that merchants "often change estate with gentlemen, as gentlemen doo with them, by a mutuall conversion of one into the other." In military parlance, the great city merchant ranked with but after the gentleman. At least the lines were finely drawn. One might even go so far as to suggest that the explanation of the celebrated English custom of absorbing risen commoners into the aristocracy is to be found in the opportunities afforded them by the great metropolis and, to a lesser extent, the provincial cities.[31]

The majority of these venturesome men, having heard that wealth could be won quickly in the metropolis, had come up from the provinces to seek their fortunes in London, where some of them found out that money could be lost as well as won. At any

---

30. Jordan, *Philanthropy in England,* 329; Harrison, *England,* Pt. I, 130–31.

31. There was no consensus about the ranking of the London merchants. Bolton insisted that "The ordinarie Citizen therefore, is of a degree beneath the meere Gentleman, as the Gentleman is among us in the lowest degree, or class of nobilitie in England." He also stated that the "true Country-Esquire" ranked ahead of the "Citie-Esquire." James Howell, in a letter to John Batty denied this latter opinion: "Nor do I see how some of our Country Squires, who sell Calves and Runts, and their Wives perhaps Cheese and Apples, should be held more genteel than the noble Merchant-Adventurer, who sells Silks and Sattins, Tissues and Cloths of Gold, Diamonds and Pearl, with Silver and Gold." Bolton, *Cities Advocate,* 45, 58; Howell, *Familiar Letters,* 362; Jordan, *Charities of London,* 55, 63; Harrison, *England,* Pt. I, 130–31; Notestein, *English People,* 108–15.

rate, one and all, high and low, scrambled to get ahead. As Thomas Nashe described the scene, it must have been a rough-and-tumble fight:

> From the rich to the poore (in every street in London)there is ambition, or swelling above theyr states; the rich Cittizen swells against the pryde of the prodigall Courtier: the prodigal Courtier swels against the welth of the Cittizen. One Company swells against another, and seekes to intercept the gaine of each other: nay, not any Company but is devided in it selfe. The Auncients, they oppose themselves against the younger, and suppresse them and keepe them doune all that they may. The young men, they call them dotards, and swel and rage, and with many others sweare on the other side, they will not be kept under by such cullions, but goe good and neere to out-shoulder them. . . . Amongst theyr Wives is lyke warre.[32]

The competition for place, and particularly the women's "warre," became the favorite subject of commentators on the social scene, who took delight in depicting the gaucheries and social blunders of the aggressive citizens. "Oh, sister Mill, though my father be a low-capped tradesman, yet I must be a lady: and I praise God my mother must call me madam," cries Girtred. When Mildred tells her not to scorn her nest, she hisses "Bow-bell," in reply. Richard Brathwaite advised true gentlewomen to avoid associating with "loose ENGLISH GENTLEWOMEN" whose gait, looks, speech, and habits reflected long hours spent "upon the Stall." [33]

As a group, the mercantile class prospered in this era; a goodly number of the merchants succeeded in gaining more than the moderate wealth normal to their trades. In their behavior, these men of substance turned out to be more truly urban than any other Londoners. They occupied most of the higher public offices as well as those in the liveried companies; they exercised social control of the metropolis; they made generous charitable bequests providing for the welfare of their fellow men in town and country alike; and

32. Jordan, *Charities of London*, 74, 76, 78–9; Thomas Nashe, *Christ's Teares over Jerusalem* (London, 1593), reprinted in *The Works of Thomas Nashe*, ed. R. B. McKerrow (London, 1904–10), II, 83.
33. *Eastward Hoe*, I, i; Richard Brathwaite, *The English Gentlewoman Drawne out to the Full Body* (1631), I, Dedication, 59.

they left large sums for civic betterment. Together with the merchants of the provincial cities, whom they dominated, the London merchants controlled and managed the economic affairs of the kingdom. Increasingly their voices were listened to by the House of Commons and the royal councils of state down to the beginning of the personal rule of Charles I.[34]

With each passing year, a greater number of the country gentry discovered that living in London offered them more access to power and privilege, more advantages, more excitement, more culture, more ease, and, indirectly, a more sociable and satisfying existence than they could ever enjoy on their own country estates. Great nobles sought pleasure, power, and pelf at the Court. "Oh, the gallant life of the court," Breton's Courtier exclaims, "where so many are the choices of contentment, as if on earth it were the paradise of the world." In his enumeration of choices, which was long and inclusive, the greatest of them was love: "And in the course of love such carriage of content as sets the spirit in the lap of pleasure, that if I should talk of the praise of it all day, I should be short of the worth of it at night." Such a comment explains why the honest citizens thought that the pursuit of love was the chief preoccupation of the Court, but some of the shrewdest heads recognized that all of the gaiety and debauchery screened a fierce and ruthless competition for office, royal largess, loans of money, profitable land transfers, and fat legal fees.[35]

The inclination of the gentry to pass more time in the urban environment steadily transformed London into one of the principal Western centers of Thorstein Veblen's "conspicuous consumption." The majority of the gentlemen were transients, and it was their need for transportation that supported the watermen and their rivals, the hackney drivers, and led to the introduction of sedan chairs in the 1630's. The handsome new houses erected for rich noblemen along the Thames bank, or later in peripheral sub-

34. Jordan treats the merchants at length in *Charities of London*, 63–78, *et passim*.
35. If the gentry had read Botero on cities, they would have found a theoretical exposition of their move to the cities under the same headings that more recent writers have used in discussing the phenomenon. Botero, *Greatness of Cities*, 4–7, 9, 11, 41, 45–6; Breton, *Court and Country*, in Dunham and Pargellis, *Complaint and Reform*, 458; Professor Stone's informative book has a long section on the Court that makes further comment unnecessary. *Aristocracy*, 185.

urbs away from coal dust and smog, provided work for countless artisans, for household servants, for coachmen, and for gardeners. Hundreds of luxury crafts catered to the wants of this prodigal gentry, and the insatiable appetite for entertainment of every kind guaranteed livings to thousands of urban workers. The lavish spending could not but invigorate the trade and industry not merely of London but of all England.[36]

Not every country gentleman who came to London could live in any such extravagant fashion. In fact some members of the gentry had left their country estates because they could not maintain them in the approved fashion. Selling all they had, and accompanied by a single servant, they moved to the city where they lived in "a few roomes in a poore Shop-keeper's Cell." Some of those who came intent on participating in the diversions of the capital forthwith spent their substance in ways that Peacham had warned against in his *Art of Living,* and not a few of these found themselves bankrupt.[37]

Royal hopes of reviving the old rural hospitality (that never again could be) and alarm at the thronging of the gentry of all degrees into London for most of the year impelled King James to issue a proclamation in 1615 requiring noblemen and gentlemen to reside at their country mansions for at least nine months of the year, and if the county lieutenants and justices of the peace wished to retain their commissions, they were to do the same. In 1622 the proclamation was extended to include *all other towns and cities,* and pertained to the entire year. The only exceptions were to be persons of quality who came on business during the law terms, and they were to leave their wives and families in the country—a restriction that greatly irked the gentlewomen. When, as a result of this measure, the price of town houses plummeted, the City authorities petitioned that the gentlemen then residing in London be excused from the order; the request was granted in 1623. In 1632,

---

36. A capital account of "The Development of London as a Centre of Conspicuous Consumption in the Sixteenth and Seventeenth Centuries," by Professor F. J. Fisher, is in *RHS Trans.,* 4th ser., XXX, 37–50; Sir Walter Besant, *London in the Time of the Stuarts* (London, 1903), 340; Barnabe Rich, *My Ladies Lookinge Glasse* (1616), 12–13.

37. Fisher, in *RHS Trans.,* 4th ser., XXX, 44; Nash, *Quaternio,* 7; Stone, *Aristocracy,* 186–7; 567–71.

however, King Charles rescinded the permission, commanded that gentlemen live at their own estates, and forbade them to make habitations in London or its environs. According to the Venetian ambassador, the proclamation was "vigorously" enforced and the City was "empty." The retiring gentry left, not without much regret and disgust at being forced to stay withdrawn throughout the winter. The net result of this ill-considered Stuart policy was that both the gentry and the citizens were angered, the latter particularly so because they felt the regulations in their purses.[38]

The traditional notions about those who ruled and those who were of gentle birth and station continued to be held without question, so too the corollary that rank had its privilege. In 1621, for instance, a royal proclamation directed the aldermen in the outwards of London to take all necessary precautions for the protection of persons of quality from insolent abuses on the streets. At about the same time, in his catalog of "Common Grevances," John Winthrop deplored the way that persons "of meane respect quallitie and condicon, whoe never keepe hospitalitie in the places where they resyde," drive about town in "Charrets, Coaches, and Caroches," endangering society. Ostentation of this kind so annoyed Sir William Vaughan that he proposed a law prohibiting anyone from using a coach who did not contribute £1,000 "towards the Plantations in America, the Nobilitie alwayes excepted." [39]

Position and fortune were never a guarantee of gentle birth, nor was gentle birth a guarantee of urbanity or humanity, for there was a great deal of passing up and down as well as in and out of the traditional ranks. "In great pedigrees there are Governors and Chandlers," was George Herbert's dictum, which was echoed by John Ward: "England hath been so often shuffled from high to low, that scarce any artificer, but may find his name, though not his pedigree, in the herald college books." Members of the impoverished gentry harassed the populace in many ways: George Barnes charged in 1613 that Robert Fuller, a gentleman of St. Mary le Strand, cozened his apprentice with false dice; Robert Coreate, a gentleman living in Charterhouse Lane, ran afoul of the

38. CSPD, 1611–18, p. 337; 1619–23, pp. 470, 484, 588; 1623–5, pp. 134, 360; CSP Venetian, 1632–6, p. 38n.
39. CSPD, 1619–23, p. 245; Winthrop Papers, I, 302; Vaughan, Golden Fleece, Pt. II, 62.

authorities "for keeping a common bowling alley . . . and allowing the King's liege people to play at bowls there" against the law. Some of the gentlewomen also debased their status by their behavior. One "virago of quality," the rich Lady Tresham, went to Newgate in 1630 for saying in open court that a thief had more friends there than an honest body. Another time the justices forced her to take back Helen Haddocke whom she had had as a servant for a year and then turned loose without wages or apparel "for no cause shewne." At the next session she was again sent to prison for abusing the court and telling Justice Long that "Your authoritie set aside, you are a scurvy companion." [40]

Prominent among the attractions of great cities, Giovanni Botero places vistas, "strayte and fayre streetes," and "magnificent and gorgeous buildings." Though Inigo Jones became Surveyor of the Works in 1613 and completed his great Banqueting Hall in 1622, his influence was not to be felt in London until the Restoration. The great inns of Holborn, built to accommodate gentle transients, were the only unusual structures to be viewed by foreign travelers, who, prior to 1642, were not impressed by the buildings of London. Even the Gothic splendor of London's "chiefest grace," St. Paul's, the great abbey at Westminster, and the 122 parish churches within a circuit of eight miles failed to arouse enthusiasm in Renaissance England, for whatever the merit we assign to them today, to the people of the Jacobean and Caroline age they appeared old-fashioned and badly run down.[41]

40. In discussing family, birth, and degree in either the seventeenth or the twentieth century, it is well to bear in mind the recent warnings of Mr. Anthony Camp of the Society of Genealogists: (1) Nearly every English family has one or more bastards among its ancestors; (2) Few families can be traced before 1538, when parish registers began; and (3) Beware of any line traced beyond 1538 to the Battle of Hastings, because only the Arden and Berkeley families can trace their pedigrees with certainty to a Saxon forebear prior to the Conquest. *The New York Times*, Sept. 1, 1964, p. 35. Herbert, *Works*, 308; Ward, *Diary*, 288; *Middlesex Sessions*, n. s., I, 102–3, 105; *Middlesex Sessions*, III, 34; Whiteway, Diary, 149 (fol. 148–9).
41. Botero, *Greatness of Cities*, 9; *CSPD, 1611–18*, p. 181; B. Sprague Allen, *Tides of English Taste* (Cambridge, Mass., 1937), I, 19–20; Fisher, in *RHS Trans.*, 4th ser., XXX, 48; Dutton, *English Interiors*, 63; Lewis Roberts, *The Merchants Mappe of Commerce* (1638), 234. For a guide to the years 1590–1640 in general, see John Summerson, *Architecture in Britain* (London, 1953), chaps. III–XI, and for London structures, pls. 10, 11, 30, 34, 41, 54, 56.

As if conscious of this insensibility on the part of Englishmen
and foreigners alike, Fynes Moryson wrote in glowing terms of the
"many stately Pallaces, built by Noblemen uppon the River
Thames," and maintained that if those fine houses "scattered
. . . in backe lanes and streetes . . . were joined to the first in
good order, as other Cities are built," London would be acclaimed
a "beautifull City, to which few might be justly preferred for the
magnificence of the building." Gentlemen and great merchants had
indeed erected some splendid houses, like that of the famous Sir
Paul Pindar in Bishopsgate, or the new town house of Sir Edmond
Verney in the fashionable Covent Garden row built by the Earl of
Bedford. Most of them were impressive double-, triple-, even
quadruple-fronted structures with gable-ends facing the street, still
in the Tudor tradition but enriched with elaborately carved bal-
conies and bay-windows. In spite of Moryson's encomium, "the re-
tyring houses of the gentry and citizens" in the "Suburbs at large
of London" did not as yet proclaim a highly developed taste in urban architecture to match the fine Jacobean achievement in country mansions.[42]

A typical London house had a very narrow front but went up as
high as five or six stories. Commonly half-timbered, with clay or
plaster filling, it appeared commodious. Fynes Moryson explained,
however, that dwellings were usually "built all inward, that the
whole roome towards the streets may be reserved for the shoppes
of Tradesmen." Similar structures, though as a rule not over three
stories high, stood in the nearby towns and villages. Wainscoted interiors and better furnishings were the mode in new houses. John
Vassall of Stepney Parish, mariner and former alderman of London, left to his son William in 1625 "all the wainscot, portals of
wainscot, cupboards and benches of wainscot," and also the dressers, shelves, iron firebacks, locks, and ironwork on the doors and
windows of his house in Ratcliffe.[43]

Away from the principal streets and lanes of London, where the
mass of the people lived, little more than the debris of the past
could be seen. Flimsy, insufficient, new tenements were being

42. Moryson, *Itinerary*, III, 496; *Verney Papers* in *Camden*, LVI, 172; Summerson, *Architecture in Britain*, 57–8, pl. 33; Fuller, *Worthies*, II, 34.
43. Moryson, *Itinerary*, III, 496–7; Clifton-Taylor, *English Building*, 31, 280;
Dutton, *English Interiors*, 27, 48, 94; Waters, *Gleanings*, II, 1314.

erected "over stables, in gardens and other od corners." A survey of householders of London parishes made in 1638 describes one parish as having "allies stuft with poor whom they maintain." With the constant influx of people, space in the cities and its suburbs was at a premium. "The desire of Profitte greatly increaseth Buyld-inges," so that "everie man seeketh out places, high-wayes, lanes, and cover corners to buylde upon, if it be but Sheddes, Cottages, and small Tenementes." Greedy property owners did not scruple to divide existing structures into one or more tenements: in 1612 George Lytchefelde, chandler of Clerkenwell, made fifteen out of one; a few years later, Richard Phillips of St. Giles without Crip-plegate had to answer for "harboring 36 inmate families in tene-ments," and such instances can be multiplied many times over. Still the metropolis could not shelter or house all its people.[44]

London officials realized even before the end of the sixteenth century that their city was so overcrowded that the convenience and health of all inhabitants were threatened. A touching report, dated June 22, 1602, states that a large part of the inhabitants were "heaped up together and in a sort smothered with many Fam-ilies of Children and Servaunts in one house . . . [and] it must needs followe, if anye Plague or any other universall Sicknes should by God's Permission enter amongst these Multitudes" (as it did the next year), it would immediately spread all over the city and eventually throughout the entire country. According to a proc-lamation of Queen Elizabeth in 1603, no new houses were to be erected within three miles of the City, justices were to pull down any such structures, and existing tenements were not to be further subdivided. These regulations only made the congestion worse, and the restrictions were but fitfully enforced. Other proclamations and rulings followed, but all of them proved futile in solving the problems created by people flooding into London and its sub-urbs.[45]

44. Lupton said of the citizens: "they live one above another; most commonly he that is accounted richest lives worst." *London and the Country*, 2; *The In-habitants of London in 1638*, ed. T. C. Dale (London, 1931), I, 4; Chamberlain, *Letters*, I, 153; *Archaelogia*, XXIII, 123–4; *Middlesex Sessions*, n. s., I, 25; II, 4, 138.
45. Thomas Rymer, *Fœdera, Conventiones, Literæ, et . . . Acta Publica . . .* [1586–1654], ed. R. Sanderson (1715), XVI, 448–9; *Bibliotheca Lindesiana*, I,

In 1632 the Lord Mayor of London complained to the Privy Council about conditions in the City which he attributed to the "extraordinary enlargement of suburbs," rising prices, forestalling of markets, contamination of the water supply, and stopped-up conduits. All of these misfortunes and more came about from the "multitudes of people of the meaner sort" who were attracted "by the new erected buildings." Additional acts were passed to restrict construction, but it was not until 1637 that a determined effort was made by the Commissioners of Buildings headed by Inigo Jones: they "watched every paltry erection, even a lean-to against a garden wall." Immediately, as the Master of Charterhouse remarked, "Much crying out there is against it, especially because mean, needy, and Men of no good Fame, Prisoners in the Fleet, are used as principal Commissioners to call the People before them, to fine and compound with them." He also declared that the enforcement of the Elizabethan four-acre act in the suburbs benefited only a few rich and influential favorites and was "far more burdensome" than the ship-moneys.[46]

The urban problems that inhabitants of all large English towns and cities had to contend with vexed Londoners to an even greater degree. The attempts to solve them were virtually the same in the capital as in the smaller cities, and equally ineffective with few exceptions. Party walls and the increased use of brick and stone construction in London after 1604 and within a five-mile radius after 1620, together with the substitution of coal for firewood as the universal heating fuel, provided better protection against the cold. The difference, however, from country conditions was merely relative. During the severest winters some provision was made to procure supplies of "sea-coale" for the poor. The coal was a mixed blessing, for the "smutty Air of London" bothered many inhabitants by the time King James first arrived. "Take me . . . out of this miserable city," cried Girtred, "carry me out of the scent of

111; CSPD, 1603–10, pp. 375, 449; 1611–18, pp. 66, 295, 557, 602; 1628–9, p. 508; Middlesex Sessions, III, 240, 256, 310–11; IV, 92, 288.
46. Gardiner, England, VIII, 288–9; CSPD, 1631–3, p. 446; 1633–4, p. 285; 1635, pp. 352, 355; 1637, pp. xv, 178, 180; 1637–8, pp. 16, 48; The Earl of Strafford's Letters and Dispatches, ed. W. Knowler (London, 1739), I, 117; Pearl, London, 13.

Newcastle coal and the hearing of Bow-bell, I beseech thee!" [47]

That the metropolis escaped a major conflagration during these five decades was miraculous. Small fires there were, but the success of the New River Company in bringing water thirty-eight miles from Camwell Springs in Hertfordshire to Islington basin in 1613 made it possible to quench many of them. The burning of the old Banqueting House at Whitehall was the only serious loss, but compensation came with Inigo Jones's glorious replacement. Not until 1638 did William Riley and Edward Mabb petition the King for permission to establish suitable fire defenses by taxation—but this implied one of the hated monopolies.[48]

The crooked and narrow streets of the capital and its suburbs presented a study in contrasts by day and by night. "Pestred with Hackney-Coaches," insolent "Carre-men," and pack-horse traffic, citizens were engulfed in a concourse of motley humanity, a scene of excitement and confusion. Thomas Randolph and his ilk found "the chargeable noise" unbearable and moved back to the country. Danger, too, was present for the pedestrian, for as yet there were no regulations or restrictions on reckless horsemen or coachmen. About the only places where the populace could relax out of doors were in such squares as Lincoln's Inn Fields, the Moorfields, or beyond the walls in the suburbs. After dark, on the other hand, not many persons ventured out on the streets: a few gentlemen accompanied by link-boys; ruffians and footpads in search of victims, whom the watch could seldom properly protect; and a well-known class of laborers called "goldfinders," who trudged along the streets carrying tubs of night soil to the Thames to be dumped. In spite of these goldfinders, piles of dung and building materials made walking dangerous in the dark and often unlighted streets.[49]

47. *Bibliotheca Lindesiana,* I, 117, 126, 137; *CSPD, 1619–23,* pp. 165, 460; *1641–3,* p. 30; Stow, *Annales,* 996, 1025; *The Elizabethan Home Discovered in Two Dialogues by Claudius Hollyband and Peter Erondell,* ed. Muriel St. Clare Byrne (2d ed., rev., London, 1930), 35; Howell, *Familiar Letters,* 216; *Eastward Hoe,* I, i.

48. Lysons, *London, III,* 164–5; Robbins, *Middlesex,* 66; *HMC Coke,* XII, I, 103; *CSPD, 1637–8,* pp. 392–3; *1603–10,* p. 411.

49. *A Character of England, As it was lately presented in a Letter, to a Noble Man of France* (1659), 27; "To Master Anthony Stafford," Ward, *English Poets,*

The general absence of rudimentary sanitation notwithstanding, the health of the inhabitants was no worse or no better than in the provincial cities. They suffered from the same ailments: common colds, "ordinarie ague," and tuberculosis, which Chamberlain termed "these popular diseases." The everlasting pollution of the air by "pestilent Smoake, which corrodes the very Iron, and spoiles all the moveables," caused throat and lung diseases. And, according to a character in *The Ordinary,* "Refin'd people feel Naples in their bodies; and an ache i the bones at sixteen passeth now for high descent." Certainly it was true that venereal diseases were far more widespread in London than anywhere else in England.[50]

When the plague appeared in a congested seaport, its incidence was bound to be high, for the rodent population rapidly spread the fever. Little could be done to aid the sick except to publish pamphlets with appropriate suggestions for their care. Two of these tracts may have aided the general public: *Certain Rules, Directions, or Advertisements for this Time of Pestilent Contagion,* in which Mr. James, an Aldermanbury apothecary, gave information intended for the poor in 1625; and Stephen Bradwell's plea in *Physick for the Sickness* (1636) that the rich stay in town and succor the miserable, sick poor. Herb-wives and gardeners throve on the sale of rosemary, which increased in price from 12*d.* an armful to 6*s.* a handful whenever the plague came.[51]

For some strange reason, visitations of the plague did not seem to last as long in London as in provincial cities, but during their stay the known death rate was staggering. It has been well said that "life was reckoned by the hour and to be safe at dawn was no guarantee of safety at sunset." "London," Charles Mullett writes,

II, 221; *Middlesex Sessions,* n. s., II, 17; *Middlesex Sessions,* III, 21, 24, 241; IV, 289; Besant, *London,* 182; Lupton, *London and the Country,* 94–6.

50. *A Character of England,* 27; *Middlesex Sessions,* IV, 62; *CSPD, 1611–18,* p. 600; Chamberlain, *Letters,* I, 300, 388, 513; II, 184, 189, 213, 622, 624; *HMC Buccleuch,* I, 269; *Winthrop Papers,* II, 307; Cartwright, *The Ordinary,* I, iii.

51. In the Bodleian Library (Gough Lond. 154) is a bound volume of eight pamphlets on the plague, which begin with the Royal Orders of 1593. See also Richard Milton, *Londoners their entertainment in the Countrie* (1604); and W. Boraston [of Salop], *A Necessary and Brief Treatise of the Contagious Disease of the Pestilence,* "composed for the benefit and comfort of the vulgar sort"; Chamberlain, *Letters,* II, 97; *Social England,* ed. H. D. Traill and J. S. Mann (London, 1895), IV, 208.

"could with some material dislocation survive the occasional loss of a fifth of its population in a year."

Deaths from the Plague in London

1592	11,505
1603	30,583–34,000
1625	35,428
1636	12,102
1637 *	2,876

* To July only.

The great mortality of 1625 took thousands of the helpless poor, but in this and other epidemics, the Lord Mayor and Common Council believed that the scourge created additional poverty by causing the decay of so many tradesmen. So completely did the plague disrupt families in the severe epidemics of 1625 and 1637–38 that, just as in lesser urban centers, thousands of ordinary individuals suddenly had to shift for themselves and begin life all over again.[52]

We have no evidence that metropolitan medical practitioners were proportionally more numerous or had a training superior to those in the provincial cities. The College of Physicians and the Company of Barber-Chirurgions attempted to keep a careful watch for unlearned and unlicensed practitioners, but in spite of their efforts there were many like Ann Dell, a butcher's wife of Shoreditch, who was detected in 1615 practicing surgery without a license. The Barber-Chirurgions managed to win a monopoly over the English way of death in 1605, and they shut out butchers and tailors from embalming. Some Londoners, ignoring the able young men, such as William Harvey and the surgeon Alexander Read, deliberately avoided "the unpleasing company of Physicians" who, it was alleged, were "more indebted to opinion than learning. . . . For it is grown to be a very housewives' trade, where fortune prevails more than skill." Perhaps the laymen classified the medicos with midwives, who, though subject to strict licensing and

52. Ola E. Winslow, *Master Roger Williams* (New York, 1957), 15; Mullett, *Bubonic Plague*, 4, 106–8, 143–4, 153–4, 171, 176; *CSPD, 1625–6*, p. 155; *1637*, xiv–xv; *1641–3, passim*.

considered quite trustworthy, were celebrated for their love of a-qua-vite and proclivity for bawdy talk.[53]

V

"In London, the ritch disdayne the poor. The Courtier the Cittizen. The Cittizen the Countriman. One Occupation disdayneth another. The Merchant the Retayler. The Retayler the Craftsman. The better sort of Craftsman the baser. The Shoomaker the Cobler. The Cobler the Carman. One nyce Dame disdaynes her next neighbour shoulde have that furniture to her house, or dainty dishe or devise, which she wants. She will not goe to Church, because shee disdaines to mixe herselfe with base company, and cannot have her close Pue by herselfe. Shee disdaines to wear what every one weares, or heare that Preacher which every one heares." Thus did Thomas Nashe proclaim the innate snobbery of the people of London, and at the same time make explicit the many groups and layers into which social position and wealth (or the absence of it) separated them.[54]

Here in the capital lived a vast population, more than half of whom had been born and reared in the countryside. Always the members of this rootless segment were in the process of making the difficult, often heartbreaking, adjustment to the strange, new urban environment. In contrast with the neighborliness and kindliness they had known in rural and small-town communities, these newly arrived folk found themselves in the society described by Nash, with group aligned against group; soon they were possessed

53. By a new charter of 1617, the apothecaries became a company separated from the Grocers, though they were not incorporated until 1624. In 1618 the King commanded that they compound medicines by the directions in the new work of the College of Physicians, *Pharmacopeia Londinensis,* if they resided within seven miles of the City. The apothecaries attempted unsuccessfully in 1625 to exclude other tradesmen from selling tobacco. *CSPD, 1611–18,* pp. 507, 536; *1625–6,* p. 204; *1603–10,* p. 189; *1619–23,* p. 418; *1623–5,* pp. 218, 258; *1627–8,* p. 78; Keevil, in *Bulletin History of Medicine,* XXXI, 423; *Middlesex Sessions,* III, 22; *Middlesex Sessions,* n. s., III, 7; "The Chirurgical Lectures of Tumors and Ulcers," in *The Workes of that Famous Physician Dr. Alexander Read* [1631–2] (3d ed., 1659); *CSPD, 1634–5,* p. 98; *Twelfth Night,* II, v, 13–14; *Eastward Hoe,* I, i; *CSPD, 1611–18,* p. 80; Powell, *Tom of All Trades,* in Dunham and Pargellis, *Complaint and Reform,* 567.
54. Nashe, *Christ's Tears Over Jerusalem,* II, 134–5.

by the same suspicions and felt the same tensions as their new-found associates admitted to. The only bonds uniting all Londoners were that they were English, and that, whatever their mutual differences, they shared the same disdain and dislike of foreigners, as the Spanish ambassador learned from the infamous incident of 1618 when one of his suite accidently rode down a small boy in Chancery Lane. Within a few minutes a mob gathered in front of the Barbican that would have torn the Spaniard to pieces if the Lord Mayor and other town officers had not arrived and dispersed the crowd.[55]

Many of the rude forefathers came from rural communities to the city, and their country speech and proverbs, which gained circulation, took on urban overtones: "It is better to live in low content, than in high infamy" applied perfectly to London's society. When citizens and tradesmen met on the street, their greeting was the old-fashioned mode of "God keep you," or "God be with you," which the vulgar reduced to "How dost do?" with a slap on the shoulder. Common speech was often earthy and rough: "I charge you in the King's name to kisse my tayle," a sturdy weaver once told the reproving headborough of Stepney, Mr. Holt. Nor were the privileged classes above using slanderous terms. William Pettit, gentleman, referred to Justice Sanders as a "man of weak understanding, not fit to be a justice," and went on to say that he "made a floute of his warrant sayinge he would not care a lowse for Sander's warrant." [56]

A boisterous, brawling, often violent people were the Londoners of every degree, and though among the great body of the middling and baser sorts were many well-behaved and decent Englishmen, the average man proved to be as far from his phlegmatic descendants of the prewar era as three centuries would permit. He was mercurial and prone to exhibit great passions—fear, grief, anger— on the slightest provocation. Even among the well-born, urbanity covered a generous amount of boastfulness and effrontery—as certain of Shakespeare's characters demonstrate so well.

Much of the rowdiness and turbulence grew out of trivial street

55. Gardiner, *England*, III, 134–5; IV, 118–19; *CSPD, 1619–23*, p. 244.
56. *The Countryman's New Common-wealth* (London, 1647), 19, 22, 23, 25, 28; Besant, *London*, 359; *Middlesex Sessions*, n. s., I, 371, III, 7.

quarrels. Because tradesmen's and artisans' shops and living quarters were confined and always crowded, people sought the outdoors, particularly during the warm summer days. Many a ruction began with name-calling, as on a day in 1615 when Matthew Foster, a carpenter, did "in a druncken tumultuous manner goe up and downe the streete calling all the women in the streete whores, and used other uncivill words to the Scavengers there and to divers other persons of creditt." Slander also led parties into court, for this was a litigious age: Hanna Mobbs sued John Ayres, a very poor man, for calling her a whore; he countered by saying she had first called him a rogue, and he was no more a rogue than she a whore; a disgruntled gentleman from Cheshire raised a tumult in the street one night by "calling the honest men cuckolds and the honest women whores"; Richard Longe and John Bubb of the Strand stood "charged with making scandalous rhymes against David Dunne of Drury Lane, cook, and his wife." It seems as if all ranks of Londoners, when unbuttoned by drink, wallowed with singular lack of inventiveness in this specific form of slander.[57]

Scurrility and vilification usually induced threatening rejoinders, which, in turn, generated brawling and actual violence. More than a hundred cases in which two or more persons were put on recognizance to keep the peace came before the Middlesex Court of Quarter Sessions in the month of October, 1615. Instances of brutality were common. Alice, wife of Thomas Porter of East Smithfield, charged Andrew Turner, chandler of Whitechapel, with so abusing her that she lost the child "which was then in her body when he did beat her." Another time, in St. Giles, John Larradd, carter, was accused of assaulting the Widow Isabel Bond and inhumanly and cruelly drawing her by her hair "wrapped about his right arm." The death of Thomas Haggett, caused, according to bystanders, by Henry Bull of All Hallows-the-Less purposely running the wheel of his cart over him, was nevertheless ruled to be death caused by the "visitation of God"! At Cow Cross, Richard Greenham and his friends made "a very notable riot . . . and pulled down a great part of the dwelling-house of George Wilkins." The brutal killing of Dr. Lamb by apprentices in 1628 was

57. *Middlesex Sessions*, n. s., III, 114, 115, 155; *CSPD, 1633–4*, pp. 287–8; *1638–9*, p. 116; *Middlesex Sessions*, I, 11.

widely reported, but the beating of the wife, infant, and apprentice of Thomas Bowell, weaver, by four "Persia merchants of great estate" received scant attention. Bowell complained to the Privy Council that the apprentice died, but because of the protection given the merchants by Sir Christopher Clitherow, the Lord Mayor of London, the merchants did not even appear at the inquest.[58]

If anyone wished to learn the news, or to spread it, the place to head for was "Paul's Walk," the middle aisle of London's finest church, which, by 1628, had become an unsavory place of rendezvous where rumors circulated like smoke:

> Paul's Walk is the Land's epitome. . . . It is a heap of stones and men, with a vast confusion of languages; . . . It is the great Exchange of all discourse, and no business whatsoever, but is here stirring and afoot. It is the Synod of all pates politic, jointed and laid together in most serious posture, and they are not half so busy at the Parliament. . . . It is the general Mint of all famous lies, which are here like the legends of Popery, first coined and stamped in the Church. All inventions are emptied here, and not a few pockets . . . a thieves sanctuary. . . . The principal inhabitants and possessors are stale knights and captains out of service, men of long rapiers, and breeches, which after all turn merchants here, and traffic for news.

Activity overflowed the portals, for a report of 1635 listed the owners of shops clustered about the great north door: nine booksellers, one bookbinder, three clasp-makers, a paperseller, a seller of points and walking-staves. Small wonder that Archbishop Laud earnestly sought to drive out the rumor-mongers along with the money changers.[59]

58. Gentlefolk of both sexes could act as viciously as the vulgar sort. Chamberlain reported "an odd fray," which took place in 1613 between Thomas Hutchinson of Grey's Inn and Sir German Poole, "who assaulting the other upon advantage, hurt him in three or foure places, and cut of[f] three of his fingers before he could draw his weapon, whereupon enraged he [Hutchinson] flew upon him and getting him doune bit a good parte of his nose of[f] and carried it away in his pocket." Chamberlain, *Letters*, I, 432; II, 11, 198; *Middlesex Sessions*, III, 51, 53, 126, 147, 293; IV, 62, 120, 142; *Middlesex Sessions*, n. s., II, 182; IV, 174, 187; *CSPD, 1628–9*, p. 169; *1636–7*, p. 471; *1638–9*, p. 621.
59. John Chamberlain regretted in 1602 that he had no news for Sir Dudley Carleton, "which may well be by reason of a new devised order to shut up the

All of the contesting for place, the violence and uproar, and the
scrambling for profit aside, contemporaries agreed with Thomas
Fuller that London was "the staple of English civilitie." From St.
Osith near Colchester in 1622, James Howell wrote to a gentleman
in town that "you must not expect from us Country-folks such Ur-
banities and quaint inventions that you, who are daily conversant
with the Wits of the Court, and of the Inns of Court, abound withal." [60]

Citizens and their wives eagerly and assiduously modeled their
manners and behavior upon the gentry and paid increased attention to etiquette, as is evidenced by a considerable library of books
on the subject printed before 1640. A most popular volume was a
translation by William Fiston of the French work *The Schoole of
Good Manners: a New Method of Vertue teaching children and
youth how to behave themselves in all companies* (1609 and later
editions). Among the new urban customs the middling citizens
adopted was "wearing a garment in bed" that was called a "night-
rail." In all probability the innovation was inspired not by prudery
or fastidiousness but by a desire to be in style, for, as one Londoner put it, "we wear more phantasticall fashions than any Nation under the Sunne doth, the French only excepted." [61]

No element of the English population underwent such a radical
and significant change in manners as the "tempestuous petticoats"
of London. Thomas Platter described them in 1599:

> Now the women-folk of England, who have mostly blue-grey
> eyes and are fair and pretty, have far more liberty than in other
> lands, and know just how to make good use of it, for they often

---

doores in Powles in service time, whereby the old entercourse is cleane chaunged,
and the traffic of newes much decayed." Chamberlain, *Letters*, I, 171, 183; Earle,
Microcosmography, 84–5; *CSPD, 1635–6*, p. 67. See also Thomas Dekker, *The
Meeting of the Gallants at an Ordinarie, or the Walkes on Powles* (1604).

60. Howell, *Familiar Letters*, 109; Henry Peacham, *The Complete Gentleman*
(1622); Richard Brathwaite, *The English Gentleman* (1630), and *The English
Gentlewoman* (1631); *A Helpe to Discourse, The Two Syrens of the Ear* (1621,
1631, and other editions).

61. Byrne, *Elizabethan Life*, 42; Thomas Coryat, *Coryat's Crudities* [1611] (New
York, 1905), I, 398; Norah Waugh, *The Art of Men's Clothes, 1600–1900* (London, 1964); C. Willett and Phyllis Cunnington, *Handbook of English Costume
in the Seventeenth Century* (London, n. d.); both of the last mentioned deal
with upper-class costume only.

stroll out or drive by coach in very gorgeous clothes, and the men put up with such ways, and may not punish them for it, indeed the good wives often beat their men . . . there is a proverb about England, which runs, England is a woman's paradise, a servant's prison, and a horse's hell or purgatory. . . .

This Teutonic visitor was also amazed that women as well as men frequented taverns, "in fact more than they." His account of their gay toasting is made the more vivid in *Well Met Gossip* by Samuel Rowlands (1619), who has three women meet to drink the best claret in town, along with some sack, and to eat "sawseges": "Then who can blame the Widdow, Wife, and Mayde, for meeting and kind drinking with each other?" [62]

This new freedom did not go unchallenged. In January, 1620, the clergy, in response to an order of the King, inveighed against women's wearing brimmed hats, pointed doublets, and even poniards. The Dean of Westminister went so far as to bar entrance to his church to women carrying yellow muffs, though it was the manly and unseemly apparel that James I said he objected to particularly. A month later the pulpits echoed continually with ministerial fulminations against the "insolence and impudence of women"; Chamberlain, commenting on the matter, sadly conceded that "the world is very far out of order, but whether this will mend it God knowes." Not every woman, of course, adopted the "phantasticall fashions." Nor did she adjust easily to her new urban freedom and city ways; we may take comfort in the knowledge that nervous disorders are not modern, for the case books of Sir Theodore Mayerne, physician to King James, reveal that he treated more than half of the ladies listed for "melancholia" and "hyperchondria." [63]

Within their households, London gentlewomen introduced new and apparently radical customs. Nowhere in the land was there such a profuse and varied diet available to persons of all ranks. Garden produce and fruits from Middlesex, Kent, Surrey, and Essex, quantities of meat at the Smithfield Market, and a long list of

---

62. Platter, *Travels,* 170, 181–2; Samuel Rowlands, *Well Met Gossip; or Tis Merrie When Gossips Meet* (1619), "To the Reader."
63. Chamberlain, *Letters,* II, 286, 289; John Williams, *A Sermon of Apparell* (1620); Roberts, *Southern Counties,* 275.

imported luxury foods and spices could be had for a price. All the townspeople, the poor included, ate "good white bread," unlike most of their fellow-countrymen throughout England. In 1621, when wheat was cheap and plentiful, Sir Symonds D'Ewes remarked that the "farmers of lands generally murmured at this plenty and cheapness; and the poorer sort that would have been glad but a few years before of the coarse rye-bread, did not, usually, traverse the markets [in London] to find out the finer wheats, as if nothing else would serve their use, or please their palates." Increased attention was given to the preparation of meals; a manual such as *Murrells Two Bookes of Cookery and Carving* went through five editions between 1615 and 1638. In it John Murrell, "by reason of the generall ignorance of most men in this practice of Catering," gave a "perfect direction" for preparing delicacies in the French fashion using wine and herbs, for making "Puf paste," and "Cheery Pye." [64]

One of the outstanding indications of London's growing civility in these years is the development of dining as an art. The many meals of the country gave way to two in the city. To begin with, the nobility, gentry, and students ordinarily dined at eleven in the morning, the merchants and citizens at high noon; the former supped at five or six, and the latter from seven to eight o'clock in the evening. Less time was spent at the table than formerly, but each meal became more of a ceremony. As in earlier times, proper Londoners washed before eating; now they also cleaned their fingernails and, once seated, kept their hands, not their elbows, on the table on either side of the china plate (china plates began to replace wooden or pewter trenchers). Correct table manners now figured prominently in the education of children, and servants in middling families received instructions about serving correctly: for example, bread should be served from a plate and not passed out by hand. In *The French Garden* by Peter Erondelle, the lady tells the butler, "You have not plate trenchers enough, Set at every trencher plate a knife, a spoone, and a silver forke." This was in

64. F. J. Fisher, "Development of the London Food Market, 1540–1640," in *Ec. Hist. Rev.*, V, 46–54; Lilly, *History of his Life*, 25–6; *The Autobiography and Correspondence of Sir Simonds D'Ewes*, ed. J. O. Halliwell (London, 1845), I, 180; Ashley, *Bread of Our Forefathers*, 45–6; *Murrells Two Bookes of Cookerie and Carving. The fifth Time Printed* (1638), title page, 1, 14, 26, 118–20.

1605, six years before Thomas Coryat claimed to have introduced forks from Italy. Turnips from Caen and mustard from Dijon were served at this meal, with native watercress which "biteth upon the tongue like pepper." [65]

The new habit of smoking, first introduced by Sir John Hawkins in 1565 and popularized by Sir Walter Raleigh, and usually called drinking or taking of tobacco, became, next to drinking, the most widespread vice of London. England spent £200,000 or more annually on "this chopping herbe of hell" by 1613, most of it in London, but Sir Robert Harcourt asserted that "the Generality of Men, in this Kingdom, do with great Affection entertain it." Barnabe Rich railed against its widespread use:

> There is not so base a groome, that commes into an Ale-house to call for his pot, but he must have his pipe of Tobacco, for it is a commoditie that is nowe as vendible in every Taverne, Inne, and Ale-house, as eyther Wine, Ale, or Beare, and for Apothecaries Shops, Grocers Shops, Chaundlers Shops, they are (almost) never without company, that from morning till night are still taking of Tobacco, what a number are there besides, that doe keepe houses, set open shoppes, that have no other trade to live by, but by selling of Tobacco.

Rich computed that if each of the "upwards of 7,000 houses, that doth live by that trade," sold but 2s. 6d. worth of tobacco a day, the annual total would amount to £310,250, "All spent in smoake." The port books of London show that imports of the weed rose rose from £55,143 in 1620 to £230,840 by 1640—from the eighth to the most valuable of all imports. An equal amount was probably smuggled in. Dozens of Middlesex yeomen and almost as many women, all unlicensed tobacco-sellers, kept shops which

65. Breton's Countryman, in 1618, says to the Courtier about washing one's hands: "But for us in the country, when we have washed our hands, after no foul work nor handling any unwholesome thing, we need no little forks to make hay with our mouths to throw our meat into them." *Court and Country*, in Dunham and Pargellis, *Complaint and Reform*, 476; Harrison, *England*, Pt. I, 162; Claudius Hollyband, in Byrne, *Elizabethan Home*, 2, 25, 28, 32; William Fiston, *The Schoole of Good Manners: A New Schoole of Vertue* (London, 1609), n. p.; Peter Erondelle, *The French Garden: For Ladyes and Gentlemen to walke in, Or, a Sommer Dayes labour* (1605), also reprinted by Byrne, *Elizabethan Home*, 73, 75; *Coryat's Crudities*, I, 236.

were, as Earle said, "the rendezvous of spitting, where men dialogue with their noses, and their communication is smoke." Increasingly, citizens imitated Payne, a tobacconist near the Savoy,
who was "drinking and taking tobacco" with Captain Neighbor
from 9 a.m. to 7 p.m.; one such day the befuddled Payne remarked that there were but four honest bishops and among the rest
were "Americans and other strange sexes." So many artisans made
pipes that King James (the leading opponent of tobacco in England) created The Company of Tobacco-Pipe Makers for Westminster. His son extended the monopoly of the manufacture to the
entire island in 1638, but every effort to license or regulate the to-
bacconists failed.[66]

While conversing with an impoverished scholar in 1614, a shoemaker explained that three occupations—alehouse-keepers, tobacco-sellers, and proprietors of brothels—gained the trade of
all London and ran ahead of the "Seven Sciences" in lucrativeness.
There was no question in the minds of contemporaries that smoking was linked with the two other social issues. A satire of 1608
told of many who "for Want of Wit, shall sell their Freehold for
Tobacco-pipes and red Petticoats"; William Vaughan regarded
drinking and smoking as companion vices; "Tobacco-taking of late
yeeres supplied the use of Preparatives, Leaders, or drawers on of
drinke, such as Caveare and salt meat were used among the Sib-
arites." Under the color of selling tobacco, many a man, and many
a woman, operated an unlicensed tippling house, while others, like
William Carpenter, who was expelled from the county of Middlesex in 1617, conducted bawdy houses. In fact brothel-keepers displayed tobacco pipes for their signs.[67]

VI

The gap between the gentry and the middling and lower sorts was
generally bridged in diversions and recreations. In the alehouse,

66. *HMC*, IV, i, 283; *Harleian Miscellany*, VI, 505; Barnabe Rich, *The Honestie
of this Age* (1614), 25–8; *London*, XVIII, 15; *Middlesex Sessions*, n. s., I, 202–3;
Earle, *Microcosmography*, 63; *CSPD, 1628–9*, p. 103; *1627–8*, p. 493; *Southampton Recs.*, III, 63; *King James's Counterblaste to Tobacco* [1604], in *Two Broad-
Sides against Tobacco* (London, 1672).
67. Rich, *Honestie of this Age*, 28; *Harleian Miscellany*, I, 184; Vaughan, *Golden
Fleece*, Pt. II, 79, 81, 179; *Middlesex Sessions*, n. s., III, 74; IV, 126, 215; *CSPD,
1633–4*, p. 479.

tavern, or inn, people of every walk of life commingled freely for pleasure or vice; more communicants foregathered every day in the taprooms in search of sociability than in the churches on the Sabbath for the minister. The alehouse or tavern early came to be the chief social institution of the great metropolis.

The inns, so numerous in Bishopsgate and Holborn, primarily supplied food and lodging for transients; alehouses were mere drinking establishments. A tavern, said Earle, "is a degree, or (if you will) a pair of stairs above an Alehouse, where men are drunk with more credit and apology." In some public houses there were partitions separating the tables so that people at one did not overlook the next, and accordingly some privacy was assured for the "knights of the Square-table" who sat at hazard or dice, or for playwrights setting down the citizens' foibles, men of business, or clandestine lovers. Those who sought mere sociability gathered in the open taprooms. Second only to Paul's Walk, the tavern was a "broacher of more news than hogsheads, and more jests than news, which are sucked up here by some spongy brain, and from thence squeezed into a Comedy. Men come here to make merry, but indeed make a noise, and this music above [stairs] is answered with the clinking below." There, too, conviviality and mirth were augmented by the popular but illegal games of cards, dice, shuffle-board, and bowling, for scores of alehouses operated quietly "in a back place, out of the eye of government." [68]

The actual number of alehouses operating in London and its suburbs at any one time bears little resemblance to the number licensed. During this period, the City had authorized only forty public houses, but as early as 1613 a comment from the Lords of the Council disclosed that "there is almost no house of receipt, or that hath a back door, but when it cometh to be let, it is taken for a tavern." In 1626, the members of The Innholder's Company, disgruntled that only thirty out of 140 publicans in London were members of the guild, petitioned the King to assist in bringing them under control. No aid was forthcoming, and by 1633 it was asserted that there existed 211 taverns in the City and liberties,

---

68. Fisher, in *RHS Trans.*, 4th ser., XXX, 48; *London*, XII, 272–3; Earle, *Microcosmography*, 31; Chute, *Shakespeare of London*, 93; *Eastward Hoe*, V, i; *Oxinden Letters*, 154–5; *Middlesex Sessions*, III, 8, 24, 33, 49, 115, 217; IV, 4, 27, 320; *CSPD, 1629–31*, pp. 10–11.

and eleven in the ward of Bishopsgate—all kept by freemen.[69]

All of the outdoor sports of the provincial towns were available to Londoners, and, in addition, there were some unusual diversions to "awake the pert and nimble spirit of mirth," as Theseus said. From time to time the London populace regaled itself with such sights as the royal lions, or the baiting of a white bear, which had been thrown into the Thames. A red savage named Epenew, captured near Cape Cod along with four others in 1606, "was shewed up and down London for money as a wonder," and some persons saw Pocohontas. Youths witnessed running races and played football in the streets; tennis, played with balls stuffed with hair, grew very popular among the gentry after John Webb taught it to the Duke of York. Within seven years there were fourteen licensed courts in London; "the meaner sort," said Strype, played tennis "in open Fields and Streets." [70]

The tales of recreations and diversions that had held the countryman spellbound and lured him to the city proved to be unexaggerated, for during his lifetime the average Londoner viewed a great deal of pageantry: the regular processions of the Lord Mayor, of the liveried companies on saints' days, military displays, and the occasional arrival or departure of foreign dignitaries. Those who looked back nostalgically on their rural youth could enjoy pastoral outings in suburban fields. Captain Quarterfield in *The City-Match* often went to Moorfields and now and then squired his sister to "demolish custards at Pimlico." On fine days, trips on the Thames drew crowds, and the watermen kept their wherries "charmingly upholstered" and laid "embroidered cushions" athwart the seats. Another favorite entertainment for citizens and their wives was driving in the newfangled hackney coaches to the liberties. More sophisticated, perhaps, were the many dancing and fencing schools. Attendants at those classes became so knowledgeable that actors had to give convincing performances and ex-

69. *CSPD, 1633–4*, pp. 138–9, 276; *London*, XII, 273; Frank Aydelotte, *Elizabethan Rogues and Vagabonds* (Oxford, 1913) 74; *CSPD, 1625–6*, pp. 472, 484.
70. On animal baiting, see Lupton's description of Paris Garden, *London and the Country*, 66–9; *Midsummer Night's Dream*, I, i, 12–14, 32–4; *CSPD, 1603–10*, p. 647; *1623–5*, p. 13; *1635*, p. 575; Smith, *Travels and Works*, II, 701; Wilson, *Life in Shakespeare's England*, 71; Stow, *Survey of London*, bk. I, 247–52, which lists the games and recreations of ordinary citizens; *CSPD, 1611–18*, p. 429.

hibit skillful sword-play and violent, spectacular dances (the gal-
liard, caprioles, and volte) in theatrical productions.[71]

Afternoon "being the idlest time of the day, wherein men that
are their own masters . . . do wholly bestow themselves upon
pleasure," plays were usually performed at that time. Many of the
gentry regularly attended the Rose, Swan, and Blackfriars; at the
Fortune and Red Ball, retail shopkeepers, craftsmen, journeymen,
and apprentices made up almost the entire audience. It was said in
1603 that many of the poor, who subsisted on alms and had almost no clothes and little food, "yet wil make hard shift but they
will see a Play, let wife and children begge, [and] languish in
penurie . . . to lay upon such vanitie." Still the Jacobean audience was no rabble, for the theaters gave to the 21,000 (13 per
cent) of the inhabitants of small income who attended them each
week the cheapest of all urban commercial entertainment. The artisan, who earned, on an average, seven shillings a week, paid from
a penny to a shilling to see a play, a treat far less costly for him
and his family than a quart of ale at 4d., two sheets of broadside
ballads at one shilling, a quart of sack at 8d., or a wherry ride at
3d.—all staple diversions of the populace. The average patron got
his money's worth in the quality of the plays presented and in the
acting, as well as first-class entertainment; and the single men and
students at the Inns of Court who crowded to the theater learned
that it was less costly and more satisfying in many ways than the
cheapest "six-penny whore." [72]

Youth rather than age characterized the audiences. Young, un-
escorted women turned out to be such avid playgoers that the
Lord Mayor and Aldermen grew concerned over the "inveigling
and alluring of maids" by young gentlemen at the theaters: "They
give them pippins, they dally with their garments, . . . they minister talk upon all occasions, and either bring them home to their
houses on small acquaintance, or slip into taverns when the plays

71. Mayne, The City-Match, II, vi; London, XII, 219; Stow, Survey of London,
bk. I, 30; Platter, Travels, 154; CSPD, 1634–5, pp. 8, 69; 1635–6, p. 168; Chute,
Shakespeare of London, 87–8.
72. Thomas Nashe Pierce Penilesse (1592), quoted by R. J. Mitchell and
M. D. R. Leys, A History of London Life (London, 1958), 108; Harbage,
Shakespeare's Audience, 37–8, 41, 56, 57, 59–64, 80; Chute, Shakespeare of London, 87.

are done." As any reader knows, plays of this period dealt freely with sex, and the young ladies laughed easily and heartily at broad jokes. It is obvious that the audiences cared more for sheer entertainment, lively dancing, and the chance for informal sociability during the several hours than for the great poetry of Shakespeare, a fact he acknowledged by putting comedy and horseplay into his productions. Later, speaking of Ben Jonson, Fuller observed that "his Comedies were above the *Volge* (which are only tickled with downright obscenity), and took not so well at the first stroke as at the rebound when beheld a second time." [73]

As playwriters inclined more and more to coarseness, the opposition to the theater grew. Parliament was induced to prohibit the use of the names of God, the Son, and the Holy Ghost in plays, and seven years later, in 1611, the Middlesex justices issued an order suppressing "Jigges at the end of the Playes" because of complaints about their lewdness. When William Prynne fiercely attacked the stage, the Puritans gradually bettered their case against it, but the people of London continued to go to the plays. When *Gondomar,* dealing with the hated Spaniard, was performed in 1624, so many persons of every degree went to see it that one had to be there by one o'clock merely to find standing room. "Time, Place, Subject, Actors, and Cloathes either make or marr a play," Lupton wisely declared in 1632.[74]

Although, like all Englishmen, Londoners were fundamentally a grave and serious people, they had their moments of gaiety and mirth (which they also took seriously), and the metropolis made available to them all of the recreations and diversions known to this age.

73. Harbage, *Shakespeare's Audience,* 77, 79; Chute, *Shakespeare of London,* 40–41.
74. Pickering, *Statutes at Large,* VII, 94; Chamberlain, *Letters,* I, 567; *Middlesex Sessions,* n. s., II, 83; *CSPD, 1619–23;* p. 7; *1623–5,* p. 330.

VI

Englishmen at Work

ONE OF THE PERSISTING historical heresies is that life under the early Stuarts was static. We have seen that this is heresy in the social sphere; so it is in the economic. The old, underdeveloped economy of Western Europe, of which England was an important part, was being gradually transformed into a new and complex capitalistic economy, a revolutionary change that was little understood at the time. Most authorities agree now that throughout our entire period, Western Europe was undergoing a serious economic crisis which was caused by the far-reaching reactions to this transformation. Though England suffered a number of crippling depressions, the nation as a whole accumulated capital and experienced what today is called economic growth.[1]

The tide of England's prosperity came in as medieval means of gaining a livelihood gave way to modern methods and as the nation experienced the longest peace in its history, 1603–24. It was revealed in the rising standard of living for the nobility and for most of the middling people. "Certainly," as Professor Haller has

1. Of "La Crise Économique" Roland Mousnier says "l'Europe est toujours dans la grande récession économique du XVIIe siècle." *Les XVIe et XVIIe Siècles* (*Histoire Générale Des Civilisations*, Paris, 1961, IV), 145, 147, 148, 161–76, 587. On Europe in general, see the suggestive work of G. N. Clark, *The Seventeenth Century* (Oxford, 1947), especially chaps. I–V; and for a formidable mass of detail on unrest in France, see Boris Porchnev, *Les Soulèvements Populaires en France de 1623 à 1648* (Paris, 1963), particularly the chronological tables and 24 revealing maps.

graphically expressed it, "the society that blazed out so brilliantly in the closing years of Gloriana was far from stable or sure either of its foundations or its direction." This insecurity was exacerbated in more ways than one under her two royal successors before 1642, and yet it is evident that, in comparison with the world of Elizabeth, the England of James and Charles grew more spacious —expanded, that is, along all lines of human activity. Many of the leading men of the age were aware of the changes taking place and grew uneasy about their extent and meaning.[2]

We are not here so much concerned with the major forces of economic growth as with observing precisely how the ordinary Englishman, caught in bewildering economic and social upheavals, improved the time. The radical changes must have dismayed, frustrated, and frequently disrupted both the rural majority and the urban minority. The lot of the average man or woman during this prolonged conversion is very difficult to assess, because the very obscurity of the everyday life and arrangements of past centuries often conceal its true nature. If we would understand the ways and conditions under which men and women made their livings, we must look at the country by region and by locality; England at this time did not have a *national* economy.

II

Agrarian England presented regional variations that had much to do with the response to the new rural economy on the part of the peasants, as well as of the yeomen and gentlemen farmers who lived and labored in the 10,000 parishes. Fundamentally, the home market for agricultural produce widened, and while the people of some areas adjusted to the demand, others doggedly clung to their old ways.[3]

2. *VCH Suffolk,* I, 660; *cf.* J. A. Williamson's brilliant estimate of the Elizabethans in George B. Parks, *Richard Hakluyt and the English Voyages* (New York, 1928), xi–xii, with William Haller, *The Rise of Puritanism* (New York, 1938), 46.

3. Slicher Van Bath, *Agrarian History,* 113, 124, 126, 195, 198–9; Campbell, *Yeoman,* 65, 69, 77–8; The best and most recent introduction to the economy of Stuart England is Charles Wilson's *England's Apprenticeship, 1603–1763* (London, 1965), 3–141.

East Anglia, properly Norfolk and Suffolk, exhibited striking variations within its own boundaries. The great marshlands south and west of the Wash were primarily sheep-raising country, which enabled East Anglia to excel in the worsted industry. Cattle, too, thrived, and the farmers found easy vent for their livestock; a dairy industry, which flourished along the east coast, produced cheese that was sold all over England and shipped to the Continent as well. In the arable hinterland, wheat and barley were the principal crops. Like the rest of England, East Anglia knew feast or famine according to the weather, and periodic crop failures with accompanying food shortages and high prices forced many poor people down to the line of mere subsistence. In 1631, during one such critical time, Margaret Winthrop wrote to her son from the Suffolk Manor of Groton: "I have bin constrayned to send to the tenants for rent wantinge monye but have receved but a little yet this week; they promise to paye. They complayne of the hardness of the tyme, and would be glad to be forborne, but I tell them that my necessityes requires it, so I hope to gette in some." [4]

Enclosures and consolidation took place comparatively early in East Anglia. It has been estimated that in Norfolk, in the decade between 1640 and 1650, over 50 per cent of the land was in the hands of thirty-five families; a similar group of lords controlled a third of Suffolk. The lesser gentry and yeomen having an average freehold of 150 acres, most of whom actively managed their own holdings, shared the land with the local aristocracy. Tenants on these properties seldom occupied over ten acres, and with rising prices, they and the landless peasants formed a depressed minority not far from pauperism. [5]

In 1594, John Norden thought that county Essex should "be called the English Goshen, the fatt of Englande, yielding infinite comodities exceding (as I take it) anie other shire, and especiallye in regarde of the varietie of good things it yieldeth." Within the county, farmers of particular hundreds specialized in certain pro-

4. J. Spratt, Agrarian Conditions in Suffolk and Norfolk, 1600–1650 (M.A. Thesis, London, 1935), 41, 101–2; Campbell, *Yeoman*, 159, 180, 204; Reyce, *Suffolk*, 14; Hillen, *King's Lynn*, I, 337; *Winthrop Papers*, III, 36.
5. Spratt, Agrarian Conditions in Suffolk and Norfolk, 29, 65, 80, 87–9, 105–6, 120; Slicher Van Bath, *Agrarian History*, 203; *VCH Suffolk*, I, 661; *Norfolk & Norwich*, XV, Pt. I, 1–3.

duce: Dunmow for hops; above Walden for saffron; oats, the main
Essex cereal, grew principally in the northern parts. Waltham Forest abounded with red and fallow deer, and the marshes supported
cows, though of "poor quality," but still, at Tendring, many
"Wyckes" (dairy houses) produced butter and "greate and huge
cheeses." Cattle grazing was pre-eminent in the southern parts—
the county raised more cattle than Bedfordshire—but Norden discovered that "Essex hath no Sheep walkes" despite its famous cloth
towns.[6]

Thirty years after Norden's visit, save in the coastal marshlands
where the cheese industry was in a slump, agriculture was still
profitable. Its primacy depended not so much on new methods of
cultivation or improved stock breeding as on the arrangements of
farms and holdings. Great landholders and a "flourishing lesser
gentry" controlled large acreages, and rich copyholders were well-
off because rents were soaring. The country appeared to be thriving, but to a numerous body of its Bible-reading inhabitants Essex
no longer resembled the land of Goshen. A serious, underlying
rural poverty existed: at least 25 per cent of the smaller husbandmen farmed holdings of less than five acres, a size insufficient to
support themselves and their families without additional outside income. The situation was aggravated by even greater distress in the
cloth towns. "Thus," as Dr. Felix Hull concludes, "prosperity and
poverty might be found side by side in Essex." [7]

Essex shared its leadership of English agriculture with Kent, a
county never wanting in praise from travelers for the capability of
its yeomen and the fertility of its soil. Here, too, most of the land
had been enclosed by 1640, and open-field culture had all but disappeared; small farms and small fields, supporting fat sheep and
good cattle, predominated—Fuller was particularly enthusiastic
over "the greatness of the Kentish breed" of cattle and poultry.
Though most farmers occupied themselves with growing cereals,
mixing their crops of wheat, barley, and oats with hops and fruit,

6. Norden, Chorographical Description, 13–14; Norden, The County of Essex,
7–8; Steer, *Farm and County Inventories of Mid-Essex,* 55, 56.
7. N. C. P. Tyack, Migration from East Anglia to New England before 1660
(Ph.D. Thesis, London, 1951), I, 93, 94–8; Felix Hull, Agricultural and Rural
Society in Essex, 1560–1640 (Ph.D. Thesis, London, 1950), 82, 117, 358, 471–
2, 503, 506, 510, 513, 518, 520–21, 528.

market-gardening was spreading rapidly in the London neighborhood and enriching many a yeoman. Indeed, diversified agriculture
brought prosperity to all Kentishmen, for it does not appear that
the husbandman and farm laborer suffered the distress so conspicuous elsewhere.[8]

The three southern counties of Sussex, Dorset, and Hampshire
were far more rural than East Anglia, Essex, and Kent, and in
them open-field farming still prevailed. In Sussex, improved management, more than any other thing, accounted for the county's
modest prosperity. Profits attributable to the increased export of
grain, sheep raising, and cattle contributed to the growing wealth
not only of great landowners but of husbandmen who were barely
above the level of the farm laborer. Agricultural operations financed by credit were not uncommon; evidence of this is found in
the striking number of inventories that list money owed to the tes-
tator. The average copyholding husbandman farmed only ten to
fifteen acres. Illegal encroachments on land, a symptom of land
hunger, mounted each year. In times of severe famine, as in 1631,
the peasants' resources were severely strained and "indigence was
a serious problem." [9]

Dorset's commodities, according to a traveler of 1611, were
"Wools and Woods in her North, where the Forests are stored with
the one and the pleasant greene Hilles with the other." Fuller believed that the county could clothe itself with its own wool. In the
interior of the shire, the cultivation of corn and grass figured
largely; flax provided much linen, and hemp-growing brought in
satisfactory returns. The produce of the countryside was bountiful
enough to support eighteen market towns. Hampshire, too, had its
woods and game, and none of its parishes lacked hills and pleasant
valleys. The meadows supplied ample feeding for cattle, but the
county's pride was "Hampshire hogs," ("allowed by all for the best

8. D. C. Coleman, The Economy of Kent under the Later Stuarts (Ph.D.
Thesis, London, 1951), vi, 18, 57, 74, 81, 90–91, 381–3; also a detailed recent
work, C. W. Chalklin, Seventeenth-Century Kent: A Social and Economic History
(London, 1965); Fuller, Worthies, I, 477–8; Barley, English Farmhouse, 41–2.
9. See articles by J. S. K. Cornwall in Sussex Arch., XCII, 48–92, and XCVIII,
118–32; and his Agrarian History of Sussex, 1560–1640 (M.A. Thesis, London,
1953), 352–3, 392, 403–6; Sussex, Arch., XVI, 21; XCIII, 79; also G. E. Fussell,
ibid. XC, 60–101.

bacon, being our English Westphalian"), which fed on acorns in the forests, going in thin and emerging fat.[10]

West of these open fields lay Devon, one of the largest shires. On its miles and miles of waste lands and vast moors, the peasants had become a pastoral people; even though the flocks were not as large as those in other counties, John Hooker thought Devon contained more sheep. Elsewhere the landscape was divided into small, irregular fields, often no more than one acre, enclosed by hedgerows, and between the rows, traversing the countryside, ran a network of country lanes. As early as 1599, a fine apple cider produced from the fruit of the many orchards was preferred to beer for long voyages into southern waters: it kept better and was cheaper than wine. In general, however, farming did not prove remunerative.[11]

The hinterland of Bristol, an extensive rural and agricultural region, included the populous counties of Somerset, Wilts, and Gloucester. Somerset farming was mixed, with sheep grazing and grains well balanced. Though the crop failures of 1622–23 created alarming shortages of corn, the peasants fared well. A country of open fields, Somerset experienced little disturbance over enclosures; in this respect it differed from Gloucester, Wiltshire, and Dorset, where the Great Rising over the enclosures of the Royal Forests took place in 1629–31. Wiltshire easily divided into two regions: the generally enclosed grasslands with small farms that produced quantities of cheese and wool, and the Chalk, where capitalistic landowners grew large crops of wheat and fodder, such as peas, beans, and tares; and where, too, arbitrary enclosing of open fields undoubtedly contributed to widespread discontent that culminated in a series of agrarian revolts between 1625 and 1640.[12]

The Cotswold country was, as Taylor wrote in 1632, "the queene of sheepe." The increasing demand for mutton offset any

10. Speed, *Theatre of Empire of Great Britain*, 17; Fuller, *Worthies*, I, 309, 400–401; Norden, Chorographical Description, 25.
11. Hoskins, Ownership and Occupation of Land in Devonshire; Hoskins, *Devon*, 71–2, 94–5; Fussell, in *Devonshire*, LXXXIII, 179–81; Hooker, in *Devonshire*, XLVII, 346–7; Caldwell, Devonshire, *passim;* Westcote, *Devonshire*, 56.
12. The widespread rural unrest is clear from the pioneer studies of D. A. C. Allan, Agrarian Discontent under the Two Early Stuarts (M.Sc. Thesis, London, 1950), and "The Rising in the West, 1628–1631," in *Ec. Hist. Rev.*, 2d ser., V, 76–83; Barnes, *Somerset*, 1–4; Willcox, *Gloucestershire*, 279–82; E. W. J. Ker-

decline in the wool trade—in 1622 Cotswold sheep were being offered in the Smithfield market. Most of the peasants lived on a noticeably lower scale than those of the richer eastern and southern shires. The old, familiar open fields, stretching eastward through the Midlands, encouraged the tendency of neighbors to encroach on one another's land; these transgressions perennially fostered local quarrels. In Derbyshire, the farmers operated fine dairies, but their "Butterie" was Nottingham and Loughborough, whence they came home with all of the malt and barley for their brewing; the common inhabitants of the county preferred oats "for delight and strength above any other graine." Actually, the Derbyshire staple was a fine and soft fleece. All over the Midlands, dovecotes could be found, some of them remarkable for their size and architectural design. One observer, calculating 500 pairs of doves for each of the 20,000 dove-houses of England, concluded that at least 10,000,000 of these birds were raised! In addition to their value as food, their droppings in the dovecotes supplied the makings for quantities of saltpeter.[13]

In the open-field country, despite regional variations, a certain uniformity did exist in contrast with the obvious diversity in other areas. The legendary three-field system was far from rigid, and we now know that the enclosure movement before 1640 has been overestimated. Where lands were fenced in, the owners of large acreages tended to improve farms quite as much as to create sheep walks. Furthermore, grazing belonged with the rest of the Midland system inasmuch as both sheep and cattle furnished the manures essential for corn tillage.[14]

ridge, The Agricultural Development of Wiltshire, 1540–1640 (Ph.D. Thesis, London, 1951), 551–607; and summary in Bulletin of the Institute of Historical Research, XXV, 75–80; Fussell, "Farming Methods in the Early Stuart Period," in Journal of Modern History, VII, 1–21, 129–40; Clutterback, in Wiltshire, XXII, 70–85.
13. Taylor on Thames-Isis, in Works, I, No. 1, p. 9; Orwin, The Open Fields, passim; Peter J. Bowden, The Wool Trade in Tudor and Stuart England (London, 1962), 9, 11; VCH Oxfordshire, V, 129; Kinder, Historie of Derbyshire, 21, 23; for dovecotes, Fuller, Worthies, II, 157–8; Winthrop Papers, I, 92; Cook and Smith, English Cottages, pls. 220–26.
14. Fussell, in Journal of Modern History, VII, 4–7, 138–40; for the Fenland of Lincolnshire and Cambridgeshire, see Thirsk, English Peasant Farming, 23, 28, 33, 45, 110, 117–19, 134.

Voracious demands for a variety of foodstuffs by the steadily rising population of London profoundly influenced the agriculture of the Home Counties. A revolutionary change was taking place in the urban diet: at one dinner in Dulwich in 1619, cauliflower, lettuce, artichokes, carrots, and turnips all appeared on the table. Some gardeners raised raspberries, strawberries, and gooseberries, as well as herbs for food or physic. Kent sent quantities of fruit, cherries above all, to the city markets. By 1635 more than 24,000 loads of "Rootes" went to London yearly, "whereby as well the poor as the ritch have plenty . . . at reasonable prices." Suffolk shipped in more butter and cheese than any other shire, while Essex attained a reputation as a fattening area for sheep and cattle destined for the market at Smithfield.[15]

After 1600 market gardening developed rapidly in the counties of Middlesex, Kent, Surrey, and Essex, and up the Thames Valley in particular. Some vegetables were planted in open fields, but ten-acre gardens in Bermondsey, Battersea, Lambeth, and the Middlesex suburbs under intensive cultivation paid best. Thomas Fuller discovered that, in Kent, where people had paid "six pounds an Aker and upwards, they have made their Rent, live comfortably, and set many people on work," for in addition to acquiring a newfangled diet, thousands of old men, old women, children, and the poor earned small wages weeding gardens and gathering vegetables. New marketing procedures were evolving as the demand for produce mounted. The Gardeners Company, incorporated in 1605, exercised jurisdiction over all market gardening within six miles of London, and by 1640, unlike the situation in the smaller cities, a substantial body of retailers, mongers of this and that food, had risen to handle the assembling and distribution of food for the metropolis. Hop growers usually sold their produce to the Salters, Grocers, and Fishmongers, because they were too busy with cultivating and drying the hops in their oast-houses to make deliveries directly to the city brewers. Middlemen also handled the quantities of flour, bread, corn, and malt that came to town by water from the mills of Kent and Essex and the granaries of other counties for the bakers and brewers of London.[16]

15. Fisher, in *Ec. Hist. Rev.*, V, 46–64; Lysons, *London*, I, 28; IV, 573; Hull, Agriculture . . . in Essex, 117, 270; Coleman, Kent, 113, 141.
16. Fisher, in *Ec. Hist. Rev.*, V, 54, 55, 57, 60; Essex Sessions, XX, 511; Fuller, *Worthies*, II, 353; *CSPD, Addenda, 1580–1625*, p. 638; Stow, *Survey of London*,

The English farmer—yeoman, husbandman, wage-earner—was a simple, rough, hard-working person who lived in a society in which custom and tradition practically dictated and fashioned his life from birth till death. Like old Thomas Parr:

> Good wholesome labour was his exercise,
> Down with the Lamb, and with the Lark would rise,
> In myre and toyling sweat hee spent the day,
> And (to his Teame) he whistled Time away:
> The Cock his Night-Clock, and till day was done,
> His Watch, and chiefe Sun-Diall was the Sun.

Anywhere in the land, crude clothing identified the ordinary countryman as easily as a cowboy's costume marks the cowhand today. A coarse, homespun woolen garment of reddish brown was proverbially his best attire, and coarser canvas his field clothes, along with the "high shoes" that Aubrey says the husbandmen wore in North Wiltshire. One gown a year was all that farm women could hope for, and shepherds had but one homespun smock. Nearer London, some peasants dressed more elaborately; it was a matter of comment when Robert Osborn of Middlesex, a market gardener charged with stealing five capons and four hens, set off his red hair and beard when he appeared at the quarter sessions in Essex dressed in a "whit jerkin" and "a pair of brownish coloured hose of fustian cut." [17]

Country gentlemen occasionally referred to poor husbandmen and wage-laborers as "men of abilitie," but, able or not, they were still landless, and their very existence depended upon the landowners. During these years, fewer servants lived in the farmers' households, and more men lived in cottages that were literally

bk. I, 51; Robbins, *Middlesex,* 25, 33. Hartlib, *Legacy of Husbandry,* 8–10, somewhat underestimates the extent of market gardening around London, but his account is still very helpful.
17. In 1609, Samuel Rowlands described the typical country fellow thus:
> . . . plain in russet clad.
> His doublet, mutton-taffety, sheeps' skins . . .
> Upon his head a filthy greasy hat,
> That had a hole ate thorow by some rat.

Quoted by Byrne, *Elizabethan Life,* 40; Taylor, "The Old, Old, Very Old Man," in *Works,* I, No. 2, p. 20; Henry Martyn Dexter, *The England and Holland of the Pilgrims* (Boston, 1905), 13–14; Aubrey, *Brief Lives,* II, 324; *Western Antiquary,* II, 16; Essex Sessions, XVIII, 308.

thrown up on the waste over night. Landowners now tended to hire laborers by the day rather than by the year, which increasingly subjected those poor souls to the caprices of seasonal employment, especially during the winter. A substantial amount of unemployment in the rural areas was normal, but during periods of crisis, such as 1622 and 1629–31, it rose noticeably. Furthermore, wages in husbandry failed to keep up with the rise in prices of necessities.[18]

Sons of landless parents had a choice of at least two ways to learn farming. Some yeomen took on youths as apprentices in the art of husbandry. George Job of Frontfield Parish, Sussex, bound himself for seven years to Thomas Page. In return for a payment by his mother of 10s. and two good sheep, he was to receive apparel, shoes, lodging, "and all things needful . . . both in sickness and in health" plus 4d. every quarter. More usual, however, was the apprenticing of orphans; in 1613 Justice Bostock Fuller signed indentures for the two sons and a daughter of "one Sparke of Nutfield," Surrey, to three different masters for periods of eleven, fifteen, and twelve years. The other method of employment was that exemplified by the case of John Mowdie of Croscombe, Somerset, who told the Court of Quarter Sessions at Wells in 1628 that he had bound himself to Robert Browne as "a convenanted servant by the space of eighteen or nineteen year." After the first year he was to have as a "sallery or wages" £3 per annum, meat, drink, and lodging. Now, since he could not sue by common law because of his poverty, he was petitioning the court for the £37.10.0 due him. The justices appointed mediators to settle the truth of the accusation by the next session. Covenanted or indentured servitude of this type was a familiar form of contract labor in both rural and urban England and, with some modifications, was widely adopted in the English colonies.[19]

Obviously, when so much farm labor was casual, and mobile

18. All laborers did not deserve sympathy or pity; some proved to be rogues and scoundrels. See the cases of Thomas James of Burton Latimer (1630) and John Mead of Great Tey (1637), in *Northampton Sessions,* 49–50; and Essex Sessions, XX, 427; Campbell, *Yeoman,* 159, 214; *Lincolnshire,* I, 16; Kerridge, Agricultural Development of Wiltshire, 562; *VCH Essex,* II, 326; *VCH Sussex,* II, 198.
19. *Sussex Arch.,* IV, 269; *Surrey,* IX, 196; *Devizes Recs.,* 84, 85; *Somerset Sessions,* II, 54, 157–8, 159; *Warwick Sessions,* I, 76.

rather than settled occupations were the rule, skilled agricultural-
ists were very rare. William Drury may have assisted Middlesex
farmers as a molecatcher, and Christopher Cockrell may have
gone from Kent to Somerset, near Glastonbury, to teach his art of
sowing and ordering flax, but most of the landless men were ordinary workers like Anthony Eire and Robert Finche, whom Henry
Lea, a husbandman of Hallinbury Morley in Essex, hired to
plough his ground, "himself sowing before the plough." Laborers
were expected to know how to harrow ploughed soil and how to
wield the shovel and hoe, but only in rare forest areas did they
know the use of the axe. Some workers commanded higher pay
than others: "Mowers of grasse" received 6d. in 1630 whereas
mowers of corn received 8d. Threshers of barley were paid 10d. by
the day while threshers of rye received 18d.[20]

The interest that some of the gentry showed in improved husbandry, which had been stimulated unwittingly by the antiquaries
and topographers of the previous century as well as by the practical needs for more production, led to the publication of several
books on the subject. Thomas Tusser's *Five Hundred Points of
Good Husbandry* (1557) went through nine editions by 1610; in
1614 the work of Gervase Markham, *Cheape and Good Husbandrie for the well-Ordering of All Beasts, and Fowles, and for the
general Care of their Diseases,* met the demand for information
about domestic animals so well that at least seven editions sold out
by 1633. The fifth book of John Norden, *The Surveyor's Dialogue*
(1607), and Markham's *The English Husbandman* (1613) taught
farmers to consider seriously "the different natures of ground" in
their agricultural practice. Evidence of a heightened interest in the
culture of fruits is shown by the publication in 1640 of *The
Country-mans Recreation, or the Art of Planting, Graffing, and
Gardening,* wherein the author stressed the ways of planting and
grafting, how "to preserve and keepe fruite, how to plant and
prune vines, gather and dress grapes, to make cider or perry." A
long account of certain Dutch practices, such as transplanting, was
also included.[21]

20. Essex Sessions, XVIII, 246; XIX, 24; XX, 346; Archbold, in *EHR,* XII, 309;
Middlesex Sessions, n. s., IV, 133; *VCH Kent,* III, 378.
21. For bibliographical comment, see G. E. Fussell, *The Old Farming Books,
1523 to 1730* (London, 1947).

Finding no agricultural manuals listed in the inventories of countless yeomen, Miss Campbell concludes that husbandry was an academic study of the gentry, whom a few alert yeomen observed and imitated. John Smyth of Nibley wrote in 1620 to George Thorpe that "Markhams and [Barnaby] Gouges books of all kynd of English husbandry and huswifery, and 2 others . . . are nowe sent" to him to take out to Virginia along with young stock and apple trees "grafted with pippins, pearmaynes and other the best apples," also apricot, "damosell" and other plum stones. At best the literate yeoman and husbandman would record local lore and methods in with their accounts in a farming book, like that of Henry Best.[22]

"Where the husband-man's acre-staff and the shepherd's hook are," one would not expect that many peasant farmers would be reading, let alone taking the advice of books on agriculture. The average "rude simple and ignorant clowne," as Markham condescendingly called the poor husbandman, "onely knoweth how to doe his labour, but cannot give a reason why . . . more then the instruction of his parents or the custome of the country." It was "custome" that moved the inhabitants of Mitcham, Surrey, in 1637 to agree in a town meeting, on behalf of all the rest, to lay open the common fields for grazing as soon as the corn was carried out. Rarely did a peasant vary from approved routines, and old-fashioned tools and implements sufficed for the bulk of them. Probably, too, more oxen than horses worked as draft animals. Of course there were exceptions: a record exists of a gardener in Brentwood being called to account for dumping ten cartloads of a novel mixture of turnip greens and dung in the public highway; he intended—eventually—to spread it on his garden. This item is of interest also because only one yeoman family in five owned a two-wheeled dung cart or a long cart for transport. In Bedfordshire inventories, wagons are never mentioned.[23]

22. Campbell, *Yeoman*, 170; John Smyth of Nibley, "Papers," in N. Y. Public Library, *Bulletin*, III, 280.
23. In some places, parochial officers (churchwardens, constables, etc.) regulated husbandry, even recasting the entire field system of the parish and hiring a surveyor to make a general enclosure. W. E. Tate, *The Parish Chest* (Cambridge, Eng., 1946), 15, 257; Fuller, *Worthies*, I, 537, 561; Markham, *The English Husbandman* (1635), 37, 95; Essex Sessions, XX, 469; Emmison, in *Bedford*, XX, 35–6.

III

Country Englishmen had daily need for the services of craftsmen and tradesmen—blacksmiths, ploughwrights, wheelwrights, and harness makers to fashion and repair their agricultural equipment —and some of these artisans could be found living in every village. Along with bakers, butchers, tallow-chandlers, maltsters, mealmen, drovers, and similar tradesmen, so essential to the conduct of rural activities, were tanners and leather dressers, turners, joiners, and lath-rivers, because leather and wood went into hundreds of common articles. During The Great Housing Boom, carpenters, masons, bricklayers, plasterers, and thatchers found regular employment.[24]

Here and there dwelt a specialized craftsman who worked all over his county. The Chappington family of South Moulton built organs for parish churches in both Devon and Wiltshire. Nathaniel Clarke and Edward Browne of Wakes Colne and Earle's Colne, dish-turners, produced a large portion of the wooden bowls and trenchers used by the plain people of Essex in 1620. When the rectory at tiny Bletchingden needed repairs in 1633, a second carpenter from Oxford, a plasterer from Shipton-on-Cherwell, and a mason from Hampden Gay worked on the job. Now and then a jack-of-all-trades, such as Thomas Upton of Wadhurst Parish in Sussex, astonished his compatriots with the list of his talents. When Upton died, the parish register stated that this "Archimedes of Wadhurst . . . was by trade a glover, a joiner, a carpenter, and an instrument-maker; [also] . . . a curious workman for jacks, clocks, stones, and vices for glaziers." [25]

Another order of craftsmen traveled through the countryside to mend household and farm equipment, for milkpails, noggins, and

24. The rural crafts in Essex alone supplied the patronymics for many families whose names became well known in America: Chandler, Cooper, Currier, Cutler, Draper, Fletcher, Gardiner, Glover, Mason, Mercer, Miller, Sawyer, Saddler, Sherman, Thatcher, Tinker, Turner, Waterman, Webster, Wheelwright. Essex Sessions, XVII–XX.
25. *Devon & Cornwall,* VI, 31–2; X, 82, 109; *Churchwardens' Accounts of St. Edmund and S. Thomas, Sarum, 1443–1702,* ed. J. F. Swayne (Salisbury, 1896), 193; Essex Sessions, XIX, 405, 441; *VCH Oxfordshire,* VI, 66; *Sussex Arch.,* IV, 276.

wooden containers often needed minor repairs that required an expert. The Devon justices licensed a man in 1603 to perform the trade and "scyence of Tynking." Among other familiar callers at cottage doors were tailors, fishmongers, badgers, drovers, "stock barbers," and chimney sweepers. One of Martin Parker's ballads about Norfolk told how "a brave lusty Cooper in the Countrie did dwell/And there he cry'd, Worke for a Cooper;/Maids, ha'ye any worke for a Cooper?" [26]

The leading English industry, the manufacture of cloth, continued, as in the past, to be centered in the chief cities and so-called "cloth towns" of Bury St. Edmunds, Bocking, Colchester, Dedham, Canterbury, Maidstone, Crediton, Tiverton, and Devizes. The yarn used by the twelve great cloth counties was made in the cottages of farm laborers and poor husbandmen whose wives and daughters spun wool into yarn to supplement the family's meager income. Artisans' families also followed this practice: Stephen Wright of Pleshey in Essex was a shoemaker, but his wife Rose was a "spinster." Some countrymen worked exclusively at looms in their own cottages while the other members of the family cultivated the four-acre plots, when they had them, to produce a little food. The great majority of these craftsmen worked under the most straitened circumstances. John Taylor described his meeting with one of them near the seacoast in Sussex in 1623:

> Within a Cottage nigh, there dwells a weaver,
> Who entertained us, the like was never,
> No meate, no drinke, no lodging (but the floore)
> No stoole to set, no Locke unto the doore,
> No Straw to make us litter in the night,
> Nor any Candlesticke to hold the light,
> To which the Owner bad us welcome still,
> Good entertainment, though the Cheare was ill.[27]

26. Hamilton, *Quarter Sessions*, 27; Roxburghe *Ballads*, I, 99.
27. Cloth workers traditionally sang away the monotonous hours; In *Twelfth Night*, the Duke alludes to this when he says to the Clown:

> O, fellow, come, the song we had last night.
> Mark it, Cesario, it is old and plain;
> The spinsters and the knitters in the sun
> And the free maids that weave their thread with bones
> Do use to chant it; it is silly sooth,

The means by which the clothiers "spread themselves all over the country" and collected the product of the country spinners is well described in a report of 1615. The "yarn is weekly brought into the markett by a great number of poore people that will not spin to the clothier for smale wages; but have stock enough to sett themselves on woorke and doe weekly buy their woolle in the market by very small parcells according to their use and weekly returne it in yarne, and make good profitt thereof, having the benefit both of their labour and of the merchandise, and live exceeding well. Theis yarn-makers are so many in number that it is supposed by men of judgement that more than half the cloathes that is made in Wilts, Gloucester and Somersettshire is made by means of theis yarn-makers and poore clothiers that depend weekly upon the woolle chapmen which serves them weekely with woolles either for money or credit." There were some spinners to whom the clothiers supplied the wool and paid wages. Once the yarn was acquired, thirty or more artisans handled it—wove it into cloth, fulled and dyed it, sheared it, and performed many other operations—before the finished product reached the market.[28]

In prosperous times, specialized crafts gave employment to thousands of skilled artisans in the provincial cities as well as in London. The division of labor within a given industry was remarkable, and on the increase. Flat round caps required the labor of a dozen or more workmen. Richard Symonds recounted the process in 1644: "First they are knit, then they mill them, then

---

And dallies with the innocence of love,
Like the old age.

Twelfth Night, II, iv, 44–9; The leading counties were Norfolk, Suffolk, Essex, Kent, Dorset, Devon, Somerset, Wilts, Gloucester, Oxford, Worcester, and York. Acts of the Privy Council, 1621–1623, pp. 132–3; Clark, Working Life of Women, 98, 145, 147; Essex Sessions, III, 2; Sussex Arch., XVIII, 138.

28. CSPD, 1637–8, p. 433; Ramsay, English Overseas Trade, 5–6; Reasons to prove the conveniencie of buying and selling Woolle in this kingdome [1615] (PRO: S. P. 14/80, No. 13); Westcote, Devonshire, 61–2; Gardiner, England, VII, 83; George Unwin, Industrial Organization in the Sixteenth and Seventeenth Centuries (Oxford, 1904), 234–5, Appendix A; J. Pilgrim, The Cloth Industry in Essex and Suffolk, 1558–1640 (M.A. Thesis, London, 1939); G. D. Ramsay, The Wiltshire Woollen Industry in the Sixteenth and Seventeenth Centuries (Oxford, 1953); B. E. Supple, Commercial Crisis and Change in England, 1600–1642 (New York, 1959); see also works of Bowden, Caldwell, Cornwall, Hull, Kerridge, Spratt, and Tyack, which have been previously cited.

block them, then they worke them withe tassells, then they sheere them." In Monmouthshire, and later in Bewdley in Worcestershire, where the industry moved after a destructive fire, Monmouth caps, as they continued to be called, were "Knitted by poor people for 2d. a piece, ordinary ones sold for 2s., 3s., 4s." These caps were sold to working men throughout the land, and, after 1607, might have been termed the headgear of colonization. Specialization was also occurring among tradesmen: in the small community of Dorchester, Henry Corbyn, baker, was made a freeman in 1621 at the same time that his brother won the privilege as a "fruiterer." [29]

London's large and heterogeneous population made it preeminent in industry and craftsmanship. Up the Thames came coal boats from Newcastle, iron from the Weald of Sussex, and tin from the stannaries of Devon and Cornwall to be used in the fabrication of consumers' goods. In the decade from 1630 to 1640, textiles stood first in importance (clothmaking, silkmaking, dyeing, feltmaking, rope- and sailcloth-making, and tailoring); next were the leather and metal trades; then came brewing and candlemaking. Nowhere did the degree of specialization exceed that in London: there were "payntor-staynors," point-makers, thimble-smiths, bitmakers, wire-drawers and pinmakers—Stow valued the pin industry at £60,000 a year! Embroiderers formed a large group. Robert Keayne, a merchant who later emigrated to Boston, Massachusetts, engaged workmen in 1627 to make liveries for the pages and footmen at Court.[30]

In retail trades, especially in the finished goods, London surpassed all other cities. Shops that had once been mere open stalls in a London market now appeared along Fleet Street, the Strand,

29. *Camden*, LXXIV, 14; Fuller, *Worthies*, II, 115, 116; *Dorchester Recs.*, 423; for trades in Exeter, *HMC Exeter*, 298–300; and *Tradesmen in Early Stuart Wiltshire*, ed. N. J. Williams (Devizes, 1960); *VCH Sussex*, II, 229.

30. We do not know how many people worked in the extractive industries before 1642; certainly they were not a large segment of the population. For both the coal and iron industries, see J. U. Nef's classic work, *The Rise of the British Coal Industry*, I, 166–88, 242; and his more controversial study postulating "an early industrial revolution," "Industry and Government in France and England, 1540–1640," in Amer. Philos. Soc. *Memoirs*, XV, 1–54; and *The Conquest of the Material World* (Chicago, 1964); for the tin mines, see George R. Lewis, *The Stannaries* (Cambridge, Mass., 1908); also Archer, Industrial History of London, 9–21, synopsis; *VCH Kent*, III, 413; Stow, *Annales*, 1038; *CSPD, 1627–8*, p. 458.

King Street, and in Westminster. Haberdashers, woolen drapers, milliners, upholsterers, perfumers, etc., established themselves everywhere. Stow complained that "the people of London began to spend extravagantly"; condemning the feverish buying of French, Spanish, and Dutch "knicknachs," he expressed the wish that Londoners would either do without those "trifles" or else make them themselves "within our own realm." [31]

The trade of milling, because of its bearing on the colonies, calls for comment. The Dutch windmill was introduced by "foreigners," but no such mills had existed in Tudor days and only a few were built in the flat eastern counties before 1640, a surprising fact because of their rapid adoption in New England by 1642, and possibly even earlier. The industrial device that the English colonists in America needed above everything else was a sawmill driven by wind or water. In 1634 Sir William Brereton marveled at the windmills of Amsterdam that drove sixteen saws at one time, but England had few sawmills before 1663 when popular opposition to them developed and some of them were given up. By this time a flourishing lumber industry in New England kept many sawmills in constant use.[32]

IV

An important and vital inland traffic went on between town and country, between towns and cities, and between all parts of England and London. Such heavy and bulky freights as coal, iron ore, stone, tin, and corn moved along coastal and inland waterways in ever larger amounts, and passengers and lighter articles passed from the head of navigation at Lechlade down the Thames to London, and along the Ouse-Cam, Avon, Severn, Trent, and other streams. Largely unnoticed, however, was the extensive highway traffic that went on at the same time, an interchange of people and goods that had social and cultural implications to match its economic importance.[33]

31. Besant, *London,* 195–6; Stow, *Annales,* 1038–40.
32. *London,* n.s., XI, 227, 236; *Country Life,* III, 348; XLVII, 194; *Chetham,* I, 62; Clark, *Seventeenth Century,* 61; Boston Record Commissioners, *Second Report* (Boston, Mass., 1902), 70; Waters, *Gleanings,* I, 463.
33. Consult the map of navigable streams in T. S. Willan, *River Navigation in England, 1600–1750* (Manchester, 1936), frontispiece; Robbins, *Middlesex,* 61;

Nearly every day in the year, Englishmen of all ranks were traveling along the lanes and roads. Foot passengers, such as servants and laborers, walked to their places of employment. With these wayfarers belonged the drovers, who regularly took sheep and cattle to market or to fattening farms, sometimes all the way from Wales to London or southern Essex. Then always there were horsemen: merchants journeying for business reasons, gentlemen riding to London and returning thence to their estates, and a few curious people, like Peter Mundy and Sir William Brereton, or humble people for that matter, who were traveling singly or in parties merely to see the country. In the 1630's too, an occasional coach passed along the roads carrying women, children, and body servants to and from London.[34]

Clothmakers, wool chapmen, and those who had bulky though light wares to transport used pack-horses more than any other form of transportation. The cloth market at Blackwell Hall in Basinghall Street opened every Thursday morning to accommodate the merchants who had left distant places on Monday morning and would ordinarily arrive in London by Wednesday night. In *Cheap and Good Husbandry* (1614) Gervase Markham gave instructions for choosing good horses fit "for Packe or Hampers," and he emphasized broad backs and long strides, "their pace being neither trot nor amble, but onely foote pace." Once a year James Skeate of Tenterden sent thirty to fifty pieces of cloth up to London by "pack-carrier." The volume of this pack-horse traffic ought not to be underestimated. Far to the north in Lancashire in 1632, the local justices of the peace stated that "commonly tow or three hundred lowden horses everie day passe over" the Ferryford between Whalley and Great Harwood, "besides great numbers of other passengers." So many pack-horse trains passed through places like Market Harborough that they became a public menace. "As I was playing in the streets, a number of pack-horses came along; and the foremost horse struck me down upon my back with his knee,"

England as Seen by Foreigners in the Days of Elizabeth and James the First, ed. W. B. Rye (London, 1865), 134.
34. A member of the Gaudy family reported in June, 1638: "The Bishop will be here next Friday in a horse-litter." *HMC Gaudy,* X, 169; *England as Seen by Foreigners,* 133; *Shakespeare's England,* I, 203, 204; and in general, Joan Parkes, *Travel in England in the Seventeenth Century* (London, 1925).

John Hull, the Massachusetts mintmaster, wrote, describing an incident that occurred when he was but two years old.[35]

In 1592 two-wheeled carts, which could "carry quite as much as waggons" and took "as many as five or six strong horses to draw them," evoked the admiration of a German traveler. Within a few years the number of these carts and even larger four-wheeled wagons, commonly used for long-distance hauling, so cut up and damaged the roads that other travelers were seriously inconvenienced. In 1605, because the King had found the roads unfit for travel, the Council ordered the justices of Hertfordshire to ban those wagons used by the carriers of Norwich and Cambridge to transport goods up to 60 hundred-weight—some of them used as many as nine horses, and the iron rims of the wheels were particularly ruinous to the roads. This restriction and ensuing proclamations on the problem were openly defied. The authorities, despite valiant attempts to repair damages, could not offset the havoc resulting from the use of heavy carts such as the six-ox teams that conveyed gunpowder from Somerset to Plymouth or the "druggs" drawn by seven to ten horses. In 1632 the Hertfordshire Court of Quarter Sessions ordered two persons to take a traffic count at Standon for a whole month and to include the names of the owners, their places of residence, and the number of their horses, as well as the number of times the drivers used the road. All owners of overloaded vehicles were to be fined fifty shillings.[36]

35. Processions of as many as fifty horses, headed by a packman or sumpter astride the first (which was belled), went along in single file, the beasts attached to one another by the halter and tail. Wicker panniers (called "dorsers" from the county of origin) or cloth packs were slung over a crude, padded saddle. Sometimes there were several sumpters distributed in a long train. At Moulton in Suffolk, on the old road from Newmarket to Clare, one can still see an impressive, narrow pack-horse bridge of four spans with pointed arches. *Suffolk*, XXI, 110–15, and illustrations; Fuller, *Worthies*, I, 31; Ramsay, *English Overseas Trade*, 7; Markham, *Cheap and Good Husbandry*, 5, 10; *VCH Kent*, III, 410; *HMC Kenyon*, XIV, IX, 50; R. G. Hedworth Whitty, History of Taunton under the Tudors and Stuarts (Ph.D. Thesis, London, 1938), 235–6; John Hull, "Diaries," *Archaeologica Americana* (Worcester, Mass., 1857), III, 141.

36. *England as Seen by Foreigners*, 14; *CSPD, 1603–10*, p. 225; *1611–18*, pp. 471, 557; *1619–23*, pp. 291, 391; *1628–9*, p. 88; *1635*, p. 458; Thomas Procter, *A Worthy Worke Profitable to this whole kingdom, Concerning the mending of all high-waies* (1607); Essex Sessions, XIX, 149, 411, 474–5, 523; *HMC Lincoln*, XIV; VIII, 92; G. S. Thompson, "Roads in England and Wales in 1693," in *EHR*, XXXIII, 234–43; Reyce, *Suffolk*, 53; *Hertfordshire Sessions*, V, 161–2.

In late Elizabethan days, the driving of wagons along set routes to and from London gradually became institutionalized. In the metropolis, every carrier, as the drivers were called, arrived and departed regularly from a particular inn at stated times—John Taylor published a useful list of them in 1637 in *The Carrier's Cosmography.*[37]

The carriers took passengers, letters, money, bills of exchange, and goods in their wagons. In 1638 Peter Noyes sent his effects from Weyhill, Hampshire, up to London to be placed on board the *Jonathan,* a ship bound for New England. The freight charges for his goods and those of eleven other emigrants to the New World came to £50.0.0. Earle observed that "A carrier is his own hackneyman, for he lets himself out to travel as well as his horses. . . . He is the Vault in Gloucester Church, that conveys whispers at a distance; for he takes the sound out of your mouth at York and makes it to be heard as far as London." Though each of the carriers acted individually, they all combined when their interests were threatened, as in 1639 when they attempted to prevent the Walloon weavers of Canterbury from setting up James Meshman as their private carrier and discharging the man the carriers had selected, who had proved unsatisfactory.[38]

It was not unusual for carriers to undertake commissions for their country customers. Most requests were simple enough, but others took an inordinate amount of time and occasionally ended unsatisfactorily for all concerned, as a tale told by Richard Richmond, a carrier of Warminster, illustrates. In 1620, Henry Bracebridge, a woolen draper of Southampton, asked Richmond to buy a piece of "Stammell bayes" for him. The carrier secured it from Richmond Cope at Taunton, Somerset, but when he delivered it on May 4, it was found to be half a yard short of the twenty-four yards ordered, and Bracebridge insisted that the price should be cut by six shillings from the asking price of £4.18.0. Richmond

---

37. Possibly the first scheduled stage coaches began to run weekly from London to St. Albans in 1637. Carriers, however, had been making scheduled trips along the main roads to London by 1630. Robbins, *Middlesex,* 72; Stone, *Aristocracy,* 512.

38. *Surtees,* LII, 36; *CSPD, 1636–7,* p. 169; *NEHG Reg.,* XXXII, 410; Earle, *Microcosmography,* 36–7; *VCH Kent,* III, 413.

tried to sell it elsewhere but was finally forced to sell it for the lower price.[39]

Unconscious evidence is always the best, and in an out-of-the-way source we have such testimony to the kinds and extent of inland trade from 1603 to 1640. From Barbados in 1647, Richard Ligon, a knowledgeable, experienced, and thrifty planter, wrote to his agent in England that one might hire "poor Journey-men Taylors" in London for small wages to make from "Canvas" and "Kentings" suitable "shirts and drawers for the Christian men and Servants" and "Smocks and petticoats for the women" of his island. He added that bespoke Monmouth caps could be made cheaper in Wales and then sent up to London "by the waynes at easie rates." Similarly, Irish stockings for servants could be brought from the West Country and oversize shoes from Northampton by carts; likewise from Sussex, one might carry iron pots to London by cart "at the time of the year when the wayes are drie and hard"—all cheaper than they could be purchased in the metropolis. He also considered it less expensive to procure nails by wagon from Birmingham instead of from London ironmongers. In other words, though freight charges for land carriage were high, the total cost of many kinds of goods purchased in the provinces was lower. It is evident too that Bristol and other lesser cities had, by 1640, succeeded in drawing on a wide inland area for raw materials and cloth, and in return supplied manufactured and imported goods. By such means foreign fashions penetrated the English countryside.[40]

Itinerant dealers served as the principal agents for the expansion of hinterland markets. Since the late Middle Ages, the peddler, or the hawker, with his wool, yarns, and cloth had enjoyed a recognized place in rural economy. In a famous sermon the vicar of Stapleford Abbots in Essex adverted to the dangerous fascination the peddler had for young people who were just making a start in life: "When our stock after a few yeares is increased, then we de-

39. *Southampton Recs.*, I, 14–15.
40. Ligon had recently emigrated from England to Barbados and knew well whereof he spoke. Ligon, *A True and Exact History of the Island of Barbados*, 109; C. M. MacInnes, *A Gateway to Empire* (Bristol, 1939), 20; A. H. Dodd, *Studies in Stuart Wales* (Cardiff, 1952), 29; *Shakespeare's England*, I, 321.

sire to trade with the merchant pedler; his packe is opened, we come to the mart, here wee buy lases and glasses, bugles and bracelets, ribbons and roses; O the most profitablest member of the Commonwealth! nothing grieves us so much, as that we have not credit, to take up money at interest, to buy these rare and excellent commodities. . . ." [41]

In the early Stuart period, the petty chapmen performed much-valued services which contributed substantially to the breakdown of exclusive town economies and cleared the way for regional and ultimately national distribution of goods. Periodically fanning out all over England, they brought the peasants what they hungered for or what they needed. No one else offered this service.

> What? dost thou not knowe that every pedler
> In all kinde of trifles must be a medlar?
> Specially in women's tryflinges.
> Those we use cheafly above all things.
> Gloves, pynnes, combs, glasses unspotted,
> Pomanders, hookes, and lasses knotted,
> Broches, rynges, and all manner of bedes,
> Laces, round and flat, for women's hedes,
> Medyls, thred, thimbell, shers, and all such knackes. [42]

The goodwife who did not wish to trudge to market relied upon badgers or hucksters, as the men or women peddlers who brought corn, meal, cheese, butter, and eggs, and sometimes fish, were called. These people covered very wide territories at times. In 1630 the Somerset justices licensed the Widow Elizabeth Dodding-

41. Ordinarily a *hawker* conveyed his wares by pack-horse and sold them by either wholesale or retail, while a *peddler* or *petty chapman* usually carried his goods in a pack on his back and sold by retail only. A writer of a pamphlet described "those that show Wares by Whole-sale, which are called Hawkers, and are not only the Manufactures themselves, but others besides [them] viz. the Women in London, in Exeter and in Manchester, who not only Profer Commodities at the Shops and Ware-houses, but at Inns to Countrey Chapmen. Likewise the Manchester-men, the Sherborn-men, and many others, that do Travel from one Market-Town to another; And there at some Inn do profer their Wares to sell to the Keepers of the place." *The Trade of England Revived; and the Abuses thereof Rectified* (London, 1681), 21; Goodman, *Fall of Man*, 184.

42. *The Four Po-Palmer, Pardoner, 'Poticary and Pedler,* a play of *c.* 1540, quoted in Stephen Dowell, *History of Taxation and Taxes in England* (London, 1884–5), III, 31.

ton of Hilbishops to use up to three horses in her work as a badger of butter and cheese in Somerset, Wilts, Hants, and Devon, and to return with corn to sell again in any market. Chapmen who exhibited capacity for shrewdness and thrift could, in time, acquire a fair substance. At the Manchester Court in 1618, James Hulme, a chapman who bought a "messuage and appurtenances" in the Milgate with his savings, appeared, swore fealty, and received admittance as a tenant. John Pit from Abington located at Reading with his wife in 1630. He "spent his tyme in travellinge from one gentleman's house to another, sellinge lawnes, diapers, and cambrickes, and suche like wares" for almost a year until, besides his wares, which he had purchased from Thomas Cope in Cheapside, and what he had brought from "home," he had amassed £40.[43]

The itinerants aroused resentment among the retailers and shopkeepers who, feeling the competition, periodically accused the peddlers of unfairness. The Company of Upholsterers of London complained in 1603 that lately there had arisen "a great company of idle and wandering persons or petit chapmen, commonly called hawksters, who pass with upholstery ware from town to town by pack-horse," whereby the petitioners were impoverished. Two years later, the brothers Pryor (one a merchant tailor, the other a yeoman) of St. Botolph without Bishopsgate stood charged in a true bill stating that they wandered abroad as "petty Chapmen, using the subtle and crafty art of buyinge and sellinge of feather bedtikes, westren coverings, doringe coverings, and other wares belonging to the art and faculty de les Upholsterers" of London. Some others, like Thomas Buckingham, had to answer for carrying their paramours about the country with them, and others were accused of fencing stolen goods. In support of the last charge, there is the damaging admission of Autolycus: "My traffic is sheets; when the kite builds, look to lesser linen. . . . Father, like A' was like wise a snapper-up of unconsidered trifles."[44]

43. For his own "trade and traffick" and also "for the use and behoofe of other resorting" to Wethersfield, Arthur Povey persuaded thirteen inhabitants to support his petition for a license to keep the cottage he had recently erected at a convenient place. Essex Sessions, XVII, 53, Somerset Sessions, II, 119; Manchester Court, III, 6; Reading Recs., III, 83.
44. HMC Salisbury, XIII, 609–10; Middlesex Sessions, I, 11–12; Essex Sessions, XX, 428, 452; The Winter's Tale, IV, iii, 8, 23, 26.

The pressures exerted on royal officials resulted in the opening of an office at London in 1618 for licensing all peddlers and petty chapmen who could produce certificates of good behavior and give the required security; no others were to pursue the trade. This measure did not bring the wanted stability, for within a year the justices of Wiltshire learned that William Hackett and some others were disturbing trade between their county and Somersetshire by compelling chapmen to compound for licenses when they already had taken them out.[45]

The pack of Autolycus contained more than trifles, as even the simple country yokel knew well: "Oh, master, if you did but hear the pedlar at the door, you would never dance again after a tabor and pipe; no, the bagpipe could not move you: he sings several tunes faster than you'll tell money; he utters them as he had eaten ballads and all men's ears grew to his tunes." Nothing could be less true than recent statements that only city people purchased ballads. "I send you likewise such pedlarie pamflets and threehalfpeny ware as we are served with," wrote John Chamberlain from the country. In 1630, James Bowle, Michael Sparke, Nicholas Bourne, and Henry Overton, London stationers, had to answer to the Ecclesiastical Commissioners for permitting more than one hundred copies of a supposedly scandalous religious work to be taken off for distribution at Oxford, Salisbury, and elsewhere. In addition to the ballads, *Guy of Warwick,* forbidden tracts, and the chapbooks which they usually sold, the chapmen offered the seventeenth-century equivalent of green stamps in the form of gossip, rumors, and true news, which assisted rural Englishmen in keeping reasonably well informed about current happenings all over the realm.[46]

Testimony to the social and economic as well as the political needs for improved communications came with the first fumbling effort to set up a postal system. At the beginning of the century, carriers were the sole means of sending letters from one place to another. In 1603, perhaps because of their remote location, the mayors, aldermen, and tradesmen in the towns of North Devon attempted to remedy "the uncertain conveyance of letters sent to or

45. *Bibliotheca Lindesiana* I, 144; *CSPD, 1611–18,* pp. 451, 551; *1619–23,* p. 84.
46. *The Winter's Tale,* IV, iv, 162, 186, 191–2, 606ff; *Chamberlain, Letters,* I, 57; *CSPD, 1629–31,* pp. 159, 166, 202, 203–4.

from London"—it took at least twenty days to get answers to their communications. They managed to cut the time to eleven days by having a "foot post" from Barnstaple make a connection with a foot post that left Exeter for London every Tuesday. Canterbury had a foot post by 1608. The Plymouth-London post regularly picked up or delivered letters at Shaftesbury, Sherborne, and Crewkerne in 1620, and by 1628 there were posts over most of England.[47]

The postal service became official in 1629, when a number of postmen on the "Westerne Stages, London to Plymouth," received orders from the Lords of the Council to deliver letters along the road and as much as twenty miles off it "if need shall requier." If the service had been poor, there was some excuse, for ninety-nine postmen petitioned the Council just prior to this for payment of their salaries, which had been in arrears since November, 1621, and amounted to £22,626.19.3! By 1635 the posts were costing £3,400 a year. It was then proposed that a "stafetto," or packet post, from London to all parts of the kingdom be established; post horses were to be provided, for it was estimated that a rider could cover 120 miles a day in contrast with the sixteen to eighteen of a foot post. Still complaints poured in. The Norwich merchants grumbled because Mr. Witherington of the Post charged more than the private carriers they had used hitherto; furthermore he interfered with private carriers: Jason Grover, common carrier of Ipswich and Yarmouth, and two of his men were imprisoned in the Fleet for seventeen days, presumably because they competed with the Post. Monopolies, it would seem, extended to more than industry.[48]

47. Somehow the news got spread abroad, even in the colonies. "Because men may doubt how we should have intelligence" of the great massacre of 1622 in Virginia, "being we are so farre distant," Edward Winslow explained that in May, 1623, Captain Francis West had stopped at Plymouth on his way back from Damariscove Island off the coast of Maine and informed the Pilgrims. Thus did the report get into *Good News from New England, or a True Relation of Things Very Remarkable at Plymouth in New England . . . Written by E. W.* (1624); *Barnstaple Recs.*, II, 215; *Oxinden Letters*, 7, 25; *Somerset & Dorset*, X, 111; *Plymouth Recs.*, 151; *NEHG Reg.*, LVII, 63; *CSPD, 1628–9*, p. 184.

48. *HMC Exeter*, 66; *CSPD, 1628–9*, p. 184; *1635*, pp. 166, 299; *1635–6*, p. 147; *1637–8*, pp. 216, 284–5; Hamilton, *Quarter Sessions*, 116.

V

"None of your Majesties Subjects dwell further than 100 miles from the Sea-side, which is no great journey," Captain Richard Whitbourne wrote in a tract of 1621 addressed to King James. More than fifty years later Sir Robert Southwell calculated for the Royal Society that the average distance of a plot of land from the sea was twenty-four miles in England, eighty-six in France, much more in Germany, and only one-quarter of a mile in Holland. Given such geographic conditions, fishing naturally absorbed the energies of great numbers of these people, for of all the trades of the Europeans of this age, this one was most important. Thousands upon thousands of Englishmen had something to do with the sea.[49]

French, Dutch, and the English unceasingly contested over the taking of herrings and pilchards in the local waters of the North Sea and the Atlantic south of England. The importance of the off-shore fishery to the English is evident from the fact that in Kent the villages of Milton, Gillingham, and Sharnwell had 2,000 persons dependent upon it. Of Essex Norden said: "The Sea is unto this Shire, a nighe and necessarie neighbour on the easte" for carriage of necessaries "but also in fish and fishing, among the reste, a kind of oyster of highest commendation called the Walfleet oyster." Complaints of foreign competition contained much truth: the fishermen of the ancient fishing havens of Rye, Dunwich, and Yarmouth charged in the 1620's that the Dunkirkers kept their boats from making the usual catches; Tobias Gentleman lamented the virtual monopoly of the herring fishery by the Dutch hoys that sailed into Yarmouth with their cargoes of fish. A Society of Association for Fishing of 1634 aimed at developing English fishing and the exclusion of the Dutch but never attained its goal.[50]

49. Giovanni Botero wrote of the "havens, which are so thicke in this countrey, that by reason of the inlets of the sea, there is not almost one house distant above twenty miles from the Ocean." *The Travellers Breviat: Or an Historicall Description of the most famous kingdomes in the World. . . ,* trans. Robert Johnson (1601), 13; Richard Whitbourne, *A Discourse and Discovery of New-found-land* (1621, 1623), 29; Thomas Birch, *The History of the Royal Society of London for the Improving of Knowledge* (London, 1757), III, 208; Wedgwood, *King's Peace,* 25.
50. *Western Antiquary,* VIII, 122; *VCH Kent,* III, 429; Norden, Chorographical Description, 16; *VCH Sussex,* II, 268; *CSPD, 1627–8,* pp. 62, 107–8, 512;

In the sixteenth century, the English joined with fishermen of other maritime nations in searching the waters off Europe, Iceland, and America for new sources of fish, which they wanted more for trading than for food at home. From 1610 to 1617 the Muscovy Company quietly engaged in killing whales and "sea horses" off Greenland and Iceland, "which yeelds above *cento pro cento,* with a short return and small charge," until the French, Spanish, and Hollanders moved in. Far more lucrative and extensive was the catching of cod on the Grand Banks off Newfoundland, which led to new discoveries and eventually to the first English settlements in America.[51]

By concentrating their interests in the ports of the West Country, using larger vessels, emphasizing the dry fishery that required less salt, and marketing their catches and procuring salt in the Roman Catholic countries, the English supplanted the French as the chief participants in the Newfoundland fishery. After they disposed of the bulk of their cod in Spain, Portugal, and Italy, the masters brought their ships home to havens in Dorset and Devon with cargoes of fish oil for making soap and pipes of wine from the Biscayan port of Viana—hence their name of *Sack Ships.* Between 1608 and 1620, according to one report, Newfoundland had come to be regarded as a "hopeful country," which yearly employed hundreds of ships and thousands of British seamen who, in turn, relieved thousands more of the needy people in the west of England and yielded a customs revenue of almost £10,000. "Fishermen are chiefly to be cherished," Sir Dudley Digges argued in Parliament, "for they bring in much wealthe, and carry out nothing."[52]

Men waxed enthusiastic over future prospects of this great traffic and published tracts to arouse the interest of ordinary Englishmen in such undertakings. In one of 1620, John Mason, fresh from Newfoundland, told of "Cods so thicke by the shoare that we

---

1628–9, p. 63; *1633–4,* pp. 25, 42, 167, 179, 191, 390. For tracts promoting the offshore English fishery to compete with the Dutch, see Gentleman, *England's Way to Win Wealth,* and I. R., *The Trades Increase.*

51. The indispensable work is Harold A. Innis, *The Cod Fisheries* (New Haven, 1940), 26–49; Chamberlain, *Letters,* I, 482.

52. Innis, *Cod Fisheries,* 50, 52, 54n, 79; J. N. Williamson, *The English Channel: A History* (London, 1959), 228–9; Russell, *Dartmouth,* 82, 83, 84; *CSP Col., 1574–1660,* pp. 25, 170; Vaughan, *Golden Fleece,* Pt. III, 14; *Proceedings and Debates of the British Parliaments Respecting North America,* I, 60.

heardlie have been able to row a Boate through them, I have killed
them with a Pike." Merchants in seaports all the way from Southampton to Poole, to Plymouth, to Dartmouth, to Fowey, and
around to Bideford and Barnstaple hastened to fit out ships for the
Banks fishery. In five small, coastal parishes of Devon, 800 persons engaged in the Newfoundland fisheries in 1635. Despite inroads made by pirates, the annual traffic from Plymouth and Dartmouth alone amounted to about 26,700 tons of shipping, and employed 10,680 mariners; these vessels returned with dried codfish
("Poor John") and more than 1,000 tons of train oil worth
£17,000. The total venture cost the backers £178,390 and netted
around £24,000, a return of more than 13 per cent on their investment.[53]

Codfish abounded everywhere in the coastal waters and along
the submerged continental shelf off the northeast parts of North
America, and the fishermen naturally moved southwestward to
take them. In the New England waters the cod were even better
and larger, but their very thickness prevented proper drying and
kept them away from the markets of southern Spain. Captain John
Smith thought hake even better than cod: "Now each hundred you
take here, is as good as two or three hundred in New Found
Land," and they can be got to market a month or so ahead of the
Banks' catch. The number of ships sent from the West Country to
New England rose from ten in 1621 to fifty by 1624. At Dorchester, in 1623, John White made plans with Robert Davy of
Crediton and other Devon gentlemen to set up a plantation "for
the better and more convenient saving of fish . . . in those parts"
and to barter Crediton cloth for beaver skins with the natives. The
venture failed, but the connection between fishing and settlement
had been made in the minds of the promoters and before long
would have momentous consequences. Sack ships bound for New
England carried both freight and passengers to Massachusetts Bay

53. John Mason, *A Briefe Discourse of the New-found-land* (Edinburgh, 1620),
5; Whitbourne's widely circulated *Discourse and Discovery of Newfoundland;*
Levett, *Voyage into New England,* 7, 9; Smith, *General Historie of New England,*
in *Travels and Works,* II, 709–10, 760, 767; Hutchins, *Dorset,* I, 40; Caldwell,
Devonshire, 139–42; *Plymouth Recs.,* 223; *Southampton Recs.,* II, 38, 39;
CSPD, 1625–6, p. 81; *1628–9,* p. 103; *1634–5,* p. 393; *1635–6,* p. 30; *1638–9,* p.
563; *Acts of Privy Council, Colonial,* I, 38–9; *Commons Debates 1621,* (New
Haven, 1935), IV, 368.

in the 1630's, and by the end of our period, Dutch ships were sailing up there from the Caribbean laden with tobacco and salt to exchange for lumber, staves, and codfish to feed the Negro slaves in the islands.[54]

It is not within the province of this work to treat the English economy with the fullness it deserves or to describe the opening of the Mediterranean and East Indian markets. Nor are we concerned about the significant accumulation of capital and noteworthy business organization achieved by the chartered companies. All these matters have been thoroughly discussed by other writers. It is pertinent, however, to note that the codfish taken in North American waters furnished the means by which England wrested a share of the New World from Spain, and it may be added that all of her fisheries enabled her merchants to extend commerce into the Iberian Peninsula and then into the Mediterranean after the peace of 1603.[55]

The activities of shipping and trading came under the aegis of the merchants of London and the outports acting singly or in concert. As a class they still await a chronicler who will, among other matters, explain just how much they owed to the examples and methods of their Italian, German, French, and Dutch predecessors.

54. Sir William Monson prepared an excellent account of the fisheries c. 1625–40, *Naval Tracts*, ed. M. Oppenheim (Navy Records Society, 1914), V, 281–2; see also an excellent cartouche of the codfishery operations on Herman Moll's *Map of North America* (c. 1715), in the John Carter Brown Library. "Dry virginea fish" and "Corr-fish" arrived at Plymouth in 1618, and vessels from Bristol and Barnstaple called at the Chesapeake from time to time. Letters from Virginia reached John Smyth at Berkeley near Bristol via Newfoundland in 1620. *Plymouth Recs.*, 151; Smyth, in N. Y. Public Library, *Bulletin*, III, 280; Smith, *Travels and Works*, II, 713; *Southampton Recs.*, III, 4, 44; Innis, *Cod Fisheries*, 72–9; T. W. Venn, Crediton als Critton als Kirton (Rev., 1960, Exeter City Library, Muniment Room), II, 307; *Winthrop's Journal*, I, 151–2, II, 89.

55. On these matters consult the thorough study by Ralph Davis, The Organization and Finance of the English Shipping Industry in the Later Seventeenth Century (Ph.D. Thesis, London, 1955); H. G. Rawlinson, *British Beginnings in Western India, 1576–1657* (Oxford, 1920); Thomas Mun, *A Discourse of the Trade, from England unto the East Indies* (1621); *A True Relation . . . of the East Indies*, in *Harleian Miscellany*, I, 258–62; Annie Marie Millard, The Import Trade of London, 1600–1640 (Ph.D. Thesis, London, 1956); Julian S. Corbett, *England in the Mediterranean* (London, 1924); and the standard discussion of trading companies and commercial activities by the late Professor Charles M. Andrews, *The Colonial Period of American History* (New Haven, 1934), I, 1–75.

"Never in the annals of the modern world," Lord Keynes wrote somewhat extravagantly of the years 1600–1642, "has there existed so prolonged and so rich an opportunity for the business man, the speculator, and the profiteer." In some measure, most rich, successful merchants revealed all of these traits. Whether they were the great merchants, such as the Reskeimers of Dartmouth, the Delbridges of Barnstaple, Sir Thomas Smyth and the Courteens of London, or the lesser men of smaller resources and renown, such as Martin Bradgate of the metropolis, Matthew Cradock of Southampton, Thomas Gregory of Taunton, or William Pynchon of Springfield in Essex, all of them figured decisively in modernizing the economy of their country.[56]

Not every merchant was successful in these "brisk and giddy-paced times." "We have many banckrupts daylie, and as many protections, which doth marvaylously hinder all manner of commerce," Chamberlain recorded in 1612. As trade extended so did the need to be well-informed. In *The City-Match*, the uncle says of his factor: "Cypher shall teach you French, Italian, Spanish, and other Tongues of Traffique." A knowledge of merchants' accounts, and even of "short hand" were considered advantageous, and several useful manuals appeared to assist the ambitious. The best one was by a former employee of the East India Company, J. Carpenter: *A Most Excellent Instruction for the exact and perfect keeping of Merchants Bookes of Accounts, By Way of Debtor and Creditor, after the Italian Manner* (1632). This work contained a list of the kinds of blank books required, provided excellent examples and illustrations, gave instructions about acting as a factor, and supplied much pertinent mercantile lore. In *Enchiridion Arithmeticon. Or a Manual of Millions* (1634), Schoolmaster Richard Hodges simplified calculating and mensuration into tables "as a special help for the sparing of much time." [57]

Equally important for merchants trading overseas or their fac-

56. J. M. Keynes, *A Treatise on Money* (New York, 1930), II, 159; *CSP Col., 1574–1660*, p. 48; R. H. Tawney, *Business and Politics under James I* (Cambridge, Eng., 1958) on Lionel Cranfield; *DNB*, LIII, 424; XII, 436; *CSPD, 1637–8*, p. 403; *Southampton Recs.*, I, Pt. II, 574; *Western Antiquary*, VII, 62; Waters, *Gleanings*, II, 867; *Merchants and Merchandise in Seventeenth Century Bristol*, ed. Patrick McGrath (Bristol, 1955); N. C. P. Tyack, Bristol and Virginia, 7–14.
57. Chamberlain, *Letters*, I, 399, 410–11; Mayne, *The City-Match*, I, iii.

tors, who resided in foreign parts, was the kind of information supplied by the several geographies—works which also appealed to the reading public. One of the more comprehensive tracts was *Geography Delineated Forth in Two Bookes,* by Nathaniel Carpenter (Oxford, 1625), which earned a second revised edition in 1635. Lewis Roberts, a merchant in the Turkey trade, produced an unusually fine manual, *The Merchants Mappe of Commerce,* which contained special instructions for travelers abroad, ambassadors, and merchants, and which the author based "upon the knowledge of Geographie and the use of Mapps and Sea-Cards in generall." He stressed the arts of merchandizing, bartering, and trucking, according to the customs in foreign parts, such as Aleppo, Agra, and Nuremberg; one of the earliest systematic books about commerce, this treatise drew on Italian, French, and German works for its information, and gave an unusually large amount of space to America, "now adayes passing by the name of the west Indies." I. B., a merchant of Bristol, issued *The Merchants Aviza or Instructions very necessary for their Sonnes and Servants, when they first send them beyond the Seas* (1640), which contained much advice that can be summed up in the phrase: Have a care, lads.[58]

As knowledge of currents, tides, climate, and trading practices increased, so too did the volume of the overseas carrying trade. To meet the demand for additional ships, the shipbuilding industry everywhere expanded, and more and more artisans turned to building vessels of all sizes from pinnaces to "tall ships" of 300 to 400 tons. Such outports as Rye and Bristol developed into shipbuilding centers: the former excelled in fishing boats and barques; the latter was known for larger craft suitable for the Irish, Newfoundland, and Virginia trades. As London came to handle treble the value of the combined commerce of the other ports, her shipbuilders naturally won primacy. Under the leadership of Matthew Baker, a "famous artist of his time," Captain Phineas Pett, and

---

58. Other geographies of the time are: William Pemble, *A Briefe Introduction to Geography* (Oxford, 1630); and Robert Stafforde, *A Geographical and Anthological Description of all the Empires in this Globe* (1607, 1618); Roberts, *The Merchants Mappe of Commerce,* 1, 13, 21–3, 46–50 (bills of exchange), 54, 57 (Virginia and New England), 57–8 (Newfoundland fisheries). On the interesting interrelationship of these tracts and their bearing on colonization and British policy, see Andrews, *The Colonial Period of America History,* I, 411n.

their fellow craftsmen, the Thames industry built most of the ships for the royal service as well as those for distant commerce. In 1618 the shipwrights of Dartmouth and "the west parts" protested their inability to conform to the regulations published by the "Company of Shipwrights of Rotherhithe," which required them to work only under the Company's supervision and rules, and to pay the Company threepence a day from their wages.[59]

Possibly it was a desire to sail on ships which they themselves had helped to build, or else a desire to see the world, but something impelled more than one shipwright to cross the seas to distant lands. With the Winthrop Fleet in 1630 sailed William Stephens, builder of the *Royal Merchant* of 600 tons and as "able a shipwright as there is, hardly such another to be found in this kingdom, and two or three others." From Devon, where he owned fourteen acres of land, Henry Cade, shipwright, crossed the Atlantic to Boston. The most famous of the many Puritan shipbuilders, however, was Nehemiah Bourne, a son of a shipwright of Wapping. He became a merchant in the Bay Town and built ships there, but later he returned to serve Cromwell as a rear admiral and then became an Elder Brother of Trinity House. Thus the most complex of colonial industries found its leaders among Puritan artisans of Stepney Parish and the Thames-side.[60]

Long voyages and the use of larger vessels presented problems of ship handling and navigation. Maps and charts were crude, but pilots and seamen had no choice but to study them. Such works as *The Art of Dialling in Two Parts* (1609) by John Blagrove and another by Edward Wright in 1614 were superseded in 1638 by a far better exposition by Samuel Foster, the astronomer of Gresham College, entitled *Art of Dialling by a New, Easie, and Most Speedy Way*. The versatile Captain John Smith brought out *An Accidence or the path-way to experience necessary for all young seamen* (1626), which he "enlarged" in 1627 as *A Sea Grammar*

---

59. Ramsay, *English Overseas Trade*, 161; Willan, *Coasting Trade*, 11; MacInnes, *Gateway to Empire*, 19; Davis, English Shipping, table, pp. 10–11; *Sussex Arch.*, XXVII, 87; XLVIII, 14; *VCH Sussex*, II, 235; Roberts, *Southern Counties*, 53; *CSPD, 1603–10*, p. 211; *The Autobiography of Phineas Pett*, ed. W. G. Perrin (Navy Records Society, 1928); Dartmouth Recs., DD 61946.
60. *CSP Col. Addenda, 1574–1660*, p. 158; Waters, *Gleanings*, I, 761; II, 1213; W. R. Chaplin in *CSM*, XLII, 28–47.

. . . with the modest disclaimer that he had been "a miserable Practitioner in this Schoole of Warre by Sea and Land more than thirty years." These books were not naval guides, but exceedingly accurate and practical little manuals that described a seaman's outfit, vocabulary, and duties—a sort of seventeenth-century version of the *Bluejacket's Manual* of the United States Navy.[61]

Many sea captains used rutters, or sailing directions. One of these by Daniel Elfryth sums up the knowledge of the Caribbean he acquired between 1607 and 1631 for the Providence Company. It includes useful descriptions of how the several islands looked from the sea, which must have been of inestimable value, plus a few diagrams and charts of harbors. In one of Heywood's plays a master remarks contemptuously:

> A Scholler in his study knowes the starres
>
>   *   *   *
>
> But set him to the Compasse, hee's to seeke,
> When a Plain Pilot can direct his course
> From hence unto both th' Indies; can bringe backe
> His ship and charge, with profits quintuple.[62]

In this age, the life of the seafarer was tedious, hard, and dangerous. Some mariners turned into "sea roughs," who brawled with each other aboard ship or on shore. This is not surprising when we realize that *Abraham,* a vessel of only 200 tons, bound for Barbados, had cooped up on board for the long journey, the master, two mates, a boatswain, gunner, and carpenter, each with his mate, the cook, the surgeon, and nineteen deckhands. Their food was seldom good, often unconscionably bad, and scurvy inevitably afflicted crews on long voyages. The *Black George,* 250 tons, out of Southampton for Cape Verde, thence bound for New England and Bordeaux in 1630, had taken on 50 tons of ship's beer made by two Southampton brewers, Christopher Benbury and Thomas Rowte. When the ship returned to her home port, seven hogsheads of Benbury's brew were "dead and sower not fitting for men to

61. Wright, *A Short Treatise of Dialling* . . . (1614); C. Saltonstall, *The Navigator* (1642); and the weighty work of David W. Waters, *The Art of Navigation in England in Elizabethan and Early Stuart Times* (London, 1958).
62. "Daniel Elfryth's Guide to the Caribbean," in *WMQ,* 3d ser., I, 273–316; Thomas Heyward, *The English Traveller* (1613), I, i.

drinke," and eleven tuns of Rowte's "did stinke insomuch that noe man was able to drinke it"—three sailors testified in the Mayor's Court that in more than twenty years on the oceans they had "never knowne any like unto it in respect of the stincke," yet they had had no choice but to drink it during their voyage.[63]

All fishermen and many mariners, save on the largest vessels, lived in the open aboard undecked craft; they knew what it was to be chilled to the bone and constantly drenched with salt spray. The loss of life from maritime accidents and disasters was very great. On November 12, 1619, a tilt-boat laden with sixty clothiers going home from Gravesend to nearby Kent was overturned by a ship under sail, with the loss of forty lives. Many a sailor was washed overboard by the tempestuous waves of the North Sea, or off Newfoundland or Maine, or in mid-ocean, and few mariners and fewer landlubbers could swim.[64]

During war times, life at sea was even more hazardous. Conditions on the King's ships for the common sailors were worse, if anything, than on privately owned vessels, but those fortunate enough to escape the naval service had to fight their own ships against the enemy. A ship's complement could rarely be put together without resort to press gangs. In 1625 Viscount Wimbledon took eight vessels out against the Spanish: seventy of his crews were "kidnapped from Lynne, 30 from Wells"; he complained that they were all sullen! He also accused these same sailors of allowing enemy vessels to escape from Cadiz. This charge seems more plausible than Sir John Coke's assertion that "our seamen generally are most resolute protestants, and will be killed or thrown overboard rather than be forced to shed the blood of [French] protestants." Some English sailors may have avoided pitched battles for one reason or another, but the loss of life was extremely heavy, and England had incalculable numbers of mariners' widows and orphans.[65]

Of all the dangers the English faced at sea, capture by the pirates of Algiers, Tunis, or Sallee was the most dreaded. Some seven thousand men sailed regularly from the outports of the

63. Worth, *Plymouth,* 60; Knyvett, *Letters,* 76; Davis, English Shipping, 110; *Southampton Recs.,* II, 82–3.
64. Chamberlain, *Letters,* II, 273.
65. Hillen, *King's Lynn,* I, 339; *CSPD, 1625–6,* p. 59.

southwest, and they all knew the risks, for the Moors had dared to push their galleys to the very shores of England and Ireland. Several times they had landed on the Devon coast and carried off women and children. They even terrorized the fishermen on the Grand Banks. What was particularly sickening was that some of the masters who piloted heathen ships were renegade, Christian Englishmen.[66]

These captures were not rare, isolated incidents involving an occasional ship and a few men, for hundreds of ships were taken and thousands of men imprisoned. On February 7, 1619, for instance, the Council told of 300 ships that had recently been captured and their crews made slaves, and for whose release the captors were demanding huge ransoms. Merchants of London and the inhabitants of the coast towns, from which most of the captives had sailed, promised to contribute large sums to finance a rescuing expedition if King James would send one out. In 1625 the Mayor of Plymouth wrote to the Council that losses were occurring daily— in one year 1,000 mariners, besides ships, had fallen prey to the Turks.[67]

The wives of imprisoned seamen, most of them destitute, added their pleas for a rescuing expedition. Nearly 2,000 of them, in 1626, vainly petitioned Buckingham to liberate their husbands, free them from torture, and, most essential of all, save them from conversion to a heathen religion. In 1635, Clare Bowyer, Margaret Hall, Elizabeth Ensam, and Elizabeth Newland headed a thousand distraught women who petitioned King Charles to redeem their husbands, some of whom, for three years, had been condemned to extreme labor, want of sustenance, and had had "no

---

66. A youthful English merchant was captured by the Algerian infidels on December 29, 1631, and kept a prisoner for seven years: "There is no calamitie can befall a man in this life which hath the least parallell to this of Captivitie." Anything that he ever experienced was "easie" when compared to the "Gallies": he slept over his oar one hour in twelve and rowed under ceaseless lashing. Francis Knight's *A Relation of Seaven Years Slaverie under the Turkes of Argeire, suffered by an English Captive Merchant* (1640) is the classic account of the galley-slaves. *Southampton Recs.,* II, v–vi; *CSPD, 1636–7,* pp. 86, 111, 141; Andrew Barker, *A True and Certain Report of the Beginning . . . and Present State of Captains Ward and Dansker, the two Famous Pirates . . .* (1609), A-2.
67. *CSPD, 1619–23,* pp. 12, 21, 25; *1625–6,* pp. 79, 81, 83, 86, 89; *Acts of Privy Council, 1623–5,* p. 31.

spiritual food for their souls" at Sallee. Finally in 1637, Captain William Rainsborough took a squadron of six vessels against Sallee, which was engaged in a civil war among the Moors, and, by promising English neutrality, secured the release of 271 prisoners. The failure of the Stuarts to wipe out the menace of the Barbary pirates probably caused misery to more people than any other delinquency on their part.[68]

Sweethearts, wives, and children left behind when mariners sailed away experienced griefs and troubles too. Edward Abbott and Elizabeth Morcome had no more than "promised each other to marry" when Edward was sent to trade in the "Streights of Aleppo." It was twelve long years before he returned and "re-

68. About 1635, the ecclesiastical authorities worked out a form for use in Exeter and other West Country ports: "A forme of Pennance and Reconciliacon of a Renegado, or Apostate, from the Christian Religion to Turcisme." *Western Antiquary*, III, 41–2, 44–5. A Shropshire lad of seventeen, Vincent Lukes [Lucas] was bound to a cook of Ratcliffe in Stepney Parish. His master "set him forth to Sea in a Cooks place," and on a voyage "for Genoway" in 1636 he was captured by a Turkish pirate and sent to Algiers, where he was sold in "the Market-place as a slave and given to the "King's" brother, who sold him to a Negro. The latter treated him "most cruelly," forced him to renounce his faith, foreswear Christ, be circumcised, and become a Muslim. Then the Negro sold him to a Grecian who put him aboard a Turkish ship as a soldier. He joined with two other Englishmen and a circumcised Fleming in seizing the ship and sailing it into a Spanish port, where their prisoners and the vessel sold for £600, out of which Lukes got £150. He then returned to England but soon shipped out for Greenland. He found himself "much troubled night and day" and unable to sleep "through horrour of Conscience for denying his Christian Faith." Once back in Stepney, he sought out his curate, who took up the case with Bishop Juxon. A "solemme, pious and grave forme of Penance" was "prescribed for admitting him again into the Christian Church," which consisted of sitting prominently in the parish church of Stepney while the celebrated William Gouge preached a sermon on the text "He was lost, and is found." The minister held that Lukes was lost when he became a "Renegado," not before when he was threatened with death but when he renounced his faith. Gouge also improved the occasion by ringing the changes on the Christian Martyrs, made famous by John Foxe, and spoke directly to his large audience: "You Mariners, Merchant-factors, and others whose calling it is to *goe to sea in ships and doe business in the great waters*, where ye are in danger to be surprized (as this Penitent was), by the moral Enemies of Christians, or have occasion to abide and Traffique among them: You may be brought to trial, and to give proofs before men, whether the habit of Martyredome be in you or no." William Gouge, *A Recovery from Apostacy, Set out in a Sermon, Preached in Stepney Church neere London at the receiving of a Penitent Renegado into the Church (1639)*; CSPD, 1625–6, pp. 516, 517; 1635–6, p. 15; John Dunton, *A True Journal of the Sally Fleet* (1637); Gardiner, *England*, VIII, 270.

newed his old love." There were many instances when one or the other of a married couple proved unfaithful: John Tucker, a Ratcliffe brewer, was charged in the Middlesex Sessions with "begetting with child Joan, wife of Richard Turbister," a Limehouse sailor, while he was absent in the East Indies.[69]

The practical matter of supporting a family concerned both the wife and her seafaring husband. Ship owners frequently neglected, or at least delayed, paying off their crews when they returned from a voyage. If a man protested too much, he might lose the chance to sign on again. Furthermore most contracts were verbal, and if the case went to trial the sailor had no evidence. If the husband died at sea, the wife was completely at the mercy of her adversary. In order to protect themselves from unscrupulous masters, the common sailors of London sought to have a registrar be resident near the Customs House in London, and others in the outports, to record their covenants. Other crewmen might find themselves in financial difficulties, like the men of the *Margaret and John,* whose master died in Virginia in 1623. When their wages were held up, they petitioned Governor Wyatt, claiming that "most of us have wiffe and Children in England whose releife and mantenance onlie [are] depending upon our wages." Fortunately the Council took care of them. Uncertainty and anxiety clouded the lives of thousands of seafaring men and their families.[70]

In 1635 the English owned 499 ships of 100 tons or more burthen, which were manned by 10,328 seamen. The need to gain a living sent most of these men and boys to sea, but some, like Edward Coxere [Coxery], who came from a seafaring family at Dover, were trained for the sea and commerce from their early days. When Coxere was fourteen, his parents sent him over to Havre de Grâce to learn French; he went with two other boys, and stayed for eleven months. Later he became a "linguister" in Dutch, Spanish, and the *lingua-franca* of the Mediterranean. For a time he worked as a cooper in Zeeland; then he made a voyage to San Sebastian: "I did then begin to grow hardy and did not think so much of home." On Dutch and English ships he had experi-

---

69. Wood, Barnstaple, n. p., December, 1602; *Middlesex Sessions,* n. s., II, 179; *Southampton Recs.,* II, 37, 56–7.
70. *HMC Exeter,* 293; *CSPD, 1635–6,* p. 16; *Recs. Va. Co.,* IV, 97.

ences aplenty, and once he made the three-cornered Newfoundland-Spain-England journey. Instead of doing scrimshaw work, he kept a journal which was unique for the fine illustrations he drew in it of incidents at sea. Christopher Newport of Limehouse went to sea as a lad, saw much of privateering in the Caribbean, and rose to be a master's mate, a master, and finally a captain whom Samuel Purchas accounted "A Mariner well practiced for the Westerne parts of America." [71]

These were the successful master mariners who, with their rough, hard-worked, wind- and sea-lashed English crews, relished an opportunity to recreate in distant parts any diversion which would remind them of home. On September 5, 1607, two ships on the way out to India (*Hester,* Captain Hawkins, and *Dragon,* Captain Keeling) lay at anchor in the road at Sierra Leone. A Portugese interpreter from the native king came aboard *Dragon* to see Captain Keeling, "wher we gave the tragedie of Hamlett." On the 30th, Keeling noted, "Captain Hawkins dined with me, wher my companions acted Kinge Richard the Second." The next day "I envited Captain Hawkins to a Fishe dinner, and had Hamlet acted abord mee: which I p'mitt to keepe my people from idlenes and unlawfull games or sleepe." [72]

---

71. *CSPD, 1634–5,* p. 531; *Adventures of Edward Coxere,* ed. E. H. W. Meyerstein (New York, 1946), xii, 3–5, 11; K. P. Andrews, in *WMQ,* 3d ser., XI, 28–41.
72. *Narratives of Voyages Towards the North-West in Search of a Passage to Cathay and India, 1496–1631,* ed. Thomas Rundall (Hakluyt Society, 1849), V, 231.

VII

The Rulers and the Ruled

O H, WHAT IS MAN Unless he be a politician?" asks Renel
in *The Revenge of Bussy d'Ambois.* Chapman here implies
that all or most of the English concerned themselves about politics.
The fact is, of course, that in Jacobean and Caroline times the business of ruling was conducted exclusively by and for nobles and gentlemen; members of the lower orders and the great majority of the
middling people in the remoter parts of the realm knew next to nothing about the conduct of foreign affairs or of the policies of King,
Court, and Parliament—which are the topics usually treated by
historians. Alien to most men, too, was any awareness of even
such widely bruited economic abuses as monopolies, pensions, the
sale of titles, and lavish grants to favorites—at least until the results of royal largess affected their own little communities. To
comprehend the attitudes of plain people toward government, we
must study the village institutions in which they gained familiarity
with the law, and only then proceed outward and upward from
these to the great game of politics at London and Westminster.[1]

A vastly different matter was the law. "Law complicated and
hazardous brooded . . . over the village, exacting public duties
from selected villagers. . . . It lay in wait for everyman. . . .
The drenching of English life and consciousness with the sense of
law, with the rights of law, with the methods of law, with the

1. George Chapman, *The Revenge of Bussy D'Ambois* (1613), I, i.

obligations of law, was very old. . . ." And going to law was a normal and not infrequent act of the ordinary man's existence.[2]

This was an argumentative, contentious, litigious age. Suing and being sued, charging and counter-charging one's neighbors, were among the conspicuous features of community life. Some people went into court for redress, others merely for the thrill of the venture. The spectators, whom no court session ever lacked, assembled for the show, most of them hoping to see some bold countryman or shrewd townsman "bite the law by the nose," while the few connoisseurs eagerly anticipated the performances of subtle men who knew how to bid "the law make court'sy to their will." In 1603, Parliament recognized that "by reason of the great increase of people, the . . . profits and perquisites of courts are grown to be of a better yearly value than in ancient times," and that an act was needed "to prevent the overcharge of the people by stewards of court-leets and court-barons."[3]

II

On hundreds of manors throughout the land, long-established judicial bodies continued to operate as remarkably vital institutions whose importance grew rather than diminished during the first decades of the seventeenth century.[4] Ordinarily each manor had both a court-leet and a court-baron, and sometimes, a customary court of copyhold tenants as well. Here and there, as at Petworth in Sussex, the judicial and administrative functions of these courts were

2. G. Kitson Clark, *The English Inheritance: An Historical Essay* (London, 1950), 26–7.

3. "The people of the southwestern counties were probably the most litigious souls of England," one authority holds, but those of the other shires south of the Humber pressed them hard. Raymond P. Stearns, *The Strenuous Puritan: Hugh Peter, 1598–1660* (Urbana, 1954), 11; *Measure for Measure,* II, iv, 172; III, i, 108–9; II, i, 1; Chute, *Shakespeare of London,* 181; Pickering, *Statutes at Large,* VII, 80–81.

4. In this chapter no comprehensive chronicle or political-science analysis is intended, because there are a number of excellent treatises on the subject. Sidney and Beatrice Webb, *English Local Government from the Revolution to the Municipal Corporations Act* is indispensable, especially the volumes on *The Parish and the County* (London, 1906) and *The Manor and the Borough* (1908). Among other recent useful studies are Eleanor Trotter, *Seventeenth Century Life in a Country Parish* (Cambridge, Eng., 1919); and W. E. Tate, *The Parish Chest.*

combined into one undifferentiated "Court of Honour" that met every three weeks on Tuesday. Similarly in Essex in 1617–18, Adam Winthrop kept both the court-leet and court-baron as one at Groton Hall.[5]

The police power of a manor resided in the court-leet. The lord or his representative, the steward, selected certain "inhabitants" for a jury and instructed them about their responsibilities. Manorial records indicate that these courts met twice a year, or oftener if conditions warranted it, to deal with a variety of petty offenses, such as affrays and bloodsheds, different kinds of thievery, drunkards, "continual tavern haunters," eavesdroppers, and "such as sleep by day and watch by night, and eat and drink and have nothing." The steward and jury also provided stocks and cuckingstools, stopped illegal games and sports, and dealt with the many cheats who were discovered giving short measure, using false weights, or making goods of bad quality or violating the assize of bread and ale. Furthermore, the court-leet investigated many civil concerns, such as disputes over walls, hedges, paths and ways, water courses, and nuisances. The high crimes of felony, rape, embezzlement, witchcraft, rebellion, and petty treason they presented to the shire court of quarter sessions. Upon the nomination of the jury, the steward appointed a constable (who executed any punishments meted out), the aleconners, and a long list of other petty officers.[6]

The number of officials appointed annually at the court-leet naturally varied according to the size and peculiar needs of a manor, i.e. if there was a market to be supervised. In 1618 at Manchester, a very large manor, Oswald Moseley, the steward, had to find ninety-six worthy men to recommend to his jury of sixteen for nomination to the many onerous posts, which included twelve "dog and great bitch officers" to patrol the streets and make sure that all canines were either muzzled or chained up, and two killjoys to stop the playing of football in the village streets. By 1630

5. Lord Leconfield, *Petworth Manor in the Seventeenth Century* (Oxford, 1954), 2, 3, 8; *Winthrop Papers*, I, 92, 99, 103, 217; Ault, in *CSM*, XLII, 177.
6. *Manchester Court*, I, ix–xv; Wilkinson, *A Treatise*, 77–80, 83–9; K. C. Newton, Proceedings of the Courts of the Manor of Wethersfield, Essex (1558–1603) [Typed calendar, Essex Record Office], Introduction, 1–3; Webb, *Manor and Borough*, 4–8.

this roll of unpaid public servants had risen to 107. In 1620 a justice of the peace, again Oswald Moseley, swore in twenty-nine
manorial officers for the Manor of Salford, which adjoined Manchester. At much smaller Clare, in Suffolk, in 1612 the eighteen
members of the court-leet confirmed the steward's nomination of
thirteen petty officials. A tiny place like Kempsey, the Worcestershire home of Edward Winslow the Pilgrim, or Scrooby or Wethersfield or the Winthrop's manor of Groton did not require the services of so many inhabitants.[7]

Anyone who reads the manorial records cannot fail to be astonished at the extensive participation of nearly every adult male in
local affairs. Sooner or later, through appointment by manorial
courts, the artificer, the copyholder, the poor husbandman, and
even the day laborer were called upon; and when they were not
serving their fellow inhabitants in unsought and time-consuming
ways, these men attended courts, for their presence was expected
at most sessions. To be sure such villagers merely served; they did
not rule, but Sir Thomas Smith had abundant reason to add: "and
yet they be not altogether neglected. For . . . in villages they be
commonly made church-wardens, aleconners, and many times
constables, which office toucheth more the commonwealth, and at
the first was not employed upon such low and base persons." In
writing about the Essex community of Stapleford Abbots, of which
he was the vicar from 1606 to 1620, Godfrey Goodman observed:

> For heere in the countrey with us, if a man's stocke of a few
> beasts bee his own, and that he lives out of debt, and paies his
> rent duly and quarterly, we hold him a very rich and a suffi-
> cient man; one that is able to doe the King and the countrey
> good service; we make him a Constable, a Sides-man, [or] a
> Head-borough, and at length a Church-warden: thus we raise
> him by degrees, wee prolong his ambitious hopes, and at last we
> heape all our honours upon him. *Here is the great governour
> amongst us,* and we wonder that all others do not respect him
> accordingly. . . .[8]

7. *Manchester Court,* III, v, viii, 1–4, 172–5; *Chetham,* XLVI, 154; *Suffolk,* II,
103–4; *CSM,* XLII, 174–98; Baber, in *History Today,* IX, 170–75, 212.
8. Smith, *De Republica Anglorum,* in Dunham and Pargellis, *Complaint and Reform,* 212; Goodman, *The Fall of Man,* 139–40 (Italics mine).

Overseeing common-field agriculture, pastures, wastes, fisheries, weirs, petty trespasses, and actions for debt belonged to the jurisdiction of the court-baron, which was an assembly of tenants under the presidency of the steward or lord. This body chose the reeve, or chief officer, and made by-laws to govern the manor. As a private court of the lord, its object was "the maintenance of the rights of the Lord against his tenants and of the privileges of the tenants against the Lord, together with the settlement of their mutual differences and the organisation of common affairs." In it we can see the link in the development between the early English township moot and the parish meeting of Stuart times.[9]

Prior to 1642, at least, the manorial courts continued to be as much organizations for local government as was the parish or the town. They were the repositories of the "Custom"—in essence, the law of the village—which operated uniformly and, upon the whole, efficiently. In the daily concerns of the mass of Englishmen, customary law figured positively; actually it assumed a greater importance in their eyes than the law of the nation. Just as the common law grew and changed in this age of economic and social instability, so too did village law grow and change. A mounting desire by the public to know more about the jurisdiction and procedures of the manorial courts was met in 1618 by John Wilkinson in *A Treatise . . . concerning the Office . . . of Coroners and Sherifes together with an easie and plaine method for the keeping of a Court Leet, Court Baron, and Hundred Court, &c.,* which reached a third edition by 1638. In this year also, Charles Calthrope published a useful work on *The Relation betweene the Lord of a Mannor and the Copyholder,* which immediately became the authority on the subject and so continued for the balance of the century.[10]

During the sixteenth century there sprang up a new agency of local government, the parish, and in the years from 1590 to 1640 the "town meeting" of the parishioners (today called the vestry) and the manorial courts frequently existed side by side, and their

9. Webb, *Manor and Borough,* 13, 18–19; Wilkinson, *A Treatise,* 113–15; Tate, *Parish Chest,* 305.

10. Ault, in *CSM,* XLII, 178; Kerridge, in *Wiltshire,* VIII, IX, for the manors of Pembroke. Another popular manual for stewards of manors was W. Sheppard, *The Court-Keeper's Guide* (1641).

functions more often than not overlapped. For instance, the records of Stretham, Isle of Ely, in the heart of Puritan Cambridgeshire, for April 29, 1614, contain a series of "Orders and Bylawes
and Paynes made and agreed upon by the Court Leet and alsoe
the Court Baron." Eight years later, those in the same series for
February 24, 1622, are headed as made "by the consent of the
Most Part and the Greatest Number of the Inhabytants of
Stretham both Coppiehowllders and Freehoullders and other Com-
muners there. . . ." Here the open meeting has taken over the
functions of the court-leet, and therefore we must turn to the
parish, for it was becoming the center of local authority.[11]

The men of the seventeenth century used the words *parish* and
town interchangeably; they were territorial designations which did
not denote a cluster of buildings but rather a subdivision of a
county. Originally a parish had been a township having its own
church and clergyman. Then the parish officers began gradually
and unobtrusively to add civil activities to their ecclesiastical employments; it must be emphasized that in the medieval view there
appeared to be no valid distinction between church and state. In
this development, there was no planned similarity discernible
among the thousands of rural and urban parishes. Instead, the
greatest diversity existed: diversity in area, in population, and in
constitutional forms. Heterogeneity, not uniformity, was their sali-
ent characteristic.[12]

Throughout Essex, and in many other places too, the parish had
absorbed many of the administrative activities of the court-leet by
1590. In such instances, the meetings of the inhabitants might consist of "the Most Part and the greatest Number" of the "townsmen," as in Stretham, or be restricted to those whom contemporaries dubbed "the chiefest," "only the principal," "the more sufficient," or "the most substantial." The size of the membership of
these assemblies ran from the many to the oligarchical few; in no

11. Some of the criminal jurisdiction of the court-leet had gone over to the
court of quarter sessions as the manor gave way to the parish. Hull, *Agriculture
. . . in Essex*, 396n; quotation from Stretham MS Records by Tate, *Parish
Chest*, 257; *Sussex Arch.*, XLVIII, 29, 30.

12. Edward Channing, *Town and County Government in the English Colonies*
(Baltimore, 1884), 9–11; Trotter, *Life in the Country Parish*, 1–3; Webb, *Parish
and County*, 6, 11, 178.

modern sense were these bodies democratic. Like the manorial court, however, the parish meeting or the "town meeting," as the inhabitants of Thornage in Norfolk called theirs, was of prime importance because it drew a very large number of parishioners into the paramount business of running their community.[13]

Town meetings of the whole parish or of a limited membership acted as quasi-municipal assemblies for the villages of rural England. It is not overstating it to label them local parliaments. Meeting as often as it seemed necessary, the inhabitants investigated ways and means of conducting the affairs of the parish: they decided the parish rate and methods of collecting it; they administered the common pastures and waste lands; and, by ancient custom, this tiny local parliament, basing its decisions upon the will of the majority of its members, made and enforced by-laws that bound the entire parish. Every year at Easter time, the vestry met in the church to elect local officers and to impose fines upon those who refused to serve. It is an impressive fact that the open-parish or town meeting was the only popular assembly in the realm other than the House of Commons that could impose compulsory taxes. By 1640 it prevailed widely in the countryside, especially south of the Humber.[14]

During the sixteenth century, a movement began in the larger urban communities of London, Westminster, Bristol, and Reading to give this primary assembly a new constitution by limiting its membership to a number between twelve and a hundred (usually

13. The Webbs point out that the word *vestry* did not acquire official recognition in the statute books before 1663. They also state that the parish never received any formal constitutional endorsement by either the Crown or Parliament; like Topsy, it just grew. Webb, *Parish and County*, 5, 14, 15, 37–9, 39n.

14. For rural town meetings, see E. J. Erith, *Woodford, Essex, 1600–1836* (London, 1950), 3; Parish of Coggeshall, Minute Book commencing 1609 (Essex Record Office, D/P 36/81), Easter Day, March 25, 1627; April 13, 1628; April 10, 1631; Ye Town Book Dom 1605 [–1642], Finchingfield, Essex (Essex Record Office D/P 14/8/1A), April 10, 1627; for efforts to get people out for town meetings at Kempsey, Worcestershire, *History Today*, IX, 171–2. For "Ordinances mad by the hole consent of the parishioners" in growing communities, see *The Vestry Minute Book of the Parish of St. Margaret Lothbury, 1571–1677*, ed. E. Freshfield (London, 1887); *Memorials of Stepney Parish*, eds. G. W. Hill and W. H. Frere (Guildford, 1890–91), 45–6; *Barking Vestry Minutes*, ed. J. E. Oxley (Colchester, 1955), 12–13, 23; *Devon & Cornwall*, XXIV, 34; Webb, *Parish and County*, 15, 19, 39, 105.

twelve to twenty-four). These persons, known variously as "the masters of the parish," "the Governors," sometimes as "the kirk-masters," "the ancients," or "the elders," and often as "the gentle-men," "The Twelve," and "the company of Four and Twenty" were, by 1641, "commonly styled Select Vestries." They were to be found across England from the tiny parish of Kilkhampton in Cornwall to the bustling puritan cloth town of Braintree in Essex. At Braintree, the twenty-four "Governors of the Town" or the "Town Magistrates" petitioned the Bishop of London for a faculty to guarantee them official status and enable them to exclude in-truders. In many ways these bodies closely resembled the manorial juries of twelve to twenty-four men who were not elected, and they may, therefore, be regarded merely as an institution transferred from the manor to the parish.[15]

In the creation of select vestries, the desire of the better sort to eliminate the influence of the turbulent "meaner sort" in parish affairs was doubtless a factor, but it is more likely that the diffi-culty of getting a large number of parishioners to attend meetings carried the greater weight. Evidence of this may be gleaned from the fact that, whether the select vestries were created by custom or act of Parliament, or sanctioned by a bishop, such a revolutionary change seems usually to have been made only after "the consent of the whole parishe to elect and chuse out of the same" a specified number of men "to order and define all common causes . . . without molestation or troublinge of the rest of the common peo-ple," as the records of Pittington in the North Riding for 1584 ex-pressed it. Contrariwise, the "whole body" of Londoners of the parish of St. Lawrence, Pountney, voted down the proposal of their vicar to limit the size of the meeting on November 1, 1615.[16]

15. Trotter, *Life in a Country Parish*, 18; Webb, *Parish and County*, 173, 175, 185, 186, 189, 195*n*, 211–12; for the process of creating a select vestry at Lambeth by a bishop's faculty, *Surrey*, XLIV, 205; Morant, *History of Essex*, II, 398.

16. The Bishop of London, in creating at least twenty select vestries between 1606 and 1626, always used the same expression: "the general admittance of the parishioners into the Vestry" had always produced "great disquietude and hindrance to the good proceedings." Webb, *Parish and County*, 91, 184, 186, 189, 190, 191, 192, 193; Sir Henry Spelman, *De Sepultura* (London, 1641), 22–3; *Pittington Parish Records* (*Surtees*, LXXXIV), 12–13; *History Today*, IX,

The danger of control by a few families in country parishes was actually no greater with limited membership than under the former constitutions of the parishes, even though some members of select vestries co-opted themselves. Furthermore, in nearly all of the older parishes of London and its environs, the new vestries had "a sort of latent power," which they exercised now and then, to summon an open meeting of the inhabitants to elect officers and reassess rates. In the parishes of St. Giles-in-the-Fields and St. Botolph, Aldersgate, in 1635, the parishioners as a whole shared the administration with the select vestries.[17]

To insist that the parishioners, irrespective of whether they met in open or closed meeting, were not an autonomous, self-governing, local unit ignores the most important point. As two distinguished historians have phrased it, the parish was "an organ of local obligation." We have seen that the parishioners elected churchwardens and inferior officers, assessed the parish rate, and framed local ordinances. To be sure, their actions were subject to some direction by the justices of the peace and the court of quarter sessions, but of lasting and incalculable significance was the knowledge of their little societies the parishioners gained by participation in the ordering of village life. Nearly all males in the rural parish, officers and servants, learned the rudiments of being governed and, to some extent, of governing.[18]

The most important parish officers were the churchwardens. Ordinarily two were elected, though Boston had three, and sometimes in particularly busy parishes two or more sidesmen were elected to assist them. In addition to their ecclesiastical duties, which will be treated in a later chapter, the churchwardens not only regulated many acts of the parishioner's life but also supervised his morals and attempted to influence his thinking. Given the responsibilities of the office, it is surprising to discover that, in communities where the churchwardens were chosen by rotation or

172; H. Fishwick, *History of Kirkham* (*Chetham*, XCII), 99–100; H. B. Wilson, *History of the Parish of St. Lawrence Pountney* (London, 1831), 167.

17. Webb, *Parish and County*, 40, 288.

18. Webb, *Parish and County*, 40, 173; Sedley L. Ware, *The Elizabethan Parish in its Ecclesiastical and Financial Aspects* (Baltimore, 1903), 12, 63, 91; Carl R. Fish, "The English Parish and Education at the Beginning of American Colonization," in *School Review*, XXIII, 434, 435.

where the occupiers of farms had to serve in turn, women became liable for the duty if they owned or occupied tenements. In Devon, Kilmington had twelve women wardens between 1556 and 1606, and during the seventeenth century, the parishioners of St. Budeau often appointed a man and a woman as churchwardens; the women who served were usually like "Jone" Holwill and Marie Collins of Axmouth, who owned land. The churchwardens of Kilkhampton, Cornwall, were elected from a list of forty-seven householders in 1616, which contained the names of four women; in 1570 eight women declined to serve; in 1567, 1580, and 1598, a woman and a man accepted the posts; and in 1599, two women took the jobs. In the West Country, at least, popular participation in parish administration had been widened to include both sexes.[19]

Next to the wardens, the most important officer of the parish was the petty constable, whom John Selden had in mind when he said, "The parish makes the constable, and when the constable is made he governs the parish." Legally the court-leet elected the constables, but there is evidence that the justices of the peace frequently relied on the nominations of the parishioners, and in many instances the town meeting or the select vestry "chose," "nominated," or more often "elected" the constables along with the other officers at the Easter meeting. The inhabitants of Horndon-on-the-Hill elected the constable in 1601 "for the vill and the parish," and he was thereupon sworn in before a justice. In 1612 the parishioners of Theydon Mount, in a petition to the Essex Court of Quarter Sessions, complained that, seven years previously, the lord of their manor, Sir William Smith, had designated as constable George Mott, "one of the poorest men in all the parish, of evil disposition, and very bad qualities, who hath wronged the parishioners very much, and made great strife amongst them." The appointment had been made "without consent of the parishioners" and, despite public protests, Mott had been continued ever since.

19. Disbursements for a variety of purposes figure in many sets of church-wardens' accounts: see, for example, Dedham Church Wardens, Accounts, 1615–1829 (Essex Record Office); *Hartland Church Accounts* [Devon], *1597–1706*, ed. Ivon L. Gregory (London, 1950), 143, 145, 166, 182; Accounts of Mellis, *Suffolk*, I, 79–83; Brears, *Lincolnshire*, 60; *Western Antiquary*, III, 197, 198; Ware, *Elizabethan Parish*, 42; *Devon & Cornwall*, XXII, 17; XXIV, 33; XIV, 165; Powell, *Puritan Village*, 14–15, 68.

For his place, the inhabitants nominated Thomas Feild, "an honest man," and "a subsidy man and very sufficient for that office." Upon learning that no court-leet or court-baron had been kept at Theydon Mount for more than twenty years, Justice Wynche overruled the lord of the manor and swore Feild in.[20]

No local official had so many and such onerous duties as the constable. He administered the statutes against vagrancy, supervised alehouses, and called the parish meeting; he also made presentments to the court and served the warrants issued by the justices; and, as "the Conservator of the Peace" in his parish, sooner or later he came to know most of the inhabitants. All too frequently he had to proceed against neighbors. Moreover, in preserving the peace, a constable stood in danger of assault: at Woodford, Essex, in 1624, Edmund Saling, victualler, and Daniel Saward, husbandman, set upon Constable John Devereux and threatened "to thrust him in the belly with a knife." In numerous instances, the constable did not live to tell his story to the justices.[21]

When Sir Thomas Smith spoke of the "low and base persons" who achieved the distinction of being constables, he glossed over the burdens placed on these poor officeholders. Indubitably there were others besides John Woodham, the constable of Long Budsley, Northamptonshire, who was summoned to appear before the

20. Channing, *Town and County Government,* 14, 15; Selden, *Table Talk,* CII, quoted in W. S. Holdsworth, *A History of English Law* (London, 1923), IV, 124n; E. J. Erith and E. P. Grieve, *Essex Parish Records, 1240–1894* (Chelmsford, 1950), 16; Essex Sessions, XIX, 92.

21. Each hundred had a "high constable," whom Lord Chief Justice Coke instructed in 1615 to attend at the opening of every assize and to be prepared "for inquiries to be made after felons, vagrants, and rescusants; as also about the decay of houses and husbandry, the tillage of land, alehouses, engrossing and forestalling, maltsters, the relief of the poor, sufficiency of petty constables, masters who have retained servants out of the general petty sessions, or given greater wages than were set down by the justices; the erection of cottages, drunkenness, whoredoms, and incontinency, discharging of servants, and thereby increasing rogues and idle persons, poulterers and purveyors who buy victuals and resell at unreasonable rates, and dove houses erected and maintained by any but the Lord of the manor, or parson of the town." *CSPD, Addenda, 1580–1625,* p. 547. At Terling, in 1630, the high constable also reported on riots and affrays, unlawful assemblies, common scolds, drunkards, Sabbath profaners, disorders in taverns, bowling alleys, gambling, annoying the highways, strangers, and neglecting to set watches. Essex Sessions, XX, 14, 275; Webb, *Parish and County,* 26, 27, 28, 29; *NEHG Reg.,* XXXVI, 274–6; *Somerset Sessions,* II, 61.

Privy Council in 1639 for neglect of office or "touching his denial of payment for ship money." Though unaware of committing any offense, the aged man trudged sixty miles in less than three days, and then, forced to await their lordships' pleasure, he sent in a written request to be informed what it was he was accused of. On the other hand, when the justices of Suffolk discharged T. Linge, the constable of Debenham, in 1640 for "insufficiency," James Freind, who was elected in his place, refused to collect the rates due to Linge. If a constable proved capable, he might serve more than the normal one-year term; of six members of the Russell family who officiated as constables in the little Sussex community of Southover, one of them held the office three times, and four held it twice.[22]

Fortunately for the constables and churchwardens, the law permitted them to pass along some of their duties to two other sets of elected officers. As provided in a statute of 1555, two to four surveyors of the highway, appointed by the constables and churchwardens upon the advice of the parishioners, summoned the inhabitants to render six days of work on the roads each year; these officers were empowered to levy and collect fines from any who refused to comply. In Essex, and possibly in other counties, gentlemen of high social standing were not averse to serving as surveyors. The other group, the overseers of the poor, provided for the parish by the Poor Law of 1597 (39 Elizabeth, C. 5), ordinarily numbered four; they acted with the churchwardens and constables to carry out the many provisions of the law, as will become evident in a later chapter.[23]

All of these offices required literate men who could read proclamations, write answers to queries from county officials, and keep simple accounts accurately. Not every man in a parish had sufficient elementary education to perform these tasks, and the trend toward oligarchical control of local administration in large mea-

---

22. *CSPD, 1635–6*, p. 9; *Suffolk*, XV, 154; *Sussex Arch.*, XLVIII, 35.
23. The standard guide for local officials was William Lambarde's *The Duties of Constables, Borsholders, Tythingmen, and other such lowe and lay Ministers of Peace* (London, 1602, 1614, 1616). Webb, *Parish and County*, 29–31; Erith and Grieve, *Essex Parish Records*, 32; Coggeshall Minute Book, Easter elections for 1627, 1628, 1634; *North Riding Sessions*, IV, 28; *Pittington Parish Records (Surtees*, LXXXIV), 81, 84; *Hertfordshire Sessions*, V, 111.

sure stemmed from this situation. The Court of Quarter Sessions of Wiltshire received a very touching petition in 1616 from a constable praying for release from his office: "forasmuch as I am unlearned, and by reason thereof am constrayned to goe two miles from my howse to have the help of a scrivener to reade such warrants as are sent to mee, and am a very poor man." Doubtless he had had to make the four-mile journey and pay a scrivener to draft his own appeal.[24]

Compulsory service for the parish was commonly exacted from unlettered folk, for poor men could not afford to pay fines for refusing to serve, and consequently they filled the posts of aleconner, town crier, hayward, and other familiar jobs to which the town meeting or the select vestry elected them each Easter. Such offices as these were among the miscellany belonging to the manorial courts which the parish had taken over. The few paid officeholders, subordinates of the churchwardens, were the parish clerk, the sexton, and the bell-ringer. We again emphasize here that upon nearly every man in a country parish fell the burdensome obligation to act in one of these capacities.[25]

The thousands of people who flocked from the country to a nearby borough or to a more distant town or city in search of a better and more exciting existence could recognize there most of the familiar features of the manor and the parish, albeit in somewhat different combinations. By custom and by incorporation, the functions of the court-leet, the court-baron, the administrative

24. At Wimeswould, Leicestershire, in 1639, Constable Martin Laren had to get Mr. Palmer (the rural vicar?) to write his notice for ship money, assize presentments, and a pass for a poor man. Parish of Wymeswould, Leicestershire, Constable's disbursements, 1628 [Robert Powell] (B. M. Add. MSS., 10, 457), ff. 37, 37b, 51b, 79. See the Ragnall Parish, Notts., accounts for the disbursements of the churchwardens and constables, 1623–1641 (B. M. Add. MSS., 36,981), ff. 69–72b; *Market Harborough Parish Records, 1531 to 1837*, eds. J. E. Stocks and W. B. Brugg (London, 1926), 51–113; *HMC Various*, I, 89.

25. Once a year, because parishes had no legally constituted boundaries, the vicar conducted a perambulation of the traditional bounds to fix them in the memories of the inhabitants. The perambulation began with a formal singing of a psalm in the churchyard, and often, to attract as large an attendance as possible, ended, as at Sarum in 1637, at an alehouse with free cakes and beer. *Churchwardens' Accounts of S. Edmund and S. Thomas, Sarum, 1443–1702*, ed. H. J. F. Swayne (Wiltshire Record Society, Salisbury, 1896); for Cuckfield, *Sussex Arch.*, LXI, 41–51; for St. Ives, *Western Antiquary*, V, 35; Webb, *Parish and County*, 32–5.

courts of the county justices, the activities derived from the guilds, and the special provisions of the charters of the municipalities had become firmly and confusingly interlaced, and they presented a bewildering variety of components and functions. The common feature of the urban centers was that each one possessed a charter confirming the customary privileges and fixing the responsibilties of the constituted municipal bodies.[26]

This is no place to rehearse the haphazard origins and development of the several hundred municipal corporations that existed in 1590. From that year to 1640, some of these petitioned for new instruments that would confer broader powers and enlarge their "bundle of privileges"; many unincorporated places sought to acquire charters. In 1596 Queen Elizabeth gave Totnes a new charter permitting the mayor and burgesses to conduct a three-day fair and set up a "Court of Pye Powder" to deal with disputes arising from the trafficking there. In 1604 the Corporation of Dartmouth received a royal grant of fresh privileges and a confirmation of its ancient liberties. Taunton Borough, one of the cloth towns of Somersetshire that was falling into decay for want of government, applied to the Crown in 1624 for incorporation.[27]

In one way or another, almost all of the functions of a town, large or small, came within the purview or the authority of the chief officers (usually a mayor, aldermen, and common council) who together might constitute a close corporation and co-opt their membership or be elected to office by vote of the freemen of the borough or city. Numerous cases indicate that popular participa-

26. In *Manor and Borough,* the Webbs have a very good discussion of municipal corporations, especially I, 260–404, though the emphasis is on the period after 1688. The "Constitution Book" of the Corporation of East Looe, Devonshire, containing the provisions for *c.* 1590 to 1628 is conveniently abstracted and provides an insight into the activities of a typical municipality. *Devon & Cornwall,* XXI, 88–96, 139–44, 184–9. For larger communities, see *Oxford Council Acts* [1583–1640] (Oxford Historical Society, LXXXVIII, XCV, 1928, 1933); and *Minutes of the Norwich Court of Mayoralty, 1630–1637* (Norfolk Record Society, XV, 1942).

27. Dartmouth continued to maintain a court-leet long after it was incorporated, as shown by presentments by the Grand Jury as late as 1613. Dartmouth Recs., DD 61821, 61830–1, 61864–5; *CSPD, 1603–10,* p. 138; *Western Antiquary,* X, 4; see also "The Town Book of Lewes, 1542–1701," for "law day" at a court-leet, *Sussex,* XLVIII, 36–7; *HMC Coke,* XII, I, 171.

tion did exist in some communities. At South Moulton in Devon on February 13, 1601, "a generall Assembly," including ten women, passed upon three articles to form a corporation by-law respecting strangers. Similarly, the *landsmen* and the *seamen* of the manorial borough of Brighton agreed—together—in 1618 that in setting the rate for governing the town, the fishermen would contribute one-fourth of the proceeds of each voyage to the town whereas the landsmen would add one-half of this total for the defraying of borough charges. The determination of any extraordinary levies was to be based upon the ability of the inhabitants to pay as decided by two fishermen and one landowner chosen by the churchwardens, constable, and "the chief of the town." Here indeed was a measure of popular control! [28]

No matter how a borough or a city was constituted, its authority was maintained and its public services rendered by a large staff of officials, whose influence was felt throughout the entire community. Because most boroughs were still agricultural communities, they had all of the familiar officers of the manor and the parish. In every sizable municipality, more than a hundred men worked in various capacities for the corporation. The daily business required the services of several kinds of searchers, weighers, and measurers; of clerks for the meal, flesh, and fish markets; and pie-powder judges. Wharves, docks, and ferries required water bailiffs, haven masters, and other functionaries, and strictly urban problems called for the services of scavengers or street sweepers, pavers, dogcatchers, constables, and often firewards. Two conditions set these corporation servants off from their rural counterparts. In the first place, they labored at their duties the year round and lived principally off fees, though some received small salaries, and in the larger communities they wore uniforms and carried wands or staves as badges of authority. Secondly, their professional status tended to bring them more and more under the supervision of the

28. *Records of Ye Antient Borough of South Moulton in Ye County of Devon*, ed. J. Coope (South Moulton, 1893), 14. For specimens of the infinite variety of municipal bodies, see the close corporations of "four and twentie" of Exeter and Kendal, *HMC Exeter*, 96, 100; *HMC Kendal*, X, IV, 310; and for the curious rate agreement at Brighton, *Sussex Arch.*, II, 42, 46–7.

corporation, with a consequent loss of the independence and authority that attended the country official.[29]

Another difference between the government of a town and that of a rural community was the high esteem in which the principal officers of a corporation held themselves and their constant insistence upon due deference and respect for their dignity by inferiors. The mayor and town council of Liskeard, Cornwall, in 1596 arrogated to themselves the right to nominate one churchwarden for the parish and arranged for their ally, the vicar, to nominate the other, both of whom the town might then "elect." The proud and sensitive Corporation of Lincoln sent word in 1615 to "the sheriffs elect [that] if they do not behave themselves well and courteously towards the mayor and aldermen and be not agreeable and conformable, [they] shall lose their allowances." Sometimes these proud burgomasters went too far, for in a letter of July 3, 1639, the recorder of Shrewsbury warned the mayor that "The assises nowe drawe neare. You know how you were blamed the last assises that you had not done fitting observances to my lords the judges of our circuits. . . . The displeasure that may encrease by the neglect may be verie prejudiciall to our towne, and confirme our censure of pride. It is unsaffe and indiscreete for us to contend with judges. I pray you consult with the company about it, and resolve on a course to recover that we have lost." [30]

The pride and arrogance of the officials may be attributed in part to the superior accommodations afforded them in the moot or town halls, which were to be found in practically every municipality. At Sudbury, Suffolk, for example, the hall, which was thoroughly repaired and "beautified" in 1607, stood on the lower part of Market Hill adjoining the shambles containing the butchers' stalls and weighing machines. The edifice had carved posts and projecting eaves; the steep, tiled roof, with gables, was surmounted by a cupola with a bell. The upper floor contained a well-

29. Some boroughs were coextensive with their parishes; larger ones contained wards or precincts, which often were parishes. The churchwardens and overseers still looked after the poor and performed other parochial duties. The influx of country people changed the character of urban parishioners markedly and gave rise to the movement for select vestries. Webb, *Manor and Borough*, I, 302–6; *Barnstaple Recs.*, I, 56–7.

30. *Western Antiquary*, I, 189; *HMC Lincoln*, XIV, VIII, 91; *HMC Shrewsbury*, XV, X, 64.

furnished, paneled council chamber, a parish room, a courtroom, and a theater; the ground floor had a watch-room, store-room, and cells for prisoners. Given such quarters and such authority, it is not surprising that the town fathers frequently suffered from inflated egos.[31]

III

The link between the locality and the nation was the justice of the peace. Though he held his commission from the King, he performed a vast amount of unremunerated service as a leader in his parish and in his county. Willing or not, he was inescapably involved in the quarrels and bickerings of friends and neighbors: John Selden made the condescending remark that justices "are but greater Constables." Sir Thomas Knyvett spent the night of January 17, 1640, with his tenants in the Norfolk village of Thorpe. "There is such a snarling and hartburning Amongst them," he wrote to his wife, "between Tollis and Dobson, and Southwells and Harrison [bailiffs all] and some of the farmers amongst them. . . . they make me so madd. . . . I carry a faier hand Amongst them and perswade them to Peace, which I know is but to little purpose." Bostock Fuller, a justice of Surrey, also played the arbitrator whenever possible; in 1612 he had to issue a warrant against one "Allingham of Nutfield, Carpenter, for brawling in the Churche and . . . striking olde Sander alias Waslyn. I agreed them." Nor was the difficulty all with the lower ranks. A Kentishman wrote in 1639 to his relative Henry Oxinden of Barham that he had spoken to Sir Thomas Palmer about Henry's going to law against Palmer's man for stealing conies. The choleric knight answered rashly that it was a great discourtesy to take a man away before the harvest, "and hee his picher." Later Henry may do as he will, but Palmer insists that "no justice of [the] peace will be so discourteous as to send a warrant for his man without writing him beforehand to settle the business, such things are us'd to clounds, never to gentlemen." [32]

31. *Suffolk,* VII, 257–60.
32. Michael Dalton, in his indispensable manual, *The Country Justice,* 6–9, asserts that fear, favor, hatred or malice, covetousness, perturbation of mind (anger or passion), ignorance, presumption, delay, or rashness could pervert

One of the duties of a justice of the peace was to empanel and charge the grand jury of the hundred, which was composed of two high constables and some others, often men with little property and less learning. According to Justice Lambarde, the Kentish antiquarian, the juries were expected not merely "to hear and receive" what others brought to their attention, but also "to inquire and present" what they themselves knew. It was not always easy to obtain presentments, for the justices complained that "in these days hardly any man is found that will inform against offenders." Juries refuse to indict their betters, favor their friends, and seek vengeance upon their enemies. Lambarde, who became increasingly critical of juries, tried to correct these postures in a charge made at Maidstone in April, 1599:

> Spare not for love, dare not for hatred, stick not for fear of any to make your presentment, but simply, as out of the sight of men and yet in the sight of God, in duty to her Majesty, for love of your country, and with care of yourselfes and yours, make faithful discovery of these evildoers, to the riddance of some of them, the amendment of others, and ease of the place where you live and dwell.[33]

William Lambarde was justly famous for his charges to juries; he told them not only why they should make presentments but also outlined the evils they should try to eradicate. He felt very strongly that a constable should be a subsidy man who could read and write warrants without having recourse to others for help, for this "discovery of his enjoined service" was the "breakneck of many a good business"; hundred juries should be the "most honest, discreet, and . . . able persons." We can learn from his charges how jury duty was one more way by which the average man learned about human nature and how local justice and government worked out in practice:

> It is you that can see, if you will, the roots and first springs of all these evils that infest and trouble the country, and in you

---

justice. Selden, *Table Talk*, 20; *Knyvett Letters*, 98; *Surrey*, IX, 192; *Oxinden Letters*, 152; Mary Gretton, *The Oxfordshire Justice of the Peace in the Seventeenth Century* (Oxfordshire Record Society, XVI, 1934), x–xxiv, lxxx–lxxxviii.
33. Webb, *Parish and County*, 319, 400–420; Read, *Lambarde and Local Government*, 58, 59, 88, 126, 139–40.

therefore it lieth to cut them off in the tender herb and before they do grow to dangerous ripeness. For if you would find out the disorders of alehouses, which for the most part be but nurseries of naughtiness, then neither should idle rogues and vagabonds find such relief and harborow as they have, neither should wanton youths have so ready means to feed their pleasures and fulfill their lusts, whereby besides all infinite other mischiefs, they nowadays do burden all the country with their misbegotten bastards. If you would complain of unlawful gaming in the day, of untimely walking in the night, and of unseemly apparelling all the year, you should hew and cut in sunder the first steps, as it were, of those stairs which do lead up to pickery [petty theft], theft, and robbing. . . . If you would present the names of regraters, engrossers, forestallers, and transporters of victual, and the faults of such as keep neither assize of weight and measure nor use any moderation of price in selling of victual, then should not the poorer sort have so just cause to complain of great want and dearth in the midst of this so blessed and counteous store and plenty.[34]

Four times a year, with impressive ceremonies, the justices met as the court of quarter sessions for the county to determine civil and criminal small causes, which were based upon presentments made by the grand jury. Most presentments dealt with the myriad problems mentioned throughout this book: licensing of alehouses, apprenticing of servants, setting wages, fining poachers, investigating absences from church, seeking out recusants, overseeing the conditions of the highways and bridges, and judging numerous felonies and moral offenses. The secret of the success of this court was the information in the list of presentments. To quote Justice Lambarde again: "So often and ordinarily do we repair to this place and for this service, good neighbors and friends, that the end of our coming hither cannot but be understood to the meanest of our assembly." [35]

34. Read, *Lambarde and Local Government*, 58, 60, 70–71, 138–9.
35. A list of counties whose quarter sessions records have been consulted is given in the bibliography of this volume. The Court of Quarter Sessions for the county of Middlesex had jurisdiction over much of London without the walls: the boroughs of Bethnal Green, Chelsea, Finsbury, Fulham, Hackney, Hammersmith, Hampstead, Holborn, Islington, Kensington, Paddington, Poplar, St. Marlybone.

At the opening of the seventeenth century, the English people stood charged with being under such "bold sway of disobedience to law that it creepeth not in corners but marcheth in the open market." Whether as a result of this "inundation of wickedness" or encouraged by the opportunities it presented, the number of professional lawyers increased conspicuously. The "multiplicitie of attorneys" were accused by Sir George Manners with "stirring uppe of many wrangling sutes of small amount," and he urged that the number in each county be reduced to the number at the time of the accession of Queen Elizabeth. Sir George had heard that when Mr. Richard Smith first became an attorney in Lincolnshire, there were only three others in the county; now, in 1621, there are "ten or twelve score." A report to the Privy Council in 1633 revealed that whereas there were 313 attorneys in the Common Pleas in 1578, the number had risen to 1,383; and the number in the King's Bench stood at 342. Whatever the merits of the rapidly expanding legal profession, its existence was the best testimony to the litigiousness of the English people.[36]

Certain criminal and civil offenses not within the competence of the quarter sessions went before the King's judges traveling on circuit three times a year at a court of assizes. Though the law contained a few safeguards for the criminal, and the prisoner often had no right to counsel and had the rules of evidence heavily weighted against him, there is very little evidence that the accused and his fellows feared the law; they regarded it more as the guardian than as the master of their liberties. Widespread literacy enabled hardened offenders to plead benefit of clergy by calling for the Book and reading "the neck verse"; it then followed that branding in the hand was substituted for hanging. Peter Mundy attended the Gloucester assizes in 1639 and admired "the Merciful Manner in Mittigation off our most severe law by giving the

St. Pancras, Shoreditch, Stoke Newington, and Stepney, *Middlesex Sessions,* n. s., I, i; Read, *Lambarde and Local Government,* 94.
36. Professional lawyers were able to make matters increasingly difficult for the unlearned justices. They bought and studied J. Rastell's *Les Termes de la Ley: or certaine Difficult and Obscure Words of the Common Law of this Realm Expounded* (1629, 1636, 1641). Read, *Lambarde and Local Government,* 143; *HMC Rutland,* IV, 214, 216; *CSPD, 1633–4,* p. 251.

booke, with the rest. There were 6 burned in the hand; none executed." This privilege was, however, for men only.[37]

Whether they lived in rural or urban England, the people were acutely aware that in the government of their parishes, ecclesiastical courts shared authority equally with the justices of the peace. "There's no such thing as Spirituall Jurisdiccion, all is civill, the Churches is the same with the Lord Mayors," was the considered opinion of John Selden in 1634. The courts held by the archdeacons paralleled and often inconveniently overlapped the quarter sessions and assizes in many ways; and they punished, as *sins,* all moral offenses, defamation, slander, drunkenness, offenses related to marriage and the family, usury, and misbehavior in church. Where the quarter sessions might convict an offender of bastardy, the archdeaconry court would convict of fornication, and though it was the same offense, the penalties differed markedly! In addition to ecclesiastical matters, the petty offenses that this court sat upon were legion; and it also probated wills.[38]

The spiritual courts did not follow common-law procedure, and they summoned no juries. In every parish they exercised jurisdiction through the churchwardens, who, aided by their prying sidesmen, regularly presented all local delinquents to the bishop or his agents for judgment in what was popularly called the Bawdy Court. When the churchwardens failed in their duty, as they frequently did through negligence or fear of their betters, the incumbent made the presentments. Furthermore, any embittered inhabitant of the parish could secretly denounce his neighbor, who would then be brought before the court. The defendant had perforce to pay all

37. George L. Haskins, *Law and Authority in Colonial Massachusetts* (New York, 1960), 49–50, 58, 94; "Have mercy upon me, O God, according to thy loving kindness; according to the multitude of thy tender mercies blot out my transgressions." [Neck verse] *Psalms* 51:1; Mundy, *Travels,* IV, 14, 14n; *Surtees,* XL, viii–lx.

38. For dualism of authority in the secular and ecclesiastical courts, George L. Haskins, in Mass. Hist. Soc., *Proceedings,* LXXII, 22, 22–23n; Ware, *Elizabethan Parish,* 9–10; Selden, *Table Talk,* 60; *Worcester Sessions,* 454; *RHS Trans.,* 3d ser., VI, 38–9; 4th ser., XXV, 93–119; John Stoughton, *Ecclesiastical History of England, from the Opening of the Long Parliament to the Death of Cromwell* (London, 1867), I, 18–20; *cf.* W. H. Frere, *The English Church in the Reigns of Elizabeth and James* I (London, 1904), 100; Hill, *Society and Puritanism,* 310–11.

fees even if the charge was a trumped-up one or the court discharged him. Such was the case of poor Peter Simon, whom some vindictive countryman succeeded in having presented at Udimore in 1603 "for baptizing a catt." The church courts also employed the *ex officio* oath by which the accused was forced to give evidence against himself, and to make matters more difficult if not incomprehensible to the ordinary person, the proceedings were conducted in Latin.[39]

The courts of the archdeacons frequently appended heavy penalties to their better-known moral and spiritual censures, which were intended to keep the English people compliant. The Archdeaconry Court of Essex fined four yeomen of Steeple cum Stangate five shillings each for failure to pay the parish rate. When churchwardens, however, were guilty of non-payment of wages to parish clerks (John Patching, the clerk of Cuckfield, charged that he had not been paid for more than nine years!), the court deemed that justice was done when it ordered payment. More potent in some ways was the courts' use of excommunication as a punishment as well as for censure, inasmuch as the individual so cut off was, in effect, excluded from society, and anyone harboring him or having any dealings with him incurred penalties also. William Howell of Streat was presented to the Archdeaconry Court at Lewes merely for selling a tenement to an excommunicant.[40]

The peccadilloes of friends and neighbors, plus the unplanned exchanges, many of them highly humorous, which occurred in the course of trials, made the sessions of the bawdy courts close rivals of public spectacles as a form of village entertainment. Not a few men, occasionally a woman too, turned out to be like John Gardiner of Ringmer, whom the court at South Malling found guilty of "dislike of the worship of God and ceremonies of the church." Nor was this exclusively a Puritan transgression. Probably the

---

39. The Archdeaconry Court of Buckinghamshire summoned "Ester Jeffes for saying that it is well her sonne in lawe Jarvis had money for the bawdy court [,] meaning the court of Mr. Cobb, at Alyesbury." Oxford Record Society, X, viii; Mr. Hill has a full discussion of "the Bawdy Courts" in *Society and Puritanism,* 298–343. In reply to Laud's pronouncement against keeping any "prophane Law-courts" in churches, cited in William Prynne's *Canterburies Doome* (London, 1646), 114, is a marginal note: "Were not their spiritual Bawdy-courts commonly kept in Churches such." *Sussex Arch.,* XLIX, 53.

40. Essex Arch., XI, 22a; *Sussex Arch.,* XLIX, 53, 58–9; L, 43, 44.

commonest symptom of the attitude was falling asleep during services. Thomas Hill of Somerby, Leicestershire, was presented in 1634 "for being Churchwarden and yet a verie frequent sleeper in the Church." Mathew Lidford of Market Harborough was presented "for disturbing the Minister in tyme of divine service, being reproved by the Minister for some offence hee had committed, saying aloud it was not soe or words to that effect." Some rude peasants of Sussex sat in the chancel with their hats on; others threw stones at neighbors during the service; one sat "disorderly in the chancel with a dog on his knee." Henry Jenner of Lindfield had to sit in the stocks for disturbing the minister by singing irreverently, after which he was excommunicated. When Thomas Prior of St. Thomas-in-the-Cliff was presented for laughing at the vicar at the Catechism, the court was told that when the clergyman asked him his name, he "sayd I know my name well enough already." Bridget Barrett, charged before the court at Lewes "for thrusting of pinnes in the wife of John Dumbrell" during the service, readily admitted it but claimed in her own defense that Mistress Dumbrell had "sate down in her lap." [41]

Entertaining as the bawdy courts were, from 1600 on resentment of ecclesiastical supervision by the archdeacons' courts mounted steadily. "The humour of the time is grown to be too eager against all ecclesiastical jurisdiction," the clergy complained. Indictments of the system increased with each decade until 1640. None of the many pamphlets more succinctly vented the anger of the ordinary Englishman who ran afoul of the "inferiour Ecclesiastical Courts" than the anonymous *England's Complaint to Jesus Christ Against the Bishop's Canons* (1640): "Item, none can be sure that his goods are his owne, when all, and *more* then all are taken from him at one Censure, and that at will and pleasure of the Board, without any and against all Law." It seemed as if one

---

41. Occasionally a shrewd character witness (compurgator) made sport of the court. In 1633 Margaret Beale of Westminster charged her husband, James, with presumed intercourse with Sarah Wood. Denying the fact, Sarah produced two compurgators, one of whom swore that James Beale was in Holland. Actually he was in Chelsea, and when the compurgator was challenged for perjury, he saucily replied that Beale was in a Holland shirt, and in Holland sheets, and wore a Holland nightcap. *CSPD, 1631–3*, p. 528; *Sussex Arch.*, L, 45; Associated Architectural Societies, *Reports & Papers*, XXIX, II, 497, 489; *Sussex Arch.*, XLIX, 53, 61, 64; L, 42, 43, 44, 45.

received less rigorous treatment from the civil than from the church tribunals:

> And be his cause never so juste, never so innocent, never so cleare, as against which no Law of the Land doth lye, yet, first of all in those Courts he cannot have any benefit of the Law at all, and consequently, where the Ecclesiasticall Judges set their Fangs, they will teare a man out of his estate, yea out of his Skin, and pull his flesh from his Bones, and break him and his all in pieces.

Obviously grumbling had given way to overt antagonism.[42]

The feature of the church courts that had aggravated the resentment of so many Englishmen was the petty interference with men's lives and conduct by, as John Milton vividly wrote, "All the hell-pestering rabble of apparitors and sumners," who had become openly obnoxious during Archbishop Laud's vigorous episcopal visitations after 1634. When Parliament abolished ecclesiastical courts in 1646, it put an end to long years of bitter, smouldering, animus of the common folk over a genuine abuse very widely experienced.[43]

42. "Articuli Cleri," Article IV (1605), quoted by R. G. Usher, *The Reconstruction of the English Church* (London, 1910), II, 82; *The Complete Prose Works of John Milton*, ed. Don M. Wolfe, (New Haven, 1953–62), I, 982; II, 279; *England's Complaint to Jesus Christ Against the Bishop's Canons*, B2; Hill, *Society and Puritanism*, 303, 305, 307, 309, 312, 325.
43. The attack on Church courts began in the press in 1641 and was continued in Parliament. *The Spiritual Courts Epitomised in a Dialogue betwixt two Proctors, Busy-Body and Scrape-all* (1641) in *Harleian Miscellany* (1809), IV, 419–21, contained a woodcut representing "the Bishop's-court in great confusion." Scrape-All speaks sadly of "Bow-Church that on a court-day used to be fuller than at a sermon on Sunday," and regrets that Archdeacon's courts that were "wont to be crowded, like money into a usurer's bag, are very quiet and peaceable now . . . No more can we send our messengers into the country, that pry into people's actions there. . . ." Busy-Body, feeling short of money recalls: "I got very well by a wench that has been undone in a dark entry; Sir John [the judge] would commute her penance into ten pounds, towards the repair of S. Paul's, and then we would share it." John Stoughton termed the abolition of these courts a "legalized revolution" that "would occasion a great social change also." *Ecclesiastical History of England*, I, 481–3. For the ordinance of 16 November, 1646, *ibid.*; *Documents Illustrative of English Church History*, eds. H. Gee and W. J. Hardy (London, 1910), 557–8; *Complete Prose Works of Milton*, III, 158.

IV

Although the lower classes had little if any actual knowledge of the designs of the King and the maneuverings of the Court circle, politics did concern the middling Englishmen whose forty-shilling freehold entitled them to vote in borough or parliamentary elections. Even in these contests, however, they found themselves ringed about by restrictions. Their votes always had to go to some gentleman or urban merchant (they themselves could not seek office), and the candidates from among whom they might choose were frequently handpicked by some influential county family or by the county justices. The burgesses of Maidstone made "Lawrence Washington, esquyer," a freeman on April 15, 1601, and respited his oath. In August they leased him a messuage with one acre of the corporation's land for twenty-one years. Then on March 9, 1603/4, at an assembly at the courthouse, he was chosen a burgess for Parliament. Things could go well for a gentleman if he had the proper interest.[44]

The prevalence of undisguised corruption at election times disturbed many voters. The mayor of Winchelsea, Sussex, procured the election of William Finch and the exclusion of Sir Alexander Temple in 1623 by threatening and illegally disqualifying certain voters; and the mayor of Arundel returned Sir George Choworth in opposition to Richard Mills by re-opening the poll after it had been taken; Sir John Suckling, the Cavalier poet, was accused of getting himself elected from Brambar by bribing and bullying freeholders. In 1625 a most reprehensible election occurred at Dorchester. Certain gentlemen had agreed at the Blandford Sessions that Sir George Moreton, Bart., should stand for Knight of the Shire, but on election day the town and county agreed on Sir Thomas Freake, and for second man, John Browne of Dorchester. Moreton's supporters "cried" for him, and confusion followed. The sheriffs, who favored Moreton, went from the Shire Hall to the George Tavern to decide upon the winners. Partisans of Mr. Browne, who pressed into their chamber, were turned away, after

44. Notestein, *English People*, 5; Barnes, *Somerset*, 9–10; *Maidstone Recs.*, 34, 35, 38, 56.

which Moreton was given one more vote than Browne and declared the Knight. Upon appeal to Parliament, Browne procured another election. Again "the cry was doubtful," and a second poll was taken. The Sheriff refused to permit the Browne faction to check the count; further skullduggery ensued, and Browne lost out to Moreton by 498 to 511 votes. The victor was carried in triumph to the George; the record does not disclose the reactions of the losing side.[45]

Every reader of English history is familiar with the story of how the members of the upper classes suffered from the "injudicious meddlesomeness of government" in the latter days of King James and, especially, under King Charles, his son. What is less well calendared but of greater concern here was the effect of the Caroline despotism on the lesser breed who did not rule. For almost two decades prior to 1635, specific acts and measures of royal authorization had been proving irritants, and despite seeming concern over the social welfare, Wentworth and Laud appeared to be getting their way. Assuredly the common people might have mused with Claudio:

> . . . Whether that body public be
> A horse whereon the governor doth ride,
> Who, newly in the seat, that it may know
> He can command, lets it straight feel the spur;
> Whether the tyranny be in his place,
> Or in his eminence that fills it up.

Eventually their hardships provoked the people, who sensed "the disease of our Commonwealth" years before the breach occurred, to execrations and resistance. These hardships must now be sampled.[46]

On December 11, 1618, some months after the Thirty Years' War had begun, a comet passed over London, causing a knight to exclaim that it was a portent of serious threats to England. Not for two years, however, did King James order "a drumme beaten" in

45. *VCH Sussex*, I, 521; *Sussex Arch.*, XX, 153–4; *Somerset & Dorset*, IV, 23–4.
46. Arthur P. C. Newton, *Colonizing Activities of the English Puritans* (New Haven, 1914), 173; Gardiner, *England*, VIII, 68; *Measure for Measure*, I, ii, 163–5. For the general case against the King, see Allen French, *Charles I and the Puritan Upheaval* (London and Boston, 1955); *Oxinden Letters*, 33.

the metropolis for volunteers to "go to the succor" of his son-in-law Frederick, the King of Bohemia. Within a few months thereafter, "a free collection made for the defence of the Palatinat" netted £200 in the town of Dorchester alone; William Whiteway heard that a total of £30,000 had been contributed by the nation but that the King was reputed to have taken a portion of it. Furthermore, James I, who deplored Frederick's policy, forbade anyone to speak of matters of state, "either of this kingdom or of any other place, upon pain of his Majesty's high displeasure." Nevertheless, among the educated ranks, concern for the fate of Protestantism continued: Tom-Tell-Troath, "One of the greatest company-keepers" in London addressed a tract to James in 1622: "I vow to God and your majesty, I can come into no meetings but, I find the predominant humour to be talking of the wars of Christendom and honour of their country, and such like treasons . . . to descant upon the royal style is not their common pastime." The justices of Somerset told the Privy Council of their awareness of the calamities in Germany, but the decay in the cloth trade and the cattle business had created a shortage of money in the West Country and rendered the populace desperate. The Mayor of Wells, reiterating the plight of the cloth industry, the increase in the number of the poor, and the threat of riots, declared that the people were willing to spend their blood but could send no more than a small sum. Primarily, this was the city's and the cultured man's cause. In *Votivæ Angliæ* (1624), a carefully reasoned bit of *Realpolitik* dedicated to Great Britain's "Great Hope," Prince Charles, the author makes a lofty appeal: "The eyes of the whole Christian world . . . are continually and curiously fixed . . . to see whether Great Brittayne. . . will couragiouslie resolve to redeeme her lost Honnor, or else cowardlie consent to lose it without any further sence, or hope of redemption." [47]

In the course of the "Buckingham Wars," however, such an intolerable burden was imposed on the average Englishman that grim and dangerous views on government in general and the per-

47. John Rushworth, *Historical Collections* (London, 1659), I, 5–8; Whiteway, Diary, 10 (fol. 20), 16 (fol. 26); Chamberlain, *Letters*, II, 307, 310, 342; *Dorset*, XIII, 60; Dunham and Pargellis, *Complaint and Reform*, 481, 482; *CSPD, 1619–23;* p. 393; *1627–8,* p. 77; *Votivæ Angliæ* (written in London, published in Utrecht, 1624), Dedication.

sonal rule of King Charles in particular began to dominate his thinking. In maritime towns, press gangs raised the seamen needed to man the ninety ships for the disastrous attack on Cadiz. Though normally freed from such compulsory service, fishermen from these communities and the watermen of London were taken up. The people expected the naval press but not the raising of an army of 10,000 men for foreign service by impressment, a device made lawful only by questionable legal legerdemain. The royal authorities set a quota for each county: that for Sussex was 450 in 1624, and 250 more the next year; in Devon the press took 300 men for the army in 1624 and again in 1625, and 400 men in the latter year for the navy. To county officers was left the disagreeable task of allocating the quota among the several communities and also of raising the "coat and conduct" money to clothe the men and get them to Plymouth for embarkation. Writing of the forced loan, Daniel Neal said: "Those of the lower sort who refused to lend were pressed for the army, or had soldiers quartered upon them. . . ." When the ships returned after a few months—they were only one week before Cadiz—the nation found out that hundreds had died on the voyage and that hundreds more had contracted dysentery and typhus. Starving and unpaid, the more fortunate of the survivors were deposited in Plymouth while the balance remained aboard ships in the Sound.[48]

The King completely failed to comprehend the effect of this fiasco upon his miserable subjects and forthwith allowed Buckingham to follow the same improvident and incompetent procedures for the expedition dispatched from Portsmouth to the Isle of Rhé in 1627. In April of that year a royal letter directed Sussex officials to press 250 men for the fleet but to take none from the train bands. In August they had to raise fifty more in Chichester and six neighboring rapes. At Dorchester William Whiteway noted in June "a third presse generall in this County, 150 to serve the King in this fleete." The press gangs scooped up any seemingly able-bodied man and many a one totally unfit or diseased. They pressed pilots,

48. Williamson, *The English Channel*, 226–7; Neal, *History of the Puritans*, I, 519; Charles M. Clode, *The Military Forces of the Crown* (London, 1869), I, 16, 17; *Sussex Arch.*, XL, 5, 7, 13–14; French, *Charles I and the Puritan Upheaval*, 70–71, 140–3; Hamilton, *Quarter Sessions*, 107; *Devonshire*, X, 228–9; *Verney Papers*, in *Camden*, LVI, 118–22 (for Bucks).

fishermen, surgeons, surveyors, and even sturdy felons from the gaols, but for the most part, rogues and vagabonds filled the ranks of the soldiers. The exasperated deputies wrote to the Lord Lieutenant on April 15, 1628, that they could not obtain more than seventy of the hundred demanded unless they pressed shepherds from their flocks, husbandmen from their plows, or poor laboring men from their wives and children. For the populace, the situation was more than grim, it was frightening.[49]

The ever-present possibility that he might be pressed into the military services inspired fear and horror in the humble man. Families would lose their means of support, for soldiers seldom got paid and seamen's rewards came late, if at all. Like Benjamin Jenkins, many pressed soldiers made their wills, for the odds on ever returning were three to one against them. Still others followed the course of William Forrest, a shoemaker of Hatch Beauchamp, and John Davies from Long Sutton, both Somerset hamlets, each of whom ran away from his captain in Middlesex, "being a prest souldier." Some despairing men preferred to risk brutal punishment meted out for desertion or to commit suicide rather than face death from dysentery or typhus, or slow starvation, or the prospect of becoming permanently maimed or incapacitated. Of 8,000 troops sent to the Isle of Rhé, only 3,000 came back, and nearly every man of them sick with some communicable disease. After watching a march of pressed soldiers on their way to Dover, John Chamberlain, showing a complete lack of comprehension, concluded: "Such a rabble of raw and poor rascalls have not lightly [often] ben seene, and go so unwillingly that they must rather be driven then led. You may guesse how base we have growne when one that was prest hung himself for feare or curst hart, another ran into the Thames, and . . . drowned himself, another cut of[f] all his fingers of one hand, and another put out his owne eyes with salt." When, in these same years, agents solicited ordinary men to go to plant in Ulster or the New World, the unknown held more promise for some than life in an England at war.[50]

49. French, *Charles I and the Puritan Upheaval*, 141–3; Williamson, *English Channel*, 227; Whiteway, Diary, 122 (fol. 126); *Sussex Arch.*, XL, 18, 24, 26, 27, 33; *CSPD, 1628–9*, p. 75.
50. *Dorset*, XLVII, 30; *Middlesex Sessions*, III, 74–5; Williamson, *English Channel*, 227; Chamberlain, *Letters*, 593.

To those families of the middling and inferior sort whose young men escaped the press, the wars still brought disillusionment and bred up a hatred of royal authority based on the inept policy of marching soldiers across country and billeting them indiscriminately on the citizenry. No one was safe along the Dover Road in December, 1624: troops marching to aid Mansfeld terrified the poor, pillaged, and committed crimes of every sort as they marched through Kent. Exactly one year later, on at least one occasion, Lyme paid the army to avoid the town. While the soldiers awaited ships to take them to Cadiz, they were billeted on the inhabitants of every community near Plymouth; the expedition failed and back they came—the sick, maimed, and starving—to batten on the householders all over again. A letter of December, 1625, describing the soldiers' pitiful condition, was written from Plymouth to Secretary Conway: "They stink as they go, and the poor rags they have are rotten and ready to fall off if they be touched. This is the general condition of the men, and some of the inferior officers are in no better plight." Six months later the plague spread from Plymouth to every parish where soldiers were billeted; in another month, two troops of soldiers and 200 families fled their homes to escape it.[51]

Heavy though the burden for the expedition to Cadiz was, the sacrifices demanded of those least able to bear the yoke multiplied several times over in the succeeding years when France replaced Spain in Buckingham's schemes. There was no letup in impressment or of billeting, and the failure of the Crown to meet its share of the expenses aroused bitterness all over England. In March of 1626, the Commissioners of Plymouth told the Council that the people had come to such a depth of extremity that they were insisting that they must thrust out-of-doors either the soldiers or their own wives and children. "The richer sort utterly refuse to receive soldiers; and the rest [are] much disabled by great arrears due for last year," was the cry of the men of Blandford in 1628. Essex justices told of being deluged with petitions of peasants who were undone for want of the money owed them for billeting. Those communities that had Irish troops foisted upon them, "much to

---

51. *Acts of the Privy Council, 1623–5,* pp. 409–10; Roberts, *Southern Counties,* 124; *Sussex Arch.,* XL, 14; *CSPD, 1625–6,* pp. 191, 350, 368.

their terror and charge," were particularly vocal in their protests. Dorcas Thurgood and others of "the poor and distressed inhabitants" of Maldon gave a lurid description of the insolencies suffered from the Irish soldiery: "They command in our houses, as if they were our lords, and we their slaves, inforcing us and ours to attend them at their pleasure." When soldiers complained about being quartered only in the houses of the poor and about the meager diet, their long-suffering hosts replied that no soldier was satisfied with any provision made, "but will be his own carver of whatsoever he likes best and can lay his hands on." Doubtless the food was poor, for the King's pay was only 3s. 6d. per man. Sir George Blundell referred to Portsmouth as "a poor beggarly place, where is neither money, lodging, nor meat for the soldiers, and no man would lend them a penny or give them any meat." The sailing of the fleet must have seemed a Heaven-sent relief to all.[52]

When the army returned from La Rochelle, the Lord Treasurer directed that it be billeted in the same places as before, and again there was an empty promise of reimbursement. After the experiences on foreign soil, the conduct of the soldiers was even more outrageous than before. During a Parliamentary debate, Sir Walter Erle of Dorset told a plain tale: "In my county, under colour of placing a soldier, there came twenty in a troop to take sheep. They disturb markets and fairs, rob men on the highway, ravish women, breaking houses in the night, and enforcing men to ransom themselves, killing men that have assisted the constables to keep the peace." From town after town came the same story: trade spoiled, roads dangerous, and private property destroyed; "Tradesmen and Artificers almost discouraged, and being inforced to leave thier Trades, and to imploy their Time in preserving themselves and their Families from cruelty." The men of Kent spoke for all of their countrymen in 1628 when they prayed to be freed from "en-

52. In 1631 the Lords Lieutenant were encouraged to promote enlistments for "the benefit which this kingdome will fynde in disburtheninge it selfe of many unnecessary men that want employment." The promise was held out that the enlisted men could claim a pension from the county where they were pressed, a claim which, upon their return, the overseers did their best to evade. *Sussex Arch.*, XL, 21, 29, 30, 35; French, *Charles I and the Puritan Upheaval*, 143; Willcox, *Gloucestershire*, 102; Hamilton, *Quarter Sessions*, 109; *CSPD*, *1625–6*, pp. 252, 291, 423; *1627–8*, pp. 41, 148–9, 549, 554, 561; *1628–9*, pp. 2, 76, 465; *Norfolk & Norwich*, I, 156.

tertaining soldiers in their houses and families, which are the foundation and nurseries of all kingdoms and commonwealths, and the only places of comfort and repose of all well-affected people, their wives and children." [53]

The callous unconcern for large segments of the lower classes by the government of the early Stuart kings was responsible more than any one thing, except religion, for the alienation of large numbers of Englishmen from their ruler and his ministers. In Sussex alone, from 1624 to 1626, a series of well over thirty orders from the Privy Council, one upon another, calling for presses, the erection of beacons, the keeping of watches, supplies of powder, billeting of soldiers, gifts of arms, loans of money, furnishing of fuel, provision of carts and draft animals—all at local charge— augmented the work of already overburdened county officials. Far more oppressive in the long run, government exactions had subjected the men who did not rule, together with their families, to treatment that drove some of them to extreme measures, even to taking their own lives. Billeting had brought nothing but trials and great fear, if not worse, to "constant residents." They had had enough of all this, and Parliament was induced to discuss their problems; Sir John Eliot graphically described the plight of Plymouth. The outcome was a clause in the Petition of Right condemning billeting. As for the soldiers, the remnant that came back, very few of them were fit to take up the life that they had led before impressment, and the authorities resorted to evasive measures to avoid paying them the pittance of a pension promised them from the county where they had been pressed.[54]

The irregular assessment of ship money in 1626 and thereafter affected men of substance, such as Sir Richard Saltonstall, whom the Sheriff of Essex reported ten years later as "one of those of rank and quality" who did not pay when due. Still, according to Richard Baxter of Bridgeworth, the rural folk of Shropshire also resented the forced loan. "The poor Plowmen understood but little

53. *Sussex Arch.*, XL, 28–9; Gardiner, *England*, VI, 253; Rushworth, *Historical Collections*, I, 548–50, 648; *CSPD, 1628–9*, pp. 49–50, 109, 117.
54. See the samples of orders and letters issued by the Privy Council to the Lords Lieutenant of Sussex, December, 1624, to January, 1631; these also went to all other counties; *Sussex Arch.*, XL, 1–37; M[ichael] S[parke], *Grievous Grones for the Poore* (1622), 15; Clode, *Military Forces of the Crown*, I, 17–21.

of these Matters; but a little would stir up their Discontent when Money was demanded: But it was the more intelligent part of the Nation that were the great Complainers." Coming as it did as a phase of the war, the plain people had little difficulty in comprehending the attitude of their betters, and unconstitutional royal financial expedients welded the gentlemen, merchants, yeomen, artisans, and peasants together, leaving religion as the single issue dividing them.[55]

Looking backward from the turmoil of the Civil War to the reigns of James and Charles, Edward Hyde, Earl of Clarendon, thought them "indeed . . . excellent times," and he wrote of the personal rule of Charles I as twelve years in which the kingdom "enjoyed the greatest calm, and the fullest measure of felicity, that any people in any age, for so long time together, have been blessed with. . . . But all these blessings could but enable, not compel us to be happy: we wanted that sense, acknowledgment, and value of our own happiness which all but we had, and took pains to make, when we could not find, ourselves miserable. There was in truth a strange absence of understanding in most, and a strange perverseness of understanding in the rest: the Court full of excess, idleness and luxury, and the country full of pride, mutiny and discontent. . . ."[56]

Edward Hyde had but a partial view of England and Englishmen, which was further circumscribed by his rank in life. For many of the middling ranks and for most of the peasants and poor urban-dwellers, "felicity" was a word seldom mouthed; and it may be argued that it was the beginning of understanding rather than its absence that impelled these people to the actions that Hyde branded perverse.

55. A Kentish sheriff reported to Edward Nicholas of the Council in 1636 that "the greatest part of the onus falles among the poorer sort who payth itt like drops of bloud and some doeth sell the only Cowe which should feed the children and most come to the Parish. . . ." Ship money was also listed as one of the great oppressions by a petition of 1641. *Somerset & Dorset*, XII, 189; *An Humble Petition and Remonstrance Presented unto both the Houses of Parliament concerning the unsupportable Grievance of the Transportation of Leather* (1641), 2; *CSPD, 1636-7*, p. 197; *Reliquiæ Baxterianæ*, 15, 17; Hull, *Agriculture . . . in Essex*, 457-8; *VCH Sussex*, I, 521.
56. Edward Hyde, Earl of Clarendon, *The History of the Rebellion and Civil Wars in England* (Oxford, 1888), I, 96.

In the seventeenth century, the simple Englishman was learning to think for himself, and there is ample evidence that by the time of the personal rule he was no longer willing to let his affairs be managed by a paternalistic, often despotic government or by his superiors, no matter how well-intentioned. Inarticulate for the most part, and without spokesmen to voice their discontent, the men and women of the lower ranks were nevertheless eager to learn the news of the world outside their own communities, to exchange opinions, and to voice their grievances. In churchyards before and after services much talk went on about the hardships that came with the wars; in the marketplaces, which had suffered gravely, the parlous state of trade, extra-parliamentary taxation, and corn prices were deplored; at manorial courts and parish meetings men spoke their minds, and the news circulated from place to place by means of the motley crowds that traveled along the roads. Sermons by both Laudians and Puritans, not only at St. Paul's Cross but at parish churches in the cities and in small villages, took cognizance of the woes of the people. In Hook, a small village of Hampshire, one Sabbath day in 1626, three men charged the rector, Mr. Nicholas Day, with stirring up sedition when he preached that the land was not governed by justice but by bribery, "that Kinges could not conteine themselves in their oone kingedoms, and that they seeke to make invasions of other countreyes . . . and commit all other villany." [57]

In the years between 1625 and 1640, revolts in Wiltshire against King Charles occurred, which sprang chiefly from arbitrary

---

57. One way of spreading popular sentiments from town to country was the ballad, and the populace had little difficulty in grasping the point of such broadsides as *England! Once Europs Envye now Her Scorne:*

> Noe help, Noe help, why then 'tis Vayne
> for to Complayne.
> (& why) Men syn with all their hart,
> & sorrow with but a part,
> & all men Crye,
> yet all is ill
> yet all doe seeke
> to mak't or keep't
> so still.

Cutts, *Seventeenth Century Songs and Lyrics,* 95; Clark, *Working Life of Women,* 51; *Somerset & Dorset,* XV, 156; *RHS Trans.,* 3d ser., VI, 26.

enclosures for which James and Charles must bear responsibility, enclosures that were "the most extensive and the most violent in their execution." Though revolts elsewhere have as yet not been studied, there is ample reason to agree with Mr. Eric Kerridge that Stuart absolutism seemed to the common man far from beneficent, and that the abuses just reviewed weighed heavily when many members of the lower classes joined in the great decision against the King. As early as 1630, many Englishmen had begun silently to nourish, and occasionally to display openly, a genuine hostility against "the demigod Authority." Archdeaconry courts, enclosures, pressing, billeting, ship money, the decline of trade had caused them to lose much of their respect for and loyalty to the King of England. The "venom of the season" increased, as the great historian perceived, until a large portion of the nation evidently grew "satiated and weary of the government itself . . ." and some of them even decided to leave the country permanently.[58]

By means such as those just described—and doubtless others of which no record survives—the ordinary men of England gained a vast amount of political experience. On many an issue they were misinformed, but upon general principles they turned out to be shrewd and astute. This mass alertness came from reading, much listening, serving, and familiarity with the practical workings of local government. How else can we explain the fecundity of political thinking these men displayed in the 1640's?

58. Kerridge, in *Wiltshire*, LVII, 64–6, 77; *Measure for Measure*, I, ii, 124–7; Clarendon, *History of the Rebellion*, I, 51; Christopher Hill, *Puritanism and Revolution* (London, 1958), 26, 204, 210.

VIII

The Faiths of Englishmen

WITH US SOCIETY is both the Church and commonwealth,"
Richard Hooker explained in his celebrated book. Englishmen accepted this view without question; in this age no one thought
about the life around him in any other than Christian terms—the
very words that he spoke or wrote came principally from religious
sources. Anglican as well as Puritan masters told apprentices that
theirs was a godly calling: "Considering (Christian Reader) how
short our time is," Richard Hodges stated in his ready-reckoner, we
must carefully space the hours we devote to worldly pursuits "to the
end we may more freely imploy ourselves in the use of all holy
meanes for the examining of our deceitful hearts, and the casting up
of our spiritually accompts." Merchants shipped every kind of cargo
"by the Grace of God"; seafarers seldom failed to mix piety with their
prognostications about wind and wave. Soldiers fought the Spaniard or the Frenchman for the greater glory of God (who was
English) rather more than for king or country. Even the *Statutes
at Large,* in many a pious preamble, reflected the mood of the day.
Indeed, Church and commonwealth did constitute society.[1]

Although it was the "cement of Society," religion, John Selden
averred, "is like the fashion, one man weares his doublett slashed,
another lac'd, a third plaine, but every man has a doublett. Every
man has his Religion, wee differ about the trimming." As John

1. Richard Hooker, *Works* (Oxford, 1865), II, 493; Hodges, *Enchiridion Arithmeticon,* preface.

Donne noticed, accidents of birth, education, and fate governed most people's religious beliefs far more than faith or intellectual conviction. Whether they were of the Established Church or of the Church of Rome, most of them agreed that there must be unity in the land: one state, one church. For the ordinary man in these days, no such idea as toleration of other than official religious opinions was admissible. The real question, then, that divided the nation was: "What Church should be *the Church?*" In 1604 King James "did absolutely conclude, No bishop, no king, no nobility." To him it was the Church of England, and it alone, "which strengtheneth the government; shake the one, and you overthrow the other. Nothing is so deeply rooted in the hearts of men as religion, nothing so powerful to direct their actions; and if once the hearts of the people be doubtful in religion, all other relations fail, and you shall find nothing but mutinies and sedition." [2]

The great and evident piety of the age notwithstanding, it was also becoming one of "stark secularism" in the urban centers, where, as Beatrice observed about Benedick, a man "wears his faith but as the fashion of his hat; it ever changes with the next block." There were some men whose thought was honestly, though usually privately, of a decidedly secular bent. Sir Walter Raleigh wrote in 1614: "And although Religion (saith he) and the truth thereof be in every man's mouth, what is it other then an universal dissimulation? We profess that we know God, but by works we deny him. . . . There is nothing more to be admired, nothing more to be lamented, then the private contention, the passionate dispute, the personal hatred, &c. about Religion among Christians, insomuch as it hath well near driven the practice thereof out of the world: So that we are in effect (saith he) become Comedians in Religion; For Charity, Justice, and Truth, have but their being in Terms amongst us." And there were more than a few persons in the metropolis who bought and read Henry Lord's *A Display of*

2. In Holland in 1634, Sir William Brereton discovered to his great surprise: "No man persecuted for religion, nor scoffed at, be he never [so] zealous." *Chetham,* I, 70; Selden, *Table Talk,* 117; W. K. Jordan, *The Development of Religious Toleration in England, From the Accession of James I, to the Convention of the Long Parliament (1603–1640),* [Cambridge, Mass., 1936], 27–8, 38–9; Godfrey Goodman, *The Court of King James the First,* ed. J. S. Brewer (London, 1839), I, 421.

two Forraigne Sects in the East Indies 1630), which catered to a rising curiosity in England about the strange rites of Hindus and Parsees.[3]

Although contention and disputes ran counter to avowed beliefs, one cannot gainsay the fact that many of the people of the generations that lived between 1590 and 1640 had undergone a spiritual quickening that made most of them less materialistic and more devout than their predecessors of the previous century. To the fear of hell inherited from the Christian past, many conjoined a gnawing sense of sin, which the Reformation, by thrusting heavy responsibility upon the individual, had heightened and exacerbated rather than assuaged. When our modern Jeremiahs attribute the uneasiness of the present day to uncertainty about the use of the atom bomb, and the manifold tensions and pressures of a technological existence that induces ulcers, mental illness, and even suicide, they might pause to reflect that all of these afflictions taken together do not attain the magnitude of the concern of the seventeenth-century man about the state of his soul. Unceasing worry and an immediate need for solace and assurance impelled even the most rugged individual to seek some form of religious knowledge. Sensing his imminent end, Sir Thomas Bitefig advised his daughter: "If ever thou hast children, teach them thrift; They'll learn religion fast enough themselves." [4]

The first recourse of the troubled soul, as of the innocent, was the English Bible, and with the steady spreading of literacy English Protestants became the greatest Scripture-readers in Christendom. To the Great Bible authorized by Henry VIII was added, in 1560, the Geneva version. Printed in roman type, divided into verses, and plentifully supplied with arguments and explanatory notes strongly tinged with Calvinism, it also included twenty-four engravings, five maps, a plan of the Garden of Eden, and descrip-

---

3. *Much Ado About Nothing,* I, i, 75; Quotation from Rushworth, *Historical Collections,* I, preface; Jordan, *Philanthropy in England,* 298–9.
4. Miss C. V. Wedgewood points to a similar state of affairs among both Protestants and Roman Catholics on the continent of Europe: "Theological controversy became the habitual reading of all classes, sermons directed their politics and moral tracts beguiled their leisure." *The Thirty Years War* (London, 1956), 17; Marc Bloch, *Feudal Society* (London, 1961), 87; Cartwright, *The Ordinary* (1634), V, i.

tions of the Holy Land and other countries and places to aid the understanding of the ordinary reader. Immediately popular with the common people because of its arrangement, this work became "the English Bible of the Elizabethan public, of the Scottish Reformation, of the English voyagers, and the first settlers in North America." To compete with the Geneva Bible, Archbishop Whitgift sponsored a new version of the Great Bible, which appeared in 1568. A copy of this edition in large folio, popularly known as the Bishop's Bible, was ordered by Convocation in 1571 to be placed in every cathedral and, as far as possible, in every parish church. In 1587 the Archbishop became uneasy because not enough village churches and chapels of ease had copies, but by 1603, 250,000 or more of the two Bibles had been sold. A Bible in English printed at Douai for Roman Catholics also won a small public.[5]

In 1604 King James I commissioned a new translation of the Bible by divines from the two universities; about fifty of them eventually undertook the work, which they completed and published in 1611. As late as 1623, however, the parishioners of Cuckfield, Sussex, were still reading the large folio Bishop's Bible; in Dorset in 1634, Queen Charlton Parish used "a faire Bible of the last edition," and Cerne Abbas continued to use its "great Bible." According to Thomas Fuller, many people who had puritan learnings did not relish the King James Bible, "suspecting it would abate the repute of that of Geneva, with their Annotations made by English exiles. . . . Yea, some complained, That they could not see into the sense of the Scripture for lack of the Spec-

5. Professor Haller tells us succinctly: "What the Geneva Bible did was to set before the reader in comprehensible terms keyed to the Scriptures a statement in the common tongue of the conception of man's inner life derived from Paul by way of Augustine and Calvin. It enabled the reader to discover for himself from the text before him that the life of man is governed from the beginning to the end of time by the design of his Creator, and that this design is revealed in the record of events. Man begins in innocent harmony with this law of his being, and this is the way of life. He contravenes the law on his own volition, and this is the way of death. From death there would be no escape, did not the Lord of life call men from time to time in their fallen condition once more to believe in Him, obey His will, and live again. Such were the elect, called out of the generality of men to strive against the spirit of disobedience, first in themselves, but then also in others." Haller, *The Elect Nation*, 73–4; H. S. Bennett, *English Books & Readers, 1558–1603* (Cambridge, Eng., 1965), 78, 142–4, 298.

tacles of those Geneva Annotations." In fact, throughout this entire period, the primacy of the Geneva version as the Bible of the
common people was never seriously threatened.[6]

It would be difficult to overemphasize the profound and varied
consequences of continuous reading of Holy Writ by people of
every rank and degree. Looking backward on this era, Thomas
Hobbes wrote in *Behemoth:* "after the Bible was translated . . .
every man, nay, every boy and wench, that could read English,
thought they spoke with God Almighty [through the marginal
notes as well as the text] and understood what he said, when by a
certain number of chapters a day they had read the Scriptures
once or twice over." The ordinary folk delighted in the Good
Book, in reading it and hearing it read or expounded, and in discussing the meaning of passages and the roots of doctrine. Here
was the new authority they all needed so much! At London, and in
other cities and towns, a Bible was kept open on the counter of
many a shop; texts were analyzed in taverns; and report had it that
some barbers even ventured to quote St. Paul while they shaved
customers. The vulgarized Bible aided mightily in stimulating literacy and improving discourse, as well as in standardizing the language. Just before his execution in 1660, Hugh Peter adjured his
daughter to read the Scriptures constantly: "Many doubtless take
up a cursory trade [in them], to read out the Cries of a defiled or
rackt Conscience: I say read with delight, not as under a load or

6. If we take Mr. Bennett's lowest estimate of 2,500 copies to each printing
of the Holy Scriptures and the 150 editions published between 1603 and 1640, a
minimum of 375,000 Bibles was printed in England. This amounts to one copy
for every 150 people, but the ratio ought to be smaller, because the usual printing
in these years was about 3,000 copies. Further, this estimate does not take into
account the unknown (though large) total of the 57 editions printed abroad,
chiefly in Holland, and surreptitiously introduced into Britain. Most of these
Bibles were the Geneva version, which Archbishop Laud tried to keep out of
circulation for theological reasons. A report of 1641, for example, mentioned
that 12,000 copies of the London roman quarto King James version, with notes
made in Holland, had been smuggled into the country. T. H. Darlow & H. F.
Moule, *Historical Catalogue of the Printed Editions of Holy Scripture* (London,
1903), I, 124–96, especially pp. 189, 190, 191–2; Neal, *History of the Puritans,* I,
469; *Sussex Arch.,* XLV, 22; *Somerset & Dorset,* VIII, 61; XIX, 98–9; *Suffolk,*
I, 80; Thomas Fuller, *The Church History of Britain* (London, 1655), bk. X, 58;
Helyn, *Cyprianus Anglicus,* 342. For convenient comparison, see the extracts
from the leading English versions of the Bible from Wyclif's to the King James,
in *Old South Leaflets,* No. 57 (Old South Association, Boston, Mass., n.d.).

as a labourer, who waits for the shadow of the Evening, which you shall never do, unless your Heart be connatural with the Word." In the very best sense, the Holy Bible was fated to be all things to all men.[7]

Second only to the vernacular Bible in forming the religious opinions and national outlook of Protestant Englishmen was John Foxe's *The Acts and Monuments of the latter and perillous dayes, touching matters of the Church, wherein are comprehended and described the great persecutions & horrible troubles, that have bene wrought and practised by Romishe Prelates, speciallye in this Realme of England and Scotland,* known as the "Book of Martyrs" after the publication of the first edition in English in 1663. In a recent work, William Haller has set forth superlatively the contribution of the Book of Martyrs both to the religious and the national sentiments of the English. "History was what Christianity was about," Foxe taught as he retold the legend of the early Christian martyrs with "an English Protestant turn and application," and continued with the modern legend of the martyrs during the well-remembered reign of "Bloody Mary." He planted in the minds of his thousands of readers the idea that the Church of Rome was the relentless foe of their country. So long as men regarded the Papacy as the main adversary of the Church of England, Foxe's treatise was the first line of defense.[8]

Before 1641, about 10,000 copies of this volume came off the presses and found ready sale among the country gentlemen, merchants, and yeomen, who read them over and over, and lent them to their friends. "I praye youe send me my boke of martors," Henry Browne wrote to the Lord of the Manor of Groton in 1593. The Book of Martyrs, as well as the Bible, was to be found in the home of any Essex yeoman who, like John George, possessed some books, and it was bequeathed as a prized belonging to one's heirs. In Dorset in 1636, Lawrence Phelps the elder left to the

7. Thomas Hobbes, *Works,* ed. Sir William Molesworth (London, 1839–45), VI, 190; Besant, *London,* 137, 139; Haller, *Rise of Puritanism,* 132; Hugh Peter, *A Dying Father's Last Legacy* (Boston, Mass., 1717), 4.
8. An enlarged edition of the Book of Martyrs, with heart-stirring woodcuts, came out in 1570, the year of the Papal Bull deposing Queen Elizabeth. By 1640 the work had reached its eighth edition. Haller, *The Elect Nation,* particularly pp. 130, 135, 138, 154, 186.

church at Thorncombe "the booke of Martyrs if it maye be had for three pounds," otherwise the money. The parish records of Stogumber, Somersetshire, indicate that Richard Hawkins bequeathed £5 to the church for the purchase of "3 bookes of Marters in folio and 1 other book called Dr. Fulks Annotation upon the New Testament." The record goes on to report on all of the books, which had "Roit [wrought iron?] chains annexed unto them; and one [was] in the possession of some of the parishioners, one in one mans hand an another in anothers. But were never as yet placed in the Church according to the Doners last will and Testament." [9]

II

We must now attempt to envisage the parts that faith and worship played in the daily round of activities of ordinary Englishmen and to indicate how for them all life was encased in religious experience. They never lived apart from their churches. Before we have proceeded far into the matter, we shall discover that their faiths and attitudes toward ecclesiastical affairs, as well as their ways of worship, differed sufficiently between county and town to warrant separate treatment, and that this fact was clear to contemporaries.

In rural parishes, religious life was more of a social phenomenon than a theological or political concern for the bulk of villagers. The entire community was organized about the church, physically as well as spiritually. As Foscarini, Mundy, Brereton, and others traveled about the countryside, the first indication that they were approaching a village or market town was nearly always the sight of a church in the distance. It might be a glimpse of a squat Norman tower, like that of St. John's, atop the hill at Finchingfield, or of St. Pancras, snugly sheltered in its valley at Widecombe-in-the-Moor in Devonshire. The same held true of most of the larger places, nowhere more notably than at Market Harborough; the Church of St. Dionysius there had one of the finest steeples in the land, and its entire structure contributed much to the remarkably successful townscape of the Square which

9. If again we use Bennett's figures of 2,500 for an average printing, it appears that about 10,000 sets were issued. *Winthrop Papers*, I, 36; Steer, *Farm and County Inventories of Mid-Essex*, 48, 82; *Somerset & Dorset*, X, 167; XVII, 77.

at closer range so charmed the visitor. In truth, in nearly every one of the 9,000 or so country parishes of England, the church edifice, set in its yard, was the most important building.[10]

Most peasants and yeomen, and even country gentlemen, Anglicans or Puritans, seem to have been indifferent to the beauty of Christian art and Gothic architecture. Perhaps the church edifice with its elaborate exterior and interior decorative detail stood as a reminder to many an Englishman of a past he would rather forget, or else the old structures were so much a part of the familiar scene that men no longer thought of them apart from their use. In view of the remarkable benevolence of the time, surprisingly few bequests were made for the upkeep and repair of church fabrics.[11]

This indifference to the structural or artistic distinction of churches, combined with declining and shifting populations, in part explains the number of decayed parish churches everywhere. Norfolk, with the most parishes (660) of any county, simply had too many structures to keep up. For decades the archdeaconry courts had been listening to presentments about dilapidated edifices. Churchwardens and vestries, who may have deplored the state of disrepair, seduously avoided raising parish rates. "Our Church is in great decay," reported the churchwardens of Swalecliffe in Kent in 1565, "for the parish is so poor that they are not able to repair the same, unless they have some help of the land within the parish, whereof we would pay two pence the acre, which would amount to the sum of £8; and we think our Church and the keeping of the churchyard will stand us more." By 1627, Thomas Vicars, the Puritan vicar of Cuckfield, Sussex, with his own hands and at his own charge, had built the vestry of the church, glazed two windows, and made extensive repairs and improvements in the parsonage. The churchwardens of Edburton were presented at the Deaconry Court of South Malling in 1620 for neglecting their church, which was "exceeding ruinous and like to fall by reason of a certayne burying place fastened unto it and leaning uppon it at the default of Thomas Hanaden, tenant of Sir Benjamin Pellatt, Knight." Archbishop Laud's determined and

10. Pevsner, *Essex*, pl. 1b; Pevsner, *South Devon*, pl. 3b; Pevsner, *Leicestershire and Rutland*, pl. 11; Sir George Clark, in *Bulletin of the History of Medicine*, XXXI, 395.

11. Jordan, *Charities of Rural England*, 65, 66, 71.

partly successful effort to improve the condition of parish churches
after the famous visitation of 1633–38 must be viewed against this
background of more than half a century of indifference and neglect.[12]

The average parish church was used for many activities besides
those of weekly worship: mid-week lectures, marriages, christen-
ings, and funerals. Frequently the schoolmaster conducted classes
in the edifice; the vestry met there once a month or oftener, as did
the justices of the peace and the overseers of the poor. When the
peripatetic archdeacon's court arrived, it convened in the building,
and the coroner held his inquests in the church. In fact most of the
parish business went on inside or right outside of the structure.
Parsons stored tithe-payments of wool or grain above the belfry,
and the trainbands kept their pikes, armor, and powder in the vestry. The latest news, lay and ecclesiastical, was read from the pulpit every Lord's Day, and all sorts of notices were posted in the
porch or nailed to the church door.[13]

If the church edifice served as an all-purpose community center
much as it had in the Middle Ages, and as it or the meetinghouse
would in North America, its churchyard was often appropriated
for even more miscellaneous religious and civic uses, and such irreverent pastimes that the rude forefathers, who were buried there,
could scarcely have slept in peace. In country churchyards from
the Midlands southward, and especially in the West Country, on or
near Whitsuntide, church-ales (or revels) began immediately after
evening prayer for the raising of funds for the church or some impoverished worthy inhabitant. The parishioners spent days fever-
ishly preparing meats and other foods for the feast. All the neighboring villagers were invited, and attendances were large because
peasants and yeomen of all ages and both sexes crowded into the
churchyard for the rare treat of eating their fill of meat. After-
wards, minstrels, drum players, and pipers provided music for
dancing, and sometimes professional bear-baiters entertained the
crowds. Because brawling and licentiousness were a frequent after-

12. A. Tindal Hart, *The Country Clergy in Elizabethan & Stuart Times, 1558–
1660* (London, 1958), 94–8; Jordan, *Charities in Rural England,* 21, Fuller,
Worthies, II, 124; *Kent,* XXVII, 218; *Sussex Arch.,* XLV, 19; L, 42, 43, 44;
Devon & Cornwall, XXIV, 38; *CSPD, 1635,* xxxiii.
13. Hart, *Country Clergy,* 80.

math, the justices of Devon, as early as 1595, attempted to restrict church-ales and other "unlawful assemblies," extremely popular though they were; and, as the years passed, other local bodies enacted restrictions. In 1633 a climax was reached in Somerset with the famous factional and political dispute over church-ales; the result was that the church-ales were allowed; later in the year, when the Book of Sports was reissued, they were regularized.[14]

During the spring and summer months, "the inhabitants and youth" gathered in the churchyards on Sundays to engage in May-games, dancing, and rough-and-tumble sports. These boisterous diversions attracted "many ruffians and drunken companions," and the ensuing racket made it impossible to conduct services in the church. In Worcestershire on a Sunday in 1617, "the youth of Langdon," compelled to cease their play during evening prayer, forced an excommunicated woman into the church and then informed the minister of her presence, "hoping thereby to put an end to God's service, that so they might again return to their sports." Over the years the inhabitants of Wimsborne Parish, Dorset, were presented for a variety of offenses against their churchyard: some of them kept hogs there; Alice Wood winnowed malt in it; and some person had stacked dirty timber in the yard. In 1615 the Archdeacon's Court of Lewes found against John Maynard, whose father had enclosed part of the churchyard in Wartling; he, the son, was continuing to work it as part of his farm.[15]

Although a wave of piety surged across England, the vast majority of the peasants, as their conduct reveals, could scarcely have been labeled devout at this time. Recently a distinguished

14. A general term, church-ale comprehended parish-ale, Whitsun-ale, clerk-ale, sexton-ale, bid-ale (for the poor), and King-ale. The churchwardens of Chagford, Devon, were called "Alewardens." A *wake* was an annual church festival usually held on the day of the local patron saint. At a "Kingale" held in Woolton Parish, Hampshire, in 1600, the total cost was £8 10*d.*, which the churchwardens laid out on minstrels, lords and ladies' "lyveries" (costumes), three calves, four and a half lambs, one sheep, "a barren ewe," a fat sheep, a ling-and-a-half, fresh fish, eggs, butter, fruit, and spices; also for suet, malt, hops, and faggots. It was later recorded: "Rec. by our Kingale all things discharged" £12 9*s.* 1*d. Hampshire,* XI, 171–5; Ware, *Elizabethan Parish,* 70–75; Prynne, *Canterburies Doome,* 128, 131–2; Barnes, in *RHS Trans.,* 5th ser., IX, 103–22; Hamilton, *Quarter Sessions,* 28–9, 73, 115.
15. Hamilton, *Quarter Sessions,* 28, 115; *HMC Various,* I, 294; *Dorset,* XLVII, 43; *Sussex Arch.,* XLIX, 59, 65; L, 43, 45.

authority has questioned whether many farm laborers ever attended church. The fact that one seldom finds any mention of farm laborers or servants in parish records seems to indicate that the churchwardens gave them scant attention; after all, laborers paid little or no tithes or parish rates, and as for servants, their families could look after them, as the Oxindens did in Kent. And surely John Walles, who was presented by the churchwardens of Stahampton, Oxfordshire, for not receiving "communyen at Easter last" was not unique. "Hee is A very poor man and saith hee had not clothes fyt to come in company then but now hee keepeth the swyne and hopeth hee shall Earne mony and will prepare him self to Receave the next communyen." [16]

As previous examples of cases presented to the bawdy courts reveal, many members of the lower ranks had little sense of the beauty of holiness. They often deliberately ignored the 18th Canon of 1604, which stated that in time of divine service, "all due reverence is to be used." "Let all things be done decently and according to order." George Herbert, Anglican parson of Bemerton, Wiltshire, writing out of experience, urged country clergymen to instruct their parishioners how to "carry themselves in divine service" and to exact of them "all possible reverence, by no means enduring either talking, or sleeping, or gazing, or leaning, or half-kneeling, or any undutiful behavior in them . . . attending to what is done in the Church, and every one, man and child, answering aloud both Amen, and all other answers . . . which answers also are to be done not in a hudling, or slubbering fashion, gaping or scratching the head, or spitting even in the midst of their answer, but gently and pausable, thinking what they say." The parish meeting of Horley, Surrey, appointed John Ansty "to see that the younge men and boyes behave themselves decently in church," but most churchwardens and clergymen hesitated to take positive action against irreverent behavior.[17]

16. Notestein, *English People*, 85; *Oxinden Letters*, 125; *The Churchwardens' Presentments in the Oxfordshire Peculiars of Dorchester, Thame, and Banbury*, ed. S. A. Peyton (Oxfordshire Record Society, 1928), X, 68; Essex Arch., X, 27b.
17. *Synodalia, A Collection of Articles of Religion, Canons, and Proceedings of Convocations in the Province of Canterbury . . .* , ed. E. Cardwell (Oxford, 1842), I, 253, 255–6; George Herbert, *A Priest to the Temple, Or, The Country Parson His Character, and Rule of Holy Life* [1632] (3d ed., 1675) 17–18; *Surrey*, VIII, 249.

Such want of courtesy, sadly enough, was not always confined to laborers. In Norfolk during 1596–97, Thomas Blenerhasset, gentleman, did "diverse and sundrye tymes" interrupt the vicar of Horsford during the reading "by lowde talkinge, laugheinge and readinge, wherebie at one time theire vicar was constrayned to leave of[f] service and go out of the church." A Roman Catholic gentleman named Southcote refused to allow the minister to say the service on Christmas day in 1598. And everywhere, country-men of all degrees squabbled over where they would sit in church.[18]

The frequency and extreme bitterness of these quarrels over seating arrangements, which not infrequently ended in court cases, reflect the concern of all those involved about their place in a rap-idly changing society; they also testify to the charge that most churchgoers went to church to be seen as much as to worship. Women everlastingly created disturbances over what they consid-ered an affront to their "respective dignities, states and condi-tions." Elizabeth Stolyon was presented in 1611 "for behaving her-self disorderly in the church by striking Katherine Rodes about a seate which they contend for" in St. Dunstan's, Mayfield. Probably the defendant felt as did a gentleman of Great Chesham in Buck-inghamshire, who complained that "Some of the meanest account had gotten the best seats, and would sit with persons of far better reckoning." Whatever else may be said about the widespread bick-ering over who should have the best seats in church, it was an Eng-lish contention of long standing, not a puritan innovation.[19]

All devout people deplored these various impieties, and many clergymen recognized them for what they were, the acts of simple-

18. *Norfolk*, XVIII, 47; Essex Arch., 22b; Stone, *Aristocracy*, 223; Essex Sessions, XVIII, 142.
19. Most country churches contained only benches for the worshipers. On a trip through Cheshire in 1626, the Earl of Huntington was surprised to find in Wybunbury "a fair country church and well seated with close pews like the manner of London churches, all of one form and height." In some parish churches servants sat in the front pews with their masters and their families; in other churches only the prominent men sat in front; their wives, children, and servants sat apart and further back. The cottagers and all strangers were usually relegated to the galleries. *HMC Hastings*, IV, 339; *Surtees*, LXXXIV, viii, 86–7; Essex Arch., XI, 7a; *Devon & Cornwall*, XI, 26–9; *Somerset & Dorset*, XIV, 158–62; XIX, 88–9; *Sussex Arch.*, XXXIV, 155; XLVIII, 28–9; L, 43; LII, 96–8; LIV, 271–2, 272–3; *Buckinghamshire*, IX, 332–46.

minded, unsophisticated countryfolk, which stemmed, for the most part, from what the Bishop of Chester, speaking figuratively of his own diocese, called "the dry and barren soyl." There were others, many of whom, as the vestry of Berkhamsted in Hampshire admitted, "through lack of devotion are idle beholders," but Richard Baxter, analyzing the common people of Shropshire and Worcestershire prior to 1640, summed them all up: "The generality seemed to mind nothing seriously but the body and the world; they went to church and would answer the parson in responds, and then to dinner, and then to play; they never prayed in their families, but some of them going to bed would say over the Creed, and the Lord's Prayer, and some of them Hail Mary: all the year long, not a serious word of holy things, or the life to come that I could hear of, proceeded from them. They read not the Scripture nor any good book or catechism. Few of them could read, or had a Bible." [20]

To a degree, the behavior and attitudes of rural parishioners mirrored the deplorable state of the conforming clergy. In all parts of the nation one heard the persistent refrain of poor vicars that their livings did not yield enough to feed and clothe them, nor could the ordinary country parson afford the few books needed for pastoral work. The real income of many a parish living failed to keep pace with the rise of prices before 1640, and the natural consequence, as Dr. George Carleton remarked, was that "preferments [were] sold to the unworthy and studious men were scouted." Indeed it has been said that only "the basest sort of people" became incumbents in the rural areas.[21]

Somewhere between 13,000 and 15,000 clergymen must have served as rectors, vicars, curates, lecturers, and schoolmasters in England's 10,000 parishes. It has been estimated that in 1640 not more than 4,000 of them were High-Church Laudians, and only about a thousand were strict Puritans; the large remainder was

20. *Camden,* 2d ser., I, 180; Powell, *Puritan Village,* 35; Baxter, *The True History of Councils,* 90, quoted in Gardiner, *England,* VIII, 124.

21. A notable exception to the generalization of poverty was Oliver Ditson, rector of Dumbleton in Gloucestershire, who left an estate of £334 8s. 8d., the twentieth largest in a list of 400 inventories. *Bristol & Gloucester,* XLVI, 187, 193. Godfrey Goodman deals with the grievances and complaints of the clergy in 1616 in *The Fall of Man,* 162. Hart, *Country Clergy,* 93, 94; Christopher Hill, *Economic Problems of the Church* (Oxford, 1957), 108, 203–4; *CSPD, 1611–18,* p. 489.

composed of middle-of-the-road men with less identifiable sym-
pathies which covered the entire spectrum of conviction. [22]

Considering the caliber of these indigent ministers, it is not surprising that some of them were guilty of the same improprieties
and evil courses that brought their parishioners up before the
authorities. Many clerics were habitual drunkards. Current London comedies, notably *The Ordinary,* by the florid Laudian
preacher William Cartwright, pictured clergymen as pothouse companions in words even less flattering than the harsh ones reserved
for puritans. More than one minister was charged with incontinence and fathering bastards. Francis Wright, vicar of the Essex
parish of Witham, went before the Court of High Commission in
1635 for committing adultery with his maidservant, Margaret
Claydon, for drunkenness, and for other derelictions from the
priestly function. He even falsified his oath! At Brompton in the
North Riding, Rowland Sewell extorted 20s. for a burial, "no such
fee being legally due." Then there were timeservers and climbers,
one of whom Andrew Marvel described mercilessly: "Hee daunct
uppon bishops, cutt capers from one preferment to another, and
vaulted from steeple to steeple." [23]

Not more than a third to a half of the country parishes enjoyed
the ministrations of properly trained incumbents. Of the 484 ministers in Norfolk in 1593, only 198 had attended universities.
Forty-two years later, Bishop Wren admitted to Archbishop Laud
that, though his diocese embracing Norfolk and Suffolk had 1,500
clergymen, only half of the churches had a clerk who could read
—a condition that led to the disuse of responses by the people.
Among the singular advantages of Suffolk, Robert Reyce noticed
in 1618, was "the great number of religious, grave, reverend, and
learned ministers of God's holy word, which are planted in this
shire." But like the author, most of them were Puritans. John Selden's dictum of 1634 was that "All confesse there never was a

---

22. G. B. Tatham, *The Puritans in Power* (London, 1913), 53–4. For the number
of clergymen in Devon, Norfolk, and the Diocese of Lincon around 1600, see
Devon & Cornwall, XV, 38; *Norfolk & Norwich,* XVIII, Pt. I, 79–81; and for
the Puritans in 24 counties, Neal, *History of the Puritans,* I, 434.
23. Wedgwood, in Plumb, *Social History,* 117; *CSPD, 1635,* p. 217; *North Riding
Sessions,* III, 270, 289; Ward, *Diary,* 292; *Sussex Arch.,* XLIX, 65; *HMC Various,*
I, 98; *Middlesex Sessions,* I, 5; *HMC Buccleuch,* I, 205.

more learned Clergy." It was true that the number of educated parsons had increased since 1590, but still a large number of unlettered clergymen failed miserably in the cure of souls.[24]

Lack of spiritual zeal seemed to be a natural corollary of the lack of education and general culture. Lay and ecclesiastical critics alike became concerned about the low repute of the clergy as charges of neglect poured in from all directions. Of Bartholomew Awdy, rector of St. Peter's at South Elmham, Norfolk, it was said: "He is unlearned and readeth not service distinctly. He doth not Catachise the yowth and readeth not service at due tyme. He practiseth physicke." The rector of Cawley, Thomas Bide, had to answer at the Archdeacon's Court in Lewes in 1626 for not preaching or reading a monthly sermon, "no not a sermon in the whole yeare." He gave himself, said the charge, to augment a scanty income, "to base and servile labour," skimped on apparel, and allowed his parsonage to fall into disrepair. Besides, "he catechizeth not at all." Some inhabitants thought their minister greedy and ruthless when he enclosed land, and more of them resented paying tithes out of their lean purses to support lazy, incompetent, negligent, and sometimes immoral parsons. William Massie, a gentleman of Springfield, Essex, expressed this sentiment very bluntly when he shouted at the rector during the service: "Parson taylor we should have had some good or goodebye sermon of you this day, but belike you are not well provided for the same." [25]

In many parishes, the churchwardens, whose office it was to assist the pastor in all possible ways, also failed to live up to the ex-

24. *Norfolk & Norwich*, XVIII, Pt. I, 80–81; *CSPD, 1636–7*, p. 223; Hill, *Economic Problems of the Church*, 207; Reyce, *Suffolk*, 21; Selden, *Table Talk*, 31–2; Haller, *Rise of Puritanism*, 39–40; Notestein, *English People*, 64.
25. In a chapter on "The Parson in Contempt," Herbert faced the problem candidly: "The Countrey Parson knows well, that both for the general ignominie, which is cast upon the profession, and much more for those rules, which out of his choicest judgment, he hath resolved to observe . . . he must be despised." *A Priest to the Temple*, 114; "Many ministers should be regarded and oftener heard, were it not that they call for tythes and maintenance." By far the largest number of citations before the ecclesiastical courts from Wimborne Minster Parish, 1570–1670, was for the failure to pay tithes or for not paying the correct amount. Nehemiah Rogers, *The True Convert* (1631), 76; *CSPD, 1603–10*, p. 49; Hart, *Country Clergy*, 86; *Dorset*, XLVII, 48; *Norfolk*, XVIII, 31, 69, 122–3; *Sussex Arch.*, XLIX, 61; Essex Sessions, XVII, 108; Hill, *Economic Problems of the Church*, 121.

pectations of those who chose them, either in their ecclesiastical or their civic capacities. Peter Heylyn pointed out in 1636 that "many times in Country Villages . . . the Church-wardens cannot read, and therefore be not employed in publishing . . . Declarations, which require more knowing than a silly villager." The "Guards" (wardens) of Great Tey once faced the Essex ecclesiastical court for "mingling beer with wyne for the Communion." A complaint was lodged in the Archdeaconry Court of Lewes that wine was brought to communion table in a bottle; that there was "no table of marriage," and that the churchyard was not properly fenced. The Archdeacon's Court at Oxford censured the churchwardens of Duns Tew in 1583 "for keeping enterludes and playes in the church and brawling in the church abowte the same with one old Poulton, and caused Poulton to be cited to D[r.] Floides courte; allso for shoting and gamming in the churchyarde upon their weekdays or evening prayer." The wardens confessed "that there was an enterlude plaide in the Church of Dunstewe upon a Saterdaye in the evening after the service was done . . . by the consent of Warden Robert Mesie." [26]

Rural parishes could have put up with a good deal of laxity in their ministers had they but preached to the people. Writing of preachers in 1571, Edmund Bunny deplored "the great lack of doctrine, and of the preaching of Gods word universally abrode in the country . . . a man may go a great way, and cannot heare the word of the Lorde preached." Seventy years later, a report from Herefordshire told of 225 churches and chapels where there never were "but twenty constant prechers that prech twice a day . . . and the nearer to the sea the worst." The Puritans dubbed the clergy dumb dogs for not preaching, but the Anglican George Herbert maintained that "The Countrey Parson preacheth constantly, the Pulpit is his joy and throne." He urged the minister to speak with great earnestness in language that his rustic listeners could understand. Country livings had increasingly passed into An-

26. Richard Purdye of Glastonbury, Somerset, repeatedly had to sue the church-wardens of the various churches for whom he had cast new bells or enlarged old ones, and for which he had never received payment. *Somerset & Dorset*, X, 352, 353, 354; Canons of 1604, No. CIX, *Synodalia*, I, 308–12; Heylyn, *Cyprianus Anglicus*, 278; Essex Arch., XII, 31a; *RHS Trans.*, 4th ser., XXV, 111; *Sussex Arch.*, XLIX, 60, 62; Hart, *Country Clergy*, 77.

glican hands after the defeat of the Puritans at the Hampton Court
Conference, and the majority of clerics preferred to catechize or
read homilies. Whatever their defenders might say, good preachers
were exceedingly scarce in rural districts.[27]

The deep-seated, dormant puritanism of large sections of the
rural population had created a ravenous hunger after the Word. A
few country parsons essayed the witty style that Lancelot Andrewes and his imitators made so popular in London and the great
towns, but humor and classical allusions did not go down with the
average man then any more readily than they do today. In the little Derbyshire village of Calke, every time Master Julines Herring
preached during the years 1610–18, "people from twenty towns
and villages flocked into Cawk Chappell (as Doves to a Window)"
to hear the Scriptures read and sermons delivered. Others stood
outside at the windows when they could not get into the building.
They arrived in companies early in the morning, either brought
their own victuals or ate "a three-penny ordinary purposely provided," stayed all day to worship, and went home in the evening
singing psalms and repeating the sermons. But this situation,
while notable, was exceptional. A long nationwide experience lay
behind the petition from Hertfordshire to the House of Commons
in 1642, praising its zeal in providing a "Preaching Ministry
throughout the kingdom, whereof this County stands in great
neede, it now abounding with insufficient, Idle, and Scandalous
Ministers, whereby the people generally are continued in Ignorance, Superstition, and prophaneness, and are ready to become a
pray to popish seducers, which Idolatrous profession hath of late
years with much boldness appeared in this County." [28]

We may conclude this survey of the country parishes with the
observation that the great majority of the rural inhabitants actually
did turn out to be mere "idle beholders." Such, of course, has been

27. Edmund Bunny, *A Sermon preached at Pauls crosse on Trinity Sunday, 1571*
(1576), sig, f. ii, verso; Herbert, *Priest to the Temple*, 20; Hart, *Country Clergy*,
69, 74; *HMC Portland*, iii, 79; Essex Sessions, 142; Curtis, *Oxford and Cambridge*,
189, 190.
28. Robert Wincke of North Ockenden was presented to the Essex Archdeaconry
Court because he refused to attend common prayer on holy days "unlesse there
be a sermon." Essex Arch., X, 28b; Tatham, *Puritans in Power*, 53–4; Samuel
Clarke, *A General Martyrologie . . . Whereunto are added the Lives of Sundry
Modern Divines* (3d ed., 1677), 191; Camden, LVIII, 227.

the case with the mass of the people in all ages. Still, even for this
large number, we can never overlook the patent fact that their village church continued to be the pivot about which revolved their
economic and social activities as well as the worship lawfully required of them. However, the winds of change were rapidly fresh-
ening. In many a community there lived "poor tractable People"
like those whom Richard Baxter discovered at Dudley, "lately
famous for drunkenness, but commonly more ready to hear God's
word with submission and reformation, than most places where I
have come." There is small doubt that, after 1620, the number of
hungry lambs in the English countryside was on the increase.[29]

III

When countrymen moved to a large town, a provincial city, or to
London, they found churches which, though they resembled those
left behind in many ways, were also strikingly different. There
were rich and poor parishes everywhere to which newly arrived
persons had either been directed or to which they naturally gravi-
tated. Most town and city parishes contained more people than
rural ones, and with the passage of years, the proportion of those
born and raised outside of the parish rose. In great centers, such as
Norwich, Exeter, Bristol, and London, a significant mingling took
place of migrants from all over the land—men and women who
were seeking spiritual sustenance at their parish churches; sociability they could enjoy in the city in many other ways. Although,
as Archbishop Laud properly pointed out, many of the city
churches, including St. Paul's, were in need of repair, they were
generally superior to and larger than country structures. All of
these differences contemporaries recognized as concomitants of
urban conditions.

That the majority of the parishioners were better behaved, preserved a greater decorum during public worship, and displayed far
more respect for the dignity of their pastors than their rural brethren is patent, but there was, nevertheless, the same incessant
wrangling over seating arrangements. In the cloth town of Cog-

29. F. J. Powicke, *A Life of the Reverend Richard Baxter, 1615–1691* (London,
1924), 26.

geshall in 1598, there occurred such "great disorder in the sytting of the parishioners in the church" that the authorities ordered the six headboroughs to seat them all "according to their discretion and according to their place, and accompt and reckoning." And if any further trouble arose, they were to present the names of the disputants to the next court. An incident at Plymouth in 1603 suggests the degree to which the struggle for position could attain. Determined to maintain the privileges of her rank, Lady Hawkins slapped the face of the Mayoress, Mistress Downname, whom she had once employed as a maid, when the latter would not consent to relinquish the civic pew in St. Andrew's Church. The incensed Corporation was not appeased until Sir Richard Hawkins presented them with a deed to a house he owned in the market place.[30]

The amenities of town life and the more lucrative livings available at some of the churches in urban centers attracted many of the abler, better-educated, more sophisticated, and usually ambitious members of the clergy. They might be such strong Anglicans as John Donne, Lancelot Andrewes, or John Cosin, or non-separating puritans of the stripe of John White of Dorchester, Samuel Ward of Ipswich, or John Davenport of London. All of these men were dedicated to their work and, whatever the nature of their convictions about church polity, they were deeply concerned about the manners and morals of their flocks. At Theobalds in 1619, the Dean of Salisbury preached before King James "against our pride and excesse in apparell" and "soft raiment" with as great verve as any puritan pastor could muster.[31]

Like their rural counterparts, not a few incumbents in the towns failed to measure up to the standards of the parishioners who provided them with comfortable livings. The town clerk of Barnstaple, Philip Wyot, preserved an instance of clerical transgression in his diary. One Friday in November, 1600, the Mayor and Aldermen were making their evening search "as usual" when they "found the Vicar Mr. Frynder in John Williams House being a Tipler with other company, and having amongst them a pipe with a tabor, a

30. Essex Arch., XII, 22b; Henry Francis Whitfeld, *Plymouth and Devonport: in Times of War and Peace* (2d ed., Plymouth, 1900), 77; Plumb, *Social History*, 60.
31. *Devon & Cornwall*, XIII, 296, Russell, *Dartmouth*, 94; *HMC Gaudy*, X, 164; Williams, *A Sermon of Apparell*.

little after nine; and because Mr. Frynder would not come down to Mr. Mayor from the Chamber upon Commandment" and for his other rude actions, the vicar was committed to ward until the next morning. He managed somehow to get a letter out to the Bishop of Exeter, in which he insisted that he had been committed without cause; the Bishop promptly took the matter up with the Earl of Bath. Rank prevailed in this case, for, after a hearing at Tavistock, his Lordship released the parson; the unfortunate mayor was "remitted to my Lord of Bath's censure." Doubtless too, the parishioners continued to be ill-served by the bibulous cleric.[32]

Townsmen and citizens of all shades of religious conviction were confirmed savorers of sermons. They listened to the preaching in London at St. Paul's Cross, or in a parish church at Warwick, Leicester, Ottery St. Mary, Dorchester, St. Mary's, Cambridge, Great Yarmouth, or Boston; they were never confined just to those of the puritan way; they simply loved a sermon. Though the "witty discourse" of Bishop Andrewes suited a cultured few in the larger communities, the "spiritual preaching" launched by John Smyth and Richard Greenham steadily won favor among the multitudes, who found the Biblical, homely qualities of the "plain style" more comprehensible—and more spiritually troubling. In commenting upon the preaching of Laudian ministers, from whom so many hearers "goe away so well contented," Thomas Hooker spoke for both town and country: "I have sometime admired at this: why a company of Gentlemen, Yeomen, and poore women, that are scarcely able to know the A.B.C. Yet they have a Minister to speake Latine, Greeke, and Hebrew, and to use the Fathers, when it is certaine, they know nothing at all. The reason is, because *all this stings not,* they may sit and sleepe in their sinnes, and *goe to hell hood-winckt . . .*" The plain preachers shot their arrows directly into the hearts of their listeners. William Lynne, re-

32. The parishioners of the populous but poor St. Botolph's without Aldgate saw in Thomas Swadlin the very opposite of a puritan curate, one whom they believed "had dealt lewdly and spent the poores stock in taverns." When a minister was preaching in his church, he spent his time in the tavern. Once he returned after the sermon, married a couple, and then returned to the tavern and said, "Come let us goe to it againe, Here is money, And so fell to drinckinge againe." Dorothy Ann Williams, "London Puritanism: The Parish of St. Botolph Without Aldgate," in *Guildhall Miscellany,* II, 31; Wyot, *Diary,* Nov. 14, 1600.

porting to Archbishop Laud, expressed the view that "people that call so for the Word, yet love not the Church." [33]

Many of the clergymen of the Church of England who were inclined to puritanism, and who, like John Cotton, changed over from the witty to the plain or spiritual preaching, published their sermons for the edification of a public that valued such works only slightly less than the Geneva Bible or Foxe's Martyrs. Peddlers working out of London or from the provincial cities under the direction of certain ministers and booksellers hawked these sermons and moral tracts in the "dark and distant corners, where Soules were ready to famish for lack of the food of the word." Near Shrewsbury, Richard Baxter lived with his yeoman parents at High Ercall. Between the ages of ten and fourteen he borrowed the works of the great William Perkins from a servant in the house, "And about that time [c. 1626] it pleased God that a poor Pedlar came to the Door that had some Ballads and some good Books: And my Father bought of him *Dr. Sibb's bruised Reed*. This I also read." Such reading matter from the towns, together with the Scriptures, in some measure made up for the absence of preaching in many a country neighborhood.[34]

To a substantial number of migrants to the cities and towns, one of the principal attractions of town life was the opportunity to hear good sermons. "But surely when I come out of the cuntry hether to the City," said Edmund Bunny, "methink I come into another world, even out of darknes into light, for here the word of God is

---

33. In the Epistle Dedicatory to four sermons printed in 1603 as *The Bright Morning Starre*, John Smyth, "Preacher of the Citie" of Lincoln, frankly stated that "I purposed to apply my style to the understanding of the simple, I indeavour to utter matter withall plainenesse of words and sentences." *Works of John Smyth*, ed. W. T. Whitely (London, 1915), I, 2; Thomas Hooker, *The Soule's Preparation for Christ, Or a Treatise of Contrition* (1632), 66 (my italics); Wyot, Diary, Dec. 1600; Haller, *The Rise of Puritanism*, 19, 23, 30; *CSPD, 1634–5*, p. 252.

34. John Smyth protested at "seeing every bald tale, vaine, enterlude, and pelting ballad, hath the privilege of the Presse, the sermons and readings of ministers may challenge the same; the worlde is full of Guy of Warwicke, William of Cloudeski, Skoggins and Wolner's jests, and writings of like qualitie; and therein men take great delight to read, and so make themselves merrie with other mens sinnes, bestowing to this purpose much vaine time and superfluous expences: and I thinke the Stationers shop, and some men's shelves are better furnished with such trifles, which deceive the minde and affection as the baite doeth the fish, then with wholesome writings of nature, art, or religion." Smyth, *Works*, 2; Fuller, *Church History*, bk. XI, 142; *Reliquæ Baxterianæ*, 1, 3.

plentifully preached. I pray God it may be as plentifully folowed."
During the reign of Queen Elizabeth, some puritan ministers, with
strong support from rich, philanthropic laymen, had introduced sermons on one or more weekdays, called lectures, which they arranged to be delivered on market days when countrymen crowded
into the towns. By such means, the "puritan Faction" deliberately
built up within the Church of England, "a veritable though unac-
knowledged and unauthorized order or brotherhood of preachers,
working in large measure independently of though not in direct
conflict with, constituted authority." John Selden was once heard
to say that "Lecturers doe in a parish what the Fryers did heretofore." [35]

The regular minister might preach the lecture himself, or a non-
beneficed clergyman might deliver the sermon and be paid by the
churchwardens, the corporation, or from funds contributed by
some local merchant, for leading residents of the provincial cities
generously supported these lectureships. In 1601 a merchant, John
Felton, left 10s. a year "forever" to continue "the prayer and lecture lately begun in the new chapel in Yarmouth." Lawrence
Bodley, canon of Exeter Cathedral, provided in his will of 1615
for what became the famous lecture that bears his name; a few
years later Thomas Mogeridge, a wealthy merchant, donated £200
more toward the maintenance of this same lectureship. Sometimes
a lucrative source of support came from the men who had gone up
to London and made large fortunes, part of which they used to
endow sermons and lectures in their native villages, towns, or
cities. Among the many good acts of Rowland Heylyn, the ironmonger, was the founding of a lectureship with an annual stipend of
£20 in the parish of St. Alkmund at Shrewsbury. At Maidstone
"the knights and gentlemen" first proposed that a "Lacter" be
established; twelve or more years later in 1640, "a Church meet-
inge" was determining "how to procure a Lecturer to preach Sun-
daies in the afternoone." [36]

35. Bunny, *Sermon preached at Pauls crosse*, sig. f. ii, recto; William Haller,
Liberty and Reformation in the Puritan Revolution (New York, 1955), 11–12,
15; and more fully in Haller, *Rise of Puritanism*, *passim;* Selden, *Table Talk*,
71–2.
36. The parishioners of Isleworth Hundred, Middlesex, began in 1600 to appoint
lecturers, whom they paid themselves. *VCH Middlesex*, III, 124; *Surtees*, LXV,
126, 128; Waters, *Gleanings*, II, 1399; W. J. Harte, Gleanings from the Manu-

Most of the lecturers had been educated in the puritan colleges of Oxford and Cambridge, particularly at Emmanuel at the latter university, where Lawrence Chaderton and John Preston profoundly influenced their charges. Master John Cotton, having served as a fellow from 1603 to 1612 at Emmanuel, accepted a call to St. Botolph's Church in Boston. Every Sabbath morning he preached a two-hour sermon. "This being done," one of Laud's minions reported in 1614, "he spends two hours more in the explanation of these his own questions and answers, soe that they keepe the same tenour all the yeare which they did when we were with them. Theire afternoone worship, as they used to terme it, will be five houres, where, to my observation, there were as many sleepers as wakers, scarce any man but sometimes was forced to wink or nod." What if many did become drowsy? The astounding fact is that this divine filled the largest parish church in England to overflowing for something like eight or nine hours every Sunday, and again for his mid-week lecture. Of John White at Dorchester it was said that "He absolutely commanded his own passions, and the purses of his Parishioners, whom he could wind up to what height he pleased on important occasions." In 1626 Mr. White's lectures were increased from two to three days a week.[37]

Sermons were much in fashion, so John Chamberlain observed, and certainly Londoners were as avid as any Englishmen in their attendance. "Let us goe see that Marriage, and then wee will goe to heare the sermon at Paules crosse," said the Gossip in Hollyband's *Campo di Fior* to her shopkeeping father one day in 1573.

script of Richard Izacke's Antiquities of Exeter (Muniment Room, Exeter City Library), 21; *Devon & Cornwall*, XX, 70–71; Jordan, *Charities of London*, 153, 236, 285; Dunsford, *Tiverton*, 126; *Maidstone Recs.*, 91, 108.

37. Samuel Ward, the famous Puritan of Ipswich, once remarked: "Of all the men in the world, I envy Mr. Cotton of Boston, most: for he doth nothing in the way of conformity, yet hath his liberty, and I do everything that way and cannot enjoy mine." (Actually Mr. Cotton had the protection of the Bishop of Lincoln, who interceded for him with King James). Samuel Whiting, in *Chronicles of the First Planters of Massachusetts Bay*, ed. Alexander Young (Boston, Mass., 1846), 426–7; Clarke, *General Martyrologie*, 75–114, 143–45; Curtis, *Oxford and Cambridge*, 189–93; Larzer Ziff, *The Career of John Cotton* (Princeton, 1962), 3–70; Pishey Thompson, *History and Antiquities of Boston* (Boston, Eng., 1856), 413–20; Associated Architectural Societies, *Reports and Papers*, XVI, Pt. I, 41; Fuller, *Worthies*, II, 233; Rose-Troup, *John White*, 36, 40–1, 43; Whiteway, Diary, 116 (fol. 21).

"I doo thinke that they be the best sermons that men may heare in all the rest of the Realme of England," and "men doo see all Sundayes and holy dayes a great and noble company in Pauls churchyeard." Invitations to preach in the open air from the pulpit in St. Paul's yard went only to the orthodox, and for the most part faithful Anglicans composed the audience.[38]

One of the truly great "preaching Ministers" of the age was William Gouge, who came from King's College, Cambridge, in 1608 to St. Anne's Blackfriars, when that church was in a very low state. Preaching twice on Sunday and at a Wednesday forenoon lecture, "which for the space of about thirty-five years was very much frequented" by parishioners, other London ministers, members of the Inns of Court, and citizens, Gouge achieved great renown for himself and prosperity for his church. It was said that when "any Country Ministers, and Godly Christians came to London about their affairs, they thought not their business ended, unless they had been at Black Friers Lecture." When Mr. Gouge published a collection of his sermons as *The Whole Armour of God* (1616), it became the bookman's and peddler's joy, for it sold 3,000 copies in three years. In 1617, Richard Sibbes, also from Cambridge, went up to London to be the preacher at Gray's Inn, where many noblemen and gentlemen attended his lectures; through their influence he was enabled to pass his summers in the great houses of worthy and powerful people. Thus through the spoken and then the printed word did these two great London preachers succeed in buttressing piety in the English countryside.[39]

Only a few London parishes enjoyed either preaching incumbents or puritan vestries before 1640, and therefore the devotees of sermons resorted increasingly to supporting unattached lecturers who would give them the serious, soul-searching kind of preaching that they so ardently desired. John Ward noted in his diary that Thomas Hooker, "the New England man, once said to Mr. Sim-

38. Chamberlain wrote to Carleton that there were "meetings of county people who dine together once a year [and] have a sermon." *CSPD, 1619–23,* p. 310; Byrne, *Elizabethan Home,* 21. M. Maclure, *The Paul's Cross Sermons, 1534–1642* (Toronto, 1958) lists the preachers and the sermons, 1590–1640, pp. 217–54; see also chaps. I–II.
39. Clarke, *General Martyrologie,* 143–5, 234–47; *Journal of Modern History,* XIV, 6*n.*

[e]on Ash, who was to preach before him, "Sym,' saye he, 'let itt
be hot.' He meant zealous." One of the most successful of these
lecturers was John Davenport, who, though no Puritan at the time,
had the reputation of a factious and popular preacher. He drew
large assemblies of the common people to St. Lawrence, Old Jew-
ry, next to the Guildhall from 1619 to 1624, when he accepted a
call to be curate and lecturer at the neighboring parish. The St.
Lawrence lectureship, be it noted, never fell into Puritan hands,
and some contributors to its endowment specifically stipulated that
the lecturer be conformable to the Church of England. The parish
of St. Stephen, Coleman Street, to which Master Davenport
moved, however, was one of the few parishes in London to have
both a general and a select vestry, and more than half of the select
vestry were puritans. Davenport preached there with marked success until November, 1634, when fear of persecution by Archbishop Laud and loss of hope for the purifying of the Church of England led him to resign and flee to Holland.[40]

King James, "Sick of a Sermon-surfeit," rightly looked upon the
lecturers as "a new body severed from the ancient clergy, as being
neither Parsons, Vicars, nor Curates." Some of them meddled in
"State-matters, and generally (by an improper Transposition) the
Peoples duty was preached to the King at Court, the Kings to the
People in the Country. Many shallow Preachers handled the profound points of Predestination; wherein (pretending to guide their
flocks they lost themselves)." In 1622, in an attempt to revive the
"primitive and profitable order of Catechizing in the afternoon," it
was ordered that no sermons were to be given at that time on Sundays, nor were they to speak on "deep points" or the prerogatives
of sovereign princes. Furthermore, all lecturers had to be licensed
by the Court of Faculties and then only upon the recommendation
of the bishop of the diocese. Any one failing to observe these rules
was to be suspended for a year and a day and subject to further
punishment if the King so determined. John Donne, Dean of St.

40. See the informative articles by Dorothy Ann Williams, "London Puritanism:
The Parish of St. Stephen, Coleman Street," in *Church Quarterly Review*, CLX,
464–82; "Puritanism in the City Government, 1610–1640," in *Guildhall Mis-
cellany*, I, 2–14, and "London Puritanism: The Parish of St. Botolph Without
Aldgate," ibid., II, 24–38; Ward, *Diary*, 131; Jordan, *Charities of London*, 289;
CSPD, 1623–5, pp. 324–5; State Papers Domestic, 1629–31, Vol. 182, no. 60.

Paul's, defended King James's orders against preaching, and "his constancie in the true reformed religion, which the people . . . began to suspect." In reporting on the sermon, John Chamberlain remarked that some listeners said that Donne "spake as if himself were not so well satisfied." Complete enforcement of these orders was well-nigh impossible, and they were very unevenly carried out. One unanticipated result of the King's rulings was that they spurred certain London Puritans on to radical action in support of lectureships by godly ministers.[41]

Something of the exhilaration and spiritual stimulation that effective London preaching imparted to English youth, especially those freshly arrived from the country, may be imagined from the experiences of two young men during the 1620's. They also testify to the existence of a genuine and large-scale discontent in the land over the state of religion. From Rayleigh in Essex, Hugh Peter went to London "to ripen his studies, not intending to preach at all." Aroused and inspired by the sermons of Dr. Gouge, Richard Sibbes, Thomas Hooker, and John Davenport, and importuned by certain friends, this spirited and volatile young minister began, in 1626, to preach hot discourses once a month at St. Sepulchure's. "At this Lecture," he tells us, "the Resort grew so great that it contracted envy and anger.," because of the deep impression "such good work" made upon his "six or seven thousand Hearers." [42]

The plague swept away all of the relatives of little William Kiffin, aged nine; four years later, in 1629, he was "put apprentice to a mean calling." Slipping away from his master one morning, he wandered up and down the city and finally joined a throng he saw going into St. Antholin's. When Mr. Thomas Foxley, preaching on the Fifth Commandment, spoke of the duty of servants to their masters, Kiffin, thinking that the minister knew about him, immediately returned to his master. Soon after, again at St. Antholin's, he was moved mightily by Mr. John Norton's sermon on Isaiah LVII, 21: "There is no peace to the wicked, saith my God," and he resolved "to attend upon the most powerful preaching" regularly for assistance in relieving his troubled spirit. At St. Steph-

41. Fuller, *Church History*, bk. X, 108–10; Rushworth, *Historical Collections*, I, 64–5; *CSPD, 1619–23*, p. 439; *1623–5*, p. 249; Chamberlain, *Letters*, II, 451.
42. Peter, *Dying Father's Last Legacy*, 75–6; Stearns, *The Strenuous Puritan*, 34, 36*n.*, discusses the size of the auditory at St. Sepulchure's Church.

en's, Coleman Street, one of John Davenport's sermons proved of "great use to my soul." I thought my heart would "close with the riches and freeness of grace which God held forth to poor sinners." Bible-reading, study of Hooker's *The Soul's Preparation for Christ,* and talking with good "Christians" brought him some solace. With other apprentices who, like himself, had little opportunity to converse save on the Lord's Day, he met an hour before the morning sermon to pray and discourse on the means of grace. Finally in 1630, Kiffin relates: "I joined myself to an Independent congregation," which met during "the heat of the Bishop's severities" on Tower Hill.[43]

The parish church of St. Antholin in Budge Row (off Cannon Street) became the vitalizing center for preaching and other Puritan activities, not merely for London but for all of England and Wales in the latter part of the sixteenth century. A lectureship founded there in 1559 had attracted the benefactions of many rich parishioners and well-disposed persons in other city parishes. After 1566 three lecturers preached in turn, by candlelight, one day a week at six o'clock in the morning. To call the people to the sermon, one of the church's smaller bells rang for an hour before the service. Laudian clergymen, gentlemen, playwrights, and the generality of the neighborhood, for whom the bell did not toll, understandably stigmatized such proceedings as "Pharisaical and intolerable"—Thomas Middleton and Thomas Dekker reached a responsive audience when they endowed Moll, their "Roaring Girle," with "a tongue [that] will be hard further in a still morning than St. Antling-bell." So many eager youths like William Kiffin joined with their elders to crowd the church that in 1623, the vestry, which administered the lectures, had to erect a new gallery and add a fifth, and, later, a sixth lecturer.[44]

43. William Lilly, the astrologer, "leaned in judgment to Puritanism," and tells that he too went "early to St. Antholin's in London." Lilly, *History of His Life,* 47, 53; William Kiffin was born in 1617, and therefore was only three years younger than John Lilburne, his friend of later years (born *c.* 1614). It seems highly improbable that a lad of fifteen would have been apprenticed to a youth of nineteen, as has been stated. *Remarkable Passages in the Life of William Kiffin* (London, 1823), 2–15.

44. Isabel M. Calder, *The Activities of the Puritan Faction of the Church of England, 1625–1633* (New York, 1957), xix, 3–4; Calder, "The St. Antholin Lectures," *Church Quarterly Review,* CLX, 49–70; Middleton & Dekker, *The*

Originally the funds for the lectures had been handled by "the Collectors of St. Antholin's" or the "Treasurers," but in 1627, the Feoffees for Impropriations assumed all responsibility for them. Founded two years previously, this unincorporated, self-perpetuating, and secretive body was composed of twelve London Puritans. Such representative divines as Charles Offspring of St. Antholin's, Richard Sibbes, John Davenport, and William Gouge associated themselves with John White, the barrister, three other lawyers, and four citizens "who commanded rich coffers." "Wanting nothing," this talented, determined group laid plans to raise funds and to acquire by gift, bequest, or purchase all of the impropriations, lay ecclesiastical revenues, and lands in private hands since the dissolution of the abbeys. The ultimate goal was to transform the Church of England from within by filling the vacancies of all the redeemed impropriations with a "preaching ministry" of puritan vicars, curates, lecturers, and schoolmasters.[45]

Immediate success in raising funds came from the efforts of Hugh Peter, John Vicars, and the other dedicated men who went through the country on "their several circuits" to solicit support from the laity. All contributions were duly recorded in "a great Leiger booke." Once, while discussing the prospect of a gift of £500 for the Feoffees from "a Lady" in Surrey, Peter contended that "if she will dispose of it that way . . . there cannot so Exquisite a way be found. . . . Oh these (Sir)," he said to Vicars, "are the times to doe good and to lay out our selves and our estates to the Service of the Church. . . ." In 1627, the 198 men and women who had subscribed a total of £1,554 13s. 4d. to buy impropriations and increase the lectureship at St. Antholin's request-

Roaring Girle (1611), in Tudor Facsimile Texts (1914), I, D3 recto; Stow, Survey of London, II, bk. 3, pp. 15–16.

45. Calder, in Church Quarterly Review, CLX, 52; Waters, Gleanings, II, 1034, 1392; Jordan, Charities of London, 286, 289, 295; Parker, in CSM, XI, 267; Calder, Puritan Faction, xv, 3–4. In 1612, a group of men in the tiny Devonshire village of Staverton offered £100 to a patron of the parish to buy in the next nomination to the living "for the good and benefit of themselves and the whole parish whereby they might have the choseinge of their owne minister, and so be provided of the able and sufficient preacher to serve the said Cure. . . ." On the practical side, this and many similar actions powerfully buttressed the contemporary theoretical development of non-separating congregationalism. E. D. Drake-Brockman, Staverton on the Dart (Exeter, 1947), 43; Heylyn, Cyprianus Anglicus, 198; Fuller, Church History, XI, 136–7.

ed the Feoffees to take over the management of the lectures. Some of the Feoffees believed that their grand scheme could be accomplished in fifty years' time; William Prynne declared in 1646 that "had they not been interrupted in this good work, [they] would in a very few years in all probability, have purchased in most of the Great Towns and noted Parishes Impropriations of England in Lay-mens hands, where preaching was most wanted, and meanes to maintain it." [46]

The Feoffees assumed the managing of the lectureship of St. Antholin's in order to use it as "a seminary" for the training of godly preachers, who, after six years at that church, would then be dispersed throughout the land in the positions acquired and controlled by the Feoffees. As a well-informed opponent put it, the Feoffees resolved "to set up stipendary Lectures in all or most Market-Towns, where the People had commonly less to do, and consequently were more apt to Faction and Innovation than in other places; and of Market-Towns, to chuse such as were Privilegded for sending Burgesses to the High-Court of Parliment." As early as April, 1626, Zachariah Symmes, who had trained at St. Antholin's, was sent to be the curate of St. Peter's at Dunstable in Bedfordshire. The trustees also increased the annual stipends of the preachers from £20 to £30, a sum much above what the average London incumbent received.[47]

As far back as 1610, King James, disturbed by the profound and incalculable influence of the London preachers and their printed books and sermons, condemned "the insatiable and immeasurable itching boldnesse of the spirits, tongues, and pens of most men; so as nothing was now left untouched from the top to the bottome, neither in talking nor writing of the highest mysteries." In 1626, in order to establish peace and quiet in the Church of England, his son declared that he would "not admit of the least innovation in the matter of doctrine or discipline of the church, nor in the government of the state," and he forbade any of his subjects, especially churchmen, to raise "any doubts or maintain any new opinions." The proclamation was but a futile gesture,

46. Heylyn, *Cyprianus Anglicus*, 198; *Essex Institute Historical Collections*, LXXI, 310–11; Fuller, *Church History*, 137; Prynne, *Canterburies Doome*, 385.
47. Calder, *Puritan Faction*, xix, xx; Calder, in *Church Quarterly Review*, CLX, 52–3; Heylyn, *Cyprianus Anglicus*, 198, 200.

but when King Charles translated William Laud to the see of London in July, 1628, he had a devoted and determined zealot to do his will in this "Retreat and Receptacle of the Grandees of the Puritan Faction." [48]

Within a year the Bishop of London submitted a set of detailed considerations on church government to the monarch wherein he stressed that "a special care be had over the Lectures in every Diocese, which by reason of their Pay are the People's Creatures, and blow the Bellows of their Sedition." Among other recommendations calculated to abate their power, he urged that Sunday afternoon sermons must give way to catechizing, but that where there had to be a lecture, the preacher was to wear the surplice and read the divine service first. Laud summoned all the local lecturers and gave them orders to conform to the regulations he had drawn up, notwithstanding the displeasure of Archbishop Abbot with "any of the Limitations concerning Lecturers to whom (as the chief sticklers in the Puritan Causes) he was always favourable." These new instructions hit the Puritans very hard, for they came just as the Feoffees had begun to have real success in purchasing impropriations and supporting clergymen of their own choice. Beginning with Laud's frontal attack of 1629, the lectures in 124 parishes of London and vicinity started to decline. The trustees seem to have understood by this time that their pious design was in danger.[49]

In the larger provincial cities, however, such as Bristol, Norwich, Exeter, Gloucester, native merchants continued to endow lectureships, which then served as models for lesser communities. Yarmouth early acquired the reputation of a strong puritan town, partly because of its close connection with Holland. The Dean of Norwich expressed the thought in 1629 that "something exemplary done upon this place [Yarmouth] may prove of great consequence with all great towns corporate," for with "the same faction . . . being more generally prevalent than were to be wished, perhaps the instance of Yarmouth reduced may prove very medicinal." [50]

Matters came to a head in 1632, after Peter Heylyn laid bare

48. Stow, *Annales*, 896; *Bibliotheca Lindesiana*, I, 173; Heylyn, *Cyprianus Anglicus*, 165, 191, 202.
49. Rushworth, *Historical Collections*, II, 7, 31–2; Heylyn, *Cyprianus Anglicus*, 190–91, 192; Williams, in *Guildhall Miscellany*, II, 34.
50. *CSPD, 1629–31, pp.* 34, 40.

the machinations of the Feoffees in a Gloucestershire lectureship in a sermon at Oxford. Moving now to stamp them out, Laud had the Attorney General institute a suit in the Court of Exchequer, which was decided in favor of the King. The Court declared the Feoffees guilty of usurping "his Majestys Regalitie" and "drawing to themselves in time the principal Dependencie of the whole Clergie, that should have rewards from them in such measure, and on such conditions as they should fancy, thereby introducing many Novelties of dangerous Consequence, both in Church and Commonwealth." The prelate had triumphed over the London lecturers, and had struck a severe blow at the Puritans, whom he often called "the most dangerous enemies of the state"—and in that he was right.[51]

The Feoffees for Impropriations thus lasted only six years. Though their funds were sequestered and their control of impropriations upset, they contributed by example and precept to inspire the godly in other cities and towns to "set up an upstart ministry of Lectures" and to continue them, as even a prejudiced Laudian supporter admitted.[52]

In spite of the Court's decision against the Feoffees, a network of lectures from the large cities to market towns continued to spread out, which eventually brought the countryside under the influence of "refractory ministers." Even small towns without markets, such as Bergholt, Debenham, Haverhill, and Little Horkesley, had set lectures. Robert Wright, Bishop of Coventry and Lichfield, told of "the running lecture, so-called, because the lecturer went from village to village, and at the end of the week proclaimed where they would have him next, that his disciples might follow." In 1637, as soon as the Vicar General left Suffolk, Edward Spar-

---

51. Miss Calder printed the accounts of the Feoffees in her complete documentary record of the suit in the Exchequer in *Activities of the Puritan Faction*, 3–142, 147–8; Heylyn, *Cyprianus Anglicus*, 199; Rushworth, *Historical Collections*, II, 150–52; Fuller, *Church History*, XI, 143; Mass. Hist. Soc., *Proceedings*, XIII, 341–2; Neal, *History of the Puritans*, I, 541. The fullest and best account of the Feoffees is by Ethyn Kirby, "The Lay Feoffees: A Study in Militant Puritanism," *Journal of Modern History*, XIV, 1–28, and Christopher Hill offers useful comments in *Economic Problems of the Church*, 261, 263, 266, 297.

52. Miss Calder does not mention the preachers sent to Barnstaple, *Barnstaple Recs.*, II, 101; Calder, *Puritan Faction*, xxi–xxii, 28–42; *Persecutio Undecima* (1636), 55.

hawk, who was neither a licensed preacher nor a curate, but a suspended minister, set out to confute his sayings. Dr. Aylett reported that he had heard Sparhawk at Kelveden on Saturday, on Monday at Braintree, and at Coggeshall on Tuesday. Matthew Wren, Bishop of Norwich, declared that "Lectures abounded, especially in Suffolke: Not a Market or a bowling green or an Ordinary could stand without one, and many of them were set up by private Gentlemen at their pleasures." It was also quite clear that the people knew beforehand who was to preach, and "if they did not phansie the man, the Church was half empty, to the great discouragement of many who complained to me." What the people wanted was someone like John Rogers, who was famous as one of the "awakening preachers" of the age. One of his hearers was reported to have said, "Come let us go to Dedham, and get a little fire." [53]

IV

From 1620 onward, the Puritan leaders devoted all of their manifold talents, wits, and energies to employing every possible means to take over the Church of England and reform it from within according to their principles and designs. With each other, these nonseparating ministers and laymen were engagingly frank about their methods; in their dealings with the world at large, however, subtlety was the order of the day. Master John Preston ever held it as his maxim "that when we would have any great things to be accomplished, the best policy is to work by an Engine which the world sees nothing of." In a similar vein, Sir John Young of the Massachusetts-Bay Company wrote to John Winthrop in 1637: "I know that the wise among you doe not expect protection from god without a mixture of the serpents wisedome with the doves in-

53. One of Laud's informers described Thomas Cotton of Bergholt as "a great depraver of government" in whose study one could find all the "discontented books" and invectives against church and state. When Cotton received news from some "peevish intelligencer" in London, he would read it in the streets of Colchester on market day, and the zealots would crowd about as they "used to where ballads are being sung." *CSPD, 1634–5*, pp. 252–3; *The Works of William Laud*, ed. W. Scott and J. Bliss (Oxford, 1853), V, Pt. II, 320; *Middlesex Sessions*, III, 107; *Devon & Cornwall*, XX, 71; *CSPD, 1636–7*, p. 513; Prynne, *Canterburies Doome*, 374, 375; Tyack, Migration from East Anglia, I, 250–51.

nocency, and that is as much wisedome . . . as may consist with
innocency; and as much innocency . . . as may consist with
wisedome." [54]

The program of quietly extending their influence and the propagating of the Word of God by lectureships held by learned, godly
preachers was probably the most successful "Engine" that the Puritans devised, and they worked it with consummate skill. A recent
study indicates that in nine counties and the two leading cities of
London and Bristol the large sum of £46,253 12s., which
amounted to 12.9 per cent of all benefactions, was given between
1601 and 1640 by rich merchants toward the founding of lectureships. What these benefactors and their clerical allies had in mind
was to eradicate ignorance by teaching the people through sermons. Referring to "the meaner ordinary sort of people," Thomas
Hooker, the suppressed lecturer of Chelmsford, wrote in 1632 that
"it is incredible and unconceivable, what Ignorance is among
them," but he went on to say pointedly that it "is not the maine
end of preaching, to instruct men: but to worke upon their hearts.
When a man hath taught men what they should doe, he is but
come to the walls of the Castle; the fort is the heart." [55]

The intention of the Feoffees for Impropriations to use cities
and market towns for broadcasting their ideas was, as we know,
not new, nor did their suppression in 1632 end the lecture movement. Lecturers continued to labor faithfully and diligently to
reach the minds and hearts of the common people, and they succeeded in large measure. The market town of Ashford, "the most
factious in all Kent," developed as an important Puritan center
through Master Udnay's lectures, until Laud silenced him. Dr.
Robert Sibthorpe of the Court of High Commission found both
Leicestershire and Lincolnshire "much overspread with Puritanism." In the Diocese of Coventry and Lichfield in 1633, Bishop
Wright suppressed a "seditious lecture at Ripon," and Essex, as Sir
Nathaniel Brent discovered in 1636, was exceedingly "factious."
Dr. Eleazar Duncon of Durham insisted in 1640 that King Charles
should not "suffer little towns to grow big and anti-monarch to

54. Mather, *Magnalia Christi Americana*, bk. III, 175; *Winthrop Papers*, III, 398.
55. Jordan, *Philanthropy in England*, 300–301, 350; Jordan, *Charities of London*,
72, 154, 237, 285; Hooker, *The Souls Preparation for Christ*, 70–71.

boot; for where are all these pestilent nests of Puritans hatched, but in corporations, where they swarm and breed like hornets in [a dead] horse's head." Contemporary observers agreed that Puritanism was strongest in the urban centers.[56]

That the Puritan lecturers of the cities managed to reach the countryfolk, however, is nowhere more strikingly illustrated than in the rural county of Hampshire, where the puritan spirit penetrated deep into the parochial life of the peasantry. Dr. Milden has amply demonstrated that not only was Archbishop Laud's brand of Anglicanism looked upon by the farmers as "an unwonted, dangerous, and unwelcome innovation," but some degree of puritanism was the normal attitude in the first half of the seventeenth century. The deepest dissatisfaction among the villagers in Hampshire, as elsewhere, arose from the spiritual failure of the Church and the decay of public and private morality and decency. To counter this, wealthy citizens of Southampton and other towns hopefully supported lectures, either by the rare preaching incumbent or by some hot, uninhibited but learned lecturer. It is impossible to measure the actual effect of the sermons on the average man or woman, but there is no reason to question the report of a Visitation of East Anglia and Essex that stated that "there are certain sectaries in those parts whose examples guide the inferior sort so affected." [57]

England, as Dr. Milden properly reminds us, "was living largely a domestic life and the principal domestic concern was religion." This concern expressed itself in family worship, Bible-reading, and attendance at church, but the surest guide to the underlying public attitude was the response to the preaching. The lecturers, as Richard Rogers of Wethersfield put it, sought in their sermons to enable their hearers to be "merry in the Lord, and yet without light-

56. "It was observed of Queen Elizabeth, that when she had any business to bring about amongst the people, she used to *tune the Pulpits,* as her saying was; that is to say, to have some Preachers in and about London and other great auditories in the Kingdom, ready at command to cry up her design. . . ." Heylyn, *Cyprianus Anglicus,* 153; Prynne, *Canterburies Doome,* 373; Rushworth, *Historical Collections,* I, 425–6; Laud, *Works,* V, Pt. II, 320; *CSPD, 1639–40,* p. 516.
57. We sorely need further critical studies of Puritanism in the counties, like the penetrating work of Dr. W. H. Milden, Puritanism in Hampshire and the Isle of Wight from the Reign of Elizabeth to the Restoration (Ph.D. Thesis, London, 1934), especially pp. 5–6, 9, 43, 61–71, 88, 100, 106, 121, 133, 134–44, 149. Prynne, *Canterburies Doome,* 103–8; *CSPD, 1634–5,* p. 252.

nesse; sad and heavie in heart for their own sinnes, and the abominations of the land, and yet without discouragement, or dumpishnesse: resting and beleeving in God, without bold presumption, and fearing their own weaknesse, but yet without dreadful and deadly despairing. . . . And [further they labored] . . . that the ungodly may see how such are blessed in comparison of other, and what they themselves goe voyde of which they might injoy, and therefore may seeke how to become not almost, but altogether Christians with them. . . . Such as would faine doe well, and yet cannot tell how, may hereby be eased and relieved." That this was a noble ideal of Christian service a great many Englishmen who could not be counted Puritans fully realized.[58]

Such sermons, delivered in the plain style, took strong hold on the laity. If the peasants' reaction proved to be more restrained and resolute than emotional, it was nonetheless sincere. Dudley in Worcestershire was one of the dark corners of the land; yet at Richard Baxter's monthly lecture, "the Church was usually as much crowded within; and at the Windows as ever I saw in any London Congregation (Partly through the great willingness of the People, and partly by the exceeding populousness of the Country, where the Woods and Commons are planted with Nailers, Scithe-Smiths, and other Iron-Labourers, like a continued Village." The "ignorant, rude, and revellinge People" of Kidderminster invited Baxter in March, 1641, "to exercise amongst us" on "a day wherein is offered the advantage of a publicque Assembly, and allso one Market day and allso a day wherein we desire a weekly lecture." When he began to preach at Kidderminster, "from town and Foreign they streamed to the Church with willing feet, some moved by spiritual hunger," others by admiration and curiosity, but all by a compelling desire to hear what he had to say. The suppressing of lectures in his diocese by Bishop Wren caused great anguish in East Anglia: "for the woorde preache is obsolete." To John Winthrop overseas, Robert Reyce (using an assumed name for security) wrote in September, 1636: "I woolde I coolde wryte unto you of any lectures contynewed, our hie contempte of the

58. Milden, Puritanism in Hampshire, 3; Richard Rogers, *Seven Treatises* (1603), "The Preface or entrance to the Booke."

woorde when wee had it abondantly, hathe begoone this presente famyn, which is feared wyll styll encrease." [59]

The highest tribute to the effectiveness of sermons, especially those delivered as lectures, came from William Laud, who considered them the direst threat to his program for the Church of England. As soon as he became Archbishop of Canterbury in 1632, he sought to extend to his whole province the prohibitions he had proclaimed for London. He went so far as to forbid merchants and tradesmen from meeting to make contributions to endowments in their native towns for the support of preachers, as John Shaw, who had served such a group in Devonshire, discovered when he went to York in 1636. There he ran afoul of Archbishop Neal after his first sermon. The hierarchy put forth every effort to prevent the people from "Gadding on Sundays to hear puritanical sermons in other parishes," or to hear weekday lectures. By 1639 the Laudian policy was beginning to show definite results, and, together with the emigration of many divines, lectures no longer caused much concern to the prelate. The next year it was reported that all was well in the dioceses.[60]

IV

It is bad history to brand puritanism as an aberration in English life, for from the days of Wyclif to the end of the nineteenth century a large proportion of the people showed themselves to be deeply preoccupied with the ethical element in human existence. In the five decades before the calling of the Long Parliament it was still possible to conjoin in the same individuals this moral concern and the old carefree attitude we associate with the Elizabethans. Fostered by Puritan ministers, by lecturers, and by unremitting Bible-reading, a welling-up of popular religious feeling took place. Everything that we know about ordinary Englishmen points to the profound truth that their Protestantism was both deeper-rooted and more sensitive than that of the prelates and clergy of the mid-

59. *Reliquæ Baxterianæ*, 14; Powicke, *Richard Baxter*, Appendix III, 294; *Winthrop Papers*, III, 306, and entire letter, 298–306.
60. Prynne, *Canterburies Doome*, 537–8; *Surtees*, LXV, 128; *CSPD, 1634–5*, p. 64; *1635*, xliv; Hart, *Country Clergy*, 91; Heylyn, *Cyprianus Anglicus*, 342–3.

dle way which had been provided by the Elizabethan Settlement and formulated as doctrine by the great Richard Hooker. And this evangelical strain, this concern with the religion of the heart, was and still is an essential ingredient in the British bloodstream.[61]

Those men and women called Puritans and the far greater number of their fellow puritans who conformed had virtually no theological differences with the Church of England. They did differ over forms of ecclesiastical polity. The essence of Puritanism, however, is only to be discovered in their states of mind. We must remind ourselves that before 1642 the overwhelming number of puritans were still conforming Anglicans. It is fatal, as we know only too well, to read behavior and attitudes back from 1660; properly we must come up to 1640 from the past. One thing is certain: by 1642 the mass of Englishmen had begun to *feel* and *reason*. These puritans of all walks of life and of all ranks were making a tremendous intellectual effort to understand God and life.[62]

61. See the important article by L. J. Trinterud, "The Origins of Puritanism," *Church History*, XX, 37–55; and for the striking similarity in outlook between a devout Anglican and a strict Puritan, *Two Elizabethan Puritan Diaries*, ed. Marshall M. Knappen (Chicago, 1933).

62. It was not required for the purposes of this work to examine puritanism as a complete culture, or even as a complex religious movement. Our concern is with the English people. Moreover, in recent years the late Marshall Knappen, William Haller, Raymond P. Stearns, Geoffrey Nuttall, and Christopher Hill have provided new information and fresh insights into this fascinating subject. It is hoped that the present study reflects the contributions of these writers and their colleagues.

IX

Educated and Cultured Englishmen

THE DAILY EXISTENCE of the Englishman was encased by his religion. But this was not all! His church also governed his education and more or less determined how much of the general culture of the age he could acquire and enjoy. It is scarcely necessary to animadvert upon the higher achievements of English culture in the Age of Shakespeare and the first Stuarts, for they have evoked a well-nigh inexhaustible literature; rather we may seek to gauge just how far the ordinary man and woman gained access to and shared in this culture. In the years from 1590 to 1640, the practical necessities of a constantly changing society, as well as the frankly realistic attitude of puritans toward education, produced an unmistakable secular drift. This shifting of standards, together with the introduction of foreign ideas and modes of thought which, as a maritime people, they were given to importing quite as much as more tangible cargoes, often confused and troubled the minds of thinking men and women of all ranks.

II

Historians of education—and others—have all too frequently restricted the meaning of the word *education* to formal, systematized schooling. Such a narrow construction blinds one to several vital kinds of training that many children and youths received before the days of compulsory, state-supported, public education. If we

define education as preparation for life, whatever the individual or
institutional agencies for providing it may be, we shall come much
closer to understanding the people of these years. It is an incontrovertible fact that every male or female infant born in England
between 1590 and 1640 was at least exposed to a minimum of
training by virtue of being a member of a family and of growing
up in some organized community. In a sense Richard Mulcaster,
Headmaster of the Merchant Tailors' School of London, was saying just this in a remarkable work of 1581 when he fixed the responsibility for educating a child so comprehensively: "The duty
of leading children to cleave to the good and forsake the bad, in
matters of ordinary conduct, is shared by all who come in contact
with them; it belongs to the parents by nature, to schoolmasters by
the charge committed to them, to neighbours as a matter of
courtesy, and to people in general on the ground of common
humanity." [1]

"There must be a good foundation and ground-work laid in the
parents house," was the dictum of Hezekiah Woodward about
1641. The introduction to nature and everyday life, to creatures,
the earth, air, sky, and seasons, was incumbent upon the father
and mother, who, more than any others, must "promote the childe
in point of information." Besides familiarizing their offspring with
civilized life, the parents must also instruct them in the rudiments
of religion and morality by means of daily worship in the household. In other words, "the good culture of the childe" was their responsibility. They should also endeavor "to give the childe instructions universally good and profitable, whereby the childe may be
capable." In rural villages and on isolated farms, such training in
agriculture as most youths acquired was by the precept and example of their elders in the performance of the daily family chores, an
experience that broadened as they grew older and as their own responsibilities increased. Indeed most of the vocational instruction
that the young people of both sexes ever received was provided by
the family. In a lesser way the family served a similar purpose in
the urban centers, where most of what a boy or girl learned during
an apprenticeship was imparted by the members of the family in

1. *The Educational Writings of Richard Mulcaster,* ed. James Oliphant (Glasgow,
1903), 32; *Mulcaster's Elementarie* [1582], ed. E. T. Campagnac (Oxford, 1924).

which he or she lived. The local community was but the family writ large; the church carried further the religious instruction begun in the home, and daily intercourse and labor played the role of the parents on the vocational side. With such matters clearly in mind, George Herbert concluded: "One father is more then a hundred Schoolmasters." [2]

The background, education, character, and aspirations of parents, then as now, largely determined the kinds of tutelage a young child received. Richard Mulcaster believed that the natural powers of children—perception, memory, and judgment—could be discerned "peering out of the little souls" from infancy, but that their successful development depended primarily upon the wisdom and determination of the parents. "Many of us . . . are poore men and simple persons, as Husbandmen, Labourers, &c.," and "many of our children are so young and raw, that they can learne little or nothing" was the lame excuse one of these countrymen made to his parson, who quickly retorted: "They learne as soon as they can speak" and must be taught "betimes." Ralph Josselyn recalled that at Bishop's Stortford, until he was ready for petty school, his father "gave mee good education, by his owne instruction" and example. In the household of a Lancashire yeoman in 1629, Adam Martindale, then aged six, taught himself to read the Bible "and any other English booke" from an "ABC." A large proportion of the youth of rural England never went any further than this. They were like Thomas Parr of Shropshire who "had good breeding (without reading)"

> But hee in Husbandry hath bin brought up,
> And nere did taste the Helliconian cup.[3]

In rural England, education was notable beyond all else for its great emphasis upon *utility*. Breton's Countryman explained this view fully to the Courtier in 1618: "Now for learning, what your

2. For details on this point, see Chapters II–VII of this work. Hezekiah Woodward, *Of the Child's Portion* (1649), especially Preface, pp. 29, 31; chap. I, 11; chap. III, 90–143, 153, 157; also Woodward, *A Light to Grammar and all other Arts and Sciences* (1641); Herbert, *Works* (1945), 344.

3. *Educational Writings of Richard Mulcaster*, 31–2; Robert Sherrard, *The Countryman with His Household* (1620), 30, 32; *Camden*, 3d ser., XV, 1; *Chetham*, IV, 5; Taylor, "The Old, Old, Very Old Man," in *Works*, I, No. 2, p. 23.

need is thereof I know not, but with us, this is all we go to school
for: to read common prayers at church and set down common
prices at markets; write a letter and make a bond; set down the
day of our births, our marriage day, and make our wills when we
are sick for the disposing of our goods when we are dead: these
are the chief matters that we meddle with, and we find enough to
trouble our heads withal; for if the fathers know their own children, wives their own husbands from other men, maidens keep
their by-your-leaves from subtle bachelors; farmers know their cattle by the heads, and shepherds know their sheep by the brand,
what more learning have we need of, but that experience will teach
us without book? We can learn to plough and harrow, sow and
reap, plant and prune, thresh and fan, winnow and grind, brew
and bake, and all without book; and these are our chief business in
the country, except we be jurymen to hang a thief, or speak truth
in a man's right, which conscience and experience will teach us
with a little learning. Then what should we study for, except it
were to talk with the man in the moon about the course of the
stars? No, astronomy is too high a reach for our reason: we will
rather sit under a shady tree in the sun to take the benefit of the
cold air than lie and stare upon the stars to mark their walk in the
heavens while we lose our wits in the clouds: and yet we reverence
learning as well in the parson of our parish, as our schoolmaster,
but chiefly, in our justices of peace, for under God and the king
they bear great sway in the country. But for great learning, in
great matters, and in great places, we leave it to great men. If we
live within the compass of the law, serve God and obey our king,
and as good subjects ought to do, in our duties and our prayers
daily remember him, what need we more learning?" To this, the
rustic might have added that, given the desire, most peasants never
had the leisure time necessary for cultivating their minds.[4]

---

4. We should recognize that the man whom Shakespeare described as "that
unlettered small-knowing soul" often possessed a shrewd, intuitive understanding
of his fellow man. In 1639 Henry Oxinden advised his brother, who was at Oxford, "to begin to studie men, for everie rationall man is a living book." *Love's
Labour's Lost*, I, i, 253; *Oxinden Letters*, 159; Breton, *Court and Country*, in
Dunham and Pargellis, *Complaint and Reform*, 468–9. For the dismal "want of
education" in county Cumberland, *CSPD, 1629–31*, p. 473; for rural Hampshire,
Gras, *Economic History of an English Village*, 150.

Emphasis upon the training of the English Renaissance gentleman in the classical languages, the liberal arts, and manly accomplishments as set forth in the writings of Castiglione and Roger Ascham has eclipsed the most exciting and significant educational achievement of this revolutionary age. This was the ever-mounting, unquenchable thirst of the commonality for improved primary instruction to prepare their children to cope with the demands of daily life. We must not take a toplofty attitude toward the peasant for tailoring education to his needs. In a hierarchical society like England's a child's requirements depended upon his rank: a gentleman's son who learned Latin and Greek for entering a university, the Inns of Court, the professions, or the public service was pursuing studies requisite for his career just as much as the son of a peasant or artisan who tried to master the English language in order to read practical manuals about husbandry, some craft, or navigation. Judged from this corner, all education was vocational.[5]

To such a view, Calvinism added the powerful sanction of the "calling"—"Man should use the place and office assigned unto him by God, in a holy manner, performing the duties annexed unto it in faith and obedience." Though they differed over many fundamental matters, the spokesmen of both the Laudian Anglicans and the extreme Puritans accepted the doctrine of the calling; it was clearly a Protestant doctrine congenial to nearly all Englishmen. Of the many works on this subject, that of William Perkins was the most influential: *A Treatise of the Vocations, Or, Callings of Men, with the sorts and kinds of them, and the right use thereof*, which first appeared in an edition of his *Works* published in 1603. Every man must have a calling "to walk in," Perkins taught, be it public or private, in the Church, commonwealth, or the family. This ensures the solid foundation of a good society, "for it maketh

5. Sir Thomas Wilson was very proud of the fact that Englishmen saw to it that their children were trained at an early age to look after themselves: "every child of 6 or 7 years old is forced to some art whereby he gaineth his own living, and something beside to help to enrich his parents or master." Wilson, "State of England," 20. Joan Simon's important and richly detailed *Education and Society in Tudor England* (Cambridge, Eng., 1966), especially 313, 315, 332, 402, 403, supersedes all earlier works on the subject. The present writer is gratified to have this view, which he arrived at independently, so completely documented.

every man to keepe his own standing, and to imploy himselfe paine-fully within his calling." Thus it followed that as early as possible parents ought to choose, with the utmost care, callings best suited to their children's gifts and inclinations.[6]

Something approaching a "system" of education began during the reign of Edward VI. Growing rapidly under his successors, it became, by 1641, the concern of both church and state. The sys-tem, made urgent by political conditions and fear of public dis-order, was consciously attuned to utility for a society with well-defined degrees, and was nourished by the benefactions of rich and pious citizens. The policy behind it was at one and the same time propagated by and reflected in the educational treatises published during the period. Their authors were not so much educational theorists as experienced men who described the best and worst conditions that they had seen over the years, and their conclusions stressed the importance of sound training in the vernacular at the elementary stage for all children of both sexes.[7]

In his *Positions* (1581), Richard Mulcaster outlined the educa-tional ideal of instructing every child; the next year he examined the thesis in detail in *The First Part of the Elementarie, Which En-treateth Chieflie of the right writing of our English Tung.* Employ-ing the vernacular himself so as to reach the widest audience of parents, he conferred a new dignity on "the very lowest" level of teaching, the primary school. He proceeded logically in his dis-course and explained that, considering the bases upon which pa-rents "do actually build," children rose to that "mediocrity which furnisheth out this world, and not to that excellence which is fash-ioned for another." Reading, writing, drawing, and music he con-sidered essential subjects—"what quality of learning is there, de-serving of any praise, that does not fall within this elementary course, whether it be connected with the higher professions, or oc-cupations of lower rank, or the necessary trades of common life." [8]

John Brinsley, a Puritan divine of many years' service, before

6. Perkins's writings went through 20 editions in two decades, *The Works of William Perkins* (1612), I, 747–9, particularly 755, 756, 758, 759.
7. Simon, *Education and Society,* 315, 369, 383, 397; Jordan, *Philanthropy in England,* 48–50; index *s. v.* Education, Schools; also Jordan's *Charities of Rural England,* 165.
8. *Educational Writings of Richard Mulcaster,* 4, 6, 11, 19, 30, 33–44.

being ejected from his mastership at Ashby de la Zouche in 1620 produced two books on "the common countrey Schooles." He urged the use of improved textbooks and emphasized particularly the worth and importance of the teacher's calling, which he equated with the minister's "charge"—was not a well-educated boy or girl a credit to the nation? He believed that "the chief endeavour" of schoolmasters should be to train their pupils so that "they may be able to express their minds purely and readily in their own tongue, and to increase the practice of it." This was of the greatest importance to the youths who were educated in the elementary schools, because "there are very few which proceed in learning, in comparison of them that follow other callings." [9]

More practical than Brinsley's studies for the recommendations of subjects and texts for the primary schools was *The English Scholemaister,* published by Edward Coote in 1596. This honest master of the Free School of Bury St. Edmunds addressed himself to "the unskillful . . . and to such men and women of trade, as Taylors, Weavers, Shop keepers, Seamsters, and such other as have undertaken the charge of teaching others. . . . Thou maist sit in thy Shop boord, at thy Loomes, or at thy Needle, and never hinder thy worke to heare thy schollers, after thou hast once made this little booke familiar unto thee." He too insisted upon the thorough grounding of all children in the fundamentals of their native tongue. Nearly two and a half centuries before Noah Webster, Coote attempted to reform spelling by eliminating useless letters from such words as *tun* for *tunne, templ* for *temple, plums* for *plummes.* He also supplied an elementary vocabulary, samples of writing, a well-composed dialogue of questions and answers, "a Shorte Catechisme," nine of the Psalms, "numeration" for arithmetic, and a chronology from the Flood to 500 A.D. ("then increased Barbarism and Papistry.") This treatise on the teaching of "distinct Reading, and true Writing our English Tongue," and how to understand "hard English words, which they shall see in the Scriptures, Sermons, or elsewhere heare or reade, and also be made able to use the same aptly themselves," met with such popu-

9. John Brinsley, *Ludus Literarius* (1612); and *A Consolation of Our Grammar Schools* (1621), 2, 7, 8, 22, 26, 45–6, 52–6; *Ludus Literarius: Or The Grammar Schoole,* ed. E. T. Campagnac (Liverpool, 1917), 22.

lar approval that by 1638 it had reached its twenty-eighth printing. Mastery of his manual, Coote assured his readers, would enable them to fit children at the ABC stage for entrance into the grammar schools, and also aid those older persons who were ignorant of Latin and "ashamed to write to their best friends." [10]

Strong support for better elementary schools came from the puritan clergy, who placed education in a religious context. "Nearest to God are ministers, and next to them schoolmasters," the celebrated Gataker asserted in a sermon delivered in 1620 during a visitation at the Tunbridge Free School. "What is their Schole but a private Church?" Warmly endorsing the study of ancient tongues, the puritan leader also tried to convince his auditors that all would go for nought if the individual were "unskilfull in Gods booke." "He that doth teach Civilitie, and not Piety withall, goeth no further" than the heathen have gone.[11]

In hundreds of little rural parishes between 1590 and 1640, petty schools, or "petties," were established to supplement the woefully inadequate dame schools. Where no schoolhouse existed, the petty school was conducted in the church, sometimes in the porch, with the incumbent or occasionally the sexton taking charge. Country boys and girls customarily started school at the age of six or seven, which was a year or so later than the children of large towns and cities. Charles Hoole, writing on the petty schools, urged that "so soon as they can read English well," they should read a chapter once a day, learn to write a fair hand, and be "exercised in Arithmatique." At Broughton near Southampton in 1601, Thomas Dowse endowed a free school at which reading,

10. In his preface, Edward Coote said that "it is lamentable to see into what ignorant handling silly little children chance, which should at first bee most skilfully grounded, which is the only cause of such woful ignorance in so many men, and women, that cannot write (without great error) one sentence of true English: let therefore Parents now be wise unto whom they commit their Children." *The English Scholemaister* (1627), Title-page, Preface, pp. 28, 32, 43, 58, 59, 66, 87.
11. Samuel Harmar of Gloucestershire called upon Parliament in 1642 to encourage the "charitable work of generall Schooling" throughout "the whole Land, for the restraining of vice, and for the good of poore mens Children" as well as to ensure "a uniformity of Religion among us." He advocated a law to rate men's estates for schooling in the same way they were rated for relieving the poor—surely one of the earliest proposals for government-supported public education. Samuel Harmar, *Vox Populi, or Glostersheres Desire* (1642), 1–10; Thomas Gataker, *David's Instructor* (1620), 16, 18, 19, 23, 31, 32, 33.

writing, and casting accounts were to be taught so that the scholars might be prepared for schools of higher learning, bound out as apprentices, or employed in husbandry. In a few places that lacked foundations for schooling, like Swarkestone, Derbyshire, the inhabitants built schoolhouses and hired teachers "at their owne paines and charges" in order to "have their children taught in good Literature." Maidstone had public rates to support an usher after 1613 and was one of the rare places where the children of all freeman were to be "frely taught . . . the Science, Art and Knowledg of Humanitie or Grammar." Whether the petty school was supported by endowments, managed either by feoffees or parish officers, or created and maintained by a parish rate or by the subscriptions of parishioners, the evidence of community responsibility for elementary education had begun to appear in the land.[12]

In the towns and cities, greater endowments and benefactions enabled the civil authorities to make better provision for elementary education. Some of the petty schools existed independently and had their own buildings. Thomas Wild left four and a half acres of land to the city of Worcester to erect and establish a free school "for the bringing up of youth in their A. B., matins and even-song, and other learning, which would make them ready for the King's Grammar School." In Devon, both the city of Exeter and much smaller Crediton maintained separate English and Latin schools. The tendency of the age, however, was to add bequests for primary training to already existing free grammar-school endowments; the result was "mixed schools," in which an usher taught the petties. In 1630, Market Bosworth in Leicestershire had a schoolhouse, master's lodging, and land for its grammar school;

12. The 27 volumes of *Sessional Papers* of the House of Commons, 1819–39, contain a mass of information about petty and grammar schools of the sixteenth and seventeenth centuries which lies behind many of the conclusions reached in this section. *Sessional Papers, 1825,* XI, 274–5;*1826,* XII, 404–5, 539–41; *1833,* XIX, 269; *et passim;* Charles Hoole, "The Petty School" and "The Usher's Duty," in *A New Discovery of the Old Art of Teaching Schoole* (1659), ed. E. T. Campagnac (Liverpool, 1913), 1–2, 25–6; *Kent,* XXV, 34; Simon, *Education and Society,* 383; *Sessional Papers, 1837–8,* 210; J. C. Cox, *Three Centuries of Derbyshire Annals as Illustrated by the Records of the County of Derby* (London, 1890), II, 287; Frank Streatfield, *An Account of the Grammar School . . . in Maidstone in Kent* (Oxford, 1915), 18, 19; *Maidstone Recs.,* 68; and on parish responsiblity for primary schools, Fish, in *School Review,* XXIII, 443.

then it was decided that the master must be an M.A. who would teach Latin and Greek in the "upper school" and that English would be taught in the "lower school" by an usher.[13]

Some urban centers and an occasional country town had separate schools for the poor, and elsewhere special provisions were made for them. When Queen Elizabeth licensed Richard Platt in 1595 to erect a grammar school in his native parish of Aldenham in Hertfordshire under the governance of the Brewers Company, his rules directed the teacher to instruct sixty children of poor people and the children of freemen of the company in Latin grammar, "purity of life, manners, and religion." In a school which Dame Elizabeth Periam founded in Henley about 1600, instruction was to be given in reading, writing, and accounts to twenty poor boys of the town; they also received clothing and apprenticing. Sir William Borlase gave Great Marlow in Buckinghamshire a school in 1628; the master was to teach these same subjects to twenty-four children. After two years' attendance, the twelve best students were to be given 40s. apiece toward their apprenticeship. A school established in 1626 by Sir John Davy would educate all poor children over five years of age in the county of Devynnock, South Wales, if they were true to the Church of England and had been born in wedlock.[14]

Most "free" schools were free only to the poor. Children from outside the community usually paid a fee to the master, and even if no tuition was charged, there were fees and gratuities required for the master and the expenses incurred for candles, fuel, and supplies. After a great fire in 1613, Dorchester built a hospital to pro-

13. By the end of the period, the reformers were well aware of the deficiencies in the primary instruction given in the private petty schools: "The Petty-School is the place where indeed the first Principles of all Religion and learning ought to be taught, and therefore rather deserveth that more encouragement should be given to Teachers of it, then that it should be left as a work for poor women, or others, whose necessities compel them to undertake it, as a meer shelter from beggery." Hoole, *A New Discovery of the Old Art of Teaching Schoole*, 28, 117, 214–15; Jordan, *Charities of London*, 145, 233; *Sessional Papers, 1824*, XIII, 76; *1828*, XI, 519–20; *1839*, XIV, 574; XV, 183, 186–7; *Western Antiquary*, IV, 59; *Somerset & Dorset*, V, 172; Izaacke, Exeter, 22.

14. A number of communities had funds to buy paper and books for poor children. Waters, *Gleanings*, II, 1034; *HMC Lincoln*, XIV, VIII, 97; Fish, in *School Review*, XXIII, 446; *Sessional Papers, 1819*, X, 78, 201; *1826–7*, X, 685–6; *1833*, XIX, 133–4; *1834*, XXII, 72; *1837–8*, XXVI, 133–4; XXVII, 350–52.

vide religious and vocational training for both boys and girls. It became known as the Free School of Dorchester. In 1623, another, known as the "New School," and later as the "English School in Trinity Parish," was founded to prepare boys for entry into the older Free School; it was placed under the supervision of Master John White and Master Robert Cheek of the older institution. In 1631 certain "Malcontents" insisted that the English school was supposed to be free for everybody. When the deed was produced and it was shown that the founder intended that the school be "free only for poore mens children," John Coke and John Paty, representatives of the protesting faction, went away "insolently" crying "a free schoole, a free schoole." [15]

In 1597 the authorities at Plymouth undertook a novel scheme when the Mayor induced William Woulfe, a serge weaver, to move there from Exeter to instruct twenty poor children in the trade of spinning worsteds. Mr. Woulfe was promised a salary of £50 the first year and £100 thereafter, a house rent free, and allowances for the food and apparel of the pupils; he was also told that he would get 100 fish from every Plymouth ship returning from Newfoundland. The experiment failed after seven years: the master claimed that the allowance given for the maintenance of the children was inadequate; the mayor charged Woulfe with gross mismanagement.[16]

Official concern about education stemmed from a law of 1563 ordering that no individual might teach without a license from the bishop of the diocese in which he conducted school, and the Canons of 1604 enjoined the bishop or his ordinary to ascertain that

15. In Hartlebury parish, Worcester, the master was to teach reading, writing, and casting accounts, and also "virtue and learning as well as a true knowledge of God and his Holy Word"; in return he was to have the profits of cock fights and potations "as were commonly used in schools." In 1639–40, the Dorchester Burgesses agreed that "all men of ability should give xxs. a yeare for every child they shall send to the frescole to be taught till the Scolemr's mayntenance by foundacion and addition by the Town be made up XI li yearely." *Sessional Papers, 1833,* XIX, 631–5; *1826–7,* X, 685–6; Fish, in *School Review,* XXIII, 443; Simon, *Education and Society,* 370; Hutchins, *Dorset,* I, 382; II, 566; *Somerset & Dorset,* III, 104; V, 172, 173; *Dorchester Recs.,* 584–5; Whiteway, Diary, 169–70 (fol. 166).

16. King Charles founded St. Margaret's Hospital in Westminster in 1633 to maintain and instruct poor boys and girls in the manual arts. *Sessional Papers, 1819,* X, 180; *Plymouth Recs.,* 215.

every schoolmaster, whether teaching in a "public or private house," be "found meet as well for his learning and dexterity in teaching, as for sober and honest conversation, and also for right understanding of God's true religion." Furthermore, schoolmasters had to teach the Longer or Shorter Catechism in English or Latin "as the children are able to bear." Additional supervision became possible with the licensing of the printing of official grammars and other schoolbooks. Under Elizabeth, the authorities allowed annually four double impressions or 10,000 copies of the official "Lily's Latin Grammar," and probably, also, the *ABC with the Cathechism* and the *Primer and Catechism* as "set forth by the Queen's majesty to be taught to children" sold even more copies. The monopoly of printing grammars and grammar books went to John Willie in 1615, but thousands of pirated copies likewise sold and circulated.[17]

It was to be expected that instances of pedagogical and moral insufficiency would crop up among the ranks of teachers. The Archdeacon's Court ordered William Asplin, schoolmaster of Great Bradfield, Essex, to ask God's forgiveness, for, as a man of inferior talents, he had taken it upon himself to tell fortunes, to give out charms, and to dispense "carectors for agues." Richard Baxter's highly colored, somewhat sour, and much-quoted condemnation of his early teachers portrays the majority of them as ignorant, immoral men; one at Eaton-Constantine was "the excellentest Stage-player in all the Country, and a good Gamester and a good Fellow that got Orders." Little R. Willis had "an ancient Citizen of no great learning," as his schoolmaster at Christ School in Gloucester. Each evening the teacher would assign several lessons to all the forms. In the morning, with all the students present, he would examine the boys of the first form, then the second, and "the rest in order . . . giving one of the words to one, and another to another (as he saw fit)." Some of the first form, called prompters, would come and sit in the seats of lower forms as soon

17. In 1615, fear of Roman Catholic training prompted a proclamation against sending children to foreign seminaries to be educated; no money was to be sent for the payment of education of those children already there, and those children were to be called back to England. *CSPD, 1611–18*, pp. 279–80, 299; *1628–9*, pp. 53–6; *Synodalia*, I, 291; Ware, *Elizabethan Parish*, 43; *Norfolk*, XVIII, 27; Bennett, *English Books and Readers*, 65–6; Simon, *Education and Society*, 316.

as they were examined and "being at our elbowes would put into our mouths answers to our masters questions." The prompters escaped correction, but we "drew little profit from lessons." The teacher at Southampton was presented to the Court in 1620 for "not geveinge due attendance to the teacheinge the Children" and for turning them over to the teaching of "a Stranger unexamined and unripe of years." [18]

Church and civic officials conscientiously endeavored to appoint properly trained schoolmasters who would perform their work dutifully, and teachers in schools maintained or supervised by the parishes were nearly always licensed and of superior attainments. The unlicensed schoolteachers, who were particularly numerous in the petty schools, often proved to be ignorant frauds. During the Visitation of the Diocese of Norwich in 1597, the officers investigated some eighty masters: most of those in Norwich (ten), Great Yarmouth (seven), and King's Lynn (six) had their licenses, but the smaller communities had few approved teachers. William Watts, the licensed master of St. Nicholas-at-Wade, Isle of Thanet, protested to the ecclesiastical court about the wife of Thomas Foster of Chislet, who "doth teach school, namely, to write and read" much to his prejudice. Mrs. Wharry, a peregrine, was presented as " a notorious wicked woman for standing excommunicate for about 2 yeares and for teaching school without a license." [19]

From 1590 to 1640 closer supervision, newer, improved textbooks, plus the availability of better trained teachers, brought about a great advance in the teaching in the parish petty schools. Readily conceding that many a country schoolmaster "never had much learning" and made his way solely by "his looks and connec-

18. Essex Arch., X, 5b; *Reliquæ Baxterianæ*, 1–2; Willis, *Mount Tabor*, 101; *Southampton Recs.*, I, Pt. II, 582.
19. Sometimes there was a "great murmuring among the Brethren" in defense of a schoolmaster. John Symons, "a petie Scholemaster" of Barnstaple, who was "not very hardly willed but one of the anabaptiscal and precise Brethren had a child brought to the Church to be christened and called it Doe Well." The vicar disliked the name, even though it was claimed that it came from "the hebreword Abdeil," and christened the child John. Not only that, but the schoolmaster was replaced by Richard, "the other Symons," a master of arts. Wyot, Diary, May 29, 1598; *Kent*, XXV, 25, 29, 32; XXVI, 18, 20, 21, 23, 25, 34, 36; *Norfolk*, XVIII, 27, 33, 34, 61; Essex Arch., XII, 35a; Associated Architectural Societies, *Reports & Papers*, XXIX, Pt. II, 490, 501, 509.

tion," Donald Lupton claimed in 1630 that "there are some who deserve the place by their worth, and wisdome, who stayed with their Mother in the University untill Learning, Discretion, and Judgement had ripened them, for the well managing of a Schoole." The country usher was usually one who had attended the university but left early, having no Greek and only Latin enough to prove to bucolic children that "he is well furnisht." Custom made him "equal to the chiefe scholers, and above the lesser boyes." The universities were now turning out numbers of young men willing to fill petty school positions, and a large proportion of these fledgling teachers went out from puritan colleges to places selected for them by their elders.[20]

The improved status of the primary teachers generally, better remuneration, not to mention the insistence of donors of funds upon a higher quality of performance, all contributed to the betterment of the teaching profession. In 1617 John Puckle willed all of his copyhold lands to maintain a schoolmaster, who had to be a university graduate, to teach "learning and good manners" to the poor children of Basildon and Laiden, Essex. Hugh Peter came from Emmanuel College, Cambridge, in 1620 to fill this position, which he held for two years at a salary of £10; and Richard Baxter taught successfully at Dudley from 1638 to 1640. Another dedicated teacher was James Weemse, who was paid £12 a year by a grateful Yorkshireman "for causing a school to be taught at Kirk Leatham for children of the poor, who work in the alum works." [21]

The background and circumstances of the parents and the recommendations of the teacher determined whether or not a lad or wench was sent to school after learning the ABC's at home or in a dame school. The Canons of 1571 suggested that after this schooling the best students should be recommended to the bishop each year, and the parents be urged to educate them further for service to the state and the church. On the other hand, fathers of sons of no "pregnant capacitie" should put them to husbandry or suitable

20. *The Corporation Records of St. Albans*, ed. A. E. Gibbs (St. Albans, 1890), 69; Essex Arch., X, 46b; *Sessional Papers, 1830*, XII, 234–5; *1839*, XV, 183; Lupton, *London and the Country*, 115–22.
21. Stearns, *Strenuous Puritan*, 25; *Reliquæ Baxterianæ*, 7, 13; *CSPD, 1634–5*, p. 220; *Somerset & Dorset*, X, 166; *Sessional Papers, 1822*, IX, 483.

craft, in order that they might be useful to the commonwealth. Autolycus talked with one, a son of "an Old Shepherd," who had been branded as unfit for more learning, and could not reckon pounds, shillings, and pence: "I cannot do't without counters," but he could read a list of things needed at the market for a sheep-raising feast. "Now if we cannot write, we have the clerk of the Church, or the schoolmaster of the town to help us . . . and therefore what need we trouble our heads with inditing letters?" quoth Breton's countryman.[22]

Many parents in the cities and great towns, and countrymen of smaller places as well, did not accept the view of the shepherd's son. "Learning is a Thing that hath been much cried up and coveted . . . by the People of all Sorts, tho' never so mean and mechanical: every Man strains his Fortunes to keep his Children at School," James Howell charged. "The Cobler will clout it till Midnight, the Porter will carry Burdens till his Bones crack again, the Plough-man will pinch both Back and Belly to give his Son *Learning*." In his will, William Bourne, innholder and portreeve of Gravesend, desired that his children be "set to scole, whereby they may have some facultie to live." Richard Furse, a yeoman of Devon, urged his descendants to "Geve yourselves to the redynge and herynge of the holy scryptures and shuche like good docteren; be lerned in the laws of the realme and have to rede the old crownenekeles and shuche like aunshyente hystoryes, rememburynge it is a common saying it is a shame for a man to be ignorante. . . ." Thus it came about that many a "whining schoolboy, with his sachel and shining morning face" crept like a snail unwillingly to school.[23]

In Chapter I of this work we noted what good listeners ordinary English men and women were. Many of them had been trained in the petty school to follow a discourse and to retain the main points of an argument. The following and memorizing of a sermon was the hardest test of the listening art, yet a surprising number of the members of the audiences could repeat portions of them at length

22. Ware, *Elizabethan Parish*, 43; *The Winter's Tale*, IV, iii, 43–6; Breton, *Court and County*, in Dunham and Pargellis, *Complaint and Reform*, 474.
23. James Howell, *Epistolae Ho Elianae*, ed. Joseph Jacobs (London, 1892), II, 523–4; *CSM*, XLII, 29; *Devonshire*, XXVI, 172; Brinsley, *A Consolation for our Grammar Schools*, 40; *As You Like It*, II, vii, 145.

—and did—despite the fact that the best preachers gave their flocks little or no intellectual quarter. The rules of many schools resembled those of Chipping Barnet, which provided that a place be assigned in the church for the schoolmaster and his pupils, and that certain designated scholars take notes "in wrighting of the sermons," which they had to present to the master on Mondays.[24]

When the great Czech educator Johann Amos Comenius first came to Britain in 1641, he was impressed by "the eagerness with which the people crowd to the services on Sunday," and was still more amazed at the discovery that "a large number of men and youths copy out the sermons with their pens. . . . They discovered an art which has now come into vogue even among the country folk, that of rapid script (tachygraphia) which they call stenography. . . . For this they employ symbols (characters) signifying whole words, and not single letters of the alphabet. Almost all of them acquire this art of rapid writing, as soon as they have learnt at School to read the Scriptures in the vernacular. It takes them about another year to learn the art of shorthand." [25]

Free classes for the petties, supplemented in many places by numerous private elementary schools, were available nearly everywhere in England south of Lancashire and Yorkshire. The surest testimony to the success of these institutions is the state of literacy. What was in 1590 by no means an illiterate English public advanced rapidly during the next half century: one authority has concluded recently that by 1640 "over half" of the males of London were literate, and something like a third of the males of the Home Counties could read. Though signatures are no absolute guarantee of literacy, almost 80 per cent of a sample of 1,000 wills and land purchases in Essex carried signatures, and about 50 per cent of the yeomen and substantial farmers could both read and write. A few young men who became apprentices after completing training in reading and writing English at the petty schools developed into writers of clear and forceful pamphlets and tracts—

24. Brinsley, *Ludus Literarius*, 255–7; Mary Briggs, *The Anatomy of Puck* (London, 1959), 6; *London*, V, 30; *Sussex Arch.*, XLIII, 79.
25. In 1558 Timothy Bright re-invented a system of shorthand: *Characterie: an arte of shorte, swifte and secret writing by character*. Bennett, *English Books and Readers*, 152; *Comenius in England*, ed. Robert F. Young (Oxford, 1932), 65.

in the two decades after 1640, John Lilburne, Richard Overton, and William Walwyn published works that were widely read.[26]

III

The founders of Latin grammar schools, which were such an important development of the sixteenth century, always stressed the classical studies and grammar along with religious instruction. The injunction to the schoolmasters of the Hundred of Bruton, county Somerset, in 1520 was to teach male children "grammar after the good new form used in Magdalen college in Oxford, or in the school at Paul's in London . . . [but] not to teach songs, or reading English, or such other small things." The scholars were to be trained to be "perfect Latin men." Sir John Deane gave as his reasons for endowing a free grammar school in 1558 in the Chapelry of Witton, Cheshire: "God's glory, his honour and the wealth publick is advanced and maintained by no means more than by virtuous education." The scholars were to be taught "good literature, both Latin and Greek," and authors of "Roman eloquence" especially Christian authors. The children were to learn the catechism and then accidence and grammar; next they were to learn three of Erasmus's works, Ovid's *Metamorphoses,* Terence, Horace, Sallust, and Virgil. Sir John probably agreed with the belief expressed in the Marlborough Grammar School in Wiltshire that "the crown of school classical studies . . . [was] the writing and delivering of a speech in Latin." [27]

In the fifty years following 1590, and occasionally even before, many small towns and rural parishes acquired free schools similarly constituted. The classics, along with religious instruction, composed the program which was intended to prepare the sons of the gentry and well-to-do for the universities and professions. At Tiverton, Devon, in 1604, Peter Blundell, a self-made merchant,

26. J. W. Adamson, "Literacy in England during the Fifteenth and Sixteenth Centuries," in *The Illiterate Anglo-Saxon and Other Essays* (Cambridge, 1946), 44–61; Ware, *Elizabethan Parish*, 31; Stone, in *Past and Present*, No. 28, pp. 43, 46, 47, 48; F. G. Emmison to author, 1962; Simon, *Education and Society*, 381.
27. *VCH Oxfordshire*, I, 457; Stone, in *Past and Present*, No. 28. p. 44; *Sessional Papers, 1824*, XIV, 380–85; *1837–8*, XXIV, 438–41; XXV, 754, 885–6; *Wiltshire*, LI, 50.

founded a school whose main goal was to raise an educated clergy.
In 1606, Sir William Paston endowed a free grammar school in
the parish of North Walsham, Norfolk: forty scholars were to be
instructed in Latin and grammar, and there were to be Thursday
lectures given in the parish church by a lecturer appointed by the
Bishop of Norwich, which were to be attended by the students. Sir
John Strode bequeathed a house and an acre of ground in 1609
for a free school in Evershot, Dorset, "wherein to instruct children
and schollars and to teach them the latten tongue, and also to nurture and breede them in learning untill such tyme as they shalbe
fitt and able to be placed abroad at the Universities of Oxford or
Cambridge or ellswhere." Unfortunately for the children of Evershot, twenty years passed before the school was actually opened.[28]

London had long been famous for its excellent schools, such as
St. Paul's, the Mercers', the Merchant Taylors', and other foundations maintained by the liveried companies. Christ Hospital,
founded in 1552 for the education of orphans, was sometimes referred to as "The Bluecoat School" because the boys wore "Azure
Liveries, and Sable head-pieces." As the seventeenth century advanced, others were established, not only in London but in Surrey
and Middlesex, many of which are famous the world over today.
Mrs. Margaret Audley left £700 in 1616 to the Skinners' Company to endow a school in Hackney Parish; a mixed school in a
new building, administered by the Drapers' Company, was founded
in the parish of St. Mary le Bow in 1617 by Sir John Jolles. According to Lupton, Charterhouse, which opened in 1611, was
principally for the younger rich; while St. Mary Rotherhithe, a
free school which opened the next year, was for the sons of poor
seafaring men.[29]

The founding of new and the strengthening of existing free
grammar schools continued apace. In the seventeenth century,
however, consonant with advancing educational demands, many of
the old established schools broadened their courses of study to include the teaching of vernacular subjects as well as Latin, Greek,

28. Simon, *Education and Society,* 313; Chalk, *History of St. Peters, Tiverton,*
22; *Sessional Papers, 1820,* IV, 135; *1833,* XIX, 318–19; *Somerset & Dorset,* IX,
252–3.
29. Lupton, *London and the Country,* 58, 63; *Sessional Papers 1819,* X, Pt. b,
94, 136–7; IV, 431.

and Hebrew, and most of the newly founded institutions, together with some of the older ones, added petty schools. At Wotton-under-Edge there was an ancient school established by Katherine, Lady Berkeley, which, when it was reorganized in 1623, became a mixed grammar school; though the scholars, aged ten to eighteen, were "to speak nothing but Latin in School," they were to be "taught to write a fair hand, to cipher and cast accounts." In accordance with the wishes of Dr. Robert Chaloner, the boys in the free schools which he founded in Yorkshire in 1611 were to be drawn from poor families as well as rich ones and were "to be educated in grammar and accidence and other inferior books." The Corporation at Gloucester used a bequest of an alderman in 1611 to appoint an usher to teach the petties. It is interesting that even though the Trinity Parish School of Exeter provided elementary instruction, the Corporation thought it necessary in 1640 to appoint Thomas Philips, scrivener, to attend at the Free Grammar School regularly "to teach such a number of Schollers as are willinge to learne to write one hour every day in the week, except Saturday" for a fee of 2s. 6d. per student a quarter.[30]

By the end of the period, every large town and most smaller ones had a grammar school. James Howell seriously wished "that there reign'd not among the people of this Land such a general itching after Book-Learning, and I believe so many Free-Schools do rather hurt than good." The opinion of Tom of All Trades was that some counties had so many schools "that it is disputable whether the universities, with the Inns of Court and Chancery, have where to receive them or no." The concurrence of Francis Osborne and Thomas Fuller in this view testifies to the large number of boys being turned out by the "multitude of Schools." Schools maintained by parishes sometimes had to compete with private teachers, as in the case of the Free Grammar School of the Borough of Reading. Andrew Bird, master of the Free School, complained first to the Corporation in 1630 about Master Greenhill and his assistant Mr. Peters whom the Bishop of Sarum had licensed to teach Latin and grammar in Reading. At the suggestion of the authorities, Bird petitioned the King, and within a few

30. Adamson, "Literacy in England," 49; *Sessional Papers, 1826–7*, X, 341; *1820*, IV, 463; *1837–8*, XXVI, 643–5; *Dorchester Recs.*, 566; *Chetham*, I, 186–7.

months, the Bishop of Salisbury revoked the licenses of the private
schoolmasters. Six years later, when Mr. Bird died, Sir Francis
Windebank requested that the post not be filled without the consent and approbation of the Archbishop of Canterbury. Laud,
who, as a graduate of the school, had a special interest in it, appointed William Page, an M.A. from St. John's College, Oxford,
and three years later donated the revenue of £200 to the town and
school. With a better building than many other schools, a library,
and even a urinal "for the school boyes . . . in a convenient
place," the Reading school merited the King's comment that the
school had become "very considerable." [31]

The regimen of seventeenth-century grammar schools would
appall the modern schoolboy. An elaborate set of rules survives
from the Steyning Grammar School in Sussex; the regulations were
read out each quarter so that students could not plead ignorance
of them. To gain admittance, scholars, who were limited to fifty
lest "the Master be oppressed with multitude," had to be able to
read English distinctly, but once enrolled, the four chief forms
were to speak only Latin. The hours from March 1 to September 1
were from 6 to 11 a.m. and from 1 to 5 p.m.; from September 1 to
March 1 the students' day did not start until 7 a.m. Scholars were
not allowed to play "above once a week." Morning and evening
prayers, catechizing for three hours every Saturday afternoon and
on holidays, plus regular attendance at church on Sundays fulfilled
the expected religious observance and promoted the principles
stated in the twenty-second article of the book of rules, namely:
"Honesty and cleanliness of life, gentle and decent speeches, hu-
mility, curtesy and good manners shall be established by all good

---

31. There were many private schools in London where subjects not offered in
the public schools were taught, such as French (by Huguenots), dancing, music,
table manners, and a variety of vocations and trades. For an intimate glimpse
of one of these schools, see M. Claudius Hollyband, alias De Sainliens, *Campo
di Fior*, in Byrne, *Elizabethan Home*, 4–22; also *CSPD, 1625–6*, p. 114; *1627–8*,
p. 54; Lawrence Stone called attention to the "proliferation of little private
schools" which brought about great growth in secondary education. Stone, in
Past and Present, No. 28, pp. 46–7; Howell, *Familiar Letters*, 525–6; Dunham
and Pargellis, *Complaint and Reform*, 553–4; Francis Osborne, *Works* (10th ed.,
London, 1701), 5; Fuller, *Worthies*, I, 32; *Reading Recs.*, III, 16, 17, 18, 26, 66,
92, 191, 227, 347, 350; *CSPD, 1629–31*, p. 339; Heylyn, *Cyprianus Anglicus*, 379–
80; *HMC Reading*, XI, VII, 225.

means. Pride, ribaldry, lying, picking and stealing, swearing, and such other vice shall be sharply punished." [32]

From the frequent repetition of orders to school authorities to instruct students "in good manners whereby to behave themselves in church, school, on street and everywhere" it is evident that multiplicity of rules and regulations did not always assure gentle behavior, even when the boys were sons of the gentry. The Lady in Erondell's *The French Garden* (1605), referring to her own boys, says to the schoolmaster: "You know wherefore they are put to your charge, which is, not onely to teach them in Grammer and Latin tongue, but also to bring them up in good maners, and to advise them of their duties." [33]

Doubtless the schoolmasters had their troubles inculcating good manners in boys whose family backgrounds were barren of the amenities of life. The experience of English youths in the grammar schools of that day ranged from severe and frequent beatings, such as Nicholas Udall administered to Thomas Tusser at Eton, to the almost paternal relationship R. Willis had with his teacher at the free school in Gloucester, "which made me also love my book." Ralph Josselyn could not recall ever being whipped, but James Howell remembered his teacher as "a learned (tho' lashing) Maser"; William Lilly, who had the good fortune to be taught at Ashby de la Zouche by the great John Brinsley, could testify how a rare conjunction of severity and capacity bred many youths for the universities—at the age of eighteen, Lilly "could speak Latin as well as English." Adam Martindale had five teachers in fewer years, and, judging by the terse descriptions he accorded them, they were a sorry lot: one was an able young man but a poor manager; another, an old humdrum curate, proved to be a simpleton and tipster; the daughter of a schoolteacher had only a "smattering of Latine"; and still another was a silly, inconstant person who treated those who could "fee" him the best. Thrown with students whom he classed as "Dullards," it is little wonder that Martindale rejoiced when he could transfer to another school. Following a dismal period at Towcester under a Welshman named Rice, Thomas Shepard told of being instructed by the eminent and holy William

32. *Sussex Arch.*, XLIII, 73, 76–80.
33. *VCH Oxfordshire*, I, 470; Byrne, *Elizabethan Home*, 80.

Cluer from Emmanuel, who "stirred up in my hart a love and desire of the honour of learning, and therefore I told my freends I would be a Scholler." [34]

Though only a fraction of the sons of the poor could attain a grammar school education, and no more than about 2.2 per cent of the youths completing a course went up to Oxford and Cambridge, still it is possible that the world had never known a time when such a large proportion of the male population of a country had access to learning. And it was in the free grammar schools that most of the sons of the country gentry, yeomen farmers, burgesses, professional men, and well-to-do tradesmen were "well seasoned" and "always after fitter for the best impressions." [35]

IV

The leaders of the English Reformation had realized that women ought to be able to read and write, and by the time of Edward VI, Thomas Becon was arguing in *A Newe Catechism* that "it is expedient that by *public authority* schools for women-children be erected and set up . . . and honest, sage, wise, discreet, sober, grave and learned matrons made rulers . . . and that honest and liberal stipends be appointed for the said schoolmistresses." In 1582 Richard Mulcaster advanced four good reasons why young girls should share in elementary training: the custom of the country, the duty owed to them by society, their aptness for learning,

34. Tusser, *Husbandry*, 156; Willis, *Mount Tabor*, 97; *Camden*, 3d. ser., XV, 2; Howell, *Familiar Letters*, 19; Lilly, *History of his Life*, 16–18, 21, 22; *Chetham*, IV, 11–15; *CSM*, XXVII, 359–60; *Winthrop Papers*, I, 145–6; II, 280.

35. The remarkable total of 909 grammar schools definitely in existence in 1640, plus 50 or more doubtful ones, indicates about 960 institutions or one public secondary school for every 5,687 persons out of a population of 5,460,000. The concentration of more than half of these grammar schools in the very regions from which came the great emigration to America is most striking. See the listings by county compiled by W. A. L. Vincent in *State Education, 1640–1660, in England and Wales* (London, 1950), Appendix A, which is by no means complete. Simon, *Education and Society*, 373, 398; Jordan, *Philanthropy in England*, 279–96; Brinsley, *Ludus Literarius*, 22; Reyce, *Suffolk*, 55–6. The most recent examinations of the state of higher education are by Stone, in *Past and Present*, No. 28, pp. 47–68; and by Curtis, *Oxford and Cambridge*.

and the excellent results already obtained. He did not recommend sending girls to the grammar schools or to the universities: "I would allow their learning within certain limits, having regard to the difference in their vocation, and in the ends which they should seek in study. We see young maidens are taught to read and write, and can learn to do well in both; we hear them both sing and play passing well; we know that they learn the best and finest of our learned languages to the admiration of all men." [36]

In contrast with these forward-looking pedagogues, there were many Englishmen who, even if they did not actually oppose grammar-school education for girls, saw no necessity for it. Even such a man as Sir Thomas Overbury could scarcely be said to be wholly endorsing education for women when he wrote:

> Give me, next good, an understanding wife,
> By nature wise, not learned by much art;
> Some knowledge on her side will, all my life
> More scope of conversation impart.

To be instructed in the ABC's at home or at dame schools along with their brothers and possibly taught the same subjects as the boys through the petty-school stage was all the book-learning that girls had need for or should expect. Anything more than that was still "by many conceived very uncomely and not decent." [37]

Ecclesiastical supervision of male teachers was extended after 1555 to schoolmistresses. In dame schools particularly the investigators turned up innumerable cases of unlicensed, unscholarly teachers, but even more shocking was the case of Magdalen, wife of William Smith of Enfield, who was put on bail by the Middlesex

36. There are three theses that treat some aspects of women's education: the most useful is Dorothy May Meade, Education of Women and Girls in England in the Time of the Tudors (M.S. Thesis, London, 1921); Elizabeth S. Bier, The Education of Women in England under the Stuarts, 1603–1715 (M.A. Thesis, California at Berkeley, 1926); and a less satisfactory one, Phyllis W. Smith, The Education of English Women in the Seventeenth Century (M.S. Thesis, London, 1921); The Catechisme of Thomas Becon, ed. John Ayre (Parker Society, 1844), 376–7 (italics mine); Educational Writings of Richard Mulcaster, 51–7; Brinsley, Ludus Literarius, 22.
37. The Miscellaneous Works of Sir Thomas Overbury, Knt., ed. Edward F. Rimbault (London, 1890), 40; Mitchell & Leys, History of London, 327.

Quarter Sessions because "shee, being a schoolmistress, intyced the childe of Thomas Warde to steal from hir father." One gets the definite impression that almost any one except wicked people such as Magdalen was considered qualified to teach little children. In 1630 in Cambridgeshire, the will of a Dr. Cage authorized the minister and churchwardens to use one-half of the bequest to engage "some poor woman in the town" to teach the children to read. Prudence Poole of Puriton, Somerset, successfuly petitioned the justices that same year to allow her to continue teaching. She had worked as an apprentice for fifteen years in Huntspill Parish, and for the first three years of the last four had been "in service" at Puriton. In the previous year, 1629, she had become unfit to carry any burdens and had therefore "endeavoured ever since to gett her livinge by instruccon of children" in the parish, but now the constable had ordered her back to the place of her birth. Herein we note that a woman "in service" had been educated sufficiently to warrant approval as a dame-school teacher. From the replies sent in from 121 parishes in Cambridgeshire, we know that women were teaching there in parish schools, and there is the testimony of Adam Martindale that he had a woman teacher in the free school of St. Helen's in Lancashire.[38]

As the new century advanced, girls as well as boys learned to read and write in the new, endowed schools of village communities, but no girl studied ciphering. The master of the Grammar School of Bunbury in Cheshire, established in 1594, was under direction from the founder to admit only a few wenches, to let them stay no longer than they needed to learn to read English, and never beyond the age of nine. Nicholas Latham, a parson, established three schools in Northamptonshire in 1619; girls under ten could attend to learn to read but nothing else; boys had classes in reading, writing, and casting accounts, and the rudiments of grammar. Fifteen years later, William Smyth of West Chiltington, Sussex, laid down more relaxed rules in the school he endowed: the schoolmaster was to teach "all youth, as well poor as rich, either male or female." On the other hand, the authorities at Uffington

<hr/>

38. Meade, *Education of Women*, 191–8; *Middlesex Sessions*, II, 82; *Sessional Papers, 1837–8*, XXIV, 131; *Somerset Sessions*, II, 111; *VCH Cambridge*, 338, 339; *Chetham*, IV, 12.

refused to admit girls, though they conceded that the practice was "the common and usual course." [39]

It is pretty clear from such evidence as we have that a goodly proportion of the distaff side could read; they read the Bible and Foxe's Book of Martyrs, and took pleasure in lighter literature. All of Shakespeare's women could read, and on the stage, women are commonly represented as being able to write—the three wives in *Westward Ho* have a writing master. In spite of the declared aims of school authorities of teaching girls to write as well as read, few women outside urban centers could spell or write with any degree of clarity or felicity, unless they had private instruction. Even such an able gentlewoman as Margaret Winthrop, who was mistress of the Manor of Groton, could not spell or match her husband's diction; and the letters of Katharine Oxinden to her son Henry reveal the inferior education provided in some communities.[40]

Fortunately for the daughters of the well-to-do and even of ordinary families of London, the provincial cities, and some of the larger towns, private schools provided girls and young women with instruction in subjects nowhere found in the curriculae of public schools. For those who could pay the fees, there was a motley crew of masters and mistresses who would essay to make young ladies out of the daughters of citizens, yeomen, and tradesmen, by teaching them embroidering, dancing, music, manners, and French. And for those in remote sections, itinerant schoolmasters toured the land; one got as far as Nicholas Assheton's Lancashire village in January, 1618: "Henry Dudley, the imbroyderer came to work and teach." The account of the accomplishments of Mrs. Susanna Perwick, daughter of a schoolmaster of Hackney, indicates the scope of instruction available. At fourteen she was acclaimed "a most rare musician" for her skill in playing the Treble viol and the

39. Simon, *Education and Society*, 376n; *Sessional Papers, 1824*, XIII, 193–4; *1837–8*, XXIV, 780–84; *1819*, X, Pt. b, 157; Mitchell & Leys, *History of London*, 327.

40. In Porter's play, *Two Angry Women of Abington*, Mistress Goursey, struggling with her husband over a letter, says: "You shall not have it, till I have read it." Master Goursey: "Give me it then, and I will read it to you," to which the Mistress replies: "No, no . . . I am a scholler, Good enough to read a letter sir." Meade, Education of Women, 244, 248, 286, 309, 317–22; *Educational Writings of Richard Mulcaster*, 55–7; *Winthrop Papers*, II, 58, 92, 98, *et passim;* *Oxinden Letters*, 150; Surtees, XXXVII, 6.

Lyre viol—she had a "rare delicious stroke"—and performed with the lute and on the harpsichord. She was also "a most curious dancer," excelled with needle, "silver, silks, straws, glass, wax, gums." What was more, she wrote a clear hand, cast accurate accounts, and was well versed in "all Arts of good housewifry and Cookery." [41]

These embellishments to secondary training aroused much popular interest, and writers of the day often condemned or at least belittled them. Robert Greene's "Shee Conny-catcher" (1592) had been to the elementary school; "after I grew to be six years old [I] was set to school, where I profited so much that I writ and read excellently well, played upon the virginals, lute, and cithern, and could sing prick-song at the first sight, insomuch as by that time I was twelve years old, I was holden for the most fair and best qualitied young girl in all that country." Through this indulgence by her parents, however, she became wanton. The play, *The Wit of a Woman* (1604), is a description of life in one of the private schools. In Act I, Balia, the "olde Schoolmistris," is scolding four "Wenches" for their poor performances in needlework, playing the lute, dancing, cushion-work, and writing. It is obvious that all the girls ever think of is men. The scene shifts, and Giro, a vintner's boy, says to Ferio, a lawyer: ". . . this writing in a wench may make ill worke with a man, which letters may convey more knaverie, then tongues may be heard to speak of." Giro's opinion of dancing and singing is in the same vein: "Pretty Qualities, the one to bee witch them, that heare them, the other to heare such as will talk with them, and under the shape of a man, to heare a Devill in a Maske." [42]

The open-handed philanthropy of the day, so fully set forth in the volumes of W. K. Jordan, permitted all kinds of educational experimentation by the donors. Most foundations for the schooling of girls, established by women of means, as well as by men, offered

41. In 1605 Peter Erondell published *The French Garden*, a French book for English gentlewomen, which Nicholas Breton praised as "a private labour for a publique good." *Chetham*, XIV, 76; John Batchiler, *The Virgin's Pattern* (1661), 2–5; *Surtees*, LXII, 8.
42. Robert Greene, *A Disputation betweene a Hee Conny-catcher, and a Shee Conny-catcher*, in Judges, *Elizabethan Underworld*, 226; *A Pleasant Comoedie wherein is merily shewn The Wit of a Woman* (1604), Act I, scene i, 1, 3, 4, 5, 7, 12.

vocational training, for if, from necessity, as Mulcaster had written, a young maid "has to learn how to earn her own living, some technical training must prepare her for a definite calling." William Borlase endowed a trust at Great Marlow in Buckinghamshire to maintain a school for twenty "weomen children" nominated by the churchwardens and overseers of the poor; the girls were to be housed in a dwelling donated by him and there taught to spin, knit, and to make bone lace. Four years later in 1630, Lady Elizabeth Hill created an endowment in Ilsworth Parish, Middlesex, to support and keep at school six or eight poor girls of eight to ten years of age under the tutelage of "a poor, modest, discreet and grave woman" who would teach them to read, work with the needle, and perform all kinds of housework "to fit them for service, and to live in the commonwealth." Remarkable as the only urban foundation for women outside of London that has come to light was one set up by John Whitson of Bristol for forty daughters of "decayed" or dead freemen. Again "a grave, painful, and modest woman" was to teach the girls to read English, sew, and some other "laudable work toward their maintenance." Known as "the Red Maids" because of their distinctive dark red dresses and white aprons, these girls were all bound as apprentices to their schoolmistresses from eight to ten years, depending upon their ages.[43]

Great numbers of boys and girls who did not attend or finish the petty schools still received an education through apprenticeship. Occasionally some kind masters or mistresses voluntarily instructed them, but the only claim an apprentice could make for lessons of any kind depended upon the terms of the labor contract. Thomas Drone, bound for twelve years in 1620 to William Bradley of Chelmsford, had in his indenture a clause requiring the master to teach him the trade of a cooper and likewise "to be learned to write and read." We have proof that many lads did learn reading and writing, and sometimes ciphering, in their masters' houses, and in rare cases some of them were sent to a private teacher for instruction. In 1637, Dorothy Leach, the servant of a Middlesex gentlewoman, left £10 for the education of three apprentices at

43. *Educational Writings of Richard Mulcaster*, 53; Jordan, *Charities of Rural England*, 56; Roberts, *Southern Counties*, 378; *Sessional Papers*, 1819, X, Pt. b, 108–9; *1837–8*, XXVI, 158; *1822*, IX, 490–91; Little, *Bristol*, 120–21.

the Stanwell Free School. A benefaction at Dedham made provision "for poor young men to be brought up in the science of clothmaking, to be assisted therein by loans." Ordinarily, apprenticed girls were taught housewifery, spinning, or sewing, but some of them learned to read and write. Orphans of the poor, who were bound out by the parish overseers and who made up a substantial proportion of the youth everywhere, seldom learned more than the rudiments of simple husbandry or household economy. The members of the Corporation of Maidstone thought it fit in 1607 to allow 25s. quarterly to "blynd Austin . . . so long as hee shall attend the free Scole . . . No attendance, no allowance." That masters and mistresses felt morally responsible for providing religious tutelage for both female and male apprentices is clear from the dozens of hortatory sermons published and several proto-Hogarthian 'prentice manuals.[44]

The presence of a puritan strain in so many Englishmen profoundly affected their attitude toward the education of their daughters. John Pynchon, a gentleman of Springfield, Essex, wrote in his will of 1610: "My said wife to keep, maintain, and bring up all my six daughters decently in good education." Their brother William, founder of Springfield in Massachusetts Bay, and others, took with them to their new home modern views concerning the education of women. Some Englishmen thundered against the *femme savante* whom a puritan fanatic eulogized in *The Magnetick Lady,* a "philosophic madam" who would crowd to lectures along with her spouse and even "dispute with the Doctors of Divinity at her own table"! In *The City-Match* Seathrift gives notice to the puritan Mrs. Semple: "No, I'll never trust again a woman with white eyes, that can take notes, and write a comment on the catechism." So far had some women of middling degree progressed with their learning by 1641 that they forgot their places and dared to read the Scriptures and then instruct their families and give counsel to their husbands. Others essayed to preach. All of this proved to be too much for the son of the great proponent of female education, John Brinsley the younger, who preached in 1645 at Great Yar-

44. Essex Sessions, XX, 199; *Sessional Papers, 1823,* IX, 308–9; Waters, *Gleanings,* II, 1124; *Maidstone Recs.,* 64; B. P., *The Prentises Practice in Godlinesse;* and A[braham] J[ackson], *The Pious Prentice, or the Prentice's Piety.*

mouth that "women must learn in silence" and must not "usurp authority over their husbands." A humorless tribute to female accomplishment in Old England, this, to a deed executed in New England a decade earlier by Mistress Anne Hutchinson.[45]

When this period opened, it was already evident that Englishmen of all degrees had been won to the belief that for success in this life, quite as much as for saving souls for the next, some education was most desirable, and that the ability to read and write was the absolute minimum for everyone. By 1641, the conviction had spread that schooling in the petties for all must be the responsibility of the commonwealth. The pamphleteers stood with pens sharpened to write up projects for educational reform and betterment. At the call of Parliament, the great Comenius came over from Bohemia. Upon his arrival in 1641, he exclaimed in surprise and admiration: "They are eagerly debating on the reform of schools in the whole kingdom in a manner similar to which . . . my wishes tend, namely that *all young people* should be instructed, none neglected." [46]

V

The surest testimony to the widespread literacy among the English people of this era is the number and variety of the titles in the *Short-Title Catalogue*. One must bear in mind constantly that what has survived is but a fraction of the output of the presses; the ephemera and popular titles passed from one reader to another and were usually worn out in a short time. Thomas Fuller condemned "the numerosity of needless books," but Sir Thomas

45. At the other extreme was the fear of such Roman Catholics as Petronella Davies of St. Giles-in-the-Fields, "who teacheth children bookes called manuells papisticall and not fitt to instruct you withall." *Middlesex Sessions*, n. s., III, 233; Waters, *Gleanings*, II, 854–5; Joseph Swetman's *The Arraignment of Lewd, Idle, and Froward and unconstant Women* (1616) went through ten English editions by 1634 and a Dutch one at Amsterdam in 1641. Quotation in Jean Elizabeth Gagen, *The New Woman, her Emergence in English Drama, 1600–1730* (New York, 1954), 19, 28; Mayne, *The City-Match*, I, i, ii, v; IV, ii; John Brinsley, *A Looking-Glasse for Good Women* (1645), 11, 16, 29, 32, 33, 35, 37, 39. See Chamberlain's comments on the "compleat women for learning" among the gentry in his *Letters*, I, 227.

46. *Comenius in England*, 65 (italics mine); Simon, *Education and Society*, 291–7.

Overbury, who was convinced that "Bookes are part of Mans pre-rogative," was allied with Shakespeare when he wrote of the dull constable:

> Sir, he hath never fed of the dainties that are bred in a book;
> he hath not eat paper, as it were; he hath not drunk ink; his
>   intellect is not replenished.

Half a century later, the bard would have discovered that the pro-portion of "unlettered, small-knowing souls" had diminished con-siderably.[47]

Contemporary critics of the English scene seemed frequently unable to describe the products of the press and their supposed effects in terms other than pathological. "One of the diseases of this age," to quote Barnabe Rich in 1610," is the multitude of Bookes, that doth so overcharge the worlde, that it is not able to digest the abundance of idle matter that is every day hatched and brought into the world." But while James Howell worried over "the general itching after Book Learning," the average English-man found in printed matter his principal source of information and education, even more than at the schools and universities. The astonishing outpouring of books, pamphlets, and broadsides by the printing press stored up and transmitted a vast amount of human experience from generation to generation which served as capital in the intellectual sphere quite as much as gold and silver did in the economic world. Referring to Sir Richard Weston, Clarendon observed that "His education had been very good amongst books and men." It would seem that in that age the reading of a book made much more of an impression on the individual than in our own day.[48]

Undoubtedly the ephemeral issues of the press reached the widest circle of readers in both town and country. "Do wee not see Pamphlets, Ballads and Play-bookes sooner sold, then elegant Ser-mons and Bookes of Pietie" was Sir William Vaughan's lament in

47. A. W. Pollard and R. Redgrave, *A Short-Title Catalogue of Books Printed in England . . . 1475–1640* (London, 1926); Fuller, *Worthies,* I, 30; Overbury, *Miscellaneous Works,* 41; Ward, *Diary,* 72–3; *Love's Labour's Lost,* IV, ii, 24–7.
48. Barnabe Rich, *A New Description of Ireland . . .* , To the Reader (1610), n. p.; Howell, *Familiar Letters,* 525–6; Chute, *Shakespeare of London,* 63–4; Clarendon, *History of the Rebellion,* I, 59.

1626; "unless a Booke containe light matters as well as serious, it cannot flourish, nor live Jovially, but like Leaden Saturne stand still in the stall." Though women were always accounted ravenous devourers of light reading matter, Richard Baxter confessed that in his youth in remote Cheshire: "I was extreamly bewitched with a Love of Romances, Fables and old Tales, which corrupted my Affections and lost my Time." According to Henry Peacham, you could "have all the news in England and other countries, of murders, floods, witches, fires, tempests, and what not in one of Martin Parker's ballads." A London wit charged that "We live in a printing age . . . scarce a cat looke out of a gutter, but out starts a halfpenny Chronicler, and presently a propper new ballet of a strange sight is endited." In the days before the newspaper, the broadside sheets or ballads supplied the human interest news to the average man, for, as Earle said, "A Mere Gull Citizen" loves to hear of acts of famous citizens such as "the Four Prentices of London, and above all, the Nine Worthies." [49]

Along city streets book peddlers also offered somewhat more serious literary and moral fare. Said Catch in *The Ordinary* (1634):

> I shall live to see thee
> Stand in a playhouse door with thy long box,
> Thy half-crown library, and cry small books
> Buy a good, godly sermon, gentlemen—
> A judgment shown upon a knot of drunkards;
> A pill to purge out popery: The life
> and death of Katharine Stubbs.

If any person desired to purchase religious tomes, practical manuals, and the like, such as Adam Winthrop lent out to his friends in 1597—Petrarch's *Works,* Lambarde's *Perambulation of Kent,* Googe's *Foure Bookes of Husbandry,* Rastell's *Les Termes de la Ley,* and several translations from the classics—he patronized a

49. "I'll now lead you to an honest ale-house where we shall find a cleanly room, lavender in the windows, and twenty ballads stuck about the wall." Isaak Walton, *The Compleat Angler* (1653), Pt. I, chap. II, 62. Stephen Vincent Benét captured the feeling and described convincingly a scene of a hawker crying his wares in *Western Star* (New York, 1943), 24; Vaughan, *The Golden Fleece,* Pt. I, 9–10; *Reliquæ Baxterianæ,* 2; Peacham, *The Worth of a Penny* (1647); *Martine Mar-Sixtus* (1591), quoted in Bennett, *English Books and Readers,* 4; Earle, *Microcosmography,* 55, 149, 150; Besant, *London,* 182.

bookseller. A dealer sent Lord Hastings "1 Shakespeare workes in folio" for £1 2s. 0d. on October 24, 1638, and during the next two years forwarded a variety of volumes on government, military discipline, and histories. Books like these, Richard Rogers held, needed pondering over and re-reading; "once or twice reading a book for practise, is not enough." [50]

Thomas Coryat frankly marveled at the booksellers' street in Frankfurt in 1611: it excelled Paul's Churchyard, St. James Street in Paris, and the Merceria of Venice; it seemed to him "a very epitome of all the principall Libraries of Europe." By 1641, however, when the well-informed Comenius explored the book offerings of London, he was astounded: "They have an enormous number of books on all subjects in their own language. . . . There are truly not more bookstalls in Francfort at the time of the fair than there are here every day." The booksellers dealing solely in old libraries totaled thirty-nine in 1628: eight of them lived in Chancery Lane and ten in Little Britain. At the great north door of St. Paul's, seven years later, nine booksellers and a bookbinder had stalls.[51]

The number of booksellers in other towns is proof that the rage for reading was not confined to the metropolis. The shop of Roger Ward at Shrewsbury in 1585 contained a stock of 2,500 different titles, among them "42 singing psalmes alone" and one "mirror of knighthood, 2 partes,"—the first Spanish-Portuguese romance translated into English. The greater part of his stock comprised unlicensed editions of the Bible, New Testaments, Prayer Books, catechisms, and more than 250 sermons. Twice a week books appeared at the market stalls of Great Yarmouth, and Michael Hart kept shop in St. Martin's Parish, Exeter, from about 1593 to 1615, when his eldest son succeeded him. His stock consisted of works on medicine and history, and volumes on religious subjects and dictionaries. At Cowcrosse, Middlesex, Henry Pyke, yeoman, stole more than seventy-five volumes belonging to John Drawater, who

50. Cartwright, *The Ordinary*, III, v; Philip Stubbs, *The Life of Mistress Katharine Stubbs* (1591) was a popular work about a godly woman. *Winthrop Papers*, I, 71–2; *HMC Hastings*, I, 389–90; Rogers, *Seven Treatises*, Preface; *HMC Coke*, XII; I, 107–8; *HMC Rutland*, XII: IV, 480.

51. *Coryat's Crudities*, II, 298; *Comenius in England*, 65; *CSPD, 1628–9*, p. 328; *1635–6*, p. 67.

was probably a petty chapman: twenty-six grammars, ten "vir-gills," twenty-four "Æsops Fables," one of Castellion's Dialogues, three "Practice of Piety," five "Delights in th' Closset," two "Learn to Live," and numerous devotional works. Before 1621 Thomas Smith had a shop in Manchester; then he moved to Barnstaple, where he sold books for five years, after which he went back to Manchester. He supplied each town with "all sorts of Latin and English books allowed by authority to be sold," and "gayned the custome both of towne and countrey." [52]

When, in the 1620's, the Puritans began to organize systemat-ically for the propagating of their views through the rural areas, they proceeded to make shrewd use of the printers and book-sellers in London and the provincial cities who were of their per-suasion. Prior to 1623, the Crown had always controlled the press in order to avoid civil dissension and for the "unity of England," but it had only exercised "a degree of polite restraint." In 1623, however, thoroughly aroused by the illegal importations from Hol-land that were critical of the laws, ordinances, etc., of the king-dom, King James issued proclamations against disorderly printing, uttering, and dispersing of books and pamphlets printed overseas. The next year he banned the publishing of seditious Roman Cath-olic pamphlets and "seditious Puritanical bookes . . . scandalous to our person and state, such as have been lately vented by some Puritanicall spirits." With the accession of Charles I, William Laud began to manage the press in order to favor Arminianism, and the booksellers forthwith complained that the writings of their best-selling authors had been stifled in the process, which presaged their ruin. But not even Bishop Laud could stop the surreptitious print-ing of works by Leighton, Prynne, Bostwick, and Burton, or John Lilburne from publishing books from his prison cell.[53]

The subtlety and skill with which "the Puritan faction" dis-persed its books, sermons, and tracts throughout the land "to nib-

52. "Roger Ward's Shrewsbury Stock," *The Library*, 5th ser., XIII, 247–68; Palmer, *Great Yarmouth*, I, 81; *Devon & Cornwall*, XXI, 36–8; *Middlesex Sessions*, II, 109; Eyre, in *Surtees*, LXV, 4, 7, 10, 23; *CSPD, 1623–5*, p. 518; *Western Antiquary*, V, i.
53. Haller, *Liberty and Reformation*, 32; *Bibliotheca Lindesiana*, I, 161, 163; *CSPD, 1623–5*, pp. 309, 327; *1633–4*, p. 266; Neal, *History of the Puritans*, I, 517–18.

ble at the Church's power" should excite admiration in the most knowing modern propagandist. At the time, an ardent champion of the Anglican clergy testified in *Persecutio Undecima* to the success of the Puritan underground: ". . . They had their mutual intelligence throughout the whole Kingdom, and engrossed almost all of the inland Trade to men of their Faction; they took up a Canting language to themselves, which they called the Language of Canaan, abusing phrase of Scripture, thereby to understand one another, to colour their seditious practices; they had their Emissaries (whereof simple Robin, the Bible Carrier was one) or Scouts to give notice where men of their tribe preached. . . ." A year before the Scottish War, this writer continues, the sectaries armed in London, and "Many Porters [were] seene in evenings carrying or conveying arms and . . . Trayterous Libels, and Observations, printed at publick charge to their Countrey Chapmen. . . ." This general indictment can be supported with less highly colored facts and more instances than that of Simple Robin, the peddler. Hugh Peter participated in distributing forbidden Bibles, catechisms, and treatises on ecclesiastical polity printed in Holland. When William Ames's *A Fresh Suit Against Ceremonies* was printed at Rotterdam in 1633, the British ambassador found out that "there is 100 or 200 bound at this time to sell to the good saintes which are in England." One Mr. Puckle, "an ignorant unworthy fellow" and "a Caterpiller to his Countrie," was a great vender of the books "as passengers go for England." Sir William Boswell also reported two recent impressions of the Bible at Delft and Amsterdam.[54]

Within England, the Londoners in the book trade dealt clandestinely in forbidden works with provincial printers and shopkeepers. James Bowler and Solomon Turner, booksellers of London, arranged with William Turner of Oxford to print and bind copies of "The Antithesis &c." and "James Giles his Haltinges"; Turner also sent copies to booksellers at Cambridge. In this same year, 1631, Michael Sparke, Nicholas Bourne, James Bowler, and Henry Overton (the servant of Mistress Sheppard), stationers of London, printed, without license, *Rome's Ruin,* which contained passages

---

54. *Persecutio Undecima,* 55, 58; Stearns, *Strenuous Puritan,* 78; *CSPD, 1633–4,* p. 213.

taxing the whole state as well as some bishops and prominent clericals with various abuses. When the Bishop of Lincoln's letter to the Vicar of Grantham about the removal of the rails in his church fell into Puritan hands, copies were made and scattered across the kingdom, especially in the diocese of Norwich where "an Advertisement" stated "they were ordinarily sold amongst the Booksellers in Duck lane in written copies. . . ." In February, 1637, Edward Penton, "a sanctified brother . . . [who] hath been already in New England," was arrested at Norwich for vending scandalous books—he admitted having seen someone reading *A Divine Tragedy lately Acted* by William Prynne in the house of Stephen Moor, "a packer of stuffs," at Philpot Lane, London, before Christmas. Shortly thereafter, fifty copies of this work and an equal number of *Newes from Ipswich* were forwarded to Penton in Norwich, and one Kipping there received eighteen copies of *Newes* and "10 Tragedies." [55]

Charles Greene, bookseller of London, got into the record books because he did not co-operate with the Puritan faction. In a petition to Laud, in February, 1638, he charged that a few years before he had suffered a great loss when he was printing a licensed book, "New Canaan." When some of the sheets had been pulled, the printing was stayed and the sheets were carried off by some agents of the New England Puritans. The book is at last printed, said Greene, and the Wardens of the Stationers' Company had lately picked up 400 copies. He prayed that Laud would order delivery of this anti-Puritan rodomontade by Thomas Morton of Clifford's Inn, gent., once "mine Host of Ma-re-mount" in Massachusetts-Bay.[56]

The issuance of further proclamations and decrees indicates that the seditious business of distributing forbidden books by chapmen and booksellers continued, apparently unabated. From the Star Chamber on July 1, 1637, came a decree, aimed at the Puritans, which reduced the number of approved master printers and forbade the printing of anything not licensed by the Archbishop of Canterbury or the Bishop of London. Charles I found it necessary

55. *CSPD, 1631–3*, pp. 3, 231; Heylyn, *Cyprianus Anglicus*, 295; *CSPD, 1636–7*, pp. 427, 487; *HMC*, 3d Report, 191.
56. Morton's *New English Canaan* (1632) is reprinted in Force, *Tracts*, II, No. 7; *CSPD, 1637–8*, p. 25.

also to issue a proclamation against the use of the press by the Scots: "For whereas the Print is the King's in all Kingdoms, these seditious Men have taken upon them to print what they please, though we forbid it; and to prohibit what they dislike, though we command it. . . ." Laud's efforts notwithstanding, the truth was that by its very smallness and mobility, the press was actually if not legally free. It was devastatingly effective, not just in exacerbating men's discontents, but telling them of a thousand troubles they had not previously realized.[57]

"Bookes are the Rivers of Paradise watering the earth; the deaw of Hermon making the vallies fertile; The Arke preserving the Manna Pot, and Moses Tables; the Monuments of ancient labours; the Baskets keeping the deposited Reliques of time so as nothing is lost: The Magazine of Piety and Arts." Thus Robert Willan exulted in a sermon of 1630 praising the donor of a library to Sion College. Urban told Countryman that what you have in the country does not advance the understanding, which is enriched in the city "by hearing, reading, and conferring" with people of like minds. We have "publick libraries," you have none . . . The Muses inhabit the city." Actually only a tiny proportion of the great philanthropic bequests of these years went to found or support libraries, especially those open to the public-at-large.[58]

Outside of London there were established nine or more "publick libraries" before 1640. At Norwich, the oldest of provincial collections could boast of sets of Hakluyt and Purchas, and most of the chronicles. Robert Redwood, a rich citizen of Bristol, provided a building in 1614 and later an endowment for books "for the furtherance of Learning" in his native city—a gesture that would be repeated in 1747 by a Quaker descendant at Newport on Rhode Island. Sometime before 1617, it "pleased God to put into the harte of Mr. [Samuel] Warde our preacher to stirre up this Corporation for the erecting of a Librarie, which being furnished with all kinde of bookes cannot but greatly further the advancement of God's Glorie, his worshippe and religion amongst us," said the will

57. Heylyn, *Cyprianus Anglicus,* 341; Rushworth, *Historical Collections,* II, 830, 834; *CSPD, 1636-7,* pp. 478-9; For a general discussion, see Frederick S. Siebert, *Freedom of the Press in England, 1476-1776* (Urbana, 1952), 107-61.
58. Thomas Willan, *Eliah's Wish: A Prayer for Death* (1630), 40; Nash, *Quaternio,* 46-50.

of Raymond George, a grocer, who left £4 to purchase books at Ipswich. A year later, Bezaleel Shermon—another grocer, interestingly enough—left "to the library of this town a book called Speede's chronicle." A moving spirit behind the library at Dorchester was John White, who urged his parishioners to support it. A catalogue of books and donors made in 1631 includes a Greek Thesaurus presented by Mr. White, the *Summa* of St. Thomas Aquinas, and many legal works, travels, and maps, in addition to a preponderance of devotional volumes. Mr. Froward, the usher at the Grammar School, had custody of the collection, which was kept in a separate room in the schoolhouse. At Leicester in 1639, a "faire library" had been established by the Corporation with the proceeds of a voluntary collection made by "a large part" of the body politic.[59]

Numerous small collections of books were assembled in grammar schools or housed in churches where people other than pupils or the clergy consulted them. The English had not yet learned to respect publicly owned books, and everywhere care had to be exercised to prevent theft or removal of books. The Redwood Library at Bristol expended £3 17s. 6d. in 1640 for "15 dozen and a half of book-chaines for the Library"; books did not circulate. Nevertheless, by the time many Englishmen set out for the New World, the hitherto novel idea of public responsibility for making book-knowledge available to all ranks of society, both for religious and prudential purposes, had made a sound and significant beginning, particularly in those areas where the puritan influence was strong.[60]

59. Some Public or Town Libraries were: Norwich (1608), Bristol (1613), Worsbrough, Yorks. (1613), Ipswich (1617), Coventry (1628), Dorchester (1631), Leicester (1632), Spalding, Lincs. (1637), Boston, (1637), Langley Marish, Bucks (1640); Edward Edwards, *Memoirs of Libraries* (London, 1859), I, 737–48; Carl Bridenbaugh, *Peter Harrison: First American Architect* (Chapel Hill, 1949), 45; Waters, *Gleanings,* I, 583; II, 1171; *Dorchester Recs.,* 581–4; *CSPD, 1633–4,* pp. 210, 392–3; Taylor, *Part of This Summers Travels,* in *Works,* I, No. 3, p. 10.

60. Jordan, *Charities of Rural England,* 47; *Yorkshire,* XXXIX, 150; Brears, *Lincolnshire,* 18; Edwards, *Memoirs of Libraries,* I, 742. For the libraries at St. Paul's and Sion College (1629), see Jordan, *Charities of London,* 254–5. Louis B. Wright supplies a wealth of data on books in general in *Middle Class Culture in Elizabethan England* (Ithaca, 1958), some of which is useful for the years after 1603.

VI

Toward the close of the sixteenth century, England led all of Europe in music. Although the oft-repeated tales of lutes hanging on the walls of every barber's shop for the amusement of waiting customers are patently untrue, there is a documented account of the English who attempted to colonize Trinidad and Dominica under Captain "Verdo Campo [Grenville] taking along "many musical instruments, 'chirimias,' organs and others, because, they said, the Indians liked music." A chancery case tells of a "chest of instrumentes of musicke" taken from Sir Francis Drake's ship after his death, that comprised "a lute, 'hobboyes sagbutes Cornettes & orpharions bandora & suche like." Furthermore English musicians crossed the Channel and journeyed southward to teach the Italians. Very few Englishmen failed in some fashion to mark "the sweet power of music." In rhetorical prose Richard Hooker gave fervent praise to music in *The Laws of Ecclesiastical Polity,* and, somewhat circumspectly, Thomas Fuller commented on its extensiveness in his *Worthies of England.* Indeed the very Puritans themselves sought through music to make a joyful sound unto the Lord.[61]

Most of the music performed and enjoyed by the peasantry and the urban poor was vocal and traditional. Here and there a man could play the tabor, the pipes, or scrape a homemade fiddle without any formal instruction. The shepherd might pipe for solitary amusement, the swain might entertain in the cottage of an evening, or, as we have seen, several musicians might provide music for wakes and village revels. Here and there in a country church, and usually in town, ordinary folk listened to choirs and organs during divine worship. Wandering minstrels appeared at taverns and at fairs, and professional waits favored most large towns with their music. Lieutenant Hammond's account of Exeter Cathedral in 1635 emphasizes the "delicate rich, and lofty Organ . . . which with their Vialls, and other sweet Instruments, and tunable voyces,

61. The essential work on popular music is Professor Woodfil's *Musicians in English Society from Elizabeth to Charles I, especially* pp. 201–3. Quinn, *Roanoke Voyages,* II, 741, 741n; Henzner, in *Life in Shakespeare's England,* 20; Fuller, *Worthies,* I, 28.

and the rare Organist, togeather, makes a melodious and heavenly Harmony, able to ravish the Hearers Eares." [62]

In England inhabitants of all degrees and both sexes could enjoy and participate in some kind of music and often together in concert. This was possible because of the availability of so many comparatively inexpensive books on music; more than 125 editions of works on how to sing, what to sing, and what to play, with the principles of music, came out between 1560 and 1600. In 1628 Coventry's free grammar school began to offer free instruction in grammar and music to the children of all the inhabitants, and it is possible that at other grammar schools youths received tutelage in music in the way that Richard Mulcaster had called for decades earlier. There were private teachers of music offering their services in places as far apart as Exeter in Devon and Audley End in puritan Essex. To the latter village went Sir Charles Caesar's music teacher, who had taught the organ and the viol for eight years, to serve a lady and her family for an annual salary of £20.[63]

London was truly a city of song and harmony during the greatest age of English music. Choir and organ music were performed weekly in the cathedral and large churches, and on special occasions there was "the King's Music." The City also had its waits, incorporated in 1604 as "The Master, Wardens, and Commonalty of the Art or Science of Musicians," whose duty it was to train up apprentices and provide musical entertainment for the populace; they were also to control dancing teachers. In 1638 a French visitor to the metropolis found "in all public places, violins, haut-bois, and other sorts of instruments are so common, for the amusement of particular persons, that at all hours of the day, one may have one's ears charmed with their sweet melody." Outside on the streets one heard "The Cryes of London," "The Country Cryes," and the cries of the chimney sweeps. Thomas Ravenscroft set down notations for these airs which came out in the collections of Thomas Weelkes and Orlando Gibbons. There were times, at night, when the sober citizens would have liked to dispense with

62. Woodfil, *Musicians in English Society*, 202–3; *Devon & Cornwall*, IX, 85.
63. Woodfil, *Musicians in English Society*, 239; Camden, *Elizabethan Woman*, 158; *Sessional Papers, 1834*, XXII, 119–20; *English History from Essex Sources, 1150–1750*, ed. A. D. Edwards (Chelmsford, 1952), 25, 34; Brears, *Lincolnshire*, 19; *HMC Exeter*, 200.

some of the sounds: trumpeters and serenaders paid by nobles and gentlemen, the scraped-out ballads or dance music performed by alehouse fiddlers, and the bawdy songs, and jiggs of inferior musicians who infested the taverns.[64]

In their homes, citizens often entertained themselves and their guests by singing "fair songes at fouer partes" or playing in impromptu concerts, for many Londoners had learned to read music and sing parts. In 1587 Thomas Morley explained why he was offering his *Plaine and Easy Introduction to Practical Music*. It arose out of an occasion when he had been embarrassed by his inability to participate in singing when he was a guest at one of these impromptu musicales: "supper being ended and the Musicke books, according to the custome, being brought to the table: the mistresse of the house presented mee with a part, earnestly requesting mee to sing. But when after manie excuses, I protested unfainedly that I could not; everie one began to wonder. Yea, some whispered to others, demaunding how I was brought up." Samuel Pepys spent many happy hours singing and tells in his *Diary* how he had listened "in perfect pleasure" as Mrs. Knepp sang "her little Scotch song of 'Barbary Allen.' " In 1609, when Ravenscroft published his *Pammelia,* the earliest assembling of English rounds, catches, and canons, Londoners who longed to sing parts but who had not yet attained the skill seized upon it immediately. By 1600, for reasons inherent in its form and not as a result of Puritan influence, madrigal singing had begun to decline; such polyphonic flights were very difficult and required elaborate musical training, which few people had either the time or the talent to acquire.[65]

In *The Merry Wives of Windsor,* Mistress Ford, comparing Sir

---

64. Woodfil, *Musicians in English Society,* 2, 14, 15, 28–9, 50–51; Sieur de la Serse, in *Antiquarian Repository,* IV, 531; *CSPD, 1603–10,* p. 106; *1628–9,* p. 203; B. M. Add. MSS 29437, fol. 40–44; *Middlesex Sessions,* n. s., I, 426.
65. Hollyband, in Byrne, *Elizabethan Home,* 26, 51; Thomas Morley, *A Plaine & Easie Introduction to Musicke* (1597, 1608), B2; earlier Morley had published *Of T. Morley, The First Booke of Balletts to Five Voyces* (1596); *Diary of Samuel Pepys,* ed. H. B. Wheatley (London, 1924), V, 175, 177; Thomas Ravenscroft also issued *Deutermelia* (1609) and *Melismata, Musciall Phansies, fitting the Court, Citie, and Country Humours* (1611). On madrigals, see the two works of John Farmer, *The First Set of English Madrigals to 4 Voices* (1592) and *Forty Several Ways of Two Parts in One Made upon a Playn Song* (1591); Mitchell & Leys, *History of London,* 309.

John Falstaff's words with his disposition, warns Mistress Page that "they do no more adhere and keep place together than The Hundredeth Psalm to the tune of 'Green Sleeves.' " As a matter of fact the juxtaposition would not have puzzled Sir John, for he was, like most Englishmen, thoroughly familiar with both religious and secular music. Nearly all citizens could have joined in when the good-humored, fat knight cried at the sky, "Let it thunder to the tune of Green Sleeves," or been in accord with him when he remarked: "I would I were a weaver; I could sing psalms or anything." Psalm-singing had figured very prominently in English musical life from 1560 onward and was given a strong impulse by the immigration of Flemish weavers and Huguenots. Edward Winslow told of the humble Pilgrims singing psalms at John Robinson's house before their departure from Leiden in 1620, "making joyfull melodie in our hearts, as well as with the voice, there being many of the Congregation expert in Musick; and indeed it was the sweetest melody that ever mine eares heard." [66]

The patent fact that Englishmen of all beliefs and conditions, not just puritan artisans, knew how to sing parts as well as melodies may be explained in large measure by the popularity of books of psalms in meter, of which some ninety-four editions issued from the presses before 1600. Orthodox Anglicans, many of whom emigrated to Virginia, Bermuda, and the islands of the Caribbean, used *The Booke of Psalmes* compiled by Thomas Sternhold, John Hopkins, and others, which, appearing first in 1560, went through many editions during the next century and a half: there are seventy-eight known editions to 1600. Sternhold and Hopkins recommended their verses "with apt Notes to sing them withall." Thomas Ravenscroft published his most popular work, *The Whole Book of Psalmes,* in 1621, and it soon replaced the earlier collections by William Damon (1579), Thomas Este

66. Elder William Brewster took with him on the *Mayflower* in 1620 a copy of Richard Alison's *The Psalmes of David in Meter, The Plaine Song being the common tunne to be sung and plaide upon the Lute, Orphorgon, Citterne or Base Violl, severally or together* . . . [for 1–4 voices] (1599); he also owned Henry Ainsworth's *The Book of Psalmes, Englished both in Prose and Meter* (Amsterdam, 1612), and other psalm-books by Johnson. Mass. Hist. Soc., *Proceedings,* 2d ser., V, 45, 64, 72, 77; *Merry Wives of Windsor,* II, i, 62–4; V, v, 21–2; *Henry IV,* Pt. I, Act II, iv, 146–7; Edward Winslow, *Hypocrisie Unmasked by the True Relation of the Proceedings . . . against Samuel Gorton* (1646), 90.

(1592), and Richard Alison (1599) as the favorite of the puritan wing of the Church of England. The *Scottish Psalter* of 1535 also won approval among the puritans in England in the later years of this period.[67]

Two misconceptions about English psalm-singing unfortunately are still widely held: the first, as we have just noted, that Puritans alone practiced it; and, second, that the psalm tunes lacked musical worth and were commonly rendered lugubriously (often through the nose). Thomas Ravenscroft, a Cambridge man and probably somewhat of a puritan himself, clearly disproves the latter belief. Frequently at divine worship, psalms were sung in unison, but Ravenscroft had in mind the Huguenot injunction: "To rejoice in God, particularly at home." The title page of Sternhold and Hopkins' *Book of Psalmes* bore a quotation from James V of Scotland: "If any be afflicted, let him pray: if any be merry, let him sing Psalmes." When the Massachusetts Puritans published their now-famous *Bay Psalm Book* at Cambridge in 1640, they retained this saying on the title page. Moreover, Richard Mather and his associates closed their labored, metrical version with the statement: "The Verses of these psalmes may be reduced to six kindes, the first whereof may be sung in neere fourty common Tunes: as they are collected out of our chief musicians by Tho. Ravenscroft." This "chief musician" knew what his readers would like, and he gave them cheerful tunes, almost folk songs, which strikingly paralleled the plain style of preaching. They were intended to be performed at a brisk tempo, and usually were. When speaking to Autolycus about the twenty-four shearers who will sing at a feast, the Clown mentions that one is a puritan "and he sings psalms to hornpipes." John Cotton, writing on the subject in 1647, stoutly denied that "the man of Sinne," or any Antichristian Church had "any hand in turning *Davids Psalmes* into English songs and tunes," or that they were wont "to make any Melody in the singing of them, yea, they reject them as Genevah Gigs; and they be Cathedrall Priests of an Anti-Christian spirit, that have scoffed

67. Robert R. Steele, *The Earliest English Music Printing* [to 1600] (London, 1903), 42–92; John Sternhold, John Hopkins, and others, *The Book of Psalmes* (1599, 1608, edns.), title page; Thomas Ravenscroft, *The Whole Book of Psalmes* (1592).

at Puritan-Ministers, as calling the People to sing one of *Hopkins Jiggs*, and so hop into the Pulpit." [68]

One needs to *listen* to the psalms sung to Old Hundred, London, Windsor, York, and Old 113 tunes, so superbly recorded by the Margaret Dodd Singers in the seventeenth-century manner, to recapture the liveliness and homely vigor with which the English families and their friends sang psalms in as many as five parts when they sought "consolation and edification," and were truly "merry in the Lord." [69]

The thousands of men, women, and children who left their island in search of a new life before 1640 carried with them a sifting, at least, of the great English tradition of secular and religious music. Some of them were cultivated amateurs, accustomed to singing madrigals, catches, and rounds from music books; more of them possessed a familiarity born of much practice in singing the several parts of psalm tunes; and a very few could perform indifferently well upon several kinds of popular instruments. Some of the youth had been grounded in music at the petty or the grammar school. Beyond all question, the Puritans gave music a large place

68. On the title page of their psalmbook, Sternhold and Hopkins described the contents as "Set forth and allowed to be sung in all [Anglican] Churches, of the people together, before and after Morning and Evening Prayer: As also before and after Sermon; and moreover in private houses, for their godly solace and comfort, laying apart all ungodly Songs and Ballads, which tend only to the nourishment of vice, and corrupting of youth." Psalm-singing was obviously as Anglican as Puritan in practice. Too much has been made of such statements as Lupton's: "Puritans are blowne out of the Church with the loud voice of the Organs, their zealous Spirits cannot indure the Musicke, nor the multitude of Surplices; because they are Relickes, (they say) of Romes Superstition." Lupton, *London and the Country,* 12; *The Bay Psalm Book* (Cambridge, Mass., 1640, J. C. B. copy), title page, preface, sig. L14; *The Winter's Tale,* IV, iii, 44–8; John Cotton, *Singing of Psalms A Gospel Ordinance* (1647), 61.

69. Historians have paid almost no attention to the role of music in either English or American life. A beginning is being made by the Society for the Preservation of the American Musical Heritage, founded by the distinguished conductor, Karl Krueger, which has issued in its series *Music in America,* recordings based upon the latest historical as well as musicological research, and performed by the best artists as closely as possible to the manner of the time. See *Early American Psalmody: The Bay Psalm Book* (MIA-102), with useful jacket notes by Carleton Sprague Smith; also imported *English Ballads in Colonial America* (MIA-97). For a less authentically performed though excellent rendition of *Catches and Glees of the English Restoration,* collected by Henry Purcell and others, see the *Allegro* LP recording, 107 (3008).

in both public and family devotions; they were not hostile to many forms of secular music. It is possible that as many of the common people of England had as much facility in singing as in writing; their literacy in music was relatively high. What would happen to this delightful common cultivation of melody and harmony both at home and overseas could not have been predicted at the time the Long Parliament met.

VII

The migrating English carried with them to the new lands overseas not just their persons, their rural skills, and their crafts; they transported their entire culture. This was a transit of civilization, which, insofar as they gave it thought, the leaders aimed to make total. Puritans of New England had this consciously in mind. Although we lack accurate figures, the evidence we have points to a rate of literacy among the emigrants paralleling that of the Mother Country, and in the special case of Massachusetts to an even higher rate. Certain it is that many of those who settled in Virginia and New England shared with Comenius the ideal "that all young people should be instructed, none neglected," as soon as conditions in the new communities warranted. The abortive college at Henrico and the noteworthy founding of several Latin grammar schools and Harvard College in Massachusetts before 1642 were visible proofs of the hold this ideal had on the settlers. The proportion of intellectuals and constant readers among the Puritans who crossed to New England was very high for any age, and books figure prominently in their surviving inventories. And we have noted that in one form or another the emigrants bore with them the common English musical heritage. One of the most remarkable features of the Great Migration was, indeed, the presence in it of a large number of educated and cultured Englishmen.

X

Insecure, Disorderly Englishmen

THE HALF-CENTURY after 1590 was a time of profound, unprecedented, and often frightening social ferment for the people of England. During these years nearly every member of the lower orders in the countryside and in the towns knew deprivation and genuinely feared insecurity; and well he might, for close to a majority of the population found themselves living perilously near the level of bare subsistence. Though in all probability few of them attempted to analyze the situation, Englishmen were experiencing the cumulative effects of long-range, persisting disturbances inherited from previous generations to which new disorders were constantly being added.[1]

Although conditions were steadily improving—these were the years in which England was developing a capitalistic economy—the old undeveloped, agrarian society did not adjust with sufficient rapidity to provide employment for the thousands of laboring poor. The period opened in a depression that lasted until 1603; again and again, from 1619 to 1624, from 1629 to 1631, and from 1637 to 1640, hard times settled down upon the countryside. The plague years of 1625 and 1636 caused further dislocation, and several bad harvests added to the widely held belief of the 1630's that adversity and evil days were the common and normal

1. Coleman, in *Ec. Hist. Rev.*, 2d ser., VIII, 280–95; Edwin F. Gay, "Economic Depressions, 1603–1660," in *The Making of English History*, eds. R. L. Schuyler and Herman Ausabel (New York, 1952), 238; Caldwell, Devonshire, 196–273.

lot of all but a fortunate few. One symptom of the distress of the poor, which required regulation, was the spawning of "counterfeit brokers, and pawn-takers upon usury," who, by 1604, had "grown of late to many hundreds within London" and the suburbs, as well as in the smaller cities.[2]

War, enclosures, political grievances, uneven application of the law, combined with depressions, epidemic diseases, and food shortages, manifested themselves like boils on an otherwise sound body politic. Reacting to their afflictions as they might have to boils, the hard-pressed people were frustrated, desperate, restive. With the loosening of family and church ties, women as well as men sought to sustain themselves by any and every means they could muster; drunkenness and immorality increased along with crime and violence as idleness and mischance forced hapless thousands down into the ranks of the defenseless poor. Ignorant of the true nature of social problems and unable to furnish costly relief or help the unemployed to find work, the royal authorities took drastic measures to avoid social revolt.

Actual inhumanity had frequently characterized those Englishmen who ruled, but now even those who themselves were sorely troubled and suffering greatly exhibited a callous indifference to the misery and anxieties of their fellow men. An Essex husbandman, Michael Weely, exemplified rural inhumanity when he turned away his servant, Bridget Purkes, without a legal order, though he knew her to be pregnant and likely to perish. In the cities, outwardly at least, the citizens who were prospering and improving their social position displayed more urbanity and made a better appearance in public life, but nevertheless, as they grew more gentle, they grew less kind, and too often their courtesy and manners were trappings they adopted only for their equals and betters. In a ballad of 1626, *A Merry Descourse between Norfolke Thomas and Sisly Standtoo't his Wife,* Edward Ford dealt with this theme. After a "thanklesse" journey to London, Sisly sings.

2. Gay, "Economic Depressions," 235–8, which, however, does not mention the crisis of 1629–1631; Thirsk, *English Peasant Farming,* 193; Wilson, *England's Apprenticeship,* 52; Pickering, *Statutes at Large,* VII, 105–6. Among the many tracts on usury, one of the most popular was that by a preacher in rural Dorset: John Blaxton, *The English Usurer: Or, Usury Condemned* (2d ed., corrected, 1634); *Plymouth Recs.,* 45.

> Nay, husband, do not you say so,
> Our cottage we'l not forgo
> For the best house that stands aroe
>   'Twixt Cheap and Charing Crosse;
> For though our house be thatch'd with straw
> We do not live, as some in awe. . . .[3]

At the same time that schoolmasters and churchmen were attempting through education to improve the language, manners, and morals of the ordinary English folk, degrading conditions of poverty and the intemperance and demoralization that so often plague a war-wearied population aggravated the traditional churlishness and incivility of the downtrodden. The rough, earthy speech and ignorance of or contempt for polite deportment among the depressed inhabitants shocked and scandalized many persons. Journeying "down over rugged wayes" from Exeter to Taunton in 1635, Lieutenant Hammond found Bradninch an ancient place, so poor that "she hath quite lost all breeding, and good manners; for I could not passe her without a Volley of Female Gun-shot, which made me hasten away . . . to a little better qualify'd Towne." Though he was speaking of Hertfordshire, Thomas Fuller, using a metaphor that cloth workers anywhere would have understood, sized up unmannerly yokels thus: "the finest Cloth must have a List, and the pure Pesants are of as coarse a thread in this County as in any other place." [4]

Every small English village had its share of women, usually wives and widows, who now and then stirred up the townspeople and broke the peace. Alice, wife of Thomas Crathorne, a victualler of Seasalter in Kent, had to face the charge in 1616 of being "a common swearer and a brawling scowld, and withal will be drunk exceedingly." When Henry Wade, fisherman, was out on the Blackwater, his wife Margaret regularly got into trouble. She was indicted as a common barrator, malefactor, calumniator, and sower of discord among her neighbors on evidence brought in by

---

3. Many citizens of London and other cities tried to improve their domestic deportment by studying *Carter's Christian Commonwealth: or Domesticall Dutyes deciphered* (1627); Essex Sessions, XIX, 421; *Roxburghe Ballads*, II, 169, 171.
4. *Camden Miscellany*, 3d ser., XVI, 78; *CSPD, 1639*, p. 341; Fuller, *Worthies*, I, 426.

them and Sir Thomas Beckingham. When the court ordered her to
answer Ann Umpton for a "misdemeanour," Margaret failed to
give satisfaction, whereupon John, Ann's yeoman husband, assaulted her near her house and tore her coat from her back. At
nearby Aveley on April 19, 1639, Susan Constable, celebrated for
quarreling with her neighbors, called Constable William Beden "a
leering knave." Later she charged, under oath, that Mary Cornwall, the wife of a yeoman, had grievously threatened to tweak her
nose and "mischief her" and demanded surety against Mary.[5]

The great majority of convictions of women were for being
common scolds, and ordinarily the punishment was a ride in the
cucking- or ducking-stool, though occasionally a fine was imposed
instead. At Northampton, Jane Withers of Weldon, adjudged a
"woman of turbulent spirit, a comon scolde and reviler of her
honest neighbours in most uncivill and unwomanly terme," had to
go to gaol in 1630 until she could find sureties for her appearance
at the next general sessions. Upon her return to Weldon, the constable was ordered to "cause her to bee brought with the cook-
kinge stoole to some convenient place within the towne and . . .
there be doused and ducked in the manner of scoulds." Later she
was required to acknowledge her fault on the Sabbath and ask forgiveness of her neighbors. In Manchester, the jury of the manor
court directed the steward to punish Isabel Richardson and Alice
Worthington, "Common Scoulds and disturbers of their neigh-
boures" in "the Cucking Stool" according to the law. Being
ducked several times in the Horse Pond in mid-October should
have curbed their tongues for a time at least.[6]

The tendency toward "slanderous and contumelious speeches"
was a common fault of both countrymen and citizens in this rude
age. Cases of name-calling and slander filled the dockets of both
lay and ecclesiastical courts in every county. Sometimes the offender paid dearly for the privilege of saying what he thought: two
surgeons of Chichester, Southcott, alias Settcap, and Thornbor-

5. *Kent*, XXVII, 217; Essex Sessions, XIX, 537; XX, 505; Dartmouth Recs.,
DD6231 (1634); *HMC Various*, I, 90.
6. *Northampton Sessions*, 99; *Manchester Court*, III, 31; Essex Sessions, XIX,
406; XX, 18, 284, 286; *Somerset & Dorset*, V, 121, 233; *Chetham*, XLVI, 159;
Sussex Arch., XLIX, 59.

ough, tangled with each other in 1633. Thornborough found himself in court to answer for reciting a rhyme he had composed:

> From Sett to South,
> From Capp to Cott,
> Who knows his name?
> He knows it not.
> At Rochester this babe was bore,
> His father a knave, his mother a whore,
> And is not he a very knave
> Who makes a privy of a grave?

When the Star Chamber finished with Thornborough, his wit had cost him £50 for the King, £20 in damages, and an acknowledgment of his ill-considered conduct to Southcott. Without any apparent provocation, John Pratt, a shoemaker, denounced and cursed the brewer Christopher Benbury in the Widow Baston's public house in Southampton: "you are one of the Assessors . . . a plague of god confound all the Assessors and the divill in hell confound him that paies a penny" of the Parliamentary subsidy. Moreover he expressed his contempt for the honorable members of the Corporation and justices of the peace in scurrilous terms.[7]

The vogue of so many yeomen associating in small groups to write and publish libels on their neighbors may have been one unanticipated consequence of improved schooling; and both puritans and anti-puritans participated in the game. An uproar occurred in the tiny Wiltshire village of Compton Bassett in 1620, when Robert Maundrell, son of a yeoman, and Katharine Farmer, servant of his father, joined the schoolmaster in framing "a very infamous and scandalous wrightinge" to disgrace Richard Miller, husbandman, and his daughters. The authors scattered copies abroad and sang the libel "in the open hearinge of divers persons"; Katharine brazenly sang it one Sunday night at Richard Miller's house, "having first placed herself upon the toppe of the table to be better heard." Nor were the clergy spared. In an Essex parish in 1616, a joiner, a laborer, and two tailors maliciously combined to

---

7. *CSPD, 1633–4,* p. 69; *Southampton Recs.,* IV, 18; Hamilton, *Quarter Sessions,* 111.

publish a libel on the curate and the churchwardens; the constable
bound them over for the court of assizes for their lines, which read
in part:

> Deliver this to the Townes Jewell,
> Whose elbow cushion is of crewell,
> To him I meane who at the poore barks,
> And eats nothing but cock sparrows and larkes,
> To him I say who no compassion feeles,
> And cries let the poore sterve and kick up their heeles.[8]

Slander and libel became more heinous when interlaced with
cursing and swearing, and it was not only the Puritans who expressed concern over the marked increase in obscene and blasphemous language. Vain attempts had been made by King James to
suppress the evil by setting a fine of 12d. for every conviction; in
1635 King Charles I wrote to the Attorney General, Sir John
Bankes, that he desired an office erected and granted for seven
years to Robert Lesley who would authorize deputies in each parish to receive the penalty money; half of it was to go to the diocese. The monarch did not endear himself to a profane people by
setting up this regulatory agency, nor did Leslie, who pocketed
twelvepence in the pound, gain any more friends than other monop-
olists. Enforcement of the statute was virtually impossible. Women
were not exempted, and they too had to answer to the charge of
"most grievously swearing and taking the name of God in vain."
Susan Seamer and Anne Hart both faced the Kentish Quarter Sessions in 1639, Susan for "common and fearfull swearing and
cursing" and also for her "most shameful and ordinary filthy and
impure speeches and obscene songs and immodest behavior such as
we shame to relate." In addition to "filthy, scolding, and impure
speeches," Anne Hart stood convicted of swearing and blasphemy.

---

8. Fortune Crewe, a woman of Crudwell, Wiltshire, was ordered to ask forgiveness in church for publishing a libel. Just as the minister was about to read the
first lesson, she strode in and called out to him: "Mr. Bradshaw, I am come to
ask forgiveness of John Comyn and his wife for publishing a libel against them."
The minister told her to wait until after the lesson, but when he asked her to
speak she answered "that what she had spoken she had spoken and would not
speak more." *HMC Various,* I, 91; *Wiltshire Sessions,* 69–70; Essex Sessions, XIX,
80, 239, 322–3; XX, 180.

The foul-mouthed fishwives of Billingsgate had many a formidable competitor in the country villages.[9]

II

It is probable that what Henry Oxinden described as "the Desperate Disease of our Commonwealth at Home" could best be detected in the evident general decline in morality brought about by the shifting standards of the multitudes of uprooted people in both town and country. "I have seldome seen the world at so lowe an ebbe, both at home and abrode," admitted John Chamberlain soberly, while Barnabe Rich uttered more strident strictures in 1614: "A general corruption hath overgrowne the vertues of this latter times, and the world is become a Brothell house of sinne. It is enough for us now if we seeke but for the resemblance of vertue; for the soveraigntie of the thing it selfe, we never troubles our selves about it." Doubtless the bulk of the people, even in the cities, were honest, moral, law-abiding, well-behaved, decent, and relatively pious Englishmen and women, and the historian must recognize that court records can give a false impression of a society. Nevertheless, after all things are given due weight, he must conclude, as did the contemporaries, that "many bewail the iniquities of the time." [10]

Cheating and many kinds of fraud seemed much on the increase. Tradesmen fleeced the poor by using false weights or short measures; John Welles and Henry Chiswicke, vintners, descended so low in 1614 as to deliver short measures of coal and charcoal to the poor of Clerkenwell. So openly did bakers flout the assize of bread in the 1630's that two tracts called attention to the practice, and taverners and brewers also cheated with small measures and adulterated their beer. Even the quality of leather goods, cloth,

9. Richard Dickson of London was fined "for 20 oaths, 1 £." *CSPD, 1633–4,* p. 238; *1635,* pp. 245, 293; *Kent,* XXV, 18; *HMC Grimsby,* XIV, VIII, 282; *Warwick Sessions,* VI, 41.
10. William Shakespeare put it best: "The web of our life is of a mingled yarn, good and ill together: our virtues would be proud, if our faults whipped them not, and our crimes would despair, if they were not cherished by our virtues." *All's Well that Ends Well,* IV, iii, 83; *Oxinden Letters,* 33; Chamberlain, *Letters,* II, 250; Barnabe Rich, *Honestie of this Age,* 2, 7.

and other articles became suspect. All ranks of society engaged in
sharp practice and, along with the authorities, did not consider it a
serious offense; indeed many hard-bitten tradesmen looked upon
well-managed knavery as but one degree below plain honesty.
Who can blame a cheat in a play for musing cynically:

> Our life, methinks, is but the same with others;
> To cosen and be cosen'd makes the age.
> The prey and feeder are that civil thing
> That sager heads call body politic.
> Here is the only difference: others cheat
> By statute, but we do't upon no grounds.
> The fraud's the same in both. . . .[11]

As meeting places for the Englishmen from all walks of life,
some taverns naturally entertained cheats of every sort, who used
the rooms, tables, and refreshments to assist them in their nefari-
ous pursuits. The public taste for gambling with cards and dice
was such that a host of male and female "decoys" cozened simple
countrymen, inexperienced citizens, and gentlemen alike. Once in-
veigled inside the alehouse or inn, the victim was relieved of his
money by "false play," often at a game honestly called "Decoy."
Bartholomew Hopkins and John Partridge of Ratcliffe used to lie
in wait along the highways to defraud honest travelers of their
goods and money "by false arts and games." In 1616, Elizabeth
Browne worked a slightly different ploy; she cozened Mary
Browne out of 22s. "by way of fortune-telling." Deception and col-
lusion were practiced throughout the realm, in provincial cities as
well as in the metropolis, though not on the scale of frauds perpe-
trated there. A really big game, which lasted two whole days, was
promoted in Maidstone in February, 1611, by John Banister,
shearman, at which false cards were used in a game called "new
cutt" wherein the gains and losses of the players ran into pounds.[12]

---

11. *Middlesex Sessions*, n. s., I, 320; John Powell, *Assize of Bread* (1630); John
Penkethman, *Artachthos, or A New Booke declaring the Assize of Weight of
Bread* (1638), published for the Privy Council; *Suffolk*, XV, 155; Caldwell,
Devonshire, 218; Cartwright, *The Ordinary*, I, v; and in general, Thomas
Dekker's classic, *The Gull's Hornbook* (1609).
12. Robert Greene insisted that his *Theeves falling out . . .* (1637) proved that
"the Villaines of Lewd Women doe, by many Degrees, excell those of Men."

"Good wine needs no bush," quoted Rosalind, but Donald Lupton believed that, as a rule, better custom could be found at taverns with "a Signe compleat." All depended, however, upon the character of the landlords. Lieutenant Hammond stopped in at the Red Lion at Portsmouth and thought his hostess "briske, blith, and merry, a handsome sprightly Lasse, fit for the company of brave Commaunders: whereof there was a great store." On the other hand, the inhabitants of Fingringhoe, Essex, petitioned the justices to "purge" the town of Robert Greenleafe's establishment because "bad husbands . . . frequent thither day and night drinking, their wives and children feling the smart thereof at home . . . likewise. . . harbouring forreners of other parishes ther to meet commonly to drink and quarell, and the saboath day by this meanes to be prophaned." [13]

The proportion of the frequenters of public houses who went there to play away their money and their time, whether cozened or not, was small in comparison with those who thronged to them because they were "bewitched with the sweetenesse of strong lycoure." Surely "this sinne of drunkenness" was the greatest of English vices. The grand jury of Manningtree, Essex, voiced the fears of decent people everywhere when it demanded that the justices of the peace suppress the alehouses within its limits, because "the town is grown to that degree of wickedness that drunkenness abounds. . . ." All too often when poor men found themselves in possession of a little money, they would run to these "sockling houses, and there join company and make themselves drunken, and their wives and children run a-begging and are ready to starve at home, and no Justice [is] near to acquaint with these things." The inhabitants of Bradford considered that they had a sufficient

Harleian Miscellany, VIII, 382, 385; *Middlesex Sessions,* n. s., II, 148; III, 182; Essex Sessions, XIX, 170–71; *Middlesex Sessions,* II, 73–4; III, 80, 148, 200, 270; IV, 105, 106, 107; *Maidstone Recs.,* 268.

13. In 1659 a French gentleman, who landed at Dover and went as far as Rochester, was startled "to see my confident Host set him down cheek by joul by me, belching and puffing Tobacco in my face . . . I afterwarde founde it to be the usuall stile of this Country; and that the Gentlemen who lodge at their Inns, entertain themselves in their company, and are much pleased with their impertinencies." *A Character of England,* 6–7; *As You Like It,* Epilogue; Lupton, *London and the Country,* 127–31; *Camden Miscellany,* XVI, 40; Essex Sessions, XVIII, 218–19; *Middlesex Sessions,* n. s., I, 241.

enough inn, good for entertaining travelers and, in 1627, petitioned the justices of Wiltshire to close thirteen alehouses to discourage drunkenness, quarreling, fighting, and absence from divine worship.[14]

One is constantly surprised at the extent and degree of drunkenness. If fewer gentlemen were sots, it was because they could
afford wines and drank better ale and not because they eschewed
the good creature. Olivia once said of Sir Toby Belch: "he's in the
third degree of drink, he's drowned: go look after him." As for
countrymen, the courts had to deal with many who came drunk to
church on the Sabbath and behaved in a disorderly fashion; in
more than a few instances the transgressor was presented for having "spued" during divine service! At the White Hart in Colchester
in 1606, Robert Fishpole "was so drunk at the fyer, if he had not
been holpen," he would have fallen into it. Church-ales and wakes
frequently degenerated into unqualified drinking bouts and de-
bauches in which participants as far apart in rank as Nicholas
Assheton and "divers drunkards" of Bunbury rubbed shoulders
and caroused together.[15]

The English people did not lack popular writers to warn them
about the dangers of drink. "The beastly Drunkard" was a favorite
theme of Barnabe Rich, and clergymen inveighed against the evil
in published sermons. Preaching at Paul's Cross in 1612, Thomas
Adams dealt with his countrymen's inordinate inebrieties: "They

14. Justices of the peace were pushed to the limit to regulate disorderly public
houses in the suburbs and environs of London. Shortly before Lieutenant Hammond crossed the Thames in 1635 to Gravesend, that town had been granted a
mayor and common council: "she hath a very great need of both, to governe,
rule, and order the multiplicity of Taverns, Inns, and Alehouses wherewith the
Town swarmes, (for the Circuit thereof there is not the like to be found in all
England), wherein there is dayly sundry Quarrells, wranglings, cheatings, and
cousenings, and all these committed by our owne Countrymen, as extravagant
[vagrant] Aliens." *Camden Miscellany*, XVI, 7; *HMC Various*, I, 85; *Essex
Sessions*, XX, 131; *Wiltshire Sessions*, 89–90.
15. In 1595, Strype said of London: "Immoderate Quaffing among Fools . . .
continueth as afore, or rather, is mightily encreased, qualmed among the poorer
Sort; not of an holy Abstinency, but of mere Necessity: Ale and Beer being
small, and Wines, in Price, above their Reach." Stow, *Survey of London* I, bk.
I, 242; *Twelfth Night*, I, v, 143–4; *Sussex Arch.*, XLIX, 54; L, 42; *Essex Arch.*,
XI, 9b; *Chetham*, XIV, 23; T. W. Barlow, *Cheshire: Its Historical and Literary
Associations* (Manchester, 1952), 150, 153.

take their fill of wine here, as if they were resolved with Dives, they should not get a drop of water in Hell." "Drunkenness . . . that hateful Night-bird," thundered Samuel Ward, the Ipswich Puritan, in 1627, "is out in sunlight at high noon, in every street, open Markets, Fairs, without fear or shame, control or punishment" to the great injury of town, church, and commonwealth. And he cited case after case from the daily life of East Anglia and Essex. What would be called a temperance tract today was published in 1617 by Thomas Young, sometime student of Staple Inn. "This vice of drunkenness," Young termed "England's Bane: because no Nation is more polluted with this capitoll sinne than ours." It has become common in villages, towns, and cities, "even amongst the very Woods and Forrests." "Nay it is mounted so high that men must in a manner blush and be ashamed as much to speake of sobrietie or to be temperate. . . . Why? he is reputed a Pesant, a slave, and a Bore, that will not take his liquor profoundly." [16]

The popular demand for alcoholic beverages became so insistent that the number of licensed alehouses grew larger every year, and the figure did not include illegal "common tippling houses." In 1608, Leicestershire had 309 licensed alehouses. With the royal grant of a monopoly to Sir Giles Mompesson in 1617 of licensing inns and alehouses in Buckinghamshire, the problem became acute; charges began to circulate that keepers of disorderly houses, because they bribed Mompesson's commissioners, procured licenses more readily than "those who refused to conform to their demands." By heroic measures the justices of the peace at High Wycombe reduced the number of licenses granted from twenty-one to nine, and eliminated one unlicensed taverner who had been "uttering Beare of an extraordinary strength" which was causing drunkenness and beggary among his neighbors. The Court of Quarter Sessions for the North Riding of Yorkshire proceeded against 259 unlicensed taverners (one of them a cleric; another a widow named Temperance). The West Riding contained about

16. Martin Parker's ballad, "Robin and Kate; or a bad Husband converted by a good Wife," probably tells the story of most conversions. *Roxburghe Ballads*, II, 414; Thomas Adams, *The White Devil, or the Hyprocrite Uncased* (1612), 17; Samuel Ward, *Woe to Drunkards* (1622), 2, No. 8 of *All in All* (1627), a volume of sermons in the John Carter Brown Library; Thomas Young, *England's Bane, or, The Description of Drunkenness* (1617).

2,000 alehouse keepers in 1638, and 500 more who brewed without permits. Excuses given for the latter were that most of them would otherwise have been dependent upon their parishes for support, and that the inhabitants were clothiers and scarcely one of them brewed his own drink. The complaints emanating from London about the multiplying of both legal and illegal taverns were irrefutable.[17]

Parliament and the local officials fought a losing battle to cut down unlawful tippling at inns, alehouses, and victualling houses, which were steadily moving away from their ancient role as hostelries for wayfarers. Every few years a new act would be passed to repress "the odious and loathsome synne of Drunkenness . . . late growen into common usage," and every effort was made to limit the dispensing of beer and wines to licensed publicans—all to no avail. Englishmen of every degree could accept the sentiment of the Royalist song:

> If thou dost not love sacke,
> And drinke whilst thou canst see,
> Thou hast a narrow wretched soule
> And much I pity thee.[18]

III

John Selden once spoke disdainfully of the vintner who "when he first setts up; you may bring your wench to his house; and do yor things there; but when he grows rich; he turns consientious; and will sell noe wine upon the Sabbath day." Certainly more than a few of the hosts at inns, taverns, and alehouses both catered to and promoted sexual immorality in their establishments; their hostelries served as places of assignation or outright bawdy houses. Rem-

17. *Hertfordshire Sessions*, V, 18; *CSPD, 1603–10,* p. 434; *1623–5,* p. 147; *1634–5,* p. 424; *1637–8,* p. 433; Gardiner, *England,* IV, 2, 4, 5; *Buckinghamshire,* VII, 305; *North Riding Sessions,* IV, 32, 33, 79; Essex Sessions, XIX, 454, 467; XX, 211–12, 371.
18. *Statutes of the Realm,* IV, 1026, 1027, 1141–2, 1143, 1167, 1216; V, 3, 26; *Sussex Arch.,* XVI, 23–4; XL, 14–15; Cutts, *Seventeenth Century Songs and Lyrics,* 190; *Somerset Sessions,* II, *passim;* H. G. Hudson, *A Study of Social Regulation in England under James I and Charles I: Drink and Tobacco* (Chicago, 1933).

ington, the host of the Angel at Mountsorrell in Leicestershire "hath had 5 or 6 bastards, and kepeth a house of such resorte," according to ecclesiastical informers; and Robert Chinnery of East Dereham, Norfolk, was guilty of harboring "diverse persons . . . some of an incontinent life and others vehemently suspected of the like crime." In 1597 the Archdeacon's Court excommunicated all of them. Nearly every inhabitant of Somerton joined in a petition to the Somerset justices in 1627 to close up Thomas Merrett's ale-house; they branded it a wicked place, "little better than a thievish and whorish bawdy house," and a scandal to the town. Falstaff, falling asleep "behind the arras" at the Boar's Head in East Cheap one night, awoke later and announced: "This house is turned bawdy-house; they pick pockets." [19]

In every age a considerable amount of sexual laxity has prevailed throughout the countryside, but the men of our period agreed that it was on the increase in the years prior to 1640. There lived in every community at least one woman whom the rude local clowns knew for "a bawdy face bitch and a hedge hore." This uncharitable label was no mere figure of speech, for the court files contain records of many instances in which men were surprised under a "hedge with a whore," or merely with some warm-blooded wench. Masters and male servants often seduced the maids of a household, either by alluring promises or by threats. Cases of incest were not unusual, though the canon law forbidding a man to marry his deceased wife's sister explained many of them; and bestiality often occurred among laborers and husbandmen, as it does in any agricultural society. Individuals of both sexes resorted to making and dispensing love philters; the Widow Sellar of Chittaway, Wiltshire, made powder and cakes out of the liver of a "Sawte Bitch" and gave it to men—the results are not recorded.[20]

Rural sports and pastimes, such as dancing, church-ales, wakes,

19. Selden, *Table Talk*, 26; Associated Architectural Societies, *Reports & Papers*, XXIV, Pt. II, 517; *Norfolk*, XVIII, 99–100; *Somerset Sessions*, II, 42–3; *Kent*, XXVI, 18; *Hertfordshire Sessions*, V, 253; *King Henry IV* (Pt. I), III, iii, 114, 179–80.

20. Essex Sessions, XVIII, 26, 320, 321; XIX, 265, 268; XX, 513, 518; *Middlesex Sessions*, n. s., II, 44; *Sussex Arch.*, XLIX, 54; *West Riding Sessions*, 24; Venn, Credition, I, 210; *Oxfordshire*, X, 163; *Wiltshire Sessions*, 104–5; Essex Arch., XII, 8a, 18b; *CSPD, 1631–3*, p. 430; Bradford, *History of Plymouth Plantation*, II, 328–9.

and other rustic revels, frequently led to youthful indiscretions, and it was this that made Sabbatarians out of so many Englishmen who were not in any other respect puritans. One character in William Cartwright's play, *The Ordinary,* berated another for his sins: "Then he answers me in the small doleful tune of a country wench examin'd by the official for the mischance of a great belly caught at a Whitson-ale: I could not help it." In July, 1617, the Somerset Court of Quarter Sessions ordered that Nicholas Ruddock and Katherine Cauker be whipped until "their bodies shall be bloody" at the tail of a cart; two fiddlers should march before it and play "to make known their lewdness in begetting the said base child upon the Sabbath day coming from dancing." [21]

Cuckolding was so common that everybody joked or versified about it. The Archdeacon's Court at Lewes dealt with Ralph Brooke of Arlington for "wearing a great payre of hornes uppon his head in the churchyard" when Henry Hall and his bride were married, "shewing thereby that the sayd Hall was lyke to be a cuckold." Taylor commented in 1632 on the virtues of a "mungrell Spaw" below Wallingford-on-Thames:

> Ah could it cure some Cuckolds of their hornes,
> It would have patients out of every climat,
> More than my patience could endure to rime at.[22]

In 1612 Thomas Dekker, the leading authority on English rogues and vagabonds, thought one of the chief reasons why so many men of his wicked generation wandered up and down the kingdom was "the free command and abundant use they have of women; for if you note them well in their marching, not a tatterdemalion walks his round, be he young [or] be he old, but he hath his most, his doxy, at his heels (his woman or his whore) . . . And this liberty of wenching is increased by the almost infinite numbers of tippling-houses, called housing kens," where rogues and thieves congregate and disport themselves. There can be little

---

21. Cartwright, *The Ordinary,* V, iv; *Somerset Sessions,* 211; *Wiltshire Sessions,* 131–2.
22. One of Martin Parker's plain-speaking ballads was *Cuckold's Haven, Or, the Marry'd man's miserie,* in *Roxburghe Ballads,* I, 148–9; *Sussex Arch.,* XLIX, 64; *Taylor on Thames-Isis,* in *Works,* I, no. 1, p. 19; *Essex Sessions,* XIX, 133.

doubt that of the thousands of men and women crowding the highways of England, few had been legally married, or that most of
their children were bastards. Seldom did the apparitors succeed in
laying hands on any of them.[23]

Bastardy was most common among the poorer sort of laborers'
daughters, but it was not unheard of among yeoman families or
even the unmarried clergy. Although Bartholomew Parsons, vicar
of Collingbourne Kingston, was "adjudged to be the father of a
bastard child . . . no corporal punishment was to be inflicted
upon him, in respect of his profession" other than being degraded
and ordered to pay 18d. per week for the child's support; the
mother was sent to the house of correction for a year. Thomas
Stocke, curate of the Durham village of Auckland in 1635, had
the temerity to suggest that "the parish should fynde him a wench,
and that he would tollerate any in his parish to begett a bastarde."
John Taylor had the knack of presenting the real cause of the
problem, no matter how poor a versifier he was:

> For from the Emp'rour to the russet Clowne,
> All states, each sex, from Cottage to the Crowne,
> Have in all Ages since first Creation,
> Bin foyld, and overthrown with Loves Temptation.[24]

Besides the obvious consequences of sexual promiscuity, such as
the cost in money, in health, in loss of character, and the ever-
present danger of catching a disease, there were other aspects
which can not be overlooked. Totally ignorant of any means of
contraception, hundreds of English prostitutes gave birth to bastards, and the rate of bastardy, already high, rose as the century
progressed. Some infanticide naturally resulted, and a great many
stillborn births occurred. Margaret Rutt of St. Sepulchre's Parish,
was charged with being "a common harborer of light weemen
great with child, suffring them to be brought to bedd in her house,
and can give no account whatt is become of the children." [25]

23. Thomas Dekker, *O per se O* (1612), in Judges, *Elizabethan Underworld*, 307.
24. *HMC Various* I, 98, *Surtees*, XXXIV, 131–2; *Oxfordshire*, X, 27, 28–9,
139–40; Essex Sessions, XX, 209; Taylor, "The Old, Old, Very Old Man," in
Works, I, No. 2, p. 15.
25. For fleeting allusions to contraception in sermons and books, see Sir George
Clark, *Three Aspects of Stuart England*, 28; *Middlesex Sessions*, II, 46; III, 168–9;
IV, 316; Chamberlain, *Letters*, II, 15.

The preamble to a parliamentary statute of 1609 stressed the fact that "great charge ariseth upon many places within this realm by reason of bastardy." Lewd women who were convicted were to be punished and set to work in the houses of correction for "one whole year." The justices of the peace were more concerned about the costs to the parish than the problem of incontinence, which somewhat explains the severity with which they punished offenders—sitting in the stocks, whipping, and exposure to public shame. In January, 1614, the Court of Quarter Sessions of the West Riding ordered that William Banks and John Leake "shall both be stripped naked from the middle upward and soundly whipped thorow the towne of Wetherby" for having begotten base children. Miles Hogg and Jennett Walker were both sent to the house of correction in Yorkshire in 1620 "for that he hath begotten three severall bastards on her bodie." Whether for money or out of pity, some midwives aided unfortunate girls to conceal their pregnancies and depart from their towns without performing penance.[26]

Public penance at the cathedral or parish church, or in the market place, for indulgence in incest, incontinence, and premarital intercourse was a part of the Godly Discipline of the primitive Christian Church; in Catholic England, Archbishop Peacham had enforced open penance for such offenses in 1281. Pre-Reformation penance, "fustigation" or a cudgelling of the penitent around the edifice to drive out the old Adam, was much more severe than that exacted by the Church of England in our period.[27]

The sons and daughters of common poor people who performed public penance were legion. The confession of Thomas Pamflett at Ramsgate in Thanet in 1613 is typical; he was ordered to appear on a Sunday during divine service penitentially clothed in a white sheet and holding a white rod. Immediately after the reading of the second lesson, he was to arise and repeat after the minister:

26. One item of expense recorded for Exeter in 1640 was "A carte to be forthwith provided for the punishinge of whores." Izaake, Exeter, 25; Pickering, Statutes at Large, II, 612; VII, 225; North Riding Sessions, III, 120; West Riding Sessions, LIV, 11, 16; HMC Portland, XIV, II, 33; Somerset Sessions, 108; Western Antiquary, I, 106; HMC Southampton, XI III, 27; CSPD, 1635–6, p. 241; Middlesex Sessions, n. s., I, 164; Sussex Arch., XLIX, 58.
27. Notes and Queries, 5th ser., III, 277–8.

Good Christian people, whereas I, through the temptation of Satan and frailty of mine own flesh, have committed the sinful act of incontinency to the offence of Almighty God and breach of the King's Majesty Laws, do here before this present congregation confess this my fault and am heartily sorry therefor, praying you to forgive me, and those that I have offended thereby to be with this my humble confession satisfied, and wishing to lead the rest of my life more honestly and chastely, which God grant I may perform.

The most fascinating example of this spectacle is probably Old Thomas Parr of Salop, aged 105, standing in the parish church of Alderbury for the sin which his "Ardent fervour had led him into with Katherine Milton":

> Should All that so offend, such Pennance doe,
> Oh, what a price would Linnen rise unto,
> All would be turn'd to sheets, our shirts and smocks,
> Our Table linnen, very Porters Frocks
> Would hardly scape trans-forming, but all's one
> He suffred, and his Punishment is done.[28]

Many writers have thought that the ecclesiastical authorities permitted rich and influential individuals to buy their way out of penance. Undoubtedly some did, but actually persons of all degrees donned the penitential garb. For entertaining Mary Worley "in men's attire" in his diggings at Oxford in 1604. Henry Bowcher was sentenced by the Heads of Houses not only to stand with Mary while his confession was read publicly in the Anglican stronghold of St. Mary's on an April Sunday but to marry the girl too! At Paul's Cross in February, 1613, a "young mignon of Sir Pexall Brocas" performed penance for illicit behavior with the knight; in October Sir Pexall himself stood at the same place "in a white sheete, and held a stick in his hand," convicted of numerous

28. Some rascal stole the newly purchased sheet from the parish chest of Rockford. W. H. Hale, *Precedents and Proceedings in Civil Causes from 1475 to 1640, from the Act Books of Ecclesiastical Courts in the Diocese of London* . . . (London, 1847), 237, *et passim; Kent*, XXVI, 35; *HMC Various*, I, 79; William Staney, *A Treatise of Penance (1617)*; Taylor, "The Old, Old, Very Old Man," in *Works*, No. 2, p. 16.

adulteries. Moll Cut-purse [Mary Frith], "a notorious baggage," managed for a time to convince the spectators of her confession at Paul's Cross that she was truly penitent until it was learned that her maudlin tears were induced by her having fortified herself for the ordeal by drinking three quarts of sack. Lady Markham, wife of Sir Griffin, appeared at that selfsame place in 1618 to do penance for marrying one of her servants while her husband was still alive. She had to stand again at other places and pay a fine of £1,000.[29]

London and, on a smaller scale, the provincial cities presented particular moral scenes that contemporaries openly recognized. City evils differ from country evils, Thomas Adams contended: "Yours in the Cities are hotter disease, the burning fevers of fiery zeale, the inflammations and impostumes of Hypocrisie; we [in the country] have the frosts, and you have the lightnings; most of us professe too little; and some of you professe too much." Each urban community sheltered a large floating population of susceptible single men and women. Where human frailty explained away most of the sexual lapses of the countryside, much of the wickedness in the cities stemmed from the conscious seeking of profit or enjoyment from sophisticated and forbidden pleasures.[30]

Young girls and women, who had gone up to London or its suburbs to better themselves, often had to take to the streets as "common Whores" through sheer necessity, or deceit. There were others who were attracted by the excitement of the life of a "Queane." At night they issued forth in large numbers in search of sporting gentlemen, mariners ashore on leave, or just any man. Others purveyed to a regular custom, like Emma Robinson of St. Botolph's without Aldgate, "a notorious Common Queene" who "sitteth up at the door til XI or XII a clock in the night to entertain lewd persons that resort to her." Only an occasional "quean" attained the elegance of Mildred Wilkinson, a spinster of Bethnal Green, who "had in an eveninge musicions at her house and certayne men at her hous unknowne." Numerous taverns, as we have noted, and

29. "I see you have heard of her, sir, Indeed she has done penance thrice," said a strumpet to a merchant in Mayne's *City-Match,* V, iii; *CSPD, 1603–10,* pp. 92, 95; *1611–18,* p. 516; *1633–4,* p. 580; *1635–6,* p. 475; Chamberlain, *Letters,* I, 334; Stow, *Annales,* 1005.

30. Adams, *The White Devil,* 27.

sometimes a tobacco shop, served as places of rendezvous for bawdy women and their pimps, and also for assignations of couples desiring to meet clandestinely.[31]

Organized vice had become an appreciable, though covert, business in the metropolis by 1598, when Thomas Nashe attempted to expose it. "London, what are thy Suburbes but licensed Stewes? Can it be so many brothel-houses of salary sensuality and sixepenny whoredome (the next doore to the Magistrates) should be sett up and maintained, if brybes did not bestirre them . . . Whole Hospitals of tenne times a day dishonest strumpets have we cloystered together. Night and day the entrance unto them is as free as to a Taverne. Not one of them but hath a hundred retayners, Prentises, and poore Servaunts they encourage to robbe theyr Maisters. Gentlemen's purses and pockets they will dive into and picke, even while they are dallying with them. . . . Halfe a Crowne or little more (or some-times less) is the sette price of a strumpets soule." Nashe even suggested that it would be better to have "publique Stewes" than to permit private ones.[32]

Certain districts of London achieved notoriety for their "houses of good fellowship (the rude and unmannerly multitude call such Bawdie-houses)." In one day, August 20, 1620, at a session of the Middlesex Court of Quarter Sessions, true bills were found against nineteen women for keeping brothels, sixteen at Cowcross and three at Clerkenwell. Within the City, Saffron Hill (Charterhouse Lane) acquired the reputation of being a district where "notorious and common whores . . . are entertained into divers houses for base and filthy lucre sake to the private benefitt of the Landlordes and Tennantes." These "infamous queanes &c," came the report,

31. In a play, the character Snarle alludes to another serious and little-known moral failing of these years: "There is such effeminacy in both sexes, They cannot be distinguished asunder." Wives of men at sea often became whores out of economic necessity or out of desire and loneliness. Shackerly Marmion, *Hollands Leaguer: An Excellent Comedy* (1632), I, i, B 1; Wyot, Diary, June 16, 1596; *Barnstaple Recs.*, I, 52; *Southampton Recs.*, II, 3; *Middlesex Sessions*, n. s., I, 162, 225, 308; III, 294; *Middlesex Sessions*, II, 47; III, 3, 4, 176; *CSPD, 1633–4*, p. 479.

32. Six years after Nashe's exposé, a German traveler, Thomas Platter, stated that the City authorities had the common strumpets under "good order," though "great swarms of these women haunt the town in the taverns and playhouses." Platter, *Travels*, 174–5; Nashe, *Christs Teares*, II, 148–54; *Middlesex Sessions*, II, 49; III, 80, 200, 242.

customarily sit at the doors of their houses and "by their Wanton and impudent behaviour doe allure . . . such as passe by that way." South of the Thames at Paris Garden, not far from The Globe and the Bear Garden, was one of the most notorious houses in and around London, which was operated by a Dutch madam whose girls were mostly of that nationality. Salacious-minded Londoners revelled in a comedy about Paris Garden and also "An Historical Discourse of the Life and Actions of Dame Britannia Hollandia, the Arch-Mistress of the Wicked Women of Eytopia." A woodcut representing the door of her establishment carries this caption:

> Where dainty Devils dressed in human shape
> upon your senses soon will make a rape
> They that come freely to this house of sinne
> in Hell as freely may have entrance in.[33]

Londoners had become so accustomed to the sight of prostitutes and the presence of bawdy houses in the City and its suburbs that worldly authors made light of them in their writings. In *Coach and Sedan* is a suggestion that if a man needs to explain his frequenting such an establishment, he can say that he hath been turning and looking over some Bookes in a French liberarie." In Thomas Nash's *Quaternio,* Urban, conceding that whores abounded in London—any child can spot them by their attire and companions —dismissed the matter almost airily with the remark: "Whores we spurne, and spit, and hisse at as they pass." There was, however, a constantly growing part of the citizenry who shared Lupton's convictions about "our degenerating Age," and Barnabe Rich heaped maledictions on "the licentious Whooremaster," "the infamous Harlot," and "Olde Mother B, the bawd." Martin Parker and Richard Climsell published rhymed advice to young men "to forsake lewd company, Cards, Dice, and Queanes." And the playwrights followed suit. Puritan clergymen could do little more than repeat the same sentiments in more unctuous language.[34]

33. *Coach and Sedan, Pleasantly Disputing,* Sig. F 3; *Middlesex Sessions,* II, 63, 72, 87–8, 139, 155–6, 171; *Middlesex Sessions,* n. s., I, 176, 186, 192; II, 170–71; III, 144; *VCH Surrey,* IV, 149–50; Lupton, *London and the Country,* 51, 66–9; Nicholas Goodman, *Hollands Leagner* (1632), Frontispiece.

34. *Coach and Sedan, Pleasantly Disputing,* Sig. F 3; Nash, *Quaternio,* 54–5; Rich, *Honestie of this Age,* 2, 3; *Roxburghe Ballads,* III, 122, 173–5, 268; Barry,

IV

In one way or another virtually every problem that confronted the English people involved the poor, for they made up almost half of the population—even more in critical times. According to one writer, "The Poor of the Nation are of severall sorts. The first such as are Beggars borne, and so live and dye, never labouring in any calling else. A godly Minister once said (Dr. Sibs by name) of them, marryed under hedges, children born in Barns and under hedges, there baptized, so continue to the Shame of the Nation. The second sort are Vagabonds and counterfeit Rogues; some dissembling lame, some one disease, or soar, some another: Will not be cured if they might . . . There are a third sort, that labor and get a little money, then will be drunk, raile, and quarrel with one another, pawn their cloaths to vex one another by law, and when all is gone, burthen the place where they live." These ne'er-do-wells also oppress "those that have been the burthen of the Nation, by their industry and labour, the blessing of the Almighty being with them, the laborious Husbandman, the Handicrafts-man, and all kind of honest Tradesmen, who would gladly live quietly." [35]

For our purposes we may reduce these classes to two: *the visible poor,* whom the poor law took into account, and *the invisible poor,* the humble, average men, women, and children of both rural and urban England who, largely unnoticed, composed the last category of Dr. Sibbes. Only an occasional writer, such as Robert Powell, seems to have glimpsed the true nature and extent of the problem of poverty: that the countryside was full of desperately poor though respectable people whom neither the administrators of the poor law nor the rapidly growing body of philanthropists ever uncovered. As Job taught, "The poor of the earth hide themselves together." One learns of the invisible poor only in times of crisis. Now and then in congested towns and cities, when, as Edward

---

Ram-Alley I, i; *Jack Drum's Entertainment,* Act II, 359, in Judges, *Elizabethan Underworld,* 509.

35. This classification of the poor derives from the Elizabethan statutes, and first Harrison, then Dalton, popularized it. J. R., *Proposals in behalfe of the Poor of this Nation* (1635), 2–4; Harrison, *England,* Pt. I, 213; Dalton, *Country Justice,* 99.

Misselden noted, "the Poore sterve in the streets for want of labour," similar unfortunates received some public notice because
such conditions might imperil the King's peace, but those sufferers
never amounted to more than a fraction of the invisible poor.[36]

It is most difficult to conjure up for the modern reader the extent and depth of the poverty and misery that passed unnoticed in
a pre-industrial society; it can only be suggested by recounting selected instances. There were the miserably housed cottagers who
frequently had no land to cultivate. In the Essex village of Finchingfield in 1600 there were "four score poor households and upwards" that produced nothing of their own, and these people had
to resort to the victualler for their bread, beer, and other food. Nor
was it unusual for many of the people living in hovels to lack even
a hearth to cook at, or fuel for a fire. Like conditions obtained at
Langham and in the larger clothtown of Halstead. This particular
form of poverty is made clear in a report of 1638 on the laboring
poor of Hitchings in Hertfordshire: "When they have worke the
wages given them is so small that it hardly sufficeth to buy the
poore man and his familye breed, for they pay 6s. for one bushell
of myselyn grayne and receive but 8d. for their days worke." [37]

There were many families who were dispossessed during these
years, and without any place to live; their plight exceeded that of
the cottagers. Parson Jefferies of Beere Hackett, Dorset, gave security to the overseers of the poor in 1625 to defend them against
charges for Christopher Sprague, "a man of no worth [property]
with 7 children and 3 apprentices." John Browne and his wife
made "his habitation . . . in the church porch of Coddenham"
until he was ordered to move to a house provided by the town, and
the justices of Suffolk licensed a resident of Brandeston in 1639 to
convert a small structure at the back of his house for a habitation
for Henry Iffe, a poor man, and his family.[38]

Whenever a depression overwhelmed the cloth areas, country
weavers suffered great privation. Rowland Vaughan recorded in
"his Booke" for the year 1604: "There bee within a mile and a halfe

36. Robert Powell, *Depopulation arraigned, convicted and condemned* (1636),
66–7; Job, 24:2; 29:12; Edward Misselden, *The Circle of Commerce, or the
Ballance of Trade* (1623), 132, 133.
37. Essex Sessions, XVII, 177, 221, 244; Clark, *Working Life of Women*, 80.
38. Roberts, *Southern Counties*, 183; *Suffolk*, XV, 152, 156.

from my house . . . five hundred poor habitations; whose greatest meanes consist in spinning Flaxe, Hempe, and Hardes. . . . There is not one amongst ten that hath five shillings to buy a Bale of Flaxe, but [are] forc'd to borrow money to put up their trade and run to Hereford (loosing a dayes worke) to fetch the same." In the depression of 1622, Somerset cottagers experienced the same unendurable hardships: "three or fower hundred poore of men, women and children that did gett most of their lyving by spinning, carding and such imployments aboute woole and cloath. And the deadness of that trade and want of money is such that they are for the most parte withoute worke and knowe not how to live." The parish accounts of Godalming and Wonersh reported 1,100 idle people in 1630 who depended on the clothiers for their livelihood, and 3,000 in the surrounding parishes. Devizes was but one community that lost population beginning in 1626 when the unemployed spinners took to wandering "upp and down begging both in Towne and Countrye." [39]

Crop failures added to rural distress by creating critical food shortages, and the surreptitious engrossing and shipping away of grain from the "blind Creeks" in Essex resulted in actual starvation for some of the destitute: from Little Braxted came word in 1631 that "divers children there are almost famished and one already dead for want of relief." Such suffering had become fairly general and must be understood entirely apart from the better-known problem of the visible poor.[40]

In the past, as Peacham pointed out in 1631, "the poore of parishes are faine to bee relieved by the Farmer, the Husbandman, and the middle rank, or else they must starve, as many upon my own knowledge did this laste Snowie-winter." A survey made locally in the small town of Sheffield in 1615 illustrates this observation. The community consisted of 2,207 inhabitants: 725 of them were "begging poor," and lived off the scanty charity of their neighbors; 100 householders, "thought the beste sort," relieved the rest, though they themselves were but poor artificers, among whom

39. VCH Suffolk, I, 676–7; Rowland Vaughan His Book [1610], ed. Ellen Beatrice Wood (London, 1897), 30, 31, 33; Clark, Working Life of Women, 118n; CSPD, 1629–31, pp. 49, 480; 1633–4, p. 387; Yonge, "Diary," in Camden, XLI, 52; Devizes Recs., 81.
40. Essex Sessions, XX, 282, 284.

"not one" kept a team of his own and not above ten had land enough to graze a cow. The invisible poor of this place, "though they beg not," obviously were unable to relieve others and could not possibly "abide the storme of one fortnight' sickness," which would drive them to beggary. Lastly, 1,222 children and servants, "the greatest part of which are such as live of[f] small wages . . . are constrained to worke sore, to provide necessaries." Few rural villages presented as dismal a spectacle as Sheffield, but during the years of almost chronic depression, 1629–41, a very large proportion of the agricultural laborers and artisans of England lived, with their families in real and bitter penury.[41]

Approximately every parish, town, and county had its difficulties with the begging poor, and it was much too big a problem to be corrected by individual efforts. Kindly people like the widow Joan Holland of Great Amwell, Hertfordshire, who took strangers into her house to live, had to be forbidden to continue so doing under a threat of penalties. Justices sent Joan Painter and her daughter Alice, beggars, back to their home in Halstead after they had been brought into court for begging up and down the county. Because James Clifford, "gent.," and Thomas Shepard, laborer, both of High Laver, appeared to be "incorrigible rogues and vagabonds" and would not settle down to any work, they had to face the Essex Court of Quarter Sessions (later both were released). In 1622 Michael Sparke told how the poor increased daily: some parishes had collected no rates for seven years, "especially in Countrie townes; but many of those Parishes turneth forth their poore, yea and their lustie Labourers . . . to begge, filtch, and steal for their maintainance." [42]

41. One indication of John Winthrop's great sense of responsibility, as well as the continuance of the old-fashioned rural hospitality in Suffolk as late as 1623, can be found in a letter he wrote from London to his wife at the Manor of Groton: "I praye thee let provision be made; and all our poore feasted, though I be from home, so I shall be the less missed: and such as are of the middle sort let alone till I come home." *Winthrop Papers*, I, 293; *Coach and Sedan, Pleasantly Disputing*, Sig. D; Hunter, *Hallamshire*, 148. The Sheffield overseers paid out only £39 10s. 6d. for their visible poor in 1636; the others apparently got along as best they could or else, as Peacham said, they starved. *Records of the Burgery of Sheffield Commonly Called the Town Trust*, ed. John D. Leader (London, 1897), 135, 136.

42. *Hertfordshire Sessions*, V, xix, xx, 10; *Essex Sessions*, XX, 334, 347; Sparke, *Grievous Grones for the Poore*, 14.

Hunger and want drove many an Englishman to poaching, though there were others, like Fielding's Black George, who preferred its excitement to some more prosaic trade. Kentish poachers, according to spies, were supposed to be catching up to a hundred hares a night near Dover in 1620, but the average nocturnal bag was closer to the twelve conies worth ten shillings caught in a warren at Berkhamsted with a "heynett." Small-time poachers usually set snares for hares and small game—possession and use of firearms was a privilege of rank and prohibited by law to the ordinary Englishman, unless he had a special license. Gilbert Wilson of High Easter had to answer at Essex Quarter Sessions in 1611 for "shootinge hayle shott in a peece at piggones in Christmas hollidayes last and divers tymes since," and Marcellus Goodwyn of Coggeshall, surgeon, came before the justices for shooting at two ducks with "a fowlinge peace." John Waylet, a carpenter, was presented, for not only did he have a fowling piece in his house but he kept a greyhound. Though poachers swarmed over the land, only a handful of yeoman Englishmen and those who did not rule possessed even the slightest knowledge of how to handle firearms, yet thousands of them were soon to depart for a new land where skillful handling of these weapons daily would make the difference between plenty and starvation, between life and death.[43]

If anyone of that day had reflected on the extreme want apparent in every village and town, he should not have been surprised at the amount of petty thievery, breaking and entering, and robbery on the highways. The justices of the peace had to sit in judgment on laborers, husbandmen, and artisans who stole livestock, clothing, and particularly such food as eggs, cheese, butter, and wheat. A laborer of Writtle named Thomas Moore drove off nineteen wether sheep worth £6 from the farm of George Allen of Chigwell, an act he confessed to at the Essex Quarter Sessions in 1597. The good people of Earl's Colne finally procured the indictment of Samuel Game, a husbandman, who for some time had been breaking into closes "to mylke their cattell in the night." Once he milked six of Henry Read's cows at Great Tey—the stolen milk was worth 10*d*. A yeoman of Walthamstow gave evidence that a vagrant of

43. *CSPD, 1619–23,* pp. 133, 136; *Hertfordshire Sessions,* V, 20; Essex Sessions, XVII, 113; XIX, 19, 63, 375, 531; XX, 90, 330, 475; XXI, 23.

Lincolnshire, Henry Goulding, had made off with four of his hens and "an old chamber pot." [44]

The courts seemingly did not take extenuating circumstances into consideration when trying these culprits nor show any mercy in sentencing them. John Wood, a laborer of Chelmsford, accused of stealing £23 7s. 8d., was condemned "To be hanged by the neck." In that same year of 1613, in an attempt to avoid the consequences of assaulting John Evans on the highway and snatching his purse, Cecily Mann, a lusty spinster of Ingatestone, pleaded benefit of pregnancy. Twelve sober matrons examined her and declared, on oath, that such was not the case, and thereupon Cecily too was hanged. In 1641, Katherine Peters, a hardened criminal of Cranford in Middlesex, stood charged with the theft of a table cloth and sheet in the Wiltshire court. When she refused to plead, the justices ordered her punished by subjecting her to the horrible "peine forte et dure" until she was dead. The corporations of Plymouth and Manchester, persuaded that laxness rather than severity was responsible for the multiplying of misdemeanors and felonies, authorized expenditures for setting up "a sufficient Gibbett or pillorye" for their respective towns.[45]

The peasants and artisans who departed from the countryside in times of scarcity and depression in search of employment and security in the large towns and cities did not always find them; indeed they merely aggravated the grim lot of their kind in those centers. It is this that has misled some writers into thinking of the poverty of those days as a strictly urban problem. Actually it was an English problem. Fortunately, in the cities, the perennially poor had their woes articulated in sermons, pamphlets, and ballads. "Poverty is but a shallow plash of misery, but Oppression breaking in, raises it to a floud: even a red sea of bloudy cruelty, deepe and deadly," Thomas Pestell preached to the judges of the assizes at Leicester in 1620 as he urged them not to forget their obligation to

44. Essex Sessions, 1590–1641, *passim,* and especially XVII, 47; XIX, 125; XX, 93, 232, 277; *Surrey,* IX, 176, 177, 178, 193; *Southampton Recs.,* II, 75–6; Powell, *Depopulation,* 38–9.

45. If a person called for the book and could read, branding was substituted for the more dreadful punishments. Essex Sessions, XIX, 125, 126, 453; XX, 277–8; *Wiltshire Sessions,* 135–7; *Southampton Recs.,* II, 55, 55n; *Manchester Court,* III, 93; *Plymouth Recs.,* 155.

the poor. The lines of a popular ballad emphasized the inequities of English life:

> That poore men still enforced are
> To pay more than they are able.
> Methought I heard them weeping say,
> Their substance was but small;
> For rich men will beare all the sway,
> And poore men pay for all.[46]

The towns and cities, already burdened with the care of their own poor, could not begin to absorb the swelling hordes of impoverished folk who streamed in from the countryside to batten on the parish rates. The cloth towns were overrun with the families of country weavers and spinners that arrived whenever the depressions blighted their industry. As early as 1608, the Corporation of Maidstone forbade any inhabitant to take in any stranger lest "the poorer sort either of their owne desyre or being for their idle and disordered life dryven out of other places do come to inhabit and settle themselves in this towne or parish." More than once Parliament attempted fruitlessly to stop this flow of people to the towns by requiring all persons who "shall come to any city or town to dwell" to furnish evidence of goods worth £5, or an estate of £2 a year, or proof that they had served an apprenticeship of seven years in some trade or craft. Otherwise they were to be returned to the parish of their origin.[47]

During hard times, what the poor of the cities needed most was food and fuel. No further proof of the sore straits the common people were reduced to in times of depression is needed than the assertion of the London chandlers in 1634 that, beginning in 1629, the poor had been buying nothing but peas, oatmeal, and horsemeat. This was a discouragingly poor fare for a folk who had grown accustomed to white bread, white meats, and sometimes red

---

46. Thomas Pestel, *The Poore Mans Appeale* (1620), 20, 28; *Roxburghe Ballads,* II, 334.
47. *Maidstone Recs.,* 65; *Manchester Court,* III, 122, 154, 163; *Wiltshire Sessions,* 85–6; *NEHG Reg.,* LVII, 63; *CSPD, 1637,* p. 535; *1640,* p. 184; *HMC Kenyon,* XIV, IV, 39; Dale, *The Inhabitants of London,* I, v, x, xi; Jordan, *Philanthropy in England,* 104; B. Kirkman Gray, *A History of English Philanthropy* (London, 1905).

meat. Coal and firewood, costly at any time, were prohibitively priced. Occasionally fuel was dispensed through charitable associations, such as the vestrymen of St. Margaret's Lothbury, who distributed wood and coal to the deserving poor of their parish, and the overseers of the poor of Paris Garden, who maintained a "Coal Yard" in 1630. A slight shift in Court plans, such as a proposed departure of the monarch from London, could derange the economy of the metropolis and throw into penury and want "many thousand soules" who had "lived in plentiful and good fashion" as tradesmen catering to the Court.[48]

A genuine desire for social betterment had produced the great poor law of 1598, which codified the legislation of the sixteenth century. In essence it placed the responsibility for the poor on the parishes and authorized the levying of local rates to relieve the destitute. The churchwardens and four overseers of the poor, appointed by the justices of the peace, were empowered to set compulsory poor rates and administer the poor law in each parish. This legislation acknowledged the obligation of the commonwealth to care for those whom we have designated as the visible poor: those who were poor by casualty (maimed soldiers, sick, or injured people), decayed householders (suffering from damages by fire, water, wind, robbery, or suretyship), and those "overcharged with children." They were to be set to work by the overseers of the poor and relieved in proportion to their needs.[49]

Proper administration of the poor law depended primarily upon the character and energies of the local authorities, and next upon the resources of the community. The accounts of the overseers of the poor in Chiddingstone, Kent, began in 1598 and indicate that the officials worked continually and seriously at relieving the impotent and worthy poor of the town. Until 1630 the annual collec-

48. *CSPD, 1633–4*, p. 489; Ware, *Elizabethan Parish*, 68; *Surrey*, XVI, 111–12, 123; *Humble Petition of Many Thousands of Courtiers, Citizens, Gentlemen, and Tradesmens Wives &c.* (1641). In Dekker's *The Honest Whore*, I, v, 223–5, one of the characters voices a rare humanitarian sentiment for the day: "Many lose their lives for scarce so much coyne as will hide their palmes, Which is most cruell."

49. The appropriate parts of all statutes 1531–98 pertaining to beggars and the poor are conveniently assembled by Dunham & Pargellis in *Complaint and Reform*, 423–55; Pickering, *Statutes at Large*, VII, 1, 30–37, 48–9; Dalton, *Country Justice*, 99; *Statues of the Realm*, IV, 962–5, 966–8, 971, 1209–11.

tions ran from £11 to £26 10s.; then from 1630 to 1639 they averaged £30, but in 1640, the overseers, in all probability prodded by King Charles's ministers, raised £40. The Chiddingstone poor, beneficiaries of humanity tempered by legalism and the fear of social unrest, fared well. This was not the case in another Kentish village, Reculver. There the two overseers of the poor did so little that "divers impotent persons and old widows" and "many fatherless children" almost perished. The overseers of the parish of Paris Garden in Surrey, on the other hand, went far to redeem the unsavory reputation of that district by the treatment of their charges. In 1611, "The Play House" contributed £4 6s. 8d., which enabled the overseers to support many weekly pensioners and care for bastard children.[50]

The establishment of almshouses for the care of the visible poor was the solution arrived at by many communities, especially those whose sons had made their fortunes in the world and bequeathed endowments for charitable services to the towns of their birth. Presented with land for such a purpose, the inhabitants of Keevil, Wiltshire, built an almshouse for the poor of their parish, many of whom had been "enforced to dwell in barns, outhouses, and other unwholesome places." A few observers contended, with some reason, that the almshouses bred as many poor as they relieved: "People in such places presume to be idle, beholding Hospitals as their inheritance, wherein their old age shall be provided for." Thomas Fuller's reply to this charge was that "it is better that Ten Drones be fed than one Bee famished." There were preposterous claims, of course. Robert Vauter, a day laborer, petitioned to be allowed to settle in the almshouse of Chiltern, Somerset, though he had been a resident of the parish but three months. His justification was that he had married an almsman's daughter, who lived there with her father. The court ordered him either to produce sureties against local charges or go to gaol.[51]

50. *Kent,* XXV, 46; LXXIII, 193–4; Parish of Wimeswould, Leicestershire, B. M. Add. MSS, 10457, ff. 37, 37b, 51b, 53, 54, 61; *Surrey,* XVI, 68–113; Essex Sessions, XX, 401–2.
51. See the interesting rules governing the poor house inmates at Sackville College, East Grimstead, Sussex, in 1631. The rules set forth by the vestry of St. Edmund and St. Thomas, Sarum, were calculated to impress on the inmates that they were objects of charity and to reveal their status to any who might come

Under the aegis of Archbishop Laud and the Earl of Strafford, the administration of the poor law was improved and better supervised from 1625 to 1642. It could be said that the concern of Charles I for the visible poor was one of the most commendable features of his personal rule. In most communities, paltry sums of money were dispensed by the overseers of the poor as out-relief to the aged, poor widows, the maimed, or the temporarily disabled who lived with families: allotments for food and fuel and even rent and clothing for those who could not be set to work. At Mayfield Parish, Sussex, the overseers of the poor paid out 4*s*. 6*d*. "for faggots for Mother Becker"; in the year from Easter, 1625, to Easter, 1626, they paid "old Browne" £3 8*s*. besides 10*s*. for rent and £1 3*s*. 5*d*. for apparel. The accounts also show numerous instances of small awards to old soldiers like William Strong, a poor man with a wife and five small children, who had lost the use of one arm in her late majesty's service.[52]

Fear of social unrest weighed equally with concern for the poor in the minds of some authorities, for there had been many occasions when mob violence had threatened the peace and security of the country. Disturbances usually broke out when desperate peasants or artisans sought redress for unalleviated grievances. During the acute depression of 1622 in the cloth areas, poor spinners "gathered themselves together by Fourty or Fifty in a company" and would fall upon the houses of those whom they thought best able to relieve them "for meate and money, which hath bin given more of feare than charitie." They also seized meat in the markets without paying for it. The outcome was not relief but the appointment of day and night watches on all the highroads to give notice of possible similar tumults. In December, 1625, a reputed 4,000 destitute people poured into Exeter, and many able-bodied citizens abandoned the town, tradesmen removed their wares and kept shop or set up markets elsewhere. Two hundred persons, representing the unemployed weavers of Bocking and Braintree, presented

---

across them. *Sussex Arch.*, XX, 161–3; Churchwardens' Accounts, Sarum, 190; *HMC Various*, I, 95; *Devizes Recs.*, 51; Dartmouth Recs., DD61633 (1600); Fuller, *Worthies*, I, 33; *CSPD, 1635–6*, p. 336; *Somerset Sessions*, II, 292.
52. *Somerset Sessions*, 162, 175; *Sussex Arch.*, XVIII, 196; Essex Sessions, XX, 201; Parish of Wimeswould, Leicestershire, Constable's accounts, BM, Add MSS, 10457, f. 92; *HMC Exeter*, 80.

a petition to the court at Chelmsford; they followed the justices about, indulging in such outcries that the latter had to abandon all other county work. Some temporary assistance was handed out, but the justices, dreading further outbreaks, implored assistance of the Privy Council.[53]

The greatest threat to the peace, however, was thought to come from those in the second category of Dr. Sibbes's listing: the riotous and the prodigal, who consumed their all in drink, play, and women; dissolute strumpets, whoremasters, and pilferers, etc., and the slothful by nature, who refused to work. To these were added those who wilfully spoiled or embezzled their work, and the vagabonds that would abide in no service or place. For all of these the house of correction was deemed the fittest abode, and those who would not work should not eat. So ran the adage.[54]

V

The "Evill of Idlenesse," as much as any one factor, drove count-less English men and women to "seeke their meate uppon Meares (As the Proverb goeth,) with Begging, Filching, and Stealing for their maintenance, untill the law bring them unto the fearfull end of hanging." This curse of sturdy beggars, rogues, and vagabonds descended from Elizabethan times, during which it had given rise to an interesting literature and produced a cant of its own.[55]

The poor laws of 1598 and 1601, supplemented by later acts or royal proclamations, defined and provided penalties for persons adjudged to be rogues and vagabonds. When the news of coming impressments spread abroad, it was expected that men would take to the woods rather than submit to military service. In December, 1624, the Lord Lieutenant of each county ordered that pro-vost marshals be appointed for securing the highways. With "6

53. Sailors, unpaid, mutinied at Plymouth in 1627, forcing the Corporation to pay out 18s. 8d. for powder and match to suppress them. *Devonshire*, XV, 162; Gardiner, *England*, VI, 218–19; Clark, *Working Life of Women*, 119; Whiteway, Diary, 42 (f. 51); *CSPD, 1619–23*, p. 441; *1625–6*, p. 188; *1628–9*, pp. 521, 524; *1629–31*, p. 545.
54. Dalton, *Country Justice*, 99.
55. Sparke, *Grievous Grones for the Poore*, 6, 10, 15; Thomas Harman, *A Caveat for Common Cursetors Vulgarly Called Vagabonds* (1567) and *The Fraternity of Vagabonds* (1575); Judges, *Elizabethan Underworld*, 307.

or 8 of the substantiallist yeomen" each provost marshall was "to perambulate his rape 3 times a week" and gather up "idle and loose persons." Again in 1628, when swarms of these people roamed "in every street of every town," the royal authorities ordered all mayors and justices of the peace to enforce rigorously the statutes against them; and in a further proclamation of 1630, the King endeavored to stop all persons from wandering about under the names of soldiers, mariners, glassmen, potmen, peddlers, petty chapmen, cony-skinners, or tinkers. Such steps on the part of the government in London suggest a resurgence of begging and vagrancy after 1626.[56]

Of particular concern to rural villages were "the Roaring Country Lads," able-bodied males who crowded the highways and, during their wanderings, infested the country towns and attended markets and fairs, where they picked pockets and stole whatever they had need of. Such a man was Stephen Worste, who, "abydeinge nowhere," admitted to the Essex Court of Quarter Sessions in 1611 that for a long time he had been moving about Norfolk, Suffolk, and Essex as a vagrant. He had been taken into custody at Braintree after he had gone to "goodman Fitche's house" because he was in want. Mary Goodwin, "spinster" of Bocking, typifies the women who were arrested for vagrancy. Immediately after her release from the house of correction in 1614, where she had been sent for leading an idle, drunken, and thieving existence, she was in court again for stealing some linen; this time she was soundly whipped.[57]

When rural vagrants associated in gangs and maintained hideouts, they often terrorized neighborhoods and even proved too

56. *Statutes of the Realm*, IV, 1024–5, 1159–60, 1161; Essex Sessions, XIX, 231; *HMC Hastings*, II, 61; Hamilton, *Quarter Sessions*, 104; *Acts of the Privy Council, 1623–5*, pp. 154–5; *Sussex Arch.*, XL, 5–6; *CSPD, 1629–31*, p. 342; *Bibliotheca Lindesiana*, 181.

57. Entire families sometimes rogued it. Richard White, his wife, mother-in-law, and children were charged at the Essex Quarter Sessions on January 6, 1639, with being "Tellers of destinyes" and wandering up and down the kingdom on a counterfeit pass. Taken up at Brentwood as incorrigible rogues, they were ordered to be whipped and returned to Yarmouth in keeping with the law. Essex Sessions, XX, 480; Dekker, *The Witch of Edmonton*, I, ii, 77–9; Essex Sessions, XIX, 23, 157–8, 244; XX, 296; Chamberlain, *Letters*, I, 159.

much for the local constabulary. Certain rogues of Berkshire gathered in sheepcotes every night until a justice, having intelligence of their "rabblement," went about midnight with the constables to their hiding place. There he discovered six couples "dauncing naked" and others lying about; he took up "divers of them" and sent them off to prison. It took the constables of six towns raiding once a week or more to break up a gang of "rogues and sturdy beggars" who had holed up in a Radborne barn in 1625; they had committed felonies of various sorts and received stolen goods. In May, 1641, the alarmed inhabitants of Much Haddam reported that Richard and Susan Haynes maintained a lodging and meeting house for vagrant persons in their barn, "sometimes to the number of 60, sometimes 40, and seldom less than 20." Such crowds were far too large for any constable to arrest, but when the parishes of Sawbridgeworth, Gilston, and Widford also sent in complaints, the Hertfordshire justices agreed to go after the rogues.[58]

Rough conduct on the part of both men and women has been shown to be a familiar feature of daily life in England, and it was crowned by crimes of violence. Edward Wilkinson of Dedham, "a quarreler and common striker of men," threatened to cut off the constable's legs when he was putting some lewd fellows in the stocks. He actually did strike one of the chief townsmen and, later, freed his friends. Finally eleven Dedhamites signed a petition to the Essex Quarter Sessions charging that Wilkinson had been so "outrageous as we do much mistrust that . . . he will offer violence unless by law he can be bridled." Salford in Lancashire had the doubtful distinction of breeding one of the most consistent brawlers, James Hartt. From 1610 to 1625, the court-leet had to deal with him time and time and time again for assaulting his neighbors and destroying other men's property. If Essex represents a typical rural society, then from 1625 to the end of the period, husbandmen, laborers, clothworkers, and their wives grew ever

---

58. In 1629, Thomas Crosfield wrote down in his diary that "at Derham in Glocestershire there's a continuall annuall meeting of these canting beggers which cannot be suppressed." *The Diary of Thomas Crosfield*, ed. Frederick J. Boas (London, 1935), 33, 78; *Camden*, XCIX, 83; Hertfordshire Sessions, V, 292–4; *Warwick Sessions*, I, 8.

more turbulent. After eulogizing the virtues in country life, Thomas Dekker became disenchanted and confessed: "I have heard of no sin in the city, but I met it in the village, nor any vice in the tradesman, which was not in the ploughman." [59]

Even though London could absorb more migrants than the lesser towns because of her growing industries, the vagabonds of both sexes who invaded the environs of the City added decidedly to the burdens of the law enforcement officers. A special effort was made in 1616 to coerce all those having no lawful occupation to repair to their places of birth and remain there. Interestingly enough, this proclamation directed the justices of the peace to search with particular care all inns and bowling alleys. The next year informers were given rewards for reporting negligent constables and headboroughs in Middlesex, but in spite of all efforts, disorders occasioned by rogues and vagrants increased. One could become an incorrigible rogue at a very tender age in London. Julius Laney, "labourer, aged seven years and more," was brought before the Court of Quarter Sessions of Middlesex and denounced as a "dangerous beggar, wandering about to the great danger of the inferior sort of people" and "for fighting in face of the Court." He was found guilty and branded with an R on the left shoulder. [60]

English crime centered about London in the counties of Middlesex, Berkshire, Hertfordshire, Essex, Surrey, and Kent; the selfsame area within a thirty-mile radius of the City wherein the influx of vagrants occurred. A summary of the true bills found in the Court of Quarter Sessions of county Middlesex in 1624 shows a total of 250 crimes, among which burglary (37), horse-stealing (16), grand larceny (84), picking pockets (15), sheep-stealing

---

59. An English precedent for the eye-gouging fights which occurred on the American frontier, and which horrified the British, took place at Little Bromley in Essex in 1618 when John Goodale was presented in court "for breaking the King's peace on Peter Clarke . . . and putting out his left eye." Essex Sessions, XIX, 306, *et passim;* XX, 42, 488; *Chetham,* n. s., XLVI, 83, 112, 128, 136, 138, 150, 161, 169, 184, 191; Essex Sessions, XVIII, 29; County Essex, Assize File (E. R. O.), 35/36/H, March, 1593/4, No. 34; *Devon & Cornwall,* XVII, 206–10; W. P. M. Kennedy, *Parish Life Under Queen Elizabeth* (St. Louis, 1914), 149–51; Judges, *Elizabethan Underworld,* 303, 510.

60. *Bibliotheca Lindesiana,* I, 140; Byrne, *Elizabethan Life,* 94; *Middlesex Sessions,* IV, 367; *CSPD, 1625–6,* p. 434; *Middlesex Sessions,* n. s., I, 208.

(15), and petty larceny (18) comprised the principal offenses. There was but one conviction for murder, another for manslaughter, and two each for rape, cow-stealing, pig-stealing, and bigamy. Among the 263 convictions for civil offenses this same year, those which probably involved the criminal element were for receiving inmates against the law (32), keeping brothels (32), and keeping unlicensed alehouses (11). Subsequent records indicate that crimes and misdemeanors increased. No wonder that a proclamation of 1630 designated London as a "nursery of burglaries etc.," where secret pawning to brokers and hucksters flourished.[61]

One of the interesting generalizations which can be deduced from the records of the Middlesex courts is that, in that county at least, more yeomen were presented for thefts and assaults than members of the lower ranks. Perhaps the fact that many of the latter were homeless vagrants made them more difficult to locate and arrest. The evidence that gentlemen, well-known gentlemen, were guilty of perpetrating highway robbery is another striking revelation. It could be that the lower orders lacked the energies, literacy, and brazen confidence that daring crimes required. At Knightsbridge on June 5, 1616, "Sir George Sandys" (poet and later treasurer of the Virginia Company) with Isaac Hawkins, also a gentleman, assaulted Anthony Culverwell on the highway and robbed him of his cloak, 40 shillings, and his watch. They also attacked and robbed John Fox, a gentleman, and, unassisted, Sir George stopped the dramatist John Marston and took his horse and much clothing. Later he joined two others in a fourth assault. A Middlesex Court judged Hawkins, who had no money to make restitution, guilty and ordered him to be hanged; Sandys was found not guilty. One suspects that this brother of Sir Edwin Sandys received special treatment. Two gentlemen robbers who, over many years, had been getting booty worth £200 to £300 on

---

61. There had been some improvement over the decade, for in the same court in 1614, of 421 persons tried, 160 had been condemned to death, but of these, 57 could read and escaped the gallows; 110 of those indicted were discharged as not guilty; 73 were whipped; 22 outlawed or transported, and the remaining 56 received minor punishments. Of 481 cases handled in 1615, 94 were executed; 61 were able to read the "Neck verse" and were branded. *Middlesex Sessions,* n.s., I, i, vi–xxvi; II, viii–ix, 312–14; III, ix; *Bibliotheca Lindesiana,* I, 190.

each job, swung from the gallows in 1628. They had many con-
federates and attendants; John Rous learned that their operations
had extended over the counties of Essex, Suffolk, Lincoln, York,
Cambridge, Hertford, Bucks, Northampton, and Bedford.[62]

London's criminal population resided in certain well-known districts: Alsatia (bounded by the river on the south, Fleet Street on
the north, and Whitefriars and Carmelite streets on the east and
west) was notorious for harboring cutpurses and murderers. The
precincts of the Savoy, Ram Alley, Salisbury Court, Mitre Court,
Fulwood's Rents in Holborn, and, south of the river, Deadman's
Place, the Mint, and Montague Close were sanctuaries where a
rogue could be safe from arrest. From Grub Street in 1614, John
Wheeler, apothecary, was summoned to advise the justices of Middlesex because he was a "wissard and tells where stollen goods
are." Crime was not restricted to thefts, however, for felonies committed by both men and women embraced assaults, kidnapping,
and arson.[63]

Toward the end of the reign of King James I, the Privy Council
blamed the laxness of justices of the peace for "the many robberies, thefts, and burglaries, besides other disorders and misdemeanors of men . . . so common as they now are growne." King
Charles and his officers also urged county officials to make greater
efforts to reduce the number of crimes. Though the age-old terror
of the beggar and the tramp did not fully disappear in this period,
certain factors did reduce bands of roving miscreants who plagued
the countryside. After 1625 impressment for the wars and the
stepped-up demand that the poor carry passes when traveling
served to restrict somewhat the activities of dispossessed persons.
We have just recounted how the justices of Berkshire and Hertfordshire took a hand in rounding up criminal elements in their
counties. In Hastings Rape alone the Sussex justices apprehended
and "corrected" 70 rogues in the first three months of 1631, and
the Worcestershire justices certified to punishing 105 vagrants in

62. *Middlesex Sessions*, II, *passim;* Mitchell & Leys, *History of London,* 97;
Middlesex Sessions, n. s., II, 150; III, xviii, 306–7; *Camden*, LXVI, 83.
63. Besant, *London*, 136; Byrne, *Elizabethan Life*, 47, 55; *Middlesex Sessions*,
n. s., I, 372; II, 27; *Middlesex Sessions*, II, 30, 51, 76; III, 9, 29, 41.

the divisions of Evesham and Pershore from January to March, 1632. At Horncastle, Louth, and Sleaford in Lincolnshire 136 wandering people were whipped, and 36 youthful vagrants were bound out as apprentices to trades.[64]

Spurred on by the same orders and proclamations of 1630 which had aroused country justices to greater efforts to search out all rogues and beggars, the justices of the metropolitan area ordered a watch to be kept in London to arrest such undesirables. Once a month the justices checked with the constables, and disturbances attributable to these vicious stragglers lessened. In October of 1632, the Corporation of London reported that 50 vagrants had been bound as apprentices to merchants to serve in Barbados and Virginia; 773 poor children were at Christ's Hospital (of which 40 had been put to trades), and more than 4,000 rogues and vagabonds had been dispatched to their native places as recommended by the statute.[65]

When one considers the absence of any effective police force in the country, the number and nature of the offenses the courts of quarter sessions and assizes had to handle are surprisingly small and generally petty. In 1628, it is true, soldiers returning from the fiasco at Rochelle committed so many robberies and other outrages in areas where they were quartered that the Privy Council took steps to curb them. Considering, too, the host of wandering, rootless men, women, and children, it is surprising that there was so little serious crime in the land. England was a safe and tranquil place when compared with a France beset by the consequences of chronic popular revolts and the terrible wanton cruelty of German against German so vividly described in fictional form by Grimmelshausen in *The Adventurous Simplissimus* (1679). The opinion of Sieur de la Serre, fresh from Paris in 1638, warrants thoughtful consideration: "The police is, nevertheless, so well observed, that they live here without disorder and without confusion; and there is so

64. *Acts of the Privy Council, 1623–5,* pp. 154–5; *Sussex Arch.,* XVI, 26; XL, 7; *HMC Various,* I, 303; *Norfolk & Norwich,* I, 167; Barnes, *Somerset,* 192; Rushworth, *Historical Collections,* III, Appendix 83; *CSPD, 1629–31,* p. 241; *1631–3,* p. 305; *1634–5,* pp. 441, 445, 447; *1635–6,* p. 137.
65. *Bibliotheca Lindesiana,* I, 189, 191; *CSPD, 1631–3,* p. 433.

much safety in the streets even during the night, that one may walk
as freely as in the day, without any other arms than those of the
confidence one has in the goodness of men." [66]

VI

By the end of the period, there is ample evidence of a recognition
of the need for moral regeneration, of a rising flood of religious
concern, both rational and emotional, and an increasing awareness
of the state of the poor. It was slowly dawning on some thoughtful
men (not all Puritans either) that the invisible poor had as much
claim upon the commonwealth as their more vocal and visible
counterparts, the impotent and disorderly. One of the hundreds of
schemes to put them to work was propounded in 1641 in *Considerations Touching Trade, with the Advance of the King's Revenue*. It pointed out that the woolen industry "imployes a million
poore People," and recommended the growing of hemp and flax
and employing more idle people in manufacturing. For the first
time, signs of a humanitarian spirit emerged. To a degree never
before attained anywhere, mercantile leaders and some of the aristocracy were creating endowments—to build almshouses, to assist
young men in their trades, and to relieve the poor in other ways.
Nevertheless "The Grievous Grones of the Poore" grew louder,
and the number of miserable people mounted. "Oh yes," sings the
crier in a ballad:

> If any man or woman,
>   in country or in city,
> Can tell where liveth charity,
>   or where abideth pity,
> Bring newes unto the Cryer,
>   and their reward shall be,

---

66. James Howell found at Paris in 1620 that one was not safe on the streets at
night and compared conditions there with the excellent nocturnal security in
London. Howell, *Epistolae Ho Elianae*, 42, 46; *Antiquarian Repository*, IV, 531.
See also Porchnev, *Les Soulévements Populaires en France, 1623 à 1648;* H. J. C.
Grimmelshausen, *The Adventurous Simplicissimus* [1669]. trans. A. T. S. Goodrich
(Lincoln, Neb., 1962); also *Courage, The Adventuress & False Messiah*, trans.
& ed. Hans Speier (Princeton, 1964), especially editor's introduction.

The prayers of poore folkes every day,
upon the humble knee.[67]

A new avenue of escape had opened for those whom William
Penn (later, in the greatest of all promotion tracts) would call
"industrious husbandmen," "day labourers," "laborious handicraftsmen," who "are low in the world" and "that are hardly able
(with extreme Labour) to maintain their Families and portion
their Children." Opportunities also awaited those whom the statutes
denominated "sturdy Beggars, Rogues, and Vagabonds." And so
desperate were many Englishmen that they were ready to listen to
suggestions that they depart the country and sail westward where
the land seemed bright.[68]

67. *Considerations Touching Trade, with the Advance of the King's Revenue*
(1641), 14–15; *Roxburghe Ballads*, II, 353.
68. William Penn, *Some Account of the Province of Pennsylvania* (1681), 6.

XI

The First Swarming of the English

I N THIS PERIOD, so notable for change as well as stability, the
English often found themselves frustrated and desperate: to
most of them "Merrie England" was but an empty phrase. In the
countryside, large numbers of people had been deprived of their
ancient rural security; they had no land to cultivate; unemployment
threatened the agricultural laborer and village artisan most of the
time; at best their housing was inadequate; in cold or wet weather,
fuel was scarce, costly, and often unobtainable. Undernourishment
and unbalanced diets sapped the strength of thousands of the lower
orders, and many fell victims to disease, notably tuberculosis. Periodically the plague decimated whole country villages. In the hearts
and minds of respectable, if impoverished men, the payment of
ship money, impressment, billeting, and similar demands by government during the years of the personal rule aroused bitterness
and alienated not a few from the Stuart King. For human and
often trivial offenses, the ecclesiastical courts meted out harsh punishments, but in spite of laws and sermons, people solaced themselves with drink, and, among the idle, bastards increased markedly. Approximately half of the peasantry lived in extreme poverty,
and depressed conditions affected townsmen and city people everywhere from 1620 to 1642.

Helpless in the midst of the bewildering changes of an economy
that never provided work for every man, beset by both private
miseries and seemingly insurmountable public problems, the com-

mon folk had no ways for redressing matters because they did not rule. Looking upward and outward from their stations at the bottom of society, the invisible poor slowly began to realize that even with the vigorous enforcement of the poor laws by King Charles's ministers, the future held forth very little for them.

Between 1620 and 1642, close to 80,000, or 2 per cent of all Englishmen, left Britain. They forsook not only their homes but their homeland in the quest for a better life. About 58,000 of them ventured across the Atlantic Ocean to the strange new lands on the continent of North America or to certain small, hitherto unoccupied islands in the Caribbean Sea. In addition, seldom-noticed and un-enumerated contingents crossed the North Sea and the English Channel to find refuge and employment on the continent of Europe.[1]

The movement to the Continent had its inception back in the time of Queen Elizabeth. Writing in 1577, William Harrison told of the men and women who had been turned off their holdings: "the wise and better-minded doo either forsake the realme altogether, and seeke to live in other countries, as France, Germanie, Barbarie, India, Muscovie, and verie Calecute, complaining of no roome to be lefte for them at home." Still others fled to Holland for religious sanctuary. One careful estimate indicates that about 2,000 Kentish spinners and weavers emigrated to the Rhenish Palatinate in search of work after Alderman Cockayne's fiasco with the cloth trade in 1616. Surely more of these artisans must have left the other cloth counties, especially Essex and East Anglia. The livery companies and the City of London began in 1611 "to plant" in Ulster, which eight years later, by the best calculation,

1. "The Remonstrance of the State of the Kingdom," approved by the House of Commons in November, 1641, contained this significant passage on past mis-government: "The bishops, and their courts, were as eager in the country [as the Court of High Commission], and although their jurisdiction could never reach so high in vigour and extremity of punishment, yet they were no less grievous, in respect of the generality and multiplicity of vexations; which lighting upon the meaner sort of tradesmen and artificers, did impoverish many thousands, and so afflict and trouble others, that great numbers, to avoid their miseries, departed out of the kingdom; some into New-England, and other parts of America; others into Holland. . . ." *Proceedings and Debates of the British Parliament*, I, 128; Newton, in *Cambridge History of the British Empire,* ed. J. Holland Rose, *et. al.* (Cambridge, Eng., 1929), I, 179–80.

contained "at least 8,000" single men of English birth or descent, together with a few women, in the six escheated counties, principally Tyrone and Donegal. By 1642, about 20,000 Englishmen had settled in Ulster.[2]

Finally, as we know so well, beginning with Jamestown in 1607 or at the Somer Islands in 1612, the promoters of the Virginia and Bermuda companies sent out colonists to the new English world. Between 1618 and 1621, they transported about 3,750 persons, including some 200 women, to Virginia alone. Thus began the Great Migration of the English, a migration whose consequences even those who participated in it did not foresee. They emigrated by the thousands, hoping to establish themselves anew overseas, from Newfoundland southward for 3,600 miles to Guiana on the Spanish Main.[3]

Why, we ask, for the first time in their long history, did such a large emigration of Britons take place? Hitherto they had been a stay-at-home folk, enamored of the smoke of their own chimneys. In 1624 Richard Eburne, who was urging miserable and unfortunate persons to abandon their wretched hovels and search for a better existence across the ocean, freely conceded that they were hard to move, "for so are all men, Englishmen especially, and of them most of all the In-Land sort, wedded to their native Soile like a Snaile to his Shell, or as the Fable in *A Mouse to his Chest,* that they will rather even starve at home, then seeke stoare abroad." In 1921 the unemployed Welsh coal miners would not accept free farms in Canada; and notwithstanding the popular cry after 1945 that "England is through," only an insignificant number of Britons went out to Australia, South Africa, or Canada. What was rotten in the state of England in the seventeenth century? [4]

Although the systematic study of demography had not yet

2. Harrison, *England,* Pt. I, 215. For a sample of the exodus to Holland in the 1630's, see *NEHG Reg.,* XIV, 324; and *Norfolk,* XXV. The exodus from Kent in the single year 1616 amounted to 10 per cent of the Puritan emigration to New England, 1629-41. Coleman, Economy of Kent, 161; T. W. Moody, *The Londonderry Plantation, 1609-1641* (Belfast, 1939), 185, 322; R. J. Dickson, *Ulster Emigration to Colonial America, 1718-1775* (London, 1966), 3. For earlier connections between Ireland and Virginia, see David Beers Quinn, *The Elizabethans and the Irish* (Ithaca, 1966), 106-22.

3. *Recs. Va. Co.,* IV, 158.

4. Richard Eburne, *A Plaine Path-way to Plantations* (1624), 59.

begun, thoughtful persons debated whether the land was over-populated. Some observers—usually those interested in colonizing —held that "the people . . . doe swarme in the land, as yong bees in a hive in June; insomuch that there is very hardly roome for one man to live by another. The mightier like strong old bees thrust the weaker, as younger, out of their hives: Lords of Manors convert towneships, in which were a hundred or two hundred communicants, to a shepheard and his dog." The writer feared "extreame famine in the midst of our greatest plenty." The figure of the bees readily occurred to other men as they sighed for the "times when our Country was not pestered with multitude, not overcharged with swarmes of people." The solution seemed to be to let them "swarm and hive themselves" elsewhere; colonizing would give the young a chance and relieve England of the unbearable burden of its poor. Dejectedly, John Winthrop recorded in 1629 that "this lande growes wearye of her Inhabitantes, so as man which is the most pretious of all the Creatures, is here more vile and base, then the earthe they treade upon: so as children, neighbours, and freindes (especially if they be poore) are rated the greatest burdens, which if things were right, would be the cheifest earthly blessings." Thousands of humble persons reluctantly shared this belief, while other men, including royal officials concerned about the number of "depopulated" communities, took the opposite view, which was that England could ill-afford to lose her sturdy husbandmen and skilled artificers.[5]

The idea of sending the nation's surplus population over-seas to colonize distant lands had been gradually germinating for half a century when the Pilgrims set out for a new home in Virginia—only to find it in New England. The slow growth of permanent colonies in Virginia and Bermuda, the quasi-permanent fishing stations in Newfoundland, and the rumored success of the Dutch plantations in the valley of the Hudson River demonstrated the feasibility of the idea. In addition, a great prose literature of

5. William Symonds, *Virginia: A Sermon Preached at White-Chappel . . .* (1609), 13, 19, 20; Robert Gray, *A Good Speed to Virginia* (1609), B 2r–v, B4r; *Winthrop Papers,* II, 114; George Louis Beer, *The Origins of the British Colonial System, 1578–1660* (New York, 1908); Powell, *Depopulation;* but *cf.* Mildred Campbell, "Of People either too Few or too Many," in *Conflict in Stuart England,* ed. William A. Aiken (London, 1960), 177–201.

colonization, made classic by the two Hakluyts and continued by Samuel Purchas, won readers in all ranks of society, though principally among the higher clergy and the gentlemen- and merchant-promoters—all of them prospective investors. Far more popular and influential in the long run, however, was a new device, the promotion tract, which was first employed systematically to propagate the work of the Virginia Company. By 1619 it was reaching a very wide audience among Englishmen of all kinds.[6]

In the year 1619 the Virginia Company circulated a large printed broadside telling about the departure of 11 ships laden with 871 passengers, 92 head of cattle, and 4 horses sent out under its own auspices, and of 390 more passengers enlisted by individual adventurers. Among those sent out by the company were 100 boys (apprenticed as servants for seven years), and 90 maidens for wives. "The aforesaid 1261 persons being arrived, will make the number of English in Virginia amount to about foure and twenty hundred Soules." Most of the males sent over on this expedition and in the next years were described as "choise men, borne and bred up to labour and industry." About 100 Devonshire men went out to Virginia who had been "brought up to Husbandry," and about 150 emigrants from Warwickshire, Staffordshire, and Sussex were "all framed to Iron-workes; the rest dispersedly out of divers Shires of the Realme" and London.[7]

The vigorous efforts of the Virginia Company to people its plantation in the years 1619–21 drew the attention of alert British shipping men to a new and highly lucrative source of profits to be garnered by transporting emigrants across the Atlantic as cargo. Thus it was that, in 1620, Thomas Weston, one of the lesser mercantile figures of London, could raise "a generall stocke" of £7,000 from a group of "Adventurers," or investors, "some Gentlemen, some Merchants, some handy-crafts men, some adventuring great summes, some small, as their estates and affection served," to fi-

6. On the slow development of "the Colonial Idea in England," of the ethos of colonization that motivated the promoters of colonies, see Howard Mumford Jones, *O Strange New World* (New York, 1964); Andrews, *Colonial Period of American History*, I–II. Several Virginia pamphlets are reprinted in Force, *Tracts*, I–IV. See also *Memorials of the Bermudas*, ed. J. H. Lefroy (London, 1877), I.
7. Broadside in PRO: C. O. 1, I, 157; *A Declaration of the Colonie of Virginia*, in Force, *Tracts*, III, No. 5, p. 5.

nance the comparatively modest expedition of the Pilgrims. When the *Mayflower* sailed from Plymouth on September 16, 1620, there were on board 131 passengers: thirty-five were Pilgrims from Leiden and sixty-one more (presumably Anglicans) had been recruited by Weston in London and Southampton. Other promoters of colonies and sea captains stood ready, greedy, and eager to seize any opportunity to enter into the profitable passenger traffic. As might be expected, among them were many Dutch skippers, ever ready to try all ports to force a trade.[8]

Many of the 3,570 English dispatched to Virginia in these years died during the ocean crossing, and others died shortly after their arrival. Only 1,140 were alive on March 22, 1622, when the natives arose and slaughtered 350 of them. The aftermath of the massacre turned out to be even more costly, for the disruption of the economy led to the death of about 500 of the survivors the following winter from starvation and a "pestilent fever" (typhoid?) introduced by new arrivals, who attributed it to the "corrupt beer" served on shipboard. These trying circumstances, together with the company's mismanagement and "aspersions from letters sent home," gave Virginia an unsavory reputation. The enemies of Sir Edwin Sandys charged in 1623 that hundreds of the 4,000 settlers he had procured for the colony were lured to their death by false information and "cozzening ballads." Emigration fell off sharply, "so much had the disgrace of the Plantation spread amongst the Common sort of people." In public-relations cant, Virginia sorely needed a new image.[9]

During the 1620's, nearly all of the discontents of the lower orders came to a head: crop failures, plague, and hardships stemming from war conditions have already been mentioned. Parliament had been dissolved, and the personal rule of Charles I inaugurated. The Bishop of London, William Laud, was proceeding relentlessly against all Puritan lecturers. The juxtaposition of social grievances with depressing economic conditions severely jarred a

8. Smith, *Travels and Works*, II, 783; Andrews, *Colonial Period of American History*, I, 268–9.
9. Powell, in *Virginia Magazine of History and Biography*, LXVI, 44, 58, 65; *Purchas His Pilgrimes* (1625), IV, 1816; Wesley Frank Craven, *The Dissolution of the Virginia Company* (New York, 1932), 96, 173, 212–13; Force, *Tracts*, III, No. 5, p. 3; *Recs. Va. Co.*, II, 397; IV, 14, 77, 135, 525–6.

home-staying people who had long suffered in silence. Once again we may recall that this was an age of listeners, and the number of readers was increasing. Most Englishmen had either heard about or read about the New World and had formed a reasonably definite idea of what it must be like. By 1629 a substantial body of Englishmen had reached the state of mind that made them receptive to the oral and written propaganda for planting, which always emphasized the light in the western sky. What the promoters told them and promised them must now be examined.

II

A conscious campaign "to educate the English public" in the wonders of the New World called America, the possibilities there for a new and better life, and especially the opportunities awaiting the average man who was down on his luck, had begun with the tracts and printed sermons to promote the Virginia Company's colony in 1609–12. Direct appeals designed to induce prospective emigrants to commit themselves irrevocably dated from a decade later, when the company, headed by Sir Edwin Sandys, resorted to the use of the ballad, the sermon, the broadside, the tract, exhortation by word of mouth, and less praiseworthy, compulsory means to stimulate settlement. Henceforth the *planting of Englishmen* in the new lands to create a new society, and not a search for gold or the Northwest Passage, not a crusade against the Spanish Papists, not even the saving of the souls of red men, became the primary goal of colonizing efforts.

The fishermen of the West Country and their home-abiding friends were stirred by the accounts of Newfoundland. In addition to making a map of the island, John Mason, a sea captain who had gone out there as governor in 1615, published *A Briefe Discourse of the New-found-land* in 1620. In it he pointed out that most of the fishermen on the Grand Banks had families at home, and that transporting planters out there in the fishing fleet would cost no more than 30 shillings a head, less than one-third of the charge of £5 for shipping someone to Virginia or Bermuda. Furthermore, in Newfoundland, people would be secure from savages, foreign enemies, and piratic attacks. Richard Whitbourne's *A Discourse and*

Discovery of New-found-land (1621), a down-to-earth discourse, gave much practical information; whereas Sir William Vaughan, in his tract of 1626, essayed a Graeco-Cymbrian appeal to the Devon and Bristol fishermen. Stressing the idea that God had ordained that "Ilanders should dwel in Ilands," and vouchsafing that "God had reserved Newfoundland for us Britains, as the next land beyond Ireland, and not above nine or tenne dayes saile from thence," he maintained that "This is our Colchos where the Golden Fleece flourisheth on the backes of Neptunes sheepe continually to be shorne." [10]

One of the most persuasive and emotional tracts of the age on Newfoundland was *A Plaine Path-way to Plantations* (1624) written by Richard Eburne, a clergyman of Somerset. Appealing to ordinary Englishmen to leave their country and venture westward, where one may have a "house . . . with fortie or threescore, with one or two hundred acres of ground," he succeeded in arousing "the poorer and common sort."

> Bee not too much in love with that countrie wherein you were borne, that countrie which bearing you, yet cannot breed you, but seemeth, and is indeed, weary of you. Shee accounts you a burthen to her, and encombrance to her. You keepe her downe, you hurt her and make her poore and bare, and together with your owne, you worke and cause, by tarrying within her, her misery and decay, her ruin and undoing. Take and reckon that for your Country where you may best live and thrive. Straine not no more to leave that country . . . wherein you were borne and bred up, for fitter places and habitations.

After all, the parson continued, the plantation to which you are going is part of England. "It be the people that makes the Land English, not the Land the People." Then came the final thrust: The sun shines there as well as in England, "so it is the same God." [11]

In a real sense, the Holy Bible was the greatest piece of promotion literature of the era of the Great Migration, yet for some unexplained reason it has been overlooked by historians. Countless

10. Mason, *A Brief Discourse of the New-found-land;* Vaughan, *Golden Fleece,* Pt. III, 5, 9.
11. Eburne, *A Plaine Path-way to Plantations,* Title page, A2, A3, B2–3.

texts in the Scriptures enjoined good Christians to leave a land which wanted them not, just as the Israelites had done. And we must not overlook the fact that Holy Writ impressed settlers headed for Virginia and the West Indies quite as much as it did the Saints bound for New England. Anglican priests of the stature of Robert Gray and John Donne, Dean of St. Paul's, joined with the leading Puritans Thomas Hooker and John Cotton in preaching from chosen emigration texts. At Gravesend in June, 1630, Master Cotton preached to the passengers of the Winthrop Fleet from II Samuel, 7:10: "And I will appoint a place for my People Israel, And wil plant it, that they may dwell in a place of their owne, and moove no more, neither shal wicked people trouble them any more as before time." As a sermon-savoring people, the English remembered well the preachers' texts. After all, God was English, and the people trusted in His Word.[12]

Inquiring men and women, many of whom had read the Bible over twice or thrice and took its every injunction seriously and literally, discovered texts for themselves as, looking for the Word of God, they pored over its pages. Very quickly they would stumble on the call to Abram in Genesis: "Get thee out of thy countrey, and from thy kinred, and from thy fathers house unto a land that I will shew thee: And I will make of thee a great nation." They read in Joshua that "Moses my servant is dead; now therefore arise, go over this Jordan, and all this people, unto the lande which I do give them, that is to the children of Israel." And again, the Lord promised them: "From the wilderness unto the great sea toward the going downe of the sunne, shall be your coast." Joshua also said to them, "If thou bee a great people, then get thee up to the wood country and cut down trees for thyselfe there in the land of the Perizzites and of the Giants, if mount Ephraim be too narrow for thee." Had not Joel taught that "your old men shall dream dreames, and your young men shall see visions"?[13]

Before its dissolution in 1624, the Virginia Company and its friends succeeded partially in countering its critics by what one of

12. *The Sermons of John Donne,* ed. G. R. Potter and E. M. Simpson, (Berkeley, 1959), IV, 255; *The Holy Bible* (Geneva version), II Samuel, 7:10.
13. *The Holy Bible* (Geneva version), Genesis, 12:1–3; Joshua, 1:2, 4; 17:15; Joel, 2:28; Matthew, 24:6–7.

them described as "varnishinge their owne actions with colourable schemes and Causeinge ballades to be printed of We knowe not what imaginarie successe of plentye and prosperitie. . . ." The news of the Massacre of 1622 had barely reached London when Michael Sparke published *Grievous Grones for the Poor,* in which he singled out Virginia and Bermuda as "now Cities of refuge for poore impoverished persons." He also praised the charity of the Virginia Company for "transporting of them to a Land, where they have Corne which they planted not, and plenty which some of them deserved not." In a tract sponsored by the company, Edward Waterhouse attempted to quicken the imagination of landless prospects with a guarantee of fifty acres of land for each individual. Even more, however, the valiant efforts of the planters themselves and private merchants engaged in the supply and passenger traffic managed to make Virginia somewhat more attractive to the average Englishman by 1629. In 1630 emigration had resumed sufficiently to warrant Governor Harvey's estimate of a population of 2,500 and upward.[14]

At the same time that Virginia was being advertised, certain men began to draw their countrymen's attention to possibilities of colonizing to the north along the coast of Norumbega. The human link between these two regions was Captain John Smith. In 1616 he brought out *A Description of New England or Observations and Discoveries in North America,* in which he narrated two voyages made to the northern coasts. In 1620 he published the first edition of *New England's Trials;* two years later a second edition came out which contained much new material. In 1624 Smith produced the most extensive and important work written thus far by an Englishman who had actually visited the places he described:

14. An informative broadside of 1622 tells of *The Inconveniences that have Happened to Some Persons which Have Transported themselves from England to Virginia* . . . and lists the kinds of clothing, food, arms, tools, utensils, and fishing tackle needed for the voyage, to which a tent must be added "for initial shelter." Approximately 2,000 persons had been transported to Bermuda from 1614 to 1629. *CSP Col., 1574–1660,* pp. 92, 117; *Recs. Va. Co.,* IV, 151; Sparke, *Grievous Grones for the Poore,* Dedication, 10; Waterhouse, *Declaration of the State of . . . Virginia,* 4, 6, 34; Surviving ballads about Virginia may be found in Firth, *An American Garland,* 9–24; and *WMQ,* 3d ser., V, 259–64, with a facsimile of the broadside *Good Newes from Virginia* (1623), facing p. 351. Stow, *Annales,* 1017–21.

The Generall Historie of Virginia, New England, and the Summer Isles, in Six Bookes. His books not only contained sound and pertinent matter, but he issued his unusually accurate map of New England (1614), which served as the best one for that region until the eighteenth century. In these works the famous adventurer had finally discovered "his true métier." He became the promoter of colonies *par excellence.*[15]

In Captain Smith's publication, the public could read a reliable report, for what he had to say stemmed directly from experience, common sense, and deep conviction. Furthermore he told his story without the usual recriminations indulged in by other writers. Readers were quick to sense the honesty of the man and placed confidence in one who could write so frankly of colonizing: ". . . it is not a worke for every one to manage such an affaire, as make a discovery and plant a Colony, it requires all the best parts of art, judgement, courage, honesty, constancy, diligence, and industry, to doe but neere well; some are more proper for one thing then another, and therein best to be imploied: and nothing breeds more confusion than misplacing and misemploying men in their undertakings." [16]

After outlining the difficulties facing would-be colonists, Smith set forth succinctly and eloquently the principal arguments used to persuade English common folk to go a-planting:

> Who can desire more content that hath small meanes, or but onely his merit to advance his fortunes, then to tread and plant that ground he hath purchased by the hazard of his life; if hee have but a taste of vertue and magnanimity, what to such a minde can bee more pleasant than planting and building a foundation for his posterity, got from the rude earth by Gods blessing and his owne industry without prejudice to any; if hee

15. These three works are reprinted in Capt. John Smith, *Travels and Works,* I, 197–229, 237–48, 253–72; 273–382; II, 383–784. The latest and soundest estimate of Smith as a promoter is by Barbour, *The Three Worlds of Captain John Smith,* especially, pp. 283–396; see also chap. I, "Promoters and Precursors," in Samuel Eliot Morison, *Builders of the Bay Colony* (Boston, 1932). The clearest reproduction of Smith's map of New England is in Bradford, *History of Plymouth Plantation,* I, facing p. 189. For the map and pertinent comments about promotion literature in general, see Jarvis M. Morse, *American Beginnings* (Washington, 1952), 44, and chaps. III–VI.
16. Smith, *Travels and Works,* II, 705.

have any graine of faith or zeale in Religion, what can he doe
less hurtfull to any, or more agreeable to God, then to seeke to
convert those poore Salvages to know Christ and humanity,
whose labours with discretion will triple requite thy charge and
paine; what so truly sutes with honour and honesty, as the dis-
covering things unknowne, erecting Townes, peopling Countries, informing the ignorant, reforming things unjust, teaching
vertue and gaine to our native mother Country a Kingdome to
attend her, finde imploiment for those that are idle, because
they know not what to doe: so farr from wronging any, as to
cause posterity to remember thee; and remembring thee, ever
honour that remembrance with praise.[17]

Reports about or coming from the first settlements did much to
familiarize men with the advantages of New England. In February,
1622, Robert Cushman returned to London bearing the manuscript of a sermon he had delivered at Plymouth in New England
the previous December. In it he told how the first care of the Pilgrims had been "to settle religion . . . before either profit or
popularitie," as in the case of the Virginians. He also had with him
the manuscript of a work compiled jointly by William Bradford,
Edward Winslow, and himself. This work, known for years as
"Mourt's *Relation*," contained Cushman's explanation of the Pilgrims' removal to America and the lawfulness of their so doing.
John Bellamy published both manuscripts at the Three Golden
Lions in Cornhill.[18]

Waiving the religious issue, Cushman bared the grim condition

17. Smith, *Travels and Works,* II, 722–3.
18. The Register of the Stationers' Company discloses the fact that 1622 was a
banner year for promotion literature. Richard Norwood's plat or map of Bermuda was entered on January 19; Cushman's sermon March 22; Patrick Cope-
land's and John Donne's sermons on Virginia, May 30 and November 8; Bradford,
Winslow, and Cushman's (Mourt's) *Relation,* June 29; Edward Waterhouse's
official *Declaration* for the Virginia Company, August 21; a poem on the
Massacre in Virginia, September 11; and Whitbourne's tract on Newfoundland
to be reprinted. *A Transcript of the Company of Stationers of London, 1554–1640,*
ed. E. Arber (London, 1875–94), IV, 25, 28–48; Robert Cushman, *A Sermon
Preached at Plimouth in New England December 9, 1621* (London, 1622), A 4v;
Cushman, *A Relation or Journall of the Beginning and Proceedings of the English
Plantations Settled at Plymouth in New England* (1622), 70–71; also reprinted
in Edward Arber (ed.), *The Story of the Pilgrim Fathers, 1606–1623, A. D. as told
by Themselves, Their Friends, and Their Enemies* (London, 1897), 503.

of the common people of England. "The Townes abound with young Trades-men, and the Hospitalls are full of the Auncient, the countrie is replenished with new Farmers, and the Almes-houses are filled with old Labourers. Many there are who get their living with bearing burdens, but moe are faine to burden the land with their whole bodies: multitudes get their meanes of life by prating, and so doe numbers more, by begging. Neither come these straits upon men, alwaies through intemperancy, ill husbandry, indiscretion, etc., as some thinke, but even the most wise, sober and discreet men goe often to the wall, when they have done their best, wherein, as Gods providence swaieth all, so it is easie to see, that the straitnesse of the place, having in it so many strait [narrow] hearts, cannot but produce such effects more and more. . . . Let us not thus oppresse, straiten and afflict one another, but seeing there is a spatious Land, the way to which is thorow the sea, we will end this difference in a day." [19]

Edward Winslow published at London in 1624 a continuation of "Mourt's *Relation*," covering the years 1621–23, under the title of *Good Newes from New England*. Painfully and accurately, he described its virtues and what "he that walketh London streetes" would want and need to know about the land and the climate. William Morrell, who had spent nearly two years at Wessagussett (Weymouth) superintending Anglican affairs under a license from an ecclesiastical court, undertook to produce a balanced account of the territory around Massachusetts Bay in good Latin and inferior English verse.[20]

John Bellamy also served the promoters when he brought out a tract entitled *An Historical and True Relation of the English Plantations in New England . . . continued from the first beginnings to 1627,* which is something of a bibliographical puzzle. Though it contains materials from two earlier pamphlets, a new letter, "To the Reader," proclaims it to be a religious work. It solicits other Englishmen to come over to New England where the society is more godly and therefore better: "For Such as are truly

19. Mourt's *Relation,* 70–71.
20. Edward Winslow, *Good Newes from New England* (1624), 65–6; also reprinted in Alexander Young, *Chronicles of the Pilgrim Fathers* (Boston, 1841), 270–375; William Morrell, *New England* (1625); also in Mass. Hist. Soc., *Collections,* I, 125–39.

Pious, shall finde heere the opportunity to put in practise the workes of piety, both in building of Churches, and Raising of Colledges for the breeding of youth, or maintenance of Divines and other learned men." Besides containing the first adumbration of higher education for New England, the letter mentions the glory experienced in erecting towns and leaving one's name to posterity, the chance to win riches, the happiness and pleasures that may be experienced; and, as for ambitious men, "Doe they aspire to be Commanders? here is the place wher they may have command of their own friends or tenants, and if they be of any worth . . ." they may participate in local government.[21]

The Council for New England, headed by that indefatigable promoter Sir Ferdinand Gorges, strove with a modicum of success to advertise New England. It published *A Briefe Relation of the Discovery and Plantation of New England,* which described the land and gave a plan for settling and governing it. The next year, 1623, the Council circulated in manuscript among prominent and influential gentlemen "Reasons shewinge the benefitt of Planting in Newe England" (with the endorsement of King James). This document stressed the value of the region both as an outlet for the poor and as a place where younger brothers of the gentry might carve out large estates for themselves.[22]

A Voyage into New England, by Captain Christopher Levett, who made no attempt to promote settlement, was memorable not only for its content but also for a bantering humor seldom encountered in promotion tracts. "To say something of the Country," the author remarks, "I will not do therein as some have done, to my knowledge speak more than is true; I will not tell you that you may smell the corne-fields before you see the Land; neither must men think that corne doth grow naturally (or on trees), nor will the Deare come when they are called, or stand still and looke one a man till he shoot him, not knowing a man from a beast, nor the fish leap into a kettle . . . neither are they so plentifull that you may dip them up in baskets. . . . But certainly there is fowle,

---

21. The unique copy of *An Historicall Discoverie and Relation of the British Plantations in New England* (1627) is in B. M. STC 18484, see "To the Reader."
22. *A Briefe Relation* (1622) is also reprinted in Mass. Hist. Soc., *Collections,* XIX, 1–25; *HMC Exeter,* 166–71.

Deare, and Fish enough for the taking, if men be diligente, there
also be Vines, Plume trees, Cherry-trees, Strawberries, Goosber-
ries, and Raspes, Walnut; and small nuts, of each great plenty.
. . ." 23

The reader may well inquire at this point whether the promotion
tracts actually reached and influenced great numbers of people,
particularly those of the lower orders. Such evidence as survives
indicates that among many persons of all ranks, even among the
"In-Land sort," the idea of colonizing or settling permanently in
communities in trans-oceanic territories, once so novel, was no
longer startling. Captain John Smith relates that when he was
planning a second voyage to the New England coast, he spent
most of the summer of 1616 "visiting the Cities and townes of
Bristoll, Exeter, Barstable, Bodnam, Perin, Foy, Milborow, Sal-
tash, Dartmouth, Absom, Tattnesse, and most of the Gentry in
Cornewall and Devonshire, giving them Bookes and Maps, shewing how in six moneths the most of those ships had made their voyages, and some in lesse, and with what good successe; by which in-
citation they seemed so well contented, as they promised twenty
saile of ships should goe with mee next yeere. . ." About the
year 1621, Smith recalled: "Now all these proofes and this relation
I now [assembled and] called New-Englands triall. I caused *two or
three thousand* of them to be printed: one thousand with a great
many Maps both of Virginia and New-England. I presented to
thirty of the chiefe Companies in London at their Hall, desiring either generally or particularly (them that would) to imbrace" the
design for raising a stock of £5,000 to finance an expedition.24

Additional evidence of the spreading of the information served
up in the promotion tracts, which proved popular as travel literature too, is the use made of Captain Whitbourne's *Discovery and
Discourse of New-found-land*. King James liked it so much that his
Council requested the two archbishops to have collections taken
up in the parish churches to help defray the costs of publication;
the prelates further charged the parish clergy with recommending
the book from the pulpit. The Bishop of London wrote in a diocesan letter to all churchwardens that because the tract tended "to

23. Levett, *Voyage into New England*, 22.
24. Smith, *Travels and Works*, II, 746, 748 (italics mine).

the advancement of his Majesties Plantation by inciting adventurers thereunto as well as for the propagation of the gospel, the clergy are required to signify unto your parishioners in so friendly and effectual a manner as possible you can, and seriously stir up and exhort them to extend their liberality herein, which you the church-wardens are to collect after the due and usuall manner from seat to seat." Among the church ornaments of Cuckfield Parish, Sussex, listed as public property on May 16, 1623, is the pamphlet of Richard Whitbourne, who obviously had not dedicated the treatise to his monarch in vain, as a second printing in 1623 confirms.[25]

Actual conditions for planting in America now appeared to be more auspicious than ever before and buttressed the claims of promoters. Virginia had recovered from the disastrous massacre and the sickly times of 1622–23: the Crown had replaced the Company; the tobacco culture flourished with a world market; and the colonists themselves had achieved self-government in the first royal colony through their House of Burgesses. Bermuda's settlers had enjoyed that right since 1620. In New England, the colonists of New Plymouth had paid off the Weston Associates, and its 500 people seemed destined to have a prosperous future. Along the shores of Massachusetts Bay there existed several small settlements, and a more important one was being established at Salem by the "old planters" from Cape Ann. To the east, in the Province of Maine, a few fishing stations could be found, and far to the northeast, Cecilius, Lord Baltimore, was attempting to colonize Newfoundland. A few Englishmen had seated themselves on the mainland of South America at Wiapoco in Guiana. Finally, and most significant of all, under the ægis of the puritan promoter Thomas Warner, the first permanent foothold in the Caribbean had been gained in 1623 at St. Christopher (St. Kitts); Sir William Courteen's men located at Barbados in 1624/5, and on Nevis in 1628.

25. At Queen's College, Oxford, Thomas Crosfield recorded on 15 April 1628: "Read Captaine Whitbournes book of the new-found-land dedicated to King James 1623, wherein he showes some motives for the encouragement of his subjects to undertake a plantation of sundry Colonyes therein; it lying about the middle way betwixt Ireland and America.—The author dwells at the golden cocke in Pater noster rowe." Crosfield, Diary, 22; Sussex Arch., XLV, 22–3; Whitbourne, A Discourse and Discovery of Newfoundland, Dedication.

By the next year these three small islands contained about 4,550 English and Irish inhabitants—almost half of the King's subjects in the New World. Those on the continent of North America numbered perhaps 3,300; and Bermuda had "above 2000" more.[26]

Here, once more, we may remind ourselves that in the seventeenth century the weight of the printed word was greater than in our own time, for books, sermons, and tracts were read and pondered, not just perused—and usually they were read two or three times over. Thus it fell out that, by the end of the year 1629, a substantial body of Englishmen had come to think and occasionally to dream about, if not to know, a better England in the strange lands to the west. Whether their knowledge of Utopia was sufficient or accurate is for the moment beside the point. The go-to-America-where-it-is-better literature, read directly, listened to, refined in sermons, or merely mentioned in diluted and distorted form in conversations, had done its work.

26. Estimated population of the English colonies, 1629:

Newfoundland	c.	100	
New England		500	(180 in Massachusetts)
[New Netherland]	c.	270	
Virginia		2,500	3,370
Bermuda			2,000
West Indies			
* St. Christopher		3,000	
Barbados		1,400	
* Nevis		150	4,550
			9,920

The figure for St. Christopher in 1629 is very doubtful. Capt. John Smith reported 3,000 settlers there *or going* there, and the Earl of Carlisle sent out a number of ships with passengers. However, the French attacked the English in August; then in September, 36 Spanish ships arrived and their soldiers burned the town at Nevis and left only 200 people alive at St. Kitts; 300 others got home to Plymouth "naked and sick." One of the latter reported that the Spanish carried off 700 men and boys. Nevertheless the population was replenished with remarkable dispatch. *CSP Col., 1554–1660,* pp. 92, 103, 105, 112, 118–19; *Acts of Privy Council, 1628–9,* p. 37; Surely Professor Andrews erred in giving the population of St. Kitts in 1629 as 6,000. *Colonial Period of American History,* I, 204, 223; II, 244, 260; Smith, *Travels and Works,* II, 903, 907, 910; E. B. Greene and V. D. Harrington, *American Population before the Federal Census of 1790* (New York, 1932), 88.

III

The swarming of tens of thousands of Englishmen—like bees indeed—is a phenomenon almost impossible to explain except as a consequence of what we may call national shock. There was abroad in Britain an uneasiness, an anxiety over the discarding of old habits and old loyalties. The people who were cut adrift in life, deprived of familiar occupations, and bereft of family and nearest of kin bobbed up and down, mentally, on a sea of indecision; the former reliance on aid from established authority in church and state no longer sufficed. Beyond all else, the Church of England had failed to provide spiritual satisfaction for many a man and woman. Such a collective change of outlook can be understood only as expressing the sum of the sentiments of each individual concerned and in the light of his immediate personal spiritual and material states. There were as many reasons for emigrating as there were emigrants.

The hardships, difficulties, and unsettling conditions which Englishmen had faced for the half-century between 1590 and 1640, and which we have rehearsed in detail, had always dogged the average man. Depressions, epidemics, wars, etc., may be designated as *propelling forces* which tend to drive people out; they were what Cushman meant when he spoke of "the straitenesse of the place." In themselves they were not sufficiently intolerable to make men leave home. Concurrently, other factors, strong *attracting forces,* from without the island drew men off. Success stories about planters in America, letters from satisfied colonists, and the compelling lure of the promotion literature picturing a better England, one lacking old England's woes, played on men's minds. Now, for the first time, ordinary folk caught a glimpse of the possibility of making a new start, and they took hope: *In Deo Speramus.* Shakespeare had Claudio say, "The miserable have no other medicine but only hope." By 1629 a new hope had become the great catalyst, and a host of ordinary Englishmen accepted in both a spiritual and a material sense the merit of Sir William Vaughan's pronouncement: "That's my Countrie which gives me well-being." [27]

The merchants who had added transporting passengers to the carrying of supplies in their own and leased vessels had to devise methods for locating and recruiting the ever-larger numbers of poor, worthy husbandmen of rural England and their artisan counterparts of the towns and cities. Bristol traders leaned on long-standing connections with Ireland: some of them had participated in the flooding of England with Celtic peasants in the first years of the century, and they had opened a considerable commerce with Derry and Coleraine after 1610. The London mercantile community concocted means to lure English artificers and husbandmen for their Londonderry plantation: in 1616 the justices of the Middlesex Court of Quarter Sessions heard from a master cutler and an instrument-maker that Richard Lightfoot, a gentleman of High Holborn, had been enticing apprentices to leave their masters and go to Ireland. This same year the Irish Society planned to send twelve boys from Christ's Hospital, with "other poor children," to Ulster to be bound out as apprentices. It is logical to assume that some of the members of the Virginia Company who shared in the Ulster experiment promptly borrowed the methods of their fellows in the city companies.[28]

Permanent and profitable planting required an abundant labor force for each colony. "Let the Planters be honest, skilfull, and painfull people," was the advice of Fuller, and his words were cogent, for it was soon evident that the visible urban poor made unsatisfactory colonists, and besides, very few of them wanted to emigrate. The dregs of society, having very little energy or ambition and being idle by habit, usually prefer to live out their lives where they are, no matter how wretched their lot. Although apprentices and journeymen from the towns and cities were much in demand in the plantations, the new colonies needed farmers most

27. James A. Williamson, *The Caribbee Islands under the Proprietary Patents* (Oxford, 1926), 7–9; *Measure for Measure*, III, i, 2–3; Vaughan, *Golden Fleece*, Pt. III, 8.

28. Although the Irish and Virginia enterprises began at about the same time and there were connections between them, it should be noted that Sir Francis Bacon remarked in 1611 that Virginia differed as much from Ireland "as Amadis de Gaul differs from Caesar's Commentaries." *Life and Letters of Francis Bacon,* ed. J. Spedding (London, 1868), IV, 123; Moody, *Londonderry Plantation,* 168, 185, 347–8; *Middlesex Sessions,* n. s., III, 175–6.

of all, and since the urban poor had long since lost any knowledge of husbandry they might once have possessed, the promoters and merchants more and more turned their attention to the countryside whence came ultimately the majority of the young men sent to America.[29]

For years the merchants had been dispatching agents into the counties to collect and distribute cloth and other goods, and now they used them to recruit emigrants. They resorted to all the familiar devices for creating and guiding opinion favorable to the idea of colonizing. To reach youths of a religious turn, their agents planted tracts and sermons, which they paid to have printed, in church porches, and they posted handbills in the public houses in the centers of towns, in the suburbs, or down by the waterside. At taverns and inns, they made contact with the non-reading element of the poor. Upon meeting wide-eyed and adventurous apprentices, fishermen, mariners come ashore, journeymen craftsmen seeking work, the idle, and the drifters, these agents (soon known as "spirits") lured them into an alehouse, plied them with drink, promised them good wages, eventual grants of land, a chance to raise a family, and a better station in life generally. They also arranged for hired hawkers to sing stirring ballads in the streets.[30]

With the great expansion of the pack-horse and wagon traffic after 1610, the highways were crowded with carriers and broggers (middlemen), responsible, for example, for taking yarn spun from wool in Dorsetshire to the clothiers of Wiltshire and Somersetshire. As colonial requirements for all kinds of manufactured articles developed, agents for the planters made their purchases in many an inland center where goods were cheaper than at the metropolis, as we noted in the case of Richard Ligon of Barbados. The news that there was a demand for men in the plantations circulated along the highroads with these carriers, who, stopping frequently and regularly at inns along the way, broadcast the message to village and farm.[31]

More persuasive with the rustics than even the carriers and pack-

29. Fuller, *Holy and Profane State*, 184.
30. N. Y. Public Library, *Bulletin*, III, 163; *CSPD, 1633–4*, p. 536; Benét, *Western Star*, 24.
31. Bowden, *Wool Trade*, 59–60; Ligon, *Barbados*, 109; Earle, *Microcosmography*, 31.

horsemen were the peddlers and tinkers, who knew rural England and its people as did few others. Traders with tales to tell mingled freely with the rural throngs at the weekly markets and at fairs. After drawing interested yokels into alehouses and giving them shillings, the occasional Autolycus who had actually been overseas could sell anything: the goods in his pack, a promotion tract, a sermon, or the idea of going down to Bristol, or up to London, or to Plymouth and signing on for a rosy future in America where, according to Falstaff, "You may buy land now as cheap as stinking mackerel." One day in Plymouth Town, a former Londoner strode along, singing "Farewell, gay Lundon," for he was going "over the water to Floryda":

> I met a frend of myne
> Who toke me by the hand and sayde
> Cum drynk a pynt of wyne;
> Where you shall here suche news, I fere
> As you abrode wyll compell.[32]

Restless youths from fifteen to twenty-four years of age were the chief targets of the spirits, who probably worked for a commission of so many shillings for each individual they sent to a merchant at one of the ports of embarkation. Some of the lads were discontented or just plain fed up; many were unemployed or else paid a starvation wage; others had no immediate families. A few of the more intelligent among them wanted adventure or the chance to satisfy their curiosity about what they had heard and read of distant lands. Most of them sought fulfillment of vague hopes and ambitions, and as always, everywhere, numbers of boys and young men who lacked any specific goal in life went along like so many aimless sheep because their friends were emigrating. When there was so little to keep them at home, the honeyed words of the emigration agents stirred their imagination, and when small sums were offered to carry them along the road, usually on foot but sometimes on horseback, off they went to the nearest seaport. For all of

32. French merchants, their agents (des rabbateurs), and peddlers (colporteurs), played a primary role comparable to that of the English promoters, in rounding up servants for French colonies. See the capital study by Debien, Les Engagés, 58, 69, 111–12, 165–9; King Henry IV, Pt. I, Act II, iv, 394; Firth, An American Garland, 7.

these, the opportunity of making a promising change was well-nigh irresistible.

Letters sent back by successful colonists helped many a countryman to make the decision to venture overseas, and returned planters on the lookout for prospective servants were even more persuasive. In July, 1623, Henry Homer encountered John Procter from Virginia, who gave such a good account of that colony that Homer decided to go there. The planter provided him with "a man servant," Richard Grove, whose "horse-hire" from London to Portsmouth Homer paid, as well as his food and lodging en route. Mistress Judith Wareham, whose husband was a gentleman planter in Virginia, somehow got to know Jacques Harding, servant to a merchant in Brittany, when he arrived at Southampton in 1634. Meeting him some time later on a street in London, she talked him into going to Virginia to serve her husband for four years.[33]

Most of the young men went to the seaports voluntarily, some of them unsolicited. Many had sufficient private reasons for leaving the country, for emigration to the New World, like the wars, afforded an escape; not a few married men cut themselves loose from family responsibilities and, incidentally, their wives. Masters now and then abandoned their trades to go overseas, leaving their apprentices to be bound out again to other artisans. Countryfolk had long since grown accustomed to seeing relatives and friends leave the farm or village to join the great internal migration of the English begun in the previous century. To go one step farther did not seem as formidable to them as we might think it would.[34]

The reception and treatment given some would-be colonists on their arrival at a port, if typical, were not calculated to encourage further enlistments. A contemporary recounts that as soon as they arrived in London, the emigrants were taken in hand "by such men as we here call Spirits" and "put into Cookes houses about Saint Katherines, where once being entred [they] are kept as Prisoners untill a Master fetches them off; and they lye at charges in

33. *Purchas His Pligrimes*, IV, 1785; *Recs. Va. Co.*, IV, 467; *Southampton Recs.*, III, 5.
34. In 1631 Richard Riall, a shoemaker of Dorchester, "being gone for New England," his apprentice Richard Greene was ordered to serve another master. *Dorchester Recs.*, 425; *Somerset Sessions*, II, *passim*; *Dartmouth Recs.*, DD 61735; *Worcestershire*, II, 337; *Warwick Sessions*, I, 215; II, 49; *CSPD, 1638-9*, p. 424.

these places a moneth or more, before they are taken away. When the Ship is ready, the Spirits charges and the Cooke for dieting paid, they are Shipped, and this charge is commonly" three pounds.[35]

The countrymen, and artisans and mariners of the cities who had also engaged to ship out, naturally chafed at being restricted to the victualing house and under the surveillance of the "Spirit." Like the *engagés* of France, they were rebellious and it was difficult to keep them together for long. John Smyth of Nibley, steward of Berkeley, made arrangements with his agent William Tracy to transport "divers persons" to a "particular plantation" in Virginia from Bristol. In April, 1620, Tracy wrote, "I am now binding my men," whom he had installed at the Horseshoe in Bristol until the ship would be ready to sail. They were still there on July 14, when he wrote in great agitation, "We lose all ouer men if we go not nowe." [36]

When the number of people going out to the Chesapeake and the Caribbean colonies began to soar, emigration agents, or brokers, established offices and announced that they would supply colonists of any age, kind, or calling. Although most of the colonists for the Berkeley enterprise had been recruited in Gloucestershire, John Smyth of Nibley had to procure a blacksmith and ten extra persons in London. For months before the departure of the *Ark* and the *Dove* for Maryland, 1632–33, Cecilius Calvert, Lord Baltimore, kept such an office at the upper end of Bloomsbury, where some Jesuit fathers managed his publicity. John Sadler, who conducted his agency at the Red Lion in Bucklersbury, furnished three servants for youthful Thomas Verney, whose family was shipping him off to Virginia as an early remittance man because of an affair with a woman of low rank. Sadler told Lady Verney that "if I was to sende 40 servants, I coold have them here at a dayes warning." Coopers were scarce, he admitted, and had to be sought in the countryside. Procter, the Virginian who procured the servant for Henry Homer, claimed "that he had dayly choice of men offered to him" by agents who provided services like Sadler's.[37]

35. William Bullock, *Virginia Impartially Examined* (1647), 39.
36. Debien, *Les Engagés,* 71; N. Y. Public Library, *Bulletin,* III, 248, 254.
37. N. Y. Public Library, *Bulletin,* III, 251, 252, 254; Andrews, *Colonial Period of American History,* II, 285, 288, 289; *Camden,* LVI, 160; *Recs. Va. Co.,* IV, 67;

In order to furnish all of the passengers requested by ships' masters, emigration agents applied to municipal authorities who were burdened with the care of orphans and abandoned children. The Corporation of London occasionally made vagrant children available for apprenticing in Barbados and Virginia instead of binding them out at home. Winchester officials once paid sixty shillings for the appareling of six poor boys destined for the Old Dominion. In 1625 the Northampton leaders seriously considered seeking a vent for their surplus poor of all ages in Virginia; the same year a Captain Baylie proposed that 3,000 poor be planted in the Chesapeake region or in New England annually—the expense to be met by voluntary contributions. The statement contained in a letter of 1627 that "fourteen or fifteen hundred children" had been "gathered up in divers places" and shipped to Virginia is probably a gross exaggeration, but ship lists do reveal that many boys aged fourteen did go out to the colonies.[38]

Competition at London and the outports for emigrants increased as the insatiable demands of the planters outran the supply. English emigration agents and ships' captains began to call at ports in southern Ireland as early as 1620 to take up peasants to fill out their passenger cargoes: it was there that William Tracy completed the personnel for the *Supply* out of Bristol for Virginia that very year. Daniel Gookin from Carrigaline, county Cork, arrived in Virginia in November, 1622, bringing about forty Irish peasants "wholly uppon his own Adventure." When he settled them near Newport News, Governor Wyatt wrote to the Company in London that "wee doe conceive great hope iff the Irish plantation p'sper, that from Ireland great multitude of people will be like to come hither." Arrivals from Erin did continue. When Thomas Anthony went there to recruit servants for his employer, he learned that a Flemish ship from Amsterdam was ready to clear outward

---

Narratives of Early Maryland, 1633–1684, ed. Clayton C. Hall (New York, 1910), 70.

38. No more than 120 to 180 felons were transported to the English colonies before 1640. Abbot Emerson Smith, *Colonists in Bondage: White Servitude and Convict Labor in America,* 1607–1776 (Chapel Hill, 1947), 90–94, 358–9; Hamilton, *Quarter Sessions,* 113; *Hampshire Notes & Queries,* IV, 82–3; *HMC Montagu,* 109; *CSPD, 1623–5,* p. 521; *1631–3,* p. 433; Edward D. Neill, *Virginia Carolorum (1625–1685)* [Albany, 1869], 46–7.

with 120 to 140 passengers for St. Christopher, and that an Irish vessel in the harbor would sail there in a month with 100 more.[39]

Information about the procuring of Irish servants is exceedingly scarce, but there exists one excellent account of 1636 describing how Matthew Cradock, Puritan merchant of London and the first governor of the Massachusetts-Bay Company, filled out his passenger list for the *Abraham*. In April of that year, months before the sailing of the ship, he sent a supercargo, Thomas Anthony, to Kinsale to round up as many servants as possible up to a hundred. Anthony asked his friends in Kinsale to make it "knowen in the Cuntry for the procuringe of servants," though he would not assemble them or pay charges for them until the ship arrived. Next he arranged for a tailor, Hugh Neal, to make clothes for the servants and to supply stockings and blankets. On the first market day after the ship's appearance on August 27, the supercargo reported to Cradock that "bothe heere at Bandon Corke and Yoghall we caused the drume to be Betten, and gave warning to all those that disposed to goe servants for Virginea shuld repare to Kinsale whear I leay and uppon Condisons accordinge to the Cuntry I would intartayne sutch. . . ." Anthony, the master of the ship, and several agents also scoured the countryside roundabout Kinsale for recruits. Once a man agreed to go, he received a glass of beer, and Thomas Belchard of Bandon was given a "pinte of wine and shugar" for his help; the supercargo also disbursed £25 at the Blue Anchor in Kinsale for the servants' diet. When the ship sailed on November 22, there were fifty-six servants on board, including about twenty of "the women kind." During the recruiting Anthony discovered that "every mans mind in thes place" was bent on going to St. Christopher, for the Irish had heard that wages were higher there than in Virginia. Actually, they were landed and sold at Barbados.[40]

39. "Tout le monde veut ganger à servir d'intermédiaire, à recruter des engagés," says Debien of contemporary France. *Les Engagés*, 62; N. Y. Public Library, *Bulletin*, 290–92; *Purchas His Pilgrimes*, IV, 1785; Neill, *Virginia Carolorum*, 36n, 54, 82n; *Recs. Va. Co.*, II, 326; IV, 105; in 1633 Edward Howes dispatched three wolf-dogs to John Winthrop in Boston with an Irish boy to tend them. *Winthrop Papers*, III, 133, 134; Smith, *Colonists in Bondage*, 63.
40. High Court of Admiralty Miscellany, PRO, Bundle HCA, 30/636, cited in Smith, *Colonists in Bondage*, 62–6.

In his *Korte Historiael* (1655), David Pietersz de Vries tells a story which reveals the voracity of some of the English in their pursuit of profits. The author was in Virginia when he learned that his settlement near Cape Henlopen had been destroyed and that his people had agreed with some Englishmen there to sail their barque to the British West Indies. It was understood that the Englishmen would serve as captains and they themselves ostensibly as "servants," but that, when the vessel was sold, they were all to share in the profits. When the ship arrived in the islands, however, the English treacherously sold the Dutch into servitude, and de Vries understandably drew the conclusion that "The English are a villanous people, and would sell their own fathers for servants in the Islands." [41]

In 1621 the treasurer and certain worthy gentlemen of the Virginia Company dispatched twelve women, with the promise of an additional fifty, to become wives of the planters. The Earl of Southampton explained to the Governor and Council of State "that the Plantation can never flourish till families be planted and the respect of wives and children fix the people on the Soyle." One hundred "young and uncorrupt" women had been shipped to Virginia in 1618, and the means used to assemble them approached kidnapping. A clerk in chancery, William Robinson, was convicted and hanged, drawn, and quartered in November, 1618, for counterfeiting the Great Seal of England. He had used his false commission "to take up rich yeomen's daughters (or drive them to compound) to serve his Majestie for breeders in Virginia." In the West of England, at the same time, Owen Evans, a messenger for the Privy Council, pretended to have a commission to press maidens for Virginia and Bermuda and used it to extort bribes at Ottery St. Mary in Devon. Forty young women fled this parish in great fear; even their parents could not find them. After this incident, Evans agreed to free Ottery from his press for ten shillings. At Weston, the pursuivant gave four shillings, as required, in the King's name for four maidens. Another hundred women were shipped to Virginia in 1622, and again the methods were such as to give the Company a bad name. Nor were the colonists all happy about the arrangements, as

41. *Narratives of New Netherland, 1609–1664,* ed. J. Franklin Jameson (New York, 1909), 196.

a letter home explained: "Women are necessary members for the Colonye, but the poore men are never the nearer for them they are so well sould, for I myselfe have ever since coming paid 3 lb sterl. per ann. for my washing, and find sope." [42]

By ruses and devices which will forever remain obscure, women were transported to America after 1629 in considerable numbers; and by 1642 some could be found in every plantation. New Providence had thirty or forty of them in 1635. This same year three ships carried 245 men and 42 women (aged seventeen to thirty-five) to Virginia, a ratio of 5.8 men to 1 woman, which was higher than the average before 1641. The sex ratio of the passengers on the *Mayflower* was almost 2.6 to 1. With the exception of reprieved felons, such as Elizabeth Cottrell from Marshalsea Prison, who asked to be sent to Virginia in 1638, few English women went willingly to any of the colonies except Plymouth and Massachusetts Bay before 1642. On the other hand, the young, lusty, and strong-bodied colleens of Ireland from seventeen to thirty-five years old appeared "Reddear to goe then men," if Thomas Anthony's findings were typical. It would be a long time before family life of the kind that many of the men and women had known in Old England could be reconstituted in any of the colonies from Maryland southward to Barbados. [43]

Most of the people assembled by the emigration agents were too poor to pay their own passages, and many of them needed clothing; they were, however, free persons. To transport them, the merchants borrowed from the apprentice system the well-known device of the indenture—a contract entered into voluntarily before departure by the emigrant with a merchant, sea captain, or occasionally another and more prosperous emigrant, who needed labor for his plantation. The indenture, which could be transferred or sold to another master, usually stipulated that, in return for pas-

42. M. Debien could find only 30 cases of unattached women (*isolées*) who became *engagées* before 1715. *Les Engagés*, 83, 85. For the first family beginnings in the French West Indies, see Jean Baptiste Du Tertre, *Histoire Générale des Antilles habituées par les Français* (Paris, 1667–71), II, 455; Chamberlain, *Letters*, II, 183; *Recs. Va. Co.*, I, 255–6, 269, 566; II, 26; III, 493; IV, 231; *CSPD, 1611–18*, p. 586.
43. Smith, *Colonists in Bondage*, 64–5; *CSP Col., 1574–1660*, pp. 217, 281–2; *NEHG Reg.*, II, 268, 374–5; III, 184, 388, 389; *HMC Exeter*, 203–4; Bradford, *History of Plymouth Plantation*, II, 399–402.

sage and clothing, the servant agreed to work for the master or his assignee in the colony for a period ranging from three to seven years, commonly four. During this time he was to be fed, clothed, and housed by the master. Further provisions, such as a promise of land, seeds, tools, or other freedom dues, were often inserted in the indenture. John Logward of Bling, Surrey, indentured himself in 1628 to Edward Hurd, ironmonger of London, to be transported to work on Hurd's Virginia plantation for four years. Logward made his mark on the documents, which were signed, sealed, and delivered in the presence of two other bound servants.[44]

Working out one's passage was a familiar and actually not inhumane way for a poverty-stricken man or woman to get to America and there enjoy a modicum of security for a few years until he or she was ready to go it alone. Sir George Peckham may have been the first to propose the adoption of the apprentices' indentures for colonizing in 1582 when he said of Sir Humphrey Gilbert's adventure: ". . . there are great numbers (God he knoweth) which live in such penurie and want, as they could be contented to hazard their lives, and to serve one yeare for meate, drinke and apparell only, without wages, in hope thereby to amend their estates. . . ." Indentured servitude became the accepted means for peopling the private or "particular" plantations in Virginia after 1620, and five years later the colony contained 487 bound servants (a mere forty-six of them females), one-third of the total population of 1,227. The practice spread quickly to the West Indies, and on June 8, 1636, the London printer Nicholas Bourne was licensed by the Stationers' Company to print two standard blank indenture forms, one suitable for Virginia and the other for St. Christopher and the Somer Islands.[45]

---

44. An indenture was a mutual covenant between two parties, executed in two or more copies all having their tops or sides correspondingly *indented*, or notched, for identification and security. By extension, it meant a labor contract by which an apprentice was bound to the master or by which a person bound himself to labor in the colonies. *Oxford English Dictionary;* Neill, *Virginia Carolorum,* 57.
45. Now and then a young man of property chose to become an indentured servant in the plantations. When Edward Dewell of Warrasqueake, Virginia, died in 1636, he left a "Hoasthouse or Inn" at Reading in Berkshire, and a sum of money. *Virginia Magazine of History and Biography,* XIII, 204; *Recs. Va. Co.,* IV, 128–9; Richard Hakluyt, *The Principal Navigations, Voyages, Traffiques, & Discoveries of the English Nation* (Everyman ed., London, 1926), VI, 70;

Not every servant entered into an indenture willingly, and this was definitely the case with recalcitrant minors and orphans. Stephen Thorpe, apprenticed to William Noone, barber of Great Bursted, turned out to be very disorderly and would not abide with his master. When the Essex justices learned in 1639 that he "runneth away and breaketh into men's houses for victuals, and will not be reclaimed," they authorized the master to either keep him or else "dispose of him to sea or some plantation beyond the sea." When orphan children were sent to the colonies, they were indentured to anyone who would pay their passages, and they were customarily bound until they attained their majority. In 1628 Governor Harvey of Virginia asked the City of London to send over 100 poor boys and girls to be bound out as servants upon reaching the plantation.[46]

IV

The highly lucrative plantation trade, which included passengers quite as much as goods in freights for the outward voyage, attained the proportions of Big Business by 1629. Here was a new outlet for investment capital where, though the risks were great, the returns, when they came, were quick and handsome. The merchants of London were the principal beneficiaries of this traffic, but those of the outports from Great Yarmouth all the way down and around the coast to Bristol entered into it to partake of the profits. The trade also stimulated shipbuilding, and, as the men of the time liked to say, it provided "a nursery for English seamen." According to one estimate, from the year 1629 onward during this period, an average of a ship a day departed from England with emigrant passengers bound for the Chesapeake, the Caribbean, or the New England waters.[47]

Perhaps the most convincing testimony to the lure of this commerce was the determined and successful effort of the Dutch to break into it. Sometimes they owed this ascendancy to the con-

Greene & Harrington, *American Population*, 144; *Stationers' Register*, IV, 338; *Proceedings and Debates of the British Parliament*, I, 291–2; Smith, *Colonists in Bondage* is the standard work on white servitude in the colonies.

46. Essex Sessions, XX, 518; *CSP Col., 1574–1660*, p. 100; PRO: C. O. 1:5, 22 f3.

47. Williamson, *English Channel*, 230–31; *CSM*, XLII, 48.

nivance of English adventurers who were seeking to increase their gains by employing the cheaper shipping from the Low Countries —two members of the Virginia Company, on their own venture, dispatched passengers in the *Flying Hart* of Flushing in 1625. At the Cape Verde Islands, during his passage to Virginia in 1630, Governor John Harvey counted "about 40 Holland ships bound to the West Indies." The height of Dutch interloping occurred five years later, when the officers of a great ship of 400 tons went ashore at Cowes and tried "to drawe as many of his Majesties subjects as they can to goe with them by offring them large conditions" for settling at the plantation of the Dutch West India Company on the Hudson River. The Privy Council hastened to order this vessel stayed, and also all English ships in the several ports, to prevent their being used in the service of foreign princes or states without a license to do so. Four of the fifteen "grate ships" that arrived with settlers at Massachusetts Bay in the first six months of 1637 were "duchmen." [48]

The Virginia Company, or the individuals who transported servants, deserved to make a reasonable profit, but the blatant profiteering of English merchants and ship captains engaged in the servant traffic evoked bitter denunciations as early as 1624 from Captain John Smith: ". . . to sell him or her for forty fifty or threescore pounds, whom the Company hath sent over for eight or ten pounds at the most, without regard how they shall be maintained with apparell, meate, drinke and lodging, is odious." After 1627 the cost of transporting a servant to the colonies settled down to £5 to £6 a head and remained there for the entire colonial period; the total charge for procuring, equipping, and sending him to America came to £10 to £12 so that there were still huge gains to be made. To these profits should be added the value of the headright, usually 50 acres of land, awarded to anyone bringing

48. Here was a grievance against Dutch competitors in the New World to match resentment of their actions in the East Indies about which the Britons were told in such tracts as *A Relation of the Unjust, Cruell, and Barbarous Proceeding against the English at Amboyne in the East Indies, by the Netherlandish Governour and Councill There* (1624), which contained a woodcut frontispiece showing a Dutchman torturing an Englishman. The copy in the Bodleian is bound with a Dutch version of the incident of June, 1624. *CSP Col., 1574–1660*, pp. 77, 113; *Acts of the Privy Council, Colonial*, I, 206; *Winthrop Papers*, III, 283; *Winthrop's Journal*, I, 151.

an individual into one of the Chesapeake colonies. Obviously windfalls such as these instigated widespread speculation in cargoes of passengers. It was the kind of commerce that was the answer to a merchant's dream.[49]

Edward Waterhouse pointed out in 1622 in his tract on Virginia that "there went this yeare, neere thirty Saile thither" for fishing along "our Coasts" and returned richly laden, and that the reports of "many hundreds now yearely coming and going" had played an important role in the growth of shipping to Virginia. After the downfall of the Virginia Company in 1624, Captain John Preen of London, merchant, became one of the principal adventurers to furnish the Virginians with servants. In September, 1626, his armed ship, *Peter and John,* 220 tons, took out 100 emigrants, small arms, ammunition, tools, and victuals. The following May he commanded the *Samuel,* 240 tons, accompanied by the *Endeavour,* a pinnace of 100 tons, both of them armed for their voyage to Virginia because of the war with France. Four times during the next year Preen supplied servants and provisions for Virginia and St. Christopher.[50]

After 1627, ship after ship began arriving in Virginia loaded with servants; and some masters were finding sale for them in the new settlements in Maryland. In February Governor West of the former colony declared that the population was approaching 3,000; and by 1634 Virginia was receiving a large share of the Great Migration. A census taken that year listed 5,119 men, women, and children. Few women came in the early days, and, as far as can be determined, females of all ages made up no more than 10 per cent of the population by the end of the period. Despite the high death rate among newcomers, especially in 1635–36,

49. Smith, *Travels and Works,* II, 618; Abbot Smith discusses the costs of transporting servants in *Colonists in Bondage,* 36–41; see also, Norwood, *Voyage to Virginia,* in Force, *Tracts,* III, No. X, p. 4; *Recs. Va. Co.,* IV, 227–8; *Minutes of the Council and General Court of Virginia, 1622–1632, 1670–1676,* ed. H. R. McIlwaine (Richmond, 1924), 160; *Acts of Privy Council, Colonial,* I, 311; *NEHG Reg.,* XLVII, 61–71, 350.

50. Waterhouse, *Declaration of the State of . . . Virginia,* 5; It is clear from the will of Miles Prickett that the "Worshipful Captain Pryn" permitted this humble baker of Canterbury (who made his mark on the parchment) to venture some goods in one of his ships in 1627; Waters, *Gleanings,* I, 206; *Recs. Va. Co.,* II, 438, 495–6; *CSP Col., 1574–1660,* pp. 81, 82, 84–5, 94, 120.

merchants found the servant traffic profitable. George Menefie, who served as an estate agent for some men residing in England, invested heavily in the burgeoning trade. Not only did he bring in servants, but he obtained a grant of 3,000 acres in 1639 for transporting sixty persons.[51]

One of the most enterprising London merchants to take advantage of the new sea lanes opened to the west was Samuel Vassall, a Puritan member of the Levant Company. Already in the eastward trade to the Adriatic by 1617, he had pioneered the vending of Surrey-made cloth at Ragusa. A decade later he exhibited toward the forced loans an unsubmissive attitude—compounded of Puritanism, commercialism, and politics—which promptly convinced the authorities to shut him up in the Marshalsea. When he declined in 1629 to pay tonnage and poundage on 4,638 hundredweight of imported currants, the Crown confiscated the currants and imprisoned him again. Yet another detention in 1630—this time over a Virginia shipload of "that drug called tobacco"—raised piteous cries from the poor Surrey weavers whom Vassall's absence from trading left "clean without work and ready to starve." These were only three of the numerous times in the span of "about sixteen years" when Vassall's independent spirit landed him inside the Marshalsea, the Fleet, or the Gatehouse.[52]

More circumspectly, in 1629, he had become a charter member of the Massachusetts-Bay Company, subscribed £50, and extended the scope of his activities to the New World. Soon, in 1630, he undertook to aide George, Lord Berkeley, Sir William Boswell, and two Huguenots in establishing a new settlement somewhere in "Carolana"—a shadowy region east of the Mississippi and north of

51. James Truslow Adams fixed the population of Maryland in 1642 at 1,500, but a report of 207 tithables for that year indicates that the number was nearer a thousand. *The Founding of New England* (Boston, 1921), map facing p. 120; Greene & Harrington, *American Population*, 123. For Virginia, *CSP Col., 1574–1660*, pp. 5, 88, 89, 201, 208, 231, 256, 264; Neill, *Virginia Carolorum*, 114–15*n*, 127, 128, 145; *NEHG Reg.*, II, 268, 374–5; III, 184, 388, 389–90; *Acts of the Privy Council, Colonial*, I, 237–8, 258–9, 288–9, 292–3; *Winthrop Papers*, III, 276; B. M., Add. MSS, 24, 516, fol. 115; *WMQ*, 2d ser., XI, 69.

52. *CSP Venetian, 1632–6*, p. 461; *CSPD, 1637–8*, pp. 104–5; Rushworth, *Historical Collections*, I, 653, Appendixes, 57, 59; *Acts of the Privy Council, 1629–30*, pp. 6, 9, 10, 217; *Acts of the Privy Council, Colonial*, I, 149, 206, 208–10, 211, 221, 222; Pearl, *London*, 74–5, 78.

the Gulf of Mexico. From time to time thereafter he engaged in the passenger traffic to Virginia, to St. Christopher in the West Indies, and possibly to New England. Eventually he tried the slave traffic from Guinea to Barbados.[53]

When the City voters elected Vassall to represent them in both the Short and the Long Parliaments in 1640, he was one of the foremost plantation merchants, one who possessed valuable interests in the three principal theaters of English colonization. It was natural that, in 1643, when he had been for more than a year a Navy Commissioner, Parliament nominated him also to the Commission headed by Robert Rich, Earl of Warwick, Governor-in-Chief and Lord High Admiral of all the Plantations in America. These absentee Commissioners, not surprisingly, favored Vassall's Massachusetts-Bay Company with a grant of all the lands in the Narragansett Country, strengthened the Providence Plantations by incorporation, and ignored everyone else in New England, thereby sowing seeds of future discord.[54]

A market for servants in the English Caribbean colonies opened promptly with the establishment of each settlement. Nine merchants joined in to send Charles Wolfenstone with sixty-four persons to locate in Barbados in 1628; thereafter the planters of this island could never get enough servants. The *Bonaventure* cleared Plymouth for St. Christopher in February, 1633, with thirty-five husbandmen on board who were bound to serve three or four years; nearly all of them hailed from Devon and Cornwall. The *Margaret* transported twenty-eight husbandmen (nine of them under twenty, nineteen from twenty to thirty years old) under the same conditions. William Whiteway noted in his Diary under April 4, 1634: "This day . . . John Harvey of Lime [Regis] went into St. Christophers Island." Such planters naturally drew on their own shires for indentured servants. Men of many trades besides farmers were soon being recruited for Tobago and the other islands. In December, 1639, the authorities licensed four ships—*Planter, Bonaventure, Love,* and *Marcus*—to carry 900 passengers to Barbados. The cargoes of the first two vessels consisted of 200 and 250 servants,

53. *CSP Col., 1574–1660*, pp. 115, 120, 190–91, 197–9, 305–6, 324, 331, 338, 339.
54. William Hubbard, *A General History of New England* (Boston, Mass., 1815), 122; Pearl, *London*, 113, 189–91.

also 550 dozen shoes, 550 shirts, 550 pairs of drawers, 50 dozen Monmouth caps, £ 80 worth of tools, 20,000 nails, oil, and "quantities of provisions." The *Victory* cleared for the same destination on February 29, 1640, with 200 passengers and a like lading of goods, plus soap, powder, balls, candles, muskets, and butter. To hasten the settling of the West Indies, a system known as "mateship" evolved, by which an English merchant entered into a partnership with a prospective planter whom he financed in the purchase of land, tools, and equipment, and whom he also supplied with servants cheaper than those purchased off the ships.[55]

Of the Earl of Carlisle's many islands, only Barbados and St. Christopher were inhabited by Englishmen prior to 1629, but during the following decade many planters and their servants settled on Montserrat, Antigua, St. Lucia, and Barbuda. Eventually Negro slaves were introduced: it was resolved in 1636 that "Negroes and Indians, that came . . . to be sold, should serve for Life, unless a Contract was before made to the contrary." By 1642 the insular population had risen remarkably, though it stretches one's credibility to accept the wild guesses which were made by contemporaries and which have been used uncritically by many writers ever since. James Hay, Earl of Carlisle, estimated the population of his Caribbean islands in 1639 at 20,000, and it is probable that when we add 3,000 Bermudians and about 300 settlers of the Providence Island Company to the cargoes of white servants and Negro slaves subsequently imported, the West Indian colonies in 1642 could not have contained more than 27,000 or 28,000 souls of all ages.[56]

55. The *Mayflower* carried 150 persons from London to Bermuda in 1641, a time when the flow of people to New England was ceasing. *CSP Col., 1574–1660*, p. 322; *Memoirs of the First Settlement of the Island of Barbados and the Caribbee Islands* (1741), 3–10; *Acts of the Privy Council, Colonial*, I, 270–71, 278; Whiteway, Diary, 210 (fol. 200); *HMC Exeter*, 203–4; Richard Pares, "Merchants and Planters," in *Ec. Hist. Rev.*, Supplement 4 (1960), 5; *NEHG Reg.*, XIV, 339–41, 347.

56. Two examples of overestimating the populations of the two most populous islands will suffice: the 4,000 people reported in 1635 to be in St. Christopher by an English merchant, who had lived there four years prior to that time, included both the English and French settlements, but Sir Charles Lucas accepted the high figure of 12,000 to 13,000 for 1637 from a secondary source. Sir Thomas Warner, who was in a position to know, reported in 1636 that Barbados contained "about 6000 English." We know that there were also some Negroes, but not their number.

Once the settlement of the West Indies began, emigration went "steadily forward." English and Irish servants sailed there in ships chartered by the Earl of Carlisle, or were transported by such traders as Sir Samuel Saltonstall, Maurice Thompson, Samuel Vassall, and lesser merchants of Dartmouth, Plymouth, and other outports. With few exceptions, the emigrants were gathered up from all parts of England; there were no families, and until the middle of the 1630's not many single women chanced going there. From the political and social confusion bordering on anarchy, it would seem that fewer men with capacity for leadership settled in the Caribbean colonies than in the Chesapeake settlements. Thomas Verney wrote to his father from Barbados that the law was "indifferent good," but it would be better "were it not for some justices that doth make laws one court, and break them the next." [57]

After the rewards of engaging in the servant traffic became man-

---

A list of 1638 gives the names of 766 persons, all of whom possessed more than ten acres of land. What then are we to make of an official statement of only five years later (1643) which gave the population as consisting of 18,600 effective men, 8,300 more landed proprietors, and 6,400 Negro slaves—a grand total of 33,300! Certain conditions of that day must be considered before any reliable judgment can be made: (1) it was very hard to persuade English youths to go to the West Indies as servants, and harder still to lure young women there; (2) prior to 1642 there could not have been much family life in the islands, and, therefore, birth-rate never approached the well-known high death-rate; (3) considering the large proportion of deaths among white servants, English and Irish, something approaching one-quarter to one-third (8,325 to 11,100) more servants would have had to be imported before 1642 to ensure a population of 33,300; and (4) inasmuch as the other colonies were receiving large shipments of human cargoes, it is extremely doubtful if enough shipping existed to transport such great numbers of people to the Caribbean, even with the aid of Dutch ships, which were also occupied supplying the continental plantations. *Winthrop's Journal,* I, 151; F. W. N. Bayley, *Four Years' Residence in the West Indies* (London, 1832), 669, 680, quoted in C. P. Lucas, *A Historical Geography of the British Colonies* (2d ed., rev., Oxford, 1905), II, 143; and in *Notes and Queries,* VI, 419; *CSP Col., 1661–8,* p. 528; For other contemporary estimates of populations in the smaller islands, see John Oldmixon, *The British Empire in America* (London, 1741), II, 227, 236 (Montserrat and Nevis); *Acts of the Privy Council, Colonial,* I, 290 (St. Lucia); *CSP Col., 1574–1660,* pp. 131, 182, 194, 217, 240, 254, 291, 295 (Association [Tortuga] and Providence Island.). There are just not enough reliable figures to permit sound estimates of the Caribbean populations; the only certainty is that they have been grossly exaggerated. On the legalizing of slavery in Barbados in 1636, see *Memoirs of Barbados,* 20.

57. Williamson, *Caribbee Islands,* 65; Waters, *Gleanings,* II, 1349; *CSP Col., 1574–1660,* I, 305–6; *NEHG Reg.,* LVII, 64; *Camden,* LVI, 192–3.

ifest, there were never enough recruits available for all those who wanted to share in it. Like their Dutch competitors, English masters from the Channel Islands hit upon the expedient of completing cargoes in France. In 1639 a Captain Jonas of Jersey and his brother-in-law Lautrey tricked 200 young Frenchmen into going to St. Servan, close to St. Malo, where they entertained them for three months—after they had signed them up for service in Barbados for five, six, or seven years. For this entire group, the English masters were to pay 900 livres' (about £45) worth of cotton goods on the ship's arrival at the island. Fate intervened and deprived the Englishmen of their hoped-for earnings, however, for the youths all died within a brief time of their reaching Barbados.[58]

The planters who went out to the Caribbean islands usually received grants of land or purchased tracts from the proprietary. In 1631, Sir Henry Colt spoke forthrightly to some of them. "You are all young men, of good dessert, if you would but bridle the excesse of drinking, together with the quarelsome conditions of your fyery spirits." He also criticized their management of their servants, whom "you keep to Idly; they continually pestered our shipp without any occasion or acquayntance, lingringe sometimes 24 houres with us . . . to avoyde labour, which I am persuaded few of you looke after." In ten days spent at a plantation, he claimed he never saw a man working. Thomas Verney, who, as a young scapegrace, had been shipped out to Virginia by his mother, returned to England and then voluntarily went out to Barbados in 1638. He considered that island "the best and healthfullest in all the westerne islands," but he penned a graphic description of the drunkenness which bore out Sir Henry's charges. It would be misleading to apply Clarendon's famous passage about the "men who had retired thither only to be quiet, and to be free from the noise and oppressions in England" to these earlier years.[59]

58. Document quoted in Debien, Les Engagés, 86–7.
59. The deaths from a burning fever and the bloody flux of Robert Hayman and, shortly thereafter, of his partner, Edward Ellman, both of Exeter, who went to settle at Wiapoco in Guiana in 1630, with 100 servants and supplies, were typical of the fates of planters who went out expecting to make a fortune. Southampton Recs., II, 65–6; III, 76; Colonizing Expeditions to the West Indies and Guiana, 1623–1677, ed. Vincent T. Harlow (Hakluyt Society, 2d ser, LVI), 65–6; Camden, LVI, 192–3; Clarendon, History of the Rebellion, V, 262.

The "western islands" had the soil and the climate to produce exotic crops, and the men who went out there hoped to carve out large estates for themselves and to reap a fortune from agriculture. Thomas Verney, soliciting aid from his father, claimed to have raised many fruits, vegetables, pepper, cinnamon, ginger, etc., but he had neither the means or the knowledge of how to ship them. Cotton and a rank grade of tobacco were exported; of the latter, John Winthrop received ten pounds from his son Henry in Barbados. It was so "verye ill conditioned, fowle, full of stalkes and even coloured" that he had been unable to dispose of it for his son. After 1641 Pieter Brouwer successfully introduced the culture of sugar from Brazil, and it was not until then that the gentlemen who went out to the Caribbean and became great sugar planters made the Caribbees the most precious of the King's overseas dominions. Before that time, the servants and small holders were the dominant element, and they often paid with their lives for the failure of their society to form as Englishmen would have liked.[60]

In their determination to make every shilling they could out of each voyage, merchants and ship captains booked more passengers than they could safely accommodate. There is no question that overcrowding and bad food were responsible for the deaths of some of the servants; John West, governor of Virginia, blamed the "great mortality" of 1635/6 on the merchants: ". . . I find with all that much imputation indeservedly lyeth upon the Countrye, by the Merchants crime whoe soe pester their shippes with passengers, that though [through] throng and noysomeness they bring noe lesse than infection among us which is so easily to be distinguished from any cause in the malignitie of the clymate, that where the most pestered shipps sent their passengers, they carry with them almost a general mortallitye. . . ." Shipboard deaths could mean heavy losses for the promoters. Lawrence Evans, a merchant of London, invested £2,000 in servants and goods in 1636, but his "factor" or supercargo died during the voyage and the whole return was embezzled.[61]

60. *Camden*, LVI, 192, 193; Andrews, *Colonial Period of American History*, II, 253; Ligon, *Barbados*, 28; *Colonizing Expeditions to the West Indies*, xxxvi–viii.
61. Neill, *Virginia Carolorum*, 130; *CSP Col., 1574–1660*, p. 258; *Winthrop Papers*, III, 276.

The emigrants to both the Chesapeake and the Caribbean were composed overwhelmingly of individuals with proportionately very few women and fewer families. In a memorial of 1637 to the Privy Council, the problem of getting certificates for the emigrants going to Virginia was brought out: "most of those who go thither have ordinarily no habitations, can bring no certificates and are better out than within the kingdom." When one recalls that the plague was ravaging the realm in 1636 and the effect that it and enclosures had on families, he should not wonder that the young and homeless survivors were ready and willing to emigrate. The sailing lists of two shiploads in 1635 reveal the comparative youth of the passengers: 87 were in the 14–20 age-group; 103 were from 21 to 30; and 17 of them ranged from 31 to 40. This concentration of youth in the human cargoes was typical of the whole migration. It also helps to explain why a petition of a few years later described the passengers who sailed on the *Rebecca* and the *Honor* "for the most part miserable poor people." These people were shipped as cargo. Secretary Richard Kemp informed Sir Francis Windebank in 1638: "scarce any but are brought in as merchandise to make sale of." [62]

In an ordinance proposed in the House of Lords in 1643, it was stated that "many thousands of the natives and good subjects of this kingdom of England through the oppression of the prelates and other ill-affected ministers and officers of state, have of late years, to their great grief and miserable hardships, been inforced to transplant themselves and their families into several islands, and other desolate and remote parts of the West Indies. . . ." [63]

The migration to colonies south of Maryland was not one of groups; no ministers led their flocks. We know, however, from the examination of life in England in the earlier chapters of this volume that nearly all of the young men and women who were lured away from their homeland held ultra-Protestant religious opinions like those of their friends at home. Where they were not avowedly

---

62. Professor Andrews (*Colonial Period of American History*, I, 207) believed that 75 per cent of the Virginians who came over before 1642 were indentured servants. For an argument for a much smaller percentage, see *Virginia Magazine of History and Biography*, VIII, 441–2.
63. *CSP Col., 1574–1660*, pp. 261, 268; *NEHG Reg.*, II, 112–13, 268, 321, 374–5; *Virginia Magazine of History and Biography*, IX, 271.

Puritans, at the very least they entertained many puritan views which were more extreme than those of their parish clergy, and very few concurred with Archbishop Laud and the Arminians. The majority of the emigrants, those who located in Virginia and established the Low-Church heritage among a population that included not a few Puritans, may be labeled non-separating puritans. Though no family or congregation existed to foster the sentiments held by the single man or woman, and their status as servants further hindered their religious welfare, the patent fact is that the hordes of emigrants were by nurture and conviction Bible-readers, psalm-singers, and, before they left their homeland, great attenders at sermons. After all, they were Englishmen. Though both the Virginians and the Barbadians earnestly solicited Governor John Winthrop and the Massachusetts elders in 1642 to send them "some godly ministers," still organized religion did not measurably affect the creation of these new societies.[64]

Ecclesiastical authorities at home quickly grew concerned about the puritan element's influence in Bermuda, and of course the Providence Island Company was promoted by such "Puritan Grandees" as Lord Say and Sele, Lord Brooke, John Pym, and Robert Rich, Earl of Warwick; the royalists charged that the company's offices were centers of sedition. Certainly no one can deny the religious emphasis in the promotion literature.[65]

The formation and growth of a stable and flourishing society in the Chesapeake Bay plantations before 1642 was profoundly limited by the fact that the settlers came as individuals and were chiefly youthful bondsmen. In that year, Virginia had about 8,000 inhabitants, and Lord Baltimore's new colony of Maryland about 1,000; and of this total of 9,000 more than three-quarters were recently imported servants. These indentured immigrants had to serve three or four years before they could set up as freeholders, and very few had a chance to marry in the first years. A longer

64. Captain Philip Bell, Puritan, sometime governor of Bermuda and Providence Island, and, in 1643, Governor of Barbados, wrote to John Winthrop complaining about "divers sects of familists" sprung up among those of "mean quality" in his island. *Winthrop's Journal*, II, 73, 142–3; Beer, *Origins of British Colonial Policy*, 263n; *Acts of the Privy Council, Colonial*, I, 241–2; *Memorials of Bermuda*, I, 397–9.

65. *Proceedings and Debates of the British Parliament*, I, 147.

time elapsed before the most enterprising freemen could develop any capacities for leadership. In 1642 the scions of the country gentry of Kent and Essex, who figured so prominently later on in the affairs of the Old Dominion, were only beginning to learn about the opportunities for building estates and rising to power overseas. Some sea captains of the tobacco and servant ships and a few merchants had already begun to acquire land by deft use of headrights, grants wheedled out of friendly governors, and occasional purchases, but this society of former servants was only just ready by the outbreak of the Civil War to receive the refugees who would determine its ultimate form.[66]

66. *CSP Col., 1574–1660*, p. 123.

XII

The Puritan Hegira

THE STATEMENT of an unknown writer on the Old Dominion of about 1650 applied to all of the plantation colonies: . . . "Its observed that Virginia thrives by keeping many servants, and these in strict obedience. New England conceit they and their Children can doe enough, and soe have rarely above one servant: and by their gross and foolish indulgence, slave themselves to their Children and Servants, giving them 2s. a day for their worke." This obviously Anglican commentator cut right to the marrow of the question by distinguishing the primary differences between the two forms of colonial societies. The soundness of his conclusion, however, can be assessed only after we examine the nature of the New England segment of the Great Migration.[1]

The exodus of the English Puritans to New England, 1629–42, was, and still is, unique in the annals of migration. This flight of groups whose members shared a religious ideal, a sense of destiny, and a firm conviction that God wanted them to depart from their corrupt homeland and settle in the New England Canaan, had no counterpart elsewhere, not even in the Puritan Providence Island experiment or the Bermuda Plantation.

In many ways this hegira differed radically from the emigration to the Chesapeake and Caribbean colonies. The Puritans who composed the movement were representative of the English people

1. B. M. Egerton MSS, 2,395, fol. 415b; also quoted in Smith, *Colonists in Bondage*, 29.

we have been studying in these pages. Save for the great nobles and the very poor, all ranks of society, both sexes, and persons of all ages, from the babe Seaborn Cotton to several octogenarians, went to the promised land voluntarily—the few servants included —and most of them paid their own way.

The suddenness with which the Puritan migration started, and its very magnitude, have long puzzled historians, largely because they have seldom examined it against the prevailing background of doubt and change in the land, or as the final phase of the entire Great Migration of the English, which, in 1629, had already been going on for ten years. The fact is that the flight of the Puritans resulted from a combination of long-range planning and daring, rapid improvisation at the right moment—the keys to success for the army of the Lord quite as much as for that of any monarch —by a group of remarkable, determined men, who knew exactly what they were doing. Spiritually, morally, practically, its leadership has never been rivaled.

The most striking fact about this remarkable movement is that, once it got under way, by dint of able leadership, it quickly generated a dynamic momentum of its own. Here was no artificially stimulated, haphazard outpouring of individual Englishmen to serve mercantile ends. The massive religious concern of the English people, and of the Puritans in particular, impelled these emigrants to abandon England to save their souls; only secondarily did economic or social considerations figure in their decisions. A majority of the rank and file, as well as the leaders, believed firmly that they had discovered the Northwest Passage to Utopia where they could be "merry in the Lord" and eventually attain everlasting salvation. A hostile contemporary testified in 1640 to the driving force of religion: "Allmost it exceeds a wonder, how manye of fair quallitye alien[ate] and sell their whole estates in their old to shuffle themselves, Wives and Children into their New England. Blinde Zeal, and more Blind Seducers doe so gull and Cheate their Conscience, that willingly they make exchange of theire Reason and Knowledge for credulous simplicitye, willful Ignorance." [2]

2. George Donne, Virginia Reviewed, B. M., Harleian MSS, 7021, fols. 312v–313.

II

Early in the third decade of the seventeenth century, certain Puritans worried about the future; they feared not only for their families and friends in the Church of England but for England itself. We do well here at Groton, John Winthrop explained to Thomas Fones (his "very lovinge Brother" in London) on January 29, 1621/2. "We might rejoyce greatly in our owne private good, if the sence of the present evill tymes, and the feare of worse did not give occasion of sorrowe." This uneasiness merged into a vague desire to leave England, for in April, 1623, Winthrop mentioned to his son John, who was at Trinity College in Dublin: "I wish oft God would open a waye to settle me in Ireland, if it might be for his glorye." Toward the end of that year, Winthrop joined Robert Reyce and others in drawing up twenty-three "Common Grevances Groaninge for Reformation," which they hoped would be redressed by Parliament.[3]

During the 1620's, a group of conforming puritans in the West Country had been active in promoting a godly fishing settlement in New England. Their inspirations and guidance came from two clergymen: Master John White, the "Patriarch of Dorchester" and a contributor to the Feoffees for Impropriations, and Arthur Lake, Bishop of Bath and Wells, and a contemporary of White's at New College. Although the experiment of fishing and farming failed completely, Mr. White and the treasurer of the Dorchester Company, John Humfry, who was married to a sister of the Earl of Lincoln and resided near Dorchester, retained their faith in the enterprise. The minister informs us that they conferred "casually with some Gentlemen of London" and urged them to add some of their number to the "Committee" for "the New England business." We can say with a certain measure of confidence that, working after the manner of John Preston "by an Engine which the world sees nothing of" (and which left few traces for later-day historians), John White, Esq., "an honest Councellor at Law," and Hugh Peter were the Londoners with whom Humfry and Master John White spoke concerning their project, and that in 1628 they com-

3. *Winthrop Papers*, I, 268, 281, 295–310.

bined to shift the Company's activities from Dorchester to London, where all Puritan operations were concentrated.[4]

When the business of promoting "a new Colony upon the old foundation" had been transferred to the metropolis, agitation began afresh. Some Puritan notables disapproved of the proposition; others showed their "good affection to the worke" by offering the "helpe of their purses, if fit men might be procured to goe over. . . ." Thus, in 1628, was formed the New England Company for a Plantation in Massachusetts-Bay, for which the West Country adventurers procured a patent to a great tract of land from the Council for New England. The undertakers were ready to establish a Puritan refuge in New England. Fourteen of the adventurers signed the strongly puritanical instructions given to John Endecott before he sailed out to govern the new colony in June, 1628. Among them were a John White (presumably the barrister), Hugh Peter, a fellow student of John Humfry at Trinity College, Cambridge, who recently had acted as agent for the Feoffees in soliciting funds and was a good friend of Master John White, and two other Feoffees, Richard Davis and George Harwood. All of them had ventured £50 in the new enterprise. Master White indicated that there were more gentlemen of substance and estate who might be brought in if the title to the land rested on a more certain foundation.[5]

To guarantee the Company's land grant, John White, the barrister, drafted a petition for a royal charter confirming the grant of the Council for New England. By using his very influential connections, White saw it through the seals. On March 4, 1629, the

4. Frances Rose-Troup's biography of John White contains a mass of material uncritically presented which must be checked with Samuel Eliot Morison, *Builders of the Bay Colony*, 21–50; Newton, *Colonising Activities of the English Puritans*, 41, 45; Whiteway, Diary, fol. 76; John White, *The Planters Plea*, in *The Founding of Massachusetts*, ed. Stewart Mitchell (Boston, 1930), 189–97 [the best edition of the prime source]; Hubbard, *A General History of New England*, 106–7, 116; Fuller, *Church History*, bk. XI, 136–7; Mather, *Magnalia Christi Americana*, bk. III, 175.

5. White, *The Planters Plea*, 195–6; Joseph B. Felt, *Annals of Salem* (Salem, 1845), I, 508–9; Thomas Hutchinson, *History of the Colony and Province of Massachusetts-Bay*, ed. Lawrence S. Mayo (Cambridge, Mass., 1936), I, 10n; Peter, *Dying Father's Last Legacy*, 101. On Hugh Peter, Stearns, *Strenuous Puritan*, is definitive.

New England Company was transformed by the Crown into the Governor and Company of the Massachusetts-Bay in New England. In April and May, a number of ships departed carrying passengers for New England.[6]

Meanwhile, when William Laud was translated to the see of London on July 15, 1628, he commenced his relentless drive against the Puritan lecturers. The Feoffees for Impropriations, reading the handwriting on the wall and convinced that the only way to oppose Episcopacy was through Parliament, astutely directed their militancy into a new channel under the leadership of the lawyer John White. Consequently, the Feoffees and merchants of London, such as the Vassalls and Saltonstalls, as well as merchants in the port towns of Dorset and Devon who had been allied with them, were dismayed when, on March 10, 1629, King Charles dissolved Parliament and embarked on his personal rule.

A concatenation of events precipitated the Puritan emigration in 1629, though Bishop Laud and his underlings looked upon the entire affair as a subversive plot to spread nonconformity and undermine the monarchy—and not without reason. At the time Parliament was dissolved, we know that the idea of emigration was in the air all over England; concurrently the French spoke of "ces fièvres d'émigration par masse." No longer, however, did the Puritans have an agency to protect them, let alone to forward their

6. The two John Whites create many difficulties, which Mrs. Rose-Troup failed to resolve by attributing all of the colonizing activities to the "Patriarch of Dorchester." I am convinced that most of the references to a John White in the records of the colonizing companies point to the London barrister, because of their legal nature. I agree with Professor Morison that the barrister, not the divine, subscribed £50 to the New England Company. He was also the one who signed John Endecott's instructions, which were issued from London, not Dorchester, in 1628. Councillor White belonged to the Feoffees for Impropriations and knew intimately most of the twenty-one members of the New England Company. He was too useful and too prominent a Puritan to be overlooked, something the Laudians never did. As the attorney who composed the first draft of the petition and also of the Massachusetts Charter, it seems incontrovertible that he knew more about the omission of the place of residence of the Company than anyone else; given White's anti-Episcopal bias and his vigorous interest in the colonizing of fellow Puritans, it may be suggested that it was his conscious effort that caused the omission, or, as Winthrop said later, the rescinding of the requirement. *Winthrop Papers*, II, 82, 82n; IV, 470; Stearns, *Strenuous Puritan*, 39. For the charter, consult Mitchell, *The Founding of Massachusetts*, 10–15, 28–30, 32–3, 60.

cause. But in no other colonizing ventures were so many men of such varied talents engaged.[7]

The role of leadership in the Puritan enterprise must be emphasized: among the merchants, Cradock and Saltonstall; the lawyers White and Humfry; the country gentlemen Johnson and Pelham; the noblemen Say and Sele, Brooke, and Warwick; and a host of dedicated ministers of whom White, Peter, Higginson, and Cotton were only *primi inter pares*. Though these men were distributed geographically from Devon to Durham, they were all known to each other by repute if not through university connections, and they were easily brought into touch by skilled managers. Some of them possessed great wealth, others had merely comfortable estates; but through their many affiliations they commanded a large amount of capital. Resourcefulness, intelligence, craft, experience, knowledge of the New World, and determination were theirs in greater abundance than William Laud could command. Unrivaled though their collective capacities and resources turned out to be, these Captains of Israel would probably have failed in their undertaking without a Moses to lead his people into the promised land. That they succeeded in uncovering this Moses in the person of John Winthrop of Groton Manor—one of the truly great men in a century blessed with so many—was what the Puritans recognized as a Divine Providence. Here was one of those rare instances where the man and the moment coincided.[8]

As John Winthrop pondered the events and changes which had taken place since Englishmen first began to emigrate, his concern about the state of affairs in the nation possessed him more and more. Beginning in February, 1628, when he suggests that his duties as attorney for the Court of Wards and Liveries are growing burdensome and that he is weary of journeying to and fro between Groton and London, it is evident that he is considering retiring to the country. In May of the following year, even more discouraged, Winthrop writes to his wife that "If the Lord seeth it wilbe good for us, he will provide a shelter and a hiding place for us. . . ." A little more than a month later he announces to her "my Office

7. See analysis of Joan E. M. Bellford, Puritan Ideas on Colonisation, 1620–1660 (M. A. Thesis, London, 1951); Debien, *Les Engagés*, 80.
8. Heylyn, *Cyprianus Anglicus*, 165; Hubbard, *History of New England*, 120–22.

gone, and my chamber," and follows with the comment that they need never part again; where they would spend the rest of their lives, the Lord in his mercy would direct them, but he takes comfort in knowing that she is willing to accompany him "in what place or condition soever." [9]

It was perfectly evident to the members of the Massachusetts-Bay Company that John Winthrop was the indispensable man for their scheme. On July 7, 1629, "many reverend Divines," attended Commencement at Cambridge. Apparently they succeeded in dispelling any lingering doubts that Winthrop might have had, for on or about August 12, he drew up some "Particular considerations" for emigrating, in which he concluded: "It is come to that issue, as, in all probabilitye, the wellfare of the plantation depends upon my assistance: for the maine pillers of it beinge gentlemen of highe qualitye and eminent partes, both for wisdome and godlinesse, are determined to sitt still, if I desert them." When he learned of Winthrop's decision, Robert Reyce tried to dissuade his friend from leaving England; he argued that "The church and common welthe heere at home, hathe more neede of your beste abyllytie in these dangerous tymes, then any remote plantation, which may be performed by persons of lesser woorthe and apprehension. . . ." But he was too late; John Winthrop had committed himself.[10]

At another meeting in Cambridge on August 26, John Winthrop and eleven other Puritan gentlemen agreed to dispose of their estates and, with their several families, prepare "to passe the Seas (under Gods protection) to inhabite and continue in New England. Provided alwayes . . . the whole governement together with the Patent for the said plantacion bee first by an order of Court legally transferred and established to remayne with us" before the last of September next. The Company readily complied, and on October 29, at a meeting in London, the freemen elected John Winthrop governor and John Humfry deputy governor.[11]

9. *Winthrop Papers*, I, 379; II, 91, 99, 100.
10. Thomas Dudley declared that Winthrop's "coming in" was "the very hinge of the great Massachusetts Movement." *Winthrop Papers*, II, 103, 105, 106, 125, 159n3.
11. *Winthrop Papers*, II, 151–2, 159–60.

III

The departure of the English Puritans was far from being the "top-secret" movement which it is so often said to have been. The royal charter for Massachusetts-Bay proclaimed the intention of the Company to settle its patent, and the ultimate objectives of "the Puritan faction" quickly became common knowledge and were talked about all over the land. Only the means by which it was set in motion remained concealed from the country at large. The Puritan leaders wisely built their campaign for emigration upon the solid foundation laid by their predecessors; upon the minds that had been prepared over a period of fifteen years, all that was required to effect a decision to leave England was a final manipulation of public opinion.[12]

A few days after the dissolution of King Charles's third parliament on March 10, 1629, there was posted on the church door at Hamel Hempstead in Hertfordshire a pseudonymous letter from "Michael Mean-well to Matthew Mark-well" at his house in "Muse-much parish." The author proclaimed his resolve, and that of others, to go to New England. A dislike of the new Laudian cere-monialism, resentment of the government of the Church of England, and rejection of some points of doctrine asserted by authority, especially on the question of predestination, were driving Mean-well and his fellows out of the land. The Star Chamber had this manifesto within a few days, which is conclusive proof that England's rulers knew about the New England scheme soon after March 20, if not before.[13]

During the spring of 1629, as we have seen, John Winthrop formulated his personal reasons for emigrating, and about August 12 he composed a first draft of general arguments, which he produced at a meeting in Bury St. Edmunds. By October 20 he had put them into final form as "General Observations for the Planta-

12. M. Debien writes that few signs of any French emigration propaganda can be discovered "parce qu'elle fut surtout orale, mais que fut efficace, n'en doutons pas." A much larger degree of illiteracy prevailed among the French engagés than among the English. Les Engagés, 165–6; Gibson, in Cambridge Journal, IV, 313.
13. CSPD, 1628–9, p. 30; Gardiner, England, VII, 41–4.

tion of New England." This manuscript he circulated among the leading Puritans. After discussing religious considerations, he proceeded to describe the discouraging English scene and the economic advantages to be derived from the new colony. To meet the objection that the "ill successe of other Plantations may tell us what will become of this," the Squire of Groton answered that the managers of the Virginia Company fell into "great and fundamentall errors" because "their mayne end was Carnall and not Religious"; furthermore "they used unfitt instrumentes, a multitude of rude and misgovernd persons, the very scumme of the Land" and they "did not establish a right forme of government." [14]

At Salem in the Bay Colony, Master Francis Higginson set down "A True Relacion of the last voyage to new England" and dispatched it to London where, by September 19, it had arrived. Within a month John Winthrop wrote from the metropolis to his eldest son: "I have sent downe all the late newes from N. E. I would have some of you reade it to your mother, and let Forth [Winthrop] copye out the observations and all that follows from the 𝆕☞: and the lettre in the ende and showe it [to] mr. Mott, and others that intende this voyage." Copies of the "Relacion" were handed about among English folk, great and small, during the rest of 1629. Higginson's description of the favorable crossing, which "we performed . . . in 6 weeks and 3 dayes" must have gone far to dispel the fears of many apprehensive souls.[15]

Although this early promotion literature reached many lay Puritans besides ministers, and produced the first efforts at colonization by the Massachusetts-Bay Company, a second campaign became necessary when preparations were being made for the departure of the Winthrop Fleet. Appeals had to be directed to the literate rank and file of prospective emigrants in tracts which, though framed with familiar materials drawn from earlier works, would contain

14. George W. Robinson settled once and for all John Winthrop's authorship (formerly attributed to John White), in *Winthrop Papers,* II, 109–11. For the General Observations, see ibid, II, 111–49, especially pp. 137, 143; *CSP Col., 1574–1660,* p. 155.

15. Margaret Winthrop wrote to her husband on October 13, 1629: "I have harde reade the Nuse from N: E: and much rejoyce in it. . . ." *Winthrop Papers,* II, 156, 158; Mitchell, *The Founding of Massachusetts,* 61–75, contains the best edition of The True Relacion.

special injunctions and instructions. The Stationers' Company authorized Michael Sparke, on March 6, 1630, to publish a continuation of Francis Higginson's "True Relacion"; this soon appeared as *New-Englands Plantation, or A Short and True Description of the Commodities and Discommodities of that countrey*. So great was the demand for copies that Sparke printed three editions (the last enlarged) during this emigration year. He also appended a letter from Master Graves, "Engynere now there resident," cataloguing such "needefull things as every Planter doth or ought to provide to go to New England": victuals, apparel, arms, tools, household implements, and spices. "Also," Master Graves writes, "there are divers other things necessary to bee taken over to this Plantation, as *Bookes,* Nets, Hookes and Lines. . . ." after which he concludes significantly: "But whosoever desireth to know as much as yet can be discovered, I advise them to buy Captain John Smiths booke of the description of New-England in Folio; and read from Fol. 203. to the end; and there let the Reader expect to have full content." In the settling of no other plantation do books figure so prominently as in the undertaking sponsored by the Massachusetts-Bay Company.[16]

Sometime before March 1, 1620, the Company also issued, in broadside form, *A Proposition of Provisions Needfull for Such as Intend to Plant themselves in New England, for one whole year*. This handbill was not entered in the Stationers' Register, nor is there any record of a London printer named Fulke Clifton, whose name appears at the bottom of the sheet. The desire to get *A Proposition* dispatched, rather than secrecy, led the Company to omit the usual permission and have it printed surreptitiously. The list, prepared by the "Adventurers, with the advice of the Planters," was designed for a family of four or five persons, not just one man. Furthermore, it included such building materials as nails, locks for doors and chests, hinges, hooks, and twists for doors, and certain luxuries for individuals of some substance. The total cost of all the

16. I have used the third edition "enlarged" of *New Englands Plantation* in the British Museum (n. p.); the italics are mine. See also Mitchell, *The Founding of Massachusetts,* 81–97. There is another edition dated 1646 in the John Carter Brown Library, as well as a copy of the 3d edition of 1630. The presence of a copy of this tract in the PRO (C. O. 1:5, p. 110) papers for 1630 further indicates official awareness of the Puritan activities.

items recommended was £17 7s. 4d. If the poorer sort could be satisfied to drink water in the heat of the summer, they could save one pound on a hogshead of malt; they might also save by not taking beef, pork, bacon, aqua vite, and hardware, and thus bring their costs down to £7 4s. 8d. There still remained the transportation charges of £5 to £6 per person. It is clear that this was to be no assisted migration of paupers under indenture.[17]

The throngs of people who were ready to dispose of their possessions and depart for the new land are proof enough of the success of the adventurers in mobilizing public opinion. In May, 1629, six vessels went out carrying emigrants to the new plantation. In 1630 it fell to the company's recently elected governor to organize and arrange for the shipping of passengers and equipment, a monumental task, for seventeen ships sailed for New England during that year. The Winthrop Fleet, so-called because John Winthrop was aboard the *Arbella*, consisted of four ships which, after a delay of more than a week while they waited for propitious winds and weather, finally started across the Atlantic from the harbor of Yarmouth on the Isle of Wight on April 8, 1630.[18]

On June 7, just two months after the departure of the *Arbella*, John Rous recorded in his diary: "I sawe a Book at Bury [St. Edmunds] at a book-sellers, conteining a declaration of their intent who be gone to Newe England, set out by themselves, and prepared for satisfaction to the King and State (as I conceive) because of some scandalous misconceivings that runne abroad." Doubtless the book was *The Humble Request*, published by John Bellamy at London, May 21, 1630. It was written "From Abord the *Arbella* rydinge before Yarmouthe April 5, 1630." The emigrants called the Church of England "from whence wee rise, our deare Mother . . . ever acknowledging that such hope and part as wee have obtained in the common salvation, we have received in her bosome. . . ." They made a plea to the "Reverend Fathers and Brethren to helpe forward this worke now in hande," and, in particular, John Winthrop and his companions entreated those

17. The unique copy of this handbill, which I used, is in the British Museum (PH2); it is reproduced in reduced facsimile facing p. 98 of *New England Quarterly,* XII, with a note by Edmund S. Morgan.
18. *Winthrop's Journal,* I, 1–12, 15; *Winthrop Papers,* II, 218, 220, 222–3, 224–6, 228, 230–31; *CSM,* XII, 202–3n.

who "through want of cleare intelligence of our course" not to despise nor desert them in "their prayers and affections" as they went to their "poor Cottages in the wildernesse." [19]

Perusal of the book evoked other memories for John Rous, for he went on to note: "Some little while since, the company went to Newe England under Mr. Winthrop. Mr. Cotton, of Boston in Lincolnshire, went to theire departure about Gravesend, and preached to them, as we heare, out of 2 Samuel vii 10" [for which he was silenced until June 24 by diocesan order]. Master Cotton's sermon was designed to assure the passengers that theirs was both a holy and a just cause, and to exhort them to cling to their holiness in the new Canaan. In discussing "liberty of ordinances," he was at some pains to point out that he did not intend freedom from a particular church, but this did not save him from Laudian censure. Nevertheless, W. Jones published the sermon on July 3 as *God's Promise to his Plantations*. Herein was no more hint of the congregationalism of a later day than in *The Humble Request,* and these two complementary publications served the purposes of placating, or at least forestalling, the critics of the New England venture and of providing important additional encouragement to those Puritans who were contemplating following the Winthrop Fleet.[20]

Five days after the Stationers approved the issuing of *God's Promise,* they authorized Jones to publish *The Planters Plea.* John White of Dorchester, a non-separating Puritan, prepared the work "For the satisfaction of those that question the lawfulnesse of the Action" of so many people removing to New England. It is a model promotion tract, for it contains none of "the dew of romanticism," and no promotion of real estate. A practical philosopher, White was well-informed, sincere, and above all devout. The chief end of all plantations, he writes, ought to be religious. "Nay, I conceive, God especially directs this worke of erecting Colonies

19. *Camden,* LXVI, 54; *Winthrop Papers,* II, 231–3. Henry Wilder Foote made a strong case for Master George Phillips rather than John Winthrop as the author of the *Humble Request in* Mass. Hist. Soc., *Proceedings,* LXIII, 193–227.
20. Master Cotton admonished his listeners in the best plain style: "Forget not the wombe that bore you and the brest that gave you sucke. Even ducklings hatched under an henne, though they take to water, yet will still have recourse to the wing that hatched them: how much more should chickens of the same feather, and yolke." John Cotton, *God's Promise to His Plantations* (1630), 18; Ziff, *Career of John Cotton,* 60–62.

unto the planting and propagating of Religion . . . from the first planting of Religion among men, it hath alwayes held a constant way from East to West . . . [and] it must necessarily light upon the West Indies [that is, all of English America]." He believed too that the English nation was best fitted to undertake the task and rehearsed all of the practical arguments previously advanced. This sacred enterprise requires "good Governours, able Ministers, Physitians, Souldiers, Schoolemasters, Mariners, and Mechanicks of all sorts," including husbandmen, of course. "It seemes to bee a common and grosse errour that Colonies ought to be Emunctories or sinckes of States; to drayne away their filth. . . . This fundamentall errour hath beene the occasion of the miscarriage of most of our Colonies, and the chargeable destruction of many of our Countrymen, whom . . . we cast off . . . leaving them to themselves either to sinke or swimme." This is not to be for New England. It is to be a godly undertaking performed by pious people who shall settle as families under the superintendence of capable and sound men. Master White also included a detailed history of the New England settlements of the previous decade in his pamphlet, and he sought to quiet any uneasiness about the orthodoxy of the undertakers, who, some critics charged, "secretly harboured faction and separation from the Church." [21]

Although he was not a Puritan, Captain John Smith, the leading advocate of settlement, brought the great prestige of his title of "Admirall of New-England" to bear in the last literary effort of his distinguished career. He had taken counsel with Sir Richard Saltonstall and many other adventurers of the Massachusetts-Bay Company prior to October, 1630, when he wrote *Advertisements for the unexperienced Planters of New England, or any where,* which was issued the following year. This devout Anglican endeavored at the outset to scotch the rumors that New England was a receptacle for "many of discontented Brownists, Anabaptists, Papists, Puritans, Separatists, and such factious Humorists," for

---

21. Mr. Mitchell collated the two editions of *The Planters Plea* of 1630, *The Founding of Massachusetts,* 143–201. In later years, William Coddington told Richard Bellingham: "And the Planters Play and John Cotton's Sermon, which was in 1630, printed by John Humphrey our Agent, to satisfy the Godly-minded of our Removal out of England, all did satisfie me to remove, as Lot out of Sodom. . . ." Coddington, *A Demonstration of True Love* (1674), 13, 14.

the principals have assured him that they will not suffer any of them, nor do they welcome any rascals trying to escape their debts or scandal at home. Of those who have gone to New England in the eighteen months previous to his writing, "the chiefe Undertakers are Gentlemen of good estate, some of 500, some a thousand pound land a yeere," all of which they say they were willing to sell to advance this pious work. Moreover, they are "good Catholike Protestants according to the reformed Church of England." The rest of them are "men of good meanes, or Arts, Occupations, and Qualities, much more fit for such a businesse and better furnished of all necessaries if they arrive well than was ever any Plantation went out of England."

"I will not say," the old soldier admitted, "but some of them may be more precise then needs, nor that they all be so good as they should be . . . and if there be no dissemblers among them, it is more than a wonder; therefore doe not condemne all for some." But if they fail, it is their own loss, if they succeed, it is "a great glory and exceeding good to this Kingdome, to make good at last what all our former conclusions have disgraced." They are not following the course of the Virginia Company, which ran everything from London, but the colonists of New England "are overseers of their owne estates, and so well bred in labour and good husbandry as any in England. . . ." This was something usually overlooked in the arguments in Winthrop's "General Observations."

In composing the *Advertisements,* Captain Smith drew heavily upon his works; he also told of the settlements at Plymouth and Salem. These accounts he followed with useful hints about building, defense against the natives, fishing, and trade. This fifth important publication of the years 1629–31 completed the most concentrated and effective promotion campaign of English colonization.[22]

22. In the continuation of Stow's *Annales* (p. 1045), published in 1631, Edmund Howes even included an account of the hasty departure of "14 sayle" with men, women, and children "to make a fine plantation." Mention should be made here of Sir William Vaughan's *The Newlanders Cure . . .* (1630); William Wood's *New Englands Prospect,* (1634; 2 eds., 1639); and the amusing satire by Thomas Morton of Mare-Mount, *The New English Canaan* (Amsterdam, 1637). All of these works contributed further toward making the New England experiment

IV

In his famous epistle to the Countess of Lincoln, March, 1630, Thomas Dudley spoke plainly about the letters that had been sent back by the colonists "wherein honest men out of desire to draw over others to them wrote somewhat hyperbolically of things here." He was right on two counts: the exaggerated claims for New England, and the compelling effect of personal correspondence from friends in the new plantations. Substantiating this assertion is the observation of Joshua Scottow made thirty and more years later, recalling the events of the Puritan emigration: "a Letter from New-England . . . was Venerated as a Sacred Script, or as the Writing of some Holy Prophet, 'twas carried many Miles, where divers came to hear it . . . and a multitude of pious Souls through the whole Nation, were in their Spirits pressed to Joyn in this Work. . . ." [23]

After the Massachusetts Bay Colony had weathered the first year or so of its existence, one of its leaders wrote to Emmanuel Downing stressing the plantation's economic advantages at the same time he asked for assistance in getting "some maysterworkmen for the ordering of our potash works." He pled with Mr. Downing to "incourage men to come over for heare is lande and meanes of lively hood suffitient for men that bring bodys able and minds fitted to brave the first brunts . . . it is strange the meaner soart of people should be soe backward having assurance that they may live plentifully by their neighbours; and that the better soart of people should not helpe the poorer, with means to transport them, that in time might returne their adventures with answereable advantage." [24]

Few letters started Puritans on their way to New England more

notorious, if not famous, throughout Britain. The entries with the Stationers' Company are in their *Register,* IV, 196, 201, 204, 205; Smith, *Travels and Works,* II, 917–72; *Winthrop Papers,* II, 111–21.

23. Emigrants who returned for their families or to settle estates often performed the same service as this transoceanic correspondence. See *Somerset & Dorset,* X, 20; Thomas Dudley's letter was first printed in *Massachusetts, or the First Planters of New England,* ed. Joshua Scottow (Boston, Mass., 1696), 20; also in Force, *Tracts,* II, No. 12; Joshua Scottow, *A Narrative of the Planting of the Massachusetts Colony, Anno, 1628* (Boston, Mass., 1694), 16–17.

24. Mass. Hist. Soc., *Proceedings,* 2d ser., VIII, 208–9; John Masters to Thomas and Lady Barrington, March 4, 1630/1, in *NEHG Reg.,* XCI, 69.

than those from dedicated ministers, such as that written in 1633 by Master Thomas Welde to his people, young and old, at Terling in Essex. In lyrical terms he told of the Atlantic crossing and the good life he and his passengers were enjoying in the new land: "in spite of Devills and stormes, as cheerfull as ever, my wife all the voyage on the Sea better then at land . . . att sea my Children never better in their lives." Never had the minister known such a wonderful land. "Such groves, such trees, such a aire as I am fully contented withall and desier no better while I live. . . . I find three great blessinges, peace, plenty and health in a comfortable measure. . . . I know no other place on the whole globe of the earth where I would rather be then here: We say to our freends that doubt this Come and see and tast. Here the greater part are the better part." [25]

A letter from the East Lothian town of Prestonpans written by John Ker in 1634 to Thomas Levistown, a tailor in the Strand, indicates very clearly that conditions were such in Scotland that some of its people were investigating the attractions of New England. Ker wrote to obtain information on what kind of success the New England colony had made since its inception, "for there be many . . . that inclyne to that countrie, if so be that the persecution by the prelates continue, I mean not so muche of Ministers that are abused as near sixty young men that are of rare gifts who cannot get a lawful entry into the ministry, also of divers professors of good meanes that labour to keep themselves pure and undefyled." [26]

By 1638 the letters sent home told of the large numbers of immigrants arriving each year and of the growth of the Bay Colony. In a report to Sir Simonds D'Ewes, who was thinking of emigrating, Master Edmund Browne exclaimed: "The plantation I found to exceede all her sisters, though her ancestours in time, as Virginia, Bermudas, and which not of theire time, in convenient buildings, settled courts, and adjacent townes." He also boasted that food was plentiful: "Mutton and Porke are usually eaten heere." [27]

A powerful impetus was given to the migration to New England

25. Welde's letter is in B. M., Sloane MSS, 922, fols. 90a–93b.
26. PRO: S. P., 16; 267: 60.
27. *CSM*, VII, 76–7, 78–9.

from 1629 onward by sermons, both oral and printed. Thomas Hooker, lecturer at St. Mary's in Chelmsford, preached a farewell sermon to his congregation in 1629 before retiring to Little Badow—he had been cited for nonconformity. If we are content with "quietnesse . . . we play mock-holy-day with God, the Gospell we make it our pack-horse," cried this master of the plain style of preaching. Then, pulling out all the stops, he declaimed: "God is going, his glory is departing, England hath seen her best dayes, and now evill dayes are befalling us: God is packing up his Gospell, because no body will buy his wares, nor come to his price. Oh lay hands upon God and let him not goe out of your coasts, he is going, stop him, and let not thy God depart. . . . Arise! and down on your knees, and intreat God to leave his Gospell to your posterity." [28]

There is ample evidence that Bishop Laud was kept informed about the preachers who were arousing resentment among the people against the ceremonialism of the Church of England, and those who, though sometimes indirectly, were responsible for the stepped-up emigration. In the spring of 1629 Laud gave a sermon preached by a Master Salisbury to Attorney General Heath for his opinion, because the minister had expressed the fear that those who could leave their callings might be persuaded to leave their country. "Such I am sure are already much troubled what to doe, whether to goe hence we heare such loud noise of transporting whole households into New England." Henry Dade, commissary for Ipswich, pointed the finger at Samuel Ward, one of the arch-Puritans, in February, 1634. Master Ward, he wrote Laud, was "the chief of those . . . who by preaching against the contents of the Book of Common Prayer and set prayer, and of a fear of altering our religion, has caused this giddiness." A few months later, two ships with 120 passengers left for New England, but Dade was afraid to press charges against Ward because of the latter's "adherents who are very potent in London and about Ipswich," so he left the problem in the Archbishop's lap. In December, Master Ward had to answer to the High Commission on his views about emigration and conditions in the country.[29]

28. Thomas Hooker, *The Danger of Desertion* . . . (1641), 15.
29. PRO: S. P., 142: 94: 551 (French Transcripts, Mass. Hist. Soc.). PRO: S. P., 16: 263: 35; PRO: S. P., 16: 278: 149; Herbert, *Works*, 235; *CSPD, 1933–4*, pp. 450–55; *1634–5*, pp. 361–2.

Printed and word-of-mouth propaganda were not the sole devices used by the projectors to rally the English Puritans for removal to Massachusetts. At Dorchester Master John White was unusually active in presenting the advantages of settling New England. John Winthrop and several of his associates personally solicited emigrants in 1629. One person to whom they gave a "Call to joyne with us," on account of his "godlinesse and abilityes in the Arte of Chirurgerie," was William Gager of Little Waldenfield, Suffolk. Six years later, John Winthrop, Jr., traveled to Ireland, crossed to Scotland, and then wended his way southward into England, and "all the way he met with persons of quality, whose thoughts were towards New England." Nor were the Winthrops and Master John White the only leaders inducing prompt action among their fellow Puritans. Vicars, curates, and lecturers joined in the drive; they used market and lecture days to further the cause; and many a family could attest that their first thoughts of joining the Great Migration were implanted by these men.[30]

It might be stated as a truism that in Stuart England when information, or news, came out in ballad form or in the speeches of current plays it was no longer secret. It was reaching the widest possible audience. The swelling numbers of emigrants going to New England must have been known to the buyers and singers of ballads and their audiences as well as to the members of the Privy Council. One such song, "The Zealous Puritan," known earlier as "A Friendly Invitation to a new Plantation," contained the lines:

> Stay not among the wicked
> Lest that with them you perish,
> But let us to New England go
> And the pagan people cherish.

William Strode, a local poet of Devonshire, penned many verses. In one entitled "A West-Country Man's Voyage to Newe England," he used his native dialect. In another, he bracketed New England with the immoral suburbs of London, but ballads baiting the "Putrefidian secte . . . the counterfeit electe," as so often is the case, served only to advertise the much-maligned movement among friends as well as foes. At any rate we can no longer harbor

30. *Winthrop Papers*, II, 97, 157, 159*n*, 183, 184, 185, 199; *Winthrop's Journal*, I, 164.

doubts about the widespread knowledge of the New England venture among people of every rank.[31]

IV

Propaganda and organization would have been insufficient to incite and sustain a migration had they not operated upon individuals and groups having special reasons for leaving England. In 1629 and for twelve years thereafter, many men and women suddenly discovered a way out of the real or fancied dilemmas that badgered and haunted them. In making a decision whether to emigrate or stay in England, the advice and pleas of the ministers of the Church of England who were Puritans often proved decisive, for, as Peter Heylyn perceived, "those who hold the Helm of the Pulpit alwayes steer the peoples hearts as they please." Some of the ministers themselves went to New England; others remained at home to manage Puritan affairs, but all the "forward-looking Grandees of the Puritan Faction" shared with each other and their followers one irrevocable commitment—the conviction that the Lord had called them to carry out this fateful mission.[32]

So many informers harried the Puritans that "no man was safe in Public company." When William Laud was Bishop of Bath and Wells before 1628, he "silenced or suspended" John Warham, Vicar of Crewkerne in Dorset. The lenient Bishop of Exeter, Joseph Hall, allowed Mr. Warham to preach a farewell sermon at St. Sedwell's outside the walls of the county city of Devon in 1629, a short time before he sailed for New England. For allowing the delivery of this discourse, the churchwardens, Thomas Hasseler and John Morefield, were compelled to do public penance by the Spiritual Court of Somerset. At Dorchester, in November, 1630,

31. "Between 1620 and 1640 not less than 20,000 persons settled in New England." Prompted by the movement, a balladeer wrote "A Proper Ballad, called the Summons to New England, to the tune of the Townsman's Cap." Firth, in RHS *Trans.*, 3d ser., VI, 37–8; *CSP Col.*, 1574–1660, p. 180; Morison, *Builders of the Bay Colony*, 344–6; *NEHG Reg.*, XXXVI, 359–62; *The Poetical Works of William Strode*, ed. Bertram Dobell (London, 1907), 114, 238; Firth, *An American Garland*, 32–4.

32. Thomas Fuller, *Appeal of Iniured Innocence*, quoted in Haller, *Rise of Puritanism*, 81, see also p. 117.

Samuel Whitcomb of Taunton and Mr. Ralph Bayly of Manchester took an oath before the justices that they had heard Thomas Jarvis of Lyme Regis say that "within this Borough that all the Projectors for New England Business are rebells, and those that are gon over are Idolaters, captivated and separatists. . . ."[33]

The Puritan clergymen sincerely believed that they were being persecuted when Archbishop Laud pressed for conformity after 1633. All of them had to resort to devious and clandestine actions in order to escape surveillance and probable punishment by the new primate. From Yorkshire, Henrie Jacie, who had been removed for nonconformity, instructed the younger Winthrop how to send letters to him: Address them to "H. Jacie Minis[ter] at Aughton in Y[ork]sh[ire]. Leave them with Mr. [Emmanuel] Downing to be given to Mr. Overton, Stationer, to send by the York Cariers to Mr. Hodshon, mercer in Onsgate. . . . So it may be safe." Dr. John Stoughton, rector of St. Mary, Aldermanbury, Laud's investigators reported, carried on a "great correspondence with the irregular, inconformable fugitive ministers beyond the seas in New England." In 1634, when he was considering crossing to Scituate where his stepson James Cudworth then lived, ecclesiastical agents seized much of his correspondence. The next year Sir Thomas Wroth had to use the subterfuge of addressing a letter to the clergyman as though it were for Lady Elizabeth Cleere in Coleman Street.[34]

33. The Puritans suffered verbal as well as physical abuse from their opponents. "Concerning the name [Puritan] it is ambiguous, and so it is fallacious," the Principal of Gloucester Hall, Oxford, charged in 1630. Some may be pure in heart; but there are evil men "who desire to seeme to be just, and holy, but in their doctrine, and discipline, they are the underminers of our True, Protestant, Reformed Church. . . . This Puritan is a Non-Conformist." Giles Widdowes, *The Schismatical Puritan* (1630), sig. A 3r–v; Charles E. Banks and Charles M. Andrews denied that the Puritans were persecuted, but my studies range me with Arthur H. Buffinton, who met their challenges: "Whether they were or were not persecuted may be a matter of debate, but it cannot be successfully denied, I think, that they believed they were persecuted," and there is ample evidence of Laud's relentless disciplining of them, fairly or unfairly, rightly or wrongly. Banks, in Mass. Hist. Soc., *Proceedings*, LXIII, 136–54; Andrews and Buffinton, in *CSM*, XXVIII, 286–7; XXXII, 311; Neal, *History of the Puritans*, I, 584; Mather, *Magnalia Christi Americana*, bk. I, 15; *Somerset & Dorchester*, XI, 309–10; *Dorchester Recs.*, 657.

34. *Winthrop Papers*, III, 128; *CSP Col., 1574–1660*, p. 194; *CSPD, 1635*, pp. 377–8; *1639–40*, p. 505; Heylyn, *Cyprianus Anglicus*, 165.

One who had experienced the Laudian persecution, Master
John Cotton, spoke for the rest of the ministers when he asserted
in 1644 that they fled to escape "Episcopal tyranny." The Court of
High Commission censured one nonconformist in 1637 for saying:
"That it was suspicious that now night did approach because the
shadows were so much longer then the body, and ceremonies more
in force then the power of godliness." Many ministers looked upon
Laud's altar requirements as being "in the Suburbs of Superstition." When an apparitor complained that the altar rail was "not
decently placed" in the church at Courtenhall, Hampshire, the rector, William Castell, refused to move it, saying "there shal be no
new tricks put upon him, and that he could live as well in N. E. as
here." So devout an Anglican as Thomas Knyvett feared that the
Puritans had been raised "to a dangerous pitch of rebellious fury"
by the suspension of "at least 50 Ministers" by Matthew Wren,
Bishop of Norwich, "forcing many . . . to deserte the Kingdome,
and fly into Holland and New England. . . ." [35]

Charles Chauncy, onetime fellow of Trinity, stoutly opposed the
regulations of the hierarchy of the Church in matters of litany,
baptism, moving of the communion table, etc. Twice he was
brought before the Court of High Commission. On the second occasion, 1635, he was found guilty of contempt against ecclesiastical jurisdiction and of "raising a schism" and was sentenced to
several months' imprisonment. After each of the trials Master
Chauncy made a "submission," but subsequent utterances gave no
evidence of change of heart. On June 12, 1637, Dr. Samuel Clark
wrote to Sir John Lamb that Chauncy had "held a fast on Wednesday last and . . . with another preached some six or eight hours.
. . . The end was, I am told, to join in prayer that God will deliver his servants from persecution. . . ." The minister answered
the prayer himself by leaving for New England (where he would
become the second president of Harvard College), for he had received intelligence of a third move to be made against him by the
ecclesiastical tribunal. A century later, his great-grandson of the

35. Fuller, *Church History*, bk. XI, 150; S. P. Domestic, April 2, 1637 (French
Transcript, Mass. Hist. Soc.); *Knyvett Letters*, 30; Prynne, *Canterburies Doome*,
167, 375; *CSP Venetian, 1639-9*, p. 305.

same name was to be just as inflexible in his opposition to the introduction of bishops to the New World.[36]

One of the most vivid accounts of the abuse that a nonconforming minister was subjected to comes from the pen of Master Thomas Shepard. He was preaching in Earls Colne in Essex in the latter part of 1630 when he was summoned to London by Laud, who was then Bishop. Never asking Shepard whether he would subscribe, but "what I had to do to preach in his Diocesse. . ."

> Dec. 16, 1630. I was inhibited from Preaching in the Diocess of *London* by Dr. *Laud* **Bp** of that Diocess. As soon as I came in the Morning, about 8 of the Clock; falling into a Fit of Rage, he asked me, *what Degree I had taken in the University?* I answer'd him, I was a Master of Arts. He ask'd, *of what College?* I answer'd, of *Emanuel.* He ask'd *how long I had liv'd in his Diocess?* I answer'd *three Years and upwards.* He ask'd, *who maintain'd me all this While?* charging me to deal plainly with him; adding with all, that he had been more cheated and equivocated with by some of my malignant Faction than ever was Man by Jesuit. At the speaking of which Words he look'd as tho' Blood would have gush'd out of his Face, and did shake as if he had been haunted with an Ague Fit, to my Apprehension by Reason of his extream Malice & secret Venom: I desired him to excuse me: He fell then to threaten me, & withal to bitter Railing, calling me all to naught, saying; *You prating Coxcomb! Do you think all the Learning is in your Brains?* He pronounc'd his Sentence thus; *I charge you that you neither Preach, Read, Marry, Bury, or exercise any Ministerial Function in any Part of My Diocess; for if you do, and I hear of it, I'll be upon your back, and follow you wherever you go, in any Part of the Kingdom, and everlastingly disenable you.* I be-

---

36. Mr. Chauncy wrote a retraction of his "scandalous submission" in 1637, but it was not printed until 1641 when its 39 pages of discussion of the "mischeife of railing about the Communion table" seemed more appropriate. *CSPD, 1635–6,* pp. 123–4; *1637,* p. 209; Charles Chauncy, *The Retraction of Mr. Charles Chauncy,* To the Reader; *NEHG Reg.,* LVII, 297. For Anglican charges of Puritan organization by "a generation of Vipers eating out the bowels of their mother Church and Country," see *Persecutio Undecima,* 2, 13, 18, 53–9.

vants who were not members of households. Overwhelmingly this was a movement of free men and free women.[40]

Pastures looked greener through the westward haze, and less pious matters naturally motivated some of the emigrants. Tales of better living conditions and the news that the General Court of Massachusetts gave land away to right-thinking people attracted ambitious people of the middle and lower orders, though the oft-quoted statement that land was one of the gods of New England does not hold; the fact that there was free land had only a secondary bearing on emigration. From Stondon Massey in Essex, Master Nathaniel Ward wrote to John Winthrop to urge him to reserve passage in his ships for two emigrants and their families, "A carpenter and Bricklayer the most faithfull and diligent workmen in all our partes . . . there is a paire of sawyers also specially Laborious, all of them will come to you upon monday or tuesday. . . ." When John Winthrop, Jr., was establishing a colony at Saybrook in 1635, Philip Nye wrote him from London: "We have sent you som servants . . . som of our husbandmen likewise are not only godlye but very skilfull. . . ." [41]

The religious malaise of ordinary Englishmen—yeomen, artisans, laborers—concealed a deep-seated social dissatisfaction which had much to do with their pulling up stakes and leaving their homeland. We have seen that though the nation was generally prosperous, many individuals failed to share in the benefits. Without question the atmosphere of change and doubt in the land upset many people, and in consequence individual laymen emigrated for a variety of reasons.

The Anglican enemies of the New England migration always emphasized the fact that debtors used religion as a means of defrauding their creditors. The levies of ship money galled those who lacked the wherewithal to pay; in fact too often the tax proved to be an unbearable burden. Numbers of the defaulters in 1636 were the very poor, and the tax collectors reported that many of those who were in arrears had gone to New England. The next year's returns of the sheriff of Suffolk indicated a similar situation: in the

40. *Devon & Cornwall,* XVII, 182–3; *NEHG Reg.,* XLVI, 128.
41. *Winthrop Papers,* II, 192; III, 211; Stowe MSS, Legal-Temple (Henry E. Huntington Library, French Transcripts), Case 70A, 70B; Andrews, *Colonial Period of American History,* I, 57n.

Hundred of Wangford, "Garrett the tanner going into New England"; at Framlingham, "Francis Baylie, gone with his family to New England, owed 4s. 6d."; like reports came in from the hundreds of Lothingland, Wrentham, and South Cone. Thomas Welsh left Bishop's Stortford without paying ship money; two years later he was living in Milford, Connecticut. The probability is that these delinquents departed because of their Puritan convictions, but in so doing, they felt no obligation to pay the tax that John Hampden resisted so manfully.[42]

Indebtedness did not preclude piety, as the letters of James Cole written from Ipswich in the Bay Colony in 1634 illustrate. Having experienced financial reverses over a period of years, he left his parents, wife, children, and servants behind in Whitechapel and departed for New England. He protested that he did not fear imprisonment for debt, "but therein should I have had little hope either to have relieved my family or to have paid my debts which now there is some hope of both." Nehemiah Wallington of London wrote to urge him to return: "you which have beene such a valliant champion in the Lords quarrel and also hath stirred mee up (with others) to stand in my place and ranke where God hath set me. . . . It was a shame to goe from home." Though dolefully homesick for his wife and family, and obsessed with the sense of guilt over flying from his creditors, Cole asked his wife not to beg him to go back, but rather beseeched her to come over to him. His son Edmund joined him later in the fall, and eventually his wife and probably the rest of the children went out to live with him. We

42. William Coddington admitted in 1674 that "I was one of those many Lincolnshire Gentlemen that denied the Royal Loans, suffered for it in King Charles the first Days." Thomas Leverett of Boston also refused to lend money or to enter into bonds for appearance. Henry Dade, one of Laud's commissaries, is quoted as saying of anyone wanting to escape debt, "he may fly to New England, and be accounted a religious man for leaving the kingdom because he cannot endure the ceremonies of the church." Far more serious in many places than the avoidance of paying ship money or debts was the departure daily of "incredible numbers of persons of very good abilities in several Counties hereabouts who have sold their land," William, Lord Maynard, advised in 1638. He believed that the exodus by Easter day would "be an occasion of for years of impoverishing of divers poor parishes, as it is found by those Inhabitants which remain behind will not be possibly able to imploy or retain their poore. . . ." *NEHG Reg.*, XXXVI, 138–40; LVII, 199; *CSPD, 1633–4*, pp. 450–55; *1637–8*, p. 88; *1638–9*, p. 64; PRO: C. O. 1: 9: 88.

do not know for certain that he paid all his debts, but in 1642 he was dwelling at "Hertford in Queneticote" and writing Master Wallington to stand fast in "the faith of Gods Elect." [43]

Mixed as were the individual layman's motives for abandoning his country, religion was the determining factor for the overwhelming majority of them when it came to the final step. Radical Protestantism was deeply ingrained in the most humble Englishmen, and for more than half a century they had disliked the hierarchy and the newfangled ceremonies; they also resented Laud's harassment of the preachers and ministers they revered and cherished. As John Cotton viewed it in retrospect, God had made the New England churches "a little sanctuary . . . to many thousands of his servants." James Cole wrote back to his ministerial friend in London that there were two congregations in his adopted town "where is neither Crosses nor Surplis, nor kneeling at the Sacrament nor the booke of Common prayer nor any other behaviour but reading the word singing of psalms, prayer before and after sermon with catichisme." Thousands of them left, so Francis Higginson believed, "meerly on Account of Pure and Undefiled Religion, not knowing how they should have their Daily Bread, but trusting in God for that." [44]

The autobiography of Roger Clap, one of six children born into a family of modest means in Devonshire in 1609, provides an excellent account of what caused a Puritan youth to go to New England. When he first left home he lived with William Southcott, three miles from Exeter. The lad attended church in the city, where he heard many famous preachers, including John Warham, whom he admired so much that he told his father that he wanted to live near him. With the parental blessing, Roger Clap went to live with one "Moussiour" [Mosier?], "as famous a Family for Re-

43. Cole's graphic and touching letters are in B. M., Sloane MSS, 922, fols. 94b–175b.
44. Henry Dade predicted that about 600 persons had left, or would soon leave, from Suffolk in 1633/4, people who were either "indebted persons or persons discontented with the government of England. . . ." PRO: S. P. 16: 263: 35; *CSPD, 1637*, p. 417; John Cotton, *The Way of the Congregational Churches Cleared* (1648), Pt. I, 102; Edward Winslow, *New Englands Salamander Discovered . . .* (1647), 23–4; D'Ewes, *Autobiography*, II, 112, 115–19; *HMC Cowper*, II, 38; B. M., Sloane MSS, 922, fol. 100a; Mather, *Magnalia Christi Americana*, bk. I, 1, 15, 17; bk. III, 5.

ligion as ever I knew." Besides the parents, the group consisted of "divers Maid Servants" and seven or eight men, to whom once a week the master propounded a religious question. "With him I Covenanted," said Clap. "I never so much as heard of New-England until I heard of many godly Puritans that were going there, and that Mr. Warham was to go also. My Master asked me whether I would go? I told him were I not engaged unto him I would willingly go: He answered me that should be no hindrance, I might go for him or my self which [ever] I would." The apprentice wrote to his father, who was twelve miles away, for permission. When his parent opposed the removal, Roger walked home to "Intreat his leave," and fortunately "now God sent the Reverend [John] Maverick, who lived Forty Miles off [at Beaworthy], a Man I never saw before: He having heard of me, came to my Father's House, and my Father agreed that I should be with him and come under his Care. . . . Mind by what I have already expressed, That it was God that did draw me by his Providence out of my Father's Family, and weaned me from it by degrees. . . . So God brought me out of Plymouth the 20th of March in the Year, 1629/30, and landed me in health at Nantasket on the 30th of May, 1630. I being then about the Age of twenty one Years." Roger Clap prospered at Dorchester, never wanted to return to England and his family; rather he "advised some of my dear Brethren to come hither. . . ." One brother and his two sisters and their husbands "sold their means and came. . . ." Clap remembered that in later years "our Hearts were taken off from Old-England and set upon Heaven" by listening to the powerful sermons of Master Maverick and others in the Dorchester meeting-house.[45]

Occasionally we get a precious glimpse of one of the many humble folk whose convictions sent them westward. *"Go whare you will, god he will find you out,"* Mistress Dane of Bishop's Stortford told her obstreperous son John, who, at the age of sixteen, was leaving home because his Puritan father, a tailor, "toke a stick and

45. Thomas Prince published the *Memoirs of Roger Clap* (Boston, 1731), "because it gives a strong and lively Image of the extraordinary pious Spirit and Design of those English People, who first came over and dwelt in this Indian Wilderness. . . ." See pp. i, 1–4.

basted me . . ." when "I went to a dansing scoll to larne to dans." At Hereford and elsewhere John Dane attended cock fights, danced, and had a rollicking good time; he also attended sermons, listening to Mr. Thomas Godwin and Mr. John Norton. He maintained himself by plying his skill as a tailor on his "shopboard." Apparently he was a personable lad, for he had to resist temptations freely offered by several young women. Even after his marriage, he believed himself to be a weak vessel. About 1636, so he wrote in later life, he decided to go to New England, for he thought he would be freer from temptation there. To secure his father's permission to emigrate, he traveled back to his home, but both his father and mother opposed his going. In the words of John Dane, he was sitting "close by a tabell whare there lay a bibell. I hastily toke up the bybell, and tould my father if whare I opened the bybell thare i met with anie thing eyther to incuredg or discouredg that should settell me. I oping of it . . . the first I cast my eys on was: Cum out from among them, touch no unclene thing, and I will be your god and you shall be my pepell . . . My first cuming was to Roxburey. . . . But mr Norton being in ipswitch, I had a mynd to live under him." John Dane's letters home must have been persuasive, for his father brought the entire family over, and in 1639 had a house lot awarded to him at Ipswich.[46]

A primary feature of this great outpouring was its group character. In many instances parishioners crossed the seas with their nonconforming ministers. That Thomas Shepard, John Cotton, and Peter Hobart of Hingham brought congregations with them is well known. In 1638 Ezekiel Rogers sailed from Hull with a large number of weavers and spinsters of his parish to found a new Rowley, where they might worship God in their own way and still fabricate cloth. Whether Rogers was a "disgruntled clergyman" or not, his flock preferred exile with their pastor to worshiping under Archbishop Neile's new favorite. Probably just as important as the desire to escape religious "tyranny" were friendships based upon an essential harmony of minds and purpose. The fact that people came from the same town or county, had the same minister, and possessed a community of spirit often transcended even a common

46. *NEHG Reg.*, VIII, 147–56, especially 154.

Puritanism and caused hard-headed men and women to emigrate in distinct companies.[47]

A most important group in English society was the family, and the sole segment of the Great Migration to preserve it from the very beginning was the planters of New England; elsewhere it had to be reconstituted. It was the transfer of Puritan families, whole and intact, that explains the uniqueness of New England. We noted that a carpenter and a bricklayer wanted to take their families with them in the Winthrop Fleet. The years 1637 and 1638 were outstanding for the number of families emigrating. Among the Norwich passengers for the Bay Colony were John Baker, a grocer, thirty-nine years of age, his wife Elizabeth, who was thirty-one, three children, and four servants; they sailed from Great Yarmouth for Charlestown in 1637 "ther to inhabitt and Remaine." Peter Noyes of Weyhill, Hampshire, rented two of his four properties to his sister in Southampton to raise the necessary funds for the passage of himself, his eldest son, daughter, and three servants, all of whom departed in the *Confidence,* April, 1638. A neighbor, John Bent, and Mrs. Agnes Bent paid him £80 to go with them. Some years later the House of Commons was told that because of Bishop Wren's "pressing their consciences with illegal oathes ceremoniall observation and many straing innovations," fifty-two families from Norwich alone went to New England at this time.[48]

Entire families could not always migrate as units. Sometimes the head of the household, either out of caution or more often because of lack of funds, went on ahead and then sent for his wife and children, or returned to get them. In describing the Puritan exodus

47. Charles E. Park, "Friendship as a Factor of the Settlement of Massachusetts," in Amer. Antiquarian Soc., *Proceedings,* XXVIII, 51; Marchant, *The Puritans and the Church Courts,* 96–102; *CSPD, 1638–9,* pp. xxii–xxiii, 430–31; Essex Institute, *Historical Collections,* LIII, 217.

48. The recruiting of families occasionally presented difficulties, especially those raised by wives who were unwilling to accompany their husbands. John Winthrop wrote of the problem he had keeping one of his employees because his wife would not join him in the colony; "she will live miserably with her children there [England] when she might live comfortable heere with her husbande." On the other hand, Thomas Shepard's wife "did much long to see me settled there in peace and so put me on it." *Winthrop Papers,* III, 87; *Norfolk,* XXV, 21; Powell, *Puritan Village,* 5; Waters, *Gleanings,* I, 10; *Proceedings and Debates of the British Parliament,* I, 104.

in which he had participated, Edward Johnson wrote: "Husbands and wives with mutuall consent are now purposed to part for a time 900 Leagues asunder, since some providence at present will not suffer them to goe together; they resolve that their tender affections shall not hinder this worke of Christ." The courts of New England dealt harshly with men who made no attempt to bring their families together: in 1643 six men were presented by the grand jury to the court of Salem for "Lieveing absent from their wyves." One of them, Phillip Crumwell, had been in the colony "seaven or eight years and in all that time not sending her any reliefe for herself or child he left with her. . . . He bee enjoyned to goe over to England to his wife with liberty to returne if he see cause. . . ." [49]

Transatlantic family connections may be traced in surviving wills. The widow Alice Torrey of Combe St. Nicholas had four sons in New England in 1640; and Smallhop Bigg, a Kentish clothier living in Cranbrook, had seven kinfolk there in 1638, including two women, to each of whom he bequeathed 20s. When Peter Thatcher of New Sarum died in 1640, he left £35 to be sent to his two sons in Massachusetts, and to one of them, Peter, he gave "Mr. Henry Aynsworthe's works and Mr. Rogers his seven Treatises." [50]

The settlement of "perhaps 4,000 families" in twelve years insured several things to the Puritan plantations that other colonies lacked. The first generations of New Englanders, wrote Francis Higginson of the heads of families, were "most of them in their middle Age, and many of them in their declining years. . . ." These men were accustomed to responsibility, and they took their charges across the water to found a permanent society. Even those for whom the economic motive was uppermost desired to establish themselves in the new land and not merely make their fortunes and then return to England. The presence of both children and the aged in most families further differentiated the Puritans from the settlers of the other two regions, where the ages ranged from sixteen to thirty years. Significantly too, like the Greeks, the wives

49. *Johnson's Wonder-Working Providence,* 53; Essex Institute, *Historical Collections,* XXXIX, 367.
50. Waters, *Gleanings,* I, 21, 549, 676, 677; Henry F. Waters, *Ipswich in the Massachusetts Bay Colony* (Ipswich, 1905), I, 759–60.

and families carried with them the civilized English mode of living, the only fundamental cultural influence that was immediately rooted in the New World.[51]

People from all parts of Britain joined in the Puritan migration: it was a representative movement in this respect. Colonel Charles E. Banks uncovered the names of 2,885 emigrants (10.5 per cent) who came from 1,194 parishes in England. Among the counties, Monmouth and Westmoreland alone failed to furnish a single person. The geographical distribution of these emigrants was as follows:

	EMIGRANTS	PER CENT
East Anglia & Essex	732	20.5
West Country (Dorset, Somerset, Gloucester, Devon, & Cornwall)	546	19.0
London, Middlesex, Surrey, & Kent	534	18.5
Southern Counties	244	8.0
TOTAL		66.0
Midland Counties	435	18.0
TOTAL	2,491	84.0
Lincolnshire, Lancashire, Yorkshire	394	10.0
TOTAL KNOWN	2,885	94.0

Thus more than four-fifths of the known total came from south of a line from The Wash to Bristol Channel, for Puritanism held little attraction for the inhabitants of the North, save in the urban centers of Lincolnshire, Lancashire and Yorkshire. The largest quota came from a circular area fifty miles in radius with Groton in Suffolk as the center—the Winthrop Country. Great emphasis has been laid upon the depressed cloth manufacture in the eastern counties, but conditions in the same trades in the West Country were even worse, and yet it sent somewhat fewer people to New England. Without doubt the difficulty everywhere of making a living played a determining part in the emigration; it was one second

51. Mather, *Magnalia Christi Americana*, Attestation, sig. A 2r.

only to religion. We may say confidently that the emigrants left the most populous regions of England, where people's ties to their homeland had been loosened by a variety of conditions, of which the religious was the most prominent and psychologically far and away the most powerful.[52]

The very same factors that induced the movement westward also produced one to the east, to the European continent. That it has scarcely been studied at all does not mean that it was not of prime significance or that large numbers of Englishmen did not take part in it. A man had to decide whether to go to New England or to Holland, and some thousands chose the latter refuge. It is clear that, from 1629 to 1642, a steady stream of Britons sought sanctuary in nearby Rotterdam, Amsterdam, and Delft, and that the prime emigration years were the same as those for New England.[53]

An entry made in a "Church Book" tells us that in 1638 "the urging of popish ceremonies and divers innovated injunctions in

52. Charles E. Banks published the following essential works on the topography of the migration: "English Sources of Emigration to the New England Colonies in the Seventeenth Century," Mass. Hist. Soc., *Proceedings*, LX, 366–73; *The Winthrop Fleet of 1630* (Boston, Mass., 1930); "The Topographical Sources of English Emigration," *New York Genealogical and Biographical Record*, LXI, 3–6, and map. Colonel Bank's posthumous work provides all the known data about the origins in England of 2,885 people, together with invaluable maps. *Topographical Dictionary of 2,885 English Emigrants to New England, 1620–1650*, ed. Elijah E. Brownell (Philadelphia, 1937). While this author's genealogical and statistical information are both admirable and reliable, his predilection for a simple and unqualified economic determinism renders his judgments unacceptable to many historians. Much the best general sketch of the social and economic origins of the founders of the Bay Colony is by G. Andrews Moriarty in *The Commonwealth History of Massachusetts* (Boston, 1927), I, 51–63. Other helpful studies are Joseph L. Bartlett, in Cambridge [Mass.] Historical Society, *Proceedings,* XIV, 79–103; Mildred Campbell, in *Seventeenth Century America,* ed. James M. Smith (Chapel Hill, 1959), 63–89; Col. Joseph L. Chester, in Essex Archaeological Society, *Transactions,* III, Pt. I, 31–47; Nellis M. Crouse, *NEQ,* V, 3–36; George C. Homans, *NEQ,* XIII, 519–29; Moriarty, in *Devon & Cornwall,* XVII, 182–3; Hunter, in Mass. Hist. Soc., *Collections,* 3d ser., X, 172; and Tyack's excellent Migration from East Anglia to New England. Useful passenger lists may be found in the *NEHG Reg.,* II, 108; XIV, 303, 338; XV, 28; LXXV, 217, *et passim.*
53. Raymond P. Stearns, *Congregationalism in the Dutch Netherlands* (Chicago, 1940), is the authority for the "English Congregational Classis"; *Proceedings and Debates of the British Parliament,* I, 104n; Prynne, *Canterburies Doome,* 375; Mundy, *Travels,* IV, 62; *The Work of Thomas Goodwin, D. D.* (London, 1704), V, xviii; Heylyn, *Cyprianus Anglicus,* Pt. II, 367.

the worship and service of God by Bishop Wren, the suspending and silencing of divers godly ministers and persecuting of godly men and women, caused divers of the Godly in Yarmouth and other places to pass over into Holland to enjoy the liberty of their conscience in God's worship; and to free themselves from human inventions." William Bridge was one of these ministers who fled from England. He had studied at Emmanuel and had served as lecturer at Colchester and later at Norwich. Bishop Wren's court had silenced him for refusing to read the Book of Sports and he had been ejected from St. Peter's per Hungate. When he learned that he was to be arrested he took ship for Rotterdam, where he became one of the pastors administering to the sizable groups of merchants, craftsmen, and soldiers residing in Holland more or less permanently.[54]

The Anglican Peter Heylyn confirmed the account of this exodus. According to him, the silenced lecturers and ministers persuaded "the people in many great trading Towns, which were near the Sea" to "remove their Dwellings and transport their Trades . . . to Holland as their City of Refuge." "So many families . . . removed out of Suffolk into Holland, and . . . set up divers sorts of the drapery" that the Merchant Adventurers petitioned the Privy Council about the danger of competition from the emigrants. Article XVI for the Impeachement of Bishop Wren in 1641 stipulated that his persecution had driven 3,000 people, mostly weavers and knitters ("some of them setting 100 poor people at work") over to Holland and beyond the seas, and that these emigrants had taught the natives of these countries the secrets of the manufacture of cloth, stuffs, and stockings.[55]

V

Although some hundreds of English Puritans sailed to New England every year from 1629 through 1642, at certain times their numbers rose into the thousands. At best, statistics for the seven-

54. Palmer, *Great Yarmouth*, II, 36.
55. Heylyn, *Cyprianus Anglicus*, Pt. II, 367; *CSPD, 1639*, p. 357; *The Parliamentary History of England*, ed. William Cobbett (London, 1808), II, 864–5.

teenth century are mere estimates and must be steadfastly so regarded, but it appears that by 1632 about 2,000 passengers had crossed the ocean bound for the new plantation. William Wood believed that the number had doubled by the next year, as did John Winthrop. William Whiteway carefully checked on the departures for New England from Weymouth and Plymouth and recorded in his diary in 1634: "This somer there went over to that plantation at least 20 saile of ships, and in them 2000 planters." An interleaved almanac contains the notation for 1638: "This year arrived 20 ships and 3,000 passengers," a figure accepted by Thomas Hutchinson in his *History of Massachusetts*.[56]

The ebb and flow of the migration was affected principally by ecclesiastical and political regulations. Immediately after the departure of the Winthrop Fleet in the spring of 1630, a royal proclamation forbade the officials in all western seaports from Bristol to Liverpool to allow any passengers to ship out without licenses to do so. In February, 1634, the Privy Council took note that "the frequent transportation of great nombers of . . . persons known to be ill affected, and discontented, as well with the Civill as Ecclesiastical Government" created "such confusion and disorder . . . especially in poynt of Religion" that it brought disrepute on both church and state. Consequently, all the ships in the Thames were stayed until their masters appeared and gave bond that, among other things, they would read the Book of Common Prayer morning and evening, and would not transport anyone who lacked a license. In this same month, Sir Richard Saltonstall, John Humfry, and "others of the cheifest of the New England Planters" were summoned before the Council and required to take oaths of allegiance and supremacy, and to subscribe to the discipline of the Church of England. They readily took the two oaths but refused to subscribe, "saying they went into New England principally to decline that. Whereupon after some consultation they were dismissed." [57]

On April 28, 1634, King Charles established by proclamation

56. *CSP Col., 1574–1660*, p. 156; Wood, *New Englands Prospect*, 49; *Winthrop Papers*, III, 166; Whiteway, Diary, April 17, 1634, (fol. 201); *NEHG Reg.*, I, 73; Hutchinson, *History of Massachusetts-Bay*, I, 76.

57. *Bibliotheca Lindesiana*, I, 189; *Acts of the Privy Council, Colonial*, I, 199, 200, 201; Whiteway, Diary, 206 (fol. 197).

the Lords Commissioners for Plantations (commonly referred to as the Laud Commission because the primate was chairman) to stop "such promiscuous and disorderly parting out of the Realme . . ." and to oversee the enlarged territories of "our Empire." In December the Commissioners issued orders that no subsidy men were to be allowed to emigrate, and none under that degree might leave without a license from two justices of the peace attesting that the applicant had taken the oaths of supremacy and allegiance, and a certificate from the minister of his parish vouching for his conformity. Further restraints came in 1635, when King Charles forbade any of his subjects save soldiers, mariners, and merchants to leave the realm without a license from him or his Council. This proclamation was designed to stop the Puritans from crossing to the Netherlands and to the plantations across the Atlantic, "whose only end is to live as much as they can without the reach of authority." In addition, lists of all persons who embarked were to be forwarded regularly every six months to the Lords Commissioners.[58]

All Laudian and other restrictions failed to prevent the sailing of the ships. The protests of the maritime interests were too loud or else some port officers winked as they cleared the vessels, so that the exodus, though occasionally halted for a brief time, continued almost unabated. Sir Simonds D'Ewes credited the deity with the persisting departures. "When in the spring-time thousands have each year prepared themselves for their passage into New England, sold their estates, shipped their goods, and were even ready to put to sea, such secret ways and means have been used, as they have been stayed for a time, and often been in danger of being prevented of their journey, to their utter undoing; but God that protecteth his, has still by one means or another disappointed the malicious and merciless plots and designs of their enemies, and opened a seasonable liberty of departure and a safe passage thither." He even argued that the enemies were benefactors, for "in making the passage so difficult," only those who go for "conscience-sake" undertake the journey, with the result that every

---

58. *Winthrop Papers*, III, 180–81; Ebenezer Hazard, *Historical Collections: Consisting of State Papers and Other Authentic Documents* (Philadelphia, 1792), I, 347–8; *CSM*, XXII, 86–7; *CSPD, 1635*, p. 286; *Bibliotheca Lindesiana*, I, 203, 210, 214.

parish in the plantation was supplied with truly pious souls and "able painful preaching ministers." [59]

The Puritan migration would never have succeeded without whole-hearted co-operation from the Puritan merchants, masters, and ship owners, as well as other men connected with commercial pursuits, several of whom were members of the Massachusetts-Bay Company at its inception. Fundamentally sympathetic with both the religious and the commercial possibilities of the undertaking, the merchants took great satisfaction in prospering in the Lord's service. James Parker, a rich and charitable haberdasher of St. Pancras, provided in his will in 1639 that £300 be set aside "for taking up out of the streets or out of Bridewell" twelve orphaned boys and eight girls seven or more years old, and paying their passages to New England where they might be bound apprentices to such persons as "will be careful to bring them up in the feare of God and to maintaine themselves another daie." [60]

The adventurers had discovered in the planting of colonies to the south that carrying passengers and provisions was highly profitable, and they were quick to enter into similar arrangements with the plantations in New England. There was sufficient money invested in the enterprise to warrant heavy purchases, which benefited the agricultural, manufacturing, and mercantile sections of the mother country. In 1630 there had been some concern about the shortages of provisions in Bristol because the emigrant vessels were taking them away. In January, 1638 there was a brief flurry over the denial of a license to export butter, cheese, shoes, and tanned hides for planters "to the number of 3,000" in Connecticut. Restrictions of this nature, like those limiting the emigrants, were not long lasting, for the merchants protested effectively. When the *Neptune* sailed from Bristol in January, 1640, with 125 passengers bound for New England, she also had on board many barrels of beef, malt, meal, aqua vitae, wine, pease, vinegar, and oil, plus quantities of hardware, iron, tools, nails, and candles. In clothing she laded 250 dozen "stockins," 150 dozen each of shirts and drawers, 20 Monmouth caps, and a variety of miscellaneous items.[61]

59. *Winthrop Papers,* III, 200; *Acts of the Privy Council, Colonial,* I, 228–9; 230–41; D'Ewes, *Autobiography,* II, 117; *CSP Venetian, 1636–9,* p. 412.
60. Waters, *Gleanings,* II, 578–9.
61. A petition from the Mayor and Aldermen of Bristol requested the Council to

By 1636, if not before, English merchants had solved the problem of procuring return cargoes for the emigrant ships. Maurice Thompson of London and other merchants from the metropolis and the West Country directed their captains to proceed from Massachusetts Bay to Newfoundland, where they took on fish to exchange for wines at Teneriffe or Malaga before they returned to Bristol, Plymouth, or London. In January, 1640, Stephen Goodyear, merchant, and Richard Russell, "Partner and Master of the Shipp," received a permit to dispatch the *St. John* from London with 250 passengers and a huge cargo to Massachusetts, then to call at Newfoundland for fish and for wine in Spain, doubtless at Malaga. This trade route became a permanent one, and because reliable agents were needed in each port of call, interesting family agencies sprang up in every port. John Trowbridge, whose family originated in Devon, was a freeman of the Fishmongers Company in London in 1630; another Trowbridge went to Teneriffe and Thomas Trowbridge, successively of Dunscombe, Exeter, and Dorchester, became an early settler in New England. Religion and commerce combined to enrich more than one Puritan family.[62]

Maurice Thompson, who had been one of the more prominent merchants of London to enter the plantation trade, arranged in 1639 with Thomas Milward and Osmyn Douch to underwrite their partnership in the New England fisheries. This scheme, which other Londoners took up about 1645, enabled Thompson to venture into the lucrative carrying trade to the Wine Islands and Spain, and links the later interest in the offshore fisheries of Massachusetts with the emigrant trade of the 1630's.[63]

From 1629 to 1642, English, Dutch, and colonial vessels carried thousands of passengers over to New England. Edward John-

ban the sailing of a ship carrying provisions to New England in November of 1630, because the "late furnishing of a ship for New England has in some measure unfurnished their markets." *CSPD, 1629–31*, p. 384; *Winthrop Papers*, III, 283; *CSP Col., 1574–1660*, p. 284; *Acts of the Privy Council, Colonial*, I, 273.

62. By 1637 Puritan shipbuilders from Limehouse, Wapping, and Stepney had built at Marblehead the ship *Desire*, 120 tons; the following year Captain William Piers was licensed to take out passengers and provisions. Apparently he went from London to the West Indies, for on his return he brought cotton, tobacco, slaves, and salt from Tortuga to Boston. *Acts of the Privy Council, Colonial*, I, 233, 273, 274, 275, 276, 281–2, 283; *NEHG Reg.*, XIV, 337; Venn, Crediton, I, 242; *Winthrop's Journal*, I, 187, 260.

63. *Note-book kept by Thomas Lechford, Esq., Lawyer in Boston . . .* (Amer. Antiquarian Soc., *Transactions*, VII), 112–13; *CSP Col., 1574–1660*, I, 274.

son, our most reliable reporter (whom Josselyn, Cotton Mather, Hutchinson, and J. F. Jameson followed), stated about 1650 that it was "supposed" that a total of 198 ships transported 21,200 men, women, and children, "or thereabout" to the new Land of Canaan in fifteen years' time. From existing passenger lists it appears that a ship brought, on the average, a hundred passengers, and if the number of ships is approximately correct, so is Johnson's number of passengers.[64]

It has been pointed out that most of the emigrants sold their lands and chattels, and they purchased the necessaries for permanent settlements before they left England. Edward Johnson also attempted to estimate the cost of the entire enterprise:

Passage	£95,000.0.0
Purchase and transporting of animals	12,000.0.0
Subsistence until crops were harvested	45,000.0.0
Building materials (iron, nails, glass)	18,000.0.0
Arms, artillery, and ammunition	22,000.0.0
	£192,000.0.0

Cotton Mather tells us that the adventurers also laid out in England "what was not inconsiderable." He then added that if it had not been for "a strange and strong impression from Heaven," which moved their hearts, they never would have faced all the costs and hazards of the undertaking. A document in the Pepys MSS at Magdalen College, Cambridge, undated but evidently belonging to 1670, repeats the figures listed above and then states that "Most of those who did not cast into this Bank were those who were in this transmigration; and their charges amount to much more than double the above mentioned sums. About 29 years ago [c. 1641] 'twas calculated to above 400,000." [65]

With the calling of the Long Parliament, hopes were renewed for a brighter religious and political future in Old England, and the Pu-

64. The usually reliable Hugh Peter reminded the Dutch West India Company in 1641 that "the English in America are about 50,000" inhabitants ("mannen") of whom 40,000 lived in New England. *Documents Relating to the Colonial History of New York*, ed. E. B. O'Callaghan (Albany, 1856), I, 567–8; *Johnson's Wonder-Working Providence*, 58, 58n, 61.

65. *Johnson's Wonder-Working Providence*, 54, 54n, 58; Mather, *Magnalia Christi Americana*, bk. I, 17–18; *HMC Pepys*, 270.

ritans suddenly stopped crossing the ocean. In his Journal for July 28, 1642, Governor Winthrop recorded the arrival of two ships, but only five or six passengers "and very few goods" came with them. The hegira had ended; and thereafter more persons returned than arrived. In estimating the English population of New England in 1642, however, we must consider certain additional factors. We know that after the first winter the good health of the planters evoked much comment. Thomas Hutchinson calculated that "about 4000 families" immigrated and they were prolific in offspring. There is no question that the American diet was both plentiful and varied, and better balanced than that of the mass of people in Old England. This accounts for the lower mortality rates among mothers and infants in the plantation. Finally, all evidence bears out the assertion that the colonial population doubled itself every two decades. When we take all of this into account, though no accurate numerical estimate is possible, we must inevitably conclude that in 1642 the population in New England must have been larger than the 21,200 people who came over from Britain—substantially so.[66]

In nearly every respect the Puritan migration and settlement were extraordinary. In an election sermon, *New Englands True Interest Not to Lie* . . ., preached at Boston, April 29, 1668, William Stoughton, whose father had crossed from Dorset to help found a new Dorchester in 1630, had good reason to declaim, "God sifted a whole nation that he might bring choice Grain over into this Wilderness." Who can candidly gainsay him? [67]

66. On the doubling of seventeenth-century population every two decades, see William S. Rossiter, *A Century of Population Growth* (Washington, 1909), Table 2, p. 10, where the estimates of growth ". . . tend to confirm the impression concerning the growth of population natural under the conditions which prevailed at this period." See further, George Bancroft, *History of the United States* (Boston, Mass., 1852), IV, 128n. It seems evident that the rate of increase in Massachusetts greatly exceeded that for the Chesapeake colonies or for the West Indies. *Winthrop's Journal*, II, 69; Hutchinson, *History of Massachusetts*, I, 82.

67. William Stoughton, *New-Englands True Interest* . . . (Boston, 1670), 19.

In Deo Speramus

THE ASTOUNDING VITALITY that Englishmen of all ranks and degrees had displayed in every form of human activity during the fifty years before 1642 has been depicted in the preceding pages. This era was not an attenuation of the Elizabethan age; it had a style and a direction all its own. Change and challenge—what men of the second half of the century would recognize as *progress*—were its hallmarks.

However, among the people who were too close to the hardships of life to comprehend what was occurring, everything seemed to be going wrong for them and their country. In rural and urban economic matters, in domestic policy and in foreign affairs, and, above all else, in the practice of their Protestant faith, nothing was as it should be. After 1620, the woes of the average man in this apparently ill-faring land mounted every year and reached a climax in the years between 1629 and 1642, when both state and church were threatened with unsought and misunderstood changes. The ordinary man and woman found all of these happenings disrupting and disturbing, and a very large minority of them came to think of themselves as supernumeraries of whom the land was weary. They were truly vexed and troubled Englishmen.

Literate and thinking persons among those who did not rule had many good and sufficient reasons for leaving the country; they lacked only the impetus or the impulse to depart. In 1619 and for a decade thereafter, the doubts about England in the minds of men, which tended to propel them away from the island, were steadily re-inforced by the attractions of distant places rosily pictured in promotion tracts, enthusiastically preached about in sermons, and expansively elucidated in conversations with friends and by a certain class of subtle men. Those of the English who followed the western star were ambitious, energetic, intelligent (often educated), and venturesome members of the middle and lower orders of the most dynamic society in the Western World—perhaps on the entire globe.

The governing facts of the Great Migration were these: the English who settled the colonies from Maryland to Barbados were assiduously sought out and recruited as individuals by spirits, or agents, who sold them to merchants and sea captains for cargo. Employing both blandishment and deception, the agents of the city merchants openly solicited youths and maidens to go as servants to the Chesapeake and Caribbean colonies. The emigrants may well have been those who read the tracts and listened to the ballads and were tempted, but they and the illiterates were either persuaded or goaded into action by the agents and spirits. Their going out of the land was a coolly calculated matter of pounds, shillings, and pence for the coffers of the shippers. Though most of them were radical Protestants, it was not faith that sent them off but some vague hope of bettering their material lot. They were talked into or coerced into departing. The colonists who went as families or congregations in the group exodus to New England did so primarily out of religious conviction. They constituted a special case of self-induced emigration.

Master William Stoughton implied a religious sifting of the Englishmen in the sermon quoted in the previous chapter on New England, but we may properly extend the sifting to other categories and to all of the settlers in the King's dominions in America in 1642. They were sifted socially because they were Englishmen who came almost entirely from the middle and lower ranks. They were sifted by religious beliefs and affiliations, whether Anglican, Puritan, or Roman Catholic. They were sifted by literacy in some degree and by education. They were further sifted by courage and hardihood, by physical vigor and energy, as well as by hopes, ambitions, and dreams about the future. Their world-view took in a wider range than that of those who stayed home. And all of this sifting was accomplished by the emigrants and their children without the paternal hand of government, which guided all other colonial undertakings.

Whatever their reasons for leaving England—a combination that differed with each individual—and without any awareness of it, these ordinary men and women had together performed the most daring and portentous act of modern history when they succeeded in planting a new nation where none before had stood.

Index